PIOTR ILYICH TCHAIKOVSKY

PIOTR ILYICH TCHAIKOVSKY

Letters to his Family
AN AUTOBIOGRAPHY

Translated by
GALINA VON MECK

with additional annotations by
PERCY M. YOUNG

Stein and Day/*Publishers*/New York

Published in the United States of America in 1981.

English language translations copyright © 1973 by Galina von Meck

Additional material copyright © 1981 by Percy M. Young.

All rights reserved.

Printed in the United States of America

Stein and Day/*Publishers*

Scarborough House, Briarcliff Manor, N.Y. 10510

Library of Congress Cataloging in Publication Data

Tchaikovsky, Peter Ilich, 1840-1893.
    Letters to his family.

    Includes indexes.
    1.   Tchaikovsky, Peter Ilich, 1840-1893.
2.   Composers—Russian S.F.S.R.—Correspondence.
I. Title.
ML410.C4A477   780'.92'4 [B]   80-6162
ISBN 0-8128-2802-X   AACR2

PREFACE

The letters contained in this collection represent a large part of those written by Piotr Ilyich Tchaikovsky to members of his family, which passed into the possession of the von Meck family. Tchaikovsky's niece, Anna Davydova, married Nikolai von Meck to ensure the union of family interests. In due course the letters which are the basis of this volume passed into the care of the Tchaikovsky Museum in Klin. Their translator, Mme Galina von Meck, the daughter of Anna and Nikolai, and therefore the great-niece of the composer, in presenting these letters in translation believes herself to be fulfilling the wishes of her family, whose interests were so closely bound to those of Tchaikovsky himself.

Mme von Meck's consideration has been so far as is possible to preserve the character and tone of the originals in the English version. This has required occasional discourtesies to syntax and to style, and sometimes appropriate unliterary expressions of the kind provided by a busy letter-writer who had little regard for detailed revision. One concession to the reader is the occasional division of passages into more paragraphs than the author of the letters allowed.

The problem of transliteration of Russian proper names has been resolved pragmatically. Rather more difficult is the use of foreign (i.e. non-Russian) terms by Tchaikovsky. For terms other than those belonging to titles and the ubiquitous word 'hotel', for which Tchaikovsky used the Roman alphabet, italics are employed. Where, however, he expressed foreign words through the Russian alphabet they stand in Roman type. Any French terms within the translator's version and at her discretion are carried in italics with inverted commas.

Tchaikovsky was not always consistent in dating letters. During his lifetime the Russian calendar was twelve days behind that of western Europe and he often gave a date in both forms. What was the date in western terms is made apparent in this edition.

Annotations of this work have been undertaken in conjunction with Mme von Meck over a number of years. Certain biographical details are contained in the first index, while the glossary explains familiar names used within the family.

P. M. Y.

CONTENTS

Page

634	Vienna	7–19 September	*to* MODEST TCHAIKOVSKY	519
635	Itter	15–27 September	MODEST TCHAIKOVSKY	520
636	Itter	[22 September–] 4 October	MODEST TCHAIKOVSKY	520
637	Klin	9 October	ANATOLI TCHAIKOVSKY	521
638	[Klin]	12 October	MODEST TCHAIKOVSKY	521
639	[St. Petersburg]	11 November	ANATOLI TCHAIKOVSKY	522
640	St. Petersburg	24 November	ANATOLI TCHAIKOVSKY	522
641	[St. Petersburg]	9 December	ANATOLI TCHAIKOVSKY	523
642	St. Petersburg	10 December	ANATOLI TCHAIKOVSKY	523
643	[Berlin]	14–26 December	VLADIMIR DAVYDOV	524
644	Berlin	16–28 December	VLADIMIR DAVYDOV	525
645	Basle	18–30 December	PRASKOVIA VLADIMIROVNA TCHAIKOVSKAIA	525
646	Basle	19–31 December	MODEST TCHAIKOVSKY	526
1893 647	Paris	22 December– 3 January	NIKOLAI ILYICH TCHAIKOVSKY	527
648	Paris	24 December– 5 January	MODEST TCHAIKOVSKY	528
649	Paris	4–16 January	MODEST TCHAIKOVSKY	530
650	Kamenka	28 January	MODEST TCHAIKOVSKY	530
651	Kamenka	29 January	ANATOLI TCHAIKOVSKY	531
652	Klin	5 February	MODEST TCHAIKOVSKY	532
653	Klin	10 February	ANATOLI TCHAIKOVSKY	533
654	Klin	11 February	VLADIMIR DAVYDOV	534
655	Klin	28 February	MODEST TCHAIKOVSKY	535
656	Klin	4 March	ANATOLI TCHAIKOVSKY	535
657	Moscow	8 March	MODEST TCHAIKOVSKY	536
658	[Klin]	19 March	MODEST TCHAIKOVSKY	537
659	[Klin]	11 April	VLADIMIR DAVYDOV	537
660	[Klin]	15 April	VLADIMIR DAVYDOV	537
661	Klin	17 April	MODEST TCHAIKOVSKY	538
662	Moscow	22 April	MODEST TCHAIKOVSKY	539
663	Berlin	15–27 May	MODEST TCHAIKOVSKY	540
664	London	17–29 May	ANATOLI TCHAIKOVSKY	541
665	London	17–29 May	VLADIMIR DAVYDOV	541
666	London	3 June	MODEST TCHAIKOVSKY	542
667	London	10 June	MODEST TCHAIKOVSKY	543
668	Paris	3–15 June	ANATOLI TCHAIKOVSKY	544
669	Paris	6–18 June	MODEST TCHAIKOVSKY	545
670	Grankino	19 June	ANATOLI TCHAIKOVSKY	546
671	Grankino	23 June	MODEST TCHAIKOVSKY	546
672	Ukolovo	6 July	ANATOLI TCHAIKOVSKY	547
673	[Klin]	19 July	ANATOLI TCHAIKOVSKY	548
674	Klin	22 July, 10 o'clock evening	MODEST TCHAIKOVSKY	548

Letters to his Family

The starting-point for the record represented by this collection of letters in reality should be the year 1825. This was the year in which Nikolai I became Czar of Russia and in which the confusion surrounding his accession prompted an insurrection of young, liberal minded, aristocrats. Because of the time of year when this took place these agents of revolution became known as Decembrists. One of them – Vassily Davydov, who for his participation was exiled to Siberia – was the husband of Alexandra Ivanovna Davydova and the father of Nikolai and Lev and their sisters, all of whom are conspicuous in the course of this book. The relationship between Tchaikovskys and Davydovs was of great importance to Piotr Ilyich Tchaikovsky and a significant influence on his musical development.

The course of Tchaikovsky's life and his outlook on human affairs were, of course, determined to a large extent by social and political circumstances. He was always deeply aware of an inner sense of passionate patriotism which, however, was not allowed to override his generally humane instincts. It was not easy for such a one to be a subject of the Czar. Nikolai I reigned for thirty years and it was in the latter half of his reign that Tchaikovsky spent his most impressionable years. Under Nikolai, whose actions were always affected by the phobias left behind by the Decembrists, the monarchy became more absolute and the system of government increasingly rigorous. The Czar maintained his government by the efficiency of army, police (of which the secret department, or 'Third Section', was the most effective and most hated part), and bureaucracy. Russia fought successful wars against Persia and Turkey in the early years of Nikolai's reign and in 1830–1 overcame a Polish uprising and eliminated Poland from the list of independent countries. The apparent stability brought about by the ruthless application of Czarist principles gave to Russia more of international respectability and in 1840 she became a member of a Quadruple Alliance engineered by Lord Palmerston for the settlement of the Middle East. Although this alliance was of short duration it brought Britain and Russia closer together at the beginning of the reign of Queen Victoria. This is reflected in this book in the acquaintance of Tchaikovsky's parents with an (un-named) English family during his childhood, in the engagement by the Davydovs of an English governess (see Letter 361), and in the English Club in Moscow (Letter 30).

Piotr Ilyich was the second son of Ilya Petrovich and Alexandra Tchaikovsky. His father was an inspector of mines, at the time of the birth of Piotr Ilyich stationed at Votkinsk. His appointment gave much authority to Ilya Petrovich and was sufficiently profitable for his family to be allowed to enjoy a comfortable standard of living. Piotr Ilyich was first taught his lessons by a governess, Fanny Dürbach (see Letter 642), who discerned in him at an early age creative talent both in music and literature. He was also more than normally sensitive and the emotional problems that plagued him later in life made themselves apparent during his boyhood. Ilya Petrovich retired from his inspectorate in 1848 and became manager of the iron ore works at Alapaievo, north–north-east of Ekaterinburg (now Sverdlovsk) in the Urals (see reference by Piotr Ilyich in Letter 559). This was far away from the important centres of culture and education and the family concentrated its main interests in St Petersburg, which shared with Moscow the status of a capital city. Here Piotr Ilyich entered the School of Law, whence he was expected to emerge in due course as a properly qualified recruit for the civil service.

Tchaikovsky graduated in 1859 and was accepted into the Justice Department in St Petersburg. He was not interested in his work, and, like many other young men of good family similarly employed, dedicated himself to a life of reasonably refined pleasure. He took a great interest in cultural pursuits – in theatre, music, and books. On 18 November 1860 his sister Alexandra Ilyinishna (1842–91) married Lev Davydov, son of Vassili the Decembrist.

The young Davydovs went to live on the family estate at Kamenka, in the Province of Kiev, in the Ukraine. This place was to become a favourite refuge of Tchaikovsky. Kamenka had its own tradition, an important one for a Russian patriot. After returning from Siberia (where her husband served a long sentence of hard labour) as a widow Alexandra Ivanovna Davydova took her daughters back to Kamenka. The property belonged to Piotr and Nikolai Davydov, sons of Alexandra and Vassili. Having been born before the Decembrist uprising they were able to inherit the estate. The original mansion had been burned down, but there was a new 'big house', and this was handed over to Lev and Alexandra Davydov in return for Lev acting as manager of the estate. Lev and Alexandra lived here until they bought their own property, Verbovka, not far away. Nikolai was said to have been something of a recluse. Nonetheless he fathered illegitimate daughters, two were adopted and their mother provided for. Pelageia Osipovna – the peaşant woman who was the mother of the girls – had a house on the estate. At the end of his life Nikolai lived in the house he provided for Maria, ̇one of his illegitimate daughters, and here he died in 1917 at the age of ninety-seven. The house in which Tchaikovsky was quartered was known as the Green House. There were many other buildings on the Kamenka site of which the most interesting were the 'Pushkin Grotto' in which A. S. Pushkin, as a guest of the Davydovs, had written *The Caucasian Prisoner* in 1821 and Sherwood's Mill, so named after the manager of the sugar factory (see p. 164) who listened-in to the Decembrist plotters and betrayed them.

In March, 1861, the correspondence begins with exciting family news. Alexandra is to have a baby. Tchaikovsky had been to Medved (a village in the Novgorod district) where his cousin Alexandra Petrovna (Sashenka) Karzova lived, on account of her husband being quartered there with his regiment.

Although it did not fulfil the hopes of the liberals in the long run, the Emancipation of the Serfs in 1861 was a political event of some encouragement. Alexander II, who had succeeded his father Nikolai I in 1855, looked forward to being able to pursue a more generous policy in domestic affairs. That Tchaikovsky was able to travel to Germany (Letter 3) was another sign of changing times. Before this it had only been possible for those who were politically trusted and influential to travel abroad.

TO ALEXANDRA DAVYDOVA   St Petersburg
                                        10 March 1861 – after dinner
                        (For dinner we had solianka and groundling.)

I have, Sasha, just read your letters to Papasha and Malia. They convey such
quiet but sombre hopelessness that I am both sorry and angry. You must
be ashamed to be in such a state of mind. Forget the past and bravely face the
future; you will see how many gentle joys, how much happiness you have in
store. In August you will be a mother! Aunt Liza and Malia will be with you.
Busy with the baby, the year will go by unnoticed; then the journey to
St Petersburg where, even if you are not there long, you will meet friends and
relatives—honestly I would like to be in your place. And what about your
husband whom you love? No, buck up, take care of your health and what is
most important, don't look back into the past. Teach yourself not to and
you will see how soon you will stop being sad.

Nothing has changed in my life since you left. Only my trip to Medved took
me a bit out of my usual rut. You probably already know everything about
Medved from Malia. Sashenka Karzova has greatly improved, her former
primness and drabness have completely gone. She is now so full of life that,
just by looking at her one feels happy. When I was [in Medved] I took part
in two plays and acted with some success. I cannot say, as yet, where I will
be in summer, it can easily happen that I will come for a few days to see you
or, perhaps, go abroad if Papasha is able to help with some money.

It is Lent – with stinking oil, meagre fish-diet, 'tableaux vivants', thaws, bad
roads, long services – pre- and post-sanctified liturgies, and horse shows. The
last week before Lent I spent in a very noisy and stupid way. Now I have
said good-bye to all masked balls and theatres and am at peace; but in spite
of that I cannot stay at home. I am off now to Piccioli's where I want
to brush up my Italian and listen to some singing. Will finish my letter when
I'm back.

                                                                12 night

Just returned from the Picciolis

They are both as kind as ever. She begged me to send you a thousand good
wishes and to say she loves you as much as she has in the old days. I returned
home early in time for supper. Alas! the meagre fried fish did not satisfy
my appetite. Out of boredom I teased Amalia – forced her to run round the
hall at least ten times. During supper there was a discussion about my musical
talent. Papasha assured me that it was not too late for me to become a
musician. It would be nice if it were so but the thing is, that if I have any
talent it is surely too late to develop it. I have been made into a civil servant
and not a good one at that. I try to perfect myself so that I can take my work
seriously, but how can I study thorough-bass at the same time.

How is your singing? I must honestly say that I do not expect anything good will come out of it. You probably never even touch the piano and have not looked at the music so carefully chosen and sent to you by Mr von Derviz. This gentleman is well again, to the great joy of Aunt Liza, all the Russian people, and the cabby Spiridon who still drives him around.

On Sunday freedom was granted [to the serfs]. I went to the parish church on purpose to see what impression the Declaration would make on the peasants. At the Opera that day the orchestra played 'God save the Czar' three times, accompanied by loud and enthusiastic shouting from the audience. Since you left, nothing of interest has been given at the opera house. Always the same old things! *William Tell* was played at least ten times. Sasha, write to Amalia (only do not mention that it is on my advice) and tell her that she must not think of going on the stage.

I have never spoken to her about it, you know how reticent I am when it concerns something serious, because I do not like to interfere. First of all, even if she has the germ of a talent I doubt if she will be able to reach a leading position in the theatre, and it is not worth being an actress like Podobedova. Secondly, even if she has an enormous talent, who can vouch for a real success. What if she does not make any impression at all! Then she will have lost everything. It is doubtful if anyone would want to marry her; and, to stay an old maid as well as being an unsuccessful actress is not a fate to be envied.

And so, Sasha, don't be sad. Summer is near! It will be glorious at your place.

For God's sake, friends, do not worry and do not write separately. I understand that it is impossible for all of you to write. It would, of course, be very nice, but I must not insist. As for me I will write as often as possible.

I kiss you Sasha, hard, hard, hard.

P. Tchaikovsky

[2]   TO ALEXANDRA DAVYDOVA   St Petersburg
                                                9 June 1861

At last I am writing to you, dear Sasha. Do not be angry with me for doing it so rarely. If I am not mistaken, I told you in my first letter what I feel about letter-writing. As you have already heard I am going abroad. You can imagine my delight, especially if you realize that the journey will scarcely cost me anything. I will be a sort of secretary, interpreter and factotum to Pisarev. . . . Naturally it would have been better without these duties, but what else can I do?

This journey seems to me to be a bewitchingly fantastic dream. I will only believe it is really true when I find myself on board ship. . . . ! In Paris, in Switzerland,—it seems quite ridiculous. . . .

I do not promise to write from abroad but will keep a detailed diary which I will read to you some day. I was thinking of paying you a visit on my way

Antwerp did not make any specially agreeable impression. Besides, I hoped to get a letter from you: did you get my first one? I gave you the Antwerp address in it. I hope that I will get some news from you in Paris. Pisarev has gone off from here for the whole day to inspect some works. I am completely alone and very bored; I do not know a soul. I tried to go for a walk but did not see anything interesting. I fear that I will have to stay here for some time. I wish we could get to Paris as soon as possible where there cannot be a dull moment.

I am sorry that my letter today is both short and boring. I am in a rather bad mood. My kind regards to all our people. When is Aunt Liza going away? Are Tolia and Modia studying hard. I dreamt of Amalia last night. Does Mina laugh a lot? And Katia eat too many cucumbers? Regards to Mashurochka. Tell Avdotia Yakovlevna that Hamburg has tempted me off the path of righteousness and also give her my very kindest regards.

P. Tchaikovsky

Better write to Paris, post restante, or to the Olkhovskys.

Ask Amalia, Tolia and Modia, to write if they have nothing better to do.

Avdotia Yakovlevna Bakhireva, the governess to Modest and Anatoli, mentioned above, was an enthusiastic admirer of Piotr as a composer.

[5] TO ILYA PETROVICH TCHAIKOVSKY   London
                                                              29 July–10 August 1861

Dear Papasha!

After Brussels, where I passed the time not very well we stayed with Pisarev three days in Ostend. It was wonderful there. I love the sea especially when it roars, and those three days it was really mad. I bathed with relish. Men and women bathe in the open sea together; I doubt if three days of bathing could do any good, but all the same I felt exceptionally well. We became friendly with a Moscow lady who travels with a doctor. She is the owner of the Shaitan works, is a Yarzeva by birth, and was married to General Kuzmin. We went together to London. This is 'a distance of enormous size' [quoted from Gogol, *The Government Inspector*].

We took rooms in a small hotel and spent all our days touring the town. Have just come back from Westminster Abbey and the Houses of Parliament. Yesterday and the day before we spent at the Crystal Palace. The building is really magnificent but inside there is a bit too much colour. We also went into the Thames tunnel where I nearly fainted for lack of air. But I would have passed the time even better if I had not been worried without news from you. London is very interesting but leaves a dark impression on one's soul. One never sees the sun, and it rains all the time.

The food here is very much to my taste. The dishes are simple, even coarse, but rich and tasty. The day before yesterday we went to the Cremorne amusement garden – I have never seen anything like it. When you enter you think it is fairyland, there I met an old acquaintance, Levtoz.

We went to a concert given by the singer Patti, who is having a tremendous success here but did not make any special impression upon me. I am leaving some space for Vassili Vassilievich. Kiss Anatoshka and Modia heartily for me, and my kind regards and kisses to everybody else. Has Aunt Liza left what is the news from her?

Your devoted son

P. Tchaikovsky

[6]   TO ILYA PETROVICH TCHAIKOVSKY   Paris
                                           12–24 August 1861

Forgive me, precious Papasha, that I have been silent for some time. You cannot help feeling giddy and forgetful in Paris. We arrived here on August 2–14 [*sic*] on the eve of Napoleon's Name Day, which was celebrated with great pomp and the next day we met [Sergei] Yuferov. You cannot imagine how glad I was to see him, how eagerly I listened to all the Petersburg news about you and all the others, dear to my heart! All that day we roamed round the Festival. The illuminations and fireworks were fabulous, and there was great enthusiasm. And these were the same Frenchmen who ten years ago were so keen on the Republic? Then I found Nikolai Ivanovich [Olkhovsky]. We had dinner together and laughed a lot. In general life in Paris is extremely pleasant. You can do whatever you want to do, and getting bored is quite impossible. You have only to go out on the boulevards to be immediately happy.

We took rooms with Yuferov and are together all day. When at home we play on a very decent piano, rented for fifteen francs a month, and all three of us pay 150 francs for our lodgings. We allow ourselves plenty of amusements which are, in general, not expensive, but we don't forget to visit the Law Courts. I will let you have all particulars about them when I see you. We are at the theatre nearly every night and have twice been to the opera (*Il Trovatore* and *Les Huguenots*). Both the performances and the theatres are definitely below those in Petersburg but the sets and the ensembles are good.

With regard to the *Bal mabille* and such like, I cannot say that it is anything wonderful. The theatres give us a lot of pleasure. Next week I am going to stay with Lidia Olkhovsky and enjoy the bathing. What will happen after that I don't know, but in any case I will be back home at the end of September.

Kiss Tolia and Modia properly from me and tell them that they are always in my thoughts. On August 16 I will be present at their examinations in spirit. Do not forget, Papasha, to tell the examiners that Tolia and Modia have been coached for the 1st senior division. Why don't they write to me?

Please kiss Mashura too, and thank her for the words she added in your letter. The same to my kind Avdotia Yakovlevna. Mina and Katia are probably back at school. Have received more letters from you.

I kiss and embrace you,

P. Tchaikovsky

[7] TO ALEXANDRA DAVYDOVA   St Petersburg
                                   23 October 1861

According to rules one ought to start a letter by asking forgiveness for a long silence, but this is too common and I hope, Sasha, you do not mind and are not hurt. What can I say about my travels abroad? Better not say anything. If I have ever made a colossally stupid mistake in my life, this was it. You remember Pisarev? Can you imagine that under the mask of that *bonhomie*, which gave me the impression that although a rough fellow he was kind, the most disgusting mental features have been lurking. Up till now I never thought there could be such vile individuals; now it will not be hard for you to understand what it was like to pass three months in the constant company of such an agreeable companion. Add to this that I spent more money than I was entitled to spend, that I did not reap anything worthwhile from the journey, and you will agree that I am an idiot. But do not scold me; I behaved like a child, that is all.

You know that the greatest desire of my life was to go abroad. The opportunity came; *la tentation était trop grande,* I shut my eyes and went. Do not think that I mean it is unpleasant abroad, or that travelling is boring. Quite the contrary! But you need absolute freedom of action, enough money, and a good reason for going. In Paris we lived with [Sergei] Yuferov and that was most comforting. What a delightful person! On the whole there were charming moments in that city. If you go to Kiev in winter you will probably meet a certain Gudim-Levkovich, who knows all the Davydovs very well, and you by hearsay. He will give you a few particulars – we met nearly every day.

You will not believe how happy I was to return to Petersburg. I must honestly say that I have a great weakness for the Russian capital. I cannot help it! I am much too bound up with it! All that is precious to me is in Petersburg and life away from it is quite impossible. Besides, when the pocket is not too empty, the soul is merry, and after my return I still had a few roubles to spare. You know my weak side, how when I have some money I spend it all on pleasure. It is mean, it is stupid, I know that. To be honest, I have no right to spend money on amusements, for I have debts which must be paid, and I have needs which must be attended to; but (again out of weakness) I do not stop to think and just have a good time. Such is my character.

How will I end? What does the future promise me? I fear to think about it. I know that either early or late in life (probably early) I will not have the strength to fight against life's difficulties and will get smashed to bits. But till then I shall enjoy life as well as I can, and sacrifice everything to enjoyment. The last two weeks I have been surrounded by difficulties: everything is going wrong at the office, the roubles have evaporated long ago, and I am unfortunate in love! But all this is nonsense – time goes on and I will be gay again. I even cry a little sometimes, but then I take a walk along the Nevsky, come back home on foot, and feel better.

I congratulate you on Tatiana. She will be a good woman!
[Then comes a short verse written by the composer on the spur of the moment in honour of his new niece.]

Not a bad improvisation. I have started studying thorough-bass, and it is going very successfully. Who knows, perhaps, in about three years you will be listening to my operas and singing my arias. . . .

Would it not have been better to pass the summer with you instead of going abroad? Aunt Liza's and Malia's accounts tempt me so much that I am ready to come and visit you at once to rest my soul, and then back to Petersburg to face life. Alas! it is not possible. Perhaps in the summer of next year.

Give a proper hug and kiss to Lev Davydov and offer Tatiana an extra suck of milk for my sake. I bless you and your dynasty.

Your respectful brother

P. Tchaikovsky

Despite his lack of interest in his official duties Tchaikovsky hoped for promotion to a higher rank. The post at which he aimed would bring a little more money and no more work. Musical classes which he attended were instituted in 1861 at the Mikhailov Palace, through the initiative of Anton Rubinstein. After a year the classes were reorganized into the Conservatoire where Tchaikovsky continued to study.

[8] TO ALEXANDRA DAVYDOVA   St Petersburg
                                                4 December 1861

Dear Sasha!

If I have not answered for so long it is because I could not make up my mind how to write. I can't find any words to thank you for what you have sent me, especially as it arrived at a moment when one has no idea how to cope with a difficulty, and also because of the delicate way you put it; I did not have that torturing thought at all which proud people get towards those who have done them a favour.

Your letter is so sweet that I felt deeply touched (please do not think I am being insincere) and never doubted that anyone had ever taken such interest in me as you have. I wish and hope that some day I will be able to repay you. My life is going on as usual. So far as my job is concerned I hope to get the post of clerk for special commissions soon, with twenty more roubles a month and less work. Please God it will happen. I doubt though that I will be able to get out of Petersburg into the provinces now. I have already told you that I am studying musical theory, and with great success; you must agree that with my real talent (I hope you do not think I am boasting) it would be unwise not to try my luck in this field. The only thing I fear is my lack of will-power. Laziness may get the upper hand and I succumb to it; but if it doesn't happen I promise to become something. You know that I have strength and certain gifts, but I am sick of that complaint called Oblomovchina and if I do not triumph over it I will be lost. Luckily there is still time.

Society life in Petersburg is at its height; I have made a few new acquaintances: the Saburovs, Mme Savelieva, Mme Gerngross, another Mme Gerngross, Mme Kozlova (not the one whom we met at the Butovskys). So I am often out, although I do not go to the theatre as often as before. Two evenings in the week are occupied by study; on Fridays I am either at Piccioli's or Bonné's, at home on Sundays, while nearly every Monday we play octets at a certain person's house, so that there is no time for the theatre.

Once more I thank you with all my heart and kiss you.

P. Tchaikovsky

Tchaikovsky's father (Papasha) had become enamoured of a Mrs Yachmeneva to whom he gave a large part of his savings to further some hair-brained scheme of hers. The Bekleshevs were involved as guarantors. When the money disappeared a law-suit was begun.

[9] TO ALEXANDRA DAVYDOVA   St Petersburg
                                         10 September 1862

Dear Sasha!

At last my dozing conscience has woken up and here I am talking to you. Now that all the Kiev Davydovs have left, you need letters from Petersburg to distract you. First I must say that I have had a boring time all this summer. I worked conscientiously and on free days I went out of town, which was my only consolation. You, I think, have not forgotten my weakness for the Golova dacha; this has not lessened at all, but it seems I am the only lover of that dacha left. You probably already know all about Aunt Liza's move from Malia.

I am now alone with Papasha, and are not bored at all. First, I dine at home every day. A certain fellow known to you by name of Gerhardt comes often to disturb our tête-à-tête, but as both I and Papasha love him as a brother it gives us great pleasure. In the evenings we often go to the Russian Theatre or play cards. Papasha spends only half as much as before on the household – and he likes it. I order the dinner and am, in general, the link between Amalia Konstantinovna and Papasha of whom she is, for some unknown reason, very much afraid.

There have been quite a lot of holidays lately so that Anatoli, Modest and Alesha have often been at home. Once we all went together to the ballet and took Malia with us and yesterday they went with Alesha to see *Nos intimes*. This young man is so good looking in his Lycée uniform that very few women pass him without falling in love. He usually arrives with Tolia and Modia and sleeps in my room. We recite poetry to each other and laugh a lot. Tolia often talks about Kamenka and tells us all about you. According to him everybody is in love with Tania.

I have stolen your photograph with Tania from Alesha and often admire it. Papasha was very disturbed when he received your news, that you had weaned your daughter. These last days he has been very worried; Mrs Yachmeneva's case at the Civil Court has been decided in favour of Beklesheva and although I am sure this decision is not by any means final, and is sure to be reversed in the Senate, he was greatly upset. Up till now he was certain that the courts would look at everything through his eyes. I managed to calm him down and the day before yesterday, in the evening, he had a letter from Derviz (the elder) who supervises the case, and it completely restored his equanimity.

I have entered the newly opened Conservatoire and the course begins in a few days' time. As you already know, last year I studied the theory of music vigorously and am now absolutely sure that sooner or later I will exchange the Civil Service for music. Don't think that I imagine myself becoming a great artist – all I want is to do what my vocation is calling me to do. Whatever I become in the end – a famous composer or a poor teacher – my conscience will be at peace and I shall not have the heavy burden of grumbling against fate and people. Naturally I will continue as I am at present until I am quite certain that I am an artist and not a civil servant. . . . I got up today exceptionally early. I was woken up by Tolia and Modia who were leaving for college. Here I want to note that my love for these little men, especially (a secret!) for the first one, grows every day. I am very proud of this sentiment and cherish it as the best feeling of my heart.

When I am feeling sad all I have to do is to think of them, and life again becomes precious to me. As much as I can, I try, by my affection and attention, to give them what they have never known – the love and solicitude of a mother. I think I am successful. Yesterday I received a long letter from Kolia, will answer him in a day or two.

Kiss the agriculturist Lev Davydov and his beautiful daughter, lady Tatiana, a thousand times.

I kiss you,

Your brother

P. Tchaikovsky

Tchaikovsky sent in his resignation, which became effective on 1 May, to the Justice Department. That he should give up a salaried post was unwelcome to his family, especially since his father had lately retired and was in general in poor financial shape. Tchaikovsky, however, worked very hard at his musical studies. During the autumn he met Alexandra Davydova's mother-in-law, widow of the Decembrist, who, with four of her daughters and a son, was now living in the city.

Rubinstein loaded him with exercises and Tchaikovsky was often compelled to work into the small hours.

[10] TO ALEXANDRA DAVYDOVA   [St Petersburg]
                                           15 April 1863

My dear friend Sasha!

From your letter to Papasha received today I see that you have no real interest in my position and that you look with distrust on the decisive step I have taken in my life. So I want to explain to you fully what I intend to do and what I hope for. You will not deny my musical capacities and also that it is the only thing I am good at; if so, it is understandable that I must give up everything else to develop and cultivate the germ that God has planted in me. It is for this reason that I started seriously to study the theory of music; up to now it has not prevented me from giving more or less proper service at the Ministry, but as my studies are getting more and more serious and difficult I must make a choice. To be an adequate official and to study music at the same time is impossible. One cannot receive a salary all one's life without doing anything in return.

Besides, it would not be allowed. Consequently, only one thing is left – to leave the service (I can always return if I like). In short, I have decided to stay attached to the Ministry, but without either set duties or salary. Do not conclude that I want to run up debts instead of earning a salary; or borrow from Papasha, whose money matters at the moment are far from brilliant.

I hope that in the next session I will get a job at the Conservatoire and I have already found a few private pupils for the next year. As at the same time I have completely renounced all social pleasures, elegant clothes, etc., etc., my expenses have diminished quite considerably. After all this you will ask: and what are you going to be when at last you finish your studies? All I can say is that I will become a good musician and will always be able to earn my daily bread. All the professors at the Conservatoire are pleased with me and say that if I work hard much can come out of me. All the above said is not a boast (I do not think it is in me) but an honest statement without false pride.

When I finish the course at the Conservatoire I would like to come and stay with you for a year, to be able to write something big in peace and quiet and then go off wandering through the world.

But enough about this . . . I congratulate you on your daughter. You cannot believe, my dear soul, how worried I was about you, and said a prayer when the telegram came about your successful confinement. Concerning what you write to Papasha, it also seems to me that it would be easier for him to stay with you and with Zinochka but I do not dare advise him about anything. If I say it would be better for him to be with you, he will think I want to get rid of him, if I say he should stay in Petersburg he may think I want to live on his money. At the beginning of July he and Tolia and Modia will come to you, but I cannot say yet where I will be. I thank you very much my dear friend, for your invitation to stay with you. Kolia is trying to stay and continue to work in Petersburg.

You have probably already heard that N. I. Olkhovsky has been appointed Director of the Mint; now everything depends upon him, and one must hope that all will be well.

The long period of Lent, with its concerts, has tired me greatly. I have been perpetually asked to accompany at different concerts. Twice I appeared on the stage of the Bolshoi and Marinsky theatres. Once I was at a musical evening at the house of the Grand Duchess Elena Pavlovna. I had the honour to attract her attention and talk to her, and two days later I received an envelope with 20 roubles (not very Grand-ducal!) in it. At present I am at home most of the time and continue to work hard.

I do ask your and Leva's forgiveness for not writing more often. It does not mean that I do not think of you, it is simply because I have not much time or any great inclination to write letters.

I kiss you hard, hard, and also dear Leva, Tania and Vera whom I am terribly anxious to meet.

P. Tchaikovsky

During the summer of 1864 Tchaikovsky – the guest of Prince Alexei Golitzin, at Trostinez in the Kharkhov District – was busy with an examination exercise set by Rubinstein. This was an overture for Alexander Ostrovsky's *The Storm*. Rubinstein, however, thought poorly of the work which was not played in public and only published by Belaiev in 1896 after Tchaikovsky's death.

[11] TO ALEXANDRA DAVYDOVA   [Trostinez]
                                                     28 July 1864

Dear Sasha!

You are wrong in thinking that I am not in Kamenka because I like it so much here and that I cannot leave Golitzin. I do not deny that I am happy here but I am certain that at your place with your husband, children, and all your family it would have been even better. But although my heart longs for you my reason tells me clearly that I must put off my visit to Kamenka until next year and then come to you straight from Petersburg for three months. That you may not think I do not long with all my heart to be with all of you, I must tell you that before leaving Petersburg I did my best to come straight to you, but circumstances were against me; then I came here hoping that I could join you without any difficulty. Thank you for your letter. It has appeased my fears that you were angry with me. The bad weather which you mention could not frighten me at all, as it is no better here. I live very quietly and do not see anyone but Golitzin. Tell Vera Vassilievna [Butakova] that my 'Storm' is progressing and that she may hear it at the Russian Musical Society.

I have not had any news from Papasha, Tolia and Modia for over a month.

Have you had any letters addressed to me? If so, send them here.

Once more I thank you, dear Sasha, and sorrow nearly to death that I cannot be with you, but I yield to my fate and beg to be forgiven for not keeping my promise. Kiss Leva and Alesha. Squeeze Tania and Vera and kiss them from me without mercy. A deep obeisance to Alexandra Ivanovna and Elizaveta, Alexandra, Sofia and Vera Vassilievna.

[no signature]

In 1865 Tchaikovsky paid his first visit to Kamenka, and also to Kiev. At that time as there was no railway between Kamenka and Kiev it was necessary to drive to the nearest station at Ostrov.

Tchaikovsky's latest exercises had been the translation of F. A. Gevaert's book on orchestration, a sequence of ballet dances which were played in Pavlovsk and later revised for the opera *Voevoda* (1868) and a Concert Overture in C minor.

In the spring of 1865 Tchaikovsky's father, now more or less moneyless, for the sake of economy decided to live with his daughter Zinaida Olkhovskaia in the Urals. At the same time he married his third wife, Elisaveta Mikhailovna Alexandrova (Lipport), who had lived with him for some years previous to their marriage.

On 30 October Tchaikovsky's String Quartet in B major (of which only the first movement survived) was played at a students' concert; on 26 November he made his debut as a conductor, directing the Conservatoire orchestra in a performance of his Overture in F later rescored for large orchestra (see p. 28); on 31 December his setting of Schiller's *Ode to Joy* was performed at the Conservatoire graduation concert, which the composer did not attend.

[12] TO ALEXANDRA DAVYDOVA   Kiev
                                                     24 August 1865

Dear Sania,

Our journey to Kiev was in the most horrible weather and if there had not been four of us I could have thrown myself into the blue water of the Dnieper. We often talked and remembered Kamenka and for some reason we could only think of it in the most sombre colours as if we had played the part of the sun there and without us it had to be cold and dark. We stayed at the Europa Hotel which was not at all bad and quite well kept. Even I do not find it too expensive although we – that is, the glutton Modia and I – had to pay 50 kopeks for a pot of coffee without cream or bread, and the pot only held two cups.

Yesterday was very dull. It never stopped raining. I tried to be a tourist and went off with Tolia and Modia to visit the ancient churches but did not go beyond St Sophia's Cathedral. A figure covered with a brocade shroud which the monk made me touch with my lips, so horrified me that I ran from there and all the insistence of my despotic brothers could not force me to continue the exploration of the Kiev churches. Alesha and Tolia left yesterday at 7 o'clock and Modia and I went to the Café Italiano where we read the papers. That was the only hour we spent without being bored. We are going now with Modosha to look for Levdik to have some photographs taken – the weather is clearing a little.

I think of Kamenka with great sorrow. I have never passed such a lovely summer before. I cannot reproach myself for having been idle but how many charming moments I remember! In one word I am returning to Petersburg with a heavy heart but with a serene conscience and the knowledge that I have not passed all my days in idleness. Vera Vassilievna who, thanks to her kind heart, did everything to make me leave Kamenka with the desire to return as soon as possible, can be sure that she has succeeded. I cannot imagine myself anywhere else but there next summer. I kiss you Sasha as hard as I can and same to Leva and the children.

My kindest regards to all your family,

P. Tchaikovsky

[13]   TO ALEXANDRA DAVYDOVA   [St Petersburg]
                                                1 September 1865

Dear Sania,

This time my letter won't be so long. The eye complaint which started in Kamenka has become much worse. In the evening I can neither write nor read. My eyes become filmed over, and in the morning I can scarcely open them, the lids are stuck together with matter. However, everybody tells me that it isn't serious. One gentleman who suffered from the same complaint, advised me to use Dr Buialsky's eye lotion. I have just bought some and after finishing this letter I will start using it.

The journey from Kiev to Petersburg was odious. Modest and I were frightfully hungry and nearly missed the train. Petersburg received us in heavy rain, and in Gatchina I witnessed such a thunderstorm as I never experienced before. My heart sank into my boots. Lightning was falling all round us. Lizaveta Mikhailovna had taken lodgings for me at an unbelievably low rent—eight silver roubles – in the house of a kind old German woman. I moved in yesterday. The room is small but very clean; my spirits are a little damped by the tiny space, after the vastness of the countryside, but it is a question of getting used to it. I saw Aunt Liza with the children – she is very pleased about her recent journey – also Aunt Katia, Piccioli, and all my friends. Aunt Katia was most touched by the few words you wrote to her in your letter to me.

Rubinstein is very pleased that I have finished the work, but he tells me I should consult a philologist about the terminology. So far I have not heard any music. Strangely enough, the day after my return they played my dances in Pavlovsk, but I only saw the announcement in the evening when it was too late to go. Laroche went and was very pleased.

I kiss you, my dear, dear Sacha, and Leva and the children as well. My kind regards to everybody. I very often think of Kamenka and its inhabitants.

P. Tchaikovsky

P.S. Tell Vera Vassilievna that I went all round Kiev without finding Levdik.

[14] TO ALEXANDRA DAVYDOVA   [St Petersburg]
                                                8 September 1865

Dear Sania,

I have been in Petersburg a whole week and still cannot get into the way of life in the capital. My lodgings, which seemed to be quite decent, I am beginning to dislike, although I must admit they are good for the price. It is only that I cannot get used to the microscopic size. The landlady is very kind and the cook has become a great friend of mine, as well as the cat she also looks after. So the future smiles at me. My eye is not better yet and I cannot work in the evenings; I fear I shall have to go to a doctor, but the very thought of this gives me the shivers. I dine alternately at Piccioli's and the house of the two aunts, who seem very cool. . . .

So far I have spent my time rather idly and feel slightly bored; this is because of my eyes, and that makes me very angry, although I know they will soon be better. I am beginning to think of the future – of what I shall do when the course at the Conservatoire ends in December, and I am more and more convinced that there is no other path for me than music. I have been' neglecting my Civil Service duties, even though with the new regulations it would be very difficult to find another job. Anyway I can't imagine living anywhere but in Petersburg or Moscow. I shall probably go to Moscow. It was Taniusha's birthday yesterday. Dear little Taniusha! How often I think of her! Kiss her, Vera and Aniuta for me – also Levushka. My very kindest regards to Nikolai Vassilievich.

I kiss you,

P. Tchaikovsky

[15] TO ALEXANDRA DAVYDOVA   [St Petersburg]
                                         1865 [probably early October]

My dear Sasha,

I am writing briefly all that has happened to me since my last letter. First of all, my eye trouble although not going *crescendo* is still no better, and all because I have not yet had the courage to go and see a doctor; but I have decided to consult Blessich on Monday. My lodgings disgust me so much that I have decided to move to Aunt Liza's, where I have taken a very decent room, cheap, but unfortunately a long way from the Conservatoire.

I work much less now than I did last year, all because of my eyes which in the evening refuse to look at notes, letters, and such work. During the week I dine mostly at Piccioli's, also at Aunt Katia's, Aunt Liza's or with Lizaveta Mikhailovna, who continues to be extremely kind and attentive; I do not know what I should have done without her: she looks after my linen, mends my coats and suits, helps me to move from lodging to lodging, visits my brothers, and so on.

In spite of some difficulties, I am feeling happier, because the ambition that gnaws at me (this is my besetting sin) has been flattered lately by some musical successes — and I foresee more ahead.

I kiss you, dear Sasha, and also Levushka and the children.

P. Tchaikovsky

[16] TO ALEXANDRA DAVYDOVA   St Petersburg
                                              22 October 1865

Dear Sania,

I got your letter two weeks ago. I did not answer because I was too lazy. I am living now at Aunt Liza's, and I am so displeased that on November 1 I am going to move. First of all, it is frightfully damp and since I have been here I have not felt well. Either I have toothache, or my arms and legs ache, and I never stop coughing. Secondly, the house is a long way from everywhere — the Conservatoire and so on. Thirdly, I never have any peace. There is a perpetual noise — bells ringing next to my room, and so on. To add to all this, I cannot bring my piano for fear it is spoilt by damp. And yet my work is getting more and more serious. For my finals at the Conservatoire I have been given the task of composing a big work. This needs peace and quiet, and also an instrument.

At the Davydovs there is always somebody ill. . . . In general, their life lately has become rather gloomy because Vera and Lizaveta Vassilievna are always ailing. She has decided not to take any singing lessons and I am afraid it will affect her morale. It is rather sad to move to Petersburg for the sake of studying music and then to watch your hopes and plans come to nought little by little. I laughed heartily over your absent-mindedness which is very like my own; I can easily imagine Papasha's astonishment when he gets your letter, in which you address him as 'mobka'. I often think of you, my loved ones, and I worry about your boredom and your desire for something else, something you cannot reach, because your wings are clipped, and you cannot fly where you wish. . .

Aunt Katia asks me to give you all her love; I very often go to see her, and whenever I want to work hard I am at her house all day long. As usual she falls ill and recovers ten times every 24 hours. Kiss Leva and the children for me. My very kindest regards to Nikolai Vassilievich.

P. Tchaikovsky

P.S. I have forgotten to give you, of all people, a hearty kiss.

Having passed his final examinations in St Petersburg, Tchaikovsky set out for Moscow on 5 January 1866 to take up a teaching position for which he was recommended by A. Rubinstein. He was to instruct in harmony at a salary of 50 roubles a month. He went without encouragement from his father who pointed out the miserable conditions likely to have to be endured. The old man quoted the cases of A. N. Serov and of M. I. Glinka, both ex-civil servants, and wished that Piotr had stayed in his safe job. H. A. Laroche, a fellow-student at St Petersburg, on the other hand, sent his friend off with good wishes and an assurance that his was 'the greatest contemporary musical talent in Russia'. At first Tchaikovsky lived with Nikolai Rubinstein who founded the Moscow Conservatoire in 1864. Five years earlier he had been responsible for launching the Russian Musical Society.

[17]   TO ANATOLI AND MODEST TCHAIKOVSKY   [Moscow]
6 January 1866
3.30 pm

My dear brothers,

Although sad my journey was without complications. You were in my thoughts all the time but I was tormented by the idea that (these last weeks) I have been worrying you by my state of despondency which has been very bad lately. But you can always be sure of my love even if I do not show it to you. I am staying at the Kokorev Hotel. I have been to see Rubinstein and have already met two directors of the Musical Society. . . .

Rubinstein was so insistent about my staying with him that I promised to do so and am moving there tomorrow. Here is my address: Moscow, House Voyeikov, flat No 9, Rubinstein. My throat is still sore. On the little cupboard in between other papers I have left the translation I was working on in the summer. Please take it, together with the scores, to the Conservatoire, to Rubinstein, to whom I had promised them before I left.

I kiss you, please do not stop loving me! Kind regards to everybody.

P. Tchaikovsky

P.S. I have just written to Papasha, write to him too.

J. A. Mann's *The Cobweb* was being played at the Malyi Theatre (with Fedotova, Shumsky, Sadovsky, and Samarin). N. D. Kashkin, the music critic, who knew of Tchaikovsky through Laroche at their first meeting, found him 'very charming and good-looking and with talent, kindness, and intelligence imprinted on his countenance'. The Overture in C minor was not accepted for performance by either of the Rubinsteins. It was first performed in 1931 in Voronezh, conducted by K. Saradzev, and published in 1952. At the time of writing the following letter Tchaikovsky's brothers – the twins, now aged sixteen – were on their way back to Law School.

[18]   TO ANATOLI AND MODEST TCHAIKOVSKY   Moscow
10 January 1866

Dear Brothers!

I am living at Rubinstein's. He is very kind and sympathetic, has none of his brother's arrogance, but on the other hand he cannot be compared as an artist to his brother Anton. I occupy a small room next to his bedroom, and to be honest, when we go to bed at the same time (which will, I think happen not very often) I feel a bit awkward. I am afraid to disturb his sleep with my squeaky pen (there is only a thin partition between us) and yet I am frightfully busy at the moment. I am at home nearly all day and Rubinstein who leads a rather dissipated life cannot stop wondering at my perseverance.

I have been once to each theatre. The opera is bad, but I do not remember experiencing such artistic pleasure as at the play. I was lucky to see a performance by the best of actors. It was *The Cobweb* which has an immense success here. I have not yet met many people but have become very friendly with a certain Kashkin, a friend of Laroche, a very good musician. One evening Rubinstein nearly took me by force to meet the Tarnovskys who happened to be very nice people. There was a popular concert here yesterday. It did not bring much profit, but was rather interesting. The orchestra was good, the chorus magnificent. I have very, very sad moments, but on the whole I feel an urge to work which gives me great satisfaction.

I have already orchestrated my summer overture and to my horror it is becoming frightfully long, which I did not expect at all; I promised Rubinstein that it will be played here first and then sent to Petersburg.

Yesterday, in bed, I thought a lot about you. I imagined all the horrors of the first night at college after the holidays; it seemed to me that Modka, with his nose stuck under the blankets, was shedding secret tears and I wanted to console him the poor boy. Not just for the sake of saying something, but, Modia, do work, work, work and make friends with Insarsky and Tolstoi not with the imbecile Lepin.

I am very much afraid you are going to stay in the same class for a second year and get into the bad graces of the administration. I am not afraid for Tolia and consequently am not giving him any advice – he works hard. My dear Tolka, I know you do not like writing letters but force yourself and write me one. You Modia, I know will do so.

I embrace you,

P. Tchaikovsky

[Moscow]
14 January 1866

Dear Tolka,

Thank you for the letter. All these last days I have not been feeling very well but am better now. Your letters give me great pleasure; yesterday I gave my first lecture, and I felt frightfully shy. But it went quite well. About my coming to Petersburg or your coming to Moscow, I must tell you that I have been wishing it as much as you have, but one cannot always do as one wishes. For nothing in the world would I agree to your spending your earnings on a journey or, what is worse, getting into debt. Besides you cannot imagine how expensive everything is here. I do not want you to be hungry or bored, but the food and the theatres will be more expensive than either you or I can afford. For the first month all my salary will have to be spent on new clothes which Rubinstein insists that I should get, saying that my present outfit is not decent enough for a professor of theory.

In other words, if one is sensible and thinks of the consequences of either my or your journey, it is better to wait until Easter, dear Tolia. Believe me that it makes me sad not to have the pleasure of seeing you, but it is wiser not to. No more for today; I have so many letters to write that I feel quite mad. I am intensely tired. I kiss you to infinity and the same to Modosha.

P. Tchaikovsky

P.S. Have just received your letter with the photographs of the Davydovs. Let me know where you found your geometry book?

[20]   TO ELISAVETA MIKHAILOVNA TCHAIKOVSKAIA

Moscow
15 January 1866

Kindest Lizaveta Mikhailovna,

Please forgive me that I have not yet written; I am extremely busy and, besides, writing letters is a real punishment for me. I have decided that it is better for me to write to Anatoli and Modest and they must inform everyone who is interested in me. All I can say is that, I pass my time rather sadly, but my work does not allow me to think about it. I experienced the greatest of pleasures here, and have twice been to the Russian theatre. I do not think that there are such good actors anywhere else in the world, and those who have not seen this company have no idea what a well acted play is. You know from my brothers that I live at Rubinstein's, and also what sort of person he is. But I doubt if I will ever get used to Moscow, it still seems to me that I am here by mistake. Everything here is terribly expensive so I must thank providence that Rubinstein has offered me a rent-free room. My lessons have not started yet, but yesterday I had to examine all the new students. I must admit I gasped at the quantity of crinolines, hair-styles, and so on. But I hope to charm all these fairies, as the ladies here are most passionate. Rubinstein does not know how to get rid of a whole army of ladies offering him their ... attentions.

I have written to Papasha.

Keep well, kindest Lizaveta Mikhailovna. My respectful regards to Sofia Mikhailovna, Alexander Mikhailovich and Ivan Mikhailovich.

P. Tchaikovsky

[21] TO ALEXANDRA AND LEV DAVYDOV   Moscow
                                                    15 January 1866

My dearly beloved Sasha and Leva!

As you know me very well you are, of course, not angry with me for my long silence; so without apology I turn to a short report of all that has happened to me since I wrote to you. I lived in Petersburg at Aunt Liza's and it was horrid – aggravated by seeing her pathetically poor circumstances, which often disturbed me. I visited your people more often than anybody else. My cantata is written and very much pleases those who had to pass judgment on it.

In general, however, I have been suffering from frightful melancholia and hatred for all mankind. This sickness has been partly, but not quite, alleviated by change of place and new impressions. What is the reason for my being in such a state I cannot say, but it has nothing to do with my finances, as some people think. First of all I have never been so indifferent to the golden calf as now; secondly, this is easily remedied and has never brought me to despair. I dream with great delight about the summer which I hope to pass with you.

Not so long ago I had an extremely vivid dream of you all and seemed clearly to hear the voice of my darling Taniusha, of whom I cannot think without a poignant love; I cannot forget how she had a fall in my room and was telling her father, half sobbing: 'I have knocked myself, Papochka!' In the summer I hope to hear her chatter away in French.

About the summer, I imagine it will not be spent in Kamenka any more but on your own estate. I hope so – passionately – both for you and myself.

There is not much I can say about my Moscow life; I am going to give lectures here on theory of music and yesterday I examined those who wish to take the course. There are lots of young ladies, and some are very pretty. I live at Rubinstein's, he is one of the most sympathetic people I have ever known. As for Moscow, I like it but doubt if I will ever get used to it. All my roots are in Petersburg, and although lately I could not stand that city any more it is still my home town.

I stay much at home, working. Sad moments come, but you get them everywhere. My brothers have written twice. They miss me but I hope to see them before Lent and at Easter; besides, summer is not all that far away. Do write dear Sania and tell me all your plans about the purchase of the new estate.

My address is: Moscow, on the Moscow [river], House Voyeikov, flat No 9, Rubinstein.

I kiss you both and also all my nieces with all my heart.

(no signature)

In both the Russian capital cities French drama and Italian opera were regularly performed. It was necessary, therefore, to distinguish the 'Russian' theatre. The eighth concert of the Russian Musical Society that season included an overture by Méhul, an aria from Mendelssohn's *Elijah*, a concerto grosso by Handel, songs by Glinka and Schubert, and Beethoven's 'Pastoral' Symphony. An Artistic Circle founded by Ostrovsky on 14 October 1865 was another source of interest for Tchaikovsky.

[22]   TO MODEST TCHAIKOVSKY   Moscow
                                       16 January 1866

Modia!

Thank you for your letter. I have nothing new to say to you, and will write about my lectures after they have started. Up till now all I have to do is to examine the new students. I went to the Russian theatre twice and enjoyed myself immensely. But these were the only pleasant moments which I experienced here. The Opera is disgusting, and the concert given yesterday at the Musical Society was also bad; in short, the music here is not to be compared with that in Petersburg. I have once or twice been at the 'Artistic Circle' and listened to Ostrovsky reading *The Abyss* and Pisemsky *The Comic*. Otherwise I am mostly at home. . . . As I have nothing more to write about and am frightfully tired (have written five letters) I am finishing this, sending you many hugs and the same to Anatoli.

P. Tchaikovsky

For God's sake let me know if you have taken my translation [see p. 15] to the Conservatoire.

A letter from Tchaikovsky to his father referred to below is not extant. The elder Tchaikovsky's reply, however, survives to show that he was now more agreeable about his son's choice of career.

[23]   TO ANATOLI AND MODEST TCHAIKOVSKY   [Moscow]
                                            23 January 1866

Dear brothers!

Do not spend all your time on letters. It is better to write once a week, but properly – something like a diary. You know how I love to hear about the college. Then I will get a clear idea about all you are doing. Now I have to make an effort to imagine you at different moments of your life. I will also write every week, maybe even twice. I have just returned from a conference of the Moscow Conservatoire Professors and a dinner given by Lanin, who is Director of the Musical Society. The Musical staff will not be as good as in Petersburg. But there are one or two decent men.

For my part I am friendly with everybody but my real friends are Rubinstein, Kashkin, Albrecht and Osberg. I have also made friends with one of the directors, the rich and well known Torletzky, and was even invited to his house a few days ago. There I was astonished to meet the former technologist Sheffer. He has grown immensely and is marrying a young lady much older than himself. I also made the acquaintance of some Tchaikovskys, ate an enormous lot, but did not take part in the dances, although I had Rubinstein's dress suit on. He looks after me like a nannie and insists on doing so. Today he presented me with six shirts, perfectly new ones (do not mention it to the Davydovs or anyone else) and tomorrow he insists upon taking me to order some new clothes. In general he is a wonderfully kind person – only I do not understand how he has earned the fame of being a great musical authority. He is a most ordinary musician and one cannot compare him to his brother.

I must also mention in the list of my friends Alexander Rubinstein's valet, a most respectable old man, and the white cat, which at the moment is here with me, and which I am passionately cuddling.

My favourite occupation is to think about summer. I have lately developed an intense love for Sasha, Leva and the children, and have decided to pass the summer at their country place with both of you. I am very happy indeed that they are going to live in their own place – but do not say anything to the Davydovs about it, they might be hurt. I also think a lot about seeing you at Easter; but concerning the week before Lent, it is better to abstain. I wrote to Papasha yesterday and have just written a long one (second one) to Avdotia Yakovlevna. I had a letter from her, full of such strong and sincere love that I was most touched and promised myself to write to her often. In my next letter I will talk to you seriously about something which is very much on my mind.

P. Tchaikovsky

Please give my love to Ippolit and tell him not to be angry with me that I did not find time to say good-bye to him.

[24] TO ANATOLI AND MODEST TCHAIKOVSKY [Moscow]
30 January 1866
Sunday

I am just back from the Zoological Gardens – which are very good here – where they gave a festival with fireworks etc. I rather enjoyed myself this week thanks to Rubinstein, I have right of entrance to the [illegible] Club which has an excellent library. I brought home a lot of good books and enjoyed reading and laughed heartily over Dickens's *Pickwick Club*, all on my own. The thought that I do it in solitude makes me laugh even more. I advise you to read that book. If you are content to read only belles lettres you should, at least choose authors like Dickens. He has much in common with Gogol, the same spontaneity and sincerity, the same gift of characterizing a whole personality in a few words, but he has not got Gogol's depth.

My lessons are getting on successfully and I am greatly admired by my Muscovite lady pupils who are most inflammable and passionate.
Here I was interrupted by the Tarnovskys who had sent for me for tea, and from there Rubinstein took me to a masquerade at the Bolshoi theatre.

My shyness is gradually disappearing. I have unfortunately met more and more people although they are all very nice. My favourites are the Tarnovskys, husband and wife, very rich people and great lovers of music: Mme Tarnovskaia is well-known as the composer of songs which are sung by Nikolsky—*I remember everything, What for,* and so on. Yesterday I was at Kashkin's house for pancakes. He has sent Laroche 10 roubles to come to Moscow for a day or two and I am happy at the thought of seeing one of the Petersburg friends. We have perpetual meetings and discussions here about our Conservatoire. The discussions are very hectic. I took part in the drafting of the Statutes and wrote a huge instruction for the Inspector which was accepted without any amendments.

Nothing much to say about yesterday's masked ball as it was exactly like all those in Petersburg. Just as impossibly boring. This week I went to the Russian theatre and saw *The Lawless Ones*, a tragedy by Pisemsky, and also a charming play, *Allegory*, by Nikolai Ivanovich Olkhovsky. By the way, my dear brothers, please visit the Olkhovskys and Lizaveta Pavlovna Ditlova (who has written to me) and go to see Apukhtin and Golitzin; I cannot understand these two, for they do not answer my letters.

The letter which Tolia mentions in the note to Modia's letter I have not received. Will you please explain to me Tolia, why you got a 5 for physical geography and will it have any bad consequences? Please let me know all particulars of how you are going to spend Shrovetide; in return I will let you know about everything of interest that takes place.

If Laroche comes I will probably spend all my time with him. I am beginning to think about an opera. All the librettos given to me by Rubinstein are extremely bad, so I have chosen another subject and want to write the words myself. It will be a simple adaptation of a tragedy. Pleshcheev, a poet who lives here, has agreed to help me. Good-bye my dears. . ..

I kiss and embrace you,

P. Tchaikovsky

The week before Lent was riotous, with dances, troika rides, and much eating – of pancakes with caviar, salmon, sour cream, and so on – and drinking. Lent itself was a period of restraint; the Imperial theatres closed for the first and fourth weeks and, of course, Holy Week. There were, however, many concerts. (Cf. p. 104f.: in 1876, unusually, the theatres were open.)

Anatoli had stated that Alexei Nikobrevich Apukhtin had written to him, saying that Piotr was complaining of his brother's behaviour to him.

[25]   TO ANATOLI TCHAIKOVSKY   [Moscow]
                                              6 February 1866
My dear Toliasha!

Forgive me for not answering at once. I decided that it would be better for you to get this letter at the college, where it would give you some sort of distraction (and not in the whirlwind of Shrovetide). This is an answer to yours of January 22 which I received on the 31st. Apukhtin ought to be ashamed! Concerning all these thoughts about 'uselessness', 'insignificance' I advise you to forget them. It is completely out of fashion. In our time such worries about oneself were fashionable and general, which only showed that our education was extremely negligent. Young men of sixteen should not spend time on trying to assess the worth of their future work.

All you must do is to see that the present is interesting and that you are satisfied with yourself (i.e. the sixteen year old Tolia), and to do so 1. you need to work and to avoid idleness so that you will be ready for hard work later on. 2. Read a lot. 3. Be honest and humble which means, that although you understand that you are not absolutely stupid it does not mean that all others are idiots and that some evil influence prevents people from understanding and appreciating your talents; in one word to prepare yourself to be an ordinary and good person – not a genius for they are above laws. 4. Do not try to please and be popular. Concerning the other fellows (which is very important as long as you are still at the college) do not be too proud, but neither must you solicit their friendship. With those who do not like you, or look down upon you, do the same, but do not start any sentimental quarrels with passionate reconciliations – and so on. 5. Do not get upset over bad marks, the unfairness of [Vassili] Schneider, all the gossip, the crazy Gorlov and Alopeus, because all this, compared with what will happen in life, is trivial. I wish you to be at the top of your class but even if you were at the bottom I would not mind, as long as I knew it was not caused by laziness. A bad 'Pravoved' [student at the college of law] can be a very nice person. 6. But the most important thing is not to be too conceited and to prepare yourself for the fate of an ordinary mortal.

You tell me it does not attract you to become a civil servant but let me tell you that I know a crowd of the most gifted, clever, educated men, who have passed their life in government offices and never imagined themselves to be unrecognized geniuses, and have consequently been perfectly happy. (For example: Pichugin, Adamov, Maslov, Satin and so on.)

I spent all Shrovetide at home. I have written and read a great deal. The frosts

here are frightful. Glad that Lent is at the door; I look upon it as the gateway
to spring and summer and I dream of summer, which I want to spend with
you at Sasha's. About the important business I was going to discuss with you.
I have decided not to; tell Modia that I will answer his letter separately.
Nothing more to tell you about, so I finish this, begging you to tell me all you
did during Shrovetide. I kiss you many times, Kiss Modia.

P. Tchaikovsky

[26] TO ALEXANDRA DAVYDOVA   Moscow
                                               7 February 1866

Dear Sasha,

I do not know if you got my first letter from Moscow. I did not post it myself,
and I have not had your reply. I should so like to have some news of you.
I am beginning to get used to Moscow, in spite of sometimes feeling very
lonely. To my astonishment the course is going very well. My shyness has left
me completely and I am beginning to assume, if I may be pompous, the
'countenance of a professor'. My pupils and especially the ladies, constantly
express their pleasure; this makes me very happy. My melancholia is gradually
disappearing, but for me Moscow is still a strange town; and it will take me
a long time to get rid of that awful thought that I may have to stay here for
many years – perhaps forever.

I am still living at Rubinstein's and shall stay here until the summer. He is a
very kind man and so in general are the Moscow people. But as far as music
is concerned Petersburg is much better. The opera here is disgusting, nor are
the concerts given by the Musical Society as good. But the Russian
Theatre here is excellent. (You have some idea of it.) Rubinstein is taking a lot
of trouble to amuse me. Twice he dragged me to a masquerade (where as
usual I was bored). He gets me free tickets for the theatres and so on. I have
completely dropped all my acquaintances except those who are musical. But
I very often go to see the Tarnovskys – a husband and wife and two charming
nieces – who are my neighbours. One of the nieces attracts me very much.
I spent Shrovetide very quietly and was at home nearly all the time. It was
not until yesterday that I went to the funfair and the circus that belongs to it.
The frost was bitter and the poor little equestrian dancers in their short
gauzy dresses were pathetic. Today is the first day of Lent and Moscow looks
absolutely dead. I am always glad when this time of the year comes, because
the 'Great Lent' makes a *trait d'union* with spring and summer. If nothing
happens to prevent it I hope to stay with you in the summer. You cannot
imagine how often I dream about this and with what delight. . . .

I get so many letters from Petersburg that I cannot find time to answer them,
but they do give me great pleasure. I am very pleased with my brothers; they
have proved that they love me sincerely and I return their affection a
hundredfold. I have received two letters from Lizaveta Vassilievna and one

from Alexandra Ivanova. From Papochka I have had no news for a long time and I am impatient to hear from him.

How are you getting on, my dear? and your lovely little girls? Kiss them warmly for me. Is Levushka very busy? and is he pleased with the way the work is getting on? Tell me all about Nikolai Vassilievich's health and moods. too. And now – my dearest, love to you all,

P. Tchaikovsky

On March 4 Tchaikovsky's Overture in F, rescored for a larger orchestra was conducted by Nikolai Rubinstein at a Moscow concert in the House of the Nobility. Although it was not noticed in the Press it aroused interest of musicians. Laroche, however, thought that the work was less satisfactory in its revised form. It was given further performances on 24 April and 1 May (see Letter 30).

[27] TO ANATOLI TCHAIKOVSKY   Moscow
                                                 6 March 1866

We are going to meet so soon that it is not worth while writing, for I shall be in Petersburg in Holy Week and all my thoughts are on the journey. Only I do not know where I should stay. Write and tell me where you think it would be best. This week has been rather stormy but very pleasant. First of all, last Sunday at the Bolshoi Theatre concert I met one Ivanov, a college friend, and went to visit him the next day. This is my first meeting with an old friend since coming to Moscow and I enjoyed it very much. On Wednesday Kologrivov arrived and this also gave me great pleasure. I frequently visit the Tarnovskys. Every evening I go to a concert and on Friday at the Rubinstein concert my overture was played and was a success.

I was called up to the rostrum and – if I may use a high flown expression – was greeted with loud and sustained applause. My *'amour propre'* was even more flattered by the ovation it was given at the supper afterwards. I was the last guest to arrive, and when I appeared the applause went on for some time. Very awkwardly I bowed all round and blushed profusely. At supper after a toast in honour of Rubinstein, he proposed one in my honour and there was another ovation. I write all these particulars because it was my first public success and naturally I found it most gratifying. (I must add that at the rehearsal I was applauded by the orchestra.) To be honest I must admit that this added a lot to the charm of Moscow. And so good-bye – answer at once, as soon as you get this letter.

[no signature]

From the middle of March until 4 April Tchaikovsky was in St Petersburg. On 4 April Karakozov attempted to assassinate the Czar – whose attempts at liberalization of the régime had brought too little too late. Rumour had it that Karakozov was a Pole. Tchaikovsky went to hear *A Life for the Czar* on 5 April. Score in hand he followed the music, unaware that everyone else in the house was only intent on ostentatiously showing patriotic feelings at those points at which the Poles were maligned. Since Tchaikovsky seemed unwilling to take part in an anti-Polish demonstration he became an object of suspicion. Uncomfortable at his predicament, he hurriedly left the theatre.

[28] TO ANATOLI AND MODEST TCHAIKOVSKY   [Moscow]
                                                  7 April 1866

Brothers!

Forgive for not writing for so long. The journey was without accidents. The news about the attempt on the life of the Czar reached us at the station where we were having tea but it was very vague; we thought the Emperor was dead and one of the ladies sitting near us shed tears while another praised the wonderful qualities of the mind and soul of the future Emperor. It was only in Moscow that I found out what had really happened. The demonstrations taking place here are indescribable. For example, when they gave *A Life for the Czar* at the Bolshoi the day before yesterday – he [the Czar] was not there at all – as soon as the Poles appeared on the stage cries of, 'Down, down with the Poles!' broke out. The chorus became confused and stopped singing, and the audience called for the [national] anthem which was played twenty times. At the end a portrait of the Emperor was brought onto the stage and the terrific noise which then started cannot be described.

I had to go straight from the railway station to give a lesson, which was a blessing as it brought me back to the everyday prose of my Moscow life. I was received here very well; there was a dinner at the Tarnovskys the same evening, then a musical evening which I opened with the overture from *Russlan and Ludmilla*. The weather is lovely and warm, just like June, and yesterday I went for a long walk in the Alexander Gardens. All conversation now revolves round the attempt on the Emperor and Komissarov has become a great celebrity in one day; at the Moscow English Club he has been unanimously elected an honorary member and he has been sent the Golden Sword of the Nobility.

I feel rather bored and, what is really silly, I think with feverish impatience of the summer, I count the days and hours, and this poisons my life and makes me afraid it will never come to pass. My journey to Petersburg, I fear, is out of the question, for from the conversation with Rubinstein I understood that the financial situation will not allow it. Last night a most awkward thing happened at the Tarnovskys; I was left alone with three women who forced me to waltz with them, each in turn, while one of them played the piano. I got so tired that I could only drag myself home with an effort.

I kiss you. Do write.

P. Tchaikovsky

[Moscow]
8 April 1866

My dear Leva and Sasha!

All Moscow is in a state of frightful excitement because of the attempt on the
Emperor's life. Demonstrations quite impossible to describe go on and on.
You will be able to read in the *Moscow News*, for example, what happened
at the Bolshoi Theatre, the day before yesterday (during *A Life for the Czar*) and
I was there. In my opinion the Moscow public has lost all sense of proportion
and reason. The opera actually did not really take place for, as soon as the
Poles appeared everybody started shouting 'Down with the Poles' and so on.
In the scene where the Poles are supposed to kill Susanin, the actor who
sang the part started fighting with the choristers – Poles – and as he is very
strong he knocked several down; the rest, seeing that the audience was
delighted about this mockery of art, truth and decency, fell down too and the
triumphant Susanin left, waving his arms, followed by terrific applause
from the Muscovites. You must agree that this was the limit.

My work is going on very well, I think I have already written to you about
my success in Moscow as a composer. On the 24th of April my overture (the
same one) will be played in Petersburg at a 'Concert-Monstre' at the Michailov
Riding School. Unfortunately I will not be there. I hope to be in Kamenka in the
second half of May (about 20th); will write again before that.

I kiss you both to exhaustion and also the children. My very kindest regards
to Nikolai Vassilievich and kindest Katerina Vassilievna; tell her that if forget
to send her my regards it is out of absent-mindedness, you know very well
how I like her.

[no signature]

Much immersed in work Tchaikovsky was seeing less of his friends than formerly,
a fact somewhat sardonically commented on by Apukhtin who observed that work
was nothing but a punishment. Tchaikovsky was also in a tense nervous state; the
'fits' to which he refers were no doubt hereditary, for his father was an epileptic
subject. Tchaikovsky found political conservatism as depressive as it was oppressive.
Count Mikhail Muraviev was Governor General in Vilna between 1863 and 1865
and notorious for his suppression of the Poles in 1863. Mikhail Katkov, an apostle of
Panslavism, was a notable reactionary publicist.

So far as his work was concerned Tchaikovsky was busy with his First Symphony
('Winter Daydreams', op. 13), which was to be finished in November; an Overture (op.
15) based on the Danish National Anthem, in honour of the State Visit to Moscow of
the Grand Duke Alexander preparatory to his marriage to Princess Dagmara (the visit
was postponed until 2 May 1867. See reference to Sokolniki Park, p. 33). The marriage
took place on 9 November and when the Overture was played on the occasion of
the visit to Moscow of the pair they expressed their appreciation to the composer.
Towards the end of the year there was hope that Ostrovsky would undertake a
libretto for *Voevoda*. This he did in the early part of 1867, when Tchaikovsky started

work on the music for the opera. In Letter 32 he notes temporarily losing as much of the libretto as he had by then received.

The reopening of the Moscow Conservatoire in September 1866 in better accommodation brought an improvement to Tchaikovsky's fortunes, and he now earned a minimum of 100 roubles a month. At this time Tchaikovsky and N. Rubinstein were living in an annexe to the Conservatoire.

[30] TO ANATOLI TCHAIKOVSKY   [Moscow]
                                                 25 April 1866
                                                 (in the evening)

I have not heard from you for some time and feel a little sad. In general I am forgotten by everybody and have no idea what is going on in Petersburg. My days are very regular and this is how I pass them. I stir between 9 and 10. Still lazying in bed I talk to Rubinstein and then we have tea together; then I either give lessons from 11 to 1 or work at my symphony (which is not getting on very well) and in that case I stay in my room until half past two; when either Kashkin or Valzek (she is a professor of singing and my new friend) visit me. At 2.30 I go to the Theatre Square to Oumetin's bookshop to read the daily papers and from there I sometimes walk to the Kuznecky Most [Blacksmith's Bridge]. At 4.0 I mostly dine at the Tarnovskys, or with Nilus (only three times in the last three weeks), or in a pub. After dinner I go for another walk or sit in my room. In the evening I nearly always have tea at the Tarnovskys and sometimes go to a club (three times to the Artistic, twice to the Merchants and once to the English Club) where I read the periodicals. I usually return home about 12, when I write my symphony, or letters, and read in bed till late.

I have been sleeping very badly lately. My 'apoplectic strokes' have returned stronger than ever, I always know when I go to bed if I am going to have one in which case I try not to fall asleep. The day before yesterday, for example, I did not sleep at all. My nerves are in an awful state because of: (1) my symphony which is not going well at all; (2) Rubinstein and Tarnovsky, who having noticed that I am easily frightened, try all they can to scare me in all sorts of ways; (3) the ever present thought that I am going to die soon and will not have time to finish my symphony. In one word I wait for the summer as one waits for the promised land and I hope to find in Kamenka peace of mind, oblivion from all failures, and good health. Since yesterday I have stopped drinking vodka, wine and strong tea.

Although I am at the Tarnovskys nearly every day and feel perfectly at home there and no one, thank God, tries to entertain me, they make me furious by their impossible old-fashioned, futile attitudes, the typical Moscow love for everything obsolete, conservative – what is called Muravievshchina, Katkovshchina, and so on. In short, I hate the human race and would love to live in a desert with a very small retinue.

My dear Tolia, I shiver at the thought that we are going to quarrel as often this summer as we did last year.

I have already ordered the coach ticket for the 10th of May.

I kiss dear Modosha, thank him for his letter and will answer him soon.

P. Tchaikovsky

[31]   TO ANATOLI TCHAIKOVSKY   [Moscow]
                                                 8 November 1866

My dear friend!

I am well, as usual, and as happy as possible. I am living in peace with everybody and think every hour about our meeting in Petersburg in the near future. I have completely finished the overture for Princess Dagmara, but it seems that her Moscow visit has been postponed until April, and there was no need to hurry. Therefore I am going to correct my symphony, and then, perhaps, I will start on an opera. There is some hope that Ostrovsky himself will make a libretto from *Voevoda*.

I have met new people, one of them being the Prince Odoevsky and another the first Moscow beauty, Princess Meshcherskaia, to whose house I went last night. I do not remember if I have ever mentioned Albrecht to you; this gentleman plays an important part in my Moscow life, consequently I must say a few words about him. First of all, he is the nicest person in the whole of Moscow. We became friends last year and now I have grown to love him and am used to him so much that I feel completely at home in his family, which is a great consolation to me. Also I have become very attached to his two sweet children who, in their turn, love me very much. His wife is expecting another baby very soon and I have been asked to be the godfather.

Albrecht has the post of inspector at the Conservatoire and also lives here. Rubinstein and I dine at his house nearly every day as paying guests. As to the Tarnovskys, I go there quite often but not as much as last year. Here is a rather amusing menu of a dinner we had at Prince Odoevsky's with Rubinstein, Laub, Kossmann and Albrecht – show it to the Davydovs. One of these days I will have my photograph taken and will send it to you. You ask why I have no money? I have sometimes plenty of it but the expenses are so large! What about Bokso [the tailor]? A new suit and a warm coat? Today I am sending my debt to Papochka. I kiss you with all my heart. . . .

P. Tchaikovsky

[32]   TO ANATOLI TCHAIKOVSKY   [Moscow]
                                                 2 May 1867
                                                 (in the evening)

I am beginning to fear that I will not get any news from you about your

32

examinations. I am most interested to know how you managed in Roman Law, what came after, and what you are getting ready for now? Do find a free moment and let me know. Nothing much to say about myself. I was upset all last week because of: (1) bad weather, (2) no money, (3) completely losing all hope of finding the libretto. There is nothing to say about the festivals here, for accounts of them have appeared in all the papers.

I did not go to the festival in Sokolniki yesterday but preferred to read *Smoke*. I read it all last evening and do not regret it. I see Laroche very often, and recently met a most interesting person at his house, Professor Bugaev of Moscow University. He is extremely learned and a very clever chap. A few days ago he kept us up half the night, talking about astronomy and all the new discoveries in this field. Oh God! What ignoramuses we are when we leave college and how horrified I am at my own ignorance when I meet a really well read and enlightened person. I will repeat to you what Postels used to say; 'Read, my dears, and reflect, reflect and read!'

Write about Modest's examinations, tell him to write himself; he will get a letter from me next week. It is up to you to decide about what you want me to do in the summer. I will be in Petersburg about the 28th of May.

I embrace Papochka and all the others. Has Sasha left?

P. Tchaikovsky

[33] TO ANATOLI TCHAIKOVSKY   [Moscow]
                                                31 August 1867

I have just returned from Ostrovsky and was given your letter brought by Teviashev. Moscow I found just as usual. There is not much to do and I wander aimlessly all day through the Conservatoire and in the town. Laroche is now living very far away with Katkov (where he has free lodgings); they have become great friends and Laroche is delighted with Katkov. Ostrovsky continues to deceive me, I read in the papers in Petersburg that he had finished the libretto but it is not true and it was with great difficulty that I got half the first act out of him. At present I am busy arranging my room and am buying a large table which will encourage me to stay at home and write my opera. I want to finish it this winter. . . .

I have not much to say about myself except for one thing: I have obviously got very used to Moscow. It is not nearly as hateful now as it was at the same time last year. From September 2 I will dine again with the Albrechts. Meanwhile I live like 'a bird in the sky'; I have been twice to the English Club, I wish I could be a member, but it is much too expensive.

I kiss you. Write. Tell Modest to write, and not to drink.

P. Tchaikovsky

In the *Russian Annals* (no. 8) Laroche published his paper, 'The historical study of music', used as an introductory lecture on musical history at the Moscow Conservatoire. An article on Glinka appeared in No. 10. These, and other of his articles gave Laroche a prominent place among Russian music critics. A song heard by Tchaikovsky at Kunzevo was introduced both into *Voevoda* and *Oprichnik*.

[34] TO ANATOLI TCHAIKOVSKY   [Moscow]
                                                28 September 1867

My dear friend Tolia,

I am perfectly well in mind and body and wish you the same. There is nothing new in my life but here are some particulars: (1) On Mondays (in fact at Rubinstein's) we have big musical evenings, with music and card playing. (2) I went with Laroche to see *Tartuffe* at the Little Theatre, excellently acted with Samarin and Shumsky in the principal parts. (3) Laroche has written and published a little article in the *Russian Annals* and for the next number he is preparing a sequence of articles on Glinka. We have seen each other very rarely all through the month but these last days we were inseparable thanks to the fine weather. (4) We spent a whole day in Kunzevo, a charming place six versts away from Moscow and wrote down a lovely song straight from the lips of a peasant girl. (5) Last Sunday we stayed in the country, sixty versts from here at Prince Trubezkoi's place, with Rubinstein, Laub and Kossmann. Tomorrow, because the weather is so wonderful I am going back there until Monday morning. The opera is getting on, and as soon as Ostrovsky is back from Petersburg I will attack him again. (7) My money matters are as bad as yours. I am expecting Papochka's arrival with impatience; I understand he will be here quite soon. I met Sorokhtin once (at the French Theatre, which is very bad), and he sends his regards. Andrei Apukhtin will probably be here; received from Lelia [Apukhtin] yesterday a tragic letter in French. What is the reason for his feeling so unhappy? Thank Modest for this letter. My regards to Vera Vassilievna and tell her I will return the play soon.

P. Tchaikovsky

Vladimir Kashperov's *The Storm* was performed on 30 October. At the first concert of the Russian Musical Society on 4 November there were works by Mendelssohn (*Melusina*), Meyerbeer, Moniuszko, Schubert, Glinka, Balakirev, and Beethoven (Sixth Symphony). Regarding (4) above: 1 verst = 3500 feet.

[35] TO ANATOLI TCHAIKOVSKY   [Moscow]
                                                [31 October 1867
                                                beginning of November]

Anatoli!

A long time since I had any news from you all. I hope you are well, otherwise you would have written. All is well here and there is nothing fresh to mention.

Our first concert will be on Saturday which makes me very happy, as Muscovites on the whole prefer physical to spiritual pleasures; i.e. they eat and drink a lot. These concerts will feed my musical needs, for without them I feel like a bear in his cave who exists only by his own strength – I mean my own compositions which refuse to come out of my head. I do everything I can to lead a quiet life but it is impossible to exist in Moscow without drinking and over-eating. These last fine days, for example, I returned home late with an overfilled belly. Still, do not think I am being idle, I am very busy every morning until dinner time.

Yesterday Kashperov's opera was given here for the first time. I think that since operas have been written nothing as foul has ever appeared; to be honest the opera had no success but it was not a complete flop thanks to Menshikova's wonderful singing (I am writing a part for her) and the noise and bangs in the third act. . . .

I kiss you. Kiss Papochka, Lizaveta Mikhailovna and Modest from me.

P. Tchaikovsky

While staying at the Baltic resort of Hapsal, near Riga, Tchaikovsky composed his *Souvenir of Hapsal* (Op. 2), dedicated to Vera Vassilievna Davydova, the unmarried daughter of Alexandra Ivanovna. Tchaikovsky had found Vera attractive company in 1863. He orchestrated his *Dances of the serving maids*, or 'characteristic dances' (to be used within *Voevoda*), which were played at the second Music Society concert on 2 December 1867 and then twice repeated. They were published in piano duet form by Yurgenson as Op. 3 in 1868.

At a reception held in honour of Berlioz, who conducted two concerts in Moscow, Tchaikovsky made an excellent, complimentary speech in French. Although his reputation was increasing in Moscow Tchaikovsky was annoyed at the slights he continued to suffer in St Petersburg. N. I. Zaremba and A. Rubinstein refused to play the whole 'Winter Daydreams' symphony, and N. Rubinstein conducted only the two middle movements at a St Petersburg concert on 11 February 1867. The dances, for which Tchaikovsky asked to be officially requested, were conducted by N. Rubinstein on 25 January 1869. The symphony was eventually played in its entirety in Moscow under N. Rubinstein on 3 February 1868. This was most successful and the composer was given a rousing ovation to which, according to his friend the Countess Kapnist, he responded awkwardly. It was soon after this that Tchaikovsky gave up seeing the Lopukhins at whose house he had seen plays performed and for some of which he had composed music (Letter 38).

On 19 February Tchaikovsky made his initial appearance at the Bolshoi Theatre as a conductor. This terrified him, as Kashin and Laroche reported. The former wrote how Tchaikovsky, having reached the podium, 'looked like a man in despair. He had completely forgotten the score, could not see the notes, and gave wrong directions to the orchestra. Fortunately they knew the dances and got through them without accident. . . . P.T. told me later that out of sheer fright he had a feeling that he could not hold his head straight, that it was bending sideways, and that all his thoughts were centred on how to keep it straight.'

[Moscow]
25 November 1867

Modest!

How are you getting on and why can't you write? You must be ashamed.

The only news I have for you is that our Metropolitan [Archbishop] has died.

Laroche is living with us now, as he has been forbidden to go out and does not want to miss his lessons. As a result I am more often at home; our friend Klimenko is also here and comes to see us nearly every day. He said he met Anatoli at Mamgig's and told us that the latter's wife is the greatest bitch on earth; tell Anatoli not to be too friendly with her.

My opera is getting on quite well. I have written the whole of the third act, and the dances from the opera will be played at the next concert; I orchestrated them in Hapsal. Do you ever meet our Hapsal friends? What is Rosen doing, does he visit you? For God's sake tell Vera Vassilievna that I beg forgiveness at her feet for having kept back for so long my piano pieces but I could not do otherwise for reasons which had nothing to do with me. Tell her that they will be published and the original manuscript returned to her.

I kiss you and Anatoli.

P. Tchaikovsky

[Moscow]
12 December 1867

.You want to know if I am coming to Petersburg? I think it wiser not to. First of all I have not enough money for the journey, secondly Berlioz is coming here during the Christmas holidays and is giving one public concert and another one at the Musical Society instead of the 4th ordinary one. I have to postpone my visit until Shrovetide or Lent. Tell Lizaveta Mikhailovna that as soon as I have any money I will send some. Which of you was at home when Rubinstein came to see you and how did you like him? Laroche lives with us because of his illness, and this has greatly influenced my way of living. It means that I am more often at home in the evenings.

On the 5th November, we had a 'Pravoved' dinner [an 'Old Boys' dinner]. I sat next to Sorokhtin. The dinner was spoiled by the behaviour of Arseniev [Vice-President of Law Court] who wanted to explain his misunderstandings with the lawyer Ourussov which brought a vehement protest from the majority of us and nearly ended in a scandal.

My dances were very successful here, and Yurgenson even wants to publish them in the form of a piano duet. I had a letter from Petersburg begging me to send them there but I answered that I will do so only if I get an official paper signed by the Board of Directors. Zaremba, via Rubinstein, told me I will get one. If so, then you will hear them. These mean individuals look down upon me too much, one has to spit at them to make them feel one's worth.

I kiss you and Modest.

P. Tchaikovsky

P.S. Not having any money I answer by post [rather than by sending a telegram]. I have already told you that I agree to everything. Have nothing against bathing in Hapsal.

[38] TO ANATOLI TCHAIKOVSKY   [Moscow]
                                      [27–28? January 1868]

Dear Tolia!

(1) . . . Word of honour I would very much like to see you. (2) Concerning money, I honestly have very little of it; but that is not important, I would have written to you 'come' but for two reasons. (3) Laroche is living with us and is occupying my room, as it is the warmest one, and I have no room of my own at the moment, and sleep where I can. Of course one could find enough place for you but I would prefer you to come when I have my own corner where we could really be together and do what we like.

(4) Also I am sorry that you cannot be here on the third of February for the concert. If this could have been possible all difficulties would have gone to the devil. . . .

The most interesting news is Laroche's engagement to a very charming Conservatoire pupil, a very poor girl, but – this is astonishing – she really loves him. All the same I think it is silly of him.

The plays, two of them, at the Lopukhins went off quite well.

I kiss you and beg to do the same to Modest.

P. Tchaikovsky

[39] TO ANATOLI TCHAIKOVSKY   [Moscow]
                                      [Beginning of February 1868]

Dear Tolia!

Sorry for not answering at once.

Here is the answer to your question:

(1) My symphony will not be played any more; the two series of concerts were

given at the beginning of the season because the big hall was not ready and one could not seat 1500 people in the smaller one.

(2) If I am not mistaken this is all you wanted to know. My symphony was a great success, especially the Adagio. Shrovetide was rather dull – not at all like last year. All I did was to eat pancakes of different kinds: 'Aristocratic, Merchant Navy, Artistic' etc. You know Klimenko is still here, he came for a week but was so charmed by Moscow that he could not leave it; he will probably soon come to stay here for good. What a delightful person he is. If I may quote Modia: 'He loves me so much that I do not know how to thank him.' He is going to Petersburg very soon and I have asked him to visit you both at home and at the college.

On Monday a big concert is going to take place here, at the Bolshoi Theatre, in aid of the starving, and I am to conduct my own dances. I am certain that it will be awful as I am more and more convinced of my lack of capacity to do so. But I could not refuse the request. Besides it is an easy piece. Today I have started the orchestration of the third act; I want to finish the opera before the summer; I have in mind another libretto.

No time to write, so I kiss you and remain,

Yours,

P. Tchaikovsky

tell Modest to write!

[40] TO ALEXANDRA DAVYDOVA   Paris
                                              20 July–1 August 1868
                                              Saturday

My dear friend Sashura!

Writing down the date I remembered that today is the birthday of our dear old man. I wish this kindest of creatures a long and happy life to the joy of all of us. . . .

You probably already know in what circumstances and how I left for abroad. So far as the material side goes, it is excellent. I am with very rich people who are also very kind and like me. This means that socially speaking all is well. In spite of that I long for my homeland where there are so many people dear to me, with whom I can only be together in the summer. I am rather angry at the thought that out of all the people who would have been glad to pass the three holiday months with me, I chose not those whom I love best but those who are the richest; but it is also true that the attraction of foreign lands played an important part.

The story of my present wanderings is very simple, and uninteresting. I stayed in Berlin a week and have been in Paris five weeks. We hoped, when we left, that we could visit the most picturesque places in Europe, but because of Shilovsky's illness and because it was important that he should see the eminent doctors here, we got stuck in Paris and unwillingly have to stay here. I pass my time as follows. I get up rather late, go down to have my breakfast, and to read the papers. Back in my room about 12 I undress completely (the heat is indescribable) and work until dinner time. At 6 o'clock I either have dinner with my fellow travellers or alone. The evenings I am at the theatre. One must give Paris its due. There is no other town in the world where you get so much comfort and so many pleasures for so little money.

The theatres here are wonderful not by what they look like, but by knowing how to achieve the best effects in the most simple way; for instance, they are so good at presenting a play without any specially talented actors that one gets a better impression than from a play at home – acted by such geniuses as Sadovsky, Shumsky, Samoilov, but produced and rehearsed anyhow, without any ensemble. By the way, Samoilov is here. I met him, he is very much interested in you and made me promise to remember him to you. As to operas, I must say again that I have not heard any singer here with a really wonderful voice; but what perfect interpretation! How well everything has been studied, and well acted, how seriously even the smallest details are handled, the sum of it all giving the proper effect. We have no idea of such perfect production.

I have seen all the different sights of Paris before, during my first visit, so I do not lead the life of a tourist, who runs round churches, museums and palaces. I am living as a man completely dedicated to his work and crawl out of my cave only in the evening. To be honest I must say that noisy, brilliant Paris is not the ideal place for work, like the Thun Lake in Switzerland or the banks of the smelly but dear Tiasmin [the Kamenka river] which has the good fortune to flow past the house where the most charming and beloved of people live. What are these people doing? How have they passed the summer? My heart aches at the thought of their solitude. My dear, my beloved Sashura, when will I see you again?

In a week's time we are going straight back to Petersburg. I want to go for a few days to Silamegy to see my brothers and your people. I embrace you and Leva and everybody.

P. Tchaikovsky

Désirée Artôt had been in Moscow since the spring but she did not make her debut there until 21 September, when the Italian company to which she belonged gave a performance of Rossini's *Otello*. Tchaikovsky was much attracted by Artôt and their relationship was one of the significant romantic episodes in his life. Their friendship became talked about and during the winter Anatoli wrote to say that people were confidently predicting their marriage. The *Romance* (Op. 5) was dedicated to Artôt (Letter 46).

At the beginning of a new session at the Conservatoire Tchaikovsky's salary was raised from 1200 to 1441 roubles. Meanwhile Ostrovsky was drafting a new libretto (Letter 43) but one which was not to be used by Tchaikovsky. On 21 October

Tchaikovsky finished the first draft of the symphonic poem *Fatum* (op. 77), which he orchestrated some weeks later (Letter 50).

[41]   TO ANATOLI TCHAIKOVSKY   [Moscow]
                                                 10 September 1868

Dear Tolinka!

Thank you for your letter, and apologies from me for having put off my answer for so long. Now I will tell you briefly and exactly what happened to me since we parted. On the day of my return to Moscow I got drunk at Rubinstein's dinner which he gave for his friends; how typical for Moscow, whose foible is gluttony. The yearly dinner was on September 1 – so more drinking. (I forgot to mention that on the 30th of August I dined at Ostrovsky's.) Lessons started on September 2 and I have more work than before. I had lost the habit of giving tuition and felt so shy during the first one that I had to leave my pupils for 10 minutes so as not to faint.

I do not remember if it was on the 2nd or the 3rd that I met Apukhtin at the theatre. The next day we had dinner together at the English Club. After dinner he fainted, which really frightened me; but I did not lose my presence of mind and with great difficulty dragged him out into the garden, where he soon recovered. He probably had too much to eat. The next evening we went to the Shilovskys and he charmed everybody with his stories. Then he stayed two days with the Shakhovskys at their country place; and last night I met him at the Opera, which was the first night of the Italian one. They gave *Otello*; Artôt sang most charmingly and a young, very good tenor called Stanio made his debut. After the opera we went to the club and had a nice evening.

This, I think, is all of any interest that happened in the last ten days.

Gedeonov came to Moscow and instructed that the rehearsals of my opera *Voevoda* should start at once. The vocal scores have been distributed. But I doubt if it will be ready for October as Gedeonov would like. With the Italians here it is practically impossible, and I reckon it will only be on from January. No real news, and I do not know what more to say. Luckily the Musical Society concerts are starting later and I will have time to cook something up.

Laroche is back and told me about his meetings with you and Modia. I went to see him the day before yesterday, with Rubinstein in the morning and with Klimenko in the evening. He and his wife live very cosily in the same flat with Yurgenson.

My darling boy, I kiss you many times and beg you to write as often as possible. Yesterday I had a letter from Modinka and will write to him soon. (Have forgotten again; I saw Glatter yesterday at the Opera he told me about you two.)

Embrace Papochka for me and Lizaveta Mikhailovna. I will also write to him.

P. Tchaikovsky

TO MODEST TCHAIKOVSKY   Moscow
                                                   13 September 1868

Dear Modinka!

I am most grateful for your rather gloomy, but kind, letter. At your age it is a
bit early to live in the past and yet you put so much value on it, as if all the
world had come to an end for you. Do not forget that you are only beginning
to live. This sounds pompous but it is true. Please work hard and finish in
the 9th grade [of the Civil Service] so as not to spoil the reputation of our
'eminent' family. Tolia has probably read my letter to you in which I describe
my life here. Apukhtin stayed twice for the night. We had dinner together every
day, and went either to the theatre or the club in the evenings; he charmed
everybody here and, to my great sorrow, left yesterday.

The Italian Opera began with the debut of the young tenor Stanio in *Otello*,
he had immense success. Begichev presented me with a reserved seat for all
the performances. I am terrifically busy. Two days ago I got a summons to
report at the theatre and to my great astonishment I found out that there had
been already two rehearsals for the chorus and that yesterday was the first
reading of the solo parts. I was present and accompanied the singers. Just
imagine, it seems that Gedeonov had ordered the opera to be ready on the
11th of October and everybody now is getting nearly crazy to please His
Excellency. I myself doubt if it is possible to learn such a difficult opera in
one month and am in fear of all the complications I will have to endure.
Rehearsals will take place every day. All the singers are pleased with the opera.
I have more work than ever at the Conservatoire. I shall get more money, but
I am so tired. Nothing much has changed in my life since last year. The plan to
live independently has evaporated. When I mention to Rubinstein that I am not
entirely at ease in his flat and that I feel ashamed to live free of charge, he
was very hurt and promised to see that I would not be disturbed by anyone.
I dine, as before, as a paying guest, at Albrecht's but very often miss going
there.

It is not true what you say that Laroche has changed towards you, he spoke to
me about you with great affection. He lives very charmingly; he and his wife
also have season tickets for the visit of the Italian Opera. I embrace you with
all my heart, my dearest friend, and am your faithful brother

P. Tchaikovsky

[43] TO ANATOLI TCHAIKOVSKY   Moscow
                                                   25 September 1868

Since I wrote last I have had plenty of worries. You know that they wanted to
have my opera played in October. The rehearsals had started, the scores had
been copied, and I was to be present at each rehearsal; although they were
only preliminary ones. Well, seeing that it was impossible to get the opera

ready in such a short time I said to the directors that, as long as the Italian Opera is here and the orchestra and chorus are being distracted by it, I will not give them the full score and wrote about it to Gedeonov. Now the rehearsals have been stopped and the Opera has been put off until the Italians have left. Hence I have more free time now.

I must say that Menshikova actually knows nearly all her own part; I had dinner with her today and she sang some of the arias not at all badly. Time flies fast and is full of fun. But, you know who poisons my life here? It is Vassily Vassilievich Davydov. He nags me to help him to be taken on as stage designer at the Bolshoi, and forces me to run about town to see Valz and others. What is even more boring, he wants me to visit him.

I have good news for you about my compositions; I had dinner with Ostrovsky a few days ago and he offered to write an absolutely new, and grand libretto. He has been thinking about it for twenty years but up till now did not offer it to anyone and, at last, has chosen me. The action takes place in Babylon and Greece at the time of Alexander the Great, who has one of the principal parts in the opera. Two classical nations of the ancient world would clash in it – the Greeks and the Jews. The hero is a young Jew, betrayed in his love by a Jewish maiden, who out of pride and ambition prefers Alexander to him. In the end the young Jew becomes a prophet. You cannot imagine what a grand theme it is. Meanwhile I am writing a symphonic poem called *Fatum*.

P. Tchaikovsky

The Italian opera has a tremendous success. Artôt is a grand person; we are great friends. . . . Why does no one write? I kiss with all my heart Papochka, Lizaveta Mikhailovna and also you and Modia.

P. Tchaikovsky

Auber's *Le domino noir* was selected for Artôt's benefit. The Italian company disapproved of spoken dialogue in an opera and commissioned Tchaikovsky to supply recitatives and add some choruses, for which he was paid 150 roubles. Artôt sang the ensemble numbers in Italian and her own solos in French.

Laroche's article on the Italian opera was very scathing; only Artôt being exempt from his strictures. Unlike some critics, Laroche was willing to try his hand at composition and he was at this time busy composing an opera – *Carmozine* – on a libretto from A. Musset (Letter 45). The overture was played on 4 April 1869 (Letter 51).

[44]   TO ANATOLI TCHAIKOVSKY   [Moscow]
                                                       21 October 1868

Dear Tolia,

It was really shameful of me not to have answered your letter at once but on the day I got yours I had no money and did not want to write without sending

you some. . . . So my dear friend, do not be angry with me. I am terribly busy
writing the recitatives and choruses for the 'Domino Noir' by Auber, which is
being put on for Artôt's Benefit, for which work I will probably get
some money from Merelli. I have become great friends with Artôt and am
very much in her good graces; I have rarely met such a charming, clever and
kind woman.

Anton Rubinstein was here. He played twice like a god and was an incredible
sensation! He has not changed at all and is as charming as ever. . . .
Lately I have been going more often to the 'Artistic Circle'. I usually play
'Yeralash' [sort of whist] when I am there, the usual stake being half a kopek,
and then have supper with Ostrovsky, Sadovsky and Yvokini who are all
charming and amusing.

Laroche has recently become a Moscow celebrity because of his two articles in
the *Moscow Gazette* about the Italian Opera. He is being very much abused
by the Italophiles, and they even talked about beating him up.

I have written an orchestral fantasia – *Fatum.*

Please, show the next lines to Papochka.

'Papochka, for God's sake forgive me for not having written. I take advantage
of your kindness but you know that I love you terribly. My regards and kisses
to Lizaveta Mikhailovna. I will write on the 1st and send part of what I owe.'

Modia, I will also write to you in a day or so. I embrace all of you.

Take the enclosed paper to Bernard or send somebody.

P. Tchaikovsky

[45]   TO MODEST TCHAIKOVSKY   Moscow
                                                      [November 1868]

Ach! Modenka! I simply must pour out all my feelings into your artistic soul.
If you only knew what a singer and actress Désirée Artôt is! In all my life
I have never before been under the spell of such an artist. And I am sorry that
you neither can hear nor see her. How charmed you would be by the grace of
her movements and even were you to see her in repose.

Why don't you write more about your daily life? I think you have plenty of
free time.

I, for my part, can only say the following about our friends in Moscow. I do
not visit the Davydovs and Katerina Vassilievna at all, sinful person that I am;
first of all, I have no time, secondly it is deadly dull. Laroche now is in a sad
state; to get the two thousand roubles promised by Khludov, he must have
the full score of his opera ready for January 1 but up till now he is far from
having composed all of it, which means that he will not manage in time in
spite of sitting at home every night. He lives happily with his wife; they gave

a dinner recently in honour of his wife's name day. He asked me to give you his very kind regards.

Volodia Shilovsky has probably been to see you so there is nothing to say about him. I am expecting a good sum of money from Merelli. If I manage to keep some of it until the first days of December I hope to come for a day or two to Peter[sburg]. N. Rubinstein has been invited to play and conduct on the 3rd of December at the concert of the Musical Society. He wants very much for me to come with him since my dances are going to be performed. What do you mean by changes in your character? I have not understood a word. Write more clearly and also let me know how you are getting on with your studies?

I kiss Papochka, Tolia, Lizaveta Mikhailovna. Write – I embrace you heartily, my dearest boy.

P. Tchaikovsky

R.M.S. concerts had taken place on 9 and 19 October and Anton Rubinstein took part in both.

In the St Petersburg concert of 3 December (repeated on 25 January, 1869) the dances from *Voevoda* were played. Otherwise the programme included works by Goldmark, Litolff, Liszt, and A. Rubinstein ('The Ocean' symphony). The concert in aid of poor students took place in Moscow on 8 December, Artôt being one of the artists, and N. Rubinstein being the conductor.

[46] TO MODEST TCHAIKOVSKY   Moscow
[Middle of December 1868]

My dear friend Modka!

It is a long time since I have written to you my Modosha, but this was because of all the circumstances which prevented me from doing so, for, all my free time I have been giving up to a person of whom you have certainly heard and whom I love dearly. Please, also tell Papochka not to be vexed at my not writing to him about what everybody is talking about. The fact is that nothing decisive has yet happened and that when the time comes and everything is decided, either one way or another, he will be the first to hear about it from me.

My musical affairs are as follows: two of my piano pieces [op. 4] will be coming out in the next days; I have made a piano duet of twenty-five Russian songs, which are also being published, and I am orchestrating a fantasia [i.e. *Fatum*] for the fifth concert of the Musical Society. A few days ago a concert was given on behalf of poor students and a certain person sang for the last time before leaving. My dances were played with great success at the same concert and Rubinstein played my new piano piece which is dedicated to Artôt.

You are proper cads for not writing; you especially – not to write a whole month and expect answers before writing!

As before, I am often at the Artistic Circle where I usually have my supper. Ach! If only you knew, Modka, how everybody loves me! Two of my great friends are the old boys Yvokini and Sadovsky. The latter shows me his love in the most original way: during supper a large apple is served which he peels carefully and cuts into small pieces; then the apple is fed to me, during which ceremony he keeps on sighing deeply and repeating: 'Oh! my dear little father. Oh! my dear friend!' Only when the last bit of apple has been eaten am I allowed to leave the club and go home.

Up till now I have not decided if I will come for the holidays to Petersburg; I will let dear Papochka know in four or five days.

Give a great hug to your beloved brother Tolia, embrace Papochka and Lizaveta Mikhailovna and remember

your

P. Tchaikovsky

[47] TO ILYA PETROVICH TCHAIKOVSKY [Moscow]
26 December 1868

My dear, my beloved Papochka!

To my great sorrow circumstances did not permit me to come to Petersburg. The journey would have cost me at least 100 roubles which, at the moment I have not got. So I wish you a happy New Year from afar. There is no need to add that I wish you happiness and all the very best. I am sure you have heard about my possible marriage and are hurt that I have not told you anything about it; so here is the full record of what has happened. I met Artôt for the first time last spring but had been at her house only once after her Benefit Concert. During the first months after she returned here in the autumn I did not meet her even once. She mentioned that she wondered why I hadn't done so; and I probably would never have gone to see her – you know how difficult it is for me to meet new people – if it had not been for Anton Rubinstein, who was passing through Moscow and dragged me with him when he went to visit her.

Since then I got little notes nearly every day from her inviting me to come and gradually I got used to spending every evening with her. Soon we were inflamed by the same feelings for each other and exchanged mutual confessions of love. Naturally the question of marriage arose. It is what we both wish and will take place in the summer, if nothing comes to prevent it. But unfortunately there are complications. First of all her mother who is always with her, has a great influence over her daughter and is against our marriage; she finds me too young and probably fears that I shall force Artôt to live in Russia. Secondly, my friends, and especially [N.] Rubinstein, are doing all they possibly can to prevent me from realizing this plan. They say that becoming the husband of a famous singer I shall have to play the miserable part of my wife's husband –

45

i.e. will have to travel with her to all the corners of Europe, live on her money, lose the habit of work and stop doing so; in one word, that when my love for her cools there will only be left hurt pride, despair and ruin. This could be prevented if she agreed to leave the stage and live with me in Russia but she says that in spite of her love to me, she could not think of dropping the career which gives her fame and money and to which she is accustomed. She has now left for Warsaw and we have decided that in the summer, I shall visit her at her estate near Paris and we shall decide our fate then.

As she cannot leave the stage, so I in my turn am not sure of being able to sacrifice all my future for her sake; as it is obvious that I shall then lose the opportunity of going forward along my own road. All of which, my dearest Papochka, makes my position extremely difficult. On the one hand I have learned to love her with all my heart and at the present moment it seems impossible to live without her, on the other, cold reason makes me think seriously about the possibility of all the misfortunes which have been described to me by my friends. I am expecting, my dear, a letter from you, telling me what you think about it all. I am perfectly well, my life runs smoothly with only one exception that she is not here any more and I miss her.

Sasha Karzova was here recently and I met her at the theatre and had dinner with her the next day at A. P. Berens's house. He, his wife and Sasha made me promise to tell you that they send you their best regards.

I embrace heartily Lizaveta Mikhailovna and wish her a happy New Year. I also kiss my brothers and am sending them a note which they must take to Bernard's shop and then have a good time each on 10 roubles (in silver); tell them that it is a shame to count letters and answers from a man who is up to his neck in work.

I am always your loving son

P. Tchaikovsky

I will send Lizaveta Mikhailovna part of my debt after the 1st.

Kashkin described how much Tchaikovsky suffered when the rehearsals of *Voevoda* started; how he would wish to correct faults in the composition when it was too late to do so, how he would discover more and more faults, how the singers were disturbed by technical difficulties, and how impotent the diffident Tchaikovsky appeared in these circumstances. Nevertheless he was already busy with another opera – *Undine* – of which a libretto had been written for A. F. Lvov, by V. A. Sollogub in the 1840's. Tchaikovsky finished sketches in April, and the orchestration in July.

In May 1870 *Undine* was rejected by the conductors of the Marinsky Theatre in St Petersburg. Tchaikovsky was very upset (see Letter 66). In 1873 he burned the score and only fragments survived to be published in the Complete Edition of 1950 (Vol. 2). In 1878, however, Tchaikovsky still hankered after the subject (see Letter 183).

Voevoda was performed for the first time on 30 January for Menshikova's Benefit.

No more than 600 roubles were allowed to the production, and the sets and costumes were borrowed from other operas. There were five performances in all. Odoevsky wrote how 'this opera [was] the beginning of a great future', but there was not any general excitement. On hearing the news of Artôt's marriage some of Tchaikovsky's friends were pleased for his sake. 'We want you,' wrote K. N. de Lazary, 'Russia needs you, but not to be the servant of a famous foreigner.' Without a word, Tchaikovsky – having only then heard of Artôt's marriage – 'went quite pale, got up and left the room'

[48]   T O   A N A T O L I   T C H A I K O V S K Y   [Moscow]
                                                            [Beginning of January 1869]

My dear Anatosha!

Yesterday I had a letter from Modia, in which he scolds me for not having written for a long time, but it is now your turn to get a letter; so tell Modka that he will get his next week. I am extremely busy at the moment as *Voevoda* is being produced, and there are rehearsals every day so that I scarcely find time even to be where it is most important. That is why I have been silent for so long. Up till now the opera has not been going very well, but as everybody is trying very hard one can hope for good results. Menshikova is sure to be very good, especially in the second act where she sings the song 'The nightingale whistles loudly!'. The tenor is also quite good but the bass is bad. If the opera is a success I will do my best for both of you to come here for Shrovetide.

I have started to compose another opera but will not tell you what the libretto is, I want to keep it a secret for a time. It will be a great surprise to everybody when it becomes known that during the summer (and I very much hope to have the opportunity to work in summer) I have written half of another opera. At the next concert they are going to play my symphonic fantasia; I think it is quite a good piece of music and the orchestration is effective. It is called *Fatum*. Concerning what happened to me at the beginning of the winter, I must tell you that it is most doubtful that I shall be tied by the bonds of Hymen. This business is beginning to go to pieces; it is too early to discuss it; you will be told when we meet. Kolia writes that he will be in Moscow for the first night of my opera (which is supposed to be on the 27th).

I will get the money for the performances during Shrovetide and shall send you the two hundred roubles (silver) which I owe you. Do not worry.

I embrace you, my dear, and I am

Yours,

P. Tchaikovsky

Kiss Modia, Father, Lizaveta Mikhailovna; what nonsense to say that I shall stop loving you because of Artôt. Even if there were ten like her I would still love you as before. Give Aunt Liza a special hug for me.

[Moscow]
1 February 1869

My dear Modinka,

Thank you for your rather frequent letters; I am very glad that you like to pour out to me the feelings that excite and worry you. I do not quite like your mood of melancholia, but understand perfectly as I suffered in the same way at your age. I only fear that, allowing yourself to indulge that sort of mood, you will stop studying; believe me the only cure for sorrow of the heart is – work. You had the misfortune to be born with an artistic soul and you will perpetually be drawn to the heights of artistic joy; but, as in spite of your fine artistic nature you have not been endowed with any talent, for God's sake, do not let yourself yield to your desires. On the other hand you have all the qualities needed to be a first class person in the field for which your college is preparing you. I implore you, Modinka, study seriously and get used to the idea that you will have to serve and make your career in doing so. If you decide to become a sad and disillusioned young man, leave off studying, and to refuse to take your future work seriously, you will make not only yourself, but all of us, unhappy. But enough of this.

My opera went off quite well, and in spite of the most insipid libretto it was a success. I was given fifteen curtain-calls and presented with a laurel wreath. The singing was good in spite of the tenor nearly fainting twice in the first act (he had not slept the two previous nights because of an abscess on his finger); and if it had not been for Menshikova who practically held him in her arms like a little child, the curtain would have been brought down.

Yesterday I received some nice letters, a few of which I shall keep until our meeting.

The episode with Artôt finished in the most amusing way. In Warsaw she fell in love with the baritone Padilla whom she used to laugh at here – and is going to marry him! What a lady! One must know all the particulars of our relationship to understand how ridiculous the end of it all is.

Kiss Papochka for me. Andrei Petrovich Berens was coming to see him to tell him about my success. I also embrace Lizaveta Mikhailovna. Will soon send a large sum of money for Tolia whom I beg you to kiss for me.

P. Tchaikovsky

N. Rubinstein conducted *Fatum* at a Russian Musical Society concert. It was badly received by Laroche, while Balakirev (to whom it was dedicated) also spoke unflatteringly of it after he conducted it in St Petersburg on 17 March. Laroche said of *Voevoda* that it had a bad libretto, that in it Tchaikovsky was too strongly influenced by Schumann's disciples, that his style wobbled between German and Italian styles, and that it was insufficiently Russian. Tchaikovsky did not take kindly to the tone of Laroche's article, and the quarrel that it started was only made up some two years later.

TO ANATOLI TCHAIKOVSKY [Moscow]
[15 February 1869]

My dear friend Tolia!

... Am writing this letter in the night after the concert of the Musical Society. My fantasia, *Fatum*, was played for the first time. This is the best thing I have written up to now, at least that is what others say (the success was considerable). Have you read Laroche's article about my opera? If you knew all the circumstances which preceded the article and the reasons for its appearance, you....

I am working on *Undine* with great energy. Nearly all the first act is ready. Unfortunately my health, lately, has gone to pieces (do not mention this to Papochka); my nerves are in an awful state of irritation, to such an extent that I sometimes feel weak to the limit of endurance. Last week I even decided to go off for a rest somewhere until September, but changed my mind. It would not have been fair to Rubinstein who would have been in a difficult position concerning the course and pupils. My kindest regards to Papochka, Lizaveta Mikhailovna and Modia and kiss them all from me. Let me know at once if you are coming for Shrovetide and on what day I am to expect you.

P. Tchaikovsky

[51] TO MODEST TCHAIKOVSKY [Moscow]
[3 April 1869]

The reason why I write so seldom is that I give up all my free time to my opera. The subject fascinates me and I want to finish it as quickly as possible to be able to orchestrate it in summer. So Modinka, if you want your glorious brother to become famous as soon as possible you must not blame him for being lazy in writing letters. I won't expect many letters from you, either, as I know you are having your examinations now! Oh! If only you were to pass them really well, how voraciously would I kiss you! There are no special facts of interest in my life. There are as many concerts here as in Peter[sburg], but I don't go to any of them. Tomorrow Rubinstein's concert takes place and Laroche is to be presented for the first time as a composer.

I have no idea about his overture but have heard it is nothing much. At the Conservatoire great preparations are made for the reception of the Grand Duchess Elena Pavlovna who is coming specially to inspect it. They are getting the whole of *A Life for the Czar* ready for her – sung by Conservatoire pupils – and I think it will not be bad at all.

My great desire is to go both abroad and to Sasha's this summer, but I do not know how I will be able to manage both; the journey abroad depends on monetary circumstances, which are not very good at the present....

And so good-bye, dear Modia, let me know how the examinations are going and do not forget your brother.

P. Tchaikovsky

[52] TO ANATOLI TCHAIKOVSKY   [Moscow]
                                                               [19 April 1869]

Dear Tolia!

A few days ago I wrote to Gedeonov asking him if my opera *Undine* could be produced in the next season in Petersburg. He answered through his secretary that if I send them the score in September it could be put on in November. Consequently I am busy with the instrumentation of the first act; the two others I will do in the summer.

Where I am going I still do not know, but in all probability abroad. The doctor says I must bathe in the sea and drink mineral waters; which means that I will come to Petersburg in the last days of May. I am very pleased with my opera and am working with enthusiasm.

Best wishes to Papochka and Lizaveta Mikhailovna for the holiday and also Modia: 'Christ is risen' I am going to the Kremlin for the midnight service. Alexandra Ivanovna can be as angry as she likes but I am not going to visit Piotr Vassilievich; I have no time.

P. Tchaikovsky

Easter was celebrated on 20 April. After the holiday Anatoli took up his first appointment in the Civil Service at Kiev, where the following letters were addressed.

[53] TO ANATOLI TCHAIKOVSKY   Moscow
                                                               3 August 1869

How are you my dear boy? I have been thinking a lot about you and am worried about your solitude. I know from experience how one's heart contracts at the thought of the beloved ones who are far away and how one does not know what to do through sheer distress and home-sickness. If you are suffering in this way, console yourself by thinking that we shall do all in our power to get you to Moscow. The journey from Kiev to Moscow was awfully boring and, although I travelled first class I suffered from all sorts of inconveniences and slept very badly. Having arrived in Moscow I was pleased to see it again; habit has made me love it as my own town.

Rubinstein is still in Lipezk, but Balakirev is here and I must be honest, his presence weighs upon me. He is a very good man and is well disposed towards me, but somehow I just cannot see soul to soul with him. I do not very much like his exclusive musical opinions and critical manner. The day before yesterday we visited Pleshcheev at his dacha in Zarizyno and stayed the night there, and last night I went to see Volodia at his dacha. On my way there I caught a bad chill and am still at his place feeling quite ill, although now, towards evening I am better. Volodia is well but such tragedies are being enacted in his family that I fear he will again lose his mind.

I did not go to Petersburg and doubt if I shall. Everybody has been saying that it is not worth while spending money on the journey when I can send the opera with someone, Balakirev for instance, who is ready to deliver it to the Director's office. . . . I am feeling rather bored but am not sorry that I left Kamenka where under the circumstances it was impossible to stay; but I am sad to have left you so early. I ought to have installed you properly first and then left. How are your money matters? I will send you a little sum on the 1st of September, but for God's sake, my dear Golubchik, if you want any now, write!

I embrace you with all my heart.

Will write to Adamov tomorrow, mentioning you.

P. Tchaikovsky

[54] TO ANATOLI TCHAIKOVSKY   Moscow
                                                11 August 1869

My dear Golubchik!

I received your letter a few days ago and was very upset at your being so sad. You cannot imagine how well I understand all you feel and how sorry I am for you. What worries me most is that you have no money and that I cannot send you any. But whatever happens I will send you something to help at the end of the month. . . .

We have taken a new flat on the Znamenka; I shall live upstairs and there is room for you. I did my best to persuade Rubinstein to let me live separately, but it was absolutely impossible. However I shall be paying for my rooms now and am going to have my own valet. My life is so dull that sometimes I do not know what to do out of sheer boredom. I often visit Shilovsky at his dacha and stay there for the night. He is going away at the beginning of September and would very much like me to go with him, but I refuse categorically, being wise enough to know that I shall get sick of him in the very first month, that being beholden to him in money matters will make me dislike him and, in one word, that in spite of all the charm Nice might have I would be sorry to have left Moscow and my position here. I have sent my opera to Petersburg with Begichev and am at peace; whether they produce it or not, I, for my part, have finished with it and can start working on something else. Balakirev is still here, we see each other often, but I understand more and more that, in spite of all his good traits, his presence would have been a heavy moral burden for me if he had stayed here for good. Worst of all

51

are his narrow-minded opinions and the stubborn way he sticks to his prejudices. All the same, in some ways he has been of use to me during his short stay. Have you seen Konstantinov? What is the tyrant Meshchersky doing? Write and tell me what your work actually is and is it difficult?

I kiss you heartily

P. Tchaikovsky

The relationship between Balakirev and Tchaikovsky was a complex one. Kashkin thought that it was at this time Balakirev suggested the subject of *Romeo and Juliet* (see p. 164) for an opera, but Klimenko thought it unlikely since at the time he was being unpleasant about the *Valse Caprice* (Op. 4).

After graduating from St Petersburg Nikolai Hubert went to Kiev to teach classes for the Russian Musical Society.

[55]   TO ANATOLI TCHAIKOVSKY   Moscow
                                                   19 August 1869

Dear Friend!

Nothing new to mention, Balakirev is leaving today. How tiring he is and yet I have to be fair, he is an honest and good man and as an artist soars above the ordinary level. We have just heartily said good-bye to each other. These last days I have been visiting the neighbourhood of Moscow with him. A few days ago I entertained Balakirev, Borodin, Kashin, Klimenko, Arnold, and Pleshcheev, for a whole evening. A daughter has been born to the Laroches, and she will be brought up by his mother. I saw him at the Hermitage, and we bowed to each other; but I have not the slightest wish to make it up with him and be friends again. Rubinstein and I have taken nice lodgings where there will be enough room for you when you come. . . .

I am in an awful hurry, so will stop, in order not to say something silly.

Write, I had only one letter from you.

P. Tchaikovsky

[56]   TO ANATOLI TCHAIKOVSKY   [Moscow]
                                                   25 September 1869

My dear boy!

No news at all from Adamov, consequently I cannot say anything new about my plans.

A certain Volkov, a student, told me that he saw you in Kiev and that he even had dinner with you. He told me you were quite happy, which gave me great pleasure. I hope Hubert's arrival and your meeting with Vera has a good effect on your state of mind. . . .

We now have an Italian opera, in which the sisters Markisio are magnificent but the rest of the singers, both male and females are very bad.

Volkov told me that your Kiev Opera is not good at all. You do not give me any particulars and yet I would like to know what the orchestra and the chorus are like, how did Hubert start his work? What impression has he made on everybody, and so on? I have lately been working very hard; I was finishing the pfte. duet score on 25 Russian songs [2nd vol.] hoping to get some money from Yurgenson. But apparently what I had obviously forgotten is that last year I had had an advance of more than 50 roubles.

Ilenka turned up yesterday morning and insisted that I should have dinner with him at the Hermitage. The dinner was excellent, but it was boring, for there is nothing more tedious than family relationships with people one rarely meets in life. . . .

I kiss you heartily.

P. Tchaikovsky

Tchaikovsky's informant Volkov, who reported on the Opera in Kiev, was a student; Ilenka, a cousin, was Ilya Tchaikovsky (see p. 60).

Tchaikovsky was not finding composition very easy. He wrote and told Balakirev so, and Balakirev, who had thought of the subject for the overture, replied on 4 November telling him to concentrate more. Taking Balakirev's advice Tchaikovsky went on to complete *Romeo and Juliet* in November.

He read in the newspapers that S. Gedeonov proposed including some new operas in the season's repertoire, one of which was to be *Voevoda* if time could be found for it. Disappointed, since he had thought a production was certain, Tchaikovsky wrote to Gedeonov for a positive answer on 12 October.

[57] TO ANATOLI TCHAIKOVSKY   [Moscow]
                                            7 October 1869

Exactly a week ago Papochka and Lizaveta Mikhailovna were here and I passed the whole day with them. They had dinner at my home, then we went to the Malyi Theatre and had supper at the Moskovsky Hotel. I saw them off the next day. The Conservatoire is already getting boring and the lessons, the same as last year, have begun to be tiring. I am not composing at all; however, I have finished 50 Russian songs and yesterday I had a letter from Bessel from Petersburg, begging me to adapt Anton Rubinstein's *Ivan the Terrible*. Balakirev writes nasty letters because I am not writing anything. No definite news about the opera – I have been told that it will be produced – but when I do not know.

I do sometimes go to the opera here. The singers Markisio are very good especially in *Semiramide* but listening to them, I am more than ever convinced that Artôt is one of the greatest artists in the world. If you will not be able to come to Moscow this winter, you will at least come for Christmas and I look forward to hearing Artôt together with you. . . .

Give my best regards to Hubert and tell him that I have done what he asked me to. I am sorry that he has a difficult time, poor fellow. You wonder if it were possible to get him out of Moscow? At the moment it is quite out of the question. I kiss you my dear Golubchik, do not be sad and write to me.

P. Tchaikovsky

[58] TO MODEST TCHAIKOVSKY   [Moscow]
                                               12 October 1869

Most charming of brothers!

I am so busy that I find very little time to make you happy with my letters. My occupations are as follows:

  1. I am making a piano duet out of Anton Rubinstein's overture *Ivan the Terrible*.
  2. Finishing and correcting the piano duet [version] of folk-songs.
  3. Am writing an overture to *Romeo and Juliet*.
  4. Preparing my new lectures on musical form.

Besides all this I have to give a lot of my time to Konstantinov, who has come from Odessa for a short stay and has taken complete possession of my free time. I stay at home much of the day. The Italian Opera is going well. The Markisios are excellent singers but after Artôt I cannot listen to anyone with real delight. Incidentally, this exceptionally charming person is in Petersburg for a month and a half, I do not know quite what for. Try to meet her and when you look at her think how I nearly became tied to her by the bonds of Hymen. I am glad that you like Menshikova. I have always been one of the Muscovites who did so.

Not a sign of my opera; I am beginning to think that it will never be produced; I have just written to Gedeonov asking him to give me a definite answer. It seems to me that if I had been more practical and daring it would have been on by now.

I kiss you my dear Modia and insist on a letter.

P. Tchaikovsky

[59] TO ANATOLI TCHAIKOVSKY   [Moscow]
                                               30 October 1869

Why is it that you have not written for so long my dear Kievite? It is true that I have plenty of news about you from Meshchersky but that is not enough. . . .

I have been working very hard; have finished what Bessel gave me to arrange, and have nearly finished an overture to the *Romeo and Juliet* tragedy in rough. Nothing is heard about my opera and I am beginning to think that it will not be produced this season. This does not worry me very much; I have become much more indifferent to my successes as a composer and am prepared to experience, most stoically, to put up with any bad luck.

Have you met Derviz recently at the theatre? He also gave me news about you and, I think, is going to Kiev in a few days. I also met his wife and find her quite sweet, much nicer than I expected.

Very soon I shall have to meet Artôt, for as soon as she arrives the rehearsals of *Le Domino noir* will begin with my choruses and recitatives and I shall have to be there. This woman has done me great harm and when we see each other again I shall tell you all about why and how; but in spite of everything I am attracted to her by such an inexplicable sense of sympathy that I await her arrival with feverish impatience. Alas! It is not real love! Tell me about Hubert, give him my kind regards, and tell him that he ought to be ashamed for allowing Famintsin to use his name. In the advert about the publication of his dirty little paper [*Musical Season*] Hubert's name is next to that of Rubez.

I kiss and embrace you. My regards to Tretiakov. The day after tomorrow, when I get my salary, I will send you a small subsidy.

P. Tchaikovsky

[60]   TO ALEXANDRA DAVYDOVA   Moscow
                                                15 November 1869

My dear Sanichka!

You thought that I would be in Petersburg in November but – can you believe it? – I do not know yet when my opera is going to be produced, or if it is to be produced at all during this season. A friend of mine was told that they have started the chorus rehearsals but as yet I have not had any official confirmation.

I am frightfully busy. I had to hurry finishing my overture which will be played at one of the next concerts of the Musical Society, besides which I had plenty of commissions to execute. So my nerves are in a state of great tension and I want to rest for a time, which means do nothing but teach. . . .

My former fiancée, Artôt, is here. Naturally I do not want to meet her but I shall have to as the rehearsals of *Le Domino noir* are going to start soon, and I have added the choruses and recitatives and shall have to be present at the theatre.

If Vera Vassilievna is still with you give her my best regards.

I kiss you and all the family.

P. Tchaikovsky

Do you know why I have not written for so long? Because I want to send you some money and cannot manage to get it from Bessel who owes me quite a large sum. The thought that you are very short makes me frantic; but, as the money has not arrived, I dare to write and beg your forgiveness. Yesterday I had sad news from Petersburg; my opera will not be produced during this season as they will have difficulties even to stage two others which were on the list before mine, i.e. *Halka* [Moniusko] and *Croatka* [Dyutsch]. I do not like this news at all as I counted very much on the money. It has also had a bad effect on my morale as, at the moment, I feel an irresistible aversion to composing and I know that at least for a month I shall not be able to write anything. Just imagine, the Petersburg management has only found out a week ago that my opera has been lying there for three and a half months! Naturally I am not going to Petersburg.

You want to know how I am going to pass the holidays. If you come to Moscow I shall stay in Moscow, but if for some reason or other you cannot come, then I shall come to Kiev for a week or two; it will give me great pleasure. I do not remember if I told you that, on leaving Moscow, Meshchersky promised to say a word on your behalf at the Ministry and I am sure that your wish to get the post of examining magistrate will be fulfilled.

Our concerts have started; and in spite of the Italian Opera performances we have 850 members and will have 1200 by the end of the season, whereas Petersburg has only 210 members. Balakirev's position is not very brilliant, for he has only just managed to cover his expenses. When one takes all this into consideration one has to thank God and fate that one lives in the blessed town of Moscow.

I have completed my overture and it will be played at one of the next concerts of the Musical Society. I think it is quite a good piece of music. How was Laub's concert in Kiev? And please write and explain why you call him an old man, when he is only 37? I was furious at your attitude to our ages; don't you know, you idiot, that he is only eight years older than I!

Yesterday your Prokhorova had her debut here with great success, under the name of dell'Greco. She sang in the opera *William Tell*. Tolia, I kiss you with all my heart and beg to forgive me for my rudeness; who knows but that the money may arrive tomorrow or the day after.

I embrace you to suffocation.

P. Tchaikovsky

[Moscow]
                                                18 November 1869

Modia, dear friend of my heart!

... I had bad news from Petersburg yesterday. The production of my opera
has been put off until the next season as they have only enough time to put on
two which were on the list before mine, *Halka* and *Croatka*. So I doubt if I will
come to Petersburg but will get you to come here for Shrovetide, as I did last
year with Tolia. The news about my opera has upset me mostly because of the
matter of money. I shall in any case, however, send you the sum I promised
to equip you. This news about my opera will have, I know, a bad effect on me;
I am sure that, for at least three weeks I shall not be able to compose. At the
moment I cannot think of writing without distaste. Fortunately the overture
you ordered on the subject of *Romeo and Juliet* is finished and will be performed
at one of the next concerts.

I am very glad that you liked Artôt, it is a sign of your artistic taste and
understanding. It is difficult to imagine a better singer. You must also take
into account that she is not a concert singer, and that not having heard her
in an opera it is difficult to have a proper opinion of her voice and talent.

Our concerts have already started and in spite of the three weekly performances
for season ticket holders for the Italian Opera, we have more than 800
members and will have over 1,200 by the end of the season. Not like your
miserable 210 members. Poor Balakirev who only just managed to cover his
expenses writes that, from all the excitement and worries he nearly had a
stroke.

When my aversion to music stops I will start composing songs.

I kiss you, Modinka, on both dear cheeks and remain,

Your

P. Tchaikovsky

[63]   TO ANATOLI TCHAIKOVSKY   [Moscow]
                                     [Beginning of December 1869]

Dear Tolia!

The day after I received your letter Vera arrived together with Piotr Vassilievich,
and on Saturday we went to the opera. They were doing *Faust* and Artôt sang
for the first time this season. She was better than ever. Vera Vassilievna and
all the others, of course, found her absolutely no good at all, and Vera
Vassilievna left after the third Act. After tomorrow I will go there again and
I mean to see Piotr Vassilievich.

My indolence did not last very long (I told you about it in my last letter) and
this week I wrote six songs [op. 6] which I want to publish. We are terribly

busy this week: Friday a concert in honour of Beethoven; Saturday, [N.] Rubinstein's Name Day [6 Dec.] there will be a serenade in the garden, later a grand dinner, and then a dance with all sorts of surprises; on Saturday Anton Rubinstein's concert.

At the moment I am at home (it is 3 a.m.) and am very worried about Nikolai Rubinstein. He was supposed to be back last evening by the nine o'clock train from Petersburg, where he played at the Balakirev concert and he has not yet arrived. Albrecht and Agafon who went to meet him, have not yet returned either and I do not understand what it can mean.

I send you 100,000 kisses, but only 15 roubles. I suppose they will be of some use.

I kiss you heartily

P. Tchaikovsky

[64] TO ALEXANDRA DAVYDOVA   Moscow
                                               19 December 1869

My dear beloved Sania!

Forgive me, my love, that I have not written for long, and have not let you know about a musical governess. I have not found anyone and am ashamed because of the definite way I spoke about it this summer. But, honestly, I did not imagine it would be so difficult. . . .

I do not know if I have told you that my opera will not be produced this season. At first I had an attack of melancholia when I got the news, but now I am used to the idea that I have been stupidly deceived – and do not worry any more. I am beginning to think a lot about another opera but meanwhile have written six songs so I will not go to Petersburg. My antipathy to that disgusting town is getting stronger and stronger.

Vera Vassilievna told me that you have quite made it up with Nikolai Vassilievich. It means that you are again tied up with Kamenka for a long time. Perhaps we may see each other in the summer; I doubt if I will be able to go abroad for a cure. All my plans have been destroyed because the production of my opera was postponed.

What a pity it is that the railway does not go as far as Kamenka, I would surely have come for Christmas; I do so much want to have a glimpse of all of you. I kiss Leva and all the children. . . .

I embrace you

P Tchaikovsky

TO MODEST TCHAIKOVSKY   [Moscow]
                                                13 January 1870

My dear brother Modia!

I suppose, dear brother, that you are not angry with me for my long silence
and that you believe in my brotherly feelings of which I have so often given
you proof. Think of all the times I gave you money, and how often you have
had all sorts of other favours from me! In one word, my dear brother, I love
you very much and although I have cheated you abominably, promising to
send you some money for the holidays and did not do so, you must remember
that I am your benefactor and I am certain that you cannot even imagine how
to thank me. Joking apart, dear Modinka, I am most ashamed for having
deceived you, and then spending all my money on a good time, and now,
having to borrow a rouble a day from Agafon. But, on my honour, I will send
you a little soon, and then what I promised for March. Tolia stayed here until
Thursday and wanted to stay longer, but shortness of money prevented him
from doing so. I scarcely saw him at all, he spent all his days making merry
with Tarasov, Gudim and another friend whose name I do not remember.

Balakirev and Korsakov have been visiting us, but their journey was in vain.
The concert which Balakirev was to conduct, did not take place because the
hall was occupied. Naturally, we saw each other every day. Balakirev seems
to love me more and more; so much so, that I do not know how to show him
my gratitude for all his affection. [Rimsky-] Korsakov has dedicated a charming
song [op. 8] to me which he sold to Yurgenson. They both like my overture
[*Romeo and Juliet*] and so do I. As well as this I have written the 'chorus' of
insects from the opera *Mandragora* the plot of which you must know; it was
written by Rachinsky. I chose it as a libretto but my friends [i.e. Kashkin]
advised me against it on the grounds that it would not be sufficiently scenic.
Now Rachinsky is writing a libretto for me, called *Raymond Lully*.

Last week Rubinstein was summoned to court accused of having shouted at
a certain Mlle Shchebalskaia, a Conservatoire pupil and telling her to 'get out'.
The whole of Moscow talks about it; the majority being against Rubinstein,
but the Justice of the Peace acquitted him.

I kiss you, Modinka, write.

I heartily kiss Papochka and the 'Bun' [Lizaveta Mikhailovna].

P. Tchaikovsky

[66]   TO ALEXANDRA DAVYDOVA   Moscow
                                        5 February 1870

Sania, my dearest!

I hear that you are not well. It has upset me more than I can say for no one
can give me any particulars. This winter seems to be especially cruel to all
the Davydovs for both the Petersburg and our Moscow ones have been ill....

I, on the contrary, am in very good health and, as before, am finding life neither dull nor specially gay, but at least it is peaceful. Only one thing upsets me at all, and that is the lack of a proper family relationship.

I often think about how happy I would have been if you had lived here and something like it would have existed in my life. I have a great desire for, and miss, children's voices, and to participate in every day family problems – in one word, an ordinary family life. Maybe you will tell me that I can have it either from Petra Vassilievna or Katerina Vassilievna? No! Why, I do not know, but I can't . . .

I am planning to write a third opera; on the tragedy of Lazhechnikov's *Oprichnik*. As to my *Undine* it will be produced only at the beginning of next season if they do not let me down. But on the whole, during this winter, I have been quite busy composing; two days ago I sent two piano pieces – one of which is dedicated to you [op. 7] – to be published. I will send it as soon as it appears.

Although spring is still very far off and we have only just got rid of insufferable frosts I am already thinking of summer and await with impatience the spring sunshine which has always such a wonderful effect on me. You, I imagine, already feel the nearness of spring. . .

P. Tchaikovsky

[67]   TO MODEST TCHAIKOVSKY   [Moscow]
                                      3 March 1870
Dear Modia,

I was upset about your illness and I rejoiced when it was safely over. You say that you were not invited here for Shrovetide because of my not *desiring* it [Cf. p. 57]. This is a lie, the wish was there but the money was not. I am rather in a muddle with money matters, having reckoned with my opera, consequently could not invite you. Do not forget, you ungrateful and thoughtless young man that I have still to send you a hundred roubles for this month! How dare you accuse of meanness the most honourable man in the world!

The court case Rubinstein-Shchebalskaia has been decided today. Rubinstein has to pay a fine of 25 roubles. You have probably heard all about it. The case is going to the Court of Appeal and if Rubinstein should lose it he is going to resign from the Conservatoire and nearly all the professors with him – including myself.

My overture, *Romeo*, is going to be played the day after tomorrow. There has been already one rehearsal. It is not a bad composition; but God only knows! For God's sake tell Alina Khvostova that my songs are nearly ready and that she will get a copy very soon; I will ask her to fetch them from Bernard's. I passed Shrovetide in absolute idleness but it was not dull. Sashenka Karzova with her husband Ilyenka, and charming daughter Liza were here for a week; I saw them every day; Sashenka is as lovely as ever in spite of having two children, but her husband Pavel Petrovich looks much older.

Where I am going to pass the summer I do not know. Shilovsky would like me very much to go abroad with him. I would perhaps go for a month but he has 'seven Fridays in a week' (he never knows for sure what he is going to do). It may happen that I will stay in Moscow. I have aged so much that I do not feel tempted to go away anywhere. All I want is peace, and more peace! I have not seen P. V. Davydov for some time but went to the circus with Katerina Vassilievna and all the family! You can imagine how much noise, joy and shouting there was. On the third week in Lent at Mertain's concert fragments of *Undine* are going to be played. It will be interesting to hear what they are like. Setov writes that it is definitely possible that my opera will be produced at the beginning of the autumn season.

I wish you plenty of success, Modinka, and good health; I wish with all my heart that you get a good job in Petersburg. Only, please do not sit with your hands folded; do what you can to get it.

Kiss and give my regards to everybody.

Your, adored by you,

P. Tchaikovsky

Romeo and Juliet, conducted by N. Rubinstein, was performed in Moscow at a Russian Musical Society concert, but without making any great impression, on 4 March. Attention was diverted from the music to the conductor, who had been fined at a court hearing on the preceding day, and pilloried in a newspaper; the audience's loyalty therefore was reserved for Rubinstein. On 16 March, a concert at the Bolshoi Theatre the Adagio from the First Symphony and three movements from *Undine* included; recital by Tausig took place in the same place on 23 March; Lavrovskaia sang 'None but the lonely heart' (Op. 6, no. 6) on 26 March; Laroche's unfinished symphony was played on the next night. By now Modest Tchaikovsky had completed his law studies.

[68]   TO ANATOLI TCHAIKOVSKY   Moscow
                                                 7 March 1870

My dear boy!

Rubinstein's case has been decided by the Justice of the Peace; Rubinstein has to pay a fine of 25 roubles; all Moscow has gone mad over the case; Rubinstein is bombarded by letters and addresses of sympathy. . . .

My overture was played at last at the Musical Society. I think this is the best thing I have ever written. . . .

At Shrovetide I took the Peresleny family to the circus.

In the third week in Lent some pieces from my opera *Undine* will be played at Mertain's concert. . . . I have been frightfully lazy, and my opera [*Mandragora*] has got stuck at the first chorus.

I embrace you

P. Tchaikovsky

[69] TO MODEST TCHAIKOVSKY [Moscow]
26 March 1870

My dear Modia!

I congratulate you on your separation from the college, which has happened by now. . . .

We have here an enormous quantity of concerts; today is the second concert with Lavrovskaia, who in a week and a half has earned over 5000 silver roubles. An enviable fate! She is a sweet girl. Tell Khvostova that tonight Lavrovskaia is singing the song which I have dedicated to Khvostova. Tausig gave only one concert and had a considerable, if not over-enthusiastic, response. Tomorrow the first part of Laroche's symphony, written four years ago, will be played at Rubinstein's concert. I do not remember if I wrote to you about my overture to *Romeo*; it is not bad at all and I am very pleased with it. . . .

On the whole I am well, and in a happy state of mind, but have been attacked by frightful laziness; have not written anything for the last four weeks.

One of my songs is having enormous success.

P. Tchaikovsky

[70] TO LEV DAVYDOV [Moscow]
[Middle of April 1870]

Dear Levushka!

I wish with all my heart that you could purchase Rebedailovka or some other country abode. It would be nice for you and a source of all sorts of delight for me. I adore country life and you. But somehow I never feel at home in Kamenka, which would not be the case if I lived on your own estate.

There is nothing much to say about my life; I am just as busy as ever at the Conservatoire and as usual compose a bit. I have started an opera on the theme of Lazhechnikov's tragedy *Oprichnik*; have only written a few scenes up till now. Now and again I get an attack of most horrid dumps which, I must say, does not prevent me from working – on the contrary – I find the best cure for it in work.

I will probably go abroad in summer which makes me very sad when I think that I will not be with you during the summer holidays. . . .

P. Tchaikovsky

On 19 April fashionable Moscow was scandalized and thrilled by the fact that Prince Ourossov, a lawyer, and the brother of Alexander Ostrovsky fought a duel in the Sokolniki Park on account of a difference of opinion that had arisen about the Artistic Circle.

[71]   TO ANATOLI TCHAIKOVSKY   [Moscow]
                                           23 April 1870

My dear boy!

... I will not say much, as nothing much has happened. A certain Rumin, a very well-to-do person, was here for nearly a month and we became great friends. He came straight from Nice on business concerning Volodia Shilovsky whose guardian he is. This Rumin is determined to make me into a religious person; he has presented me with a lot of books on religion and faith which I have promised to read. In general I have gone in for a God-fearing life and in Holy Week Rubinstein and I went to Confession and Communion.

My opera is going feebly; the reason for it is the subject, which, although very good, does not really attract me. Although the libretto of *Undine* was roughly stuck together it was something for which I had much more sympathy and its writing went fast and easily.

I passed the holidays very pleasantly....

On the 17th I am going abroad. I am partly pleased, partly upset; pleased, because foreign countries have always charmed me; upset, because I will not see you for a long time and also because I fear that Shilovsky will poison all my pleasure by his mad behaviour, in spite of promising and swearing in his letters that he will look after me, spoil me and generally pamper me....

All that people talk about here is the duel between Ourussov and Ostrovsky's brother – a vulgar business.

I read in the *Musical Season* about Hubert's concert. I am happy about his success; give him my very kindest regards.

I embrace you and kiss you a million times.

P. Tchaikovsky

[72]   TO ANATOLI TCHAIKOVSKY   Soden
                                           1–13 June 1870

My dear Tolka!

I apologize most humbly I had no time to scribble a note to you before leaving Moscow and because of Petersburg and Paris, I was running about so much all day that I did not find a minute to write. . . . I am sure that I will meet Misha abroad and naturally will talk a good deal about you and Modia. Misha will tell you what I did in Peter[sburg], so I will not mention it here. But you can imagine how I felt, having the double weight of Meshchersky on one side and Balakirev on the other pressing upon me. It felt like being between two blazing fires. Modenka was very sweet and I am very pleased with him; and also glad that he is happy and is going to the provinces without any fear or misgivings.

I travelled from Peter[sburg] to Paris non-stop. I got very tired and my nerves were on edge when I arrived. I feared to find a dying Shilovsky but although he is very weak, I expected him to be worse; I cannot say how delighted he was to see me. We stayed in Paris for three days and then came here. As I love Paris these three days passed happily; I went to a theatre each night and for walks all day long. Was very frightened by Volodia fainting, but all ended well.

Soden is a small clean village situated at the foot of the Taunus range [in western Germany]. The country is beautiful and the air wonderful; but the multitude of people suffering from consumption makes it look a bit dismal which, on the day of our arrival made me feel so miserable that I had to make a big effort not to have hysterics. Now I feel better and am taking the task of watching over Volodia very seriously. He is hanging on a thread, the doctor says that the smallest carelessness can develop into T.B.; but if he responds well to the cure he may be saved. He is so grateful, and shows me so much love for my joining him that I have accepted with pleasure to be his Argus – the saviour of his life. What made me unhappy at first was the thought that I would not see either you or Modest or Sasha for so long. This thought still tortures me but I hope that at the end of the summer I shall be able to return to Moscow from the south and pass through Kamenka and Kiev. We shall stay here five weeks and what will happen next – I don't know. I shall of course, write several times more, both to you and Modia. I am sending the next letter straight to Modia in Kamenka; he then will pass it on to you to be read.

Yesterday we went with Volodia for a donkey ride; I did not think it great fun; the animals kept up their reputation – they are so lazy and stupid that if you do not smack their bottoms they refuse to move forward. The view on the mountains is wonderful. I wonder what will happen to me in Switzerland, where I am going with Volodia.

There are plenty of Russians in Soden. I do not try to know them, and thank God that I have not met any one I know from Moscow or Petersburg. I do not intend to work hard but will do a little. For God's sake write, my Golubchik, and tell Modia, when he passes by, to write with all particulars what he has been doing since we parted.

If he has already gone, send him this letter to Kamenka.

I kiss you especially hard.

P. Tchaikovsky

Soden
7–19 June 1870

My dear Modenka!

In passing through Kiev, you have, I hope, read my letter written to Anatoli; a week has gone by since then. My sadness which was severe at first is gradually getting better. I have found some things here that are not only worth noticing but also worth admiring. Soden is situated in a valley of the Taunus mountains, and it is this Taunus [range] which is the object of my raptures. It is not particularly high but the slopes are all covered with thick forest and charming castles, compared with which the Hapsal ruins, praised and sung by me and immortalized by your poetical effusions (when we went there) are pure trash.

This mountain range should be of great interest to tourists. The most striking [feature] is the Castle of Königstein, built in A.D. 967 and still a stronghold in 1800. We climbed up to the top of the tower, Volodia and I, and the view spread before my enchanted sight was truly magnificent. When we came down we went with a guide to inspect the cellars and dungeons. Absolutely frightening! Every morning I go to a place called 'Drei Linden' and either compose there or read – alone, surrounded by the austere mountain scenery, with a view stretching across about two hundred versts.

As to life in Soden, it is very simple. We get up at six. Volodia drinks the mineral waters, and I, on the doctor's advice, take alkaline baths. We have our coffee at eight and then I either go for a walk or sit at the 'Drei Linden'. At four o'clock we listen to quite a decent orchestra; from six we go for walks until eight, drink tea and go to bed at ten. There are moments where I long to see you, when the insufferable desire to pass even a few days in Kamenka brings me to the verge of tears and the memory of last summer with you at Sasha's tortures me. But I wage an energetic battle against my sad thoughts, consoling myself that by my severe watch over Volodia I am surely saving him and that life here in Soden will also be good for me. The good results of the cure are already noticeable. Volodia has an excellent appetite, sleeps well, has fresh colour in his cheeks, he can, again, go for long walks once more, and is even beginning to get fat. There are a lot of Russians here and although I did my best to avoid them, it became impossible to do so completely. We have dinner in the restaurant, which lasts a long time but is (according to my taste) quite good. On Thursday the Russian Military Band played here, the one that got the first prize in Paris, and it is wonderful, I have never heard anything like it.

We are planning to go to the Opera in Frankfurt, but what they give there is quite vile; I never expected it from the Germans. Just imagine the singer Minny Gauk, who had been hissed during a whole season in Moscow is creating a sensation here in Frankfurt.

I cannot say how long we are going to stay here; not longer than the middle of July; from here we shall probably go to Switzerland. . . .

P. Tchaikovsky

My address: Soden (Nassau) neben Francfurt [sic] am Main, Kurhaus.

Soden
24 June–6 July 1870

I do not understand my Golubchik why you do not write. I am beginning to
think that my letter did not reach you. Now that a whole month has gone by
that I am abroad without any news, I am beginning to get worried. As for
Modest, he makes me angry. I heard from a third party that he was still in
Peter[sburg] in the middle of June; but he himself made no effort to write.
I wrote him a letter to Kamenka; is he there? And you – are you also there?
Has anything happened? I am getting quite worried.

Life in Soden is monotonous and dull but my health is excellent. I take mineral
baths which are very good for me and in other ways, the life I lead here is most
wholesome. I get up at six, wake up Volodia, and then he goes to drink the
waters, and I to take my bath. Coffee at eight after which I go for a walk, or
write letters, or read. Dinner at 1 p.m. in the restaurant. At four we go to listen
to the music, then walk from 6–8; drink tea, play and to bed at 10. You can
judge by all this that I lead an idle life and, to be honest, have no desire to
work.

A few days ago, in Mannheim (about two hours away from Soden) there was
a great musical Festival in honour of Beethoven's centenary; it lasted two days
and we were there. The programme was most interesting and the performance
wonderful. Several orchestras from the Rhine towns took part; the choir
was four hundred strong; I had never heard one so magnificent and well trained.
The conductor was the well-known composer Lachner. It was the first time
that I heard Beethoven's *Missa Solemnis* – terribly difficult to perform – which
is one of the greatest of musical compositions. But apart from this one there
are very few musical pleasures here. The Soden orchestra is not large, plays
quite well but the programmes are awful. Volodia and I made them learn
Glinka's *Kamarinskaya* which they are going to play tomorrow for the first time.

I went to Wiesbaden to meet N. Rubinstein, and found him without a penny
in his pocket; he has lost everything at roulette. This did not prevent us from
having a very pleasant day. He seemed quite happy and is positive that he will
not leave Wiesbaden without having broken the bank. I feel frightfully lonely
without you and all our dear ones, and think continuously of the charming
days in Kamenka last year. How I wish I could again go on a picnic to the
big forest, with tea, a bonfire and all the rest. We are going to stay here for
about another week and a half and are then going to Switzerland where I
expect to find inspiration and much pleasure. When I will be coming back to
Russia I do not yet know. Write to this address, if I should have left, they will
send it on.

Scold Modest, when you write to him, but also kiss him. Good-bye my dearest
Golubchik.

P. Tchaikovsky

Interlaken
12–24 July 1870

Dear Modinka!

Thank you for the letter I got in Soden. It gave me great pleasure as it made me see that you are in good health and good spirits. I do not understand why Tolia is silent.

This is our third day in Interlaken where we shall probably stay for a month, and from where I plan to take excursions all over Switzerland. The news about war made everybody run away from Soden to Switzerland; the rush was so great that the trains and hotels were full to overflowing. To avoid all the confusion which was caused by the trains carrying troops as well as passengers, Volodia and I took a roundabout way by Stuttgart and the Lake of Constance. But even that route was both uncomfortable and annoying. Bavarian and Württemberg recruits who were going to Ulm were picked up by our train which made it late; the carriages were so crammed full that it made it very difficult to get anything to eat or drink. But, thank God, we have at last reached Switzerland and here everything is absolutely normal.

Modenka, I find no words to express my joy at finding myself in this magnificence of nature. There is no end to my ecstasy; I run about like a madman from morning to night, and do not feel tired in the least. Volodia, who is absolutely indifferent to the beauties of nature, and has not stopped asking where the Swiss cheese can be found ever since our arrival, just laughs at me. . . . I wonder what he will say in a few days time when I start roaming about the mountains, glaciers, and gorges! Interlaken itself is nothing more than a row of excellent hotels where people from all over the world crowd together, for this is the very centre of the beauties of Switzerland. The town lies between two lovely lakes, Thun and Brienz, and is surrounded by enormous mountains of which the most magnificent one is the Jungfrau. What is a bit annoying is that there are a lot of English people here; wherever you turn you come face to face with a son of Albion.

I am returning to Russia at the end of August. You will already be in Simbirsk. For God's sake, when you get there do not let yourself be miserable. I will help you if you should need money. Let me know if Insarsky is there.

I kiss you a thousand times.

Peter the Great

Kiss Sasha's dear eyes and hands for me; also kiss Leva and the children.

My address is: Suisse, Canton de Berne, Interlaken.

Cendrillon, a projected ballet, was never completed. During the previous June Tchaikovsky had revised *Romeo and Juliet*, which was accepted for publication by Bote and Bock, of Berlin, on the advice of Karl Klindworth.

[Moscow]
5 October 1870

Modia!

Your last letter did not please me at all as much as the first. What pleasure do
you get making presents of boxes of chocolate, and paying court, to the
Simbirsk ladies of the aristocracy when you cannot afford it? And why don't
you say anything about your work? All the same, I was pleased to get such
a long letter from you. I would like to answer you in the same way but so
much work has accumulated and I am being worried from all sides, that there
is no time to write from the heart. Besides I have undertaken to write the music
for the ballet *Cendrillon* and the enormous four act score must be ready in
the middle of December.

I rarely see Bibikov; he always asks me to give you his kind regards. Yesterday
he and I had dinner with Kondratiev. Konstantinov has taken complete
possession of me, and makes me dine with him almost every day. Generally
speaking, everybody adores me, though I really don't know why.... The
latest news is: (1) Laroche has a son. (2) To my delight the Prussians have
been completely smashed near Paris. (3) Tamberlik has been hissed here and
I have written a protest which has been signed by all the professors of the
Conservatoire.

Good-bye, Modichka. I kiss you as hard as I can. Write. Forgive me, the money
will be sent a little later, I had a few unexpected bills to pay.

[no signature]

[Moscow]
[5?] October 1870

My dear Tolka!

This letter will be very short; I still have not summoned up enough energy to
write you a long one. I am exceedingly busy. I was silly enough to promise a
score for the ballet *Cendrillon* cheap. The ballet has to be ready for December
and as I have signed an agreement I cannot back out; although there are only
two months left to do it in and I have only just begun to write the music....

A few news items to finish with: (1) Krivoshein came to see me but I did not
return the visit. (2) My overture is being published in Berlin and will be played
in several towns in Germany. (3) My friend Kondratiev is here and I see him
often. (4) I rarely see Hubert, who is a great favourite here. (5) I often visit
Konstantinov.

Let me know if, in case you will not be able to settle here, you could come
at least for a short time.

P. Tchaikovsky

TO ILYA PETROVICH TCHAIKOVSKY   Moscow
26 October 1870

My dear Papochka!

I am taking advantage of your permission to write a rare letter to you;
especially as you had recent news of me from the Davydovs; that is why I did
not personally let you know about my life. Well – all I can say is that I am
happy and well; I work a lot and am beginning to get so used to my duties at
the Conservatoire that I do not find them tedious any more. At the moment
I have not done much about composing but from the month of November
I shall get down to it properly. Anton Rubinstein is here and I am happy at
seeing him every day. He played at the opening night of a series of our concerts,
which have started most brilliantly; we have already 1100 members.

I do not see the Davydovs very often, and am not very keen on visiting Lizaveta
Sergeevna; she is most kind to me but I just cannot get used to her. I went
twice to see Andrei Petrovich Berens, who always sends regards to you. I kiss
you my dearest and sweet, your eyes, nose, hands; kiss Pyshka properly. If you
see Lida Olkhovskaia kiss her lovingly from me.

P. Tchaikovsky

During that season the membership of the Russian Musical Society comprised fifty
permanent members, ninety-two active members, and eleven hundred and fifty-one
guest (non-active) members. At that period the affairs of the Conservatoire were
in a state of uncertainty, because funds had been almost exhausted by the move
from the Vozdvizhenka to the Nikitskaia (see p. 31) and the directors had to remind
the city that without help the Conservatoire would not be able to survive.

The 'little sister' mentioned below was Tchaikovsky's cousin Anastasia Vassilievna
Popova.

TO ALEXANDRA DAVYDOVA   [Moscow]
20 December 1870

My dearest!

Your letter touched me greatly and at the same time made me ashamed. But
I do wonder how you can have any doubts about my deep love for you, even
for a moment. My silence is partly due to laziness, partly because writing
a letter requires a peaceful state of mind which I rarely manage to acquire.
Either I am at the Conservatoire or feverishly trying to use a free hour
for composing, or being tempted to go somewhere, or someone comes to see
me, or I am so exhausted that all I can do is – sleep. And so my life is such
that I do not know how to find enough time to correspond with people as dear
to my heart as you are, my dearest, kindest Sania.

Anyway I have already told you that although we live far away from each other you play a most important part in my life. In difficult situations my thoughts instinctively turn to you. I always think: 'If things get really bad I will run to her.' Or; 'I am sure I will do as Sasha would have told me.' Or; 'Should I write to her? What will she say?' But in spite of everything, life goes on unrolling and carries one off into its abyss, without giving one any time to stop, to get strong, or to think things over.

The society in which one lives catches one in its web, and ties one up from head to foot; and it is a rapturous dream to be free from it all, even for a short time, and to breathe air that is different, and to feel the warmth of your dear, loving heart. I hope to come for sure, to stay with you this summer, for I do not think I shall go abroad. With what delight I shall embrace you and all your family. Thank you for the photographs. All your girls are charming, each in her own way. Tania's serious face is most attractive.

I live according to a settled plan. I compose a little – a new opera – and have an established way of life and set of people around me. However, I am getting more and more used to Moscow, and life anywhere else seems impossible. Modia arrived here two days ago, on his way to Petersburg. I am not quite pleased with him for not knowing (as I do) how to manage on a small income. But on the whole I liked him. My only fear is that he will not give enough attention to his work – it is very important he should, but, he has not enough ambition. Tolia is going to be transferred here in winter.

I see your people now and again. Today Modia and I had dinner at Katerina Vassilievna's. She is as nice as formerly. I am beginning to get used to Lizaveta Sergeevna, who is most kind. I also visit Derviz. On the anniversary of your wedding we had dinner at his house and drank your health. The letter from 'Sestriza' [little sister] is very touching, but what can one do when life brings people together and then, against their wishes and hopes, separates them. I shall write to her. It was wonderful of you to invite her to Verbovka.

I kiss you my dearest darling, also Leva and everybody. A happy New Year! Modia also sends his love.

P. Tchaikovsky

At about this time Tchaikovsky was busy with a translation of J. C. Lobe's *Katechismus der Musik* into Russian. On 16 March there was an all-Tchaikovsky concert in Moscow, at which the attendance of I. S. Turgeniev created a stir. Tchaikovsky's Quartet in D major (Op. 11), which was given its first performance, was highly praised by Laroche. After this the composer worked for a time at *Oprichnik*. During the summer holidays the idea of a *Swan Lake* ballet began to shape itself around the choreographic wishes of the Davydov children at Kamenka. In August Tchaikovsky finished a text-book on harmony and in the autumn, in a restless frame of mind, he returned to the Conservatoire.

TO ANATOLI TCHAIKOVSKY   Moscow
                                   2 December [1871]

Dear friend!

... I must inform you that, because Shilovsky has asked me most insistently
to join him, I am going abroad for a month about December 15 but as nobody
in Moscow (except Rubinstein) is to know about it, everybody must think that
I am going to Sania's. Tell no one, even Sasha Gudim, that I am going abroad.
If Papochka leaves Kamenka before getting my letter, warn him that he will
not find me in Moscow after December 15, but I will see him, in Petersburg,
on my way back.

The position of our Conservatoire is very uncertain. But I can assure you
that although for its sake I shall be sorry if it comes to an end, I will be
delighted for my own. I am absolutely sick of giving lessons. I get so tired and
upset that any change will be welcome. I shall not die of hunger, I suppose,
if it happens, for we shall organize daily lectures and classes, or else I shall
move to Petersburg if the Conservatoire there offers me a good salary. Who
knows? I may even go to Kiev!

My opera is moving very slowly and I doubt if I shall manage to finish it by
Lent. Nothing of interest to report; that I have become a newspaper
correspondent you probably already know. I am doing it out of pure altruism,
Hubert is too lazy to do it and we do not wish outsiders to meddle; tell
Modest that everything I hear about him gives me great pleasure.

P. Tchaikovsky

Tchaikovsky had been writing for the *Contemporary Annals* since 1868. He now
joined the critics of the *Moscow News* to which he contributed until 1876 (see
Complete Works, 1950).

Alexandra's new baby, Vladimir (Bob), became Tchaikovsky's favourite nephew and
his heir.

Tired of living with Rubinstein and of 'being completely in the hands of Agafon
[Rubinstein's valet]', Tchaikovsky took an apartment of his own near the Granatny
Pereoulok, one of the smaller residential streets off Spiridonovka Street. Both streets
were known for their charming private houses.

[81]   TO ALEXANDRA DAVYDOVA   [Moscow]
                                   9 December 1871

My beloved and dear Sania!

I received the news that a son has been born to you and a nephew to me with
great joy. I am always worried when your time of confinement draws near
which makes me rejoice more than ever when I hear the happy news.

My letter is going to be short as I have nothing of great interest to report except for the fact that I am extremely happy to be living alone now, but I must add that I get more tired from hard work than ever before. Besides my work at the Conservatoire, I am in a hurry to complete my opera by the spring and have also promised to write some articles on music; this is something I have never done and find a little difficult. As a result of all this I am thinking of perpetrating the following subterfuge.

I have the chance of going abroad for a month at little cost, and for several reasons I have decided to leave about December 15, in about a week's time. But because of my Conservatoire commitments it must remain secret (except to Rubinstein). I beg of you, my angel, not to write about it to anyone except the Moscow members of your family. Everybody here must think I have gone for a rest with you. My brothers have been told about my journey. I am not sure that this letter will arrive before dear Papochka leaves; if he is still with you, warn him that he will not find me in Moscow after the 15th and that I will see him when I return.

So that I shall know his new address in Petersburg before my return about February 1, please send it to me. I shall write to you from Nice – you, in your turn write me a few words there to the following address, Nice, France, Place Masséna No. 4.

P. Tchaikovsky

[82] TO ANATOLI TCHAIKOVSKY   Nice
                                      1–13 January 1872

Tolia!

... My journey was without any complications; I stayed a day and night in Peter[sburg] (at Meshchersky's) and the same length of time in Berlin and Paris. Although Paris is still brilliant and animated it is not as it was before. I have been in Nice about a week. It seems queer to be transferred out of a deep Russian winter to a place where you don't need to wear a coat, where oranges grow, roses and lilac bloom and all the trees are bright green.

The place is charming but what is awful is the worldly way of life. All the idle rich from all over the world come here in winter and I have to make a great effort not to be sucked into this whirlwind. You know how I love this sort of life and can imagine how I enjoy it. I must tell you something odd. I awaited the day of my departure with such intense impatience that towards the end I lost sleep over it. But already on the day I started I was enveloped in severe home-sickness which did not leave me during all my journey and has still not left me in this glorious countryside.

There are, naturally, delightful interludes, as when I sit quietly alone at the seaside in the morning, under the rays of the bright, hot – but not scorching – sun. But even these delightful moments are not free of a touch of melancholy. And what is the reason for all this? That old age has come and nothing brings joy any more. You live in the past or hoping. Hoping for what?

From Shilovsky's manager's letter I understand that Modest is in Moscow, I would like to know what for? Did he get the job about which he wrote to the Davydovs?

As it is impossible to live without hoping for a sweet future I am already dreaming of going to Kiev for Easter week and of the summer when we shall be together in Kamenka.

This time I will not finish the last page, as I have nothing more to write about.

I kiss you

P. Tchaikovsky

[83] TO ILYA PETROVICH TCHAIKOVSKY Moscow
31 January 1872

My dear Papochka!

I arrived here three days ago and want to apologize for not giving any news about myself for so long. I hoped to be in Petersburg on my way back but was forced to go straight to Moscow. Rubinstein wrote that my presence was indispensable, so from Vienna I went on to Smolensk. By the way, I still do not know your address and where to write. Alexandra Ivanovna kindly agreed to send this letter over to you.

My trip was pleasant and comfortable; I went to Berlin, Paris, and Nice, for three weeks; also to Genoa, Venice and Vienna. The weather in Nice was rather bad; the rain and wind for a time were so strong that the sea flooded nearly all of the town; a train fell into the sea (the railway line runs along the shore); a whole cliff came down destroying an enormous building with a lot of people in it. However, there were also fine days as hot as it is in June at home. All the same, however much I enjoyed my trip, idleness was beginning to weigh upon me and I returned to Moscow with great pleasure. Modest was here during my absence – why and what for I do not know, but I presume for the sake of the Davydovs. He did choose a queer time, when I was away – which he knew perfectly well. I have no news of Tolia; there was a telegram from him to Rubinstein today asking for news about me. I want to write and tell him to come here to consult a good doctor, I do not think that his position would suffer from him coming here for a few days. I have been told that the Kiev doctors are no good at all. Alexandra Ivanovna told me you look much younger which makes me very happy.

I kiss you heartily, my dearest. Give a great hug to the 'Bun' [see p. 59] and let me know how you are pleased with your new lodgings.

P. Tchaikovsky

Tchaikovsky had commenced his Second Symphony at Kamenka in June, 1872. It was dedicated to the Moscow section of the Russian Musical Society and first performed on 26 January, 1873 (see Letter 89). The work was revised in 1879 and 1880. The D Major String quartet had been played at a chamber music concert of the Russian Musical Society on 24 October.

At this time Tchaikovsky, with his newly engaged valet 'Misha' (Mikhail Ivanovich Sofronov), moved to a flat in Kudrinskaya Ploshchad (Kudrinsky Square – now the 'Square of Revolution'). Worried about the prospects for *Oprichnik* he wrote to Klimenko on 12 November complaining how the St Petersburg authorities would probably prefer *Sardanapal*, an undistinguished opera by the 'completely ungifted' Famintsin. However, in January he was to be pleasantly surprised after he had played through *Oprichnik* to the operatic committee of the Marinsky Theatre (see Letter 88). In December–January he composed the six songs of Opus 16.

[84]   TO MODEST TCHAIKOVSKY   [Moscow]
                                      2 November 1872

Modia!

My conscience tortures me for not writing to you – but what can I do? My symphony, which I am finishing, has engrossed me so deeply that I am not able to do anything else. The writing of this work of genius (as Nikolai Kondratiev calls it) is coming to an end and it will be performed as soon as the orchestral score is ready. I think this is my best creation, so far as perfection of form is concerned – a quality which I have hitherto failed to achieve. I wish you could hear it. . . .

I have just read if not a beautiful, but a most finely written thing by Droz called *Babolain*. I advise you to get this novel from the College secretary. My quartet had an enormous success in Petersburg.

P. Tchaikovsky

[85]   TO ILYA PETROVICH TCHAIKOVSKY   Moscow
                                          22 November 1872

My dearest Golubchik Papochka!

Although you do not openly blame me for not writing more often I still torture myself and am sure you are angry with me. Forgive me my dearest, you know how lazy I am at letter writing. Also, I have been working hard at my symphony which I have now finished, thank God. All the same it is your own fault that you have such lazy sons – blame yourself! And so I cover with loving kisses your grey head, and your hands, and once more beg forgiveness for my laziness.

You say in your letter you hope my flat is warm. Well, up till now I am perfectly satisfied with it. Besides, the weather at present is so warm here that it is even

annoying. One wishes for nice crisp frosts instead of misty, damp rainy days!
I stay at home quite a lot but also go for long walks. If I do not do so my belly
will grow enormous and that God forbid! Now that I have finished my
symphony I am resting. . . .

My health is in order, only my eyes worry me a little; they are strained by
hard work and my sight has weakened so much, compared to what it used to
be that I have acquired a pince-nez. People say it suits me greatly. My nerves
are not in order, but nothing can be done about it – anyway this is not
important. Who in our position has got good nerves, especially artists!

My brothers, too, do not write; I have no news to tell you about them and
heard about Kolia's wedding from the Davydovs. For the holidays Rubinstein
and I are going to Kiev where he wants to give a concert and I will go to keep
him company. But, it may happen that the administration of the Mariinsky
theatre might summon me to Petersburg concerning the production of my
opera, which will give me the opportunity to kiss and embrace you properly.
My symphony is going to be played in Petersburg and I wish very much that
you could hear it. Good-bye, my Golubchik, I kiss your hands and eyes and
also hug the 'Bun'. My Misha begs to give you his humble regards.

P. Tchaikovsky

[86] TO ILYA PETROVICH TCHAIKOVSKY   [Moscow]
                                                9 December 1872

My dear Papochka!

Piotr Vassilievich Davydov told me a few days ago that he got a letter from
Petersburg for Alexandra Ivanovna. For some reason I imagined that it was
from you and that you had not received my last one. I thought, perhaps, that
you were angry with me or that I used the wrong address. Please let me know
at once, to allay my fears. Anatoli and Modest write very rarely, the former
has not written since he is back from abroad. I hope to go with Rubinstein to
Kiev during the holidays and see my brothers.

Nothing much to say about myself. I am well, but my nerves often worry me.
At the moment I am being lazy and am not writing anything. I hope to have
my new symphony performed before I start composing again as I look upon it
as my best work. As regards my opera, I am nearly sure it will be staged next
season. Two censorships, the theatrical one and the dramatical one have given
their sanction. Only the musical committee is left and I am told it will give
its approval.

All the Davydovs are worried about the health of Vassily Vassilievich who has
a bad cold which aggravates his illness. All the others are well. The weather
is mean in the extreme. Strong frosts and no snow. Nilsson is a regular
sensation at the theatre. I saw her yesterday in *Hamlet*. She is very charming,
sings beautifully although her voice is not as sonorous as Patti's; she acts

to perfection. Do you ever go to the theatre, my dear? Write and tell me how you are in general; whom do you see; where do you go? – How is 'Fatty' getting on? . . .

And so good-bye, my dearest, and make me happy with a letter. I kiss you heartily and Lizaveta Mikhailovna.

Your most loving son

P. Tchaikovsky

[87] TO MODEST TCHAIKOVSKY   Moscow
                                                     10 December 1872

I got both your letters a week ago, my gracious Modestina, and am most grateful. In your first letter you mention that I had a slight attack of the spleen. Nothing of the sort, only – as before – that I sometimes get a fit of sadness and despondency. This comes partly from my nerves getting irritated without reason, but also partly because I do not exactly find my work as a composer particularly soothing. But on the whole nothing has changed very much.

I have already told you that my new symphony into which I have put great hope, is finished. It will be performed in January but not before. Now, because I have neither desire to work nor any inspiration I am being quite idle. I tried to compose a few songs but they come out somewhat ordinary and I cannot find any words I really like. Why don't you write me a list of good poems? Baikova has scribbled over a whole lot of paper with poetry, but so bad that I found it all unworthy of music. Nothing special is happening at the Davydovs. Vassili Vassilievich is getting better slowly.

Nilsson here is having a terrific success. I heard her twice and must say that, since I heard her in Paris her talent has taken a great step forward. On the vocal side she is quite unique. When she starts singing, you do not at first think she is anything out of the ordinary but then when she suddenly takes a high 'C' or lingers on a middle note the whole theatre bursts into applause. All the same, in spite of all her wonderful qualities I still do not like her as much as Artôt. If the latter decided to come to Moscow I would jump for joy.

If you have time to answer tell me if you are coming to Kiev for the holidays where I want to go for a week with Rubinstein and Hubert. It would be nice! I want to have a change, see the Kiev opera and the town, and see Anatoli who, by the way, has not written once since he is back from abroad. . . .

[incomplete]

[88] TO ALEXANDRA DAVYDOVA   [Moscow]
                                                     9 January 1873

Forgive me, my dearest, that as usual I am too lazy to write. You probably must have heard from Papochka that I had to go to Petersburg quite unexpectedly during the holidays. I was summoned to be present when the committee was deciding the fate of my [*Oprichnik*]. I was so sure that would be rejected that I did not dare to go first to see Papochka, fearing to upset him by my distracted appearance.

The day after the committee meeting, which was a real torture but ended to my greatest satisfaction, I went off to see Papochka and stayed with him for a whole week. I cannot say that the week passed very happily for I was being torn to pieces. Every day there were musical evenings and dinners so that in the end my only wish was to sneak away from all these pleasures, and get back as soon as possible to my dear and blessed Mother Moscow. There is much less bustle and more peace here.

After this visit to Petersburg I have at last come to understand that my ties with Petersburg are completely severed, and also how much I have come to feel at home in Moscow. However much I am being pampered and spoiled in Petersburg and whatever success I experience there I will, to the end of my days stay a real Muscovite. It seems to happen after a time, to all who live in Moscow. My greatest and sweetest wish is – that you too, one day settle here, my dears, in the 'First Capital'.

Yours

P. Tchaikovsky

The day after tomorrow my new symphony is going to be played.

'Pelmeny' derives from 'pell-mell' and designates a Siberian dish: fine pastry stuffed with finely chopped beef and pork, cooked in salt water, and eaten with the resulting juice flavoured with vinegar and with butter on each piece.

The article on Beethoven (*The Citizen*, 1873, nos. 7, 8, 11, 18) was unoriginal and unfinished. Nor were Ilya Petrovich's memoirs completed; so far as they went, they were used by Modest in his biography of his brother. The old man was delighted at the success of the Second Symphony, played under Rubinstein on 26 January (it was repeated on 27 March after some changes in instrumentation), and wrote to his son to say so on 8 February. Laroche had nothing but praise in his notice in the *Moscow News*, 1873, No. 33.

[89] TO ILYA PETROVICH TCHAIKOVSKY   Moscow
                                                      5 February 1873

My dear Papochka!

Time flies so fast that it seems only a week ago that I was eating your 'ideal Pelmeny' and sleeping in your little dining-room. But actually it is more than a month ago and my conscience is torturing me again that I am so unpunctual in my letter writing to you. Time flies so quickly because I am very busy. I am working on the scoring of my opera, am writing articles on music in one of our papers, and am compiling a biography of Beethoven for the *Citizen*. I stay at home every evening and behave in the most peaceful and respectable manner, as a Muscovite should. The winter has come at last and it is so cold today that the Muscovites are threatened by frostbite and 'swellings' but I who mostly sit at home, am snug and warm in my little flat.

Not long ago, thinking about you I had the following idea. As your literary language is very good, why don't you in your idle moments, let us say, in the mornings, write your reminiscences about all the different interesting, well-known people you have met, about any special events relating to your work, and, even earlier, your school years at the Mining Institute. Do think about it. I am sure it would interest you and you could have it published either in the *Russian Archives* or any other periodical. Let me know what you think of the idea.

My symphony was played here last week with great success; I was called for many times and cheered repeatedly. The success was so great that the symphony is going to be played again at the tenth concert and a subscription has been started to make me a present. Also I received 300 roubles from the Musical Society. Laroche came here for one evening to hear my symphony; in one word (Oh base human soul!) I am delighted with all the success and the material profit that has accrued from it. I hope that my opera will be as lucky next year! ...

I embrace you as hard as I can, my dear, and beloved one and kiss your hands. I also heartily kiss the Bun and repeat to her again: she must walk, walk, walk and not sit at home all day dozing, getting fat and out of breath.

Your loving son

Peter Tchaikovsky

The Ukrainian folk-song, 'The Crane', the basis of the last movement of the Second Symphony was truly popular. One day, according to a recollection of the Davydovs transmitted to the translator, the composer was playing a variation on the theme when old Mrs Davydov's butler came up to him. 'May I interrupt you, Piotr Ilyich,' he said, 'you are not playing "The Crane" properly. This is how it should be sung. . .', and started to sing it. Tchaikovsky asked him to repeat his version, which turned up in a variation in the symphony.

In the spring Tchaikovsky was asked to write incidental music (Op. 12) for Ostrovsky's *Snegourochka* (*Snow Maiden*), which he did in three weeks. The play was produced at the Bolshoi Theatre on 11 May, and the music, on the whole, made a better impression than the play itself. Tchaikovsky found it rather irksome that for some time he had to attend the theatre daily for rehearsals.

[90] TO MODEST TCHAIKOVSKY   Moscow
                                               13 February 1873

Dear Modia,

You say that I have become quite silent! But did not Sasha get my letter written last month? I meant it for both of you and will be upset if it did not reach you. . . .

You probably have read in the papers about my symphony; I may add to what they say that it did have great success, especially 'The Crane' which got the most flattering notices. The honour for this part of my composition must go not to me but to the real composer of this piece of music – Piotr Gerasimovich who, whilst I was playing 'The Crane' song, came up to me several times and hummed this:

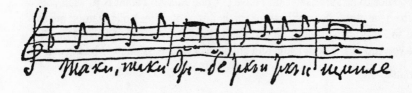

When I was in Petersburg and played the finale at an evening at Rimsky-Korsakov's house all those present were so enthusiastic that they nearly tore me to pieces. Mme [Rimsky-] Korsakova implored me to allow her to make a transcription of it for a piano duet. She may if she likes. For this composition I get back my credit note for 300 roubles from the Musical Society and in the concert it will be given again (the symphony not the credit note) and a gift and a reception are being got ready for that day. Naturally with my angelic disinterestedness I want to refuse the present but I doubt if they will allow me to do so. Ah! How hard it is to submit to the tyrannical demands of the public; they do not understand that we artists live at such empyrean heights that money for us is – a base metal.

Soon the time will come when Kolia and Tolia and Ippolit and Modia will not be Tchaikovskys any more but only the brothers of Tchaikovsky.

I cannot deny that this is the great aim of all my endeavours; to rub into dust everything around you – is that not the greatest delight! So tremble, for my fame will soon crush you.

The 'charming and amusing' tone of my letter has been inspired by my seeing a lot of Apukhtin who is here now, in a better frame of mind than ever before, in spite of having lost everything he had won at cards. A few days ago I was a witness at his Andrei Apukhtin's wedding; he married his own aunt. Lelia [brother] as the *chef de la famille* does not recognize this marriage, but was present at the ceremony, insisting that he had come only because he saw lights in the windows.

You want to know about my plans for the summer. I do not know, honourable sir, I do not know at all, but I am sure not to miss coming to Kamenka.

I kiss you hard, Sasha, Leva and all the others.

P. Tchaikovsky

TO ILYA PETROVICH TCHAIKOVSKY   [Moscow]
                                                    7 April 1873

My dear, my beloved Papochka!

For a whole month now I have been working very hard at my desk. I am
writing the music to the fairy tale *Snegourochka [Snow Maiden]* by Ostrovsky,
and just had no time to write letters. Besides, two days ago, I had a slight
accident; I cut my hand so badly that it took two hours for the doctor to stop
the bleeding and to bandage the wound. Hence I cannot write very easily and
beg you not to be surprised that I have not done so. All I want is to wish you
and the dear 'Bun' the very best for the holidays. Brother Kolia wanted me to
come and stay with him but unfortunately I cannot. And so: 'Christ is risen!'
I kiss you thrice and your 'Bun' and am always your passionately loving son

P. Tchaikovsky

My dear one, let me know when you will be coming through Moscow and what
your plans are.

[92] TO ILYA PETROVICH TCHAIKOVSKY   [Moscow]
                                                    24 May 1873

My dear beloved Papochka!

My heart wants me to fly off to you but for the moment I have to be content
with written expressions of my unending love. The fact is that I am planning
to travel this summer; first to the south – to Kiev and Kamenka, then, in the
second half of June, abroad via Elisavetgrad, Jmerinka and Volochinsk. It would
be too expensive to go to Petersburg which is why I will be deprived of the
pleasure of embracing you. What a pity that you have decided to stay in Peter
[sburg] and that we shall not be able to pass a few days together in Kamenka!
I will not fail to write from Kamenka and from abroad, and shall probably
return by way of Petersburg. All these last weeks I have been hectically busy,
with the production of Ostrovsky's play with music; the transcription of my
symphony for the publishers; examinations; and a reception given by the Grand
Duke Konstantin Nikolaievich. He was most kind to me, delighted with my
symphony, and full of compliments.

My health is in order except that my nerves are irritated, I am frightfully tense
and exhausted, and the best cure will be travel. Excuse the scrap paper I am
using, it is four o'clock in the morning and I seem to have run out of writing
paper.

I kiss your hands and embrace dear Lizaveta Mikhailovna.

Your son

P. Tchaikovsky

TO ILYA PETROVICH TCHAIKOVSKY   Paris
23 July–4 August 1873

Dearest Papochka!

As usual my conscience tortures me for not giving you any news about me but
I do not know your address in Pavlovsk. Am writing to Petersburg hoping it
will reach you. Perhaps one of you will be there and fetch it. I left Sasha the
day before my name-day and have, since then, been wandering over Europe.
Went to Breslau, Dresden, Cologne, Zürich, Lucerne, Geneva, Milan and the
Lake Como, and at last I am in Paris where I have been for the last three days.
In Switzerland I did a lot of wandering around and went up to the top of the
Rigi mountain by a newly built railway of the most extraordinary construction.
I also went to Vevey where I got all the information Sasha wanted and send
it to her. She can get very good and cheap accommodation there. The
boarding-schools for girls in Vevey are excellent and she will be able to send
all the three eldest girls as day pupils for 30 francs a month. Vevey is
beautifully situated, although at first one feels a bit awed by the high giants
towering around one.

From Switzerland I went off to Italy hoping to travel up and down all over
the country but, even in Milan, the heat was so intense that I did not dare to
travel further south and turned my steps towards Paris which is charming at
any time of the year. One cannot really describe how comfortable and
agreeable Paris is and how delightfully a man who wants to have a good time
can pass it here. Even walking along the streets and looking into the shop
windows is interesting and amusing. And then the theatres, drives out of town,
museums — all this takes up so much of your time that you do not notice how
quickly it goes.

Please tell Lida Olkhovskaia that at every step I have memories of our stay
together in Paris twelve years ago. I hope to stay here a week and then back
home. It is doubtful whether my finances will allow me to travel via Petersburg,
so I fear I shall not see you this summer. But the consoling thought is that
when my opera will be produced I will have to be in Petersburg for quite a long
time.

I embrace you with all my might, my Golubchik. Kiss for me Lizaveta
Mikhailovna and Lida and give my regards to Katerina Ivanovna.

Yours

P. Tchaikovsky

TO ILYA PETROVICH TCHAIKOVSKY   [Moscow]
9 October 1873

My dear Papochka!

I am deeply ashamed and kiss your dear cheeks and hands and beg again to be
forgiven for being so lazy. However, I think you will understand: I get so

tired. I have so much to do that when I return home to rest there is no energy left for letter writing; these last days I have not been well. My throat was sore, I had a temperature, and I am still bothered by a nasty cough. But none of this is really serious and otherwise my health is good. Life goes on as usual. There is no time to be bored, but I would be happier if I had some news about my opera. I have just heard that there is nothing certain and it may not be played this season; but I am so sick of waiting and also need the money.

I am like a mother who hopes to get her daughters married and looks everywhere for the most eligible suitors. Not only do I want to hear my opera performed, but I would like, above all, to pass three or four weeks in Petersburg with you. It is so long ago since I had the opportunity to taste your lovely soup, sleep on the comfortable couch under the warm eiderdown, listen to the high-pitched laugh of our dear 'Fatty'; in short, to enjoy the charms of life with you, of which the most important is to be with you and kiss you as often as possible.

I am very angry with Modia. He could, at least, write me a short letter to let me know what he is doing and how he is settling down to his work. Please, box his ears for being silent – the Davydovs also worry about him. I go to see them every Sunday.

I kiss your hands and embrace dear 'Bun'.

Your son

Piotr

The Tempest (Op. 18), conducted by Rubinstein, was given its first performance on 3 December, and was repeated at an 'extraordinary' concert of the Russian Musical Society on 7 April, 1874.

    Tchaikovsky's new flat was on the Malaia Nikitskaia (now Kachalov Street). The Second Symphony was performed in St Petersburg on 23 February 1874, and was conducted by E. F. Napravnik.

[95]   TO MODEST TCHAIKOVSKY   Moscow
                                                       28 November 1873

My dear Modia!

I do not think that anybody has been so badly treated by me as you have; how proudly I promised you the subsidy of a hundred roubles a month and how meanly 'my Government bank' pays them to you. But, in a few days my finances will improve and then – honestly, joking apart – my debt will be paid. This change for the better will come, because next week my *Tempest* will be played and, as usual, I shall get 300 roubles from the Musical Society. This payment will buck me up a lot. I am very interested to hear my new composition into which I put great hopes, and am very sorry you will not hear it.

I have moved to another flat which, although smaller, is cosier than the previous one, and life goes on according to its usual pattern. The death of Vassili Vassilievich Davydov was sad news indeed. I went to the funeral – altogether a very sad and tragic occasion – and I think that, although it had been expected, his death was an awful blow to Alexandra Ivanovna.

Of all my friends I miss Kondratiev more than any one, he was here for five weeks and is now in Kharkov for the elections. I often dine with Shilovsky but it is not easy to find anything in common with him, for he gets more unpredictable and difficult every day. I have only lately come to the conclusion that I am actually rather lonely here. I have many friends but none like Kondratiev with whom I could have a heart to heart talk. Sophia Lvovna is a great source of help, but she is more a sort of living accessory to, or attribute of, my establishment than a proper friend. However, all is for the best, even the most charming friends, in numbers, interfere with one's work and I, thank God, am not being idle. To stop this little lament I must be honest – actually everybody loves me and I do not know how to thank them for it. . . .

I hoped to see you very soon but the performance of my symphony has been put off until the month of January. When the rehearsals of my opera start in Lent I shall come to Peter[sburg] and stay for some time.

I kiss you heartily, Tolia also and beg both of you let me know all about you. I kiss Papochka's hands and press to my heart Lizaveta Mikhailovna.

Yours

P. Tchaikovsky

On 16 December, 1873, Napravnik wrote to Tchaikovsky suggesting some changes and cuts in the score of *Oprichnik*, as well as some names for the cast. Three days later Tchaikovsky wrote back agreeing to make the alterations proposed; nonetheless, he was not altogether pleased with Napravnik. Bessel was given the rights of publication, but on terms very hard on the composer (Bessel was to receive a commission of 33⅓% of the composer's earnings on every performance in consideration of his trying to arrange performance at the Marinsky Theatre). Tchaikovsky was discouraged at the first rehearsals of the opera, confessing to Taneev on 25 March 1874 that 'there was nothing good in this opera'. The premiere was on 12 April, 1874, under Napravnik. Laroche praised the opera, Cui castigated it.

The first performance over, Tchaikovsky immediately went abroad, and in Milan wrote a notice of Glinka's *Life for the Czar* for the *Moscow Gazette*.

The Quartet in F major (Op. 22) was played by F. Laub, I. Grjymali, V. Fitzenhagen, and Y-G. Gerber, at A. Rubinstein's house. According to Kashkin, Rubinstein 'with his usual bluntness declared that the style was not that of chamber music and that he could not understand it'. The performers and other guests – Kashkin, Hubert and Albrecht – were delighted with it.

TO ANATOLI TCHAIKOVSKY   [Moscow]
                                            26 January 1874

My dear Tolia!

Today I saw Sasha Gudim and he gave me all sorts of news about you and told
me that you are very interested to know about my visit to St Petersburg. First
of all I stayed in the awful Hôtel Victoria with my valet, Mikhail; secondly,
I went straight to Napravnik with whom I had made an appointment by letter.
I decided to charm him by agreeing to all his demands and by being courteous
and respectful. This I succeeded in doing most brilliantly and we parted the
best of friends. All the four days I worked, shortening and changing the score.
I dined mostly at my father's and also worked there; whatever I did to run
away from everybody, I was still found and attacked at my hotel; I saw Bessel,
all the complications with the censor have been eliminated; to all intents and
purposes the opera is completely finished: rehearsals will start in the second
week of Lent, and go on every day and I know for sure that Napravnik will get
out of his skin to do well.

I have written a new quartet and will hear it one evening at Rubinstein's house.

A few days ago I went to see Fedotova, with whom I passed a whole evening;
she seemed to me to be an unnatural and affected bore. She declared that she
hated me, and that I cannot be compared to you. She talks about you with
such superlative enthusiasm that I am sure she is in love with you. . . .

The Royals are here and I have just been watching the drive from the
Kremlin to the Bolshoi Theatre for a 'Festival Gala'. Most imposing but
frightfully noisy.

Dear Tolia, I am very sleepy but to keep to the custom of writing four full
pages I am doing so in large letters.

GOOD-BYE TOLIA, TOLIA GOOD-BYE, GOOD-BYE TOLIA, WRITE TOLIA,
GOOD-BYE TOLIA, MY REGARDS TO JEDRINSKY, TOLIA GOOD-BYE TOLIA,
GOOD-BYE TOLIA.

Your brother

P. Tchaikovsky

TO MODEST TCHAIKOVSKY   Venice
                                            17–29 April 1874

There! Look at the paper and burst with envy! I have been walking about this
square all day. I got very tired and decided to chat to you, Modinka. . . . I was
in a very sad mood, and why? – for many reasons, one of which that, my going
away was not fair to you. Instead of spending all this money on foreign travel
I ought to have paid your and Tolia's debts, not go off at full speed to enjoy
the south. The thought of having been so mean and miserly tortures me

abominably and it is only when I express it on paper that I begin to feel some relief. So, dear Modia, forgive me that I love myself more than I love you and all the rest of humanity. I am also ashamed of my behaviour to Lizaveta Mikhailovna. I ought to have forced 100 roubles into her purse for the trip to Paris she has been dreaming about. You may think, perhaps, that I am acting the part of a self-denying person? Not at all; I know that this self-flagellation is futile, for here I am travelling and you are stuck at home with your debts. But at least I feel more at peace after confessing my sins.

I am back in Venice now. I do not mind the cold which is awful, after having experienced the hot weather in Italy last year. But because the town was full of foreigners I only found a small and dismal room – and this with the greatest difficulty. Venice is a town where you cannot stay more than five days unless you want to hang yourself in the end. Everything is concentrated on St Mark's Square. Anywhere else you get lost in a tangle of narrow passages which lead to nowhere, and only by hiring a gondola can you get out of them. It is worth going along the *Canale Grande* for you pass palaces, palaces and more palaces built of marble, each more beautiful than the other, but also more dilapidated and dirty. In one word, like a shabby setting to *Lucretia*. But the Palazzo of the Doges, on the other hand, is the crowning beauty, and invested with all the romanticism of the 'Council of the Ten', the inquisition, tortures, dungeons and similar delights. For the sake of a clear conscience I went all round the town again; and to two or three churches with a multitude of paintings by Titian, Tintoretto, statues by Canova, and other artistic gems. But I repeat, the town is gloomy, as if it had died; not only no horses but I did not even meet a dog.

I have just received a telegram from Milan in answer to mine. *A Life for the Czar* will not be on before May 12 (new style) and I have decided to go to Rome and then to Naples where I will expect your letter. I kiss Papochka, you and Lizaveta Mikhailovna.

P. Tchaikovsky

[98] TO ANATOLI TCHAIKOVSKY   Rome
                                 19 April–1 May 1874

Dear Tolia,

To ease the state of despondency my soul is in, I am writing to you; solitude is a good thing and I like it but only up to a certain point. It is now a week since I left Russia but I have still found no one with whom to exchange a single word; except for the hotel servants and railway guards I have not spoken to anyone. In the morning I wandered around the town and saw such marvellous things as the Colosseum, the Thermae of Caracalla, the Capitol, the Vatican, the Pantheon, and lastly the summit of human genius – the Cathedral of St Peter. I then had dinner and afterwards went to the Corso, and here I had such an attack of spleen that I only hope to get saved from it by writing to you and a cup of tea that I am waiting for.

I travelled from Petersburg to Venice without stopping; but had to stay the night in Warsaw as the twelve o'clock train from Petersburg has no direct connection with the foreign one from across the frontier. The journey tired me but had a salutary effect upon my very tense state of nerves. I only stayed in Venice for a day and a half and did not specially enjoy it. You who have been in this queer town, will agree with me that it gives a dismal impression. From there I got in touch with Milan by telegraph and finding out that *A life for the Czar* will not be given before May 12 (April 30) I decided to go to the south, by-passing Florence. I am trying to take advantage of the cold weather which in Venice was so severe that I was freezing in my room. In Naples this change of weather, which has affected the whole of Italy, is of great advantage, for when the hot weather comes, half the pleasure of being in Italy will disappear.

Except for the historical and artistic sights of Rome, the town itself, with its narrow and dirty streets, lacks interest, and I do not understand how one can live all one's life here (after our vast and free countryside), as some Russians do. I have plenty of money and can, if I wish, travel all over Italy without refusing myself anything. I took in Venice what is called a *billetto circolare* which cost only one hundred and seventy three francs and allows me to travel to Naples and then back to Milan – very cheap.

Concerning money! – From the first day I left I have been blaming myself for being hard and selfish. Instead of travelling around Europe I should have helped to pay your and Modia's debts. Here I am, I say to myself, walking about the Vatican when poor Tolia is trying to find a way of paying one of his creditors. If you could imagine how bitter is my repentance! But I wanted madly to go to Italy; this was really silly, for I ought, for a change, to have gone to Kiev or the Crimea – cheap and good.

My dear Tolia, I embrace you as much as I love you, and I really love you deeply.

P. Tchaikovsky

I would gladly give much to have you here.

[99] TO MODEST TCHAIKOVSKY   Florence
                                       27 April–9 May 1874

I am sure you think – what a lucky fellow! First he writes from Rome, then he was in Naples and now, all of a sudden, a letter from Florence. In spite of that you could not imagine a more home-sick person. In Naples I was in such a state that I shed tears out of sheer longing to see my home country and all my nearest and dearest. I would have given much at such moments of black melancholy to at least have had Nikolai Lvovich with me.
Everything in Moscow seems especially sweet. . . . I think of you and some of the Peter[sburg] friends with delight, but Petersburg is really the reason

for my melancholy. I am tortured by my *Oprichnik*; this opera is so bad that at rehearsals (especially the 3rd and 4th act) I used to run away so as not to hear so much as one sound of it; and I wanted to disappear through the ground at the first performance. The extraordinary thing is that when I wrote it I thought it really charming. But, what a disappointment! From the very first rehearsal, no movement, no style, no inspiration! All the applause and curtain-calls at the first performance meant that there were a lot of friends in the audience and that I had already built up a good reputation. I know the opera will not be on for more than six performances and that is killing me. Also I am very worried about what I said in my first letter and, to crown everything, the weather is awful.

The Italians say they do not remember such a bad spring. I stayed in Naples for six days, but it is as if it was not there; for without any sun it is nothing. I did not see the blue sky once during my stay, and the last two days I never went out. I ran away from there as fast as I could hoping to go straight to Sasha's, missing out Milan where, for important reasons, I did not want to be. I heard from Shchurovsky that the way *A Life for the Czar* is produced there is impossible. If I went I would have had to interfere and give advice which I fear would be not very enthusiastically received.

I stayed in Florence only for the night, thinking to stay two days at Sasha's, then straight back to dear Moscow. However, I may pass through Peter[sburg] where I only want to see you, Papochka and Lizaveta Mikhailovna; so do not mention to anyone that I may come. We will perhaps see each other soon after this letter, but not for sure; I am drawn to Moscow not only by home-sickness but because of my classes that are worrying me. I received your letter, and also letters from Ania Malozemova, in Naples; actually I am only writing to relieve my soul by talking to you. I went to Pompeii, which made a strong impression on me.

Good-bye Modia, until very soon.

Your

P. Tchaikovsky

I only had time to run through the streets of Florence and like it very much. I hate Rome – and as to Naples – let it go to the devil! There is only one town in the world – Moscow, and, maybe, also Paris.

A few days later Tchaikovsky went back to Moscow and started work on *Kuznez Vakula* (*Vakula the Smith*), Op. 14, for a competition of the Russian Musical Society. The libretto, by Y. Polonsky, was based on a story by Gogol. Tchaikovsky finished the opera by 24 August 1874. Piotr and Modest had stayed with N. D. Kondratiev during a summer holiday they took together in 1871. Kondratiev, a dilettante and friend of Piotr, owned much land in Kharkov, including the estate in Nizy.

Nizy
18 June 1874

You wrote your letter a month ago and I got it when still in Moscow, but have not answered up till now. Life here is organized in such a way that there is no place in it for letter writing. First of all I drink Carlsbad waters, secondly, despite your boldness in trying to stop me from doing so I am busy composing *Vakula*.

The order of the day is as follows: I get up at 6.30 and drink five glasses of mineral water from seven to nine. Then we have tea; then piano playing (mostly Schumann) and reading until 12, then lunch. From 12–3 I work, i.e. composing *Vakula*; from 3–5 first game of bezique (which attracts me greatly) then bathing and dinner; after dinner a solitary walk which lasts about two hours, then a rest on the porch, and then tea at nine in the evening, after which we have another game of bezique until bedtime at 11 or 11.30.

This orderly life, with scarcely any variation has been going on for two weeks. The two of us live quite alone, only the doctor calls sometimes or one of Nikolai Dmitrievich's brothers. I am immensely pleased with this sort of life and, what with the mineral waters, expect much benefit from it so far as my health is concerned.

The harmonious current of our life and its peaceful flow have been disrupted recently (luckily not for long) by the visit of Saveliev, Julie's youngest son. This young man rejects all kind of authority, from morning till night, cuts aesthetics down to size, and annoys me with discussions on music. At the same time he hints that he has no respect for me at all, while roundly abusing Beethoven and Schumann. In short he discusses everything in an impossibly presumptuous manner which makes me fly into a rage.

J'ai pris le parti de ne pas talking to him. As soon as he starts I either leave the room or keep absolutely silent. Luckily he is going away tomorrow.

Nikolai Dmitrievich and I often talk about you. He begs me to say that he will not write until you do. It would be a good idea if you did let us know how you are getting on yourself, and with Tolia, and if you are thinking of coming here? . . .

I embrace you both and am yours.

P. Tchaikovsky

Modest Tchaikovsky wrote a long letter to his brother on 24 October, 1874, after having heard a rehearsal of the Second Quartet at the Davydovs and the first public performance. At the rehearsal Davydov said that it was Tchaikovsky's best work; Auer that it had the force of Beethoven (according to Modest the only composer most Russians would listen to); Malozemova wanted to send a congratulatory telegram. During rehearsal Auer and Davydov disagreed over the tempo of the Scherzo, the former wanting it faster, the latter slower. In the end Davydov's views prevailed and Modest found the slower tempo at the concert less than convincing. However, the slow movement was played marvellously, so that some of the audience called out 'bis!' at its conclusion. The finale was absolutely convincing. Modest heard Rimsky-Korsakov unreservedly praising the work to Cui, as also the Grand Duke Konstantin Nikolaevich to whom it was dedicated, and Count Litke.

Disheartened that the competition for which *Vakula the Smith* had been intended would offer no hope of performance for another year, Tchaikovsky hoped that he might be able to arrange privately for its production at the State Theatre.

Although Tchaikovsky was very critical of Mussorgsky he reckoned him to be the most talented of the 'Five'.

[101]   TO MODEST TCHAIKOVSKY   Moscow
                                        29 October 1874

Imagine Modia that I am still sitting over the piano score of my new opera. I gave it to Langer and Razmadze to do, and both said they would, but did not do much and what they did was so bad that I have to do it all over again. That is why I am so busy and do not answer any letters. I am most grateful for both of yours more so because you write as elegantly as Sévigné. Seriously I think you have a literary gift and I sincerely wish you could develop it enough to make you into a real writer. At least then I would be able to get a decent libretto, and not have to look and look without finding one. Berg the poet offers to write a libretto about the Hussites and Taborites. I asked if he had any plan. No, none at all, he said – he just liked them because they sung hymns. I would give a lot to have a good libretto from foreign history!

I am glad that you, Malozemova and all those who sympathize, liked my quartet; I look upon it as my best composition; none of my works flowed out of me so simply and easily. I wrote it practically at one go and was astonished that the public did not like it, for I find that compositions written spontaneously have every chance of success.

My life is in order, as much as it can be when the lack of money is great, as it has been since I have returned to Moscow. It is hopeless to wait for the competition as it will take place not on the 1st of January but only on August 1, next year. At the moment I am not contemplating writing anything new; I would like to start a piano concerto but somehow I have neither ideas nor inspiration.

I stay at home a lot but unfortunately I do not read. Either I work or I play. I have studied *Boris Godunov* and *The Demon* thoroughly. Mussorgsky's music I send to the devil; it is the most vulgar and vile parody on music. There are charming bits in *The Demon* but a lot of ballast. The Russian quartet performs here on Sundays and played my D major quartet. Go to hear Kraus, she is a good singer. Give my regards to Malozemova and tell her I will write to her.

I kiss Papochka's hands and embrace him with all my heart; and also Lizaveta Mikhailovna. Tell Papochka that I shall write to Bessel about *Oprichnik*.

I kiss you.

P. Tchaikovsky

Do write more often, you make me happy with your letters.

The Tempest (Op. 18) was played in St Petersburg on 16 November, 1874, the conductor being Napravnik. This work was much approved of by Stassov. On 9 December Tchaikovsky was in Kiev for a successful performance of *Oprichnik*. In those days the train journey to Kiev from Moscow took two nights and a day.

[102] TO ANATOLI TCHAIKOVSKY   Moscow
                                                 21 November 1874

Tolia! Your silence worries me, I wonder if anyone is ill or something else has happened; Modest especially astonishes me. I know that my *Tempest* was played a few days ago, why doesn't he report to me about this work. After the quartet he wrote two charming letters, Malozemova also and now no one except Stassov who wrote after the first rehearsal quite queer!

You told me to let you know when I am going to Kiev; I execute your order: I had a letter from Setov saying that *Oprichnik* will be played on the 19th. I begged Setov to have a performance on December 1 (providing the opera is not unsuccessful) and I am waiting for an answer; if I get a positive one I will leave on Friday (29th November) by the evening train and will return on Wednesday. So if you can come, be here on Thursday. But please do not miss your work just for the sake of a short trip.

I am engrossed in the composition of a piano concerto and want Rubinstein to play it at the concert; but it is not coming easily and well. I have, as a duty, to force my brain to invent piano passages, with the result that my nerves are very strained; that is why I want to go to Kiev although now that Tolia is not there any more it will lose 90% of its charm; also I hate *Oprichnik* with all my soul. In short, I need a trip and would love to have you with me. . . . At tomorrow's concert the overture to my *Vakula* is going to be played – called 'Overture to an unfinished opera'. Answer as quickly as you can.

I kiss you hard.

P. Tchaikovsky

Moscow
26 November 1874

My dear Modia!

Forgive me for answering your kind, long letters by short notes; last week, just before your last letter arrived I was getting worried without any news from you; especially after the performance of my *Tempest* and wrote to Anatoli to find out how you all were. A week has passed since and I still have no answer. Now I am worried.

What do you mean by saying that you do not want to be on the attached list? You must do all you can to reach a proper position in the service and make an effort to be on the attached list. Your wish to become an actor is absolute nonsense. Literary work is different, providing it does not interfere with your service for, however humble your position is at first, it will in the end give you a standing in life.

I am, down to the very depths of my soul, stuck with the composition of a piano concerto; the work is moving very slowly.

As to my other compositions I am very disappointed with the cold reception of my *Tempest*, not only by the general public but by my friends. You do not say a word about how you liked it. Malozemova is also as silent as the grave. Laroche's article made me furious. He is so insistent on saying that I am copying Litolff, Schumann, Glinka, Berlioz and some others. I am not hurt that he does not particularly like *The Tempest*. I expected it and am grateful that he, at least, praises some parts. But I protest against the general criticism that I have been filching from all the existing composers. However, I read his address to Rostislav with great pleasure. It is witty and elegant without Cui's coarseness and fierceness.

I congratulate you about entering the company of published writers. Would you, perhaps, like to write reports on the musical life in Petersburg, about both opera performances and the Musical Society concerts? I could have them published in the *Russian Gazette* and you would be paid by instalments (so much the line). What do you think? Let me know! Do not belittle your capabilities. . . .

If I get a telegram from Setov I might go to Kiev when *Oprichnik* is on.

P. Tchaikovsky

At about this time Anatoli was transferred to St Petersburg. According to Modest the overture to *Vakula* did not arouse much enthusiasm. Laroche's article in the *Golos* (*The Voice*) was not published in his collected writings. The article from Modest referred to in this letter, 'Musical News from St Petersburg', was published in the *Russian Gazette*, 1874, No. 274, on 20 December. Because Laroche was going abroad Modest was entrusted with the editing of the music page of the *Golos*, on condition that he invited well-known people to contribute. Having had a refusal from Piotr in respect of an article on Anton Rubinstein's *The Demon*, (St Petersburg, 25 January, 1875), Modest set to and wrote it himself.

On 24 December Tchaikovsky played his First Piano Concerto (Op. 23) to N. G. Rubinstein and Hubert. Three years later, angry with Rubinstein through some other cause, he told Mme von Meck of Rubinstein's reaction on that occasion. 'I patiently played the concerto to the end: it was greeted with silence. I got up and asked, "What do you think of it?" Suddenly a torrent of words gushed from Rubinstein's lips, getting louder and fiercer every minute until he sounded like a thundering Jupiter. According to him my concerto was no good at all; impossible to be played, with many awkward passages . . . so poorly composed that it would be impossible to correct them. The composition was vulgar, and I had stolen bits from here, there, and everywhere. . . . I was not only astonished but offended by this scene.' Instead of dedicating the work to Rubinstein the composer inscribed it to Hans von Bülow. In the course of time, however, Rubinstein was often to play it.

In January, 1875, Tchaikovsky composed his *Sérénade Mélancolique* (Op. 26) for violin and orchestra, dedicated to Auer, and he completed the scoring of the Piano Concerto on 9 February (see Letter 110).

[104] TO MODEST TCHAIKOVSKY   [Moscow]
                                          [Middle of December]

I work at my concerto without stopping and must finish it this week; so do not expect more than a few words from me, dear Modia. I am very, very, very pleased about your writing for the *Golos* [*Voice*]; read the first article and liked it. It is the right kind for Moscow and I shall send it to you as soon as it comes out – either Thursday or Friday. I would have placed it earlier but mine will be out tomorrow and articles about music on two consecutive days won't do. Your fee will be sent to Petersburg straight from the paper. I have told them they should pay you 4 kopeks per line; the article will be signed with the letter N.

I kiss you.

P. Tchaikovsky

[105] TO MODEST TCHAIKOVSKY   [Moscow]
                                          6 January 1875

My dear Modia!

I could not possibly satisfy your request concerning *The Demon*, because I know very little of it and what I know I do not like. I advise you to ask Malozemova; out of personal sympathy for the composer she naturally thinks well of *The Demon*. You know yourself that it is looked upon as the right thing to praise Anton Rubinstein. All you can do is to write a short article describing the plot and mentioning the best bits in the opera. You must not give any technical details, for, by now, everybody is aware that you are the author of the articles.

You complain that you find it difficult to write and have to sit quite a long time over every sentence. What else did you expect? Did you imagine that one can do things without any effort or hard work? I often sit for two long hours biting my pen and not knowing how to begin my article, then, quite unexpectedly, others praise it and discover it to have been written easily and spontaneously. Remember how difficult I used to find it to do my work for Zaremba. Just think how I ruined my nerves in 1866 at Miatlev's dacha, sweating over my symphony which would not come out properly, however hard I tried. Even now, when composing, I have to bite my nails sometimes, smoke an enormous amount of cigarettes, and walk up and down the room before discovering the main theme. Sometimes, on the other hand everything is easy and thoughts are born and push each other out as fast as they can. Everything depends on the mood and humour you are in. But even if you are not in the proper mood you have to force yourself to work. You will never succeed otherwise. You write that you are in a bad mood. Believe me it is not worse than mine. All to do with my accursed nerves.

What you write about Laroche pains me greatly, I felt with all my heart what they must have felt when they had to leave their children behind. And the poor little girl, she is also to be pitied. Give me Laroche's address: I want to write to him. Kiss Papochka's hand for his lovely letter, and kiss him, besides, all over and tell him how I love him.

Yours

P. Tchaikovsky

[106]   TO ANATOLI TCHAIKOVSKY   [Moscow]
                                                9 January 1875

... I hate holidays. During the week you work in an appointed time and everything runs in an even flow, like a machine; but during the holidays your hand does not hold a pen properly. You want to be with people who are near to you, and to have a heart to heart talk, and you get a feeling, probably exaggerated, of being an orphan, of being all alone. Honestly I live in Moscow slightly like an orphan; because of which I had a real attack of the spleen during the holidays. At the Davydovs it is boring and I have no close ties of friendship with my Conservatoire colleagues and their wives. What I really wanted was to go to Petersburg but I had not enough money. Besides not having anyone here whom I could call a real friend (like Laroche had been and Kondratiev is now) I could not get rid of the blow to my composer's pride which I got from, of all people, Rubinstein. When drunk he likes to say that he feels a sweet passion for me but when sober he knows how to irritate me to tears and sleeplessness. I shall tell you personally what happened.

Your Hubert too did not behave any better; these gentlemen cannot stop looking on me as a beginner, needing advice, severe criticism and opinions. It stems from my piano concerto which, laboriously and with much effort, I have been writing for the last two months. But this unfortunate composition did not have the honour of pleasing Messrs Rubinstein and Hubert who expressed their disapproval in a most unfriendly, hurtful, way. If one takes into consideration the fact that they regard themselves as my friends and that in all Moscow there is not a soul who would accept my work with love and attention, you can imagine how upset I was. It is quite extraordinary that people like Cui, Stassov and Co., who sometimes behave nastily to me, often make me feel that they are much more interested in my person than my so-called friends. Quite recently I had a very charming letter from Cui. Today I received a letter from Rimsky-Korsakov which greatly touched me.

I am very, very lonely here and if it had not been for steady work I would have got into a profound state of melancholia. . . . Please, do not imagine that I am not well physically, I am quite well, sleep well, eat even better – this is just a sentimental mood in answer to your letter.

P. Tchaikovsky

[107] TO MODEST TCHAIKOVSKY   [Moscow]
                                      [Middle of January 1875]

Modia! Run at once to Kraevsky and ask him to publish in the *Golos* part of my article as marked. I promised it to the Kiev artists who are very hurt that they are not mentioned in the Petersburg papers. Please, do it at once so that the article may appear before the holidays.
I kiss you.

P. Tchaikovsky

I saw Aladina yesterday, she is in raptures over you.

[108] TO MODEST TCHAIKOVSKY   Moscow
                                      [End of January 1875]

Modichka! I have sent an article to the *Golos*. Run to their office and beg them to have it published as quickly as possible. Do the corrections yourself, they must be done very carefully.

P. Tchaikovsky

[109] TO MODEST TCHAIKOVSKY   Moscow
                                      3 February 1875

Modia! I find it quite impossible that my article – written with pleasure and love, an article which is filled with real humour, wit, brains, erudition and such like good things – should be published without my signature. Honestly it will lose all its sense if it is not signed by me. I wrote to Bilbasov that I refuse to let *you* rewrite it. So, please send me the article back, at once, and, although it is a pity, I will have it published in the *Russkie Vedomosty* [*Russian Gazette*]. I would not mind it being published in the *Peterburgskie Vedomosty* [*Petersburg Gazette*] but it would be awkward as I mention Cui.

Tell me, for God's sake, why Kraevsky is afraid of Makarov objecting to my article but not afraid to publish it if you had rewritten it? Makarov will object to you just as much. I think the real reason is that either Makarov is a good friend of Kraevsky or, what you say about these gentlemen being delighted with my article is a lie and – they really find it indecent, badly written etc., etc., which is a pity, for the statistics at the end of the article are very interesting. I have nothing interesting to write about.

I am well. . . .

I kiss you

P. Tchaikovsky

[110]   TO MODEST TCHAIKOVSKY   Moscow
                                                 13 February 1875

Modia! I agree with you that writers are rabble. But what about it? Musicians too are often the same; must I therefore hate music? I do not in the least wish for you to become only a music critic. Your work for the *Golos* I look upon merely as a little window through which you are cutting your way into Russian literature. Your sphere is the novel.

You may not have a real talent but you have a positive gift, of taste and understanding, which Laroche esteems so much in you. Understanding is very important, many very clever people are devoid of it. Thanks to it you will never write anything vulgar or insincere. This may be only a negative quality but important in a writer. So do not lose heart and continue your work for the *Golos*. I am most displeased with that paper and it amuses me how, after a refusal to publish my article without giving any reason for it, they dare say they are offended by my telegram. I do not understand one of your sentences. You say that for the sake of my dignity it would be better not to have my article published – do you mean now, because of the snub I got from the *Golos* or later? Tell me about it.

Forgive me for writing so little. I am very tired. I have finished my piano concerto and have written a violin piece that I promised to Auer. I leave some space for Alesha who is very touched by your remembering him. I kiss you, Papochka and Lizaveta Mikhailovna.

P. Tchaikovsky

On 7 March 1875, Anatoli wrote: 'I grieve sometimes that when you are upset for one reason or another, and wish to pour out your sorrow into a sympathetic ear you forget about me, who certainly loves you more than myself – more than anything in the world. Meshchersky [see p. 52] told me you wrote to Kondratiev about feeling very lonely. If so, I think a visit from me would please you, but if I am wrong please let me know whether or not I should come – without any fear of hurting me.'

Tchaikovsky was in any case upset by the death of Ferdinand Laub, to whom he dedicated the Third Quartet (Op. 30). This work was completed on 18 February, 1876 (see Letter 119) and performed on 18 March.

[111] TO ANATOLI TCHAIKOVSKY   Moscow
                                                9 March 1875

Tolia! Thank you for your note. What you say about your love for me I know; as I love you no less it would be more than ever wonderful to have you near me when I am sad. Unfortunately cruel fate for the last ten years has behaved in such a way that those whom I love most in all the world are far away from me.

I am very lonely in Moscow, not because there is no one to pass the time with but because there is not a soul around me that I could call a close friend. I am sure you have noticed that my friendship with Rubinstein and my other Conservatoire colleagues is founded only on the fact that we all work in the same place. I have definite reasons for saying that none of them has any feelings of real friendship for me which I need so much. In one word there is no one near me to whom I can pour out my heart. Partly it is my own fault. I do not easily make friends with people. However, whatever the reason, whenever I have one of my attacks of hypochondria the absence of people really near to my heart is most upsetting. All this winter I have been sometimes more, sometimes less, in an awful state of despondency and disgust with life; sometimes to such an extent that I longed and called for death. Now, with the coming of spring these attacks have completely disappeared but I know that as the years go by – to be exact, during every future winter they will come again more acutely than ever.

I have, therefore, decided not to be in Moscow all next year. Where I am going to be and where I shall go I do not know but I must change both the place and the atmosphere I live in. We will discuss it when we meet; I shall ask you and Modest to come here for Holy and Easter weeks; also *Oprichnik* will be on, and it is worth having a look at it if only out of curiosity. . . .

You probably already know from the papers about the death of poor Laub. The day after tomorrow Flotow's *Martha* is going to be performed for the Grand Duke. Just imagine, I have several times been a juryman at the Law Courts.

Yours

P. *Tchaikovsky*

TO ANATOLI TCHAIKOVSKY   Moscow
                                                    12 May 1875

Dear Tolia! Thank you for the passport, I want it for it may be that I shall go
abroad for a short time. This, of course, depends on money which is always
short. Such is my never satisfied appetite, the more I have the more I need.
Since you left I am in good health and state of mind. I have been to many
rehearsals of *Oprichnik* and stoically endured the systematic disfigurement of
this unfortunate opera; ugly as it is in any case. However, last Sunday's
performance, to my astonishment, was much better than I expected. Everybody
did their best. It seemed to me that the audience was very cool which did not
prevent my sympathizers from yelling, applauding and presenting me with
wreaths, one of which, as I found out later, came from Derviz.

All my thoughts are now concentrated on my beloved child, my dear *Vakula*.
You cannot imagine how I love him. It seems to me that I shall go mad if
I have no success with this opera. It is not the money I am thinking of – I just
spit on it, although it is not to be despised. I want *Vakula* to be staged in
a good theatre. The score is ready, I am correcting it and will then send it to
Petersburg. I do not know at all how I am going to plan my summer days;
but in any case the first half of August I shall be with Sasha, so as to be able
to see you. . . .

And now, Good-bye, my Golubchik. I kiss and embrace you and think with
delight about my stay with you at Sasha's in the country.

Your brother

P. Tchaikovsky

In August Tchaikovsky began the music for *Swan Lake* (Op. 20, see p. 70) which
he finished on the following 10 April. (Concerning first performance, see p. 115). At
this time he was busy with articles for the *Russian Gazette*. Taneev played the Piano
Concerto at a Russian Musical Society concert on 21 November, 1875.

TO MODEST TCHAIKOVSKY   Moscow
                                                    14 September 1875

Do you know, Modia, that I have completely lost the capacity to write letters.
It took me nearly two hours to force myself to sit down and write one to you
and another to Kondratiev. I have lost all power to fight my laziness. Actually
there is nothing to be astonished about: I work at the Conservatoire, and
afterwards am hard at work composing a ballet. Then I write the music
articles. Is that not enough? I am accommodated as before, the only difference
being that I have moved up to the next floor; and live a little more
sumptuously. . . .

The Italian Opera has started; *Oprichnik* is going to be on in a few days with
the same abominable cast. I often see Taneev. If you only knew how

magnificently he plays my concerto. Thank you for the news about *Vakula*. I get the same reports from everywhere but am still worried about the fate of this opera. But if I do get the money for it you and I will go abroad to see Sasha. Let me know what you think about it and if you will be able to get leave. After which, being tired to the last degree I am coming to an end of this note, begging to be excused for not filling the usual four pages. . . .

I kiss you

P. *Tchaikovsky*

Skvorzov begs you to write the reports on music from Petersburg to the *Russian Gazette*. I embrace Papochka and Lizaveta Mikhailovna.

In the *Russian Gazette* (10 December, 1875, No. 252) Tchaikovsky answered the writer who accused him of being unfair to the singer Slaviansky. Tchaikovsky had said that the singer was principally concerned with obtaining the good opinion of the Moscow citizens, mostly well-to-do, and conservative, who lived across the river in the Zamoskvorezk district. The polemics of music criticism drove Tchaikovsky to retire from this activity. His last article appeared in the *Russian Gazette* 1875, No. 268, although he wrote five articles about the Bayreuth Festival which he attended in 1876 (see Letters 125–7).

[114] TO ANATOLI TCHAIKOVSKY   Moscow
                                                11 December 1875

My dear Tolichka!

I have been very busy lately and, with great energy, have also written to the papers about Slaviansky. There is a paper here, the *Contemporary Annals* which has been abusing your brother – who, as you so rightly say, has shamefully forgotten Tolinka and does not write to him! – in several of its leading articles. But after writing articles, giving lessons at the Conservatoire, dealing with the instrumentation of my ballet etc., etc., it is difficult to find enough time to have a proper chat with you. But the less I write the more I love you my dearest and best of all the assistant public prosecutors.

You most probably know already that because of the impossible cold in my rooms, I had to move to another flat and live now near the Vozdvizhenka – House Schlesinger in the Krestovozdvibzhensky Pereoulok. I pay 500 roubles per annum (in quarterly instalments) and have three very cosy rooms, with an entrance hall, kitchen, and toilet with water laid on. Of all the recent events in my life the most important is that I have become friendly with Saint-Saëns, a nice clever Frenchman who could be of great help to me in making my compositions better known in Paris. On December 6 *Der Freischütz* was performed at the Conservatoire after which there was a dance and supper. At the ball I danced like a madman and consequently was ill the next day.

Artôt made her debut here yesterday, she has become awfully fat and has nearly lost her voice but her talent helped her out and after the fourth act she was called back more than twenty times. A few days ago I received an official letter saying that my opera will be on at the Marinsky Theatre [Petersburg] in the next season. I am very glad.

I am expecting Modest here on Monday. Has he taken the situation at the Konradis? I would very much like to know. Good-bye my Golubchik! I shall be back from abroad on the 15th January; how happy I would have been if you had come with us!!

Yours

P. Tchaikovsky

You will get the photograph in a few days.

Modest and Piotr left Moscow on about 20 December to join their sister and her family in Geneva. Modest went with the intention of learning about the 'Gugentobler' method for dealing with the deaf and dumb so that he could apply it to the case of his pupil Nikolai Hermanovich Konradi. Modest stayed in Geneva after his brother had left. The latter broke his homeward journey in Paris, where he heard Bizet's *Carmen* for the first time. This work made a great impression on him.

[115]   TO ANATOLI TCHAIKOVSKY   [Geneva]
                                                 31 December 1875 –
                                                 12 January 1876

My dear Tolia!

. . . Modest and I took the route via Smolensk and Warsaw and were naturally a day and a half late arriving in Berlin. Modia liked Berlin very much and we stayed there two days. He went to hear *The Huguenots* and then we both went to the performance of *Around the World in 80 days*. We stayed at the Hôtel St Petersbourg, and arrived here exactly a week after we left Moscow.

Leva and the girls met us. We thought of going to an hotel but Sasha would not hear of it and we are with them although it is a bit tight. We pass the time very pleasantly but mostly stay at home and have had only a few walks around the town. I do not like Geneva but it is nice to be in a cosy atmosphere. Sasha's tummy has grown but she is quite well and merry. The children are as nice as they were in Verbovka. Tania has lost the style of an idle young Miss and makes a much better impression. Bebinka has grown; he is a dreadful tyrant so far as Modest and I are concerned and we carry out all his commands with delight.

I very much like the Norov family, especially Mme Norova. Tomorrow, for the New Year, I am giving a dinner at the Hôtel National to all our family and the Norovs. On Sunday we are leaving. I want to pass a few days incognito in Paris; so be good enough not to mention it in musical circles. The fact is that I do not wish to have anything to do with music during this trip and shall not go to see either Saint-Saëns or Viardot or anyone else. Consequently these people must not know I am in Paris. Thank you for the news you sent me, it is most gratifying. In general your letter has warmed my soul. I shall be in Peter[sburg] about the 15th.

I kiss you as hard as I can.

P. Tchaikovsky

Please, kiss Papochka and Lizaveta Mikhailovna.

[116] TO MODEST TCHAIKOVSKY   Berlin
                                            11–23 January 1876
                                            11 o'clock in the evening

My dear Modia!

If you only knew how I miss you. I cried all yesterday evening and today. When I think of you my heart aches and my eyes are full of tears. This sorrow, for a person whom I have not left in the middle of a wild desert, but at the centre of civilization seems highly exaggerated. Obviously the sickness I suffered from in Moscow and which had subsided during our journey together had not completely disappeared and now that I am alone again I plunge into the blackest thoughts.

If I had a little more money I would have rushed off to Paris to be able to have another day roaming around with you. I travelled to Cologne in a magnificent sleeping-car, more luxurious and comfortable than anybody could imagine. In Cologne I had to change and took a seat in an ordinary first class carriage. I arrived here at 7.45 and got to the hotel only at 8.30. Imagine my disappointment! *Lohengrin* was being performed today with Mallinger and Niemann, but it was impossible to get there in time, after having washed and changed. I would have been at the theatre after nine and the opera started at 6.30! Out of sheer disappointment I rushed off to Bilse's and had to listen to a quartet for four cellos, variations for a cornet-à-piston, and such-like horrors. And all this in a huge hall with small tables around which sit Berliners smoking stinking cigars. But it was impossible to stay at the hotel where not so long ago we had been together, full of pleasant anticipation about Paris and Switzerland.

Tomorrow, after a good night's sleep, I shall probably be in a better mood but at this moment I can only quote Katerina in [Ostrovsky's] *Storm*. 'Oh! How lonely I am without you!' Tomorrow morning I shall send you a telegram; writing this letter and the idea of sending a telegram has consoled me. The only good thing about separation from a beloved person is that it is possible to measure the strength of one's love for him.

After Bilse's I had supper at a dirty little restaurant and am back at the hotel now. My room is on the same floor as the one we had together. I have asked for tea and am writing to you.

I embrace you heartily.

Yours

P. Tchaikovsky

You will get the photograph in a few days.

[117] TO MODEST TCHAIKOVSKY

St Petersburg
20 January 1876
Monday

My dearest Modia!

I arrived here last week but am still sitting in Kanonerskaia [Street]. The reason for this is that my symphony is going to be played this week and I find it important for me to be present at the rehearsals; and as it made no sense to go to Moscow and back again, I decided to stay here. On the last day in Berlin I saw in the papers that the Andante from my quartet was going to be played at Bilse's, but, as it could be expected, Bilse was ill and the whole programme was cancelled.

Only since I am in Peter[sburg] surrounded by my family have I stopped being upset about our separation. Here is how I pass my time: (1) Wednesday evening: arrival, sauna bath, tea and supper with Papochka and Lizaveta Mikhailovna, and then to [meet] Tolia who returned late from a dance. (2) Thursday: various business meetings, dinner and tea at Meshchersky's. (3) Friday: business meetings, dinner at Dusseau with Tolia and Laroche, the opera *The Huguenots*, to the baths with Kondratiev, then tea with him and the Sheikh [Mirza Riza Khan]. (4) Saturday: business meetings including Napravnik. All in a dither – should I leave or not? Dinner with Azanchevsky, circus with Kondratiev and Meshchersky, evening at Apukhtin's. (5) Sunday: visits in the morning, loitering along the Nevsky Prospect [Main Street] with Laroche, dinner at home, visit to the Porokhovshchikovs, opera *(Tannhäuser)* supper in a pub. (6) Monday: various visits, dinner at Adamov's, [Serov's] opera *(Rogneda)*, tea at home. Today I am at rehearsal of [Cui's] *Angelo*, dinner with Meshchersky, in the evening my second quartet and later at Mme Davydova's. You see for yourself how much bustle there is.

I shall stay here until Sunday; the moment has come when I am being pulled about so much that I do not know any more where to hide from all the invitations. Besides the rehearsals I stayed here longer to discuss details of the production of *Vakula* which is going to be performed at the beginning of next season. I have no idea to whom I could give the part of Solokha. Kadmina will not be here, Kamenskaia is no good, Krutikova is coming to the end, and I have no idea who else I can get. Yesterday I had a serious talk with Azanchevsky about sending me abroad for two years. It may happen next year. I wish it and

E

fear it at the same time for, in spite of everything I love my Holy Russia and am afraid I shall get frightfully homesick.

We often talk about you and all of us, i.e. the Kanonersky inhabitants think that you ought to decide to stay at the Konradis. Just think, according to the agreement, you are to be with the boy only four hours a day. All the rest of the time you will be free to do what you like. I hope to find a letter from you in Moscow. Everybody at home is delighted with our presents. The gloves for Kondratiev are too small and I have given them to Tolia and Laroche. Dear Modia, I kiss you hard and implore you not to feel lonely and give way to sadness.

P. Tchaikovsky

I need not add that everybody sends their regards and kisses.

The Third Symphony (Op. 29) was played on 24 January, 1876, and was conducted by Napravnik. It was received with moderate enthusiasm by Cui, writing in the *St Petersburg News*, but without reservation by Laroche. Cui's *Angelo* (libretto by V. P. Burenin after Hugo) was first performed in St Petersburg a week later.

[118]   TO MODEST TCHAIKOVSKY   Moscow
                                                 28 January 1876

I returned the day before yesterday and found a mass of letters including yours, which gave me a lot of pleasure. I can vividly imagine what you felt when you found yourself in the centre of the Parisian 'Bohemia'; but it will do you good to have met all these people; there is nothing sillier than to travel, and to avoid meeting the people of the countries where you go, as I usually do. However interesting may the museums, theatres and restaurants be, people are always more interesting...

I do not remember where I stopped in my last letter (addressed *poste restante*) describing to you how I passed the time, but by the end of my stay in Peter[sburg] things were becoming impossible because people never left me in peace. My symphony was quite successful. I was much applauded and recalled. As to Taneev his success was no less than mine; he played brilliantly, especially Liszt's *Rhapsody*. At the quartet evening before this and during the concert I was happy to meet [Duke] Georg of Mecklenburg and found this young man very charming; I was also introduced to his mother and sister who were both most gracious to me. A. A. Davydova had two evenings with Apukhtin. who was the chief attraction and I enjoyed them very much.

I saw Laroche quite often, the circumstances of his life are very bad but he does not lose heart. Twice I went to rehearsals of *Angelo* with Laroche; he was chucked out of the second one and I left with him. I do not like the opera at all. Cui and I saw each other very often and once had dinner with Taneev at his house – Cui never stopped showing me his affection. I visited all *'mes cousins et mes cousines'* and had dinner with Laroche at Annette's.

I travelled to Moscow with Kondratiev and Meshchersky.... Good-bye, dear Modia. Your letter gave me indescribable pleasure and I am with impatience expecting letters from Lyon. Please do not lose heart.

I kiss you very very hard.

Yours

P. Tchaikovsky

Hans von Bülow wrote directly after the concert from Boston saying that on 13 January (Western style) the 'First Quartet was played finely and with perfect feeling and was received by the audience with enthusiasm'. With regard to Laroche's article Tchaikovsky misread it. Laroche did not say that the composer repeated himself, but that he 'was moving forward. In his new symphony the art of form and contrapuntal development stands at a height not reached in his previous works.'

K. S. Shilovsky wrote a libretto for *Ephraim*, the music critic K. I. Zanzer (1825–90) one for *Francesca da Rimini*. Neither subject finally attracted Tchaikovsky (full of enthusiasm for *Carmen* at the time), nor did suggestions by Stassov in respect of *Othello* and Alfred de Vigny's *Cinq-Mars* (see Letter 158 about Gounod's opera on this subject, of 1877). The theme of Francesca, however, became the inspiration of the Fantasy (Op. 32).

[119]   TO MODEST TCHAIKOVSKY   Moscow
                                             10 February 1876
                                             1 am

Dear Modia!

I got your letter from Lyon two days ago, and was interested in your descriptions and pleased with your general attitude of mind. I see that you are getting used to the new way of life. You have quite a talent for writing letters; you describe the people who surround you in a few words and I see them perfectly. About myself, quite honestly, I have nothing interesting to say.

Nothing unusual has happened; although my life is full of work, worries, feelings and impressions; but to tell you about them I need time which I have not got. At the moment I am busy finishing my quartet, started, as you know, in Paris. It is ready but not yet quite ready in score. I am also hard at work correcting my opera [*Vakula*]. I have absolutely refused to write any more articles and, mostly sit at home in a pleasant state of mind....

As to music I report as follows: I heard *Aida*, and am absolutely in raptures over it, especially over Artôt in the role of Amneris. A few days ago a letter came from von Bülow enclosing numerous articles about my first quartet played in America. Here the public's reaction was rather cold, including Laroche. Everybody agreed that there was nothing new in it and that I am beginning to repeat myself. Could it really be so? After this quartet I want to have a rest, to finish my ballet, and not write anything new until I start on an opera. I am wavering between *Ephraim* and *Francesca* and think that it will be the latter. As you remember I have been unfair to this, very cleverly written libretto – now I am beginning to like it.

I embrace you with all my might, dear Modia.

Yours

P. Tchaikovsky

[120] TO MODEST TCHAIKOVSKY   Moscow
                                                          3 March 1876

Dear Modia!

Your letters are a great joy. You will not believe how interesting all particulars of your life in Lyon are to me. . . .

My quartet begun in Paris is finished and was played yesterday evening at Rubinstein's. It has been greatly praised but I am not entirely satisfied. It seems to me that I am repeating myself and cannot invent anything new. Surely my song has not come to an end and will continue to go forward? If not it would be unfortunate. The best thing is not to work at all for a time to get my strength back.

I am still correcting the score of *Vakula* which is being published and will come out in a few weeks. We had an interesting concert in honour of Rubinstein who was presented with 26,000 roubles; if you add to this another 4,000 from the box office takings it will come to the nice round sum of 30,000 roubles. However, this Lent concert season is not very interesting because the theatres are also open. By the way, do you get the Russian papers? and are you in touch with what is going on in Russia?

You do not say anything about your latest plans and when you expect to be back in your homeland. . . .

I kiss you heartily

P. Tchaikovsky

[121] TO ANATOLI TCHAIKOVSKY   Moscow
                                                          17 March 1876

My dear Tolia!

I am up to my eyes in the orchestration of my ballet which must be ready by St Thomas's week. As I still have to finish two and a half acts I have decided to work at this most boring task both in Holy and Easter Weeks; to be able to do this I must get away from here. I know plenty of people who, knowing that I will be free of my Conservatoire duties will wish to exploit me, as for example Lyshin, who declared that he is purposely coming to Moscow in Holy Week to get better acquainted with me and make me listen to one of his creations. A lady from Dünaburg writes that she is coming to Moscow at the same time to ask me for advice about her studies on musical theory – and so it goes on . . . and on.

So as to be free from all these people and be able to finish my work in peace I have decided to go off for two weeks into the country to stay with Konstantin Shilovsky. But I am worried when I think that you wanted to come here then. Let me know if you have definitely decided to do so, my Golubchik, then I shall stay here, if you cannot come in St Thomas's week. It would make me very happy. You must know that my ballet would never make me lose the opportunity of having you here with me. Do not be afraid to be truthful and let me know. Moscow may have a special attraction for you in Holy and Easter Weeks, I understand that perfectly and shall stay with pleasure. In one word do with me what you like best.

The Grand Duke [Konstantin Nikolaievich] passed last evening with us; my quartet was played to him and he liked it very much. Today he was at the dress rehearsal of *Der Freischütz*, it is delightful, especially the orchestral and choral parts, absolutely lovely! Write as soon as possible.

I kiss you very tenderly. Kiss Papa and Lizaveta Mikhailovna.

P. Tchaikovsky

[122] TO MODEST TCHAIKOVSKY Moscow
24 March 1876

My dear Modia!

Why on earth did you ask Saint-Saëns about when my overture is going to be played? This made me angry; he may imagine that I am dying for it to be performed in Paris. This is true, of course, but Saint-Saëns need not know anything about it. Spring is with us, the streets even have dust on them. At the end of this week, and for the next two, I am going away to stay with Kostia Shilovsky in the country. I want to get rid of all the bustle of Holy Week in Moscow and give all my time to the ballet which must be ready as soon as possible.

If you could have seen how comical the ballet-master looked, composing the dances in a most serious and concentrated manner, to the accompaniment of a little fiddle. At the same time it was a pleasure to watch the male and female dancers smiling at the future audience and looking forward to the possibility of jumping, pirouetting and turning about in the execution of their holy duty. Everybody in the theatre is delighted with my music.

These last days my new quartet was played three times; the first time at the Conservatoire, for the Grand Duke, then twice in public. Everybody likes it. During the Andante [Andante funebre e doloroso] many people (so I was told) cried. If it is true it means a serious success. But my poor *Oprichnik* which is being given here again is executed in the most shameful way and spoils my reputation. . . .

I kiss you heartily

P. Tchaikovsky

Yuri Lvovich Davydov, the youngest of the Davydov children, was born in Geneva. He spent the last years of his life as Curator of the Tchaikovsky Museum in Klin. He died in April 1969.

Modest had now given up his other work to become full-time tutor to Kolia. (See p. 102.)

[123]   TO MODEST TCHAIKOVSKY   Moscow
                                       29 April 1876

My dear Modia!

You can imagine how happy I am that Sasha's confinement did not have any complications and everything is in order. I was very worried about her, had dark premonitions which, as usual, were wrong. I was also worried about you. I heard from Hubert that your Kolia has gone to join you. How was the first meeting; how did the first difficult days pass? I am certain that they will be the only hard ones for you. . . .

Now I have to talk about myself – but what about? Have not been quite well, having as yet not got rid of a cold I caught at a hunt in the country. Periodically I run a temperature, the last attack of which was so bad that the doctor thought it was the beginning of typhus. However it came to an end and I think it will not come again. The weather is awful, just imagine a bitter cold down to 5° [*Réaumur*] after hot June weather. I can't look without pity on the trees which had all blossomed out and now the leaves are shrivelled and brown. What is going to happen? What would happen if the trees stayed bare in summer. As I am short of money I have no definite plans for the summer.

Today I am going for one day to Petersburg, as I have been summoned by the directors concerning my opera. The piano score is published. Among my friends *Vakula* is causing a considerable stir. Taneev has memorized it from beginning to end, which pleases me greatly as *Vakula* is my favourite progeny.

A certain Lyshin, known to you, is here at the moment. A few days ago he played me his opera, *Count Nulin*. Oh! God, what a horror! And besides that this individual disgusts me by his self-confident dilettantism, vulgar jokes and arrogant manners. . . .

I kiss you.

P. Tchaikovsky

Dear Tolichka!

Here is a short report on everything I have been doing since I left Kamenka.
I arrived in Vienna on June 20 (our style); waited there for Sasha for a whole
week and was impossibly bored. They arrived at last and we had a lovely day
together. They left on Saturday the 26th and after seeing them off I went to
Lyon on the same day. It was a great pleasure to see Modest and meet all the
Konradi family. I found them putting little Kolia to bed. The little boy has
enchanted me from the very first sight I had of him. Later Modest and I went
to a café and chatted until midnight.

The two and a half days were spent as follows. In the morning Modest and
Kolia came to see me on their way to Gugentobler's [see p. 99]. I was alone
until twelve and then passed the day with Modest and his charge.

My love for little Kolia, called to life by his sweet disposition and temperament,
together with my deep feeling of pity, has been growing in geometrical
progression with every minute, and he has become one of the most cherished
beings in my life. As to Modest, I am astonished at the clever, tactful and
conscientious way he is doing his work. To my love for him I have now added
deep respect. The love between the teacher and the pupil is most touching and
several times I was near to tears. I have also come to love Sophia Alexandrovna,
good and kind creature who is a good friend to Modest.

The day before yesterday in the evening I arrived in cursed, horrid, disgusting
Vichy. Everything here has conspired to make my stay impossible. Up at
five to get a bath, crowds round the well where one drinks the waters,
worldly way of life, absolute lack of natural, beautiful surroundings and
complete loneliness – which poisons all my life. I feel so melancholy that I
doubt if I shall stay for the whole course. For all I know I will run away to
Lyon.

Ach! Tolia if you only knew how I hate foreign lands. The first performances
of Wagner's *Ring* will be given on August 1–4. The very next day I go full
steam back to Russia, straight to Verbovka, and hope you will come there too,
for certain. Do not fail me Tolia; I only live by hope. Oh! cursed, cursed, cursed
Vichy.

I kiss you heartily

P. Tchaikovsky

Write here, in any case, Hôtel Bellevue. If I leave before, I will tell them where
to forward.

Laroche wrote of the quartet in *Golos* (10 June, 1876, No. 159) and expressed his
displeasure thus: '[the last movement] is a pretty bolero suddenly turning into a
learned fugue. The first and second movements are interesting – meaning that they

are complicated and fine, but devoid of warmth and sincere charm . . . the third movement [andante] is one of the best inspirations of Mr Tchaikovsky.' He had written of the Piano Concerto on 5 November, 1875, that it took 'a very, very secondary place in the Tchaikovsky compositions'. A. S. Razmadze and A. S. Famintsin were music critics.

[125]   TO ANATOLI TCHAIKOVSKY   Vichy
                                                   6–18 July 1876

I hate Vichy deeply. Besides it being boring here and I am lonely, I have to get up at five o'clock otherwise I am not able to take the prescribed bath, as all other hours for baths have been booked.

However, I am not quite so lonely as I was, as I have met some nice people in the dining-room, especially the jolly, fat Antonin Kniajevich, and also because I have managed to deceive my doctor in quite a crafty way. I pretended that I had urgent news from Russia and could not possibly stay in Vichy more than eleven days. He told me it did not matter as the most important part of the cure could be done in that time and, that instead of the other ten, he would prescribe me Vichy water in bottles which I could take on my journey back or anywhere I wished; this would replace the time I shall miss here. You know Tolia, I have completely lost the capacity of living in a foreign land on my own. This will be a lesson to me. Next year I either will have to find a travelling companion or take Alesha with me. And so, I am staying another five days here and then will join Modest in Lyon. I will be there till my journey to Bayreuth and then straight back to Russia, to Kamenka, where I hope to embrace you.

I forgot to answer your query if I liked Laroche's article. On the whole – especially the first part – it is very good, I mean the brilliant and witty way it is written, but the part that concerns me is sickening. Tell Laroche (to whom I shall write myself) that I did not expect from him such a *Razmadze-Famintsin* lack of understanding which he has shown about my second quartet. I do not think that in all my life I have ever written anything more sincere and coming straight from my real deep personal self, as the first part of the quartet and he calls it elaborate and insincere. If his general attitude to my work which, although not always quite fair, is at least flattering then I am most grateful. However, lately when appraising my compositions he has been making such queer and incomprehensible mistakes that they have shaken my belief in his understanding as a critic. For example his disdainful attitude to my piano concerto. It is awfully strange!

If it had not been for Wagner's operas I would have gone off back to Russia at once, Russia which I adore the more I have to be in these disgusting foreign lands. If you are going to write (I implore you to do so) write to: Deutschland, Bayreuth, *poste restante*. I embrace you hard.

P. Tchaikovsky

[126]   TO MODEST TCHAIKOVSKY   Bayreuth
                                                  2–14 August 1876

Modia, you will understand that in all the bustle I am in at the moment
I cannot write a proper letter. I have just received yours. I too, but much
more than you, have gone through all the phases of anguish and distress which
you describe. As to my illness, it has come to an end only now. In Paris on
the day I wrote to you I had such attacks of colic that I got frightened,
I rushed to the chemist, bought the strongest laxative he had, drank a large
dose, and had an awful night, but was nearly well towards the evening of the
next day; this forced me to stay for another, very boring, day in Paris.

On my way here I was terribly nostalgic for you, for Kolia, for Russia, for
Moscow, and for a multitude of other things. I stayed the night in Nürnberg,
and arrived here on the eve of the performance, on Saturday, [August] 12/
[July] 31. I was met by Klindworth. I saw a lot of acquaintances and instantly
dived into a gulf in which I have been tossed about since then. Completely
dazed.

I have met many new people; visited Liszt who was most kind; and Wagner
who at the moment does not receive anyone, and so on. . . . Out of those whom
you know: [N.G.] Rubinstein is here – we are staying together – who also
arrived on Saturday; Laroche, who is drunk from morning till night; Cui, whom
I brought together with Laroche, but with the only result that two hours later
they had quarrelled again.

The *Rheingold* was performed yesterday. As a theatrical performance it
interested and attracted me by its marvellous stage settings and production – as
to the music, it is an impossible medley through which extremely beautiful
and extraordinary details shimmer.

Bayreuth is a tiny town where several thousand people, cramped by lack of
accommodation and insufficiently fed, have now assembled. We had booked
our lodgings in advance and are very comfortable. As to food, I got supper
with great difficulty on my arrival and had dinner yesterday only thanks to
a slice of good luck. I am not in the least bored but not really enjoying myself,
as all my thoughts are concentrated on how to run back to Russia, via Vienna,
which I will probably do on Thursday. You really cannot imagine how I love
you and Kolia, how I am always thinking of you, and how sweet and, at the
same time, sad, I felt when reading your letter.

I kiss you both hard. My regards to Sophia. Answer to Verbovka,

P. Tchaikovsky

[127]   TO MODEST TCHAIKOVSKY   Vienna
                                                  8–20 August 1876

I do not know why, but I think that by now you are no longer in Palavass
so I address this to Lyon. Bayreuth has left a dismal impression although my

artistic pride was very flattered there. Apparently I am much better known in Germany than I thought. The dismal memory is the result of the indescribable activity there; then on Thursday all came to an end and with the last notes of *Götterdämmerung* I felt free at last. Maybe the *Ring* is a great composition but I have never heard anything so boring and so drawn out as this. A collection of the most complicated harmonies, the singing parts colourless, unending dialogues; a hellish darkness in the theatre, lack of interest and poetry in the subject – all this is excessively tiring to the nerves. And is this what Wagner's reform is leading to? Up to now one tried to charm people by music, now one tortures and exhausts them. There are, of course, beautiful parts but the whole thing together bores me to death.

The day after *Götterdämmerung* everybody left except Laroche who stayed for the second series. Laroche is in such a state of nerves that I sometimes feared he was going out of his mind. He hasn't got a penny and although [N.G.] Rubinstein and I gave him each 100 roubles he found it was not enough. From Bayreuth I went to Nürnberg where I stayed the night and wrote my report to the *Russian Gazette*. What a charming place Nürnberg is!

I arrived in Vienna this morning, tomorrow I travel to Verbovka. . . .

I kiss you hard, dear Modia! Kiss Kolia's eyes and his little palm! How I love the little fellow!

I embrace you. Regards to Fofa.

P. Tchaikovsky

[128] TO MODEST TCHAIKOVSKY   Moscow
                                          17 September 1876

. . . I pass my days as colourlessly as usual, but it has its own charm: I cannot properly describe that feeling of sweet peace and of near happiness that I feel in my small but cosy flat, when I come home at night and take a book in my hand. . . . Only my composing is at a stop. Since my return I have scarcely written anything. I am slightly apprehensive at not having heard from Petersburg if my *Vakula* is being produced. Are they rehearsing the choruses? I have not heard from anybody. Anyway, even if *Vakula* will not be produced at all I will accept the fact stoically. I have become a frightful philosopher.

I kiss you lovingly

P. Tchaikovsky

[129] TO ANATOLI TCHAIKOVSKY   Moscow
                                          20 September 1876

. . . of course I would like *Vakula* to be performed as soon as possible. I do want to hear my favourite child. But if fate decides that [A. Rubinstein's] *Maccabees* must be given first I will not get upset. All I want is to be sure that

Vakula is going to be produced during this season. If you see Bessel you may tell him he is a son of a bitch, if he intrigues against *Vakula*. You can also tell Anton Rubinstein: 'My brother informs you that you are a son of a bitch!' My God! how I have grown to hate this man lately! He has always behaved to me in a condescending manner. No one has hurt my feelings and my self respect and honest pride in my own capacity (sorry Tolia, for boasting) as this arrogant Peterhof houseowner. And now he pushes forward his scurvy operas to be in my way! Surely this stupid and most bombastic of all humans should be content with his fame abroad! Is Berlin, Hamburg, Vienna etc. . . . not enough. If it had not been for the Penal Code Volume XV, I would go to Peterhof and with the greatest of pleasures set light to his dirty dacha. I feel better now after having given vent to my anger. I kiss you and embrace you with all my love.

Yours

P. Tchaikovsky

What do you think, I have just received an invitation from the Vienna Philharmonic Society! An invitation to play at a concert there! Quite a joke!

[130] TO MODEST TCHAIKOVSKY   Moscow
                                                   14 October 1876

Dear Modia!

After wondering about your long silence for two weeks I became worried, and then my worry turned to fear and distress. If when I am back from the Conservatoire tomorrow I do not get a letter I shall send a telegram. Either one of your letters has been lost or you are ill! . . . But if it is just laziness you should be ashamed. . . .

Have just finished my new composition, the fantasy *Francesca da Rimini*. I wrote it with love and love has come out well. As to the hurricane, one could have written something more like Doré's picture but it did not turn out as I wished. Anyway it is impossible to give a proper judgment on this composition so long as it is neither orchestrated nor played. I have already told you about the Serbian [Slavonic] March. As to *Vakula* I have no definite news about it but I know it is just about in rehearsal. Have I told you that I am taking cold baths in the morning – like Tolia? It has an excellent effect on my health. I have never felt better (please spit three times). This (I mean the cold water) had and will have influence on my work. If *Francesca* is something fresh and new, it is to a great extent due to water. . . .

I am most interested in Strusberg's case which is on at the Law Courts and often go there. Good-bye dear Modia, am expecting news with feverish impatience. Kiss Kolia a million times.

Yours

P. Tchaikovsky

War with Turkey did not break out until April 1877, but relations between Russia and Turkey were acutely uncomfortable as from August 1876 when a new Sultan, Abdul-Hamid II, was installed. The reason for war was a common concern about the balance of power in the Balkans, which was greatly affected by a developing sense of pan-Slavism. As a result of the Turks seeking an armistice in the spring of 1878 the Congress of Berlin took place, at which the pursuit of self-interest by the great powers ensured the certainty of future disasters in the Balkans. Tchaikovsky was caught up by the general pan-Slav fervour. (See Letter 177.)

On 24 November *Vakula* was produced for the first time at the Mariinsky Theatre in St Petersburg. Great care was taken with the production, and the cast included the great singer Ossip Petrov and Fyodor Stravinsky, the father of Igor, but the reception of the work was discouraging. Tchaikovsky wrote to Taneev that it was his fault, because there was too much detail, a too dense instrumentation, and too little that was truly operatic.

[131] TO ALEXANDRA DAVYDOVA   Moscow
                                               8 November 1876

I am sure, my sweetest girl, that you were not quite well when you wrote, for your letter sounded sad. When I read it I recognized one who is bound to me by the tightest of bonds. The melancholy, of which your letter is full, is well known to me. Sometimes for hours, days, weekends, months, everything looks black; it seems that you are abandoned by everyone, left alone and no one loves you. But I explain my state of despondency, and my weakness and sensitivity, by my bachelor state and absolute lack of self-denial. To tell the truth, I live following my vocation as well as I can, but without being of any use to individual people. If I should disappear from the face of the earth today, maybe Russian music would lose something – but surely no one would be made unhappy. In short, I live the egoistic life of a bachelor. I work for myself, think only of myself, aspire only for my own welfare. This is very convenient, but it is dry, narrow, and deadly.

But how you, who are quite indispensable to so many people, so useful to many others, and a consolation and treasure to all of us – how you can allow yourself to get despondent, I do not understand. How can you doubt that everybody with whom you have anything to do loves you! It is impossible not to love you. I am sure that even these silly idiots, the ladies Bulatova and Druzkaia, however much they gossip, adore you in their innermost hearts. Please, do not worry any more about it, there is no one in the world more beloved than you. And you deserve it. Not only because of your charm but the whole of your life, which has never been anything but a blessing, even to those who had only a slight connection with you.

As to myself, it would be useless to assure you again that I love you. If I do love anyone it is certainly you, your family, my brothers, and our old man. And love you I do, not only because you are the nearest and dearest people to me but also the best people in the whole world. . . .

112

Unfortunately there is a delay with the piano: until the end of the mobilization no goods are accepted on the Kursk railway. So you will have to wait a little and get the piano over from Verbovka. As soon as it is possible the piano, which is ready for the journey, will be sent off to you.

Any day now I am expecting an invitation to Peter[sburg], where my opera is being produced at the end of November. Last Saturday my Serþo-Russian March was played and brought a storm of patriotic enthusiasm. I am sure to be with you for Christmas; the hope of seeing you and all your family keeps me going and consoles me.

I embrace you with all my strength.

Yours

P. Tchaikovsky

Tchaikovsky, flattered by Tolstoi calling on him, arranged a concert of his chamber music at the Conservatoire for the great writer. During this concert Tolstoi, sitting next to the composer, burst into tears while the slow movement of the First Quartet was being performed. In subsequent meetings, however, Tchaikovsky found his reverence for Tolstoi diminished because of the dogmatic manner in which Tolstoi projected nonsensical views on musical matters. On 24 December Tchaikovsky acknowledged receipt of some folk-songs which Tolstoi sent to him from his estate at Yasnaia Poliana; but the folk-songs were without merit or authenticity. For Tchaikovsky's first impression of Tolstoi's *Anna Karenina* (1875–7) see Letter 142.

[132]   TO ALEXANDRA DAVYDOVA   [Moscow]
                                                  23 December 1876

My Angel!

I presume that Alexandra Vassilievna has already brought you my letter saying why I cannot come. I am very upset about it especially now that Christmas is here. The town is full of people now who are pulling me to pieces – just as in Petersburg, and I had hoped to be able to work during my free time! My God! How gay it will be on Christmas day in your new cosy house and how I envy you. The memories of last year also upset me, for I then had one of the most delightful trips in my life with Modia.

I have no idea what to do with the piano. It is still impossible to send it by freight and any other way it will cost 60 roubles. But rest assured that it will be done as soon as the opportunity comes. I have not yet had any money from the Plesskys. . . .

A few days ago Count Lev Tolstoi was here. He came to see me several times and passed two evenings with me. I am very proud and flattered by his interest in me and am completely captivated by his personality.

And so I have to wish you a Happy New Year by letter. Shall think about the lovely time we had together on that evening last year.

I embrace you with all my strength.

P. Tchaikovsky

[133] TO MODEST TCHAIKOVSKY   Moscow
                                                  2 January 1877

Most honourable Sir Modest Ilyich!

I do not know if you still remember my existence. I happen to be your own brother. I hold the position of professor at the Moscow Conservatoire, and have written several compositions: operas, symphonies, overtures and so on. There was a time when you condescended to take an interest in me. We even took a trip abroad together last year which has left an unforgettable memory in my heart.

You often used to write charming and interesting letters to me! But now it all seems to me nothing but a sweet dream. Oh yes – you have forgotten me and do not want to know me any more!! But I am not like you. In spite of my antipathy towards keeping up a correspondence, in spite of my being very tired (it is midnight now), here I am sitting writing to you to remind you of my feelings of great love for you. And so, dear brother, I wish you a Happy New Year, health, happiness and success very soon in all your new ventures. My deep regards to your pupil Nikolenka whom I beg you to kiss with all my love. Also, please, dear brother, let me know how everybody is, if they are happy, and if they remember me?

As for me, dear brother, the holidays passed idly and not very happily. I wanted to work but was disturbed by friends. And now my relative Misha Assiere is on leave and staying with me. I must say, he is a very nice and sweet boy, and I, dear brother, stay at home with him every evening. Also, dear brother, an acquaintance of yours named Kotek often comes to see me, someone you like very, very, much.

Before the holidays I became very friendly, dear brother, with the writer Count Lev Tolstoi and am now in possession of a very nice letter from him. And he listened, dear brother, to my first quartet and during the Andante even shed real tears and this, dear brother makes me very proud.

And you, my dear brother, do not be so presumptuous to forget that I, dear brother, am a 'bird' of certain importance.

And now, good-bye, my dear brother.

Your furious brother

P. Tchaikovsky

In 1875 Saint-Saëns had urged on Tchaikovsky the desirability of giving a concert in

Paris with the Colonne orchestra and during the next year Taneev had talked to Saint-Saëns about the idea on Tchaikovsky's behalf. It was, however, not until Mme von Meck was able to help that such an enterprise was undertaken.

The first performance of *Swan Lake* took place at the Bolshoi Theatre on 20 February, 1877, that of *Francesca da Rimini* (Op. 32) at a Russian Musical Society Concert on 25 February.

[134]   TO ANATOLI TCHAIKOVSKY   [Moscow]
                                                12 January 1877

Dear Tolia!

I got your letter this morning and am quite upset by it. Why, suddenly, this unhappy tone? I really do not understand it. Women fall in love with you, your work smiles at you, all who know you love you! You only lack one thing – money! Surely money is not the reason for your dark mood? If so I should drown myself for you cannot imagine financial affairs in a worse muddle than mine. Anyway, Tolia, I would love to see you.

Perhaps you can manage to come here for Shrovetide? Actually, because of Papochka's illness I ought to go to Petersburg but after *Vakula* this capital city has become obnoxious to me, and you know very well that you will see much less of me there than if you come here. Naturally your stay here will not cost you a penny. Please, answer. If you prefer to come before Shrovetide so much the better; I do want to see you very, very much.

I will not go to see Glamsha unless she asks me to. I have met her several times and have been most attentive. She is a very pretty woman but . . . to be honest I would prefer to do without any visits to her. I have accumulated plenty of work and am also thinking day and night about a trip to Paris in March, to give a concert there. I have been advised to do this both here and from Paris. But I need no less than 2,000 roubles for this! Where can I get them? All the preliminary steps have been taken but if I do not get any money it will have to be put off. It is impossible to waver and wait any longer. Please, do not mention it to any one but Modest. Come, dear Tolia!

Your

P. Tchaikovsky

[135]   TO ALEXANDRA DAVYDOVA   Moscow
                                                22 February 1877

My dearest, beloved Sania!

I am deeply in debt to you. I have been trying to answer your and Leva's letters for quite a long time but I have been prevented by laziness and a general state of confusion. The latter came about, not only from urgent work but from the fact that I have been nursing a plan – as you know – to give a concert in Paris. Now this plan has dived into oblivion or, at least, has to be put off to a more favourable time. I would have needed 2,000 roubles for its realization. I did not manage to find this sum. Let us hope that next year will be luckier.

I went to Petersburg for Shrovetide and spent several most agreeable days there. Papochka made me really happy, he is again so full of energy, fun and kindness. It was his loving ways that I missed most during his illness. Lizaveta Mikhailovna, however, has been complaining somewhat about him. He sometimes gets really fierce. All last week to my great delight, Tolia was here. He came on purpose to be with me and, at the same time, to hear the music of my ballet, which has been produced at last.

Unfortunately Moscow in general is overflowing with my music; it is being played practically every day and with great success. In spite of trepidation and uncertainty I conducted my Russo-Serbian March at the Bolshoi Theatre, with great success. I have decided to find as many opportunities as possible to conduct my own works. I must get rid of my stupid shyness, since if my plan to go to Paris matures I shall have to conduct there.

I hope to come to Kamenka at the beginning of Holy Week and stay until the end of Easter Week. Besides – I will get some money soon. Is there anything you want me to buy for you? If not I shall send you some money. I am most grateful to Leva for allowing me to wait in respect of my debt. Last week I had a wonderful present from the Director of the well-known piano firm of Bekker – a new, first-class, piano. What did you think about yours? I hope it did not get spoiled by frost, first here and then on the way to you.

Thank you for the photograph of Tania and Anna, they are having a fine time.

I embrace you with all my heart, my angel.

Yours

P.T.

[136] TO ANATOLI TCHAIKOVSKY   [Moscow]
                                                 18 May 1877

My dear Tolia!

Your letter has completely stunned me! Surely these 170 roubles 60 kopeks are not for two performances? If so it means that at both performances the theatre was nearly empty; this kills me because it shows that interest in the opera has suddenly waned. Please, let me know at once. If this money is for two performances then I will send you 150 roubles so that you can pay back both Malia and Papochka. I returned last evening from the country. Stayed two night with Kostia Shilovsky. I went to see him to ask him to put the libretto of my future opera into shape.

Tolia, I am going to write a charming opera which is absolutely in keeping with my musical character. You will be astonished when you hear what it is.

116

All those to whom I have mentioned it at first are astonished and then delighted. And do you know who suggested it – Lavrovskaia. And the opera is going to be *Eugene Onegin*. The libretto is charmingly constructed.

The last examination will be on the 28th and the next day I am off to stay with Kostia Shilovsky who has got a suite of rooms and a piano waiting for me. There I will feverishly write my opera until I feel that I want to rest and refresh my soul at Sasha's. This will probably be at the time of your leave; so you can come and join me in Glebovo from where we will make our way to Sasha.

If you agree, here is how to reach Shilovsky. Very simple. You get out at Kruvkovo station between Klin and Moscow where you hire a carriage and horses which will drive you for 30 versts through charming country to Glebovo, where I shall meet you with open arms.

Yours

P. Tchaikovsky

Modest had submitted a libretto based on *Inès de las Sierras* (1837), by Charles Nodier (1780–1844).

[137] TO MODEST TCHAIKOVSKY   [Moscow]
                                                18 May 1877

Dear Modia!

I did not answer at once as I went to stay with Konstantin Shilovsky at his place in the country for three days and had a lovely time there. What I have to say about *Inessa* is: The idea does not appeal to me at all and I have no desire to start working on it – a sure sign that this libretto has not got the basis of a good opera. Inessa's sufferings are romantic-dramatical, very much in the style of a cheap novel. No proper characters in the plot; Pedrina is an interesting figure but she appears only in the first act. The 'disguise' scene in the second act is unnatural and tedious. The whole thing is unpoetical and has no continuity! No Modia, my friend, you are no good as librettist but thank you all the same for the effort.

Last week I went one evening to see Lavrovskaia. The conversation came round to operatic subjects. Her stupid husband was talking awful nonsense and suggested all sorts of impossible librettos. Lizaveta Andreevna was silent and smiled condescendingly when she suddenly said: 'What about using Eugene Onegin?' The idea seemed wild to me and I did not say anything but later, while eating alone in a pub I remembered about 'Onegin' and started thinking. I thought the idea of Lavrovskaia possible, then became captivated and by the end of my meal I had decided. I ran at once to get Pushkin at the library, found the book with difficulty, went home, read the poem over again with rapture and passed a sleepness night, of which the result was a charming plot with words from Pushkin. In the morning I went off to Shilovsky's and now he is arranging the libretto for me at full speed.

Here it is in short: Act I, scene one – as the curtain rises old Mrs Larina and Nania are remembering the past and making jam – the old women's duet – singing is heard from the house. It is Tatiana and Olga singing a duet on Zhukovsky's words, accompanied by a harp. Peasants arrive with the last sheaf of corn of the harvest, they sing and dance; suddenly a servant announces: 'Guests!' Eugene and Lensky come in. Ceremony of Lensky presenting his friend and the young men are given drinks (bilberry water). Eugene and Lensky and the women discuss their ideas: quintet à la Mozart. The mother goes to get supper ready. The young people stay – walking in the garden in two couples. They come and go in turns (as in *Faust*) Tatiana is shy at first and then falls in love. Scene 2: With Nania and then Tatiana's letter. Scene 3: Onegin's conversation with Tatiana.

Act II. Scene 1: Tatiana's name day. Dance. Lensky is jealous, accuses Onegin and challenges him to a duel. Horror all round. Scene 2: Lensky's last aria and duel with pistols.

Act III. Scene 1: Moscow – ball at the Club of the Nobility – Tatiana meets all her aunts and cousins – they sing a chorus. The General appears and falls in love with Tatiana. She tells him all about herself and agrees to be his wife. Scene 2: In Petersburg – Tatiana is expecting Onegin – he appears – a huge duet. Tatiana gives way to her love for Eugene but fights against it. He implores her – her husband appears – duty takes upper hand – Onegin runs away in despair.

You cannot imagine how passionately keen I am about this plot. How glad I am to get rid of Ethiopian princesses, Pharaohs, poisonings and all that sort of pompous convention. Onegin is full of poetry. I know very well that there will be no scenic effects and little movement in this opera; but the lyrical quality, the humanity, and the simplicity of the story, and a text written by a genius, will compensate more than enough for these failings.

On the 29th I am going off to stay a month with Kostia Shilovsky; write to me there: Government of Moscow, District of Zvenigorod, the town of Voskresensk, from there to Glebovo.

P. Tchaikovsky

[138]   TO LEV DAVYDOV   [Moscow]
                                                    19 May 1877

Dear friend Leva!

First of all, of course, I am to blame for not having written since I returned to Moscow. Secondly 'merci' for the kind invitation. I shall come in the second half of the summer, not now. The reasons are as follows: Sixty versts from Moscow there lives the eldest of the brothers Shilovsky, a very talented and charming person, whose wife I also love very much. This Shilovsky, according to my instructions, is writing a libretto for an opera. As soon as the examinations are ended I am going to visit him and will then start writing my opera. I shall live at his place in a large cottage away from the main building, so that no one and nothing can disturb me.

When I am composing an opera it means, that (1) I must not see a soul during certain hours of the day, and know that no one can see or hear me; I have a habit, when composing, of singing very loud and the thought that someone could hear me disturbs me very much. (2) A grand piano is at my disposal near me, i.e. in my bedroom – without which I cannot write, at least not peacefully and easily.

Now, in Kamenka I could not have these two conditions. The fact is that I simply must compose this opera, I have an irresistible urge to composition and cannot lose a minute of the precious time. Levushka, you know that if you collect all my friends into one pile, including the Shilovskys, my love for the lot of them will not be even a hundredth portion of my unlimited love for Sasha, you, your children and all the Kamenka Davydovs; in Kamenka all the objects of my deepest feelings are concentrated. But you must agree that in Kamenka I should not have the conditions favourable to composing a complicated work like an opera. It would have been easier in Verbovka.

And so, my dear soul, I shall come to you in the second half of the summer to give a real rest to my heart, soul, and mind. To see and be with you is indispensable to me. In all probability I will come at the time when Modest, and Kolia, and Tolia, will also be there.

I am frightfully tired of Moscow and the Conservatoire and am impatiently waiting for the end.

I doubt if I shall go abroad, although it would be a good idea to go to Vichy. Shall drink the waters at the Shilovskys.

And so good-bye, my Golubchik. I kiss you all with all my love.

Your

P. Tchaikovsky

[139] TO MODEST TCHAIKOVSKY   Glebovo
                                            9 June 1877

I got your letter yesterday dear Modia, I was furious at first at your criticism of my choice of *Onegin* but it only lasted a moment. Let my opera not be scenic, let it have too little action but, I am in love with the image of Tatiana, I am completely charmed with Pushkin's poetry, and am writing music to it because I am drawn to it and am engrossed in the composition of the opera. One must also agree that there could not be a more favourable setting than the one by which I am surrounded.

I have the full use of a whole, separate, beautifully furnished house; no one
– not one human soul, except Alesha – appears in the house when I am busy,
and, what is most important, I have a piano, of which the sound, when I am
playing, does not reach anyone but Alesha. I get up at eight, have a bath, drink
tea (alone) and then work until breakfast. After breakfast I go for a walk and
then work until dinner time. After dinner I go for an enormous walk and
spend the evening in the big house. Besides my hosts only the two old Yazykova
spinsters and myself are staying here. Scarcely any guests come to visit us.
So – it is all peace and quiet around. The countryside is exquisite but the
weather – absolutely awful. There is frost every morning and it is frightfully
cold during the day, not one proper summer day yet.

Thanks to all that is described above my work is moving very fast, and if
I could stay here until August I would be sure to finish the opera in rough,
probably leave here and I doubt very much if I shall come to Grankino. I must
spend a few days with Kotek in Moscow, then go to Sasha's, where I hope to
see you and then, if only for a short time, abroad would be a good idea. I have
a great longing to go abroad again.

Good-bye, my dear Modia. Please cultivate an interest for this opera of mine
that is being born. The whole of the second scene of the first act is finished
(Tatiana with Nania) and I am very pleased with it. Most of the first scene is
also written.

I kiss Kolia tenderly. My regards to the owners of Grankino and also Sophia
Alexandrovna.

Yours

P. Tchaikovsky

Anatoli replied to the following by reiterating his doubts: 'I just cannot imagine
an opera on *Eugene Onegin* could be any good, and am very upset that you have
chosen this subject.'

[140] TO ANATOLI TCHAIKOVSKY   [Glebovo]
                                                 15 June 1877

Dear Tolichka!

I received your letter today and am answering at once. I have already been
here for two weeks, where I am accommodated in the best possible way for
work. I live in a separate house, Alesha serves me, and I have a piano in the
sitting-room; in brief, one could not have more comfort than this. The society
here is very much after my own heart, the library excellent, the countryside
incomparable and there is nothing to prevent me from taking long walks.
I have arranged my time-table meticulously, and work at appointed hours;
so, as there is nothing whatever to stop me from working, my opera is getting
on successfully. The whole of the first act, in three scenes, is ready; I started

the second act today. If I could have stayed here for the whole summer there is no doubt that my opera would have been finished by the end of the summer, but I cannot stay for so long and for various reasons, do not want to. I am not even sure, Tolia, that you will be able to come and fetch me from here. It may well be that after St Peter's day I shall leave for Moscow, and await you there. In any case I shall let you know where we shall meet, here or in Moscow.

You can say what you like about *Eugene Onegin*, it does not prevent me from writing with great pleasure, and I am sure that the poetic subject, and the indescribable beauty of the text, will prove effective. The scene between Tatiana and Nania is charming (what a way to boast!) and in general I am very pleased.

Tolia! Kiss Papochka and Lizaveta Mikhailovna and tell them that I am not writing because I have asked you to tell them that I am well and happy. I am on the whole well, but as before I am worried with my stomach and with perpetual heart-burn. I have decided, come what may, to take a cure at the end of the summer.

I kiss you heartily

P. Tchaikovsky

[141]   TO ANATOLI TCHAIKOVSKY   Kamenka
                                                     27 August 1877

It is Saturday today, my dear Tolia!

The day after tomorrow it will be a week since you left. Although I miss you most awfully I still do not at all want to leave Kamenka. Thanks to Modest being here time goes by very nicely. Sasha wants to go to Odessa, and Modest and I decided to accompany her. It was decided that we would go today, but neither she nor we have any desire to move. I put off my journey until Tuesday but do not know as yet if we shall go to Odessa or straight to Kiev. About the way we spend our time – nothing special has happened.

I am still madly interested in hunting and shoot up to thirty bullets a day. The very day after you left we went with Modia to Makhor. We saw a multitude of quail, and banged, and yelled, and were most excited, but we didn't kill anything. On Tuesday we – i.e. Sasha, Leva, Modia and I – went to Verbovka for dinner. Modia and I went off to shoot ducks, plenty of them flew about, and at first our banging was ineffective. At the end of the day, however, I shot one on the wing. You can imagine how proud and delighted I was. Modia nearly burst with envy. After this we went several times to the big garden and the Bakai and did shoot a few birds. . . .

I have finished the full score of the first scene and am now writing the piano score. Tolichka! Go and see Kotek at once or send him this letter. Tell him that I think of him a lot and dearly love him. My not writing to him is due to the fact that all the news I have here in Kamenka is of interest to you but not to him. Ask him to write to Moscow. I on my part, will write once more from here or from Kiev.

I embrace you heartily, my Golubchik.

Yours

Piotr Tchaikovsky

Do not send my letter to Kotek. I shall write to him myself, at once.

[142]   TO MODEST TCHAIKOVSKY   Kiev
                                                        9 September 1877

Dear Modia!

We arrived here yesterday morning and Alesha and I found your kind letter awaiting us. Your description of the gentleman who, at every opportunity, gets all heated in public places is so well written that it proved to me again that you have a literary talent which you ought to develop. If you are too lazy to write whole novels full of entanglements and disentanglements you can, at least, write short stories or sketches like the one you wrote about that man. It would be fresh, and original, and would bring you some money. Think how pleasant your life would be if you could divide it between teaching and literature; how full and rich it would become! I advise you to think seriously about it as long as you are still young and *le pli du dilettantisme* has not taken hold of you. I know that if I had been in your place I would not have left such ability dormant. Since you left I have read more of *Anna Karenina* – how can you be enthusiastic about this vulgar nonsense which pretends to give a deep analysis of characters. Devil take this analysis, which leaves one with a feeling of emptiness and insignificance; just as if you were present at a conversation between Alexandrine Dolgorouky with Nikolai Kondratiev about all sorts of Kittys, Alinas and Lillis. I find your sketch about the man at the station more interesting and serious, than all this high society artifice. But enough about literature. . . .

Tania's name-day was celebrated with pomp. In the morning – presents; I wrote some verses and presented her with 25 roubles. At mid-day there was a short service and we all drank chocolate. In the evening there were a lot of guests, dancing, and a magnificent supper. I have forgotten to tell you that the day before I dined at the Plesskys and that I paid them a visit before then. At 7 o'clock on Wednesday I left. Naturally I was seen off by everybody and Vishnizky was so full of kind feelings that he accompanied me to the Bobrinsky Station, that 'it should be more gay for me', as he expressed it. We arrived in Kiev at noon instead of nine o'clock. Had a bad night as the train was full. After having had some dinner I sent Alesha off to the Lavra and went for a walk on my own. In the evening I went to the opera. *Traviata* was performed, with the principal part very well sung by a certain Pavlovskaia.

The rest was no good. This morning, after a good night, Alesha and I went to St Sophia's Cathedral, to St Michael's, the Lavra, the grave of Askold and then to the delightful beautiful Vydubezky Monastery. . . .

I kiss you, dear Modia. I am delighted that everything is well with you and that Kolia loves you so dearly.

Good-bye, my Golubchik.

Your

P. Tchaikovsky

The following letter gives the first reference in this book to Mme Nadezhda Filaretovna von Meck, the wealthy patroness who was to support Tchaikovsky – but whom she was never to meet – for the next fourteen years. Tchaikovsky had complicated his life in July by marrying Antonina Ivanovna Milyukova, a not very intelligent girl of twenty-eight who had become infatuated with him. The fact that Tchaikovsky had informed Antonina, who had been a Conservatoire student, that he lacked the proper qualifications for marriage did not deter her. The marriage was a disaster. In Letter 144 Tchaikovsky apologizes to his sister for the worry this had brought to her and her family. Alexandra had indeed entertained Antonina at her home and had attempted to explain the situation to her.

By October Tchaikovsky was in a state of absolute depression – to the extent of walking one night into the icy River Moskva, a potential suicide – and in a short time Anatoli Tchaikovsky, accompanied by N. Rubinstein, visited Antonina to tell her of the medical advice that there should be a divorce. Antonina, however, was not to be dismissed in this way and in the future was to cause much concern to Tchaikovsky. To avoid unpleasantness, and indeed to save his sanity, Tchaikovsky himself, who was the subject of much gossip in Moscow, went abroad. Before his departure he received a special stipend from the Russian Musical Society in token of his services to that Society and to the Conservatoire. This was due to Rubinstein's prompting.

[143] TO MODEST TCHAIKOVSKY   Rome
                                          10–22 November 1877

Modichka!

I would like to have a proper chat with you but I have so little time. My journey to Italy has been the most idiotic thing I could have done. Money thrown away.

Tomorrow, we are going to Venice, with Tolia, where I hope to have a rest from the mad life of a tourist. It was absurd for me to run about museums clutching a Baedeker in one hand! ! ! From Venice on about the 20th (our calendar) we shall be going to Vienna where I will wait for Alesha to whom I have already written to come and join me. From there Tolia will go to

Kamenka, Moscow and Petersburg and I shall go to Switzerland, to my beloved Clarens.

Here is a brief account of our trip. We left Paris exactly a week ago. Next day at 10 o'clock we arrived in Florence where we passed two boring days which nearly killed me. I just could not enjoy the beauties of Italy, for I was upset about spending too much money. At the same time, however, it was imperative that we should go to Rome where I was (1) expecting some money and especially (2) a money order by registered post from Mme von Meck; and (3) my symphony which was to arrive in Clarens a day after I left and forwarded to me here.

Very bad-tempered, we arrived in Rome at 6 in the morning. I changed, and went to the Post Office, but there was nothing there. We roamed round the town all day, went to St Peter's Cathedral, and in the evening to a horrid opera. The next day we took a guide and went to the Vatican where we looked at the Museum of Sculpture.

Just think of my having to gaze at three thousand statues in the mood I was in! From there we went again to the Post Office and got several letters, some from Kamenka! All letters from Kamenka are always disagreeable. When I heard there was nothing for me in the registered letters department of the Post Office I was nearly desperate. I decided to telegraph to Mme von Meck the next day to say that her letter had not reached me. It seemed clear from her letter that the money had been sent 10 days ago. Passing by the Post Office again, however, I went in and begged them to look again. They did, and found two letters, one of which was from Albrecht. After this we went to the Vatican again and saw the paintings and the frescoes of Raphael. When we returned to the hotel, what I had been avoiding all the time happened. Massalitinov having found out from the papers that we were in Rome, came to see us, and left his card with an invitation to dinner.

Oh God! I did not want to see him at all! But I had to go. Golitzin is in Paris. Massalitinov behaved very nicely and tactfully. He did not pester me with questions, and gave us an excellent dinner, after which he took us for a drive to the Coliseum. He 'got out of his skin' to please us! Today, Tolia and I went to the Capitol, after which I had difficulty in finding the symphony but got it in the end. Then we went with Massalitinov and Lady Hamilton (sic!), née a Russian, to the *Palais des Césars*, had dinner at Massalitinov's with the lady, changed the money at a bankers, and at last here I am at home, writing a letter to you whilst Tolia is at the opera with Massalitinov. Tomorrow we are off to Venice. Do not write there but to Vienna, to Leopoldstadt, Hôtel Goldenes Lamm.

And now I must tell you of an idea which I cannot get rid of. . . . What if Konradi could arrange for you and Kolia to come and join me for a month in Clarens? I know the exchange is awful, but things are cheap there. For an excellent flat, with linen and full service, Tolia and I paid 13 francs a day. Which makes 6½ francs per head. If you came with Kolia I could get you accommodation for 12 francs as Kolia is small. This makes 360 francs a month, i.e. 150 roubles even at the worst exchange!!! For me it would be such bliss, such happiness, of which I dare not even dream! On the spur of the moment I wanted to write about it to Konradi himself but Tolia would not let me.

I must add, although you should not mention it to anyone else, that I think it would be better for Kolia not to be at home during his mother's confinement. What do you think of the idea? I do not dare to hope but, my God, what kindness it would be to me!!! If, however, you find the whole idea silly, don't take any notice.

Frightfully tired. Good-bye, my dear one.

Your

P. Tchaikovsky

If only you could come. I want to see you so much. I will look after Kolia like a *nania* [nurse].

[144]   TO ALEXANDRA DAVYDOVA   Venice
                                                18–30 November 1877

My very dear Sasha!

I got your letter about six days ago, it had the best and most reassuring effect on me. I started working; and I have masses to do. As well as other things I must finish the scenes of my opera which are to be performed at the Conservatoire evening, and which Tolia must take back to Moscow. I got down to work and in six days did more than I expected. This work so engrossed me that it is only today that, at last, I am answering letters. . . . I know only one thing: that if there are good, kind, and absolutely irreproachable people in this world, they are you and Leva. His letter has done me a lot of good. I cherish your love much more than you think. Whatever I think about, whatever plans I make, at the end I always come to wonder what you would say about it, how you would act and would you be pleased with me and not cease to love me. Thank you both for everything. I have given you a great deal of worry and many bad moments.

Tomorrow Tolia and I are going to Vienna, where we shall stay a few days together and from where Tolia will go to Kamenka at the end of November. After saying good-bye to Tolia I shall return to Venice. It is very quiet here The separation from Tolia frightens me. My last letter to you was written in a state of nerves and irritation. Forgive me if I expressed myself as I should not have done.

Good-bye my angel! I am very tired and am writing with effort; have been working all day at a hard task.

Your

P. Tchaikovsky

I embrace you all with all my love.

It is hard for a Russian to live abroad at the present time. My God! How everybody hates us! Tolia will tell you how excited and angry we got every night at the Piazza St Marco when the newspaper boys called out: 'Grande vittoria dei Turchi', and this is the same every day over each Turkish communiqué after every little skirmish; they never cry out 'Vittoria dei Russi'.

Writing to Taneev on 12 November, 1877, Tchaikovsky wondered whether it was, as was being said, that 'in Wagner music has found its first and most important representative. . . . Is this really the last word in art? Are the generations to come going to enjoy this pretentious, heavy, ugly absurdity. . . ? If so it is frightening. I also heard *Sylvia*, by Delibes . . . this is the only ballet I know where the music is of the only and vital importance. . . . If I had known this music earlier I would not have written my *Swan Lake*.' From the beginning of 1877 at least Tchaikovsky had been working on the Fourth Symphony (Op. 36), which was finished on 26 December. Dedicated to 'my beloved friend' (Mme von Meck) this work was first performed at the Russian Musical Society concert of 10 February 1878, the conductor being N. Rubinstein.

[145] TO MODEST TCHAIKOVSKY   Vienna
27 November–9 December 1877

Modia!

Why no letters from you in Vienna? I hope that this means you are coming to join me with Kolia. But I am still afraid to believe it. *Ce serait trop de bonheur!* [It would be too much happiness.] You cannot imagine what it would mean to me! Although Alesha is coming and I shall not be alone I still need you and Kolia!

I have much to discuss with you but as I have decided to write several letters I will not go into any particulars now. Especially as I hope this will be my last letter to you before we meet. Oh God! How wonderful, what bliss it will be! I shall feel absolutely resurrected! . . .

We sit at home nearly all the time, play duets with Kotek and the three of us chat. In the evening we often go to the theatre. We have heard *The Water Carrier* by Cherubini, *Sylvia* by Delibes, *Valkyrie* by Wagner, and *Aida* – which was very bad. Out of all these the most delightful were *The Water Carrier* and *Sylvia*, which were given together. Yesterday and today no theatre for us. Modia, do not write any more, for I feel we will see each other soon.

I kiss you hard.

Yours

P. Tchaikovsky

TO ANATOLI TCHAIKOVSKY   Venice
                                                3–15 December 1877

Tolichka!

I feel much better today. I slept very well and sat down to work at my
symphony as soon as I was up. After breakfast Alesha and I went to see the
palace of the Doges and then wandered around the town. From two until five
I wrote again. Now I am back home. Alesha is going to bed. I have just
written a long letter to Karlusha in answer to his, which was sent on to me by
Mme Mayor from Clarens. I hope that with the help of the symphony I shall
get used to the hard separation from you and shall manage to exist till the
end of the month. . . .

I must say that Venice disgusts me. It has something nasty, repellent which
I shall never get used to. My lodgings are rather high up, very small but quite
cosy. It is good for me to have breakfast and dinner with Alesha. He is
behaving charmingly. He is not at all bored; he consoles and tries to amuse
me when I am sad, reads, studies arithmetic, and writes as many letters as
I do. He was enraptured by the Palace of the Doges. In all respects I am very,
very pleased with him. Tomorrow I will address my letter to Petersburg.
I wanted very much to go and hear Patti in *The Barber of Seville* but did not
have enough money. I kiss you my Golubchik and please forgive me that you
have so much to do for me.

Yours

P. Tchaikovsky

[147] TO MODEST TCHAIKOVSKY   Venice
                                             [Beginning of December 1877]

Modia!

Lenka is a proper fool! He wrote a long letter without a word about the joys
in store for him and me. I am perfectly happy and will work hard until you both
arrive here. Expecting something pleasant is an excellent stimulus for work.
My symphony is definitely the best work I have written so far, but it needed
some hard work to compose it; especially the first part. I kiss you with love
and am expecting a letter with all details about what, when, where and how!

Yours,

P. Tchaikovsky

[148] TO ANATOLI TCHAIKOVSKY   Venice
                                             Saturday
                                             [10–22 December 1877]

. . the first part of my symphony is coming to an end. I have done a lot of work today and am very tired. This morning I heard from Modest; he wants to live in San Remo near Menton. I agreed with his choice and sent him a telegram saying so. At the end of the week I will go to San Remo to get everything ready; I hope it will be possible to find similar accommodation to that in Clarens. I shall not be sorry at all to leave Venice. Last night I felt a desire to have a good time; so went off to the *Birreria di Genova* where every evening there is singing and acting – something like a *café-chantant* – but it was only boring. The singing was only a mock parody of something serious, and the beer – bad. I had one mug full and returned home.

Today the streets are crowded with people. Christmas day will be in three days time; in all the shops they have displays of goods for presents, the shopkeepers shout to entice you in, and you can scarcely push through the crowds. I have just bought a huge volume of a French illustrated *Life of Napoleon* at a second-hand bookseller's. Now I am drinking tea, looking at the book, and feeling perfectly well, peaceful, and happy. Good-bye – a sweet kiss to you! The next letter will be sent on Wednesday.

P.T.

[149] TO ANATOLI TCHAIKOVSKY   [Venice]
                                                 11–23 December 1877
                                                 Sunday

This morning I finished the first, the most difficult part of my symphony. After breakfast we went to the Lido, drank coffee in the same restaurant as we did with you, and then collected sea shells. Alesha put so much energy and delight into this activity (he collected nearly a whole *pud* [40 pounds]) that I felt happy too. The journey back was quite an adventure: a fog came down suddenly and was so dense that you could not see anything even two steps away; this caused us to leave the main canal, lose ourselves, nearly bang into a barge, stop, get stuck on a sand bank, and so on . . . as a result it took us not half an hour but over one hour to get back. The cold is awful. No answer from Modest to my telegram of yesterday. . . .

For your most reassuring letter received today, I have left my thanks to you *pour la bonne bouche*. I was happy reading it! It promises me so much that is good. I am not accepting Sasha's offer to live in Verbovka – you must agree with me that it will be neither one thing nor the other. Besides, at the moment, there cannot be any question about my returning to Russia: Modest is coming here! – It will be different in summer, the possibility of my living in Verbovka then pleases me greatly. Until tomorrow Tolia!

A hearty kiss

[no signature]

128

[Venice]
12–24 December 1877

... I have decided to go on Friday to San Remo to find good and cheap accommodation, and will stay for one day in Milan. Nothing of consequence happened today. I worked as usual, and went for a walk at the usual time. I have not yet told you about the pigeons. I feed them every day and they know me so well that they perch all over me. They even quarrel, and fight, sitting on my head.

I shall leave Venice without sorrow. However I must say that it is probably thanks to the peace and quiet here that I feel so well (spit, spit, spit) these last days. My nerves are wonderfully improved. I sleep perfectly but must add that before going to bed I drink beer, or two small glasses of brandy. As usual my appetite is excellent. All this is a result of my symphony, but it is only thanks to the monotony of Venetian life and lack of all distractions that I could work so hard and intensively.

When I was writing the opera I did not have the same feelings as when composing the symphony. There I took a risk – perhaps it will do, or maybe nothing will come of it. But this symphony I am composing I know is not just an ordinary piece of music, but in form the most perfect of all my compositions up to date.

I am still reading *Pendennis* and the history of Napoleon, and before going to sleep I always read two daily papers; *Italie* and *Gazetta di Venezia*.

Until tomorrow my dear.

13–25 Tuesday

It is a great holiday today and, just as we are doing, everybody else is staying at home. The streets are quite empty. After two weeks of perfect weather it is raining today. As usual I have been working. I wanted to go to the theatre in the evening, but to go alone is dull and Alesha did not want to go. I stayed at home, therefore, and had tea, and then went for a short walk. Now I am going to read. This is the time of day I like best. When the shutters are closed the stillness is complete. Alesha is asleep. It is so perfectly quiet that one can hear the lamp burning. I can think, dream, read, remember; in one word – rest. Again there is no letter from you, which worries me a bit. But there were two letters from Kotek.

Good night.

[no signature]

Venice
15–27 December 1877

Venice Milan

I have finished the Scherzo and am very tired. All day the fog has been so dense that you could see no further than a step before you. I am going to bed. It is ten o'clock now, and we must get up at 6.00 tomorrow. Everything is packed and the bill paid. How glad I am that I shall not have to eat any more the filth they serve us here. We are the last inhabitants of the hotel . . . tomorrow it will be empty.

Milan 16–28

We started at 8.00, arrived at 4.00, and are staying at the Hôtel d'Europe. We went for a walk and then dined. Now I am off to the theatre and will give you my impressions tomorrow. Am feeling perfectly well.

Milan 17–29,
in the morning

Slept beautifully. Last night's theatre made me angry, not pleased. They gave *Ruy Blas* by Marchetti; this opera has been played all over Italy, I expected to find it interesting, instead of which it is banal, vulgar, and a poor copy of Verdi. It was so badly produced that, presented in this way in Moscow, it would have been booed throughout. Although the leading singers tried hard their voices were awful. Costumes, settings, choruses, the orchestra, were all very poor. And this is the best theatre after La Scala; but that was closed.

L'Africaine is on today and I would like to stay and hear it, but Alesha says we spend too much money. Alas! he is right. After the opera there was an amusing ballet (with harlequins, disappearing acts, transformation scenes, just like at our fun-fairs) and Alesha laughed so loud that the whole theatre heard him. I too could not help laughing. Oh! Oh yes, I have forgotten to mention how the audience behaved during the opera – in positive raptures! The huge theatre was crammed.

If I decide to stay I shall continue my letter on the same sheet of paper; if I go on to Genoa I shall finish it tonight. We will arrive there at 11.45 pm. Now, at this moment, we have decided to go to the Cathedral and to climb up to the top. Did you go up the tower of the Milan Cathedral in 1872? I went today for the first time; the weather was not bad but not clear enough to see the Swiss Alps. The Tyrolean Alps, on the other hand, shone in all their glory. I think that the Milan Cathedral is the most beautiful thing I have ever seen.

Anyone who has not climbed to the top and has not studied it in all its details is in no position to judge its vastness and its beauty. I enjoyed this sight-seeing very much. Then we went to a gallery and had some lunch. After the filthy and rotten food in Venice everything tasted wonderful! Now I am back at home and in a few minutes we shall take another walk.

At 6.40 pm we travel on to Genoa where I expect to stay the night. I am sending a telegram at once to Modest; with the address at San Remo. I have decided to stay at the Hôtel Victoria, but to be on the safe side address your letters *poste restante*.

Yours

P. Tchaikovsky

TO ANATOLI TCHAIKOVSKY   San Remo
                                                      19–31 December 1877
                                                      9 o'clock in the evening

Tolia!

Here are first impressions of San Remo! They are awful! I do not mean its climate and surrounding country. Although I arrived late and could not see anything I could judge by the lovely views on the way that it must be beautiful. No, I mean the hotel. Having found a Hôtel in Baedeker, situated a long way from the town centre, I chose it for the first days, as I imagined it sumptuous, empty, and cheap. But it happened to be absolutely full. We were given a tiny room with no more than the bare necessities; no desk and I am obliged to write my letter on a small dressing table. A list of prices hangs on the wall: (1) Room – 8 francs. (2) Dinner, if not table d'hôte, 8 francs, and if you want it served in the room – 10 francs. (3) Coffee in the morning 1.75 francs and 2 francs if you want it served in your room. So you are supposed even to have coffee in the restaurant, and so on, and so on.

When I went with Alesha to the dining-room the dinner was coming to an end and the guests were coming out. There were at least a hundred dressed-up ladies and gentlemen who looked at us with an air of hauteur and astonishment. You can imagine how much it all pleases me! And Baedeker says there are no furnished rooms here at all. I do not know what I am going to do, all I know is that life here is 'much bigger than the size of our pockets'. All the same, tomorrow, when it is daylight I shall go and look for something else. With what regret and affection I think of Clarens, of the kind and honest Mayors! It is a pity that Modest chose this place!

I owe you reports for two days: The day before yesterday we left Milan, arrived in Genoa at 11.45 and stayed at the Hôtel des quatres Nations. Just the sort of hotel I like, i.e. an old, very old house with thick walls, doors several inches thick, the house full of crooked passages and absolutely empty. We had a large suite with a fire burning brightly in the open fireplace. After tea we went to bed but for some reason I slept badly, shivering and shuddering all through the night.

All the next day we wandered around. We climbed a church tower, with a beautiful view of the whole town. In the evening we went to the theatre where they were giving *L'Africaine*, which was boring and badly performed. The rest you know from the beginning of the letter. We continued our journey today at 1 o'clock. The views are beautiful but I doubt if I shall stay unless I can find a comfortable and cheap habitat! But how warm it is here! We had to open the window wide because it was so hot in the room and a mosquito flew in and bit Alesha. But warmth is no great pleasure when one has to write on a dressing table and pay 8 francs for one's dinner. I wrote a letter to Papochka from Genoa.

I kiss you and Lizaveta Mikhailovna.

P. Tchaikovsky

TO ANATOLI TCHAIKOVSKY

San Remo
20 December 1877–
1 January 1878

Tolia!

This morning, quite early, I went looking for lodgings. I hoped to find one floor in a villa but there was nothing like that. Whole villas are let for two or three thousand francs. I came across small lodgings which a Frenchman (un réfugié, Monsieur, un condamné à mort, Monsieur) was trying to make me take, and I only just managed to rid myself of him. Anyway it would have been much too small for us. At last I came upon the Pension Joly where I found more or less possible living quarters. Modest and Kolia will be in one room, I alone, and also Alesha, and we will have a sitting-room too. The price for the lot is 38 francs per day. Not too much according to the prices here. My first condition was that we should not have our meals in the dining-room. We shall be served in our rooms – lunch at 1 o'clock, dinner at 7.00. In comparison with the Pension Richelieu neither the rooms nor the food here are so good. The furniture is poor but clean; the host very kind.

Tolia! My dear! I am today in the grip of an awful melancholia! The palms, the orange and lemon trees do not make me happy; I am frightened and sad. How I long to go back to Russia. How can one live a whole winter without frost or snow? It is as warm here as it is in June at home and this at the end of December! Let us hope I shall feel better tomorrow. No telegram from Modest. No letters from anybody. Today is a holiday and the Poste Restante is closed.

The address is: Italie, San Remo, Pension Joly.

I kiss you lovingly, your eyes, your cheeks.

Yours

P. Tchaikovsky

Tchaikovsky was invited to be a delegate to an International Exhibition, to take place in Paris during the summer. After worrying himself and everybody else he decided not to accept the invitation – to the annoyance of his colleagues at the Conservatoire. (See Letter 162 and 163.) He was also feeling very homesick.

TO ANATOLI TCHAIKOVSKY

San Remo
21 December 1877–
2 January 1878
In a Coffee House

This morning when I went to the Post Office they gave me a lot of letters. One was from you which made me very happy. Then an official one from Butovsky, to inform me that the Minister of Finance has appointed me a delegate with a pay of 1,000 roubles a month! This was a real thunderbolt. I had forgotten about the delegation and was sure in any case that I wouldn't get a penny. And now this blow! I was going today to start working on the Finale of my symphony and wait here for Modest! Besides I do not know where Modest is or if he is coming. In brief – the most awkward and unexpected state of affairs. I do not really know what to do. On the one hand it would be wrong, and may not be profitable to refuse, on the other the whole thing repels me! And, in the state I am in at the moment, should I go and tie myself down for the whole of spring and summer?

After relaxing a little I sent you a telegram asking where Modest is. Then I went into a café to drink beer. The waiter came up and said something which I did not understand, and said, 'Yes!' He brought me paper and envelopes and ink; this made me start writing to you. What should I do? – I do not know at all! – Oh, Lord! When shall I find peace? . . . I will finish this letter tonight. Perhaps by then I shall be able to decide what to do.

Evening 8 o'clock

Back home I stretched on the bed and lounged until dinner, thinking, dreaming, longing, and in my thoughts covering you with kisses (how I love you, Tolia) and complaining over my fate which makes me ill at ease; and thinking of dear Russia whose snowy wastes I prefer a thousand times to the palms and cypresses here. Then we went for a walk, I went to a café, had some brandy, continued my walk, and returned home determined not to be a milksop, and to go to Paris on the 10th (Butovsky wrote that between the 10th and the 18th there will be Committee meetings which I must attend). I still do not know what I shall do with Modest.

If I understand from your telegram in reply to this that he is in Paris I shall telegraph to the Hôtel de Hollande. My function in Paris will be most difficult and complicated. In his letter Butovsky says that the Government will not allot any more money. Judging by the questions which are to be discussed, we shall have to decide whether the Russian orchestra is to give Russian concerts, whether one should engage the national choir at the Committee's expense, and so on.

I am going to write at once to Tahl, the president of the Russian Department, that I will come on the 10th. I have decided to do so because I know that you and all my friends would advise me to. . . .

Yours

P. Tchaikovsky

[155] TO ALEXANDRA DAVYDOVA   San Remo
                                            24 December 1877–
                                            5 January 1878

Sasha, my very dearest!

All these last days I have been ill, upset, unhappy. On the day of my arrival here I found an official letter saying that I have been appointed music delegate to the Paris Exhibition and must be there on January 10 and stay there to the very end.

I cannot tell you how stunned I was. In the state I am in it would be impossible to go to Babylon, be under orders of Privy Counsellor Tahl, attend sittings of all sorts of commissions, get acquainted with a crowd of people, drag myself to dinners and musical evenings, pay calls, and live in Paris until the end of the Exhibition, i.e. eight long months. I swear to you that all I hope for is to return to Russia in the spring and pass the whole summer with you! !

But now, all my plans have been destroyed at one blow. At the same time I somehow imagined that I must accept this offer, that all of you – brothers, friends, all who feel kindly towards me – will hate me and look upon me as despicable if I refuse. I decided to go. But no words can describe what I went through all these last days! I did not eat or sleep and got drunk several times out of sheer grief.

Then, today I saw it all! I have paid dearly once before when I acted against my nature and took something for my duty that was no duty at all. Why should I accept a task which disgusts and frightens me. What am I going to do with Modest who is bringing Kolia here? He cannot stay in Paris and never see me. Also, I am not well, I cannot stand crowds, new acquaintances and so on.

I have sent an official refusal and now with an effort am writing to those whose judgement I fear. For God's sake if you, Leva, and all the Kamenka people find that I lack character and am spineless, forgive me. I cannot, I cannot go to Paris; the thought alone makes me sick.

I have not yet seen San Remo properly. Everything seemed disgusting, abhorrent and all I wanted was to die. The beauties of nature did not appeal to me at all.

Modest is on his way from Berlin to Paris. Tomorrow or the day after I shall write a saner letter.

I kiss you all with all my love.

P. Tchaikovsky

Italie, San Remo, Pension Joly

[156] TO ANATOLI TCHAIKOVSKY   [San Remo]
                                      24 December 1877–
                                      5 January 1878

Yesterday, I was so afraid of your being angry at my refusal to be a delegate that I exaggerated my condition. I have been drinking lately but only enough to feel in a better mood and to sleep better. I slept well, my health is good, only my nerves are in a bad state at the moment. But all this will soon end. I promise that as soon as Modest arrives all my worries 'will be swept away by one sweep of the hand'. But the most important thing is to know that neither you nor all the others are angry with me for my refusal.

Today I worked at my symphony all day from early morning and am very tired, so do not expect a long letter. Tonight I am going to the theatre. *Faust* is on and one Ludmilla Raievskaia is singing. She interests me.

I kiss you times without number.

Your

P. Tchaikovsky

Papa, our dear old man, and Lizaveta Mikhailovna I kiss with all my love.

[157]   TO ANATOLI TCHAIKOVSKY   San Remo
                                        [28 December 1877–]
                                        9 January 1878
                                        Pension Joly

A telegram came from Milan tonight. Modest says that he is penniless because he cannot get Russian money changed, and that Kolia is not well. I am so worried that I have decided to go myself to Milan in the morning instead of sending money and waiting. Yesterday and today I worked at my dear symphony without stopping and have finished it. Health perfect. Humour good. Will write tomorrow from Milan.

I kiss you

P. Tchaikovsky

[158]   TO ANATOLI TCHAIKOVSKY   Milan
                                        [January 1878]

The day before yesterday I had a telegram from Modest; yesterday at seven in the morning I went off to meet him and at seven in the evening I was in Modest's arms. Difficult to describe how wonderful it was. We passed a lovely evening, chatting, and interrupting each other, and I heard everything about everybody and you in particular. I slept wonderfully well. This morning, in spite of the horrid weather and snow, we went to the Cathedral and were all very happy. We had lunch together. Then I worked, for I had taken the symphony with me. It is now ready, and I am marking it and want to send it tomorrow from here to Moscow. We had tickets to the Scala where they were going to give the first [Italian] performance of Gounod's *Cinq Mars* [see p. 103].

After dinner (having paid 20 francs for second best seats), we went only to

135

find the theatre closed on account of the death of the king, who had died the same morning. They promised to return our money tomorrow. So we went home, had baths and are going to have tea now.

We leave tomorrow at 2 o'clock and will stay the night at Genoa. Write!

I kiss you with all my love – my dear joy.

Yours

P. Tchaikovsky

[159] TO ANATOLI TCHAIKOVSKY   2–14 January 1878
                                          11 o'clock in the evening

Today I have started the orchestral score of the opera. I am happy, my heart is warm and serene but I still do not like San Remo. Yesterday I read the following passage in a book: 'The climate on the Ligurian coast is not appropriate for full blooded people with highly strung nerves – they get wearied by the blinding motley of colours and the richness of the atmosphere.' Probably that is why I did not enjoy myself either in Rome, or Venice nor here. At the moment Modia and I are both writing under the dim light of the same lamp. He – tasks for Kolia, I – a letter to you. Until tomorrow my Tolichka. Had a nice letter from Kondratiev.

3–15 Tuesday

Very tired. Shall not write today. Anyway nothing special to describe. Took a long drive into the mountains. No wonderful views. Everything shut in by trees. Roads abominable. Am reading *Alexander I* by [S. M.] Soloviev. Good.

4–16 Wednesday

... After all said and done, about the way I am living now, I shall easily be able to stay here about three months but, in spring, shall be irresistibly drawn back to Russia, and this is my sweetest dream. Alas! When I turn my thoughts from Russia in general to Kamenka in particular I am not so sure. I will find it difficult to be there without you or Modest. But this is all in the far distant future! Our immediate plans are: to go in two or three weeks to Nice across the Corniche (mountain road to Nice), then on to Lyon and Paris, where Modest must go, and then to the bosom of the family Mayor. As much as I hate Venice, Rome and San Remo I have the warmest memories of the Villa Richelieu.

Two days without letters. I write exactly three letters a day. And now good-bye, until the next letter which will end with Saturday.

I kiss you a thousand times, my dearest.

Yours

P. Tchaikovsky

[160]   TO ALEXANDRA DAVYDOVA   San Remo
                                                 5–17 January 1878

We have already been in San Remo for six days, my dear, beloved Sasha, and
I often think of how you stayed here. We are not luxuriously but quite
comfortably accommodated and stick to the order of day that was agreed upon.
The meeting with Modest and Kolia made me very happy. I love Kolia more
and more every day. Modia as tutor also pleases me; although sometimes
I get angry with him when he is severe but I understand that it cannot be
otherwise.

Kolia has grown to love Alesha very much and as one can entrust the boy to
him perfectly it gives Modest the opportunity to go for evening walks with
me, which are lovely as the moon is full. I must say the climate is charming;
the country is beautiful but I am still not attracted to San Remo very much.
I get so easily depressed; the first days here I was very upset and still cannot
get rid of this feeling. However it does not matter; I am ready to live anywhere
with Modest and Kolia. All the same, San Remo is expensive which is a good
thing for it will force us to leave soon and go to Switzerland to Clarens where
I long to be and where it is twice as cheap.

I am well, except for my nerves which are a constant worry. Time, time, and
time, is the only remedy. I work a lot. I have finished the symphony and am
getting to the end of my opera. I will return to Russia having finished these
two large works. To Russia! I get a happy tinkling in my heart just at the
thought of it. You have to be forced to live abroad to understand how much
you love your own country. But my return is still far away, not before three
months. How are you all my beloved? Will this letter find you in Kamenka?
How is Anna, dear Anna? What have you decided about her? I kiss and
embrace everybody.

P. Tchaikovsky

[161]   TO ANATOLI TCHAIKOVSKY   [San Remo]
                                                 5–17 January 1878
                                                 Thursday

Today I caught myself counting the days and hours which we have to spend
here. I just cannot force myself to like San Remo. Or is it that I have reached
the state of mind which will prevent me from ever finding a place where I can
be happy. Will I ever be in expectation of something, and yearning for the
unknown? We went for a delightful long walk along the sea shore, the scenery
was really beautiful but despite that I am not contented and feel irritable.
Please do not think that I am in a despondent mood. Not at all. I have written
quite a lot today and have orchestrated your favourite, Gremin's aria.

It is quite extraordinary, no letters from anyone. Kashkin for instance, who says
he loves me has not answered my Vienna letter [26 Nov.]. None of my Moscow

friends, despite my repeated requests, has written to say how my classes are getting on and not a word about *Onegin*. Is it going to be produced? And this after Rubinstein asked me for the opera and wanted to know how to distribute the parts. . . .

I kiss you

P. Tchaikovsky

[162] TO ANATOLI TCHAIKOVSKY   12–24 January 1878
                                                          Thursday

The mistral is blowing. The sea is so rough that it frightens you. After lunch we went to the harbour and walked along the sea-wall. Several times the waves whipped up and soaked us. . . .

Tonight they are giving *The Barber of Seville* and Modest and I wanted to go and hear a Russian, one Raievskaia, who is singing Rosina. The papers were full of predictions that she would not be able to sing the part, that she would be hissed, and so on. We wanted to leave Kolia with the maid Margarita who was willing to stay with him but the storm howled, and rattled the windows so much, that we were afraid to leave the boy with her, without us being there, for so long. I really expected the whole house to collapse. In the end Modia persuaded me to go [to the Opera] alone. I went but did not feel happy and ran home after the first scene of the second act. I found Modest worrying about me – and true enough the wind was so fierce and strong that it was difficult to walk. (Raievskaia was good and had plenty of success.)

                                                 13–25 January
                                                 Friday

I had an awful night. I cannot tell you what the wild wind was like. My window creaked, banged, and rattled, so that it took me a long time to go to sleep. But, just when I managed to do so, first the window opened with a fearful bang, and then the door. I jumped up in fright, shut the window and the door, and went to sleep, when the same thing happened again. And so it went on until 4 o'clock in the morning. At last I closed and fastened the shutters, left the window open and then went properly to sleep. The wonderful thing about the wind was that it was quite warm and I did not suffer at all from the window being open.

Today the wind has stopped but the sea is still rough. It is hot outside just like in summer. How kind Modest is. He gives lessons to Alesha every day and is most conscientious. It is 8 o'clock in the evening now. Kolia is sawing something; Modest is reading the *Daily News* [sic], while I am writing to you. I had a photograph taken of Kolia. What a dear boy he is. Until tomorrow my dear. I kiss your lips, eyes, neck. And again I kiss you.

A letter from Rubinstein arrived in the morning which made me furious. I was
very upset and answered at once, and Modest was pleased with the manner
of my reply. How right I am not to love the man. How heartless, dry and full
of self-importance he is when he plays the part of the benefactor! I have told
him once and for all that I am not as beholden to him as he imagines. I hate
the thought of getting back under his yoke in Moscow. This is to be a short
letter. The orchestration is ready; the day passed as usual. There is no change
in Alesha. I embrace you, my dear boy.

Yours

P. Tchaikovsky

I enclose Rubinstein's letter

[163]   TO ANATOLI TCHAIKOVSKY   [San Remo]
                                                  15–27 January 1878
                                                  Sunday

Modia and I have just been laughing our heads off. He said I was like the old
woman in Pushkin's fairy tale [*The little golden fish*], who wished to become
the queen of all the seas. We were discussing my future. I said I wanted to
become a rich landowner and live on my own estate; the reason which brought
about this wish was Rubinstein's letter which provoked all my anger against
this General of music who continues to look upon me as a subaltern completely
under his command.

All the elements of antipathy and hate for him which lay dormant at the roots
of my being boiled up with tremendous force and I cannot imagine how I shall
manage to continue working at the Conservatoire under orders from His
Excellency! What makes me furious is that he still wants to be my benefactor.
Having understood that what he did for me in the autumn was actually not
really important, and that it is only a normal act of decency to help me, he
now imagines that I must be solely grateful to him for Mme von Meck's
money and adds that I am not worthy of it: 'I have taken advantage of
the generosity and magnanimity of my Principal, am lazy, forgetting how
to work, I must take myself in hand!' Oh, God, how vulgar, brazen and
insolent it all is. He does not understand that I do not really need the
2,700 roubles which I practically forced him to send me, and that if I wished
I would get more money elsewhere for less work! But no! He imagines that
I would not be able to continue my work without his help. . . .

Do you wonder that I want to get rid of this burden? This morning, while
still in bed, I even thought of begging Leva and Sasha to take me as a piano
teacher and stay with them forever. Away from all this meanness! Even the
kind-hearted, sweet Karlusha wrote silly nonsense which I cannot forget. He

also thinks I have been wrong in refusing to be a delegate and said: 'I fear that Nikolai Grigorievich will cease to like you, and what will Davydov think of Rubinstein who begged him to recommend you? – He thinks he can frighten me when he says that Rubinstein will cease to like me! It makes me sick! And they want me to believe that Davydov recommended me as a delegate solely thanks to Rubinstein's intervention!

Disgusting!

Tolichka my dear! I must tell you that I feel well, my health is excellent. Rubinstein is actually right when he says that I am playing the fool.

It is quite true but my only sickness is that I am playing the fool and am not able to stop doing so. From the physical side I am perfectly well. Even my nervous twitches have disappeared (spit, spit, spit). Today Modest, Kolia and I took a donkey trip to the little mountain town of Cola, where there is an interesting picture gallery. On the way back I picked a large bunch of violets.

16–28 Monday

... this morning a photographer came and took a group of the four of us. How silly that we had no pictures taken in Clarens and Venice! As soon as this photograph is ready I will send it to you. As usual I felt awful while the picture was being taken.

After lunch, with note-paper and pencil, I went alone into the mountains to finish the scene of the duel, which is not yet all composed. I found a solitary nook with difficulty, but worked successfully. . . . Tolia! It seems to me that you are displeased with my refusal. But just imagine me, my Golubchik, in all the excitement; with new acquaintances (people who do not know and do not care for me as a musician), surrounded by the most insipid Russians, who pretend to be good musicians, surrounded by all the disorder and mess. How could I stand it? For eight whole months! !

What a beast your Rubinstein is, I still cannot get over his letter.

[no signature]

Modest at this time was writing a novel, *The Drones*, which was never published. At the end of 1877 Tchaikovsky had accepted a commission from Yurgenson to translate the Italian words of six songs by Glinka into Russian.

[164] TO ANATOLI TCHAIKOVSKY   [San Remo]
                                        17–29 January 1878
                                        Tuesday

Yesterday after having written my letter, Modest read me two chapters from his novel which he has been quietly writing for some time. I was immensely surprised. It is so good, clever, fine, interesting and new that I could not believe, at first, that the author was facing me. It seems to me that Modest has a real, a definite talent. If he could have added to it my patience, hard work, and perseverance, he would have, long ago, written several first-class works. I made him promise to finish it here. Modest has forbidden me to mention his work to any one but you. Keep it quiet, please, and do not say anything to Laroche. I am pleased that I was right about Modest's literary talent.

I slept badly, with a pain in my stomach. Took a cold shower in the morning. No baths here. . . . In spite of the bad night I feel really well today. My work is getting on and I have started to compose the last and most difficult part of the opera – the Introduction. I felt so happy that I could not help thinking that something unpleasant was sure to happen later.

Just as I thought, letters arrived after lunch. One from Yurgenson who writes that he still has not received the Glinka pieces which I sent from Venice, I am appalled. My work lost! Worst of all – the manuscript for which Yurgenson paid 2,000 roubles. I sent a telegram to Venice. To add to this I see from Taneev's letter that my symphony, sent from Milan three weeks ago, has also not reached Moscow. I have telegraphed to Albrecht. I expect answers tomorrow.

We went to the opera today and left Kolia with Margarita the maid. *The Barber of Seville* was on, Rosina was sung by a Russian, very charmingly. The tenor was very good. The rest of the cast was beneath criticism, but worst of all is the behaviour of the audience – screams, whistles, mad shouts.

18–30 January
Wednesday

Thank God! Had an answer from Venice saying that the parcel was sent in time, and from Moscow that the symphony has arrived. I am at peace.

The weather is cold and grey. Which does not prevent me from feeling happy. I have just finished the Introduction, there is only enough work left for two weeks.

[165]   TO ANATOLI TCHAIKOVSKY   Nice
                                                  22 January–
                                                  3 February 1878
                                                  Sunday

This morning at 8.30 we took a very comfortable carriage and went off towards Nice along a very picturesque road. We arrived in Mentone at twelve, had lunch, went for a walk and then continued our journey at 2.00 pm. From there on the scenery became really lovely. The road runs along immense cliffs, the view changing round every bend. The sun was bright and warm and sometimes we climbed so high that we had to drive through snow. At last at 5 o'clock we arrived in Nice where we took rooms on the eighth floor of the Hôtel de la Paix. I had time to go for a short walk. We had dinner in the restaurant, after which Alesha and I went to have a bath, for which the arrangements in the hotel are splendid. Modia went to the theatre and returned early.

23–4 Monday

Slept very well. After morning coffee we had our photographs taken with Kolia, at Mme von Meck's request! By the way, send me at once one of yours, as I have promised it to Nadezhda Filaretovna. Do not forget to do so, my Golubchik. After lunch we went to see everything that is of interest and beauty in Nice. At 4 o'clock I took Kolia to the Zoo to see a female lion-tamer. Dinner has just come to an end. Am going to the theatre. Goodbye. Have been to the theatre. Mlle Kushnik sang Angot.

San Remo
24–5 Tuesday

In the morning I took a beautiful walk to the Château. You must remember it. From there you have a great view of Nice and its surroundings. The weather was as in May. After lunch we left at 2.30, and returned to San Remo at 7 o'clock. How foul San Remo seemed after beautiful, glamorous Nice. How dull it is here in San Remo. There is nowhere to go for walks except along the beach. Wherever you go in the mountains everything is exactly the same. Never-ending olive groves which shut out the views, and women, old men, and boys, collecting olives.

Found a lot of letters waiting for me including your short one. I forgot to ask you to kiss Leva, Sasha, Tania and Anna. When are they going back? I am not writing to them to Petersburg because you will give them all the news.

I kiss you.

25 January–6 February 1878
Wednesday

Tolichka! As a punishment for your short letter this also will be short. Today I swear at San Remo more than ever. A filthy, horrid, little place. After Nice it looks miserable. Nowhere to go for walks. One cannot tramp forever up and down the sea front. As soon as you go up into the mountains all you see are the dull monotonous olive groves, shutting out the views which are not beautiful anyway.

P. Tchaikovsky

This letter should have been dated (old style) 26, 27, 28 January. The death of Tchaikovsky's half-sister, Zinaida Ilyinishna Olkhovskaia (see p. 15), took place on 13 January. His mother had died on 13 June, 1854, and the coincidence of days of the month certainly impressed him. Anna Davydova (later to marry N. K. von Meck) had lately been accepted as a student at a royal boarding school on a special grant.

Anatoli at this time was in love with Alexandra Panaeva and was anxious for her to sing Tatiana's 'letter' song from *Eugene Onegin* (Op. 24) at a Conservatoire concert. (See also letters 222 and 228.)

TO ANATOLI TCHAIKOVSKY   [San Remo]
                                   27 January–8 February 1878
                                   Thursday

Nothing special has happened. Alesha is much better. The weather is gorgeous.
The sea like a mirror, but all the same San Remo is boring. I notice that Modia
is also beginning to feel bored and would like to go somewhere else. I am hard
at work on my opera and hope that in three or four days it will be finished.

                                   28 January–9 February
                                   Friday

I have just received your letter. Zina's death has upset me very much. I am
sorry for the younger children. But what worries me even more is how
Papochka will react to the news. I fear it will upset him frightfully. Although
you do not say exactly when she died, if you got the telegram on the 14th it
must have happened on the 13th. A curious coincidence of dates which is sure
to impress Papochka. Please let me know how he took the sad news.

I have finished the piano score of the opera. However dull it is in San Remo
we cannot but admire the lovely weather. We found a lot of flowers during
our walk. Birds sang with all sorts of different voices. I am a bit angry with
you. Why could you not give me more particulars about Sasha? Where are
they staying? What are they doing? How does Tania pass the time? How does
Anna face her fate? Believe me all this interests me very much more than my
overture being played at a concert! When is *Francesca* being played? How
do you pass your leisure, whom do you meet? What are Apukhtin and Laroche
doing? Make up your mind to write me a letter twice a week in the form of
a diary, just as I am doing. If there is nothing interesting to report just say
so. But I am sure you will find plenty to write about.

Please, as soon as you have read this letter go downstairs and give our dear
old man a great hug. My God! Somehow I fear that I will not be able to
embrace him alive, something warns me that it can happen (that he too may
be taken from us). . . . However my presentiments often fool me.

There is no separate Tatiana's aria, there is the 'Letter scene' so you are wrong
in wanting Panaeva to sing it; it has no end of its own and would not do for
a concert. The scene with Nania starts immediately after it. It would be better
if she sang Oksana's song [from *Vakula*].

P. Tchaikovsky

TO ANATOLI TCHAIKOVSKY   [San Remo]
                                   29 January–10 February 1878
                                   Sunday

Last night I went to the opera and heard *The Barber of Seville*. The Russian
singer Raievskaia was quite good.

30 January–11 February
Monday

Slept badly, and worked all day. Am copying out the libretto. In a day or two all will be ready. Had a letter from Rubinstein in answer to mine. All these despots become tame if you growl back at them. The ruder my letter was, the kinder his answer. My new symphony will be played on the 10th (old style) of February. Most interesting to know the result.

1–13 February
Wednesday

Today I finished my opera, packed it and sent it off. As a consequence of this, I am in the best frame of mind. . . .

Rubinstein is offended at the telegram from Davydov demanding the score of *Eugene Onegin*. Why did he ask for it? For Panaeva? Or did he want it for other reasons? Beg Panaeva, from me, to sing Oksana's aria instead of Tatiana's which is not suitable to sing at a concert. I would be very grateful. . . .

Your

P. Tchaikovsky

[168] TO ANATOLI TCHAIKOVSKY Florence
12–24 [February 1878]

Tolia, my dear!

Although I am late with my diary I will continue from where I left off. My last letter was from Pisa on Tuesday 7–19th.

8–20 Wednesday

I went for a tour round Pisa, and saw the famous 'Leaning Tower', the cathedral and the adjoining cemetery. Most impressive! I liked everything I saw, especially the tower. We climbed to the very top and admired the view. How glad I was not to have to look at the sea and olives any more. I was thoroughly sick of both. After lunch we went to Cascino, which is far away from the town. The weather was gorgeous, not a soul around – it was wonderful. We took a walk through the woods, which are surrounded by a high wall and are full of wild goats, hares, antelopes, etc. which belong to the King. Kolia was thrilled with them. The hotel dinner was long and dreary. The rest of the evening we stayed at home.

9–21 Thursday

Having spent a lot of money at the hotel, we left at 11 o'clock and arrived in Florence at 2 o'clock and went to the hotel Citta di Milano, where rooms had been booked in advance. A very nice hotel. Modest and Kolia have a magnificent room facing the street, with sun streaming in all day. We also use it as a sitting-room. Next to it, separated by an arch, is their bedroom. Then comes Alesha's room, with a bathroom next to it. Across the corridor is my room, cosy and well furnished. After the poor furnishings in the Pension Joly everything here seems grand and luxurious! I was happy the whole day.

The dinner was very good. There are not too many people here, but those who are are English. This is a nuisance but at least it insures against boring dinner acquaintances. We all went for a walk together before dinner. I started by going to the Arno to think of you. How different everything looked then. What a miserable being I felt and how well I am now. After dinner I went for a walk alone. As it is spring now the town looks quite different: flowers everywhere, crowds of people on the streets, little lit-up tents with cheap goods being sold on the squares. All this gave me great pleasure.

All the evening I wrote my answer to Nadezhda Filaretovna's letter which was waiting for me here, it is eight pages long, and is more than usually kind and thoughtful. So I had to write a long answer to her. Modest, after having put Kolia to bed, went for a walk and then to the theatre to see Salvini, Rossi's rival – in *Othello*.

10–22 Friday

In the morning we noticed the difference between the climate here and San Remo. It is also spring but by far not so warm as there. I went to the Uffizi Gallery, but very quickly got tired. Modest admired everything but only very superficially. He wants to go again, without Kolia. They went back to the hotel afterwards and I went off to roam on my own. After lunch I took Alesha to the baths; then I went to Cascino where I met Modest and Kolia. For some unaccountable reason I was in a bad humour and irritable all day. I even did not feel very well in the evening and went to bed early.

11–23 Saturday

In the morning we went to see the Palazzo Vecchio. I was quite touched to see again the same old man who took us around when I was with you! Do you remember? *'Vedez, Moussou, la cole de Raphael, Moussou!'* He showed us round again. Between lunch and dinner I composed a song, and then went for a walk to the Boboli Gardens which belong to the Palazzo Pitti. In the evening Modest and I went to the theatre. Salvini was playing *Hamlet*, but I did not like him. He is old, ugly and full of mannerisms. Rossi is better.

12–24 Sunday
Just got up. I kiss you heartily.

Got a telegram yesterday from Moscow concerning the symphony which was played on the 10th.

[no signature]

The Fourth Symphony had been played in Moscow at the Tenth Concert of the Russian Musical Society. Tchaikovsky had congratulatory telegrams from Mme von Meck and from N. Rubinstein. The silence of his friends and colleagues in Moscow hurt Tchaikovsky, as he explained in a letter to Albrecht. Mme von Meck's letter (see Letter 170) has not survived, but it prompted the recipient to write: 'How infinitely happy I am that my symphony pleased you – that when listening to it you experienced those feelings that I was full of when I composed it, that my music has reached your heart.'

According to Modest his brother had written the last of his piano pieces comprised in Op. 40 on 12 February. This piece – 'Interrupted Reverie' – used a song that Tchaikovsky heard sung beneath his window in Venice every night as the middle section. The whole set was dedicated to Modest. The songs of Op. 47 were dedicated to Panaeva, but these did not appear until 1881 by when Anatoli's love for the singer had subsided.

[169]   TO ANATOLI TCHAIKOVSKY   Florence
                                       14–26 [February 1878]

On Sunday, the day before yesterday, we went for a charming drive out of town. The monastery *des chartreux* left a special poetical impression. In the evening I went along the river hoping again to hear that wonderful child's voice.

To meet that heavenly boy and to hear him sing again has become an obsession with me. Where has he disappeared?

Composed a piano piece yesterday morning. I have decided to write one every day. After lunch we went to the Palazzo Pitti. In the evening I walked to exhaustion along the river hoping to see the lovely boy. Suddenly I noticed a crowd further on, heard voices, ran, but oh! disappointment! A bewhiskered man was singing, very well too, but how can one compare! ...

If Panaeva loves you I shall write her a whole sequence of songs, and will, in fact, become her devoted slave....

Yours

P. Tchaikovsky

TO ANATOLI TCHAIKOVSKY   Florence
                                                  [February 1878]

Just as you have started at last to send me your diary I on my side am getting slack. It is Saturday today and I have not written since Tuesday. All the same I will keep my promise and give a day by day description of what has happened.

16–28 February
Thursday

Nothing out of the ordinary. After lunch a delightful drive to Cascino. You would never recognize it now. How charming it has become – simply lovely. The trees are coming out and the birds are singing all the time. There are delightful solitary, shady walks. In the evening I went to the popular theatre and enjoyed myself. Try to imagine the most intense tragedy – acted by naïve and well-intentioned actors – in which in spite of all that is horrific Punchinello plays a big part. A most amusing mixture of melodrama with an impossible harlequinade. The audience was in raptures. Quite impossibly cheap. We had a magnificent box right over the stage which made it even better. The box cost four francs. Modest arrived at the very end.

17 February–1 March
Friday

Also nothing out of the ordinary. Received a letter from Mme von Meck who is enthusiastic about my symphony. What a charming person she is! How warm and kind her letter is. Notice, that none of my Moscow friends has yet mentioned my symphony. . . .

18 February– 2 March
Saturday

Slept badly. Went to see the church of Santa Croce in the morning; where Machiavelli, Michelangelo and many others are buried. Just returned from an enormous walk in S. Miniato. Went alone. The view of Florence from there is beautiful. I do not know why, but I am in a bad humour today. . . . However on the whole I feel well.

In a week's time, not a day later, we are off to Switzerland. I would gladly stay here a little longer but money flows away like water and we have to retreat as fast as we can.

So the address will now be: Clarens, Villa Richelieu, that is where I will think of you at every step.

I kiss you.

P. Tchaikovsky

I was very upset about the death of Shumsky.

Florence
                                                      [February 1878]

Once again I have not been regular in keeping my diary. Forgive me! Too much
has happened these last days. I lived – not merely existed. Was I really happy?
I do not really know. But I lived intensely.

                                            18 February–2 March
                                            Saturday

In the evening I was to meet the boy-singer. . . . Exactly at 9 o'clock I came
up the bridge where the man, who had promised to find him, was to wait for
me. The man was there. A small crowd of other men stood looking at me with
curiosity and in the centre stood our boy. I noticed at once that he had
grown slightly and that he was beautiful, although when I was with you we
thought he looked insignificant. Because the crowd was growing larger and
the place was very central I moved on towards Cascino.

On the way I said I was not sure if he was the same boy. 'You will hear that
I am when I begin to sing. You gave me a half a franc in silver.' All this was
said in a sweet voice that stirred one to the very depths of one's soul. But
what happened to me when he started singing! I find no words to describe it.
I am sure you do not get as much satisfaction when listening to Panaeva!
Enraptured, I wept. I was in ecstasy. Besides the songs you know, he sang
two new ones, one of which, *Pimpinella* is delightful. I thanked both him and
his acolytes liberally.

On my way home I met Modest and was sorry he had not been with me. I hope
that on Monday we shall hear him again. . . .

                                            19 February–3 March
                                            Sunday

Nothing special. Did not feel well after a bad night. In the evening we went
with Modia to a masquerade in the best theatre, the Pergola. I expected it
to be full of excitement and fun. But it wasn't, at all. Very few people, poor
costumes, scarcely any ladies, so few that men had to dance with each
other. . . .

                                            20 February–4 March
                                            Monday

Because of the carnival he [the boy] appeared in fancy dress, as also his
acolytes. Only now could I have a proper look at him. He is really beautiful,
has kind eyes and a charming smile. But I prefer listening to him out-of-doors,
not in a room. He felt shy, and did not use his full voice. I have written down
all his songs. I then took him to have his photograph taken, which will be
ready only after we leave. When I get one I will send it to you.

                                            21 February–5 March
                                            Tuesday

The evening was free, and Modest and I went to the theatre where there was
a carnival play, with Harlequin and Colombine and so on. Quite amusing.

This morning I had a letter from Sasha which touched me greatly. I went to the Museo Nazionale, which was very interesting, and had lunch with Modia and Kolia at 'our restaurant', do you remember (*Gille e Leta*)? Then I went to Cascino alone – a long way – and picked some violets. After dinner he will come and sing. I am looking forward to it. Tomorrow evening we go straight to Geneva – to Modest's great sorrow, who likes Florence. But we cannot stay any longer, money flows like water. . . .

[no signature]

[172] TO ANATOLI TCHAIKOVSKY   Clarens
                                       25 February–9 March 1878

Once again I have missed a few days.

22 February–6 March
Wednesday

Vittorio, my little singer came, but with a sore throat and could not sing. I was very upset.

23 February–7 March
Thursday

We were sad to leave. Of all the foreign towns I know Florence is the one I like best. We left at eight in the evening, having said a hearty farewell to everybody. . . .

24 February–8 March
Friday

The journey was comfortable and pleasant. We arrived in Geneva at seven in the evening and took rooms at the Hôtel de Russie. We bathed and then had tea. Slept very badly like all these last days.

25 February–9 March
Saturday

Wandered round Geneva. How dull, prosaic, and commonplace Geneva seems after Florence which, during the last days of our stay, and thanks to the spring weather, turned into a fairy city. And Vittorio! He alone made it full of charm. At every step you come to my mind. Nearing Clarens I felt very tense. (We started at two.) Were met most kindly by Mme Mayor and Marie. I shall live in our former sitting-room. . . . I kiss you with all my love.

Your

P. Tchaikovsky

The G major Piano Sonata (Op. 37) was being sketched at this time, but Tchaikovsky turned aside from it to concentrate on the Violin Concerto (Op. 35). The concerto, completed on 20 March, had been subjected to the critical scrutiny of Yosif Kotek (for whom Tchaikovsky was trying to obtain a teaching post in St Petersburg see Letter 179), who was helpful in matters of violin technique. Dissatisfied with the andante he had written, on 24 March Tchaikovsky composed another slow movement (see Letter 179). The original andante became the first item of Op. 42.

It had been the composer's intention to dedicate the concerto to Leopold Auer, who was to give its first performance. Auer, however, refused the work on account of its difficulty and its 'radicalism'. In due course it was dedicated to Adolph Brodsky, who gave the first performance but not until after the passage of some years.

[173] TO ANATOLI TCHAIKOVSKY   [Clarens]
                                                 3–15 March 1878
                                                 Friday

Again a freezingly cold day. After a morning walk I composed. I am working on a piano sonata. (Keep it quiet.) I worked quickly and without any success. After dinner we went to the Righi Vaudois. Every bend of the road reminded me of you. If I had been alone I would have got an attack of melancholia; luckily in the numerous and pleasant company I was, I found myself remembering you which made the walk specially charming. In respect of companions and intimates – I cannot think of the moment when I shall have to be separated from Kolia. My love to him grows with every hour. I have never loved a child so deeply and tenderly.

On our way back we experienced some frightening moments. We decided to return, not along the main road, but along a steep and narrow path; and we came to a place where we could neither move backward nor forward. I feared for Kolia. One minute was quite horrifying; I slipped, fell and started rolling down the slope which ended in a sheer drop, and I was holding Kolia by the hand. Somehow I managed to hold on, crawled up but was badly shaken.

In the evening before and after supper we made music. Kotek who is here, brought a lot of music with him and we are expecting another lot of piano duets from Berlin. I liked very much Lalo's *Symphonie espagnole*. After tea we played for Modia my fourth symphony which he has not yet heard.

                                                 4–16 March 1878
                                                 Saturday

I slept well, and went for a walk. I forced myself to work, but found no pleasure in it. I do not know, cannot understand why, in spite of my present favourable situation, I am not disposed to work. Am I drying up as a composer? I have to squeeze out cheap little ideas and sit thinking over each phrase. But I shall not give in and hope that inspiration will come back soon. I thought of you at dinner. We had *bouilli* with horse radish. We are just as well fed as when you were here. How sick I am of our mysterious ladies! You have to talk and talk and only in French. Luckily their guest, a gentleman, is a man of the world and quite clever. Went for a walk to the Châtelet and Crêtes. Again memories of you everywhere. After our walk I received two charming letters, one from Nadezhda Filaretovna the other from you. I could not tear myself away from yours it was so interesting. Now I know all about what you are doing and the company you keep and it pleases me greatly. I continue to worry concerning Alexandra Valerianovna [Panaeva]. I fear that if you come across any complications you will lose heart. Also, you are wrong to be worried about looking so young; that cannot do any harm. Mme von Meck is delighted with your photograph. Had a bath and again thought of you. Made plenty of music. Will go to bed now. I kiss you with immeasurable love.

Your

P. Tchaikovsky

[174] TO ANATOLI TCHAIKOVSKY

[Clarens]
5–17 March 1878
Sunday

The weather is a little better. Kotek and I went to Songier – where we had often been with you – to drink a glass of wine. We went along the Gorge de Chauderon; you wouldn't have recognized it. It was risky to walk in some places, for during the winter huge boulders had rolled down, broken the railings – even the metal ones – and filled the path with stones. On our way back we had a rest in your favourite place, and in the evening played piano and violin duets.

6–18 March 1878
Monday

The weather is awful; it is impossible to go for a walk. It is raining and snowing which does not make a walk very attractive. All the morning I sat working at a violin concerto and became so keen that for the present I have put my sonata aside. I want to take advantage of Kotek's presence here. This is a new and difficult task for me but very interesting. . . .

7–19 March 1878
Tuesday

Again I worked all the morning at my concerto. Please, do not mention to anyone what I am composing and how. I hate it when people are expecting something from me. Received from Yurgenson several scores, including *Francesca*. By the way, has it been played in Petersburg or not? Could it be that it has passed as unnoticed as my symphony in Moscow? Not one of my friends in Moscow has written even a few sympathetic words about it. Poor idiot that I am to expect appreciation and enthusiasm for my work! This morning I got a parcel of books from Nadezhda Filaretovna. I had asked her to find me some good poems for songs, in response to which she sent me a whole lot of books of poems and *Russia of Old* [a periodical] for the whole of this year. It has been snowing all day and was so cold that I wore my fur coat indoors. In the evening I played *Francesca* with Kotek. Both he and Modest were generous with their praise. Am worried about you. How are things? Are you well?

8–20 March 1878
Wednesday

Again I worked very successfully. The concerto is taking shape – not too fast, but it is moving along. After dinner we went for a lovely walk where we had not been with you. The weather is better today, damp, and the roads dirty, but warm enough not to wear a coat. I remembered former days, and danced a grand *Pas de Deux* with Modest, which was greatly applauded by the audience – i.e. Kotek and Kolia. Naturally my dancing and pirouettes had more success than my compositions.

I received a lot of piano duets from Berlin, including *Francesca*, and we played all the evening. And the result of everything is: excellent health and perfect humour. There is only one little cloud on the horizon – you! I get so worried when I have no letters from you. I do not think too much about the future, Kamenka does not exceedingly appeal to me. It will be difficult for me to stay there especially when Modest and Kolia leave. But all the same I must go.

I kiss you lovingly.

Your

P. Tchaikovsky

[175]   TO ANATOLI TCHAIKOVSKY   [Clarens]
9–21 March 1878
Thursday

Tolichka!

The days are so full that I only find enough time to write letters in the evening (I am writing this on Saturday). I have several others to write, so this will be very short. Forgive me! The weather is perfect. After dinner I went to Vevey along a new and delightful road, and returned by train. Played duets for piano and violin. Laughed heartily all through supper. We have become great friends with our two ladies. They are most amusing.

10–22 March 1878
Friday

I was not very well this morning. Worried over rheumatic pains, and no appetite. I instantly imagined that I had caught a severe illness. After dinner Kotek, Modest and Kolia went off for a boat trip on the lake and I went to give my legs a sunshine cure. I went to Montreux, sat down near the church, and stayed there quietly for a long time, and then returned by another road parallel to the lower one. The sun helped, and I returned home perfectly well. I watched the sunset from our balcony and enjoyed it deeply. In the evening I wrote a letter to Nadezhda Filaretovna and read Jacolliot who is, at the moment my favourite author.

11–23 March 1878
Saturday

Again the weather is awful; it is raining and snowing with no sign of its stopping. Have started work on the Andante of the Violin Concerto. . . . Now, here is what I have been thinking about! As I want to see you very much why not try and join me for Easter Week in Kamenka? Think about it, my dear, you would make me so happy, answer as soon as possible. . . .
So, to end this, I beg you again come at Easter to Kamenka, if you want to make me happy.

I kiss you

P. Tchaikovsky

Napravnik conducted *Francesca da Rimini* in St Petersburg on 11 March, 1878. When Tchaikovsky did have some news of the performance, it was good news. Anatoli wrote how the applause went on 'for ever', Napravnik was decorated with a wreath, K. Y. Davydov considered *Francesca* the greatest of modern works; while Taneev, though observing Napravnik's comment that the work could with advantage be shorter, also wrote his congratulations. Cui praised the introduction; Rimsky-Korsakov was critical of the themes but on the whole liked the work; Laroche said some pleasant things in *Golos* but noted a too close resemblance, perhaps, to Liszt and gave it as his opinion that symphonic poem was not Tchaikovsky's metier.

On 3 March, 1878, the Treaty of San Stefano was signed after the Russian capture of Plevna, Sofia, and Adrianople. The Turkish Empire was all but destroyed and if the terms of the Treaty had been carried out its power would have been quite ended. The other great powers, however, distrusted Russia and some made aggressive moves. The British Navy sailed into the Sea of Marmora, Indian troops were put onto Malta, and the Austrian Army was mobilized. As a result of such confrontation the Czar drew back and agreed to revision of the San Stefano Treaty at Berlin. After the diplomatic defeat he had suffered the Czar put the brake on liberal ideas once more. Both Tchaikovsky and Mme von Meck were gloomy about the political future in Russia. The manner in which Russia had been frustrated at Berlin by the British, particularly by Lord Beaconsfield, did not endear the British to the Russians. (See Letters 181 and 225.)

[176] TO ANATOLI TCHAIKOVSKY Clarens
15–27 March 1878

There is nothing much to report about the last few days.

(1) Sunday 12–24. Went for a walk to Villeneuve. Modest met an acquaintance, a Mme Kablukov.

(2) Monday 13–25. All day the weather was vile, and it never stopped snowing. I am continuing to work, with great enthusiasm, on my concerto. . . .

(3) Wednesday 15–27. The weather is cold but clear; thank God for that.

I worked as usual, and went for a solitary walk after dinner. I had four letters from you, from Nadezhda Filaretovna, from Kostia Shilovsky, and from Leva. There was nothing disagreeable in any of them; nevertheless I am upset and in a bad humour. First of all I worry about you. If you want to make me happy do come to Kamenka.

I still have had no news about *Francesca*. Was it unsuccessful? Or was it badly played? Did no one think it worth while to let me know that it had been played and was successful? I do not mean the audience, but all the Davydovs, Malozemovs, Konradis etc. Is it possible that they thought *Francesca* unworthy of their attention? How bitter this is. If no one liked it, it means that Napravnik is to blame. If played properly it must make a strong impression.

Except for all that you write about your relationship with Alexandra Valerianovna [Panaeva], your letter has given me enormous, unbelievable, pleasure. After which I kiss and pray for all the blessings of heaven to descend on your head.

Yours

P. Tchaikovsky

[177] TO ANATOLI TCHAIKOVSKY   Clarens
                                                       16–28 March 1878
                                                       Thursday

The days have been so much the same that it is difficult to keep up a diary. The concerto is finished in rough. After dinner we all went to Chauderon. The snow has made the roads so dirty that we only got about half-way there. The weather continues to be horrid. In the evening I wrote to Nadezhda Filaretovna, and tried to make her appreciate the beauties of Mozart's music which she does not understand.

                                                       17–29 March
                                                       Friday

A good, still a bit cold, but fine day. I have started to copy out the concerto. After dinner Kotek had a letter from Malozemova in which she said that *Francesca* had been successful and was well played. I hope she has not invented this for my benefit. Yesterday we had supper with our mysterious half-Russian ladies for the last time, as they left today. Now the only stranger at our table is a pompous German woman, ugly, old and deaf. Yesterday during dinner she started talking in German with Modest. I suffered in silence as long as I could but in the end I burst out laughing, to such an extent that I almost couldn't stop. Luckily the German woman was not offended. Modest speaking German is the greatest farce on earth.

                                                       18–30 March
                                                       Saturday

Again the weather is beastly. It is getting quite impossible. I slept well but could not go to sleep for a long time after having read in the papers that war is inevitable, this is awful! The only good thing about it is that I will be back in Russia and will not have to experience what we did when the Venetian newspaper boys yelled 'Vittoria di Turchi!'

In the morning I copied out the concerto. After dinner I went for a walk in pouring rain. . . .

Forgive the uninteresting letter.
I kiss you, my dear one,

Yours

P. Tchaikovsky

[178] TO ANATOLI TCHAIKOVSKY   Clarens
                                                 19–31 March 1878
                                                 Sunday

Today has been quite exciting. First of all Mme Mayor's eldest son, a student, had dinner with us and our hostess made a wonderful meal in his honour, the like of which I have never eaten before. In the afternoon we went up the woody hill at the foot of which you and I rested on the grass – do you remember? The walk up was full of amusing episodes – we slipped, fell, pulled each other up and so on. . . .

                                                 20 March–1 April
                                                 Monday

I expected a letter from you, but in vain. Why, Tolia, must you upset me and make me sad? If you have no time for long letters, write short ones. I have finished copying out the first part of the concerto, and in the evening I played it. Modest and Kotek are both delighted with it. I was very gratified at their approval. The weather is simply horrible. My soul is sad. . . .

                                                 21 March–2 April
                                                 Tuesday

Slept rather badly. . . . Weather awful. An attack of melancholia is creeping over me, especially on account of the political situation which makes me sad and angry. I also feel ashamed that the money Nadezda Filaretovna sends me, which I badly need to get away from here, will cost her such a lot because of the unfavourable rate of exchange. All day I was grumpy, irritable and nervous. If I could I would have got drunk. Went for a walk alone.

                                                 22 March–3 April
                                                 Wednesday

Again no letters from you. If none arrive tomorrow I am going to send a telegram. Kotek has copied out the violin part of the concerto and we played it before dinner, to the complete satisfaction both of composer and performer. Kotek, indeed, played it so well that it could have been performed at a concert there and then. We all went for a long walk after dinner and, returning by our favourite path, rested in our favourite place (do you remember?). The papers seem to be a little less glum today. In the evening I played the Andante which was not so well thought of as the first movement. I myself am not very pleased with it.

How cold it is! I am sitting right in front of the fire but cannot make my feet warm. I kiss you lovingly.

P. Tchaikovsky

[179]   TO ANATOLI TCHAIKOVSKY   [Clarens]
                                               23 March [–4 April 1878]
                                               Thursday

I have had your letter. You do not write very often but jolly well. Your letter was more interesting than the best of novels. *Merci*, Tolichka! Nothing of any interest today except for a letter from Nadezhda Filaretovna which was as kind and as interesting as ever. The Finale of the concerto is creating a stir. The Andante, however, has been adversely criticized, and tomorrow I shall have to write another. The weather – horrid.

                                               24 March [–5 April]
                                               Friday

Have been remembering with pleasure our last year's journey to Kamenka. It was exactly a year ago that, after passing the night at Bobrinsky station, we made our appearance in Kamenka. I have written a new Andante with which my kind but severe critics are pleased. Kotek has been glum and silent all day. . . . All the same he is a dear person. What devoted attention he gives to my concerto! I could never have done anything without his help. He plays it beautifully.

                                               25 March [–6 April]
                                               Saturday

Modest, Kolia and Alesha went to church in Vevey. I worked intensively at the orchestration of the concerto. The weather is lovely and I decided to go for a long walk after dinner. Do you remember the *chalet* Blumenthal where you tried to take me but I never went? Now I have been there several times and love it. Today Kotek and I went even further and reached Les Avants where, as you did, we had some wine and enjoyed the delightful, clear air. The snow is still there but on the way fresh green grass is coming through and masses of wild flowers; the walk was perfect but I am so tired I can scarcely write.

I still do not know when we are leaving, but I have hardly any money left. As soon as I receive some from Nadezhda Filaretovna I shall let you know! But in any case I will be in Kamenka in Holy Week and hope to embrace you there.

I have just had a charming letter from Taneev; he writes from Riga about the different comments on *Francesca*. I find them most queer. Try to talk to Davydov about Kotek. Did they get our letters? I embrace you a thousand times.

Yours

P. Tchaikovsky

On 24 March Anatoli wrote to his brother, saying how Cui had been telling him how good the Piano Concerto was and how he regretted that he no longer wrote for the papers. 'I was,' said Anatoli, 'very touched with all he said about you.'

[180] TO ANATOLI TCHAIKOVSKY   Clarens
                                        26 March–7 April
                                        Sunday
                                        29 March–10 April 1878

The day was absolutely perfect. I do not think I remember one like it. After dinner we hired a carriage and went to the Aigle. There we walked in the forest full of spring flowers, and returned when it was getting dark.

                                        27 March–8 April
                                        Monday

Nothing to mention except for the rain pouring down all day, which makes it dull. I worked for a long time on the instrumentation of the concerto. It is moving on well.

                                        28 March–9 April
                                        Tuesday

The bad weather continues. I felt so unwell all day that I thought I was going to be ill. In the evening I could neither read nor write. I sat over the fire and warmed myself. The maids – Marie, Annette and the porter Emile gave us a surprise; in the evening they appeared in our sitting-room in fancy dress. Annette as a young man; Marie as a bride; and Emile in a woman's dress. We all laughed like anything.

                                        29 March–10 April
                                        Wednesday

The weather as bad as ever. It is getting boring here and the wish to leave grows stronger. I got your letter. We shall leave for Geneva either on the 2nd or 3rd. From there Modest will go to Lyon for a day or two to see Gugentobler. As soon as he returns we shall go to Vienna and stay there one or two days. And I shall be in Kamenka, in your arms, either on Wednesday or Thursday of Holy Week. On Saturday I shall write to you from here as usual and then I will telegraph on the day of departure from Geneva and also from Vienna.

I am going back to Russia with joy but also with a certain amount of apprehension. With joy because, apart from the wish to be back in my native land I rejoice at the thought of seeing you. The apprehension is because of Kamenka. What am I going to do there when both you and Modest have left? It amused me to read that you were impressed by Cui's kind manner. I too always get caught by it. I had a nice letter from Sergei Taneev from Riga, describing a concert of his where the audience consisted of 40 people and the deficit was 10 roubles.

After which I kiss you. Soon I shall be able to plant a personal smacking kiss on your cheek. Good-bye, my dear.

Your

P. Tchaikovsky

I am enclosing a power of attorney in case you would like to collect the money from the tickets if you wish to use it.

[181] TO ANATOLI TCHAIKOVSKY   [Clarens]
                                                   30 March–11 April 1878
                                                   Thursday

I was honoured by a visit from General Shenshin, my creditor. Oh God! what an idiot he is. I suffered agonies until he left. I have lost the habit of meeting strangers, keeping silly conversations going, and putting up with the arrogant way in which they insist on my playing something. And here this son of a bitch turns up to state that as he has now left the accursed slum that is Russia, he can breathe freely at last.

He says everything in Russia is disgusting, that Russia's politics are filthy, that we are called thieves in other countries, that our soldiers are bad, and that England is perfectly right. And all this is pronounced by a money-lender who is inferior even to Bochechkarov in brains and education. At the end of his peroration he added: 'I shall not leave, my friend, until you play me something new.' Shenshin's visit was to me a first taste of those encounters with vulgarity and stupidity that I shall not be able to avoid in Russia.

The nearer the day of our journey approaches the more frightened I feel. I have – I must be honest – experienced many sad moments abroad, but there have also been many that were delightful; what is most important, I was absolutely free. Today, I have finished my concerto. I have cashed the cheque sent me by Nadezhda Filaretovna.

                                                   31 March–12 April
                                                   Friday

The weather magnificent but not all day. At five o'clock we had a thunder-storm. I am enjoying being idle and resting. Kotek has received a refusal from

Davydov, a polite and kind one but a refusal all the same; this has upset him very much. I am sorry for him. Why did Davydov promise in the first place; he is losing a lot by refusing. They may find as good a violinist as Kotek but it will take them a long time to find such a good musician.

1–13 April
Saturday

A wonderful day. We have not had one like this before. In the morning we went to Chillon by steamer and returned in (a small) boat. A certain Kablukova had dinner with us today. In her honour our host caught a huge, and delicious, trout. Mme Kablukova is quite charming and so is her daughter. I went to Chauderon with Kotek who felt a little happier. How lovely it is today! . . .

Tomorrow we are going to the Gorge du Trient. The day after tomorrow Modia is going to Lyon and will join us in Geneva on the 5th. From there we shall all go to Vienna, probably on Thursday.

I shall send you a telegram from Geneva.

I kiss you my Golubchik.

Your

P. Tchaikovsky

Tchaikovsky left Clarens on 5 April and arrived in Kamenka, where he had his own 'Green House', six days later. He was joined on 13 April by Anatoli. Tchaikovsky's birthday was on 25 April (old style). He was currently working on the Piano Sonata, and also on other piano pieces for Op. 39 and Op. 40.

[182] TO ANATOLI TCHAIKOVSKY   Kamenka
                                                     27 April 1878

Do you know, Tolia, I only realized today that I must still write to you although I am not abroad any more. I could not get rid of the feeling that I had just seen you, would see you again shortly and consequently did not need to write. Please, forgive me. I had your letter last night. It was read out loud (nearly all of it) and created a sensation. We counted up that before you reached Kursk you had met twelve acquaintances. Extraordinary! I am expecting your next letter with impatience and excitement. . . .

We were all very sad that you had left. But I hope to see you again soon. Sasha's name day passed quite happily. There was a real ball with an orchestra. . . . I started dancing, with some initial hesitation, but I got gradually carried away, as it always happens in Kamenka, and then went on dancing passionately – quite tirelessly and with all kinds of fun and games. The next morning Leva left for Chigirin with Vassiliev (the hero of the ball) to attend a meeting of Justices of the Peace and he only returned yesterday.

These are the only things worth mentioning; everything else is uninteresting. My life has acquired a proper pattern. After tea in the morning a short walk; then work – which is getting on very well – until dinner.

Since you left I have written three movements of the sonata, a waltz, and another short piece. For a long time I have not had such a perfect setting for work. No one disturbs me. After dinner I go back to write letters or work on proofs and corrections sent to me by Yurgenson. Then I go for a solitary walk. In the evening I am in the big house with the family and play quite a lot. Yesterday at A. Shidlovsky's request I played for so long that my arm aches today. I had an awful letter from Kotek, for since he had not heard anything from me he had got it into his head that I hate and despise him. He has accepted a post at Joachim's school. Judging by his letter he is very unhappy. I had a letter from Nadezhda Filaretovna inviting me to stay for a few days at the end of May at Brailov in absolute solitude. She will not be there. She will only come in June. I am determined to accept her invitation.

There were two telegrams on my birthday. One from you and the other from the Conservatoire professors. I suppose you saw and reminded them about it, otherwise I do not think they would have remembered.

Have come to the fourth page and now, except for the fact that I love you passionately I have no idea what to say next. Unless I mention my state of health. It is perfect. What a great happiness it is to be able to devote all of oneself to a congenial occupation! My head is always full of musical ideas...

Yours

P. Tchaikovsky

[183] TO ANATOLI TCHAIKOVSKY   [Kamenka]
                                                 1 May 1878

... Except for disgusting weather and incessant wind there is nothing out of the ordinary. In spite of the weather I go out for walks. I am composing a lot and well. Yesterday I had a very long letter from Kotek. He had received my letters, is in better spirits, and the tone of his own is quite bright. He is beginning to like the school, the new friends, the attention he gets from Joachim and so on. He refuses the money I offered him and which, anyway, I am not able to send to him at the moment. His letter gave me great pleasure.

Everybody is well here and life runs according to plan. I continue to be pleased with my cottage and have grown so accustomed to the distance from the house that it is no inconvenience. Modest has still not received an order to start on his journey. I have given him some work to do. He has been ordered to write a libretto for the opera from *Undine* – by Zhukovsky. I have again a great desire to write an opera on this subject and this time really will.

I kiss you millions of times. Do not forget about my commissions – a *pince-nez*, and manuscript paper from Bessel.

Yours

P. Tchaikovsky

[184]   TO MODEST TCHAIKOVSKY

Brailov
17 May 1878
Wednesday

After getting into the train and leaving you behind, as you may imagine I started a prolific tear-shedding operation. To make things worse our last meeting in Milan came to my mind; how happy we were then, during the journey from there to Genoa, and further on. . . . To think that this was half a year ago! At which point there came more torrents of tears. And so it went on until, quite suddenly, I fell fast asleep. Actually there was nothing to get upset about; I suppose it was Kiev with all its bustle that tired my nerves.

I woke up near Jmerinka in view of Brailov and a steam plough that was at work in a field next to the railway line. One of the passengers on the train, wishing to impress me by his knowledge of the district, told me that Brailov belongs to a certain von Meck, a banker, had cost three millions and brings a yearly revenue of 700,000 roubles!! As we approached Jmerinka I felt nervous. In the waiting room I was met by the friendly young waiter who served us our supper (do you remember?). I sent him to find out if there were any horses from Brailov, and two minutes later Marcel appeared. He is not a Frenchman at all but a local fellow who was nicknamed Marcel for some reason. He is exceptionally courteous and helpful. His coat and hat are better than mine, so when I got into a magnificent carriage, drawn by four magnificent horses, and Marcel climbed onto the box and sat down next to the coachman, I felt most uncomfortable and continued to be so up to Brailov. It took us about an hour to get there.

The house is a real palace. My room is the epitome of comfort and luxury. After a wash I was escorted by Marcel to the dining-room where a meal awaited me. A huge silver samovar was simmering on the table, next to it a coffee pot kept warm on a spirit burner, the tea-set was of beautiful china, and there were eggs, butter, exquisite tea and coffee. . . . I noticed at once that Marcel had been warned; he did not start any conversation, did not stick in the room all the time, and after serving he disappeared at once. He asked me how I would wish to plan my day. I ordered dinner at one, tea and a cold supper at nine. After coffee, I went round the house which consists of many separate apartments, all beautifully furnished. The enormous brick annexe, built specially for guests, is just like a hotel. A long and wide corridor with rooms on both sides, kept ready to receive people at any time. As to the ground floor, where I am living, there is no end to the utmost refinement of comfort here.

In my room all the toilet accessories – brushes, combs, nail brushes, tooth brushes, soap, powders, etc. – are all new. Pens, ink and paper are prepared for me on two tables. There are book-cases full of books in several of the rooms, and interestingly illustrated volumes lying about everywhere. In the music room there is a piano, a harmonium and a mass of music. In Nadezhda Filaretovna's study there are several paintings, but that of St John about which she wrote I did not like; the marble figure of the sleeping boy is delightful. At one o'clock I paraded once more to the dining-room for dinner. It was excellent but a little too light. The zakuskis [hors d'oeuvres] were gorgeous; the wines too. The menu consisted of: soup printanière, asparagus, chicken, and a sweet dish made of cream (I asked to have no more than four dishes). After dinner I poked my nose round the music library and then went for a walk. At 4 o'clock I ordered the horses and was taken to the 'rock', where a fast-running river flows between two high rocky banks covered by thick forest. There is a summer house standing in the most picturesque nook. I took a long walk there and returned by another road. Brailov itself is not very interesting. There are no special views from the house except of the magnificent trees in the garden, which is large, rich in variety, with lilac bushes, rose bushes, etc. But it is not shady and picturesque enough for me.

Of all I have seen I like the house best. I have been told that the surrounding country is charming but not in the immediate vicinity to the house. In that respect I think Glebovo is superior to Brailov. All the same I could enjoy myself perfectly here had it not been for your Honour! I was not sad before dinner, I had no time, but during my drive, and walk, and at this moment, I am aware of a sense of sadness and awe. Not that I wish you would be perpetually with me, but I feel sorry for you and ashamed. Here am I enjoying freedom in this quite exclusive environment, whereas you will have to leave the dear Kamenka people in order to go to a place you are going to find hateful. If I could be sure that after leaving here and returning to Kamenka you would still be there I would be at peace and happy.

Modia, to make me perfectly content you must swear to come to Kamenka in July, or at least in August. I cannot think without a shudder about the two last days in Kiev. It was all so sad, and made worse by petty complications. Give a special kiss to dear Verousha. Also everyone else, beginning with Sasha and Leva I embrace passionately and with all my love. You I want to suffocate in my arms and also dear Kolia, Ouka, Bobik, Mitia, Tanka, Taska, in one word the whole lot of them. Alesha has not yet arrived. Write to me here.

Yours

P. Tchaikovsky

[185] TO MODEST TCHAIKOVSKY
Brailov
18 May 1878

I will send this letter straight to Grankino. It will make me happy if when you arrive you find my letter waiting for you. My dear, dear Modia, how marvellous it would have been for me here if I had known for sure whether you were happy. But although you are in Kamenka I fear that your stay is spoiled by the thought that you must go to Grankino and that I am not with you. This shows how conceited I am to imagine that my absence has poisoned your stay in Kamenka as much as your not being here with me has poisoned mine.

But in my case time is a great healer. Today I am not as sad as I was yesterday; tomorrow I shall probably feel better than today. Alesha arrived yesterday and that made me feel much better. All particulars about last night and today you will know from my letter to Sasha. If you have left before it arrives they will send it over to you.

19 May
7 pm

Just as I returned from a walk and feeling happy I was handed a telegram from Kamenka saying that the one I sent from Jmerinka two days ago did not reach them. I am both astonished and upset about it.

It is quite extraordinary, Modia, that although I am completely free to do as I like I still do not find enough time to do all I want to do, which makes me angry. Today I was going to copy out a violin and piano duet and did not manage to do even half of it. Then I wanted to write to you, to Kotek and Nadezhda Filaretovna, and I will not even finish this letter, because I want to go for a walk before sunset, then have my supper, then play and then – to bed. How will I find time to write three letters?

I continue to be very pleased with Brailov. It has no special charm or character, nothing that could remind one of old times. Everything is perfect and the house is more like a town house, large, luxurious and very comfortable. I like the garden more and more. Today I climbed over the garden wall and on the other side found a small square wood which I immediately explored.

It happens to be what is left of a garden which had been planted by Catholic monks who had a monastery here until 1840. Of the walls that surrounded the monastery only the ruins of the gates are left; the trees are old and large, the grass thick and luscious. Of all I have seen here I like this charming little wood best. Plenty of scope for imagination. . . .

20 May
9 pm

I went to inspect the factory which is magnificent; took Alesha with me. The director of the factory (Count Scipio) took us round all the factory and behaved as if I was his superior. I felt uncomfortable. From there we went to the woods but no sooner had we reached them than a thunderstorm started. I got frightened and decided to return home but the little cloud went by scarcely wetting the ground.

I would be perfectly happy were it not for you. I wonder when this letter will reach you? I worry because I know that as soon as you arrive in Grankino you will have to make decisions, and I fear unpleasant complications. All I want and ask for is to see you in July. If you want me to come to Grankino I shall do so but we must first stay in Verbovka together. For God's sake come!

I embrace you with passion.

Yours

P. Tchaikovsky

Count Scipio, who ran the sugar factory on the Kamenka estate, was not all that he seemed to be and the Davydov family had reason to doubt his honesty. During this period at Brailov Tchaikovsky composed the three pieces of Op. 42, for violin and piano, which were dedicated to the place.

Despite his misadventures with *Undine* (see also pp. 365–9) Tchaikovsky found it hard to escape from a story (Berthalda and Hugo, named below, are characters in that story) that had attracted him from boyhood, according to Modest's testimony. On 23 May Tchaikovsky wrote to Mme von Meck stating his intentions regarding *Romeo and Juliet*. 'The operas by Bellini and Gounod do not frighten me; in them Shakespeare is completely distorted. Don't you think that this drama of genius must attract a musician? I have already discussed it with Modest. I will think seriously about this opera, to which I shall give all the ability I possess.'

[186] TO MODEST TCHAIKOVSKY   Brailov
                                                            25 May 1878

Today is the Feast of the Ascension. I have just returned from the convent where I passed a very pleasant hour. The church was crowded out, not only by local people but also by many who had come from afar as the church is dedicated to the Feast of the Ascension. We only managed to get in with the help of a nun who took us upstairs to the gallery. The architecture of the church is a mixture of the Catholic style with Byzantine additions which makes it interesting and gives it quite a character of its own. There are still a few Latin inscriptions on the ceiling. These consist of names of virtues such as *Scientia, Fortitudo*, etc. The choir also sang from the gallery which gave me the opportunity to study the expressions of the choristers.

The conductor, a very old little lady with a beautiful, expressive face, was particularly interesting. She is a masterly conductor. In some cases the singers sang from copies, which means that the old lady knows something about music! I wonder where from? I made up a romantic story about her. I came out of the church before the end of the liturgy. Outside a most picturesque and lively scene was taking place. I want to mention the way the people dress here which I like very much. The men's clothes are similar to Polish costume. But their heads are shorn with a long tuft of hair left in the middle of the head, in the manner of the Cossacks in the south (see *Taras Bulba* by Gogol).

The costumes of the women are also much more picturesque than those at Kamenka. Nearly all have magnificent coral necklaces. Even the blind beggar women who sat on the grass in a row singing their own peculiar songs in chorus had beautiful corals and pretty dresses. The blind men played on lyres and sang as they do at the market in Kamenka. One of them was prophesying the coming of the Last Judgment: 'Brother against brother, neighbour against neighbour!' he sang.

The people coming out of the church distributed cakes to them. At the church gate pedlars, both male and female, were selling their cheap goods. Groups of people sat around eating thick slices of pork lard with bread or a sort of liquid with cabbage in it, or just bread. Young girls, pupils of the convent school, walked around between all these people. All together it was most interesting and picturesque.

My love of order and punctuality has made my life here run so smoothly that one could think I have lived here all my life. Sometimes I even have the feeling that all this belongs to me, the house, the garden, the woods. . . . My excursions are wonderful whether on foot or when driving – with tea [provided]! At first I felt really uncomfortable when behind my carriage came a cart with samovar, crockery, table, chairs, carpets. However, everything is done with such kind, unassuming attention that I do not feel uncomfortable any more.

Every day I am being taken to a new place. The most beautiful was where I went the day before yesterday – so lovely that I felt tears welling up in my eyes. It was on the high bank of the river, surrounded by a thick forest, and with a fine view to the other side. Yesterday we went to the 'faraway' forest where, as in Pisa, there is a fenced-in part for fallow deer. At home a surprise was awaiting me; a boat moored near the bridge took me to the summer house in the middle of the little lake where I had tea and angled for carp. In general I am living on the fat of the land. 'I am rolling like a cheese-cake in butter.' However, the future slightly worries me. I must go to Moscow I must see Tolia, but can't decide anything for lack of money, for which I am waiting, or for an indication from Nadezhda Filaretovna as to when I shall get some.

I am expecting your news from Grankino with impatience. Send your answer to this letter to Moscow, to the Conservatoire. It is quite certain that I will be in Moscow at the beginning of June. Shall I see Kondratiev, I cannot say? Modia – since I have read *Romeo and Juliet* all these Undines, Berthaldas and Hugos seem silly and childish. Enough of them, I am going to compose *Romeo and Juliet*. Anything you say will not stop my enthusiasm. It will be my very best work. It seems queer to me now that I did not realize long ago that I was chosen to write the music to this drama. I cannot imagine anything more appropriate to my musical talent. No kings, no marches, nothing that belongs to a Grand Opera. But there is love, love, and love. And what a delight are these secondary parts: Lorenzo, Tybalt, Mercutio. Please do not fear monotony; the first love duet will be completely different to the second. In the first one everything will be bright and clear: love! love not frightened or stopped by anything. In the second – tragedy. From being children full of love Romeo and Juliet have become people, loving and suffering, caught up by tragic, hopeless circumstances. Now I wish to start this opera as soon as possible.

Forgive me, my dear, poor libretto writer, for having tortured you with *Undine*. To hell with her. And what is there so wonderful about it? It does seem silly for her to have 'wept' her idiot to death. It is all so trivial. I must have been an ass to . . . I would never have written anything decent if I had chosen *Undine*. I think of you every hour! I remember with pleasure our life together and worry about how you feel! I wish you would be as excited over your novel as I am over my future opera. Only interesting work, captivating work can reconcile you to reality. Kiss Kolia from me.

Yours

P. Tchaikovsky

[187] TO MODEST TCHAIKOVSKY   Brailov
                                                27 May 1878

What a disquieting way fate has of adding 'a drop of tar to a barrel of honey!' Nothing would be better for me, who loves solitude now and again, than to take advantage of the opportunity to enjoy such a lovely place and wonderful surroundings without any worries; however, there must always be some poison about. The first days I was worried about you . . . now Tolia makes me angry for not letting me know if he will wait for me in Moscow, where he is at the moment. . . . Outwardly everything goes on as if I were perfectly happy. I go for walks, eat, go for drives to the forest (always with tea), drown in luxury and comfort.

But in spite of that the worm of worry gnaws at me. There are minutes when it becomes quite horrible. Pessimism takes over, and I start making myself unhappy about everybody and everything. But none of this is important; the real reason for my worry is Tolia. It is impossible to let him come here, and anyway there is no point as I shall get some money soon, and start on my journey before he could join me here.

I am doing nothing; not even copying the piano pieces for Nadezhda Filaretovna. Either I read – there are so many interesting books here – or I wander round the garden and the countryside, or eat, or sleep. It is a pity that for the last two days the weather has been bad. Two days ago towards evening as we just arrived in the woods a terrific thunderstorm started which made me hide in a shed in the bee-garden with eyes shut and hands over my ears. The day was cold yesterday but we had tea in the woods in spite of it. Oh, God! how happy I would be if not for this drop of tar. For instance yesterday it was so lovely in the forest, looking for stone mushrooms which are plentiful here, and then coming to the little meadow where tea was waiting for me.

Last night I played nearly the whole of *Eugene Onegin*; the composer was the only listener. I am ashamed to say so, but I must tell you in secret that the listener was impressed to tears by the music and paid a thousand compliments to the composer. Oh! If only all the other members of the future audience could be so impressed and touched by this music as the author was. . . .

I kiss you, my dear Modia.

P. Tchaikovsky

The following letter was mistakenly dated '16 August' by Tchaikovsky, at which time he was at Verbovka (see p. 169).

[188]   TO MODEST TCHAIKOVSKY   Brailov
                                                  [End of May 1878]

My stay here is coming to an end. I have decided to leave not on Saturday night but Friday morning. I have come to the conclusion that I will find full contentment in life only in the country and solitude. If it were possible I would agree once and for all to pass my life somewhere in a lonely part of the country. But, from time to time, I would want to be able to entertain close friends and relatives at my home, and enough money in my old chest to be able to visit great cities, foreign lands, and neighbouring villages. I was made for just such a life. Glinka was wrong when he called himself a 'mimosa tree'. It is I who am a mimosa not he. Only in the peaceful, quiet, vast countryside can I open my leaves and live a normal life. How I dream of it! How often I imagine myself in a cosy country house, expecting you, receiving you, chatting with you! How much value there would be in such occasions. How much I could have read! To read in town when you have definite duties to perform is practically impossible.

By the way, talking of books, I am mad about Alfred de Musset. Today I was ready to scream with delight when I read *Les Caprices de Marianne* and, of course, I immediately decided to make it into an opera. What do you think? There is, unfortunately, one important fault in it: the fact that Coelio and Marianne would never be together on the stage. All the same, the story is charming, I am in love with Coelio. . . .

I hope that I shall find a letter from you in Verbovka. In spite of the bad weather I drive to the forest every day. The bathing is delightful. I must say that on the whole I am very pleased with Brailov. No letters from Nadezhda Filaretovna.

I kiss you and Kolia – sweetly.

P. Tchaikovsky

Nizy
6 June [1878]

I have no time to write a long letter, Modia, my dear. Here is a résumé of all that has happened. *Tuesday* 30th: Departure from Brailov. *Wednesday* – 31st: Journey. Disgusting humour. *Thursday* 1st: Arrival in Moscow, meeting Tolia, Taneev, Nikolai Lvovich, evening at Yurgenson's with musicians, supper with Tolia and Nikolai Lvovich at Patrikeev's. Nikolai Lvovich looks much older, was very charming, and I was glad to see him. *Friday* 2nd: Lunch with Rubinstein to celebrate his birthday. . . . *Saturday* 3rd: Running round on business and talk with Rubinstein. Dinner at Bernard's and meeting with Mashenka Golovina who is dying of consumption. Then – evening with all the musicians at the Hermitage.

Sunday 4th: Departure from Moscow – bliss and delight. We decide to pay a visit to Kondratiev. *Monday* – arrival at Kondratiev's. Very jolly! Have just written a large business letter to Nadezhda Filaretovna. Am being called for lunch. Good-bye my dearest, I kiss you. Why no news from you? Either in Moscow or here.

Expect letter with more details.

P. Tchaikovsky

Kamenka
15 June 1878

Modia!

We arrived here the day before yesterday. As I drew nearer to Kamenka I felt a great joy. In spite of all its faults I was coming home – 'It is nice to stay with friends, but better at home'. . . . My cottage is charming, especially with all the flowers around which are already in bloom. Alesha who came here two days in advance has put everything in order. Vera brought a cartful of flowers. Today I have started work, i.e. copying out my sonata. I went for a walk in the evening but was caught in a thunderstorm. The last three days thunderstorms have been practically incessant. All your letters have been received and I enjoyed them immensely.

I will take your advice concerning *Page d'amour* later. At the moment all novels, and specially Zola, make me sick.

I have quite a selection of 'ancient' books and cannot tear myself away from the eighteenth century. We are planning a theatrical performance and none of us can imagine you not taking part in it. You must come here in July. I am so glad that you have such a good relationship with Alina.

Modia, where should I send my letters so that you get them sooner? I fear that at the moment they take a roundabout way via Ekaterinoslav, Novomoskovsk etc. I embrace you a thousand times and Kolia too.

Yours

P. Tchaikovsky

Tchaikovsky wrote to Mme von Meck about his playing *Eugene Onegin* to his family and said 'I enjoyed the music no less than they did, and there were moments when I could neither play nor sing because of the impact the music made on me.' But he worried that its only production would probably be at the Conservatoire. Work on the Suite No. 1 in D Major (Op. 43) was halted and only resumed in November. The subjects from Shakespeare and de Musset were taken no further so far as opera was concerned. Soon Tchaikovsky turned to Schiller's *Die Jungfrau von Orleans*.

[191]   TO ANATOLI TCHAIKOVSKY   Verbovka
                                                  3 August 1878

What would you like to hear about? Nothing of special interest has happened. Sasha and Leva are back from Kiev. Every evening we go to Vyssokoie where we have tea prepared by ourselves, i.e. we get the samovar ready etc., and it is Natalia Andreevna [Plesskaia] who works hardest. Up till now the weather has been glorious but today the strong wind and the dust have started. Rain would have been better. Leva says that he would gladly give 3,000 roubles for rain. My health is perfect but I do not enjoy the *dolce far niente* to which I have full right now that I have finished everything I have been working on. Even the correcting of the *Onegin* proofs has come to an end. I played them the whole opera and the effect was wonderful. I myself like the music very much.
Why do I not enjoy this state of doing nothing? Because of my horrid nature which is perpetually expecting some extraordinary pleasure or delight and is never satisfied. Yesterday I could not wait for dinner to be served. After dinner I waited impatiently to go for a walk. During the walk I was longing for tea. After tea I wanted the moon to rise as soon as possible. Then I just could not wait for supper, and then – the right to go to sleep. And then I slept, and very well too.

Sleep is probably the greatest boon in life. It gives us strength every morning to hope and to expect that things will go well. And now I have already started worrying that I shall have to leave here soon, and I know that only after I have left I shall appreciate in full all the charm of the peaceful, carefree life here.

To be sorry for the past, to hope for the future, never content with the present – that is my life.

My morose attitude to life, of course, is a result of the disgusting weather;
the wind and the dust are terribly depressing.

I kiss you, my dearest, with all my love.

Yours

P. Tchaikovsky

Au revoir, we shall see each other in three weeks' time.

[192]   TO MODEST TCHAIKOVSKY   Verbovka
                                                   21 August 1878

Today is my third day here...

Leva wants me to stay until Sunday to take part in a beat in the forest. I shall
probably stay and leave on Monday. In Brailov I wrote an orchestral Scherzo.
Here I am composing an Introduction and Fugue. Both these pieces are
movements for a Suite which I want to write, I shall leave aside symphonic
music for a long time as I wish to start on an opera. What will it be? *Romeo*
or *Caprices de Marianne*. Let me know your opinion about the latter.
Sasha says that she will send you everything you have asked for on Thursday
and that she is going to write.

I kiss you and Kolia.

P. Tchaikovsky

[193]   TO MODEST TCHAIKOVSKY   Verbovka
                                                   28 August 1878

This week passed like a dream. It was merry and altogether pleasant, and
warmed my heart so much that I often had tears in my eyes at the thought
that I shall soon be obliged to leave for Moscow. Nearly every day we went
on a picnic to the great forest, and in the morning I worked. Inspiration,
Modichka, has descended on me. In Brailov I composed a Scherzo, here an
Introduction and Fugue and an Andante. All this, with an Intermezzo and
Rondo, will be part of a Suite. Both of these are germinating in my head.

I ought to have left the day before yesterday – Saturday evening. But a big
beat was planned for yesterday in the forest. Thirty-two people (hunters) took
part, with 75 beaters. I was tempted and put my journey off until today,
which is Monday. But unfortunately I did not enjoy the hunt, because I caught
a chill a day before and felt so bad in the forest that I was ready to cry and
all I wanted was to return home. (Anyway the hunt was not much good, and
very little game was killed.) At last I got into bed at 9 o'clock and woke up
at 5.00, perfectly well. It is now 7.00 in the morning and I am in a hurry to

write to you, Nadezhda Filaretovna, and Kotek. I dare say you can notice it from the way I am writing. . . .

When do you think we will see each other?

I kiss you and Kolia a thousand times.

Yours

P. Tchaikovsky

[194]   TO ANATOLI TCHAIKOVSKY   [Moscow]
                                            18 September 1878

You lazy boy, why don't you write? I am in a most extraordinary state of mind and lead a strange life. It is not that I am desperately unhappy, or have a burning sense of dissatisfaction. No! – not at all. But I feel completely bored and cold too, and contemptuous of everything that surrounds me. Moscow has become absolutely repulsive but, since it has been decided that I am not going to be here for long anyway, I could not care less. I try to evade society and meeting people. Except for Nikolai Lvovich, I cannot stand all those whom I see. This includes Kashkin, Albrecht, Yurgenson and Laroche, who, God only knows why, is stuck here, eating and drinking too much every day.

I feel like a visitor at the Conservatoire; it has become so alien to me that I do not get angry or boil over any more as I used to do during classes; but have a numb disgust for my male and female pupils and their work. The professors with their servile attitude to Rubinstein, with their petty quarrels and trivial interests, seem to be some sort of foreigners with whom I have nothing in common. I come to the Conservatoire only to give lessons, leave at once after them, and try not to meet or speak to anyone. When I hear someone say, 'Hallo!' or 'See who is here!' I disappear round the next corner as fast as I can.

After the Conservatoire I go every day either to the Neskouchny Sad [the 'Garden Without Boredom' outside Moscow] which is nearly always empty, or to Kunzevo, where today I enjoyed myself immensely, and where you will not even meet so much as a dog. After a two hours walk I go home for dinner where Nikolai Lvovich usually joins me. In the evening we either go together for another walk or I go to church. On the eve of Holy Cross Day we went to the Cathedral of the Dormition in the Kremlin, and stood by the altar where Nikolai Lvovich was greeted as 'Your Excellency'.

As to my health, it is good and my digestive organs *on ne peut plus* regular. My apartment looks very much like a temporary establishment. It is not at all cosy and has one great fault – I hear the traffic day and night. I have no desire at all to write music, and all I do is to correct proofs. *Eugene Onegin* has been delivered at last. I feel happy when I think that you will come to see me in

October and Modest likewise. I presume I shall stay here until November, certainly not later than December. . . .

Yours

P. Tchaikovsky

[195]   TO ANATOLI TCHAIKOVSKY   Moscow
                                                  23 September 1878

Rubinstein arrived yesterday. He was given a suitably pompous reception at the Conservatoire. At 6 o'clock we gave him a dinner at the Hermitage. At the dinner several speeches were made; the first, by Rubinstein, was in my honour. He said that my music had made a deep impression in Paris, and how proud the Conservatoire must be that I honoured it by returning to its fold again. Everybody congratulated me, and Samarin was touched to tears. You can imagine how much I enjoyed it all.

I decided that I just could not speak to Rubinstein about my resignation; and yet during these last days my decision to quit has become stronger than ever. I came home very upset and got up this morning in despair at the thought that I shall have to put off my resignation until next year. Fortunately when Rubinstein met me at the Conservatoire he asked me to give him a few minutes in which we could talk things over. I was very nervous but had enough courage to tell him, privately, that I would only stay as professor until 1 December.

The conversation was most friendly and at the end of an hour we separated good friends after hearty embraces. And so, in a little over two months I shall be a free man. A heavy load off my shoulders. Now I feel happy and at peace Definitely I could not live in Moscow any more. Please, keep all this secret for the present. I shall leave here without any complications or ceremony so that no one will notice. Laroche has just left me, he is going tomorrow.

I kiss you with all my heart.

Yours

P. Tchaikovsky

I am writing this late at night; I cannot find your letter with the address, so am sending this to the District Court.

[196]   TO ANATOLI TCHAIKOVSKY   Moscow
                                                  2 October 1878

My dear Tolia!

I have just got your letter, from which I gather that you did not get one of mine. I wonder why. Anyway that is not important. Very soon now I shall stop writing from here. It was only yesterday that I had the brilliant idea that since there is someone at the Conservatoire to take my place I need not carry on with my boring occupation until November. I am not any more compelled to be tied to the Conservatoire and behave with particular delicacy. So I told Rubinstein today that I am leaving at the end of the week. Only imagine how delighted I am. Please, my Golubchik, as I have now decided to stay in Petersburg the whole of the month of October, go down to the Numera Residential Hotel and see if there is a comfortable room that is free. If not I shall have to stay with you.

I would be pleased if you could come to meet me on Saturday.

Keep all this a secret.

Yours

P. Tchaikovsky

On 7 October Tchaikovsky wrote to Mme von Meck: 'I gave my last lessons yesterday . . . I am a free man now! This feeling of freedom gives me an indescribable pleasure. . . . My conscience is perfectly at peace. I am leaving with the complete assurance that the Conservatoire will not suffer in any way and that I need not worry about being ungrateful although some people may accuse me of being so. When I recall my work at the Conservatoire I see that nothing at all was done to help me in that side of my work which is the only one that makes sense and gives meaning to my life.'

In 1885 he returned to the Conservatoire, as Director of the Russian Musical Society.

While he was in St Petersburg Tchaikovsky was offered a post at the Conservatoire there by K. Y. Davydov (no relation of Lev Davydov). This would have meant twice as much salary as in Moscow and only four hours' teaching weekly. Tchaikovsky thought about it but rejected the idea when he discovered that it was Davydov's intention to spite Rubinstein (see Letter 237). N. G. Rubinstein was in trouble at this time. He had given concerts at the Paris Exhibition but had not done anything to advance the claims of 'The Five'. The instigator of criticism in the newspapers on this head was Stassov. From St Petersburg attacks on Rubinstein were transferred to Moscow. Tchaikovsky was furious. (See letters 228 and 230.)

[197]   TO LEV DAVYDOV   [Moscow]
                                                     7 October 1878

. . . From yesterday I am a free man; tonight I am leaving for Petersburg. I am very happy. No time for letter writing. Tell Tania that her letter has given me great joy and that I will answer her sweet scribbles from Petersburg.

I kiss you all with all my love.

Yours

P. Tchaikovsky

TO ANATOLI TCHAIKOVSKY   Moscow
                                     29 October 1878

Tolichka!

Yesterday I received a letter from Nadezhda Filaretovna in answer to my question
if, in her opinion, I was right in wishing to leave the Conservatoire. As was
to be expected she wrote that that had been her wish for a considerable time,
and she was sure I would soon stop looking upon my work here as a duty.
Her letter was most reassuring and made me more than content. She also
finds that I am perfectly right in not agreeing to Davydov's offer and says
that I must be absolutely free and these words are underlined which means
that she has no wish ever to stop my subsidy.

I am more than pleased and happy. Another reason is that [N.] Rubinstein is not
displeased with my resignation and has already found a substitute. He has
invited Taneev to take my place but to say nothing about it for the time being.
Taneev will be used at first as a piano professor. However, he has been told
to get ready to take the theory classes. So I can leave without any misgivings
at any time I like; and this will be much sooner than you think. So do not be
astonished that I promised Kotek to join him in Berlin in December. This is
certain, provided that nothing intervenes.

I do want to go abroad and do you know why? As long as I am in Moscow
I shall not write one note, in spite of a great desire to work – partly to
vindicate myself in my own eyes and also to efface the disgustingly stupid way
I have been behaving here. You must agree that it is easier to work in Clarens
than in Petersburg where it is noisy, crowded and restless and where I shall
never be able to find a place where I can work in peace, without anyone
disturbing me. . . .

I have decided, therefore, that I shall stay in Petersburg, just to enjoy your
company, either for the whole of November or part of it and of December,
then I shall go abroad, shall work hard and return to Petersburg at the
beginning of spring.

Yours

P. Tchaikovsky

TO ANATOLI TCHAIKOVSKY   Moscow
                                     [2 November 1878]

Am in a hurry so this will be short; the journey was most comfortable. Kariakin
and his wife were in the next compartment and we chatted. Alesha met me at
the station. I am staying at the Loskutnaia Hotel. Yurgenson appeared and
we had lunch together; then Rubinstein joined us, very upset and morose. He
is deeply hurt by systematic attacks in the papers and is contemplating leaving

the Conservatoire for good. I am very sorry for him. At 5 o'clock he left, after checking the proofs of the Liturgy [music] for two hours. By the way, your *clever* Akim forgot to pack the proofs for the twelve piano pieces in my case. Please, my dear, send them off at once to Osip Ivanovich Yurgenson to be forwarded to Piotr Ivanovich. . . .

I paid a short visit to the Kondratievs, who were surprised to see me. There was a supper at the Hermitage at half-past ten with Rubinstein, Albrecht, Hubert, Kashkin, Yurgenson, Taneev, Zverev. We did not feel happy, I do not know why. . . . All the same we stayed until 3.00 am. It was nearly four when I got back home. It is eight in the morning now and I am waiting for Karlusha who is going to take me through secret passages to the gallery to attend a rehearsal of the concert.

Leaving at 1.00 pm. [for Kamenka].

Once more a loving embrace from me.

P. Tchaikovsky

[200]   TO ANATOLI TCHAIKOVSKY   Kamenka
                                                   [4 November 1878]

After the rehearsal where I had been taken to the gallery along secret passages and sat there all alone, we went to Patrikeev's for lunch – Rubinstein, Yurgenson, Taneev and me. At half-past one I was already on my way; the journey was uneventful and ended by my arriving today in Kamenka. . . .

Tolia! Please do find out, my Golubchik, what Akim, or my landlady, or the maid, has done with my sketch-book covered with notes written in pencil; this is of utmost importance to me as it contains three parts of my new symphonic work. I only noticed today that the book was not in my travelling case and will send you a telegram about it tomorrow. For God's sake, find it and send it to me as soon as I will give you my Florentine address. Akim has also forgotten to put in the *proofs* which I beg to be sent to O. I. Yurgenson for Piotr Ivanovich. I am so tired that I do not find enough strength to write properly.

I am very happy here. During the journey I was a little bored but felt at peace. I want you to stop being unhappy, and I want to start composing again, for I am beginning to worry lest I shall never be able to any more.

Write: Italie, Florence, *poste restante.*

I kiss you and embrace you

P. Tchaikovsky

Kamenka
9 November 1878

Here is some good news. Thanks to my 'intriguing', and to the fact that Leva
wants to be in Moscow for the Jubilee of his Cadet Corps, Sasha, Tania, and
Vera are going with him to Moscow and Petersburg. They will stay there
until the middle of January. I am glad for your sake and also for mine. I am
so happy here that I hate the thought of leaving Kamenka, but now that they
are going away it will not be so sad for me to leave. Now that the woods are
bare and the cold air is not impregnated with farm smells Kamenka appeals
to me greatly. The routine is just what I like, but I do not want to stay here
without the family.

I even did some work, i.e. finished the proofs of the twelve piano pieces, a few
corrections to the score of *Vakula* and I shall at last complete the score of
the Suite. . . .

As soon as you get the score of *Vakula* which I am dispatching today, please
take it to Napravnik yourself. You will always find him at home before eleven
in the morning. My regards to Velina and tell her to cherish, and spoil, you
and not to annoy you with her tantrums. If she behaves I will give her a good
part in my next opera. Write at once to Florence, *poste restante*, so that I
have news from you as soon as I get there. I kiss you thousands of times.

Have you found my sketch-book?

Yours

P. Tchaikovsky

Kamenka
13 November 1878

You cunning Modia!
Surely you could have made an effort and written to Kamenka. I am writing
my second letter to you, from here. Tomorrow I am going abroad. In a letter
which I had today, Nadezhda Filaretovna offers me the choice of two
apartments, one in town, the other out of town on the Viale dei Colli. I chose
the latter, which means that I can give you my address now, and will you please
let Tolia have it? Italie, Florence, restaurant Bonciani, M. P. Tchaikovsky.
The week and a half I stayed here was like a passing dream, and I was
extremely happy. My soul was at peace as never before. Only one thought
bothers me, it is that you and Tolia might be envious. Oh! Nasty, envious,
cruel men! Inspiration has descended on me here and my Suite is nearly finished
in the rough. But I am worried that the first three movements, which I have
left in Petersburg, may be lost. Here I have composed the last two. The whole
of this short (and if I am not mistaken) charming Suite will consist of these
five movements:

(1) Introduzione e fuga
(2) Scherzo
(3) Andante Melancolico
(4) March of the Lilliputians
(5) Dance of the Giants.

If the manuscript is not lost I shall start working on the orchestral score in Florence. After that I shall seriously start to consider an opera. I think I have decided on *Joan of Arc*. Please tell Tolia that, as soon as the manuscript is found Akim is to pack it – sewn up in oil-cloth and linen – and send it off at once to Florence (here is the address once more) Viale dei Colli, restaurant Bonciani. . . .

I have no right to grumble about anything at all and can think of myself as the luckiest man in the world. Sometimes though like Sobakevich I fear that it is not to the good!

Your

P. Tchaikovsky

[203]   TO MODEST TCHAIKOVSKY   Vienna
                                            18–30 November 1878

Oh dear! What a huge piece of paper! I have to write on it because Alesha is out and without him I can't find my own. Don't be angry if I do not fill it all.

I am in Vienna in the same hotel, Goldenes Lamm, which is full of memories of you and Tolia. May be that is why I am feeling so desperately sad. Everything here reminds me of you and both the landlord and the servants want to know about you – but you are not here! – Alas, I must say that since I left Kamenka I have felt terribly sad. Never before have Kamenka and all the people there been so near to my heart as during this stay. It is a long time since I felt so perfectly happy (I mean spiritually, for I was by no means well physically) as during these two weeks. I think I may say with confidence that it is only country life, with near and dear people around me, that can really satisfy me. However, to keep up the traditions of youth, foreign countries still fascinate me but as soon as my craving for 'foreign-countriness' is satisfied they lose their fascination and I begin to feel bored. But I have never been as sad as at this moment, particularly if one takes into account the absolute absence of any good reason. For the circumstances of my life are more than favourable and I have no right whatsoever to complain.

I will soon stay a day in Venice and then go on to Florence where Nadezhda Filaretovna has reserved an apartment for me which is sure to be excellent. Now I am my own master and can go where I like and stay abroad as long as I like. I ought, therefore, to be absolutely carefree and happy. All this I realize perfectly, but nevertheless I am ready to cry. I may add, however, that I have always disliked Vienna.

I was a real martyr all the way here. First of all I had toothache and a swollen cheek, secondly I felt awfully tired and was painfully hoping to arrive as soon as possible. Probably I am just sick of travelling and spend too much time in trains. We got here yesterday at dinner time. The dinner tasted as good as before; the best of all the hotel dinners I have ever tasted. Afterwards, as *The Sicilian Vespers*, which does not interest me at all, was on at the Opera House, I went with Alesha to Renz's Circus. Bad company, boring programme and not one of the artists had a nice face. . . .

Yours

P. Tchaikovsky

Today I am going to the Opera to hear *Robert* [*le Diable*] and tomorrow afternoon I am leaving.

[204]   TO ANATOLI TCHAIKOVSKY   Florence
                                    21 November–2 December 1878

My dearest, my very good boy!

I arrived here last night straight from Vienna without stopping in Venice. If the first part of my journey down to Vienna was tiring and disagreeable because of a bad tooth and my not having been well in Kamenka, this last lap of my journey was most comfortable. The weather was lovely, and the trains were nearly empty; in short, everything was perfect. I was met here by Pachulsky (the heir to Kotek at Nadezhda Filaretovna's), who took me to my apartment which I found warm, bright with lights, and expecting its surprised and delighted tenant.

The apartment consists of a row of magnificent rooms; drawing-room, dining-room, bedroom, dressing-room, toilette and Alesha's room. The drawing-room has a lovely piano, and there were two gorgeous bunches of flowers on the desk, and all one needs for writing and composing. The furniture is beautiful. I am quite enchanted with it all and what makes it perfect is that the apartment is out of town, with a lovely view from the windows, and absolute quiet outside. Yet it is only half an hour's walk to the centre of the town. I am absolutely happy and well. On the way here I feared that N.F. being so near we would have to meet and I even thought that she might invite me to visit her. But her letter, that I found waiting for me on the table, has completely reassured me, Everything can be organized in such a way that we need not meet at all. She will be leaving Florence in three weeks time, and, I am sure, we will not meet even once.

In Vienna I felt as sad as here and now I feel happy and content. One could not find anything more comfortable and perfect for working in than my lodgings. Lunch will be at twelve and then I shall go to town to collect my letters. I shudder to think that my manuscript is lost after all. If you have not sent it yet, please send it to: Florence, Viale dei Colli, restaurant Bonciani.

On the eve of our departure from Vienna I went to the opera with Alesha. It was *Robert* [*le Diable*] with an excellent cast and beautiful settings, I was very pleased. . . .

I embrace you and Modia and will soon write again. I kiss you as heartily as it is in my power.

P. Tchaikovsky

[205] TO ANATOLI TCHAIKOVSKY   Florence
                                    23 November–5 December 1878

I am happily living in peace and luxury, but I cannot deny that the proximity of Nadezhda Filaretovna slightly disturbs me. She often drives and walks past my windows. What if we meet? What ought I to do? She does not seem to be afraid of it as she has even sent me a ticket to the theatre for Saturday, where she is also going. She asks if I would like to come and have a look at her villa saying that when I come not a soul will be there, but all the same I am a bit frightened.

Sometimes I even get the idea that perhaps she does want a personal meeting, although I do not find any hint of it in her letters. All this makes me feel a bit uncomfortable and at the bottom of my heart I want her to leave as soon as possible. Actually she is leaving on the 9th according to our calendar.

I have just come back from a long walk. I went on foot to the town, wandered around it for several hours and walked back. The weather is ideal. The view down to the town and the whole valley of the Arno, together with the Viale dei Colli, is wonderful.

The routine of my life is as follows. I get up about eight, work after coffee until twelve o'clock when my lunch, consisting of two courses and a sweet dish, is served. After lunch I go for a walk and when I am back home again I play the piano, or read, or do a little more work. At 6 o'clock a six course dinner is served, very long, but rather tasteless. After dinner I play, write letters, read, loiter on the magnificent balcony, and go to bed at midnight. Tonight I am breaking the order of the day by going to the theatre. My health is perfect. I have no definite plans. However it is Paris that really attracts me. I wanted to go to Rome and Naples but as one cannot work in either of these cities I have given up this idea. . . . I embrace you with all my might and kiss you.

P. Tchaikovsky

The Fourth Symphony, conducted by Napravnik, was given its first performance in St Petersburg on 25 November, 1878. It was an enormous success, as Modest reported to his brother: 'I will be the first to give you an account of your symphony for I am only back from the concert ten minutes. I didn't stay to the end, because I couldn't listen to anything else after the symphony. . . . After the first movement the applause was as after something by Beethoven or Schumann. There was more after the second movement and Napravnik had to take a bow. After the Scherzo there were fortissimo shouts, applause, stamping feet, and demands for an encore. Napravnik bowed once, twice, three times – but the noise never stopped until he lifted his baton. Then the noise did stop and the pizzicato started. At the end of it there was more terrific noise, with Napravnik bowing; and at the end, even before the last notes of the Finale had been heard, the audience went mad again. . . .'

For the rest of the month Tchaikovsky fumed at his brother on account of the non-arrival of his MS.; it did not reach him in fact until after the beginning of 1879 (see Letter 223).

[206] TO MODEST TCHAIKOVSKY   27 November–9 December 1878
                                      Florence

Dear Modia!

Just imagine, I do not remember to which of you I last wrote, but it is not important. I am writing now to you to thank you for sending the telegram about the symphony. I was very pleased to get it. I did not know the symphony was to be played so soon. On the same day, after yours arrived, I had another telegram – from Velinskaia.

I have become so accustomed to the Villa Bonciani [Mme von Meck's villa], to my solitude, and to the lovely peace and quiet of my apartment that I am never bored or lonely. The evenings, particularly, are so delightful. I have plenty of books, and plenty of scores sent by Nadezhda Filaretovna; but I also have my own. I have bought Massenet's opera *Le Roi de Lahore* and play it with the greatest pleasure. The devil take those Frenchmen, they do have proper taste and chic. I advise you to get it. The telegram and other letters have stopped me from worrying about you both, but you are a bit too lazy. Actually if you will always write as full and interesting a letter as the last one, you need not write too often. So, I am happy here, and do not feel bored, because I know I can change both place and mode of life whenever I wish. Unfortunately the nearness of Nadezhda Filaretovna puts a strain on my life, for I do not feel quite free. . . . I went to the theatre with Alesha but it was not very amusing, even though a little girl of ten, nicknamed 'la piccola Ristori' had a part. Tomorrow I am going to the Pergola to hear the new opera *Il violino del Diavolo* [A. Mercuri].

I have finished the orchestral score of the two last movements of the Suite but have still not received the first three. I am not bored but I would give anything to have you and Kolia here as last year!

I kiss you and Kolia; I have thought a lot about him today. I also kiss Tolia and will soon write to him.

Your

P. Tchaikovsky

TO ANATOLI TCHAIKOVSKY   Florence
                                      29 November–11 December 1878

Had it not been for your telegram and Modest's letter I would not have known why you were silent. Now, judging by what Modest wrote in his last letter, you have been too busy courting Panaishna, which leaves you no time to write. Tell me why the manuscript is not here yet. Akim must have perpetual hiccoughs from my swearing at him.

I am perfectly well and have got so used to my cosy corner that I rarely feel sad. My work is getting on so well that at the moment I have nothing to do. I am waiting for the parcel from you and do not want to start anything new. My life here is very well ordered. I rarely go to town. Yesterday Nadezhda Filaretovna sent me a ticket for the theatre, for a new opera, *Il violino del Diavolo*. The only interesting thing in it was that the prima donna Ferni is at the same time a famous violinist. In the third act she played an excellent violin solo.

Nadezhda Filaretovna was also in the theatre which embarrassed me as I feel embarrassed in general at her being so near. I have a feeling she wishes to see me; every morning, for instance, I can see how when she passes my house, she stops and tries to get a glimpse of me. What should I do? Come out to the window and bow? But in this case I might as well call out of the window 'Zdravstvouite'! [Greetings!] However, in her daily, long, charming, clever, and wonderfully kind letters there is not even a hint that she wishes to meet me.

The weather yesterday was so magnificent that I was mad with delight. The roof of my villa is a terrace where you get a magnificent view of the town and the surrounding country. I stayed on the terrace nearly all the afternoon. I always remember you at luncheon and dinner for I am mostly served with lamb, brains, sausages, and veal! What would you have done with those, my poor boy?

All the same I am beginning to await with some impatience your sloping scribble. Write, my Golubchik, even a few lines, do write! There are no special plans for the near future but I am not staying more than two months abroad, and will come and join you at the beginning of Lent. I embrace you, my dear, lazy boy! My kind regards to Volodia, kiss Modest, and also Sasha, Leva, and Papochka, to whom I owe a letter.

Your

P. Tchaikovsky

[208] TO ANATOLI TCHAIKOVSKY   Florence
                                    3–15 December 1878

The last letter I got from you at the *poste restante* was dated 12 November. Today is 3 December, which means that I have had no letters from you for

3 weeks. I sent you my present address from Kamenka, begged you to write and send me my manuscript but – no manuscript. All this made me sad, upset, and irritable, and now I am furious.

The orchestral score of the last two movements of my Suite is finished and here I have to sit, with my hands folded. And as I live in an absolute desert doing nothing it is boring, especially as I never start a new work before having finished the one I have been working on. Should I be angry with, or worried about, you? But from Modest's letter I know you are perfectly well.

However, silly thoughts have started up today, and I wonder if Modest is hiding something from me. All right, the parcel could have been lost in the post, but not a line for three weeks – that is incomprehensible. As to your famous Akim! What a Ukrainian idiot he is. I am beginning to think he takes your letters to the Nikolaev railway station and sends them by freight.

I have just come back from town where I sent you a telegram. Am saying nothing more. I am very upset and angry.

I kiss you and do not want to think that you are ill.

Yours

P. Tchaikovsky

[209] TO MODEST TCHAIKOVSKY Florence
4–16 December 1878

The devil take it! I am like a man who has been running over an open field and suddenly banged against a wall that rose up out of the ground. I still have not got my manuscript. During my first week here I have most enthusiastically orchestrated and even made a piano duet of the two last movements of my Suite while waiting for the first three. But the days go by and no parcel. So I am forced to exist in absolute idleness. You know very well that I do not start a new work before getting the old one off my hands. All the charm of my life here is lost without work.

Luckily I had a letter from Tolia yesterday which made me a little happier, he writes that he took my manuscript to Yurgenson two weeks ago. Now what is the old idiot up to? In short, I am angry, and in as bad a humour as a man, who in general is content and happy, has the right to be. Moreover, the weather is foul. The streets and the roofs of the houses are covered with snow which comes down intermingled with rain. Most depressing! But when it clears up it is so lovely that one is, inevitably, happy.

Your

P. Tchaikovsky

I am going to Paris on the 16th–28th. Send your letters to Hôtel de Hollande, but I hope that one more will reach me here.

182

Florence
5[–17] December
Tuesday 9 pm
Villa Bonciani

Last night when everyone in the house was asleep, and I was sitting alone in
front of the fire reading about dogs in [A. E.] Brehm's book on animals, there
was a loud ring at the front door. Then there was a sound of opening doors and
a telegraph boy came in with a wire from you. The telegram surprised me
greatly, but it did not make me cross. I had used up all my anger in the
previous days, and was glad to know that the manuscript was safe. I there
and then decided not to lose any time, to start composing the opera from
today and I have begun the venture with much efficiency. I somewhat feared
that after my desperate letters you would imagine my being furious, so to
stop you from worrying I sent you a telegram.

I have just returned from town where besides telegraphing you I sent one to N. G.
Rubinstein with congratulations. How queer and beyond comprehension is the
human heart. I have always, or at least for a long time now, thought that
I did not love Rubinstein. Quite recently, however, I dreamt that he had died,
and that I was in the depths of despair. Since then I cannot think of him
without a pang in my heart and a positive feeling of love. This is of course
easily explained; barring a few exceptions I do not love people too near me,
and, in general, dislike the company of people. But as soon as I can move
away from them, and contemplate them from a certain distance, it appears to
me that I do love them. I sent him a most kind and loving telegram.

And now let us talk about how I spend my time. The three or four days that
I passed expecting my manuscript to arrive were not happy. One cannot be
without anything to do when living in solitude especially when one is keen
on one's work, and hates any obstacle which comes in the way. Having
nothing to do I played cards ['dunces'] with Alesha; no luck, got furious and
in spite of Alesha begging me to stop I would not and went on playing, losing,
getting angrier every minute. The weather is horrid except for rare moments
of sunshine which are lovely. Besides long walks I take binoculars on to the
roof and stay there for a long time enjoying the view. I rarely go down town,
it is too far. The nearness of Nadezhda Filaretovna does not bother me any
more.

I have become quite used to the everyday exchange of letters, one must give
this wonderful, clever, woman her due; she arranges things so well that there
is plenty of material for correspondence. Every morning I get an enormous
letter from her, sometimes on five pages, as well as Russian newspapers and
the *Italie*. I answer in the evening. Exactly at 11.30 in the morning she passes
under my windows, trying to see me, but not able to do so because she is
shortsighted. I see her perfectly. Once we saw each other at the theatre. Not
the slightest hints from her that we might meet; so I am perfectly safe.

In one word, my life here could not be more appropriate to my misanthropic character, even the waiter who serves my dinner is very courteous but otherwise silent. Provided that I have letters from you both I am happy. I kiss you – my dearest.

Yours

P. Tchaikovsky

Wallon's book *Jeanne d'Arc*, a present from Mme von Meck, is preserved in the Museum at Klin. This was a period of intensive reading. The correspondence between Catherine the Great and Friedrich Melchior von Grimm – who associated with the Encyclopaedists – was published in *The Russian Archives*, 1878, vols. 9–10.

Presumably Tchaikovsky knew, or knew of, Verdi's unsuccessful *Giocanna d'Arco* (1845), although he particularly names A. Mermet's *Jeanne d'Arc* (1876) and Gounod's incidental music to Jules Barbier's drama with the same title (see also Letter 222).

[211]   TO MODEST TCHAIKOVSKY   Florence
                                        10–22 December 1878

Modia! The last days were full of inspirational fever! I have started *The Maid of Orleans* and you cannot imagine how difficult it is. Difficult not because of lack of inspiration but, on the contrary, because the pressure was too great. (I hope you will not say I am boasting.) I was in a real state of frenzy; these last days I was tortured and worried at the thought of the immense amount of material and so little time and strength to use it in. I wanted to accomplish all in one short hour as it happens in a dream. My nails are bitten, my bowels won't work; in order to sleep I had to increase the usual dose of wine, and last night, reading the book on Joan of Arc, a present from Nadezhda Filaretovna (a magnificent edition which must have cost at least 200 francs), when I came to the denial scene and the execution (she screamed all the way to the scaffold and implored them to cut her head off but not to burn her) I burst into tears. I suddenly felt so sorry for the whole of mankind and so miserable. Besides, I began to imagine that you were all ill, or dead, that I had had to come here because I am such a poor pitiful being. In a word, in a state of high nervous tension I needed an outlet. After having wept I went peacefully to sleep and woke up blissfully happy when Alesha came in, opened the windows, and let the sun pour its rays into the room. The weather was glorious; I decided at once to go out for the whole day and did so. Alesha went to the Russian church and I went to S. Miniato after which I could not resist temptation and went down town. I went into the magnificent Church of S. Croce where only a little Low Mass was being celebrated at one of the side altars. Back home to lunch then, hired a carriage and went with Alesha first to Bello sguardo where we thought of you and Kolia and from there to Cascino. The trip was marvellous.

Nadezhda Filaretovna is leaving on Thursday the 14th–26th and I on Friday

the 15th–27th. I go straight to Paris, providing the cursed Suite arrives by
then. I have been pondering over the libretto all the time without having
decided upon a proper plan. I like Schiller's play but the way he despises
historical facts puts me rather off. If you are interested to know what scene
I have written I shall tell you. It is when she enters into the king's presence
and he makes Dunois take his place but she is not fooled. She then tells her
story – after which comes the ensemble and the great finale. Nothing new,
am leaving here with neither special pleasure nor much regret.

I kiss you hard.

P. Tchaikovsky

[212]   TO ANATOLI TCHAIKOVSKY   Florence
                                            11–23 December 1878
                                            Monday

Tolia!

Only a short time ago I gave you a scolding for indulging in an attack of
unreasonable *khandra* [Russian = spleen] – and now, during these last days,
I have been suffering from an attack of the same sickness. It is true that the
day before yesterday it was the result of madly intensive work, but today
there is no reason whatsoever for my nerves to be so tense – unless it is the
bad weather that makes me somewhat depressed. Besides, I have still not
received that famous manuscript which forced me to do nothing all day, and
I do hate sitting with my hands folded.

I must also add that I have been lately specially selective in my reading. I have
lost for ever the taste for novels and such like literature. Nadezhda Filaretovna
recommended me to read Daudet's short stories. I tried but could not force
myself to go on. I also twice started in vain to read *Une page d'amour*. I am
constrained to read only historical books and articles but here too it is the
eighteenth and, perhaps, also the seventeenth centuries that really interest
me. With what pleasure I read the two volumes of the *Russian Archives* – the
correspondence between Catherine the Great and Grimm. I am also reading
with the same great pleasure *The Life of Animals*, by Brehm. I bought his six
enormous volumes before leaving Moscow.

Every day I get the *Moscow News* from Nadezhda Filaretozna and the *Golos* if
it has one of Laroche's articles. But what I read with breath-taking interest is
the book *Jeanne d'Arc* which Nadezhda Filaretovna gave to me. I have already
told you that I have chosen *The Maid of Orleans*, after Schiller, as a libretto
for my next opera, but I am not quite happy with his interpretation and am
going to dig into history and also get the librettos of the two unsuccessful
French operas on the same subject. That is why I want to go to Paris.

Am writing with difficulty, to dissipate my morose humour. I ate too much
for dinner, which rarely happens, as the food is bad. Nothing from either of

you for some time. P. Yurgenson has sent me several of my new pieces including your songs [op. 38]. Have you seen them? Tell Sasha that the children's album with a dedication to Bobik has been published. It is three weeks today since I came here. In four days time, that is Friday, I am going to Paris. Kotek will arrive three days after I have left and will stay a week. I kiss your eyes, your lips, nose, and the beauty spot on your ear.

Yours

P. Tchaikovsky

The *Children's Album* (Op. 39), dedicated to Vladimir Davydov, had illustrations by A. Stepanov at the head of each piece.

[213]   TO LEV DAVYDOV   Florence
                                           12–24 December 1878

How sweet of you Levushka, to have written to me! ... Tell Bobik that the music has been published with pictures, that it was written by Uncle Peter, and that on the front page it says: 'Dedicated to Volodia Davydov'. The silly little man will not know what 'dedicated' means. I am writing to Yurgenson to send a copy to Kamenka. The only thing that worries me is that Mitiuk might get offended. But how can one dedicate music to him when he says he does not like it? Whereas Bobik's charming little figure, when he sits at the piano looking at the notes and counting, is worth dedicating whole symphonies to.

The day after tomorrow I am going to Paris. I have chosen Paris because to compose an opera I need some distraction, such as going to the theatre, strolling along the Boulevards, and so on. A few days ago I got so tired after working on the first scene of the opera that it caused an attack of hysterics. The advantage of an enormous city like Paris is that my moods will pass unnoticed. Besides I need to be in Paris to collect some material for the opera. My address will be: Rue de la Paix, Hôtel de Hollande. This, of course, is only for the first few days, after which I shall look for a cheap *garnie* [boarding house]. But letters will reach me anyway.

The weather here has been bad all the time – rain and even snow. But now and again the sun shines and it is glorious. To my astonishment I have not been bored at all in spite of being completely alone and living in a wilderness. I need solitude now and again, when my state of mind is normal. ...

Now, this is what I would like to discuss with you. I do not expect to settle for ever either in Moscow or in Petersburg. In all probability I shall pass the greatest part of the year with you and the rest of the time travelling. Although I am perfectly satisfied with the wing, it is a bit cramped; and besides, in summer with the windows open it is not always convenient for working. Where can I live when I come now? I am going to write an opera. I must be completely free of all noise; I need something like last year. I wonder if it would be possible to build a small annexe to the wing or something of that sort? Please, Golubchik, let me know what you think about it. (How much would it cost to build a *khata* [a peasant's cottage]?)

I do not know how long I shall stay in Paris. I shall return to Russia during Lent for sure; but I doubt if I shall come to you before Easter as I have to be in Petersburg for a few weeks. Anyway I cannot say anything definite now. I kiss you, my Golubchik, and stifle the children in my embrace.

Your

P. Tchaikovsky

[214]   TO MODEST TCHAIKOVSKY   [Florence]
                                        15–27 December 1878
                                        Villa Bonciani

My dear Modia!

Yesterday, I cannot say why, I remembered during my walk how you and I went for a little drive to the Zrubanec Forest to pick lilies of the valley. Was it because the weather was so bad, or because I felt sad that I had a sudden desire to sing a song of praise to lilies of the valley in the form of a poem. I spent all of yesterday and this morning composing this poem and here is the result.

I am very proud of it. For the first time in my life I was able to write a poem and one that is full of feeling. Although I found it hard I got as much pleasure in doing so as I get from composing music. I would be grateful if you would make this creation of mine as well known as possible – read it to Lelia, Laroche, to the Davydovs, to Sasha, Tania, Alina Ivanovna, Jedrinsky and Tolia, and so on, and so on. I want everybody to be surprised and to admire it.

I had planned to leave today but as the parcel has still not arrived I had to stay on, which is no fun. Nadezhda Filaretovna has left and to my astonishment I miss her greatly, and have a feeling of loss. Tears come to my eyes when I pass by her empty villa and Viale dei Colli has become dull and dark. I became so used to being in touch with her every day, and to seeing her pass beneath my window with all her retinue, that what at first embarrassed me I now sincerely miss. Oh God! What a wonderful woman she is! How touching her solicitude was, even over the most trifling details which made my life here so delightful in every way.

I have been waiting for a whole month now for the Suite and this hopeless waiting has made my blood boil with anger – especially at Akim and Osip Yurgenson. The thought that this precious manuscript is lost has upset my nerves. Tolia's explanation about the delay is not very convincing – and, honestly, Yurgenson's reason that he had no time to send it within a fortnight are rather silly. I do not want any reasons, I want the manuscript. Why has it still not arrived by now? I am furious. What is the explanation? If I do not get it by tomorrow I will tear up the rest. Anyway I am going to Paris tomorrow. No I have lied, I shall not tear up anything. All I shall do is to have it sent to Paris.

I kiss you with all my love

P. Tchaikovsky

LILIES OF THE VALLEY by P. Tchaikovsky

When at the end of spring I gather once again
The flowers I like best – an anguish fills my heart
And to the future I address my hopes and prayers,
I beg to see the lilies of the valley just once more.
Now they have finished flowering, the summer has flown by,
The days become much shorter, the feathered choir is still,
The sun is thrifty with its gifts of light and warmth
And all the woods are covered in a leafy carpet.
Then, when the time will come for winter cold and stern,
And the snow-shroud envelops all the woods and trees,
Unhappy will I roam and wait with wakening longing
For the spring sun to shine and light up the blue sky.
No book brings me content, nor peaceful talks with friends,
No fast sledge drives, nor glitter of a dance.
Not Patti, not the theatre or finest food at dinner,
Nor when the smouldering logs fall crackling in the stove.
I wait for spring. Enchantress, here she comes at last
The forest takes its shroud off, shady grow the trees,
The rivers flow again and woods are full of sounds,
And then, at last, the long awaited day arrives!
Quick to the woods! . . . I take my favourite narrow path,
Can it be true? Reality my dreams?
Yes, look! – and bending low I with a trembling hand
Pick up the wonder gift of the Enchantress Spring.
Dear lily of the valley why do you please us so?
The other flowers grow much more luxurious,
Their colours are much brighter, varied their design
But your mysterious charm and loveliness they lack,
What is your secret spell? Your promise to my soul?
What do you lure us with and make our hearts rejoice?
Or do you wake the ghost of bygone happiness?
Or is it future bliss that you are promising?
I do not know! But your sweet smelling fragrance
Warms and intoxicates like a long drink of wine;
Like sounds of music it brings anguish to my breast,

And like the fire of love it feeds my blushing cheeks.
And I am happy when you blossom, modest lily,
All trace of winter boredom disappears for good,
Gone all dejected thoughts, my heart in tender languor
Through you will now forget all evil and bad luck.
But you have faded, and monotonous as before
The days will slowly pass, again but much more fiercely
Tormented will I be by my besetting anguish
And poignant dreams of happy days in May.
But then one day spring will be here again
And tear all bounds to bring the world alive. . . .
Maybe my hour will strike, no more between the living,
Like all before me I will meet my destiny.
What will be there? Whereto on wings of death
My spirit on command will silently depart?
There is no answer – be silent my unruly mind,
'Tis not for you to guess eternity's kind gifts.
But we are just like nature full of thirst for life,
We call and wait for you most beautiful of springs!
The joys of earth are near to us, familiar,
The grave's wide open jaws are much too dark.
P.S. As I am no poet but only a 'versifier', I may be wrong but it seems to me
that a poem can never be absolutely sincere and be poured out straight from
the heart. The laws of versification, especially regarding rhythm, call for
artifice. I find then that music is on a much higher level than poetry. Naturally
music also has, what the French call *remplissage* but you are not so much
aware of it. When analysing a poem you will always find lines which are there
only for the sake of the rhythm.

[215]   TO MODEST TCHAIKOVSKY   Paris
                                              18–30 December 1878

I arrived this morning. The journey was comfortable; to Turin a *coupé-lit*
[sleeping compartment], then from Turin to Paris, without changing, in
a *sleeping car*. But it was expensive, and the golden coins diminished so fast
that I dare not stay here. . . . I was pleased to be in Paris again but not as
much as before. Maybe because the Hôtel de Hollande reminds me of you
and Tolia, or because I am not used to the noise any more, I do not feel
happy.

By the way I must tell you something queer. Have you noticed that every
place has its characteristic smell? I feel it very strongly. Moscow has its own,
Berlin its own, and so have Clarens and Paris. The smell of Paris is quite
special and I have always loved it; but for some reason today, in spite of
sniffing and sniffing, I have not yet felt it.

Had lunch at the Diner de Paris. How can I live in Paris and eat anywhere else but at the Diner de Paris? However, if I stay here a month and a half, it will not be possible. I must live in a pension. Most boring. I'd better go off to my dear Mme Mayor! I wanted to go to the Gymnase tonight where they are giving a very good play, but for Alesha's sake I shall take him to the Châtelet where they are giving a fairy play, *Rothomago*.

I kiss you. Next time, I shall write not to you but to my adorable boy Kolia.

Yours

P.T.

[216] TO MODEST TCHAIKOVSKY   Paris
22 December 1878–3 January 1879

I am in a bad temper and have no wish to write about the theatres . . . but all the same I will. Alesha and I went:

(1) to *Rothomago* a fairy tale given at the Châtelet, which bored me immensely.
(2) to the Comédie Française – *Le dépit amoureux* and *Andromaque*. The part of Andromaque was brilliantly acted by Sarah Bernhardt. Unfortunately I had to translate the play to Kotek which spoiled all my pleasure.
(3) to the Matinée at the Gymnase to see *Grande Duchesse*. I went to the Gymnase again and saw a charming, well-acted new production of *L'Age ingrat*. This was the only show I really enjoyed.

Yesterday we went off to the Hippodrome for, as we thought, an interesting musical festival, but I made a mistake in the dates and read not *Jeudi 2* but *Jeudi 9 Janvier*, so instead of music we had to watch a display of horsemanship.

Life as usual: Lunch and dinner for three at the Diner de Paris. Between meals we wander round the streets and visit the Louvre and the *Jardin d'aclimatation*, while in the evening we go to the theatre. Tonight we go to see *Polyeucte* [Gounod] at the Opéra. They say that it is boring, but that the sets are beautiful. . . .

Send me your articles on the Mikhailovsky Theatre. I have managed to get a copy of Mermet's *Jeanne d'Arc* and am gradually coming to the opinion that it will be best to keep as near to Schiller as possible despite his disregard for the historical truth. I do not know what I am going to do in Clarens. The manuscript has still not arrived. I do not want to start working seriously on the opera before finishing the Suite.

It is Friday today. I will leave on Sunday. A letter from Mme Mayor said that everything is ready.

I kiss you and Tolia and Kolia. Will write to the boy when I am in a better mood.

Yours

P. Tchaikovsky

Mood much better. I have decided to have a good time.

[217] TO MODEST TCHAIKOVSKY   Paris
                                 26 December 1878–7 January 1879

Modia!

I am still in Paris ... but glad to be leaving for Clarens tomorrow. . . . I have been to the Comédie Française twice, the first time I saw *Le Fils naturel*, and the second time *Les Fourchambaults*. I expected as much pleasure as I got from *Le Gendre de M. Poirier* but was very disappointed in the second piece. Not a bit interesting. Got acts in it as well but you cannot compare his wonderful rendering of Poirier with the way he plays the part of an extremely honourable young man who gets his face smacked at the end of the play. But I would give all I have to receive a hundred boxes on the ear a day from the hand of the divine creature who does it to Got in the play! The hand belongs to one Boucher whom we both admired at that memorable performance in 1876.

Do you remember Got? What a charmer and what a first-class actor! I was delighted to have seen him in both plays. Worms played in *Fils naturel*, and very well indeed. It is interesting that both comedies are built on similar plots. In both there are illegitimate sons who live with their mothers, from whom they find out who their fathers are. After all sorts of complications they eventually show themselves as good sons to both parents. It is also interesting to note that in both plays the mothers are played by actresses who usually have a *jeune première* role. In the first play Favart has the part of the mother, in the second Agar.

Thanks to Boucher my impressions of the plays are very poetical – what a voice, what a smile, movements, posture, how he walks! Yesterday we did not go to the theatre at all.

P. Tchaikovsky

[218] TO ANATOLI TCHAIKOVSKY   Dijon
                                          [28] December 1878–
                                          [9] January 1879

Tolia!

You are sure to wonder why I am writing from Dijon. It all happened this way; yesterday we left Paris, and as Alesha and I had a compartment to ourselves

I very soon went to sleep. When I woke up it was morning and we were standing in a little, God-forsaken, station. Naturally I rejoiced that in three hours time we would be 'home'. The cold was so bitter that the windows were completely covered with hoar frost and one could not see anything. I opened a window and saw to my amazement that the fields and mountains were covered with thick snow. Not a railway guard to be seen, but I found out from other passengers that we had been at this station since 4 o'clock in the morning. As it seemed that the train would stay there for a long time, and as we were hungry and cold Alesha and I decided to look for food.

At last, in a little inn, we found the engine driver, the guards, and a few passengers. We were told that snow storms and deep drifts had stopped all the trains and that we would continue our journey only when the lines were cleared. After lunch we warmed ourselves and about 2 o'clock we were told that the train would start in a few minutes. Cheered by the news we ran knee-deep through the snow to the train, which brought us, an hour later, to Dijon. At Dijon station, since no one told us anything, we stayed in our compartment; first in the station for about five minutes, then, after being shunted backwards and forwards, our carriage stopped in the middle of a mass of other carriages and trucks.

Three hours went by. It was getting dark, and the cold became so intense that it was impossible to stand it. With difficulty I climbed out of the train and, up to my waist in snow, went to find out what had happened. There was not a soul around. At last I found a railway guard who told me that there would not be any trains running and that we need not have sat in the train so long. I was staggered! The guard took me to the station where the stationmaster was amazed that we had sat so long in the train and most apologetic that no one had told him we were there. They had never experienced anything like it before, and had all lost their heads. Dijon station was crammed with trains from everywhere, none of which could be moved. When I asked when we could continue our journey the answer was: 'We cannot say, perhaps the day after tomorrow!'

All we could do was to find a hotel; which I did in the end. The town is small but the hotel very good and I was delighted to sit down in front of a blazing fire. I then had a wash and an excellent dinner. As all my belongings were in my inaccessible travelling case I had to buy myself a shirt before dinner. To crown it all the waiter spoke Russian as good as ours. He was born in Petersburg, lived in the Province of Kiev, and how he got here I could not make out.

Tomorrow I will probably write to Modia. After dinner I went round the town. To cross the streets I had to walk knee-deep in snow, and the drifts are six feet high. Popped into the theatre. I kiss you.

P.T.

TO MODEST TCHAIKOVSKY   Dijon
29 December 1878–10 January 1879
Friday

This letter is a continuation of yesterday's to Tolia. I never expected anything
like this to happen to me. To sit in Dijon in a frightful, 'cracking' frost, with
the streets three feet deep in snow, and high walls of snow along the pavements.

All this in the south-east of France!

The room is impossibly cold. However, I am not at all upset. On the contrary,
I am glad to be able to get an idea of a French provincial town. Dijon is sweet
but reminds one very much of the weekly picture in the *Illustration* – 'Nos bons
gens de provinces'. There is scarcely any traffic in the streets; the houses are
small and narrow; the clothes, after Paris, look drab. But still a gulf divides
Dijon with its 40,000 inhabitants from Kursk, for example, where the
population is about the same.

I went to the theatre last night. It is very nice, and although the actors and
actresses are not first-class they are quite good. I have just returned from the
Art Gallery where they have several Guido Renis, Carlo Dolcis, Peruginos and
quite a collection of contemporary paintings of the French School. The famous
tombs of the Dukes of Burgundy are also there. I went into the church of
St Michel – lovely ancient church.

The shops are wonderful, and our hotel, although it does not look like
anything much, is comfortable and the food first class. In general one feels that
one is in a country where centralization is strong, for the gulf between Paris
and Dijon is wider than that between Petersburg and Kursk – but one is in
a more civilized country than our homeland.

I went to the station to find that order is being restored and that we shall be
able to leave tonight at 1.45 am. A minute ago a horse-drawn passenger sledge
passed under our windows, greeted by cries of wonder from the inhabitants. . . .

These last days I have been remembering all that happened last year. A year
ago today you and I left Milan for Genoa. At the very moment that I am
writing to you now we were waiting for the train in Alessandria. *Nessun
maggior* and so on. . . .

Yours
P.T.

The quotation from Dante is:

> Nessun maggior che ricordarsi
> del tempo felice nella miseria.

(There is no greater woe than, when in poverty, to remember happy times.)

   In his correspondence with Mme von Meck, Tchaikovsky refers to a private
performance of *Eugene Onegin* organized by Julia Abaza, singer and wife of a
minister.

In *Golos*, 31 December, 1878, Laroche wrote an article on this opera preparatory to its Moscow production at the Conservatoire.

[220]   TO MODEST TCHAIKOVSKY   Clarens
30 December 1878–11 January 1879

I have to write to you today instead of to Tolia. Here I am at the Villa Richelieu in Clarens, in the same room that you shared with Kolia. I seem to see you both every minute of the day and feel sad. Then it was spring and you were here with me. Now it is the height of winter, with people driving about in sledges – and you are not here! Everything is as it should be; the characteristic smell of the villa pervades the corridors; Marie; and the same splendid dinners as before. All is as it was except that you are not here! We are alone in the Villa. Mme Brandt who lived underneath us is dead, the sick man who lived downstairs is also dead, and their ghosts roam through the empty rooms. And where are the charming Baroness Fecht and her sister? If they had appeared today at dinner I think I would have screamed with joy. All the same I am glad I came here for I know nowhere could be better for working.

My sad mood will be away by tomorrow and I am sure I shall enjoy the peace and quiet just as I did in the Viale dei Colli! Oh memories! How sweet and at the same time how bitter they are! If I do not take care I will start talking in rhyme. By the way, although I am proud of my *Lilies of the Valley*, it is not good enough to be published, so please do not take your offer further. I am sure that you are wrong, Modia, when you say that the *Annals of Europe* and *Russian Annals* will quarrel over the honour of publishing the nonsense I have written. There are many degrees in artistic values. My poem is excellent for me because I am no poet. But one could not compare it, for instance, with Apukhtin's poetry. No! Advertise my poetical talent as much as you like but do not dare have it published. Write more about your novel. What are your heroes and heroines doing? I implore you not to lose heart and write.

And I, after all, never wrote to Kolia. Kiss him from me, his eyes, nose, neck, everywhere.

Yours

P. Tchaikovsky

[221]   TO ANATOLI TCHAIKOVSKY   Clarens
1–13 January 1879

I must be honest, after Paris, Clarens – especially as it is so full of memories of all of you – seems empty and dark. Last night I longed to fly over to Petersburg and celebrate the New Year with you. On the other hand I am grateful for solitude, for my work is going full speed and I shall return to Russia with a great part of the opera in my pocket. This time, if I am staying

with you I am not going to trust Akim, but will pack my manuscripts
myself. . . .

Villa Richelieu is empty and a bit sad but my rooms are very cosy; I have a fire
day and night, the lamp burns brightly in the evening and *en somme* I feel very
well. Today I do not miss you as much as yesterday and the day before, and
my work is getting on well. The order of the day is as follows: In the morning
coffee, then later a light breakfast, after which a walk while the room is being
put in order; up to dinner-time composing my opera; after dinner a long walk;
back from the walk reading, and writing the libretto. I have surrounded myself
with a multitude of sources (I have collected a mass of books on the subject)
and am putting the libretto together myself. It is nearly ready. In the evening
I prepare a certain scene, with text for choruses and arias, to work on the next
day. In this way I work on music and text at the same time. After which tea
and supper, letter writing and reading; to bed at eleven.

Let me know, my Golubchik, how *Onegin* is going to be performed at Abaza's.
Is it to be on the stage with choir or in a concert hall and only the solos?
I would very much like to know.

My plans are as follows: I shall stay here for a month, then, providing Nadezhda
Filaretovna keeps her promise I shall go back to Paris for two weeks and then
straight into your arms. But, if I do not go to Paris I will come straight to
Peter[sburg], after staying a short time in Berlin.

I kiss you.

P. Tchaikovsky

[222] TO MODEST TCHAIKOVSKY   Clarens
                                                2–14 January 1879

. . . I must say I do love solitude. Today I am quite at peace with the dear
Villa Richelieu. Naturally if you or Tolia were suddenly to appear I would be
madly happy – but the burning feeling of loneliness I felt the first day here has
gone, and again, as in the Viale dei Colli, I enjoy that absolute lack of noise
which surrounds me. This is quite natural. I am full of enthusiasm over my
work, and think of it all the time; thus the day is full, either of it, or of my
preparations for it.

The day's routine is as it was when you were here, only supper is not at
seven but at eight. I compose in the morning and for an hour or two before
supper I work on the libretto. It will not be bad at all; if not completely
according to Schiller; I have used bits from Mermet and Barbier and added
some of my own. There will be some very good scenes. I am going to write
carefully, and without hurrying.

I do not understand how Tatiana's aria could be sung at a concert? And how could Kamenskaia sing a soprano part? You must have made a mistake – it must have been Olga's aria she sung.

Good-bye, my dear Modia. I love getting letters from you.

Yours

P. Tchaikovsky

[223]   TO ANATOLI TCHAIKOVSKY   Clarens
                                                4–16 January 1879

Imagine my mad joy, my dear Tolia!

At last I have just received the manuscript which has been travelling around for so long. At first I could not believe it when I saw that precious little parcel. Although I had accustomed myself to the idea that it was lost, my joy was immense. You ask me to write a diary, but that is what I practically do by writing every day either to you or Modest. Actually there is not much to say about days which are so much alike, but I shall try; and, if you find it more interesting this way, I shall [write as follows]. Am starting from yesterday.

                                                3–15 January 1879

Up at the usual time. Had cold lamb for lunch and thought of you my dear, beloved mutton-hater. After lunch I took my usual walk, to the left out of the gates to the Post Office, then past the Russian pension and along the lake, where, as usual, I sat awhile on the bench nearest to the wharf. Sitting and admiring the beautiful mountains covered with thick snow, I came to the conclusion that I am, indeed, a very lucky man. For example: at the moment I am composing an opera, and where could I find a more appropriate place than Mme Mayor's empty house where one can play and sing without being hampered by the thought that someone will come and stop you? True, it is sad that I am far away from all the people who are near to my heart but this is not for long! And I shall return to Russia with a good supply of 'scribbled paper', and shall be able to enjoy their society with a contented heart. Full of these happy thoughts I went back home, worked with pleasure on the scene in the first act where the chorus of peasants, fleeing from the English, appear.

Dinner, as usual, was perfect. After dinner I went for a long walk with Alesha, first to the church in Montreux, then towards Glion, and then down to the main road through Veytaux. On the way we made huge snow balls and rolled them down the slopes. Back home letters from Yurgenson and I. Bochechkarov were awaiting me. He is a good fellow this Piotr Ivanovich! On the first day here I sent him a telegram asking him to lend me two hundred roubles and felt most uncomfortable after having done so. Well, he wrote in his letter, which was sent the day before I telegraphed, as if he meant it. 'Do you want any money? If you are in need of one or two thousand francs. I am ready [to help].' Then back home, and played 'dunces' with Alesha. I won, which happens very rarely to me. Then I worked on my libretto and wrote a letter to Nadezhda Filaretovna. After supper I wrote to Yurgenson, read *Old Russia* for the year 1875, which I found in the local library, and *Little Dorrit*, and went to bed at midnight.

4–16 January 1879

. . . Sat down to work. At first it went very slowly but after a time I got into a frenzy and never noticed how time flew until called for dinner. The dinner was wonderful; in spite of heartburn which I have been suffering from lately I could not resist a glass of kirsch which brought back the heartburn during my walk. Went to the seat on the other side of Châtelet, my favourite place here. Very tired after my walk. At home found a letter from Nadezhda Filaretovna and a short one from Tolia. *Golos* was brought in (I get it every day), in which I read Laroche's article. Received the parcel in the evening just before supper. Am frightfully glad. Will read now and then to bed.

Yours

P. Tchaikovsky

[224] TO MODEST TCHAIKOVSKY

Clarens
6–18 January 1879

Modia!

Tolia suggested I should write in the form of a diary, and I decided I would. However, my diary may not be interesting enough – we shall see.

5–17 January
Friday

Got up about nine. Had a good laugh at Alesha who looks very funny with a swollen cheek. After coffee I went for my usual walk . . . then worked with success and finished the great ensemble of the first act – before the end scene of Joan alone and chorus of angels. At dinner I was in a good mood and joked with Marie about the carrots she served me; I asked her what she liked better, carrots or kisses – from men? The short answer was – kisses. Went alone for a walk after dinner as Alesha is not quite well. Back from my walk I had two laborious hours, having to prepare the text of the important scene between Joan and the Angels for the next day. This sort of work does not come easily. Then I got worked up at the thought that there is still so much to do before this task is finished; this is my usual difficulty! I am always in a hurry, burning with impatience to live up to the minute when everything will be finished. Later I played cards with Alesha and, tortured by an attack of appetite, I waited with impatience for supper where they served us macaroni. Poor Lenia, not feeling well, went to bed directly after supper. I wrote a letter to Nadezhda Filaretovna and then enjoyed reading *Little Dorrit* until midnight. What a delightful book! Did not sleep very well.

6–18 January
Saturday

Alesha woke me up at nine. His cheek is so swollen that I cannot help laughing when I look at him. Although he said he was well again one could see by his eyes that he was not telling the truth. My work today was very successful and I laughed a lot with Marie at dinner. Went for a walk – alone. The weather is glorious. Frost and a clear sky. It is great fun to go for walks now, for whenever you go up higher into the mountains at every step you meet boys and girls and even grown-ups sliding down the snow slopes in little sledges. . . . Went to the Clarens cemetery. It has many more new graves. Sat long on the seat near the Montrésor church and enjoyed the peace.

Back home found a letter from Kotek and another from P. I. Yurgenson with a cheque for 500 francs. Worked on the first scene of the second act. Alesha is not feeling well at all. I am going to put him to bed and give him some hot tea. He has a temperature but I am not unduly worried since it does not look like anything serious. It is past seven now. Am waiting for supper with impatience.

On the whole I am pleased with myself. Work, appetite, and sleep (except for rare occasions), are in perfect order.

Good-bye, I kiss you Modia!

Yours

P. Tchaikovsky

[225] TO ANATOLI TCHAIKOVSKY   Clarens
                                           7–19 January 1879

I wanted very much to go to church in Vevey. The church you saw being built has been consecrated and services are held there. Unfortunately Alesha has a hideous swelling instead of a cheek and I was reluctant to leave him. In consequence everything went according to the usual order, the only difference being that dinner was better than ever.

After dinner I went for a walk alone. You remember how glum this place looks on a Sunday. All the shops are closed. The inhabitants pass you on the way to church dressed in their ugly Sunday clothes. Boredom permeates everything, even the air itself, but today I liked it. At the end of my walk I went along the shore where you and I sometimes walked in the mornings, and sat down to rest on a bench. The silence was absolute. One could hear voices singing far away; gulls flew around me in their amusing way, screeching loudly, and not a soul passed by.

The Dent du Midi and the Savoy Mountains shimmered through a light haze; sitting on that seat I dreamed, and suddenly felt at perfect peace! Unfortunately this did not last long, for as soon as I returned home, I started worrying about the scene between Dunois and the King in the second act.

I felt desperate about the literary work I had to do in connection with the text and the usual anxiety and impatience settled on me again. It is ridiculous! I always work as if everything must be ready by the next day, or else I shall have my head chopped off. Hurry, empty fears, bustle, the killing thought that you are composing a piece of music which will be completed and played you do not know when, as usual poisons the pleasure of writing what your soul desires. As long as I compose in the mornings, time passes by unnoticed, but as soon as I have finished worries and silly fears start again.

That is why I think that it would be better, when working so intensely, to live in Paris or in any other large town rather than in Clarens, which is charming, but devoid of any sort of entertainment. That does not mean that I am bored here, or discontented. Everything, in fact, is perfect. After tea I wrote letters (that is another thing that tires me, I write not less than three letters a day) to Yurgenson, Kondratiev and Natalia Andreevna.

Before going to sleep I read *Little Dorrit*. Tolia, have you read this book of genius? Dickens and Thackeray are the only two men that I forgive for being Englishmen. One ought to add Shakespeare, but he lived at a time when this dirty nation was not so mean.

8–20 January
Monday

Worked with great success. Tomorrow the first act will be completed. Alesha has recovered, but I now have a frightful cold, which I don't mind because it gives me such enormous pleasure to be able to sneeze all the time. Went again for a solitary walk. The bill was sent up for eight days; the rooms, wine, heating, food, everything, came to the sum of 170 francs. What could be cheaper? Say what you like, but it is nice to be able to be received here with open arms at any time and to live here so comfortably and cheaply. I kiss you to suffocation. Am waiting for your diary. Kiss Papa and everybody.

Yours

P. Tchaikovsky

On the day before this letter was written Tchaikovsky reported to Mme von Meck: 'I am very pleased with my work. But the libretto is sure to take several days of my life away. It is difficult to say how tired I get, how many pens I gnaw in the process of my work, how many times I jump up in despair at not being able to find a rhyme or a rhythm, or not knowing what word this or that person should use.'

[226]   TO ANATOLI TCHAIKOVSKY   Clarens
                                                  9–21 January 1879

... I will tell you about today, and start with the night. Because of a slight cold I had a disturbed night and saw the oddest things in my dreams, which I cannot really describe. One dream was especially queer because in it a play of words seemed very important.

I dreamt that I was present at a meeting where Renan made a speech which he finished with the following curious doctrine: 'Four things are to be cherished on earth – *France, rêve, tombeau, roi*'. I asked my neighbour what he meant. He said that Renan was a Royalist, had been shot for it and does not dare to speak about it openly but only in riddles, these four words mean: 'France, dream about *ton beau* [thy king].' In my dream I was deeply impressed by the deceased, speech-making Renan. After his speech the barrister Gerke came up to him, and they started drinking beer and speaking German. After which I woke up and for quite a long time I was amused by Renan's pun. . . .

Finished the first act. After another solitary walk (Alesha is still afraid to go out), I found four letters waiting for me at home. Two from you (how glad I was) one from Modia, one from Nadezhda Filaretovna. Queer, no letters for three days and then four at once. How glad I was to see from your letter that charming Volodia Jedrinsky has completely recovered, dances, takes part in theatricals and so on. Sat and sweated over the scene between the King and Dunois and worried over rhymes. My cold is gone. Am perfectly well. I kiss you.

Yours

P. Tchaikovsky

[227] TO MODEST TCHAIKOVSKY Clarens
10–22 January 1879

It is difficult to write a diary when life is so monotonous. It was very cold and I found it difficult to get up, but I worked well and profitably. I am writing the duet of Dunois and the King and am so delighted with one of the melodies in the King's part that I am singing it all the time with my usual passion and feeling.

The words are as follows:

>Moments full of wonder,
>Languors full of sweetness!
>I have no more thought now
>For my throne and power.
>Tender sweet confessions,
>Passionate embraces,
>Brightly have illumined,
>Blinding by their brilliance,
>Concealing from my sight
>My poor land's disaster.

My poetry is rather hewn with an axe, but it is not as bad everywhere, and in some places it is quite good.

Alesha is not quite well yet. His face is still swollen and again I went for a walk alone – along the Vevey road, then turned into the mountains, walked along solitary paths, and came out near the Château des Crètes. . . .

Having read Yurgenson's charming letter I sat down to continue work on my hateful libretto. It took me three hours to finish the words of the duet between the King and Dunois but I have been victorious. At supper I laughed a lot with Marie. I continue to feel a strong inclination towards this charming girl. In the evening my nerves were very strained from being tired after my morning's work and writing a letter to Nadezhda Filaretovna who wanted to know all the details of the libretto. I feared that I would have a sleepless night (have stopped a long time ago drinking wine before going to sleep) but went off very quickly and slept excellently.

11–23 January
Thursday

At last I have finished the duet which did not come easily but nevertheless I am pleased with it. That I have finished the first act I have told you. Now I have to compose the first, shorter, part of the second act – the other part I wrote in Florence. This means that in a few days I shall have two acts ready. Not bad at all, but, although I am content, it does not prevent my being terrified of the endless labour! I came to the conclusion that I am just lazy. I wish to win the right to do nothing as soon as possible. When I have finished the second act Alesha and I will go to Geneva for an outing, just for one day. Went for a walk with Alesha and gave him a French lesson. Then we played 'Dunces' before supper – everything is usual in fact.

Supper has just ended. I am writing this letter and will read *Dorrit*. Oh God! How wonderful it is! If you have not read it yet, get the book at once. I kiss you frightfully hard. Please write as usual. I am very pleased with your last letter.

Yours

P. Tchaikovsky

[228]   TO ANATOLI TCHAIKOVSKY   Clarens
                                                   14–26 January 1879

Tolia!

I do not know what to do. I have to give you a report for three days but nothing happened which could distinguish one day from another. The only difference is in the menu for dinner. I could of course, write that down but it would be a little too trivial. Therefore I shall describe all the three days together.

Yesterday I went to the baths. The work is getting on so well that the second act will be finished tomorrow without fail. And now I want to discuss something which interests me but has also upset me and made me rather angry. I saw in the *Novoe Vriemia* [*New Times*] the programme of the Musical Society Concert and found in it to my great astonishment the Letter Scene from *Eugene Onegin*. Modest has already written to me that he had heard this item at a concert but I was certain that he had made a mistake and meant Olga's aria. Now I see that Mme Kamenskaia was really silly enough to sing this aria twice. Please try to see, or beg Davydov to see, Napravnik and tell him that the Letter Scene, not having an end, cannot be sung separately, and that if it is it makes absolute musical nonsense. It can only be sung together with the next scene with Nania.

It makes me angry that, without asking for my permission, Moscow gave them the score and allowed them to make such a musical blunder. It may be that Kamenskaia will want to sing this aria again (though I doubt if she can have any success with an aria which does not end). She must be stopped in good time, but without hurting Kamenskaia's feelings; for I cannot be otherwise than thankful to her for wanting to perform my music. And now this is enough about it!

Why no letters from you or Modest for a long time? Kotek too makes me wonder, even worried, for with his exactness I cannot understand why he has not written for more than a week.

I think it a great mistake to read Russian papers every day. In each of them I find something to upset or anger me. I have not the slightest desire to know anything about what is going on in our country except for what concerns my nearest ones and I am quite happy to have only myself and you to deal with. As soon as I start reading about what is going on in our Fatherland (beginning with the low rate of exchange, plague, and the invectives which the beastly *Novoe Vriemia* pours over N. G. Rubinstein) I am angered and distressed. It would be nice if one could manage *not to know* all the mean and negative aspects of what is going on there, and to live exclusively in the circle of one's own family and interests.

However, in spite of all this I am perfectly well, and pleased that I have nearly come to the end of the second act of my opera. I have decided to be in Paris on 1 February, and to come to Peter[sburg] (which is dear to me because the people whom I love so much live there, though in other respects I hate it), not later than 1 March.

I kiss you, my Golubchik. Please, write. A hug from me for Papochka and all the others.

Yours

P. Tchaikovsky

TO MODEST TCHAIKOVSKY

Clarens
16–28 January 1879
10 o'clock in the morning

It is rather a wild idea to write a letter in the morning, but I do so because I never remember getting so tired working, at this time. Yesterday I did not feel at all well and decided to give my head a rest, and not even to write any letters. The result was that I slept beautifully and woke up today quite refreshed. In an hour's time I am going to Geneva with Alesha. We will stay for the day, go to a concert in the evening and return tomorrow. I am looking forward to this trip like a child.

I refuse to write a diary any more; it is quite impossible to vary it. I shall give you the libretto of my opera in my next letter. I think I have done it quite well but, oh dear, how much effort it has cost me! How difficult it was to plan the action using Zukovsky, Mermet, Barbier and myself, Barbier helped a lot. I am using him for the last scene of the fourth act. Joan is going to die on the scaffold, not in the field from a wound as in Schiller's tragedy.

I am so pleased with the first two acts that after having played through them two nights ago I got into a nervous state at the thought of the opera never being produced, never being played properly, of there never being a suitable Joan and so on, and so forth. If this opera is not going to be looked on as a *chef d'oeuvre* by the general public, it will be so by me! The simplicity of the style is absolute, and the form clear. In one word a complete contrast to *Vakula*.

I kiss you, Modia, why no letters? Why doesn't Kolia answer?

Yours

P. Tchaikovsky

TO ANATOLI TCHAIKOVSKY

Clarens
19–31 January 1879

On Wednesday we went off to Geneva at 12 o'clock. As I had decided to have a good time I drank quite a lot of wine and kirsch with my lunch. In Lausanne I had some more and by the time we arrived in Geneva I had frightful heartburn, and was in a bad humour.

I took a room in one of the best hotels and went at once for a walk. But Geneva is a most extraordinary town! After strolling along only one or two streets one is afflicted by an awful sense of boredom – a characteristic of Geneva. I bought some manuscript paper and little presents for the family Mayor and was at the hotel at five. Dinner was at 6 o'clock, but not very good. Only eight people were there. After dinner we went at once to the concert; the programme was as follows:

(1) Symphony by Spohr,

(2) Dances from the *Cortez* by Spontini,

(3) *Euryanthe* by Weber.

The hall was a miserable barn. At 8 o'clock the orchestra (about 20 men) came in followed by a tall, lanky conductor, a real clown. He gesticulated in such an 'acrobatic' manner that Alesha could not stop laughing. I would have laughed too if it had not been for my heartburn, a result of too much kirsch. Back at the hotel I took some bicarbonate of soda, read *Little Dorrit*, and went to bed with the earnest wish to leave Geneva as soon as possible the next morning. I slept well. Asked for the bill. Our two little rooms cost 18 francs, dinner, 12 francs, and so on. For an 18-hour stay at the hotel I had to pay 50 francs.

We left at once, roamed round the streets, absorbed plenty of Geneva's boredom and with the greatest of pleasure, I got into the train and went off to my dear Clarens. We were met with great pomp. Little Sophie, whom I had promised a toy tea set, came a long way from her home to meet me, and so did Marie. When I gave Mme Mayor the presents (a locket for her, another for Marie, the tea set for Sophie, a geographical game for Constant and cuff links for Gustave), she wanted to kiss my hand. I felt awful. With tears in her eyes she asked: 'My God, what can I do for you?' It took some effort to stop this scene. Dinner, which tasted a hundred times better than that in Geneva was served, and it was so nice and jolly to chat to Marie, read the papers which had been waiting for me, sit by the fire, and then go for a walk. I am deeply attached to the Villa Richelieu. . . .

I have forgotten to add that last night I did what I wanted to do for a long time! Having heard from Yurgenson that N. G. Rubinstein is terribly irritated by the attacks on him in the papers, I wrote to Stassov trying to make him understand that, for the sake of the great services Rubinstein has given to music, he must insist that Suvorin orders his Moscow correspondent to stop that mean persecution. I wrote the letter in a most convincing manner. Do not mention it to anyone but Modest.

Good-bye, a thousand kisses.

Yours

P. Tchaikovsky

[231] TO MODEST TCHAIKOVSKY   Clarens
                                       20 January–1 February 1879

The Maid of Orleans

An Opera in 4 acts

the plot:

Act I

Peasant girls are sitting under an old oak tree, decorating it with garlands of flowers – they sing – *chorus*. Joan's father Tibeau enters with Raimond – Joan's suitor – and Joan. Tibeau says that it is not the time for dancing and singing, the fatherland is in danger and the enemy can be expected at any moment. It is the time for a woman to get a brave, reliable husband, and he wishes Joan to marry Raimond. She does not say a word. Her father insists. Raimond begs him not to force her. *Trio*. At last Joan says that her destiny leads her in other directions. Tibeau is angry, thinking she has another lover.

On the horizon the sky is suddenly lit up by fire; the tolling of bells is heard. Peasants from neighbouring villages fleeing from the English, run in and ask for asylum. The chorus expresses horror and fear. Tibeau asks where the army and the king are. Old Bertran tells them of the awful state of the country. Everyone is numb with horror. Orleans is surrounded and Salisbury, the invincible leader, is attacking the town. Suddenly Joan steps out and, inspired, sings that the end of the calamity is at hand, and she prophesies a French victory. The people (*chorus*) are astonished and do not believe her. 'Miracles do not happen any more', they say. 'There are miracles!' exclaims Joan. 'One has just taken place, for Salisbury has been killed!' No one believes her. Tibeau decides that she is in conspiracy with the devil. A soldier from Orleans, who was with a company which escaped from the English, enters. They ask him if is it true that Salisbury has been killed. 'Yes', he says, whereupon everyone believes in Joan. *Ensemble. Prayer*. Joan is left alone. She says it is time to act but she feels sad at leaving her home and village. *Aria*. One hears the church bells ringing. Her sadness grows, she wavers. Suddenly she hears the singing of Angels (*chorus*), who tell her that the hour has come. She implores that the cup should pass her lips; the Angels inspire her, she makes her decision, *sings* and, in a state of ecstasy, makes prophecies.

Chinon Castle, Act II

The King sits sadly, in company of Dunois and Agnes. Minstrels sing. When they have finished he orders food for them and presents each with a gold chain. Dunois says that you cannot make chains out of words, that there is no money, and that the treasury is empty. Agnes says everyone should help. She goes out to fetch her Jewels. The King suggests that one can suffer anything for the love of such a woman. Dunois retorts that this is no time for love, and implores the King to lead his army to save France. The King wavers; he would do so, but he does not wish to leave Agnes. *Duet*. The wounded knight Loré, accompanied by soldiers, runs in and reports that the battle is lost, and that the King must either flee or fight and be killed on the field of battle. The King, who a minute ago was ready to go and fight, gives the order to flee.

Agnes enters with a casket of jewelry. The King gives her the bad news. She is thunderstruck, but tells the King how much she loves him. *A short love duet*. Fanfares are heard outside. People come in. Dunois runs in and says that a miracle has happened, the English are fleeing. The Archbishop enters, saying how at the last moment a girl had appeared to rally the French, and that the English were in flight.

Act II

The cheering of crowds, the ringing of church bells is heard. Joan enters with a group of knights. The King has hidden himself among a crowd of courtiers and has told Dunois to take his place. But Joan goes straight to the King; then (according to Schiller) she tells him about her three prayers. The King and all present believe in Joan. 'Who are you?' they ask. She tells them. When she has finished everyone is impressed and people weep. An ensemble, full of enthusiasm, but melodious, begins. When it ends the King puts the army under her command and all present sing praise to Joan.

Act III, Scene 1

Near Rheims in a forest glade. Joan meets Lionel. They fight, she is victorious; she lifts her sword to slay him, but a ray of moonlight illumines his face. She falls in love with him – he with her. *Duet*. 'Run,' she says, 'they are coming.' 'I will never leave you.' he answers. She implores him, and Dunois appears. Lionel runs to him and says he wants to fight for the French (he is a knight of Burgundy) Dunois rejoices that a famous leader wants to be on their side and receives him in the name of the King. Joan faints. She is wounded. 'The wound is light but the blood flows. Let it flow and take away my life!' (According to Schiller.)

Scene 2

Coronation (according to Schiller). *March*. The King announces to the people that Joan is the saviour of France. Tibeau enters. He says that Joan's victory came through the help of the devil and not through that of God. No one believes him. Dunois and Lionel want to prove it with weapons. 'Let her answer for herself,' says her father. She is silent. The Archbishop challenges her three times. Thinking herself a sinner, she does not answer. Thunder rumbles. *Ensemble*. Everybody leaves. She is alone; then Lionel comes up to her. 'Everybody has forsaken you,' he says, 'but I will never do so.' She faces him and tells him he is her worst enemy and runs away.

Act IV, Scene 1

In the forest. Lionel follows Joan. At first she curses him but then cannot resist her passion. She forgets everything. *Love Duet*. English fanfares are heard. 'Let us run,' Lionel says. She comes to her senses and curses him and herself. *Chorus of Angels* tells her that although she did not keep to her contract and allowed sinful love to touch her heart, she will be forgiven but will not be able to fulfil her task. She must accept her unhappy fate with contrition for she will be recompensed by everlasting bliss. The English are approaching. Joan refuses to flee. Lionel implores. The English appear, take Joan prisoner, and kill Lionel who tries to protect her.

Scene 2

Rouen, the scaffold. *March.* Joan is brought in. The people (*chorus*) want to stop the execution. The order is given to hurry. For a moment she loses heart at the sight of the wood pile. The *Chorus of Angels* which does not stop singing until the end, keeps up her spirits. She is led to the pile. The priest makes a cross out of two twigs and holds it before her. They light the wood – Curtain.

The first two acts are ready. Am writing the first scene of the third act. If you do not like the plot, please keep it to yourself. It is too late to change anything and I do not want to be upset by thinking that the libretto is bad. . . .

Yours

P. Tchaikovsky

[232]   TO MODEST TCHAIKOVSKY   Clarens
                                      24 January–5 February 1879

You must be ashamed of yourself, Modia, for thinking that I am angry because your letters are not interesting enough. I read them with indescribable pleasure and it was only once that I was upset because your letter was so short. The last two were delightful. Don't mind if mine is a bit insipid. I'm frightfully tired. I have been writing the duet of the last act with great intensity, and at this moment my brain is scarcely functioning. I have jumped from the first scene of the third act to the fourth act as it is more complicated than the former, especially the scene between Joan and Lionel which I want to get off my chest. But as I am a bit tired I have decided to work on my Suite when in Paris – which will be a respite from the opera – and finish the two missing scenes of the opera in Russia. I am going to Paris next week on the 30th, but cannot yet say where I am going to stay; I am not very keen on the Hôtel de Hollande; it is dark, and sad, in spite of its pleasant memories.

I have decided first to take a room anywhere and then look round for something comfortable – besides, Nadezhda Filaretovna does not know either where she will stay. All she wants is for me to live near her, and it would be wrong not to take her wishes into consideration.

The weather yesterday was marvellous – as warm as in summer. The sun shone so brightly that I went out and sat on the balcony, without a coat, and Marie and I found some violets in the garden. Although I hate them I thought I might as well pick some!

I have a new pleasure in life, I bought some piano scores of Mozart and Beethoven quartets in Geneva and I play one each evening. You will not believe what a joy it is, and how refreshing they are. Nadezhda Filaretovna has sent me Goldmark's opera *La reine de Saba*, which I find lacking in talent, and pretentious. But I am quite in love with Massenet's *Le roi de Lahore*. I advise you to get hold of it and play it. I would give a lot for my *Maid of Orleans* to be as good.

As I cannot give you a definite address, write – Paris, *poste restante* and tell Tolia about it. Do you know, Modia, if it had not been for Nadezhda Filaretovna I would not have thought of going to Paris but stayed here for another two weeks and then moved slowly back to Russia.

I kiss you without counting.

Yours

P. Tchaikovsky

[233]   TO ANATOLI TCHAIKOVSKY   Clarens
                                     26 January–7 February 1879

Tolia!

First I must let you know about the weather; I had never dreamt of anything so beautiful. As warm as in summer, and there is snow only on the summits. The air is so clear that one can see the smallest cracks on the Dent du Midi. And to crown it all, it is full moon, so when I come out on the balcony at night, or open my window before going to bed, the scene outside is fantastically beautiful. The day of my departure is drawing nearer, and less than a week is left of my stay here. Tears well up when I think of my coming separation from the Villa Richelieu. I can honestly say that this was a life in 'Christ's bosom'. It is impossible to imagine anything better than living under Mme Mayor's wing.

Had it not been for Nadezhda Filaretovna I would not think of going to Paris for a whole month – I would have gone there for about five days and then returned, and stayed here until the end of the month. Ah well! It cannot be helped. My work is going steadily on. Provided that, with God's help, I can work in Paris in the same way, you will find me perfectly happy and content at the beginning of March, for I will have the complete score of *The Maid of Orleans*, but, naturally, as yet not orchestrated. I hope to stay in Petersburg for a month and orchestrate the Suite and in Kamenka work exclusively on the orchestration of the opera.

For God's sake, Golubchik, don't be angry because I only write short and uninteresting letters in answer to yours, which are so delightful. But, honestly, I am so tired that when evening comes I can only move my hand with difficulty. But for God's sake go on writing your diary, and, until I let you have an address, please write to: Paris, *post restante*, P. Tchaikovsky. I have no idea where I am going to live.

A thousand kisses to our wonderful Papa and also to Lizaveta Mikhailovna.

Yours

P. Tchaikovsky

[Clarens]
27 January–8 February 1879

My very dear Modia!

Actually I ought to write this letter to you tomorrow but as I have a very difficult job in front of me, and my brain is fresh, not overtired, I want to get rid of you today. My Golubchik, how wonderful these fine days are. Back from my usual after dinner walk I found several letters waiting for me, and sat down to read them on the balcony. After I had finished reading them I looked up at the beautiful scene, bathed in the warm rays of the spring sun, and suddenly felt a surge of that incomparable inner ecstasy which only nature can bring. I stayed on the balcony for over two hours without moving, and it had a marvellously pacifying influence.

Lately I was much too engrossed in my opera to take any notice of nature; but today I took my fill of the endless bliss which it can give. Do you know that I feel I want to cry when I think that I must leave Clarens. I have rarely felt as happy and at peace as I have here. It is true that my nerves get tense from intensive work, but how many beautiful moments it brings. How wonderful it is to feel assured that nothing can take me away from my work during the hours set aside for it. How nice it is to be the sole inmate of the villa (except for the first days when I missed you, Tolia and Kolia so much). How I enjoyed the *repas* with Alesha, and served so charmingly by Marie! I like supper-time best. It comes precisely at 8 o'clock, with a samovar simmering on the table. This is so *gemütlich*. I enjoy writing about the delights of the Villa Richelieu to you, since as you do not like it, you will not feel envious.

I have no wish at all to go to Paris. I would not mind going there for a few days and then return here. Especially now that the weather is so glorious! What is more, the day's routine, which has been so well kept, will have to be broken, and everything will have to start all over again. The routine, indeed, is kept pedantically. For instance: in the evening exactly at 6.30 a French lesson for Alesha, punctually at 7.00 I sit down at the piano (not to play my own music but that of Beethoven and Mozart, and operas by Massenet and Goldmark); then at twenty to eight a game of 'dunces', supper at eight, and so on, and so on. . . .

I think I shall leave on Thursday the 1st. Write: *poste restante*. At the beginning of March I shall have the joy of embracing you. Only God knows how happy I'll be to see you, Tolia and Kolia! But how I fear Petersburg!

I kiss you.

Yours

P. Tchaikovsky

Am very pleased with your article on the *Age ingrat*.

TO ANATOLI TCHAIKOVSKY   Clarens
                                          29 January–10 February 1879

I am very pleased with myself. The first act, the second act, the first scenes
of the third and fourth acts are ready and the introduction practically so.
I hope that in Paris I will be able to do the remaining two scenes and shall
arrive in Russia with a contented soul. I have received an answer from Stassov.
He expresses his great love for me, and tells me he was glad to get a letter
from me, as he thought that after the articles from Paris I would be too proud
to take any notice of him.

In answer to my voluble calls for help he writes about Rubinstein's crimes,
saying that if he leaves Moscow, music will not perish, and it would be better
than to allow Rubinstein to corrupt young musicians by teaching them
servility, to encourage the incompetent and untalented, and to oppress all
talent! ... And he adds that I can ask him for any favour I wish except to
intercede on behalf of Rubinstein. This letter, in spite of all the compliments
he pays me, has worried me greatly. It is so full of vulgar lies (perhaps
involuntary ones), so childish in its attacks on Nikolai Grigorievich, that I felt
a great desire to answer with a thundering protest but realized that it would
not help. It would not affect Stassov! Please, Modichka, do not mention it to
anyone but Tolia. Do you know that I get a feeling of disgust when I think of
all the advances Davydov has made to me. Believe me it is all a campaign
against Rubinstein. I am glad to say that since all these attacks on poor
Rubinstein have started I have forgotten all my little grievances against him
and appreciate his good qualities.

The money has not yet arrived so I cannot say for sure when I am leaving.
Most likely on Thursday the first. I would not like anyone but my nearest to
know that I am in Paris. Tell everybody else that I am in Switzerland. How
awkward it is to go to Paris with the exchange standing at such a low rate
and it looks like continuing to do so for a long time. ...

Yours

P. Tchaikovsky

A complete Edition of the works of Prince Piotr Andreevich Viazemsky was issued in
two volumes (Vol. I, 1810–27, Vol. II 1827–51) in 1878.
    On 3 February Anatoli had written to say that his feelings towards K. Y. Davydov
had changed because of Davydov's refusal to let him have a free ticket for a concert
in which Maria Savina, in whom he was at the time interested, was taking part.

[236]   TO MODEST TCHAIKOVSKY   Paris
                                      7–19 February 1879

On the whole my time here is not very rewarding, for, missing the dear Mayor

Villa, I am bored. On Sunday Berlioz's *Damnation de Faust*, complete, is on at the Châtelet, and I am looking forward to it. *Merci* for your letter received yesterday, and read with infinite interest. I kiss you and Kolia.

Yours

P. Tchaikovsky

P.S. After sealing the letter I suddenly remembered I had forgotten to mention two more things.

(1) I have not thanked you for Viazemsky's book, which is not very interesting, though you are right that it is to my taste. It would have been much better if this quite intelligent old fellow, instead of complaining in the preface – that he has been ignored by contemporary literature and attacking everything new – had written his own reminiscences, for they could have been so interesting. He knew Zhukovsky as a young man, was a pupil of Merzliakov, remembers all the Moscow 'aces' of the past century, and had personal acquaintance with all the outstanding figures of the beginning of this century. But how little he says – his articles written in the twenties are simply naïve.

(2) Your article about *The Marriage of Figaro* is well written but a bit à la Laroche, slightly too flowery. What do your corrections in ink mean? Or is it only a proof? I would like you to continue writing as well as this, but in a simpler style. One other fault. You have not mentioned at all the historico-political significance of Beaumarchais. He was not only witty; his jokes were political.

I am getting old, Modia! I have no desire to go to a theatre, and do not look forward to seeing *L'Assommoir*.

Have no desire at all to work!

P.T.

[237] TO ANATOLI TCHAIKOVSKY   Paris
                                                8–20 February 1879

... I have not even once been to the theatre, but tomorrow I shall go to the Opera to hear *Freischütz*. At this moment I am sitting at home in my dressing-gown, writing to you and feeling very well. In the morning both before and after lunch, and until dinner, I worked. What is more to the point, I worked well. So I have nothing to worry about. I see by your letter that you have the same feelings towards Alexandra Arkadievna Davydova as I have. I cannot say why, but lately her husband's kindness to me, and all her attempts to persuade you to influence me to work under her husband put me off. I do not believe it is in recognition of my talent and I ought not to have been affected by Davydov's offer.

This only stems from a cruel and heartless desire to hurt Rubinstein's pride to the core. I must say that since this hunting down of Rubinstein started, in which Alexandra Arkadievna plays the part of the fiercest, most tenacious blood-hound, I have been completely on Rubinstein's side, and have quite got rid of that secret feeling of antagonism I had for him. And as to those attacks from Karl Yulievich – who woke up and became alive solely when an opportunity arose for intriguing, quarrelling, for inciting some, and crushing others – how he has fallen in my esteem.

I kiss you, my dear, very hard. My very kindest regards to Velina. I am glad you have made it up.

Yours

P. Tchaikovsky

[238]   TO MODEST TCHAIKOVSKY   Paris
                                        10–22 February 1879

Dear Modia!

I went to the Post Office today, sure that I would have something from you, but – not a word. I went to the Opera yesterday and heard *Freischütz* and [Métra's] *Yedda*, a new ballet. *Freischütz* I enjoyed very much, and several times during the first act I had tears in my eyes. In the second act Kraus who sang Agatha was very good. The 'Wolf's Glen' was not as brilliant as I had expected. The third act was a typical example of the easy-going way of the French of including something alien to the play, like the *Invitation à la Valse* with the most stupid dances, and at the same time to exclude the part of the hermit who appears at the end as a conclusion to the play. As to the ballet *Yedda* neither the much boosted Sangalli [*sic*], nor the much boosted music of Mr Métra, nor the much boosted richness of the costumes and sets satisfied me in the least, and I left after the second scene. Such a mug as Sangalli I have never seen on the stage before. In comparison Vazeme is a Venus of Milo. I must honestly say that the Grand Opéra has greatly deteriorated.

I have worked hard these last few days, and successfully, and have finished the big ensemble of the second act. . .

I got used to Paris but, if I could, would instantly fly away to my dear Clarens of which I cannot think without a pang. There I lived as you express it: 'Not as I wish but as God wills.'

About God: out for a walk today the following thought came into my mind. Can a sincere and conscientious man of faith painlessly reconcile himself to the idea that God, whom he has worshipped from early childhood in *his own church*, who speaks to him in *his own language* – keeping to all the customs of his own country, investing him with the concepts which belong to the ikon paintings of his people, can he then believe that this God is the same to which the nasal catholic Fathers and all the other foreign priests address themselves?

I just cannot agree that our Russian Lord is the same as the one who is worshipped at the Madeleine.

I kiss you, Modia, and also Kolia.

Yours

P. Tchaikovsky

Recently at the Café de la Rotonde I read in the *Golos* one of your articles about the Benefit of Dica Petit. I found the news in it interesting. For example, that there is a famous dramatic author named Octave Oreiller! ! ! ?

Modia, you must correct the proofs yourself ! ! ! !

Tchaikovsky wrote to Mme von Meck also on 12–24 February:

'I am not an absolute admirer of Berlioz. There is something incomplete in the organization of his music, a lack of knowledge of how to choose harmonies and modulations. There is an element of "wanting to please" in him which I cannot accept. But this does not prevent his having the spirit of a fine artist and sometimes he reaches the greatest heights. Some of the Scenes in *Faust* – especially that on the banks of the Elbe are real pearls of his. Yesterday when I listened I only stopped my sobs with difficulty. Mephistopheles's recitative is charming, and so too the chorus of sprites and the Dance of the Sylphides. As one listens to this music one feels that he was full of poetic inspiration. . . .'

[239]   TO ANATOLI TCHAIKOVSKY   Paris
                                                 12–24 February 1879

As I was writing the date on this letter I realized that it will be twenty years since I ended my studies at the College. What an old man I am, Tolia! But (spit, spit, spit) the old man's health is good. . . .

Last night I had a most enjoyable artistic experience. I heard the whole of the *Damnation de Faust*, which is one of the miracles of art. Several times I had to suppress my sobs. The devil only knows what a curious man Berlioz is. On the whole his musical nature does not attract me and I cannot agree with the ugliness of some of his harmonies and modulation, but sometimes he reaches extraordinary heights. If you do not know the music I mean, ask Laroche – it is one of his favourites.

As Alesha has been behaving very well I promised to take him to the circus, in spite of being tired; but I could not put it off as it was the last day of Shrovetide. We got seats with great difficulty, had to sit very high up, and breathe a tropical atmosphere. The dear clown, Billy Haiden (the one you liked so much), was very funny. But I could not endure the whole performance and went home long before the end. The greatest pleasure I have in Paris is to sit at home in the evenings and enjoy absolute quiet in my back-yard.

Nadezhda Filaretovna sent me a mass of books. Today I simply had to get a ticket to the Théatre Français where they are showing my favourite comedy, *Le Gendre de M. Poirier*. We saw it with Modia in 1876 and enjoyed it immensely. Tell him that the actors are the same as we saw then. I am going to the Post Office to see if there is a letter from one of you. There ought to be one from Modest. Tolia! It will be heavenly to get out of here and meet both of you, my dear ones. I am staying here only two weeks more. Judging by the way work has been going I will be able to finish the opera in the rough. Have you read [Nikolin's] story *A Specialist* [or *A page from a woman's life*] in the *News of Europe*? If not, get it and read it. It is about a divorce case. Very interesting. I kiss you with all my might.

Yours

P. Tchaikovsky

[240]   TO MODEST TCHAIKOVSKY   Paris
13–25 February 1879

Modia!

Two days running I have had wonderful pleasure in works of art. On Sunday I heard Berlioz's *Faust*, and yesterday at the Comédie Française I saw three plays: (1) *Le Mariage forcé*, (2) *Le Petit Hôtel*, and (3) *Le Gendre de M. Poirier* The second play is new, by Meilhac and Halévy, which is quite enough to recommend it. A charming play and how well acted! What a good actor Thiron is (the one who played the part of the cook in the *Gendre*) and Coquelin – delightful, and Samary! the new *sociétaire* (new member of the Comédie Française) is a charming actress. As to the *Gendre* all the actors were the same. I saw Got at Christmas in the *Fourchambaults*, in which he had the part of the son. I did not like the play then and especially disliked Got. As I watched him I thought there must have been two Gots at the Comédie Française, for the one who played the part of Fourchambault had nothing in common with him who acted Poirier.

I looked in the shops for photographs of both, not thinking it possible that one and the same person could act so differently, as a scrawny, funny-faced old man at one moment and then a good-looking young man at the next. But yesterday when I looked at him carefully through my binoculars I saw that it was one and the same man; and you know what, I think he is a genius, for to play these completely different roles he has to be reincarnated. All the actors are wonderful! I feared that seeing this play for the second time I would not like it as much as before, but not a bit of it, I enjoyed it immensely.

Croizette does not completely satisfy me. She is an actress who (like Medvedeva) performs but does not act the part. When she has to say something passionate, forceful, and out of the ordinary, she does it well but when she is silent or says ordinary things one feels she means: 'This is all sham, make-believe, you must not think I am a Marquise, I am only Croizette.' Besides, she has grown very fat and her looks remind me so much of Alesha Davydov and her manners of Vera Boutakova that all my illusions disappear. She even blinked her eyelids like Alesha. However, enough news about the theatre. . . .

Yours

P. Tchaikovsky

[241]   TO ALEXANDRA DAVYDOVA   Paris
                                            15–27 February 1879

I am in Paris for the sake of Mme von Meck who expressed a wish for me to come here. I must say that I greatly miss my dear Clarens where I lived so peacefully and happily a whole month. I am most comfortable here and have everything I need but the fact is that I have completely lost the capacity to live in a big city – even in magnificent Paris.

I need country solitude, no town noise and bustle. My health (spit, spit, spit), is excellent, and my work getting on so well that I shall bring with me the whole opera which I shall orchestrate during the summer [see p. 222]. As this kind of work does not need much solitude or quiet, please do not bother to arrange anything special for me. I can easily work at orchestrating either in the Verbovka or Kamenka wing, without any fear of being disturbed, for when doing this work neither noise nor conversation get in the way. So my dearest dove, you need not worry about any permanent living arrangements for me. I shall definitely come to you in the spring, but do not know if it will be for Easter, as for the sake of my brothers I must go to Petersburg for two or three weeks; I hope to be there at the beginning of March.

There is not much to say about my life here. I do not quite understand why the kind Mme von Meck wanted me to come here. In Florence we lived next to each other and although only saw each other from afar, at the theatre, there was friendly intercourse. Here we are as far apart as if we lived in different towns. However, there is one good side of Paris life; when I get very tired from my work I can amuse myself by going to concerts, theatres, and walking about the streets. This does not prevent me from living the same solitary life as in Clarens. I sit at home much of the time, do not see anyone I know, and most evenings I stay in with a book. I have been to the theatre only twice in ten days. I kiss and embrace everybody. My God! How happy I will be to see you all.

Yours

P. Tchaikovsky

Petia (i.e. Piotr Emilievich) Henke, named below, was a nephew of Tchaikovsky. He was born in 1862, served as an officer in the army, and died at the beginning of the twentieth century.

The Brothers Karamazov, by Dostoevsky, at the time being published in *The Russian Annals*, made a great impression on Tchaikovsky. On 16 February he wrote to Mme von Meck: '. . . there appear curiously wild people, sick, and highly strung – figures more like beings from dreams and hallucinations. . . . There is in this book something heartbreaking, dismal, hopeless, but also there come moments of genius – of great and unaccountable revelations of artistic analysis'. But Tchaikovsky's enthusiasm for Dostoevsky lessened as he read more of this book. He was frightened by the theme of madness.

[242]   TO ANATOLI TCHAIKOVSKY   Paris
                                         15–27 February 1879

. . . Do you know that I am beginning to count the days and hours until my departure? After all is said and done Paris does not suit me. . . . I do not enjoy life enough not to wish for a change. You will say, of course, that nothing stops me from leaving now, but I would not like to return home before my opera is completely finished and I have only enough work for about two weeks. What I really would like to do is to go back to Clarens for two more weeks! But it would not be fair to Nadezhda Filaretovna! I will have to stay here until 28 February. On the same day or not later than the next I shall go to Berlin and stay there for two days. Anyway, I shall be in your arms in less than three week's time, Tolia!

But I shall not be able to live at your lodgings, I have become too exacting, too irritable to live anywhere without my own private corner. Remember that I must orchestrate the Suite in Petersburg and also finish composing a few bits for it. As it is there is not enough room even for you two. Where will I and Alesha fit in? And as you and I will be busy in the mornings it will not make any difference if we have separate lodgings. For dinner and in the evenings we shall be together all the time. I hope to be in Peter for three weeks or perhaps for a whole month! Please, my Golubchik, think where you can find me somewhere to stay. I should say that La Paix where Sasha stayed, would be the best. Do not forget that I have a yearly income of 8,000 roubles and it would be silly to economize on such trivial things.

Today I had a letter from Sasha; just in time, as I had an earlier one from Petia Henke, who writes that Vera fell seriously ill during the journey. You can imagine how worried I would have been if Sasha did not say in hers that Vera is out of danger, but that Tania is now ill, and Sasha thinks all of the children will be ill. This worried me so much that I sent them a telegram with the reply prepaid, to discover how the children were. Yuri has measles! One cannot think of that without tears.

And, to make it worse, I am at the moment so much under the influence of Dostoevsky's *The Brothers Karamazov*. If you have not yet read it, run and get the *Russian Annals* for January where there is a description of Father Zosima receiving visitors in his monastery. In that episode a woman is struck down by sorrow because all her children have died. After she lost the last one she left her husband to wander, full of anguish, all over the country. When I read about this, and the woman's words, and her hopeless agony after the death of her last child, I wept as I have never wept over a book before. It has made the deepest impression on me.

I have not been to the theatre lately. There are plenty of interesting plays one should see but I do not have the strength to do so. It is extraordinary how my interest for the theatre has cooled down. I only feel happy when at home in the evening, wrapped up in my dressing-gown, neither hearing any sound nor seeing anyone. Every day I have dinner at the Diner de Paris. I have a new hobby in place of the theatre; that is, buying things. Today I bought eight neckties!!!

I kiss you, my Golubchik.

Yours

P. Tchaikovsky

[243]   TO MODEST TCHAIKOVSKY   Paris
                                      17 February–1 March 1879

... Modia! How pleased I was to hear that you like the plot of my opera. I am working, keeping to my usual strict routine, and I hope to finish everything before leaving. This will be in less than three weeks. ... My attitude to Paris has now become quite clear. My enthusiasm has cooled off. Since I went to see the *Gendre* I did not go to the theatre again, and I have no desire to go anywhere. The shops, asphalt-paved streets, restaurants, electric lights, brilliance, bustle – all this has lost its fascination and although, as in Clarens, I am mostly at home I do not have those wonderful feelings of happiness and joy that I had there practically every day and every hour.

Why didn't you write that you were short of money? I could always arrange a little loan from Yurgenson. We shall see each other in about seventeen days.

I kiss you.

Yours

P. Tchaikovsky

[244]   TO ANATOLI TCHAIKOVSKY   Paris
                                       20 February–4 March 1879

Here is a short diary of everything that has happened lately.

Sunday

Worked in the morning. After lunch went on foot to the Pasdeloup concert.

Very interesting programme. Main work. Berlioz's *Symphonie fantastique*. The soloists were the son and daughter of Viardot; he is a violinist, she a singer – neither is at all bad. I did not stay till the end. The weather was lovely and I enjoyed my walk home. On my way I had great pleasure in admiring the beautiful town so full of life and brilliance. All the rest of the day was in a trance. . . .

Monday 19

Worked, had lunch. Bought a ticket to a play which is supposed to be amusing. I needed some distraction. I am very tired of perpetual work and tension, and I was angry with (1) Bochechkarov who wrote a vile letter to Modest, and (2) Nadezhda Filaretovna!

Yes, with her! The saying that a woman 'has long hair but a short brain' is perfectly true; just imagine – this woman, who is clever and refined, and to whom I have written of myself at length, asks me in her last letter: 'Why do you never go to see Turgeniev and Viardot?' This made me furious, because now I shall have to explain all over again my love of solitude, my dislike for new acquaintances. I enjoyed myself at the theatre only moderately well, left before the end, and came back to write a long letter to Nadezhda Filaretovna. Slept well, and when I woke I thought with pleasure that in a week's time I shall have finished my opera.

Tuesday 20

Worked. Went after lunch to order some clothes. At two o'clock as usual (twice a week) gave a lesson to Pachulsky. Then worked again. I had dinner at 7 o'clock, went for a great long walk, and then worked again. It is midnight now and I am very pleased with what I have done.

My dear Tolia!

After getting this letter you need not write here again – better to write to Berlin where I am going to stay for three days. The address is as follows: Berlin, Linkstrasse 18, II Treppe, Herr Josef Kotek P.I.T. And after this we shall meet in Petersburg! If only one could do without all the relatives and acquaintances. Write to Berlin to say where you want me to stay in Petersburg.

I send you a thousand sweet kisses.

Yours

P. Tchaikovsky

A typical example of his realism but a diatribe against drunkenness – *L'Assommoir* (1877) by Emile Zola – had been dramatized by Guillaume Busnac and Octave Gatineau and was first staged in January 1879. The performance of *The Tempest* and the notice in the *Paris Journal*, 10 March, disappointed the composer intensely. His letter of thanks to Colonne was published in the *Revue et Gazette Musicale* on 16 March.

Paris
                                          22 February–6 March 1879

Dear Modia!

Yesterday was a red-letter day in my life. Quite unexpectedly I have completely
finished my opera. When you have written the last sentence of your novel you
will understand what a relief it is to have 'this mountain roll off your
shoulders!' Say what you like but to squeeze music out of your head for nearly
three months – sometimes with ease, at other times with difficulty – is a tiring
business. How wonderfully I can rest now, for instrumentation is merely
mechanical! Like embroidering on a given pattern. Today I put my notes in
order and will finish the Suite. Tomorrow I will put the last touches to the
fugue of the Suite, and then, beginning from the day after that, right up to my
arrival in Petersburg, I won't do anything!

For a man of studious habits who perseveres in an unswerving pursuit of his
great aim, the right to be idle is a real triumph! Last night I walked about
Paris in an entirely different frame of mind. I was an idler and all the love of
my youth for this city came back as strong as ever. This also came from hearing
that my *Tempest* is going to be played at the Châtelet on Sunday. Seeing my
name on the big posters and in the windows of the music shops I felt at home
in Paris. But, I must say that at the same time I am somewhat ill at ease.
I know beforehand that they will play badly and the audience will hiss, as is
usually the case when my compositions are given abroad. I would prefer it
to be played after I left. However, it cannot be helped, and I will have to
suffer slight torture on Sunday, only very slight, for I am a wise old bird and
know very well that my time will come in the future. But so much in the
future that I will not see it in my lifetime.

Anyway, yesterday and today I have been walking about Paris like a dandy,
nursing the sweet knowledge that I am entitled to be idle, and that you would
not have recognized your dear brother sauntering along the streets of Paris
in a new coat, top hat and elegant gloves.

Tonight I am going to the Variété to see a play called *Le grand Casimir* which
has been very successful. I have no desire at all to go and see *L'Assommoir*, but
I shall have to. Will be in Berlin in a week's time.

I kiss you.

P. Tchaikovsky

[246]   TO ANATOLI TCHAIKOVSKY   Paris
                                          24 February–8 March 1879

I have quite made my peace with Paris, and am passing these last days very
pleasantly. There are two reasons. (1) I have completed both the opera and
the Suite, and so can enjoy complete idleness. (2) The weather is sunny and

bright, quite like summer. I get frightened when I think that in Peter I shall find winter or, what is even worse, a poor spring. Only all my love for you and all my other dearest people can destroy the unending, ineradicable loathing for Petersburg. If it had not been for all of you I would not even show my nose on the shores of the Neva. . . .

During my walk today I booked a place in the *wagon-lit* to Cologne for the 28th, which means that I will be in Berlin on the first (Thursday) and leave on Sunday evening. So I shall suffocate you in my arms on Tuesday. . . .

Yesterday, at last, I went to see *L'Assommoir*, a play which creates interest, since everyone likes the bit in the second scene where the washerwomen are seen at the wash-tub. In the sixth scene everybody is drunk; in the eighth a man dies of D.T.; and the presentation is excellent. All the same, the play is doubly 'inartistic': first of all because it has been made out of a disgusting, if talented, novel; and secondly because the novel has been distorted, and melodramatic elements (which are very funny), have been added solely in order to please the 'boulevard' public. In the play Virginie becomes the personification of perversion, and revenge. In the last scene, as a punishment for her vice, she is stabbed in the back by her husband. *L'Assommoir*, in brief, is a play of scandal and its success is founded on the taste for scandal.

I have disliked Zola for some time. But since I have seen his photograph in all the shops, with an unusually repellent, arrogant and self-complacent face, and since I have seen this play in which this priest of realism has allowed completely unrealistic additions for the sake of more powerful effects, he has, so far as I am concerned, become quite disgusting and I shall never waste a moment of my time reading his filthy stuff. Two days ago I went to the Variété and saw a very amusing play, *Le grand Casimir*. The plot – a new idea – centres on the world of the circus: riders – male and female, animal tamers, clowns etc. Very amusing.

Today I am going to a concert of Berlioz's music, and tomorrow I shall hear my *Tempest*. If the performance is good I will have great pleasure in listening to my own music, for, besides Nadezhda Filaretovna, there will not be a soul who will know that I am there. But if they play it badly I shall be angry. As to success or failure I don't give it a thought. One can say beforehand that there will be no success; anyway I will have nothing to do with it. On the posters it says under my name: *Professeur du Conservatoire de Moscou*. So I look on myself as being in Moscow and from there a Paris failure will seem of secondary importance. Today it is Saturday. On Monday I shall write to Modest, perhaps a short letter to you and then no more letters from me.

I embrace you and kiss you. Have bought you and Modest three ties each.

Yours

P. Tchaikovsky

Paris
26 February–10 March 1879

Yesterday was a most exciting day. In the morning there was a concert at the Châtelet where they played my *Tempest*. The way I worried proves more than ever that I should not live anywhere but in the country. Even what up till now gave me enormous pleasure – to listen to my own compositions – has become a source of frightful torture. I ought to have been quite calm before hearing *The Tempest*. But nothing of the sort! Already on the day before I was sick and had diarrhoea; up to the very first notes, my excitement rose in a *crescendo*, and through the whole performance it seemed to me that I was going to die, the pain in my heart was so bad. And all this, not because I feared it would not be successful but because every time I have listened to any of my own music of late I have been terribly disappointed.

To make it worse they played Mendelssohn's 'Reformation' Symphony before *The Tempest* and despite my emotional state I appreciated his skill. I have no skill. I still write like a gifted youth who is promising but gives very little. What astonishes me most of all is that my orchestral parts sound so poor! True, reason tells me that I am exaggerating my faults but that does not console me. *The Tempest* was played well but not perfectly. The tempi were definitely wrong. It seemed to me that the orchestra tried hard but without enthusiasm and love for the music. One of the players, a cello player whom I watched all the time, never stopped smiling and glancing at someone as if saying: 'Sorry for presenting you with this queer stuff. It is not our fault you know, we have been ordered to play it – so we play!' When the last notes ceased rather meagre applause was heard. Then, just as it grew louder there were three or four loud hisses, then a few cries of, 'Oh!' as a condescending protest. Then silence.

All this I suffered without getting too much upset but what was killing me was the thought that *The Tempest* which I had regarded as a brilliant work sounded so trivial! I left at once, and the weather being glorious, I walked for two hours. Then I returned to the hotel and wrote a letter to Colonne in which I lied, saying that I had been only one day in Paris and could not have attended the concert. The note thanked him for the performance – it was true that he had studied *The Tempest* very well. . . .

I must get away, without putting it off, and am leaving on Wednesday, that is the day after tomorrow. As to the failure of *The Tempest* it is relegated to the back of my mind and worries me very little, I mean the lack of success I feel, not that apparent at the concert. I hope that after the Suite and the opera I will, at last, write a first-class symphonic composition. To my very last breath I will aspire to absolute mastery, and I shall never reach it. There is something lacking in me, I feel it, but cannot help it.

My head has stopped aching. The weather is lovely and I feel better for my walk. Had lunch at an elegant restaurant. Am sending you a cutting about yesterday's concert; it is from the *Paris Journal*.

I kiss you.

P. Tchaikovsky

The premiere of *Eugene Onegin* by students of the Conservatoire took place in Moscow on 17 March. Tchaikovsky reached Moscow in time for the dress rehearsal with which he was generally satisfied. N. Rubinstein and Taneev were both overcome by the beauty of the music. After the first performance, at which his brothers were present, Tchaikovsky had to attend a party organized by N. Rubinstein and the staff of the Conservatoire. The reception of the opera was somewhat reserved, only the critic of the *Russkiye Vyedomosti* prophesying its probable future fame – on account of 'its national subject and excelling music'. From Moscow Tchaikovsky went to St Petersburg, where he had to endure an hysterical visit from Antonina Ivanovna, who continued to persecute him and to press for money. He sought sanctuary, therefore, in Kamenka where he worked on the full score of *The Maid of Orleans*. Later in the summer he accepted Mme von Meck's invitation once more to stay at Brailov.

[248]   TO ANATOLI TCHAIKOVSKY   Paris
                                     28 February–12 March 1879

I am leaving today my dearest, beloved brother and in a few days I shall be in your arms. I am travelling in the best of spirits in spite of being short of money! . . .

I had a telegram from Yurgenson two days ago, saying that the first rehearsal of *Onegin* with full orchestra took place on Saturday. Everything is going well and the first night will be on 17 March. I have decided to be there, but incognito. Naturally you and Modest shall come with me. Do not forget.

Here is a newspaper cutting from which you can judge that, as usual, I have been exaggerating; for my *Tempest* did not do as badly as I thought. There was only one person that hissed and he also hissed Saint-Saëns. I have become quite reconciled to it all. . . .

One complication I fear is that I will not have enough money to get to Berlin. It is a long time since I have been in such circumstances.

I am reading *Les Confessions* by Rousseau for the first time. What a wonderful book! Some of the passages are really marvellous. He expresses thoughts which I understand so well and of which I have never spoken to anyone, not knowing how to formulate them, and here I find them all said by Rousseau! !

I will telegraph from Berlin to let you know the day and hour of my arrival in Petersburg.

I kiss you, my dear.

P.T.

[249]   TO ANATOLI TCHAIKOVSKY   Kamenka
                                                  12 April 1879

How happy I am here, Tolichka! The weather is lovely and every day I go to Trostianka. The forest is beginning to put on its vestments, nightingales are singing everywhere, and the sky is clear and pure! It is a pity that there are so few good walks at Kamenka, that Trostianka is so far, that one has to hold one's nose and shut one's mouth tight every time one goes through the [Jewish] settlement! Time passes as follows: Up at eight, and after tea I work in my pleasant little study. Lunch at 12.00, then I work again. At 3 o'clock I go for a walk. Dinner at 5.00, after which I wander in the vicinity of the house and enjoy the lovely early evening – my favourite time of day. We have tea at 8 o'clock in the drawing-room, then chat, and play cards until, at about 12.00 we go our separate ways. I sleep beautifully.

Yesterday my things arrived; I mean books, music, pictures and so on. Now everything is in its right place. . . .

Have started working, my Suite is coming nearer to the end. Am impatient, expecting news about your leave. Yesterday I received your big letter, and read it with pleasure.

I kiss you my love.

Yours

P. Tchaikovsky

[250]   TO ANATOLI TCHAIKOVSKY   Simaki [Brailov]
                                                  9 August 1879

I must tell you all about my first impressions; they are most pleasant. The house is very old, the garden full of century-old oaks and lime trees, very overgrown and lovely as a result. The river is at the end of the garden. The house itself, far from the factory and the little town, is absolutely quiet, and extremely comfortable, consisting of a large drawing-room, an enormous study, my bedroom and Alesha's room.

Everything suits my taste and habits to perfection. There are fields and woods on the estate where one can wander without meeting anyone, and this I have been doing with much pleasure. To crown it all I am being served by an old valet, Leon, with whom I need not stand on ceremony, a cook (a man) whom I never see, and the coachman who looks after the carriage and four horses which I can use as much as I like. Don't you think it is wonderful? But alas! It is spoilt by the nearness of Nadezhda Filaretovna and her family and retinue. Although I am perfectly certain that no one is going to disturb me, this proximity worries me.

Pachulsky met me yesterday – I feared it would happen – and we did not only meet but he came back with me to my house and stayed all the evening. However, when he was leaving I told him honestly that I would like to be completely alone for the next seven days and promised to invite him after that. In that way I insured myself against intruders for quite a long time.

Am expecting a letter from you with indescribable impatience. You are a 'spoon of tar' for me. I feel a bit ashamed to enjoy all this luxury when you, my poor boy, have to suffer in Petersburg. I embrace you with infinite love.

Yours

P. Tchaikovsky

How wonderful Nadezhda Filaretovna is!!!

[251] TO ANATOLI TCHAIKOVSKY   [Simaki]
                                                   12 August 1879

Just a few words so as not to miss my promised letter. I am too tired to write much.

Everything is the same – delightful, indeed perfect. My work is getting along fast, but I am very tired and will be glad to have it finished. I await your letter with some impatience to know if you are going to let me visit Modest first. Then I will make a decision and will let you know when I shall be leaving, for where, for how long I shall stay with Modia, and approximately when I shall reach Petersburg. I hope to get a letter from you to hear how Sasha got home and if they are all well.

I have just returned from a walk in the forest, and am wet through with perspiration. I now intend to go and have a swim. After which, supper and then – well I have made it a rule not only not to work but not even to write letters after supper; that is why I am in such a hurry now.

Have enough work only for a week.

I kiss you without end.

Yours

P. Tchaikovsky

On 12 August Tchaikovsky wrote to Yurgenson that he realized that all the movements of the Suite were in duple time. 'As No. 4 (Miniature March) is not very good I have quickly written another piece in waltz rhythm which is much better.' In the end, however, the Miniature March was also kept in the Suite. The intention not to go to Shilovsky's (see letter 253) was the consequence of Shilovsky having spread rumours about concerning the money he had given to Tchaikovsky and Tchaikovsky's ingratitude. All this had led Tchaikovsky, having heard what Shilovsky was supposed to be saying, to write an angry letter to him in May.

[252]   TO ANATOLI TCHAIKOVSKY   Simaki
                                                       13 August 1879

... I am so happy, comfortable, and content here, that if I see from your letter that you are not missing me too much I would like to stay in Simaki for at least two more weeks. It is difficult to describe all the joys of life here in a letter – I never dreamt of such felicity. Lesha and I yesterday went by boat to a wonderfully picturesque forest. There I wandered about looking for mushrooms, drank tea, and returned when it was quite dark. The bathing is wonderful. The weather has been perfect up till now, but today it is beginning to frown.

My work is getting on perfectly. I will have my opera ready in about ten days' time, in addition to finishing which I want to change one of the movements in my new Suite. I composed it yesterday, and it will only take me a day to orchestrate. I must also copy out the libretto. All this will take no more than a fortnight. I think of my trip to Petersburg with great joy; I want to see you so much and Papochka too; but to be honest I would prefer to arrive after Sasha leaves so as not to get straight into a state of confusion after the peace of country life.

Please continue to write letters just as interesting as the one I got today. How is it you did not have enough money for first class; I do not understand. Very tired, consequently contrary to usual regulations I am not finishing this letter on the last page.

I kiss you most sweetly....

P. Tchaikovsky

[253]   TO MODEST TCHAIKOVSKY   [Simaki]
                                                       21 August 1879

When I received your letter of 11 August I was astounded at your complaint about my silence. I have been methodically writing once a week. It is quite clear that one or even two letters have been lost!

I was also quite astonished to hear that *Onegin* is to be produced at K. Shilovsky's and that they are expecting me. I have never heard anything like it. Of course I shall not go. Here I shall stay another week and a half. First of all I must finish absolutely everything and then start on my travels. I am ashamed to leave. A whole house with new furnishings and so on has been put in order for my benefit. I really cannot leave for at least another three weeks. I am working feverishly fast, to be able to get rid of it all and rest. The orchestration is done; but I still have somewhat less important jobs – which you called endless in San Remo. I have written a new movement for my Suite, and that has to be orchestrated and fair-copied.

From here I shall travel to join you but will probably go and see Kondratiev, who is insistent that I should, on my way. However, I shall not stay there more than two days. Then I'll be off to join you. Shall be with you at the beginning of September – the very first days. Since I shall be able to report personally, then, I shall not say anything about my way of life at this moment.

Conditions are ideal but I cannot say that I am enjoying it as well as could be expected; there are several reasons why I don't. I want so much to see you.

I kiss you and Kolia. Good-bye.

Yours

P. Tchaikovsky

[254] TO MODEST TCHAIKOVSKY   Kamenka
                                                 10 October 1879
Modia!

It is a week since you left but I cannot say that the days have been flying. On the contrary they have been dragging and during these last few days I had some symptoms which I could not understand. I felt a vague sense of displeasure with myself, an irrepressible desire to sleep, a sort of emptiness and then – boredom. There were hours when I did not know what to do. At last, yesterday I knew quite well what was wrong: I must do some work. It is absolutely impossible for me to live without work for long. Today I started to compose, and at once boredom vanished.

And the weather! Wonderful – absolute summer. Yesterday and today I celebrated! Especially as there was none of that everlasting Kamenka wind. How I would have loved to have been in the real country in this weather – in Simaki or Grankino.

Everything is in order here and everyone is well. . . . Good-bye, dear Modia! I kiss Kolia. Write.

Yours

P. Tchaikovsky

Vladimir Sergeevich Soloviev, son of a well-known historian (see Letter 159) was eventually to present the first comprehensive system in Russian philosophy. Basing his system on a Christian humanism he was to exert influence on modern history by his insistence that the Churches of east and west should reunite. Tchaikovsky began his Second Piano Concerto (Op. 44) in between reading Soloviev. He finished it at the end of April, 1880. On 29 October he reached St Petersburg, whence he travelled to Berlin. Here he reported on a performance of Ambroise Thomas's *Hamlet* (1868). From Berlin he went on to Paris, where he heard two concert performances of excerpts from Berlioz's *Les Troyens*, the first conducted by Pasdeloup, the second by Colonne. The second performance was better than the first, but Tchaikovsky still refused to acknowledge the work as one of any significance. Indeed, in comparison with *Faust* and *Romeo and Juliet* he found it 'feeble'. So he wrote to Mme von Meck, who was in Paris at the same time. From Paris Tchaikovsky travelled to Italy, Mme von Meck, however, back to Russia.

[255] TO ANATOLI TCHAIKOVSKY   Kamenka
                                                 12 October 1879

Tolinka!

I had your letter, with one from Kozlova enclosed, yesterday. How delightful it is! What you say about *Vakula* has been said many times by you, myself and everybody else. But what can I do? If I write and tell them to give the parts to other singers no one will take any notice and Komissarjevsky and Raab will become my fiercest enemies. The initiative in this case cannot be either mine or yours.

Here, thank God, everything is in order. The weather these last days has been wonderful – absolute summer. Every day I go for a long walk and pick mushrooms which are very plentiful here. Thanks to me we have mushrooms for dinner every day. Started working. I was getting bored doing nothing. I am reading a lot. Besides other books the philosophical articles of Soloviev in the *Russian Annals*. Health perfect. Yurgenson writes that Lukashevich, whom he went to see to tell him that my opera has been submitted to the Directors for approval, behaved in a frigid and pompous manner and very clearly had no desire to help towards the acceptance of the opera.

When the score has been sent to the Directors do you think it would be possible to ask Panaeva to talk to Adlerberg and seek his help?

Yours

P. Tchaikovsky

[256] TO ANATOLI TCHAIKOVSKY   Kamenka
                                                 17 October 1879

... I have started writing a piano concerto in a leisurely sort of way. I only work in the mornings before lunch, but composition is something of an effort. I do not feel any great desire to write but experience on the other hand has shown that I cannot live without work. I read a lot and have read the philosophical articles by Soloviev in the *Russian Annals* with some pleasure.

Health excellent, sleep good. In short, I can boldly say that I feel very happy and would have been even more so if my nearest ones had been pleased with their lot. . . .

Yours

P. Tchaikovsky

It is not worth writing to me here any more. I shall leave not later than on the 25th.

[257] TO ANATOLI TCHAIKOVSKY   Berlin
                                      12 November 1879

At 7 o'clock I went to the theatre with Alesha, where Kotek was to join us after a concert. There was a performance of *Hamlet* at the theatre. Since I like that opera the evening passed very pleasantly. The performance was good but less than excellent. The baritone who sang Hamlet was an awfully vulgar lump of a man, and the basses were bad; but the women, especially Ophelia, were perfect. The chorus and orchestra were good but not to be compared to Vienna.

Yours

P. Tchaikovsky

[258] TO ANATOLI TCHAIKOVSKY   Paris
                                      25 November–7 December 1879

What a frost! We do not get anything like this even in Russia. Paris has acquired the looks of Petersburg, with the difference that there one knows how to cope with, and get rid of, the snow, whereas here it is lying in great heaps everywhere. It was only since yesterday that it became possible to drive along the streets again. I do not suffer from the cold outside and enjoy breathing in the frosty air, but indoors it is awful. I have just come back from the concert at the Châtelet – the first complete performance of Berlioz's *La Prise de Troie*. The French have become quite mad and enthuse over every note he composed. The President, Grévy, was there today, and when he appeared in his box the audience applauded and gave him an ovation.

I am still without news of Modest. It must be because all the trains had to stop or are frightfully late, on account of the snow. I cannot therefore say when I shall move from here. Quite honestly I have no wish to leave Paris which I love passionately, to travel to Rome for which I have no liking. On the other hand one spends too much money here and there are too many temptations. . . .

Yours

P. Tchaikovsky

228

TO ANATOLI TCHAIKOVSKY   Paris
                                    3–15 December 1879

These last days of my stay in Paris I am passing just as peacefully and
pleasantly as before and, in spite of looking forward to the coming meeting
with Modest, I think about Rome with dread. . . . Two Berlin publishers have
been pestering me to sell them all my future compositions. However flattering
it is, I had to refuse out of loyalty to friend Yurgenson. You see now how
famous your brother is getting! The Berlin Quartet Society has announced
that its second evening will be devoted solely to my compositions. Unfortunately
it will take place after I have left for Rome.

Am leaving on Wednesday, the day after tomorrow. . . . Write now to Rome:
Via Babuino, Hôtel de Russie. . . .

I kiss you most frightfully.

Yours

P. Tchaikovsky

[260] TO ANATOLI TCHAIKOVSKY   Turin
                                    7–19 December 1879

Unexpectedly I found myself in Turin for 24 hours. The train I took was three
hours late and we had to stay the night to catch the next through train. The
journey was awful. I had reserved sleeping-car accommodation a week in
advance, but for unexplained reasons there was no sleeping-car on the train
the day we travelled, and we had to travel in an ordinary coach. It was bitterly
cold. We were forced to change twice, and at the frontier were obliged to take
a slow and impossibly crowded train which stopped at every station. By the
time we got to Turin I was completely exhausted and glad to find a good
hotel, and have a proper meal, for I had not had a bite all day. I slept well
and today took a stroll round this beautiful town, which is quite original in
plan. Original, because all the streets run radially, straight from a central
square where are the palace, the cathedral, and the best hotels.

What surprises me is the incredible cheapness of everything Italian, after Paris.
Alesha and I had a magnificent lunch at the best restaurant. With dessert,
coffee, and wine, it cost five francs, i.e. liras, which are cheaper than francs.

At 7.00 pm we continue our journey and have booked seats in a sleeping-car.
I hope that this time we shall get them. . . . During my last journey I cursed
my wandering life and deplored my not trying to settle somewhere for good.
I do get tired through all this travelling.

I shall expect a letter from you in Rome. Shall arrive there at 7.00 p.m.

I kiss you lovingly and embrace you.

Yours

P. Tchaikovsky

I

Rome
9–21 December 1879

Dear Tolichka!

I arrived yesterday in Rome, which this time has made an excellent impression on me. The reason is good weather. What sun! What sky! What warmth! After Paris where the weather was as severe as in Petersburg – with the difference that they do not know how to protect themselves from it as one does in Russia, the Roman 'summer' seemed to me fairy-like. One goes about without a coat. The Hôtel de Russie is both expensive and uncomfortable, so this morning we went to look for something better, and found it. Tomorrow we move. The address is: Hôtel Costanzi, Via San Niccolo di Tolentino.

The rooms will be quite modest, but Modest's and Kolia's is large and sunny, which is important for Kolia. He is charming: healthy, jolly, kind, and interested in everything and in love with Rome. Modest is also in a very good mood. I am going to stay with them here, therefore, without any other particular consideration, for about two months.

I kiss you my Golubchik, also Volodia.

Yours

P. Tchaikovsky

The First Suite, conducted by Rubinstein, was given its first performance at a Russian Music Society Concert on 8 December. Taneev wrote to the composer on 19/31 December saying that it had been well received both by public and press alike.

Rome
18–30 December 1879

My very dear Tolichka!

There is nothing much to say. Life is in its regular rut. I am up by nine, when I go down to have tea. Back in my room I write and then go for a short walk before lunch at 11.30. Then another walk; either all of us together, or Modest goes off on his own (I send him for a solitary walk to have a rest), or it is I who leave them to wander on my own. Back at 4.00 I write letters and play. At six o'clock we go down to dinner; there I stubbornly refuse to be dragged into conversations but eat enough for three. After dinner I take another walk, or get into my dressing-gown and start reading. Modest goes to bed at midnight but I never go before 2.00 am. I sleep perfectly until Alesha comes to wake me. I do not go to the theatre. Today was my turn to go for a walk alone. I went to see Massalitinov for a minute and greatly regretted it, for he stuck to me and I was obliged to walk about the Villa Borghese with him for two hours. There he took his hat off to practically every carriage we met, explaining to me that this was the Duke of so and so, the Marchioness of something or other and the Cardinal of something else. But, one cannot be angry with Massalitinov, he is so kind, so helpful and loving.

Had a letter from Yurgenson who writes that my Suite was successfully performed in Moscow. This would have pleased me if he had not added that Rubinstein said he had never met with anything more difficult. All I try to do is compose simply and easily and the more pains I take – the worse it is.

That comment has greatly upset me. I have written to Taneev in Moscow and asked for an explanation. What about Petersburg? Has it been played there? Tolichka, please, kiss Sasha, Tania, Vera, Anna and Tassia for me. How I sometimes long to see you all. Would fly to you if I had wings. It is warm today like in summer; the sirocco is blowing from Africa.

I kiss you lovingly and Volodia too.

Yours

P. Tchaikovsky

[263] TO ANATOLI TCHAIKOVSKY   Rome
                                        23 December 1879–
                                        4 January 1880

Today, without any good reason, I am in a bad humour, and a bit tired of town noises. I had a great wish to go out of town somewhere, and after lunch we did. And what was the result? The noise, the rumbling of carriages and carts, beggars (Rome's pest) were worse than in Rome! And this in perfect weather when one longs for the countryside. Deep in my soul I sighed for the peace and solitude of Clarens and Kamenka.

But I have no right to grumble about Rome. For example, two days ago we went for a walk which gave me great delight. First to the church of Santa Maria Maggiore, then to another church (S. Pietro in Vinculo), where Michelangelo's famous statue of Moses is to be seen, and from there to the Colosseum. We climbed to the top and watched the glorious sunset. Yesterday I went to the Capitol and studied the statues of the Emperors. This was of particular interest as I am reading an excellent book by Ampère, *L'Empire romaine à Rome* [1862–4], in which the emperors are extremely well characterized and presented.

Tomorrow we are going to have a Christmas tree. It would have been very jolly if only Modia had not mentioned it to Massalitinov. Because of this Massalitinov was invited, then, because of him, Golitzin, then because of Golitzin, the painter Giulio who lives with them, and after that young Amici, who recently delighted me by his singing of folk-songs, and also Amici's brother who accompanies him on the mandoline. Which means that we are going to have a large party, the very thought of which makes me shiver. Each of us is giving a present to each of the others including Kolia and Alesha. We are all keeping our presents a secret, so you can imagine what conspiracy and hiding from one another is going on all day. Even Kolia, the dear boy, went off alone to do his shopping in town. He loves it all.

Tonight I am dining with Golitzin who is back from Naples. He is a good and kind fellow, but why doesn't he prefer the Neapolitan climate to that of Rome? If he had I would have dined at home. I fear people so much that in anticipation of the Golitzin dinner my legs are aching just as if a new work of mine were about to be presented to the public. However, his dinners are excellent and I am a bit tired of the hotel kitchen. Had a sweet letter from Nata. Yesterday one from Nadezhda Filaretovna. She is in Brailov and very glad to find herself at home.

I kiss and embrace you heartily. Also Volodia.

Yours

P. Tchaikovsky

[264] TO ANATOLI TCHAIKOVSKY   Rome
31 December 1879–
12 January 1880

Today the weather is bad. A cold north wind is blowing, and that, maybe, is why I feel a bit sad and long for my own country and my beloved people from whom I am separated by such a vast distance. Tolichka, I am very worried about Tania and Sasha. Please let me know how they are. During the last weeks I have been visiting Museums and Art Galleries with more pleasure than before. In the Vatican some of the paintings – Raphael's *The Transfiguration* and Domenico's *St Jerome receiving the sacraments* have made a particularly great impression on me. The Michelangelo frescoes in the Sistine Chapel have also ceased to be incomprehensible, and I am beginning to be full of astonishment at their original and powerful beauty. I also went to the Casino of the Villa Borghese where there are several wonderful statues. I left very pleased.

However, my attitude to Rome has not changed. I cannot get rid of my inexplicable antipathy to this city. But what is becoming quite impossible are the dinners in the hotel restaurant. Up to now Modest and I managed to ignore our neighbours but two or three days ago *la glace a été rompue*. The ladies and gentlemen sitting next to us made conversational openings which could not go without acknowledgment, and now we have to keep up an impossibly banal chatter, and all the time put up with the most awful ideas about Russia and the Russians. Our relationship with Golitzin is also awkward. I rarely go to see him and torture myself with the thought that he may be offended. This is very wearing. Oh dear! How I sigh for Clarens, or Paris, where you can get away from all attempts by people who want to get to know you. Already there are some who feel hurt that I do not wish to make their acquaintance; one of them is the musical 'ace', Sgambati. But with Modest and Kolia I am ready to live even in Hades and am not grumbling. We have passed many wonderful hours together in our intimate circle. . . .

Yours

P. Tchaikovsky

[265] TO ANATOLI TCHAIKOVSKY   Rome
                                     22 January–3 February 1880

My dear Totosha!

I am waiting for your letter with impatience so that I can decide about my future plans. To a certain extent Modest also depends on them. If I decide not to go back to Russia now we shall go to Naples together, but if I turn my steps from here to the North he will stay in Rome. I have plenty of money and am completely free. In any case I shall stay abroad only during the month of February and about March I shall be in Petersburg. But please, a letter as soon as possible. . . .

Received from Bessel a rather cleverly worded answer but am not going to make any decisions now; will leave it until I see him.

The Carnival is in full swing. I am not the least attracted by all this excitement but am glad to have seen it. We have a balcony over the Corso from where we can see everything perfectly. It would be difficult for you to imagine how far this madness goes. It is quite an agony to walk along the Corso. From all sides you are being bombarded by little balls of flour, in your face, on your head. Some really hurt, but God preserve you from getting angry, for if you do you will be bombarded to death. I came back covered in flour like a flour merchant. But what is really wonderful – the weather, absolute summer; it will be funny to see snow and sledges in Petersburg. I kiss you, my Golubchik, and also Volodia.

Yours

P. Tchaikovsky

It was intended that on 19 February 1880 there should be a series of *Tableaux vivants* performed in St Petersburg, illustrative of the history of Russia since the accession of Alexander II. Rimsky-Korsakov, Cui, Napravnik and Borodin – as well as Tchaikovsky – were among the composers invited to contribute illustrative music. Tchaikovsky's music was to accompany an episode dealing with the Declaration of War on Turkey on behalf of Montenegro (see p. 153). The performance, however, never took place, and the score did not survive.

Colonne sent a telegram on 13/25 January announcing that the Paris premiere of the Fourth Symphony had been a great success. In a follow-up letter, however, he made it clear that the success was only a qualified one. The composer was not pleased that the letter telling him of the fact of the performance arrived only one day before the performance.

On 16/28 January a start was made on the *Italian Caprice* (Op. 45). The sketches were completed within a week and the scoring by 12 May.

[266] TO ANATOLI TCHAIKOVSKY   Rome
                                    28 January–9 February 1880

I had your letter and was very glad that all is well and everybody all right. Two days ago I had a letter from Davydov with an offer to contribute something to the music for some theatrical performance or other that is to take place on 19 February. It was impossible to refuse and I telegraphed my acceptance. These last two days I have been working hard and fast, for everything must be ready as soon as possible. So there is only a short letter for you today.

My head is so full of music, the noisy Roman sounds of the Carnival, and all sorts of bustle, that at the moment I can't tell you exactly when I shall be with you. It depends on all sorts of things; especially on Modest's plans for himself and Kolia, when he has a letter that he expects from Konradi. I can only say one thing for sure; that is, that I shall be in Petersburg by 1 March if not earlier. Forgive me, Tolichka, that I am not able to be more exact. You can't imagine how sick I am of the Carnival and how little it fits in with my moral views. Thank God, tomorrow will be the end.

One more thing prevents me from deciding about my return. Colonne writes that my symphony will be repeated at one of his last concerts, and there are only three left. He promised to let me know in time, and I may go to Paris to hear it. You know that I have not yet heard my symphony, and I don't want to miss the opportunity of doing so; on the other hand I would like to be in Petersburg on the 17th. How am I to manage both?

Wait until the next letter. I kiss you and Volodia.

Yours

P. Tchaikovsky

[267] TO ANATOLI TCHAIKOVSKY   Rome
                                    31 January–12 February 1880

The Carnival is finished to my great relief. The last day the madness and devilry of the crowds surpassed everything imaginable. It was all so exhausting and irritating so far as I was concerned. But the weather was glorious.

During the whole of the Carnival I had to sweat over a boring commission from K. Y. Davydov. Last night, at last, I finished and sent it off. It goes without saying that I could not write anytsing but a lot of noise and banging.

On the other hand I have written a delightful *Italian Fantasy* for orchestra!
– Delightful! He's boasting, you will say! . . .

I still cannot tell where I shall be in February, can only promise that I shall
be in Petersburg by 1 March.

I kiss you hard and lovingly. I embrace Volodia.

Good-bye, Tolichka.

Yours

P. Tchaikovsky

The 'stanzas' (It. *stanza* – room) referred to below are rooms in the Vatican decorated
with paintings by Raphael; a Pinacoteca is a picture gallery.

[268]   TO MODEST TCHAIKOVSKY   Rome
                                     26 February–9 March 1880
                                     12 o'clock

I had to take Amici to Condotti and talk to him. Then I went to the Vatican.
I sat for a long time in the Sistine Chapel and – a miracle happened.
For the first time in my life, maybe, I felt a real artist's enthusiasm for painting.
This comes from getting gradually used to that form of art. I remember when
it all seemed ridiculously ugly to me. However, after Michelangelo the
Stanzas and Pinacoteca seemed a bit pale although I looked at everything
most attentively and with interest. It made me very tired. I hired a cabby and
bought some cigarettes and a pair of gloves on the Corso. At the moment
I am sitting in a cosy corner at Falcone, having ordered a dish of macaroni.
As you are going to Naples and the weather is ideal, and as I have booked a
seat on the train and everything is arranged, my soul is quietly sad when
I think of my dearest and unendingly sweet ones – but without the anguish
I feared. The macaroni has arrived!

I embrace and kiss you all three. Write, Modia, dear.

P. Tchaikovsky
(Ricciardo Luck)

[269]   TO MODEST TCHAIKOVSKY   Paris
                                     1–13 March 1880

Last night when I returned home, your letter arrived, my dear Modia, and
I read it with interest and pleasure. In response to it I will tell you all about
the last days. The day before yesterday, after writing to you, I went for a walk

with Sasha to the Champs Elysées. I had dinner – it was not good – with Kondratiev at the expensive Café de Paris. From there we went to see [Daudet's] *Le Nabab*. The first two Acts seemed so boring that I preferred to miss the third Act to take a walk round the boulevards. I walked, and walked, until 3.00 am. . . .

In the morning I read the papers and chatted with Kondratiev. Then I had lunch alone and went for a walk. At 4 o'clock Nikolai Dmitrievich and I drove to the Bois [de Boulogne] and then we had dinner at the Taverne de Londres. We had tickets to the Opéra Comique, and I promised myself a lot of pleasure from Delibes's *Jean de Nivelle* the score of which I had bought in the morning and played through. But fancy my disappointment – the prima donna was ill and the performance cancelled. Instead I went to the Variété for *La petite Mère* by Meilhac and Halévy, and I was not sorry I went.

The play is adorable. The hero, long-haired and very sensitive, is a young composer of symphonies. I never saw anything so amusing and in spite of it being something of a caricature it is very true. In one scene, where he is sitting at the piano in a dressing-gown, and composing the second part of his symphony, I nearly burst myself laughing. Dupuis who is playing this part, is a magnificent character-actor.

After the theatre I had some punch with Nikolai Dmitrievich and then went to bed. Slept well. Starting on my journey tomorrow; the seat is booked. The weather is getting worse.

I kiss you and love you, Kolia, Alesha.

Yours

P. Tchaikovsky

[270] TO MODEST TCHAIKOVSKY   Berlin
                                   4–16 March 1880

The worth of things in life depends on comparison. Yesterday as I was nearing Berlin, gradually turning from the southern to the northern winds, and looking at the bare fields and the grey Prussian landscape I appreciated much more the delicious and everlasting Italian summer. Do not forget, Modichka, when you are enjoying life in the Kingdom of Spring, that I am compelled to walk the Berlin streets in my thick overcoat (which has been lying in Rome unused for three months); that at night I try, with difficulty, to get warm under an enormous eiderdown; and that at every step, I meet fur collars, and see neither trees in bud, nor flowers. What will it be like in Petersburg?

The journey was perfect, and the last day in Paris very nice; I mean without Kondratiev who was really beginning to get on my nerves. . . . But this did not prevent me from going to see him after having been at the Comédie Française from 1.00 to 5.00. I saw a fine performance of *Polyeucte* and [Molière's] *Les Femmes savantes*. We parted good friends. Modia, I am in love with Racine, or is it Corneille (which one is the author of *Polyeucte*? [Corneille]) What poetry, what beauty, what force! Even more, what artistic and lofty truth there is in this tragedy, although at first it seems both false and quite impossible! In the last act, where Felix, weighed down by his accusing conscience, is enlightened by the ray of Christ's light and, suddenly becomes a Christian, I was greatly moved. And what a performance! Although the actors were not in the top class they were very good. As to the *Femmes savantes* the principals were Madeleine, Brohan, Got, Coquelin Lloyd (a charming *jeune première*), and Leopold Barrès; to tell you the truth I have only seen comparable acting at the Malyi Theatre in Moscow 15 years ago.

How can one but love Paris? The Comédie Française alone is priceless! Every time you come out of that theatre you have a feeling of satiety as though you had been hungry for a very long time and then, at last, could really satisfy your hunger. In the world of the theatre the Comédie Française is the nearest you can get to the ideal. It is true that they have not got an actress like Rachel nor an actor like Sadovsky – I mean there is not one genius, but an ensemble of a number of first-class abilities, and excellent second-class actors who could not be any better.

I travelled all the way to Cologne in a sleeper, and from there to Berlin quite alone in a private, magnificent compartment. At the hotel I found Anatoli's letter waiting for me; it was short but happy and gave me a really good impression. He writes that on the 6th both he and Volodia will have to do the summing-up at the District Courts and advises me to stay an extra day in Berlin. After having a look at the programmes which showed that *The Flying Dutchman* was on – something I have wanted to see for a long time – I decided to stay in Berlin for an extra day. After Italy Berlin looks vulgar and funny, after Paris, it looks pitiful and provincial, but my old weakness for it is still strong and I have nothing against staying here a little longer. . . .

Went off to Bilse's. This enormous, magnificent hall makes a curious impression, impregnated as it is with the smell of food and stinking cigars, full of women knitting stockings and men drinking beer. After Italy where we practically lived in the fresh air all this seems disgusting. However, there are a magnificent orchestra, excellent acoustics and a good programme. I heard the overture to *Genoveva*, by Schumann, and to *Mignon*, and an amusing pot-pourri, and was very pleased. . . .

I embrace you, my dear, many many times.

Will write again tomorrow.

Yours

P. Tchaikovsky

I passed the day not without pleasure, but at the same time I was rather bored.
In the morning I went to the Zoo, and was enchanted by a chimpanzee that
lives as a friend with a little dog. How they played and frolicked together!
How the chimp jumped and laughed when it ran away from the dog and
beyond his reach! Wonderfully clever! It looks upon the keeper as its nanny.
I enjoyed it all greatly.

At 12 o'clock I had coffee and a cake. Then I went to the museum, which you
wouldn't have recognized again. You remember how the pictures used to
hang, in no sort of order and without any system? Now everything is perfect.
I note that I have made a great step forward in understanding painting. Many
of the pictures gave me great pleasure especially the Flemish School –
Teniers, Wouverman, Ruysdael – more than the highly praised Rubens
who paints Christ with fat pink legs and an unnatural pink complexion. For a
moment I felt I was becoming a real connoisseur. I recognized Correggio by
his manner even before I saw his name in the catalogue! ! Marvellous! !
However, Correggio must be an artist with definite mannerisms, for all his
faces and figures remind one of the Christ at the Vatican and all the females of
the Danaë at the Villa Borghese. I did not look at the sculptures, but will go
today. . . .

The Dutchman I found dull and noisy. The singers were bad, the prima donna
(Mallinger) is voiceless and below average; I did not wait for the end and went
to Bilse's. . . . I kiss and embrace you and also Kolia and Alesha.

Yours

P. Tchaikovsky

Don't be angry with me Modichka for writing infrequently and erratically.
I cannot do anything sensible in Petersburg. Life here is one everlasting worry,
and all my thoughts are centred solely on one thing – how to leave as soon as
possible. Now just listen to what I did yesterday and today.

13 March. Thursday. Up late (stayed at Meschezsky's until 3.00 am). After
tea I had to run and tell Kolia that I had made a mistake when I promised to
dine with him the next day, for I had previously promised Konradi to go to
a restaurant with him. The muddle happened because when I went to see Kolia
I was met by reproaches and there was a scene on account of my not having
been before. From there I went to see Malia who was very hurt, even tearful,
accusing me of not wanting to know her etc. Then I was not sure if I ought to
go and see Napravnik or not. I know I should but I do not want to do so since,

for some unknown reason, I am afraid of him. After vacillating painfully
I decided to go home to do some work. Here I remembered that I had not
so much as a penny and sent Akim to Bessel for money.

I did only a little work before it was time to go and have dinner with Vera
Boutakova. But before getting there I had to find Jedrinsky to give him an
invitation from the Butakovs. I looked for him in two inns, but in vain. At
the Butakovs I suffered another annoyance, Vera told me that the Grand Duke
Konstantin Konstantinovich wished to meet me at his house. This frightened
me beyond description; Apukhtin suggested that Vera Vassilievna should invite
the Grand Duke to come after dinner. I only just managed to persuade her to
put it off. At ten o'clock – after dinner and tea – I wanted to go home, but
Tolia who had not been for a walk, wished to do so, and we did. At home we
found Volodia thoroughly upset, because his pains and constipation had
started again. Tolia was worried about an explanatory letter which he had
to write to Saburov in answer to some question that upset him. When at last
we went to our rooms mine had been heated so much that I had to sit with
both the window and the flue open for two hours. When finally I could go to
bed I slept well (thanks to a bottle of beer) but heavily.

This morning Bessel came and stayed for quite a long time. He brought only
half of my fee and bored me with his small talk. Suddenly a letter arrived
from Napravnik with an invitation from the Grand Duke Konstantin Nikolaevich
to dine tonight. However I had promised Apukhtin and Konradi to eat oysters
with them. What is more I have no evening dress and my throat is sore. But
Napravnik says it would help my opera. Painful and long deliberations! At
last I answer that it is impossible today but that I will come next Friday.

Being upset I take a walk. Lunch at Palkin's [restaurant], when I drink more
than I intended, get heartburn, and feel sleepy. Go for a stroll. My legs can
scarcely move. Cross the Neva over boards towards Peter the Great's little
house. The wind blows strongly, the frost quite bitter, the sky leaden. At the
Church of the Saviour a Service is going on. Praying women, the scent of
incense, the reading of the Gospels – all pours peace into my soul; I pray
fervently and cross the Neva again; turn home still suffering from heartburn.
At home I try to work but in the end throw myself on the bed and go to
sleep at once with twitchings and my heart beating. Fight sleepiness and
feel refreshed. Work successfully. But it is time for dinner. Konradi, Lelia, and
I meet at Chesnokov's [restaurant]; we eat and drink quite a lot but
conversation flags.

After the second bottle Konradi and Lelia start a political argument; both get
excited and are rude to each other. Tolia comes in from the Law Courts, where
he has been prosecuting. He is tired, fed up, and full of complaints about
something or other. After having eaten a little he says he has nausea and does
not feel well. Nevertheless he suggests we go to the opera. I refuse, fearing
to meet Napravnik to whom I had written in the morning saying I had a sore
throat. Tolia is displeased and goes off alone. We stay a little longer and then

Lelia accompanies me home. Thick snow is falling. The streets are quiet for the snow deadens the sound of passing carriages.

At home I get so bored that I go to the Alexandrinsky theatre. I arrive for the third act of the *Dame aux Camélias*. Savina is disgusting, and the actors who play the French gentlemen are mere lackeys. In the interval I meet Pyleev and Averkiev and talk to them. I leave for home. No one there. I beg sleepy and glum Akim to put on the Samovar. What do you think of this 'wonderful' life?

All the same I am perfectly well and can put up with another fortnight of this sort of life, but after that I shall certainly leave. Thank you for your letter. Went the day before yesterday to our College, and enjoyed it immensely.

I kiss you heartily.

P. Tchaikovsky

[273]   TO MODEST TCHAIKOVSKY   Petersburg
                                                              19 March 1880

Modia!

It is impossible for me to keep up a proper correspondence from here. It gets worse every day. I am being torn to pieces, and only shreds are left. I feel horrible. To crown it all I have to correct the piano score of *The Maid* which had been given to the Directors by Yurgenson in such an awful state that I need to correct every phrase. . . .

I have to make many sacrifices for the sake of my opera. It has gone so far that, on Napravnik's advice I am paying visits!!! He insisted that on Friday I must attend on the Grand Duke Konstantin Nikolaievich. On Tuesday a concert entirely of my works is being given here, arranged by Issakov, with Panaeva and the orchestra of the Russian Opera. Yesterday I had an invitation to the Quartet Society where Auer and Davydov played my quartet, and I was given an ovation and a bouquet. It was very flattering, but, oh God, how tired I am, how disgusting everything seems here, and how I long to leave Petersburg. I dream of this prospect as of an unattainable state of bliss! Madman, how little did I appreciate the boundless joys of freedom when I was abroad. Here I must go somewhere to see someone from early morning till late at night. A tyranny of the most disgusting order.

And Vera Butakova! I implored her to release me from the torture of meeting Konstantin Konstantinovich, but she refused. And today I have to be at her house to be "exposed" to the Grand Duke. I know he is very nice but I hate new acquaintances. I hope to write a more interesting letter next time.

I kiss you.

P. Tchaikovsky

The concert given by V. Issakov on 25 March included the Letter Song (Panaeva) and Lensky's aria (Issakov) from *Eugene Onegin*, the Andante for violin from the First Quartet (A. N. Alferaky) and the First Suite and *Romeo and Juliet* (Opera Orchestra, cond. Napravnik).

Napravnik conducted the extra concert of the St Petersburg Russian Musical Society on 23 March.

[274]   TO MODEST TCHAIKOVSKY   Petersburg
                                                                 22 March 1880

As I cannot write properly, will give you a brief account of what has happened. . . . There was an evening at Vera Butakova's with Lelia Apukhtin and the Grand Duke Konstantin Konstantinovich – a charming youth and we were all enchanted by him. Yesterday I dined with his father the Grand Duke Konstantin Nikolaievich, who was kind and charming. I paid a visit to Lukashevich, and was amiably received, but Napravnik warns me not to trust his ingratiating ways.

Issakov gives a concert of my works on Tuesday, with orchestra, the singer Panaeva, and so on. The papers and the public call it "my concert" (Tchaikovsky Concert) – you can imagine how pleasant it is. Yesterday I heard Lavrovskaia as Amneris and found that her singing is as good as her acting is absurd. . . . Tomorrow I'm going to a Musical Society Concert, with Lavrovskaia, Auer, Brassen, and my *Romeo* overture. All my life is one mad rush from one place to another, and trying to find a minute to check the piano score of the opera. I have no time to orchestrate the Piano Concerto as I have to look through the score of the opera. It seems they are going to produce it but nothing has been properly decided yet.

I shall leave in the fifth week of Lent, stay in Moscow for two days, and then go full speed to Kamenka. I await the journey to get free from this mad life.

I kiss you, my dear, beloved Modia, and Kolia and Alesha.

Yours

P. Tchaikovsky

[275]   TO MODEST TCHAIKOVSKY   [Petersburg]
                                                                 27 March 1880

Modosha!

Things have got to such a pitch that I have no time even to write a few words. The so-called 'my concert' went very well. *C'était très aristocratique* and created a sensation. . . . Every day I lunch in three places, dine in five, sup in ten, and am as tired as a dog! But perfectly well.

Tuesday I am leaving for Moscow – *definitely*. I will stay there incognito for two days to finish my work. Then I will spend a few days with Moscow friends, and may wait for Anatoli and go with him to Kamenka. If he cannot come, I will go alone and he will have to come later. I hope to see you soon in Kamenka. How wonderful!! No details, too many of them. You will hear all about it when we see each other.

I think the opera is going to be produced.

I kiss you very hard and also my dear Kolia and Alexei. . . .

Yours

P. Tchaikovsky

[276] TO MODEST TCHAIKOVSKY   Moscow
                                                    7 April 1880

Here too, just as in Petersburg, it is impossible for me to write properly. I tried to stay incognito my first day here but that very afternoon I was unlucky; for when taking a walk on the other side of the Moskva river I met the Grand Duke Konstantin Nikolaievich who, while dining at the Governor General's house, described our unexpected encounter.

Work, i.e. correcting proofs has accumulated so much that I am obliged to stay until Friday, 11 April. I can't believe that the day at last will come when I won't any more have to think from the moment I wake up until I go to bed whom – damn it – I must go and see, who – damn it – is coming to see me, etc. I am sick of the everlasting, chronic, celebrations and parties that went on in Petersburg and go on here. . . .

There are moments when I feel depressed, especially when I return home in the evenings, but I must say that Moscow in spring is charming.

I kiss all of you.

P. Tchaikovsky

[277] TO ANATOLI TCHAIKOVSKY   Kamenka
                                                    15 May 1880

All these days I have been suffering from nettle rash – all my body itches and little white pimples have erupted on my skin. They say it is a cold. But the rash does not prevent me from being well and full of energy. These last days I have been working like a madman. The proof corrections of the opera hang round my neck – the most disgusting occupation in the world. But in order to get it done I must first finish the *Italian Caprice*; so I am sitting here and working so hard that I get very tired. Luckily the *Caprice* is nearly finished; please tell Yurgenson about it. . . . Every day I go to Trostianka and always alone. Today on account of Misha's birthday everybody is going to Verbovka.

Tolichka, as I have not much material for letters, and too much work, please permit me to write not more than once a week!

I embrace and kiss you. My regards to Rubinstein.

Yours

P. Tchaikovsky

[278] TO MODEST TCHAIKOVSKY

Brailov
4 July 1880

This is my third day here, my dear and precious Modichka! This time my journey was distinguished from the others by my meeting acquaintances all the way, and suffering unbearably from them. There was not one of them who did not ask me, 'Are you going to give us something new?' That is what is called the charm of life in society and of mixing with people!!! In Fastov I met (luckily not for long) Setov, Orlov and Barzal – three tenors.

The last named spoke to me about my opera, *Oprichnik*, and took me to task for its faults. Setov advised me to become a bandmaster. Orlov condescendingly interrogated me as to my new opera, and I humbled myself and, with the unnaturally sweet smile of 'Peter the Stranger', begged him to sing the leading part. . . . Talking to them and allowing 'Peter the Stranger' to play the fool – to my disgust – I thought all the time: 'I wish the flies would eat you! Won't you go soon?' They went at last.

Everything here is as grand and cold as before. If this house were not the house of someone very dear to me, like Nadezhda Filaretovna, there would be nothing to touch the heart. All this is too new and reminds me of Petersburg. I will only stay about five days in the big house and then go on to Simaki where everything is ready for me and where much has been changed and improved. Yesterday I drove to the Cliff, one of my favourite places. This is the high bank of the river covered with woods. Below, the river flows fast and on the other side is a dense forest of oaks. I am doing nothing. I read, play, swim, and catch crabs in a net with Alesha, eat all day, and enjoy myself. I am not bored for a single second. On the way here, however, I longed for Bobik, Yury, and Kamenka in general. I made the discovery that N.F. has a complete collection of my works.

Oh God! how much I have written and how much of it is imperfect, weak, below the highest standard. And how badly most of my works have been published. Disgusting! I have decided not to write for a time but, instead, to correct and have republished everything that I have ever done.

Tolia writes that he will leave Moscow on the 20th so I can easily stay here another three weeks, which I will do. I kiss you and Kolia with all my love.

Yours

P. Tchaikovsky

Brailov
7 July 1880

... I feel very content here. There is plenty of space, peace, and quiet, so much
so, in fact, that it is somewhat frightening in the evenings. I found a mass of
new music in Nadezhda Filaretovna's library; for instance, several numbers
from *Judith* (I played them and remembered my one time enthusiasm with
amusement and pleasure); *Le Roi l'a dit*, by Delibes; *The Maccabees*, by [A.]
Rubinstein; and much more of interest. There is also plenty to read, but I am
a queer person! The habit always to be in a hurry to do something even now,
when I can be idle, starts to worry me from early morning; I fear I shall not
have time to read the book I want to read, or to write a letter to a certain
person. How short the day is and how little time one has to do things in!
To be always in a hurry, in a turmoil, and continuously reproaching myself
for not having achieved anything, is my particular disorder.

Alesha and I drive to the forest every day and two days ago we got lost and
nearly had to spend the night there. It was getting dark when, at last, we
came out on to the right path and found the place where tea and the horses
were waiting for us. I go bathing three times a day with infinite pleasure.
Tomorrow evening I am moving to Simaki, where everything is ready for
me. ...

Yours

P. Tchaikovsky

Tchaikovsky is busy reading proofs of *The Maid of Orleans* and the drama of
Sákuntalá (from Kâlidâsa, a Hindu poet of the post-Vedic period of Sanskrit
literature). He did not find inspiration in this work (F. Weingartner's opera *Sakuntala*
was produced in Weimar in 1884).

The proofs of *The Maid of Orleans* were sent to Yurgenson on 18 July.

Life in the country gave opportunity for more reading. Tchaikovsky was both
attracted and repelled by Victor Hugo and Zola. Napravnik recalled once how he
visited Tchaikovsky in Klin to find him reading Edmond Bire's *Victor Hugo après
1830* and complaining of Hugo's lack of depth and of sincerity. In the first volume
of this work (now in the museum in Klin) Tchaikovsky noted Heine's negative
attitude to Hugo. On the other hand he thought highly of French music, but in so
doing had no intention of allowing his appreciation of Russian music to be diminished.
On 15 August 1880 he wrote to Taneev saying: '. . . European music is a treasury
to which every nationality brings something of its own for the good of all. . . . If
you hear Russian national traits in my compositions I find a typically French flavour
in those of Massenet and Bizet. . . . In general I want our music to be of its own
kind and Russian songs to bring a fresh impulse to music, as the songs of other
countries have done in their time.' Fifty years later Ravel was preaching the same
doctrine in a speech delivered at Houston, Texas, U.S.A.

Simaki
8 July 1880
10 pm

I expected a lot from Simaki but the reality surpassed my expectations! What a delightful little corner of the world it is and how uninteresting Brailov in comparison. The house is as it was last year, but the furniture and wallpapers are new; it is superbly comfortable, and the surrounding countryside is absolutely adorable! The garden is full of flowers. I am swimming in an ocean of happy impressions.

There was a moment, an hour ago, when walking in a field of wheat, next to the garden, I was so overwhelmed with joy that I went down on my knees and thanked God for this ecstasy. I am extending my experiences. I was on a little rise and could see my cottage peeping out through thick, green foliage, and all around were hills covered with woods. On the other side of the river was the village, whence came the homely sounds of village life – children's voices, bleating of lambs, and mooing of the returning herd of cattle. In the west there was a magnificent sunset, while on the opposite side the full moon was rising in the sky. All around beauty and space! Oh! Oh! What moments come to one in life! Everything is worth forgetting for the sake of them.

10 July

I swim in waves of unending delight. Probably like you did last year in Skalonovka. Yesterday I again watched the sunset and the rising of the full moon. I went to the forest, where it's lovely, and in my little house, everything is charming, cosy, countryfied. One thing more – Marcel Karlovich, the Brailov butler, is not here to serve me at dinner and stare at me all the time making me feel uncomfortable. I am waited on by old Leon, a Pole, who does not frighten me a bit.

Have received the third proofs of the opera and am going to work on them properly. Sasha is passing here on her way home and if she lets me know in time I shall go to Jmerinka to meet them. . . . I kiss and embrace you and Kolia! I still hope that we shall stroll in winter over the Corso, you and I.

Yours

P. Tchaikovsky

During this month Tchaikovsky was once again disturbed by a communication from Antonina Ivanovna in which she stated her readiness for a divorce refused to agree to this being based on a charge against her of adultery (the only grounds on which divorce was possible in Russia). She also accused her husband of spreading rumours about her. There might appear to be some significance in Tchaikovsky's reaction to the relationship of Mary Magdalene and Christ as hinted at in the following letter.

Simaki
                                              18 July 1880

Dear Modia!

How sick I am of my *Maid of Orleans*, and how glad to have sent it off. She
is at this moment flying to Moscow and up to the time that she will be
produced I need not worry about her anymore. To refresh myself last night
I played *Carmen* from beginning to end and all my wonder and love for this
wonderful opera flared up again. I even mapped out in my mind an article in
which *Carmen*, in spite of its modest pretensions to be only an *opéra comique*
and not grand opera, is shown as really one of – if not the most – prominent
lyric-dramatic creations of our time. Under the influence of this idea I even
wrote a few words to Nadezhda Filaretovna which are the essence of my
imagined article. So as not to tire myself by a new version of my thoughts
I am going to copy them into my letter to you, which I have not yet posted.
I want you to know my opinion. As to the article I shall never write it. I have
too little of skill or knowledge – all that Laroche has got in plenty. A pity in a
way, for I am ready to swear on oath that in a few years *Carmen* will be looked
upon as a perfect *chef d'oeuvre*. Here is what I have written to Nadezhda
Filaretovna:

'In my opinion *Carmen* is an absolute *chef d'oeuvre*, i.e. a work which is very
much the reflection of the musical taste and aspiration of a whole epoch. It
seems to me that the epoch we live in differs from its predecessor by reason
of this characteristic trait – that composers pursue (what Mozart, Beethoven,
and Schubert never did) pretty, piquant, musical effects. What, for example, is
the new Russian school if not a cult of spicy harmonizations, original orchestral
combinations, and all sorts of superficial effects. The musical idea has been
pushed into the background. It has become not the aim but only the means;
that is, the reason for the invention of this or that combination of sounds.
This, purely brainy process of musical reasoning makes contemporary music,
however amusing, witty, curious, and even "tasty" (an expression invented
by and most characteristic of the new Russian school), at the same time cold,
not warmed by real inspiration. But, suddenly a Frenchman appears (whom I
can really call a genius) whose piquancy and spiciness do not result from
ingenuity but flow in an unhindered stream, to flatter your hearing, to excite,
and to touch you at the same time. As if he means to say: "You do not want
anything grand, mighty, and strong, but prettiness – here it is!" He has, indeed,
given us an example of the element which is called pretty – *le joli*. Bizet is an
artist who, in spite of paying tribute to the decadent taste of this century is
full of sincere feeling and inspiration.'

That is the newspaper article chatter which will give you an idea of what
I think. But I have not enough guts to write a proper article. I would have to
prove that not only the Russian school but Wagner and Liszt are also pursuing
prettiness and 'tastiness', and that the last of the Mohicans of the Golden
Age of Music were Mendelssohn, Chopin, Schumann and Glinka; but in their
music, too, you can see a move away from the great and beautiful to the
'tasty'. In brief, I have not enough of what it takes to write a proper article.

All the same *Carmen* is worth writing about, so if you like I give you the right to use my ideas for an article. You could, with my help, in respect of musical terminology. However, you had better write your novel! ...

I had another letter from you yesterday, what a good boy you are! Thank you, Modichka. As to your advice to read *L'homme qui rit* I also thank you; but ironically. Don't you know my relationship with Victor Hugo? I will tell you how it ended. In Oussovo I once started to read *Les travailleurs de la mer*. As I read and read I got angrier every minute at all the affectation and grimacing! At last one night after having read a whole row of meaningless noisy phrases which consisted of exclamations, antitheses, omissions etc. I became furious and started spitting on the book, tore it to shreds, stamped on it with my feet, and finally threw it out of the window.

Since then I cannot even look at a book with Hugo's name on it, as to reading one, you could not tempt me with the most tasty morsel. And believe me your Zola is also only an actor in a new style. I am not so sick of him as of Hugo but am getting that way. He disgusts me as young women do who, pretending to be simple and natural, are, in fact, flirtatious and full of tricks. I must say as much as I like the latest French music I find their literature and journalism disgusting.

19 July

Yesterday I praised Bizet, today I am going to be enthusiastic over Massenet. I found in Nadezhda Filaretovna's library Massenet's *Marie Madeleine*. Having read the text and what is said about the relationship between Christ and Mary Magdalene, and Judas, and also about Golgotha and the Resurrection, I felt prejudiced against the composition. But when I started playing it I understood that the opera is by no means trivial, and that the duet between Christ and Mary Magdalene is a masterpiece. I was so impressed by the music in which Massenet showed how he knew to express the eternal purity of Jesus that I shed floods of tears. Wonderful tears! Hail the Frenchman who knew how to make them flow. What a pity that I cannot play and sing this apparently simple but wonderfully gifted work to you. No! definitely – the French have placed themselves at the head of music. Today I have been full of this duet and under its influence I composed a song to words by A. Tolstoi [op. 47]. The tune is inspired by Massenet.

Yours

P. Tchaikovsky

[282] TO LEV DAVYDOV Simaki
22 July 1880

Levushka dear,

What a fright I had yesterday! We had three thunderstorms, one a particularly bad one. The like of the second I had never seen before. I must describe it to you.

I was having tea on the balcony at 6 o'clock (luckily I had returned from my two hour walk by then). The sky was clear but one could hear an incessant rumbling like the noise of a train in the distance. But as one normally cannot hear it from here I could not understand where it came from. The rumbling sound grew gradually stronger and came nearer. Suddenly, from the south, from out of the horizon, a cloud appeared, moving at a terrific speed. It consisted of a front part as of a black hairy substance, with a dark red and whitish rim, followed by a solid, dark grey mass and was coming straight at us. The front part flew at a terrific speed, growing louder and fiercer every minute. The extraordinary thing was that there were no separate thunder claps or lightning, but the sky glimmered, throbbed with incessant light, and rumbled loudly and menacingly, but evenly like the roll of a colossal drum. It was really frightening, but in spite of the terror I felt I stayed by the window, for the scene was so magnificently wild and fiercely beautiful.

When the front part of the cloud had passed over our heads and the grey mass had reached us there came a terrific hurricane and a hailstorm like nothing I had ever seen. Everything trembled, moaned and howled. Trees were felled, the air was full of flying branches, twigs and leaves. Through the noise of the storm one could now and again hear the branches cracking and trees crashing down; and, to crown all my fears, the hail smashed a window pane in the dining-room. Honestly, 'my heart went down into my boots'. But there is an end to everything, and the storm gradually spent itself.

At about 9 o'clock, however, another dark cloud started coming from the west. An hour later it was over us, and hail again drummed on the roof while blinding lightning criss-crossed the sky. The storm may not have been as bad as the one before but several flashes of lightning hit the ground near us and our little house trembled from the crashes. My old fear of thunderstorms, from which I suffered long ago but which comes only rarely now, afflicted me. I hid my face in my pillow, instructed Alesha not to leave me for a single minute, and all the rest of it. At last about 1.00 am everything was quiet, although, at the open window, I watched the flashes of lightning and listened to the far away rumbling of thunder for a long time. I embrace you, Sania and all, all of you.

P. Tchaikovsky

[283] TO MODEST TCHAIKOVSKY   Simaki
                                                      26 July 1880

I hope this will reach you by Thursday! I want once more to repeat that nothing could have given me more pleasure than your letting me know that you hope to be at Kamenka all September and October. It is clear that I increasingly feel the necessity to live with you and Kolia as often as I can. We shall not be able to go to Rome; this is definite. Hermann will not let you go and without you and Kolia Rome is nothing to me. Besides, I doubt if you will be able to go abroad this year. Before December I shall have no money and I must also wait to know if Alesha will be called up. Then, I hope, the opera will be staged and I shall have to be in Petersburg. Perhaps later, but that will not be a winter abroad. In general, the future worries and frightens me and I try not to think about it.

So far as the present is concerned, staying here in Simaki, I am more than pleased. I am leaving on the 29th – Tuesday – and not at all happy at the prospect. On the other hand it may be bad for me to stay here too long, for the continual state of ecstasy I am in has a bad effect on my nerves. I react painfully to all sorts of things, often cry for trivial reasons and especially when I think of something irrevocable in the past – I really mean irrevocable. I have written several songs. I like one of them so much that I can't play it without shedding tears. Write to Kamenka.

I embrace you and Kolichka with all my love. Did he get my answer?

P. Tchaikovsky

The songs referred to above are those of Op. 47, dedicated to Panaeva. Bonifazi Sangursky, brother of a servant of Modest, was sent to Moscow to study painting. Several of his paintings are in the Tchaikovsky Museum in Klin. Y. A. Plushch had sent a letter to Anatoli about the engagement of a singer for the title role in *The Maid of Orleans.*

[284]   TO ANATOLI TCHAIKOVSKY   Kamenka
                                                 7 September 1880

Tolia!

Thank you for your help, 300 roubles a year is a bit too much for Bonifazi [Sangursky] but it can't be helped! I hope that Nikolai Vassilievich will put up 200 while I contribute 100 – which will not bankrupt me.

Concerning Plushch, I entreat you not to answer his enquiries, if he nags, tell him that it is the custom now to engage two performers for an important part, and that Napravnik and I have chosen Raab and one Makarova. I find the point made by the principal singers about the piano score a good one, and asked Yurgenson to send several copies.

Yesterday we celebrated Tania's birthday. . . . I presented her with 25 roubles and a poem.

The weather is quite like summer, and I have donned my Chinese silk suit, but still sweat and suffer. The nights are bright and magnificent with the full moon. Yesterday I had tea in Trostianka. I kiss you hard,

P. Tchaikovsky

P.S. Who all are going to sing *Onegin?* If you find out, let me know!

[See Letter 295.]

On 9 September Tchaikovsky wrote to Mme von Meck saying that he had started sketches for a new symphonic work, and that this exercise had relieved his sense of depression. Away from music – even when trying to enjoy a holiday – he was restless and unable to find a satisfying mind-filling occupation. What started as a symphony changed into a suite and then into a Serenade for Strings (Op. 48). The sketches were completed at the beginning of December. One of the composer's favourite works, the first performance took place in Moscow on 4 January 1882, conducted by Max von Erdmannsdörfer.

On 18 September Rubinstein asked Tchaikovsky to write music for an exhibition of Art and Commerce that was to take place in Moscow. Not very willingly he undertook this commission, and produced the *1812* (*Solemn Overture*, Op. 49).

Modest meanwhile was busy on his comedy *The Benefactor*.

[285]   TO ANATOLI TCHAIKOVSKY   Kamenka
                                          21 September 1880

Dear Anatosha!

How are you? Why no letters from you? Everything here is fine and everybody well. . . . I am well and happy and just think! In spite of having decided to stop my composition mania for a whole year I have started to write again. For as soon as I have no composition in view I begin to get bored. A pity really! It would have been a good idea to refresh my creative powers. The mushroom season is at its height and every day I bring masses of them home, some of which are fried, some pickled, but all eventually devoured.

Modest is very pleased with his lodgings, and is writing his comedy. Do you know, it is going to be a splendid play if he sticks to his plan. Yesterday he read me the first half of the second act and I was absolutely delighted. I am trying to make him finish it before I leave Kamenka.

I kiss you my dear, my own Tolichka.

Yours

P. Tchaikovsky

[286]   TO ANATOLI TCHAIKOVSKY   Kamenka
                                          1 October 1880

Dear Anatosha!

I definitely do not wish Krutikova to sing something out of *The Maid* before it has been produced at the theatre, and I cannot give my permission. There are very fundamental reasons for my refusal, which are too long to explain now. . . .

You asked about my plans. For the present they are as follows: the Litkes will come here in the second half of October; and as they have a private railway

carriage I want them to take me back with them when they leave. But, even if
they do not come I shall travel with Modest to Moscow. I want to arrange
a reading there of Modest's comedy and have it produced in Moscow this
season. It will be important to invite Samarin and Begichev etc., and ask them
to look after the play which is really wonderful. In any case we shall be in
Moscow not later than at the beginning of November.

After staying with you for a little I will either go abroad – as Nadezhda
Filaretovna wishes – or go back to Kamenka before January. Anyway all my
plans depend upon my finances which makes it difficult to decide anything in
advance. But in any case, I shall see you in a month's time.

I kiss and embrace you.

Yours

P. Tchaikovsky

[287]   TO ANATOLI TCHAIKOVSKY   Kamenka
                                                17 October 1880

Tolichka!

You say that I should change the last scene of *Onegin*. Although I do not really
agree – because Pushkin by a hint here and there gives the right to finish the
scene more or less as I have done – in response to your request I have tried
to change it, as you will see from the notes I am sending.

First of all, on page 242, instead of the note saying that Tatiana throws herself
into Onegin's arms I have written: 'Onegin comes nearer.' Then he sings
what is on the same page, still using the formal 'you'; then everything goes
on without change until the very end where I changed Tatiana's words: she
will not weaken and be drawn to him but continues to assert duty. Onegin
will not try to seize her; he will only implore her. Then instead of the words,
'I am dying!', Tatiana will say, 'Farewell for ever', and disappear. As to
Onegin, after a few moments of bewilderment, he will say his last words. The
general must not appear.

I am sending these changes to you. Take them to Klimentova, see Begichev and
Beviniany or beg Nikolai Grigorievich to see to it all. I think that everybody
will be pleased with the changes. I kiss you and will write again soon.

Yours

P. Tchaikovsky

The notes which were sent with the preceding letter have not survived. On 22
October Anatoli expressed his pleasure at the changes made, observing that 'every
time one mentions *Onegin* someone immediately starts to accuse you of distorting
Pushkin'.

Among Tchaikovsky's worries at this time was the calling-up for military service of his servant Alexei and the distressful tone of communications to and about him suggest a closer relationship than is usual between employer and employee.

Instead of staying in Moscow for the premiere of the *Italian Caprice* Tchaikovsky went to St Petersburg where he stayed for two weeks.

[288] TO MODEST TCHAIKOVSKY

Moscow
17–29 November 1880

The longer I stay in Moscow the less I see an end to my tortures. It seems that I shall not be able to leave before the beginning of next week; for on Friday night there will be a solemn performance of my Liturgy [Op. 41] at the Conservatoire and I have promised to attend. On Saturday I must talk to Beviniany about *Onegin* which he is having performed for his Benefit. On Sunday Klindworth is giving an official dinner in my honour, and next week my *Italian Caprice* is to be played, and I want to hear at least one rehearsal. After all this the rehearsals of *Onegin* are going to start, and so on, and so on . . . to be precise, I will either come to Petersburg for a few days in between all this (for example at the beginning of next week), or much later. However, I have not yet quite decided. Proof correcting is accumulating. . . .

Yours

P. Tchaikovsky

[289] TO MODEST TCHAIKOVSKY

Moscow
8 December 1880

Last night back in Moscow I hoped to get a letter from you. I am terribly interested in the fate of your comedy. The news that Savina has chosen it for her Benefit has made me extremely excited and happy. Am waiting for news. The rehearsal of *Onegin* is today, will you arrive in time? I think, though, that if your comedy is to be produced you might be too busy and will not bother. I shall see Begichev at the rehearsal, and talk to him about your *Benefactor* and let you know at once. Kamenka has left the saddest of memories; but still it was a great blessing for me to have been there. I did have a rest in spite of everything.

No time to say any more. Am off to a rehearsal. I kiss you hard.

Yours

P. Tchaikovsky

TO MODEST TCHAIKOVSKY

Modia!

Having arrived here I was met by a messenger from Albrecht, and in spite of
my wanting to stay in a hotel I had to give in to Karlusha's insistent invitation
and am living with him. I am quite comfortable and it is very quiet, for up to
dinner time no one disturbs me and I am working hard. The changes in the
opera are ready; I am obliged to stay here until the 21st. Next week there will
be a special concert of my setting of the Liturgy – by the Russian Musical
Society, and on Saturday the 21st, my *Italian Caprice* is to be repeated in
response to public demand. Although both concerts interest me greatly it would
be bliss to leave; but Rubinstein promises me mountains of gold and I have
decided to stay. I need some money badly. On the 21st I am off to Kamenka –
Anatoli too. I am passing the time as before – often in an inn – but I have not
seen anyone yet and am keeping my incognito quite well.

I saw Strepetova in two roles on the same day. In the prologue to the
Pskovitianka [Princess] and in *Grusha* [*You cannot live as you would like*].
In my opinion she is an actress of genius and I was immensely impressed
by the tremendous force of her talent. But the audience is vile! As Grusha . . . is
not a moral young maiden, she has no success. Samarin has your play. Will
see him tonight.

Good-bye – I kiss you.

P. Tchaikovsky

TO MODEST TCHAIKOVSKY

My dear Modia!

You beg me to telegraph how the reading of your comedy went off. This
means that, either you did not get my letter, or you have forgotten its contents.
I have up till now only given it to Samarin to read. I saw him yesterday, when
he had only had time to read the first Act. He finds it extremely effective and
original, but added that in his opinion the Princess in the play should speak
either French or, as the actresses can't speak proper French, plain Russian,
not Russian mixed with those gallic expressions you put in their mouths. I find
this comment a little strange but am passing it on to you exactly as it was
said to me.

When Samarin returns the comedy I shall take it to Begichev and then arrange
a reading for Tolia and all our Conservatoire chaps who are very interested
in it. Do not think that I am not trying hard enough to help your comedy,
which is just as dear to my heart as it is to you, and you may be sure that
I shall not leave Moscow before its fate is settled.

And it seems that I shall not be staying here for much longer! Today I have been at a rehearsal of *Onegin*. Was delighted with the performance of the soloists in the first act and could not refuse Beviniany his insistent request to be present at the orchestral rehearsals and the performance. As it is due to be on the 11th I shall have to be here at the beginning of January. Is it really worth while going to Kamenka? Kamenka's every-day life, as now, is what attracts me, and not the holiday periods there, which are not to my taste. So here I am not knowing what to decide and fearful of what is in store for me; this week's solemnities, the holiday visit to Kamenka; my opera in Moscow; my opera in Petersburg! It is all so tiring and uncongenial. But, 'if you like a sledge-drive you must know how to pull it'. . . .

As to the comedy Modia, do not worry. Will keep you *au courant* about it and also about myself. I kiss you and Kolia.

P. Tchaikovsky

The *Moscow Gazette* said of the slow movement of the First Quartet (performed, 15 December at Russian Music Society concert) that it was '. . . one of the most wonderful pages of Russian music', adding, 'the impression was such that several moments after the music had ended the listeners sat silent, afraid to disturb the charm of the Andante'. The Liturgy (see p. 175) was sung by the Sakarov Choir at an extraordinary RMS concert on 18 December. The Accounts of the RMS for 1880–81 detail payment of 1000 roubles to Tchaikovsky.

Taneev did not write an oratorio on the subject of Christ but his *John of Damascus* (text from A. K. Tolstoi) dedicated to N. Rubinstein, was performed in 1884.

While at Kamenka Tchaikovsky had chanced upon a bundle of letters which he had written to his parents in 1850–51. All his grief of twenty-five years earlier at the death of his mother was reawakened and the thought of the consequences of this loss drove him to an extreme of depression. Thus, in Letter 289, he refers to the 'saddest of memories' at Kamenka.

[292] TO MODEST TCHAIKOVSKY   Moscow
                                                      18 December 1880
                                                      2 am (in the night)

. . . My successes! On Monday the third performance of *Oprichnik* was most enthusiastically received. I was incessantly called for, but I was not there. The same evening my First Quartet was played at the Society concert with the Andante repeated and calls again for the composer. Two hours ago, this day, the special Musical Society Concert of Church music including my Liturgy took place. The hall was packed and in spite of applause being forbidden, there was a terrific, totally unexpected, ovation with a presentation of a wreath in the form of a lyre from some unknown person. The Board of Directors of the Musical Society wishes to give me a substantial sum of money which I need very badly. In the morning I heard a rehearsal of the *Italian Caprice* which sounded magnificent. At the same concert Borodin's Second Symphony will be played, he came specially to Moscow for the occasion and appeared at the rehearsal in his General's uniform with the Cross of St Vladimir round his neck.

This is the usual pattern of things: a mass of unfinished proof corrections; every day dinners, suppers, lunches, with a lot of drinking, and sometimes a game of vingt; state of mind – depressed, a great desire to get away as soon as possible to a totally uninhabited island, and sometimes even to go down to Tartarus. Samarin has not yet returned your comedy because, he explains, he has too many new parts to learn. He promised to bring it back tomorrow morning. I will then take it at once to Begichev and the reading will have to be postponed until my return from Kamenka. I shall be back on the 5 January, for the last rehearsal of *Onegin*. I could not refuse Beviniany's request to be present at the rehearsals and first night which is to be on 11 January.

Modia! Forgive me! I cannot possibly finish all the business about your comedy before I leave. But for God's sake, do not worry, I will do everything I can.

I received your and Kolia's letter an hour ago. The news that our dreams about going abroad could come true is wonderful. Is it possible that we shall meet in February on one of Rome's seven hills? I dare not hope for such luck! Modia! Please, will you do as follows: Find out from A. A. Davydova Pleshcheev's address or, even better, Polonsky's; go and see either of them and on behalf of Taneev ask if one of them would write the text for a short Cantata on the subject of Christ! Send the answer straight to Taneev addressing your letter to the Conservatoire. For God's sake do that! I am off to Kamenka on the 21st. Tomorrow or the day after I will let you know the result of my meeting with Samarin and Begichev.

I kiss you heartily and also Kolia.

Yours

P. Tchaikovsky

This is the first evening I did not have supper out; came home straight after the concert, drank tea with Tolia and Karlusha, and am now writing to you. In spite of my mad mode of living I am perfectly well.

[293]　TO MODEST TCHAIKOVSKY　　　　　　　　[Moscow]
　　　　　　　　　　　　　　　　　　　　　　　　　　　[21 December 1880]

Dear Modia!

Samarin has returned the play. He talked about it for a long time, and without much sense, but this is what I understood. He finds the parts of Sonia, Nastia and the Baron Torf excellent. Miller, according to him is not clear, one cannot understand if he is an aristocrat or democrat!!! The language he finds perfect. But there is not enough action and there is a lack of theatrical experience in the play. The first act, he says, is not a comedy but a story, and the way in which you present your idea cannot be acted on the stage. It is not possible to portray such finely thought out details in a theatrical performance.

On the whole, neither I nor Kashkin, who was present, understood clearly and definitely what Samarin meant. Now Begichev has the play. I will see to its definite fate in January.

Yesterday the *Italian Caprice* was played with great success.

At the Huberts' the day before yesterday, I quite unexpectedly had an awful attack of nerves. I never had one as bad before. . . . This obviously was the culmination of all my Moscow and Petersburg tortures. Now I feel relieved and well. Luckily Anatoli was not present, he does not know anything about it. Please, do not mention it to anybody. Am on my way now, very happy to be alone. I need solitude. I kiss you and Kolia. For God's sake keep me *au courant* about the trip abroad.

P. Tchaikovsky

[294] TO ANATOLI TCHAIKOVSKY   Kiev
                                                        22 [December 1880]
                                                        Midnight

I travelled comfortably, and slept a lot. This blessed capacity for sleep is a real boon. I feel wonderful. I stayed at the Hôtel Francia, and after dinner went to two theatres. *Lucia* was performed at the Opera, but the theatre was empty. The singer Nebelskaia (Serov's daughter), is not bad, but soulless and cold. At the Theatre I saw something I had never seen before, an absolutely empty theatre, so much so that the policemen were the audience. . . . I have decided not to go to Simaki and have written about it to Nadezhda Filaretovna. . . .

I am devoting my time tomorrow to buying presents for Kamenka's Christmas celebrations and will leave in the evening.

Good-bye, my dear Tolia, I kiss you hard hard.

Yours

P. Tchaikovsky

Expecting a letter from you in Kamenka.

[295] TO MODEST TCHAIKOVSKY   Kamenka
                                                        2 January 1881

I was going to leave tonight but a blizzard blew up and so much snow has fallen that there is no doubt that the trains have stopped running altogether, or at least they will very often be brought to a halt. In fear of getting stuck in some small station I have decided to wait until it is known how big the snowdrifts are. I shall leave when I am sure that the line is cleared. The blizzard is still blowing. With a great effort, and up to the waist in snow, I just now went out to see what the railway looked like. The line is many inches deep in snow. If it is as bad tomorrow I shall send a telegram to Moscow telling them not to wait, and to start the rehearsals without me. In any case, I shall arrive in time for the first night. . . .

Because you are not leaving Petersburg the journey abroad has been put off. If Leva and Tania get well in time they will go to Moscow and Petersburg for the performances of *Onegin* and *The Maid of Orleans*. But this is not yet certain and still vague. I had your letter today. Poor Modia! You are living through a hard time both as a human being – tied to such a cad as Konradi – and also as the author of a comedy. Authorship brings the best moments of human happiness but only at the cost of many difficulties and sufferings. I know from experience. But you must never lose heart, and write, and write, and write. I wish I knew what Outin will say. It may be that here also you will find no sympathy. But please, do not get upset. As to the situation in Moscow, believe me all will be well.

Are you coming to Moscow for the 11th? If so send me a telegram to the Conservatoire.

I kiss you and Kolichka with all my love.

P. Tchaikovsky

Eugene Onegin was first performed in Moscow on 11 January, 1881, at the Bolshoi Theatre. *The Maid of Orleans*, dedicated to Napravnik, was performed at his Benefit at St. Petersburg on 13 (not 11) February. Tchaikovsky went abroad the day after the premiere of the opera.

Modest's *The Benefactor* was performed for Maria Savina's Benefit on 6 and 9 February.

[296] TO ANATOLI TCHAIKOVSKY   Petersburg
                                                  1 February 1881

Tolia!

Modest's play will be performed on 6 February at Savina's Benefit. My opera on Wednesday 11 February. If you find you can manage both, come on Thursday evening; if this is not possible take into account that the Benefit will be repeated in the same week, and that the opera will also be performed again.

As we shall see each other soon I will not go into details. The rehearsals of the opera are getting on very well. Kamenskaia is wonderfully good. But the sets are awful! I get a bit tired at the rehearsals but this time I feel well thanks to declining all invitations and visits.

Come Anatosha! I am at present at Konradi's but he is coming back on

Wednesday and I shall probably take a room at the Europe hotel. I kiss you. Am off to see a new ballet [*Zoraiya*, by L. Minkus].

Yours

P. Tchaikovsky

[297]   TO ANATOLI TCHAIKOVSKY   Vienna
                                        16–28 February 1881

My Golubchik Anatosha!

Thanks to Nike [Litke], and in spite of feeling dreary and bored all the way, I had a wonderful journey. It was sad that I had to leave you, and I was upset that I had not kept my promise to Napravnik, and frightfully worried about the possible failure of the opera, and about all kinds of things concerning your life, Modest's, Sasha's, and Tania's. Also I missed Alesha all the time – in short, there were only disagreeable things creeping into my mind.

In general I felt as if I had committed some awful crime, and was fleeing from Russia. In spite of that the further we moved to the south the more it smelled of spring and here I found lovely spring weather. I am writing this letter with my window wide open. I am staying at the Goldenes Lamm, where I had an excellent dinner and immediately afterwards went to the opera. Weber's *Oberon* was on. What marvellous sets! One just cannot compare them with those of the Mariinsky theatre productions! The music is a bit boring but there are charming bits. I did not stay until the end but went back home. Am drinking tea as I write to you and Modia.

On the way here I read a telegram from Petersburg in the *Neue freie Presse*, saying that my opera had been produced with immense success but, in spite of that, it is bad, boring and monotonous. Abuse has already started to pursue me!

I am staying here all day tomorrow and on the morning of the day after I shall probably go on straight to Rome. I could have left tomorrow but must finish correcting an urgent proof and write a few letters. . . .

I embrace you with all my strength. Kind regards to Rubinstein and Yurgenson.

P. Tchaikovsky

[298]   TO MODEST TCHAIKOVSKY   Vienna
                                        16–28 February 1881

I do not remember ever being in such a state of spiritual depression as I was during my journey, and I am still suffering from it! It was painful for me because of my separation from all of you; because of the imaginary failure of my opera (I know this is mad but cannot help it!); because I did not keep my promise to Napravnik; because of fear of bad reviews to come; and because Vienna makes me sick. In one word, for a thousand reasons. Even now, at this

moment, I am ready to burst into tears. How stupid it all is. I waited longingly
for this trip and now have nothing in my heart but anguish and distress, as
though, having committed some awful crime, I was fleeing from Russia. This
is the best way of expressing what I feel.

Thanks to Nike I travelled in perfect comfort, and was alone all the way to
Vienna. I read Pisemsky's novel with some interest but mostly I thought, and
thought, and thought – about what disagreeable things the devil only knows.
I thought a lot about you and would have given anything to have had you and
Kolia (and my poor Lenia), here with me. We were not far from Vienna when
I bought the last number of the *Neue freie Presse* and read, in the article from
Petersburg, more or less as follows:

> Yesterday the opera, *The Maid of Orleans*, by Tchaikovsky was performed
> for the first time with great success; but it is quite obvious that the critics
> will not be as lenient as the public. The opera is very poor in respect of
> action, monotonous, and boring. Except for the 'Maid' herself it is lacking
> in characterization. The choruses are bad, and the sets miserable.

This made me even sadder. However it will all pass away by tomorrow. The
weather is lovely, and I am writing at the open window of the Goldenes Lamm,
where I am staying. After an excellent dinner I went to the opera and saw
Weber's *Oberon*. The production was fairy-like; what wonderful scenery!

I leave the day after tomorrow at seven in the morning – on the best through
train. Probably straight to Rome. I want to write many more letters. I kiss you
with love. For God's sake, write, but not a word about the opera. I embrace
you.

P. Tchaikovsky

[299] TO MODEST TCHAIKOVSKY   [Florence]
                                      19 February–3 March 1881
      Modia!

The second day of my stay in Vienna there was a terrific unexpected snow
storm which blew fiercely all day and made me more miserable than ever.
I managed to get through the day somehow and the next morning, still
pursued by the same howling storm, I left at seven in the morning.

The trains to Italy do not now go via Trieste as before but by a much shorter
route and at six o'clock in the evening I had crossed the Italian frontier. It
was such a relief to see those 'kind Italian mugs' and hear all this sort of
thing: 'Pronti, partenza che commanda, si cambia le vitture' etc. I had to
change carriages in Udine, then again in Mestre near Venice, after which
I slept, waking up an hour before reaching Florence, where I experienced a
delight which I shall not describe, to prevent you from bursting with envy.

Imagine after yesterday's snow storm a complete change of scenery. Green
fields, blue skies, and blindingly brilliant sunshine, which filled my compartment

with light and warmth after the cold and hungry night! I now feel that I really love Italy and have learned to appreciate and understand its charm.

When I came here before I used to be disappointed because the truth did not live up to my dreams. Now I felt that I had come home; but where frost still reigns, the seal of death lies on nature, and where my opera had no success (I just cannot get rid of that idea – an unnatural and morbid symptom) there I am only a passing guest. I cannot say why, but I have not taken rooms at the nice Hôtel Milan. I am at the Hôtel New York and regret it. Shall dress now and go and wander round the town, and then, in the evening leave for Rome.

I embrace you and Kolia with indescribable love.

P. Tchaikovsky

Please do not say a word about the opera.

On March 1 the Czar was returning from a military parade in St Petersburg when a bomb was thrown at his carriage by an unknown assailant. Unhurt the Czar left his carriage but as he descended a second bomb was thrown, by which he was fatally injured. He died a few hours later in the Winter Palace. The heir to the throne was the second son Alexander, whose elder brother had died in 1865. With the accession of Alexander III there was an immediate return to liberal policies.

[300] TO MODEST TCHAIKOVSKY   Rome
                                     25 February–9 March 1881

I have already had two letters from you dear Modia! The second one this morning. How well I understand your pains of authorship – that curious false shame and repentance that you write about. Be sure that all these feelings are only sick manifestations of a soul exhausted by recent excitement and agitation. They only prove that you will go on writing and travel uphill. Only half-wits without a grain of talent are always satisfied with their works, and as to Mr Nikolai Potekhin, he is completely devoid of such fine and delicate feelings.

I hope that the *Benefactor* and everything you had to experience to bring him to life will retire into a far-off past, and that two obvious truths will stand: (1) that, without any doubt, you have a real and big talent; and (2) that a budding author always makes technical mistakes and the production of your *Benefactor* has, in this respect, been a very good lesson for you. . . . All three of us must pass next winter abroad! ! !

But Rome frightens me! I lead a social life here and fear that next winter may even be worse. On the other hand, Rome is so charming and pleases my soul! . . .

I kiss you hard.

P. Tchaikovsky

During February Yurgenson, acting as a private detective, reported to Tchaikovsky that Antonina Ivanovna had had a child by one Bolkov with whom she was living in Moscow. Yurgenson urged Tchaikovsky to sue for divorce. This, however, he was not prepared to do – neither now nor at any other time in the future – being fearful, no doubt, of the revelations which might come from Antonina. He continued, at least partly, to maintain her until his death. Antonina died in a mental institution in 1917.

At this time Tchaikovsky was also disturbed at the reported deterioration in the condition of N. Rubinstein. He wrote an article on the last days of Rubinstein's life for the *Moscow News*, 1881, no. 82 (see Modest's Life of his brother II, pp. 463–5).

[301]   TO ANATOLI TCHAIKOVSKY   Nice
                                                 11–23 March 1881

My Golubchik Tolia!

I had a telegram from Yurgenson saying that Nikolai Grigorievich was very ill. I wanted to leave at once but would not have got a through train and the Kondratievs persuaded me to wait until tomorrow morning. At the same time I sent a telegram to the Grand Hotel and have just had an answer from Tretiakova, that Rubinstein's condition is hopeless. I cannot say how upsetting this news is. I have no wish to write about anything. I am perfectly well, but have started to long to get back to Russia quickly and I do not think that I shall stay long in Paris. Kondratiev and Sasha are coming with me. Will write at once from Paris.

I have prepared myself not to find Nikolai Grigorievich alive, but I still hope.

I kiss you hard.

Yours

P. Tchaikovsky

[302]   TO MODEST TCHAIKOVSKY   [Paris]
                                                 13–25 March 1881

Dear Modia!

In Nice I found out first from Yurgenson's telegram that Nikolai Grigorievich was very ill and then by means of telegrams to and from the Grand Hotel that (1) there was no hope and later (2) that he had passed away. On the next day I left Nice with Kondratiev and Sasha. The journey was a devilish nervous torture. To my great shame I have to own that I suffered not so much from the knowledge of a terrible and inconceivable loss but from the fear of seeing in a Paris hotel – the Grand Hotel of all places – the body of poor Rubinstein distorted by a fearful illness. I was afraid that by whatever efforts I tried to stop my shameful fear something would happen to me. But my fears were unfounded.

At 6 o'clock this morning the remains of Nikolai Grigorievich were taken to the Russian church and at the Grand Hotel I found only E. A. Tretiakova who was with Nikolai Grigorievich, day and night, for the last six days of his life, and she told me all about it. One consolation is that Nikolai Grigorievich did not once show any awareness of his approaching death and talked about his plans for the future to the last. He lost consciousness three hours before his death and died without agony; and so quietly that Tretiakova, whose hand he tightly clasped to the end, did not know if he was still alive. He suffered from T.B. of the bowels. According to the doctors here it was an act of madness to send him abroad.

The Service for the Dead will take place tomorrow morning. I have not yet decided when I shall leave but I think very soon. Write me at least a short letter to Berlin, Hotel St Petersburg, where I shall stay for a day about 20 March.

I kiss you hard! Am terribly anxious to see you.

P. Tchaikovsky

[303] TO ANATOLI TCHAIKOVSKY   Paris
                                               17–29 March 1881
Dear Tolichka!

You will hear from S. A. Bernar and Yurgenson all about the sorrowful days through which I have been living. Last night the body of poor Nikolai Grigorievich went to Moscow accompanied by Anton, Yurgenson, Sophia Alexeevna and Zadonskaia. Anton Rubinstein in my eyes has completely lost any right either to love or to respect. It would be hard to describe the disgusting impression he made during these last days. He is not only not at all stricken by the death of his brother but seems even to be somewhat pleased. Yurgenson, to whom I mentioned this, explains the incomprehensible fact by the jealousy and envy that Anton always felt for Nikolai.

Why, how, and what for, I do not understand. And if it is a fact, what can be more disgusting than such envy? You know that although I always valued Nikolai Grigorievich for all he had done for me, I didn't, especially of late, have any warm feeling of love towards him. Now, however, everything is forgotten but his good qualities, and there were more of these than of their opposites – not to mention his importance to society. Horror descends upon one at the thought that he is irreplaceable.

Anatosha! I am leaving with Kondratiev on Saturday the 21st of March. I shall stop off in Berlin for a day or two and then go on to Peter where I will stay for a few days. For Easter I hope to go to Kamenka. I shall probably also stay a few days in Moscow.

I have much to tell you, but we shall see each other soon. Why no letters from you? How is Sasha? How are your *affaires du coeur*?

P. Tchaikovsky

Paris
17–29 March 1881

Modia!

We shall see each other very soon; so I am not going to tell you all about the sorrowful days I had to live through. Generally speaking, this last trip has been so unsuccessful that it may possibly lessen my affection for foreign countries.

My life is going through a drastic change which will play an important part in relation to my whole future. First of all there is Rubinstein's death, which is of great significance to me; in the second place, N. F. von Meck has lost nearly all her fortune. I heard about it when I was in Moscow and wrote to ask her to tell me honestly if it were true. From her answer I see that it is. But she writes that the sum of money I receive from her is very small in comparison with her losses and she wishes to continue paying it. She asks me not to mention it again. You will understand, however, that this allowance is neither stable nor secure any longer and that, if not during this season, then in the next, I shall probably be obliged to toil again somewhere, as before. This isn't much fun.

I wrote an article about the last days of Nikolai Grigorievich for the *Moscow News* and had only just sent it when I had a note from Mme Tretiakova begging me to stop its publication. I shall have to do this by telegram. When we meet I will tell you all my latest impressions, especially of Anton Rubinstein whom I now have the full, and lawful, right to despise. A mean and nasty little soul! Good-bye, my Golubchik. Shall see each other in a week's time.

Yours

P. Tchaikovsky

Tchaikovsky, whose edition of the *Liturgy of St John Chrysostom* (Op. 41) had been published in 1878, now undertook to edit the *Vigil (Vesper) Service* (Op. 52) for Yurgenson.

[305] TO MODEST TCHAIKOVSKY

Kamenka
24 May 1881

Dear Modichka!

I have the opportunity to talk to you quite openly. Today is Sunday and as I did not feel well yesterday I have decided to do nothing today. Lately my work has consisted in getting acquainted with the 'regulations', or laws, of old church music and making choral arrangements of some ancient church melodies; those sung during a Vigil Service (e.g. as in Kamenka church). Great chaos reigns over all. Many lovers of the old want to return church music to its original purity and character. I do not know the history and alas! I have come to recognize that this is impossible. In the last century European habits have forced themselves into our church in various vulgar forms as, for example, the dominant seventh chord etc. They have sent down such deep roots, that even in the most remote corners of our land the cantors, after studying in town seminaries, sing something far removed from the original form of the music. This is written down in accordance with old rules, but the singing is much nearer to what is sung in Petersburg, at the Kazan Cathedral. Let us, for instance, take the eight original 'modes', etc. Every cantor knows them and sings the troparion appropriate to the day, the Song to the Mother of God, and the Sedalion to the appropriate 'mode'. But the most recent methods of singing only faintly remind you of those that are traditional. In respect of harmony, what comes from a choir assembled by chance (as in Kamenka) is nothing more than the most awful and vulgar conglomeration of European commonplaces.

On my part it would, I think, be merely quixotic to compose new church melodies after the manner of the old ones, as Potulov and Odoevsky do. One cannot change history. In the same way as it is impossible to resurrect the singing which Ivan the Terrible heard in the Cathedral of the Dormition in Moscow. You cannot change a contemporary congregation – in suits, frock coats, uniforms, etc., and all the women's hair styles and 'German clothes' – into Boyars, Oprichniks etc. etc. – Why am I actually telling you all this? I wanted to say only a few words but instead my letter has been turned into an introduction for my coming *Vigil Service*, set to music by P. Tchaikovsky.

I would like to remove excessive Europeanization from church music and make it more dignified, not so much according to theory but after the feeling of an artist. I am going to be an eclectic – something between Bortniansky and Potulov. But the *Vigil Service* will be much less European than my *Liturgy*. This will partly be the case because in the *Vigil* there are fewer opportunities for getting carried away and for 'composing'. In this case I shall only transcribe the prescribed service and sequence, no more – not a freely creating as an artist.

Yours

P. Tchaikovsky

[306]   TO MODEST TCHAIKOVSKY   [Kamenka]
                                                24 June 1881
                                                Sunday

For the *Vigil Service* I had to delve deep into church books (with and without music). If you only knew how difficult it is to understand it all. Each service has some unchangeable hymns and others that are changeable. Those like 'Praise the Lord' – the great Doxology or hymn of praise – do not present any difficulties but the canons, the canticles, on 'I beseech you, O Lord!' etc., have complexities that require more than a lifetime of study. I would like to transcribe at least one Canon to our Lady ('Open my lips'). Just fancy even with all the church books I have collected, I cannot find either the proper text or the proper melody. I went to Father Alexander [Tarnovich] for help, but he told me honestly that he himself is not quite sure and that he conducts the service by routine and custom without checking it with the Tupikon and the statute.

I am completely lost in this ocean of Eirmos, Sedalions, Theotokions, Troparions, Kontakions, etc. first and secondary ones, and sometimes I feel I am going off my head. When I asked Father Alexander again how his cantor manages when he sings the canon with the stichiras and how he does know what he has to read and sing (for the church has extremely exact rules about what to sing and read on particular days, in what mode and how many times); he answered: 'I don't know, before each service he looks something up in the book.' If the clergy don't know, what am I, a sinner to do?

I kiss you and Kolia with love.

P. Tchaikovsky

[307]   TO MODEST TCHAIKOVSKY   Kamenka
                                               23 August 1881

On the evening you left I had a long letter from Taneev concerning church music and also about my becoming a Professor at the Moscow Conservatoire. He insists that it is my duty to do so. This worried me so much that I hardly slept all night and when I did it was only with the help of wine. No! it is better to perish in poverty than make a stupid sacrifice. It would not be so bad if the Moscow Conservatoire was an important and indispensable establishment! Although I love it as a place to which I belonged for some time, it is really a colossal bluff created by Rubinstein's energy but on feeble and unsteady foundations. No! No! and No! ...

Modia, as soon as I think of the coming month my head goes round. Help me to decide it all. . . . I still do not know if I should go to Petersburg now or later but in any case I shall go at the end of September or the beginning of October. We could meet in Kiev and then I shall either see you off or come to Odessa and Naples with you.

Am reading the *Karamazovs* and long to finish it as soon as possible. Dostoevsky is an author of genius but I find him antipathetic. The more I read him the more he weighs me down.

I kiss you.

Yours

P. Tchaikovsky

Modest wrote on 29 August advising Piotr to refuse the post offered to him by

Taneev. Acceptance of such a post would destroy both his health and his talent, he opined. The following letter was written en route from Moscow to Kamenka. The idea of a *Romeo and Juliet* opera came to nothing, but some sketches for *Mazeppa* ('V. P. Burenin' from Pushkin) had been made during the summer. Tchaikovsky laid this project aside, to return to it in May 1882. The opera was finished in the April following.

[308] TO ANATOLI TCHAIKOVSKY   Kiev
                                                    2 October 1881

Dear Tolichka!

Having arrived in Kiev I took a room at the Grand Hotel and went at once to see the family. After staying with them a bit I went to the opera *La Juive* for half an hour and then returned home. Am writing with an awful pen. Shall finish the letter tomorrow; will tell you then why I am in such a good humour.

                                                             3 am

... I promised to tell you why I am well and happy; doubts about the fate of my *Maid of Orleans* have been like a 'sharp knife' for me during the last days in Moscow and on my journey. But the best way out of a difficulty is to start another, and on my way I thought about what subject I should choose for a new opera (I do not fancy Mazeppa, for I couldn't get enthusiastic over it), and after thinking things over I came to the conclusion that *Romeo and Juliet* would suit my capabilities best of all – an old but always young subject. I have, therefore, quite decided that I am going to write an opera on that subject. I feel that if I take enough pains it will come out well, and this has quite calmed my fears concerning all the uncertainty about the *Maid*. I shall leave tonight or, if the [Davydov] boys press me to stay, tomorrow...

I kiss you with love. Write, love to Sasha Gudim.

P. Tchaikovsky

Not a word to anyone about *Romeo and Juliet*.

As well as the edition of the *Vigil Service* Tchaikovsky was preparing a complete issue of Bortniansky's church music. He found this work boring in the extreme and when the publisher told him that it was 'good for him' retorted: 'If you imagine that I am afraid of hard work you are quite wrong. I fear *stupid* work of no artistic value that brings no benefit to whoever takes it on. If you make me transcribe 40 Bach cantatas, and prove to me that it is important for Russia then I will do it without complaining of the difficulties. . . . But for a musician capable of doing something better . . . to transcribe 40 miserable platitudes by Bortniansky is not proper.'

   Vera Davydov, Tchaikovsky's niece, was to be married to Nicholas Rimsky-Korsakov – a naval officer later to become an admiral, and a distant relative of Rimsky-Korsakov the composer.

[309] TO MODEST TCHAIKOVSKY

Kamenka
12 October 1881

Modia you bad boy!

Why don't you write? Nadezhda Filaretovna who arrived in Rome at the same
time as you did has already written, but not you! ... About myself I can say
that I do not feel in any particularly euphoric condition, but just jog along,
thinking only how to finish my work as soon as possible. Just think, in eight
days I have transcribed 20 large Bortniansky motets for two choirs. I still
have much to do but the work is getting on. I get quite numb with fatigue,
stop understanding what is said to me, and when I go to the big house I am
irritable with everybody and everything. Generally speaking, the more hours
I spend with them and the less we talk, the more I love them.

But sometimes there are delightful hours, when – putting aside the eternal,
gnawing, vague, feeling of dissatisfaction – I can contemplate the whole,
immense, spiritual beauty of these three angels. I mean, of course, Alexandra
Ivanovna [widow of Decembrist Vassily Davydov], and Lizaveta Vassilevna and
Alexandra Vassilevna [daughters of Vassily Davydov]. In that mood I want to
weep and fall at their feet. My life has a proper framework, and everything
that intrudes into it makes me furious. Vladimir Andreevich [Plessky] sometimes
comes for a chat during my working hours. How I then hate him! I do not
allow myself to think about Rome for the present. ...

I must finish my work, and go to the wedding. I shall probably have to go to
Moscow and only to Rome after that. Hope to join you about the 10th or 15th
of November. ...

P. Tchaikovsky

[310] TO ANATOLI TCHAIKOVSKY

Kamenka
25 October 1881

Anatosha!

Because we shall see each other soon, I am late with my letter. Everything is
going smoothly, with my work moving swiftly, and my health perfect. I think
that I shall have pleasant memories of the month passed here. ...

I am so tired of Bortniansky. He makes me so sick and I am so bored with
him that I just cannot occupy myself exclusively with him. (Do not tell Piotr
Ivanovich about it. He is angry that I am complaining about the hard work.)
But the arrangements are nearly ready. I have also corrected a few proofs – but
after the 1st I want to refuse this sort of work for the next two months. Not
a word to Piotr Ivanovich; I shall write to him myself.

In Kiev we shall stay with you at the Grand Hôtel. If I arrive first I will reserve
a room for you. Good-bye my Golubchik, I embrace you hard.

Good-bye.

P. Tchaikovsky

Writing to Yurgenson, Tchaikovsky thought he might be able to write 'good music, full of feeling' on the subject of D. Averkiev's *Vanka the bartender*. He did not pursue the idea but started to compose the Op. 50 trio in memory of 'a great artist [N. Rubinstein]'. The medium of violin, cello, and piano had already been proposed to Tchaikovsky by Mme von Meck.

The first performance was at the Moscow Conservatoire on the anniversary of Rubinstein's death by J. Grjymali (violin), V. Fitzenhagen (cello), and S. Taneev (piano). The notice by S. V. Flerov (pseud. Ignotus) in the *Moscow News*, 1882, no. 290, which was sent to Tchaikovsky by Taneev, gave him no pleasure at all. (See Letter 332).

[311] TO ANATOLI TCHAIKOVSKY   Venice
                                                  16–28 November 1881

Anatosha!

May I report to you that I arrived safely in Venice? The journey was terribly tiring as I had to get up at 5.00 am (afraid of being late I did not sleep all night), catch the train at 7 o'clock, and travel in a packed carriage, non-stop, till 11.30 pm. Maybe because I was so tired I was pleased to get into a gondola, and then into a bright room, surrounded by that Venetian stillness – as of the grave – which I find so attractive this time in Venice.

This morning when I got up and opened the window I found the day was beautifully clear and the air soft and sweet. After dressing I went for a walk and had lunch at that little inn where we were with you, and then wandered through the funny little narrow streets. As I passed every greengrocer's and butcher's shop – each with its own stink – I remembered how angry it made you. I went to Santa Maria dei Frari (where Titian and Canova are buried – do you remember?). Then I sat on the Piazza and enjoyed the lovely day, and the noise of the crowd which was attracted by the playing of a military band in the middle of the Square and which filled the Square.

I feel so happy and well here that I have decided to stay another day and only go to Florence tomorrow evening. I shall also stay there for two days. I have just written to Piotr Ivanovich to commission Averkiev himself, or someone else, to write a libretto for *Vanka the bartender*. I feel I could compose good music on this subject, in which there is something that attracts and excites me.

If only you could see how carefully I am spending my money! For example, all I spent today was three francs for my lunch. Tonight I will go to the circus. The dinner bell is ringing! . . .

I kiss you, regards to Sasha Gudim.

P. Tchaikovsky

[312] TO ANATOLI TCHAIKOVSKY   Rome
                                                  1–13 December 1881

My dear Anatosha!

At last, yesterday, I moved into my proper lodgings, a really cosy room where

I have my piano, a large table and two armchairs. Next to me on one side is Grisha [Sangursky's] room which also serves me as a dressing-room, and Modest and Kolia are on the other side.

I started working but in spite of having very few acquaintances, and complete freedom, I do not find enough time. Before I have started working properly luncheon is served, then we go for a walk, then dinner, then comes the evening, usually spent with the Kondratievs and then bed.

Last week there were solemn celebrations to mark the canonization of new saints. Modest managed to be present at the actual ceremony but to take advantage of the ticket he had only obtained with great difficulty, he was obliged to sit motionless from 8.00 in the morning to 3.00 in the afternoon. He came back with a headache; but had had a perfect view of the whole, curious proceedings. As for me, I only attended the High Mass on Sunday – at which the Pope was the celebrant – in honour of the new Saints. That was rather tiring too, but the procession and the entry of the Pope were magnificent and I am glad I did not miss it. These are the only out-of-the-ordinary events of these happy and peaceful days. I feel very well here. Am beginning to love Rome more and more. . . .

3–15 December

Today I managed to get free of old acquaintances and am not making any new ones. I got rid of the Bobrinskys by pretending I was ill. Also, under the same pretext, of a certain Princess Bariatinsky who was very insistent.

I kiss and love you, Golubchik.

Yours

P. Tchaikovsky

Tchaikovsky never forgave Auer for refusing to play the Violin Concerto that had been dedicated to him in the first place. Subsequently A. Brodsky, who gave the first performance in Vienna on 4 December, was the dedicatee. Because Kotek seemed influenced by Auer not to play the concerto Tchaikovsky broke their friendship, only relenting when Kotek was dying (see Letter 376f.). At this time Napravnik relinquished the conductorship of the Musical Society in Moscow to be succeeded by K. Y. Davydov, who also disliked the Violin Concerto.

[313]   TO ANATOLI TCHAIKOVSKY   Rome
                                                   12–24 December 1881

. . . I had to fight a real battle against all sorts of people, men and women, who wanted to meet me – Princess Bariatinskaia, Count Stroganov, and so on. But I am victorious and think I am free from any more such attacks. Started to work. Something like an inspiration is coming, but shy and uncertain. I am not sure of myself – not as I was before.

Anatosha, I do not think I ever told you how I live here, and I want you to know. We get up at 8.30 when tea is served; after which, while the rooms are being done, we go to the Kondratievs for his *levé* [*sic*] – I in my dressing-gown. Then I work till 12. I lunch with Nikolai Dmitrievich precisely at mid-day, Modia and Kolia having theirs later at 12.30. Then a walk. Mostly I go alone, but on Sundays we take Grisha with us and do some sight-seeing. From 4.00 to 6.00 I read, write letters, play the piano. At 6.00 we dine, but Kondratiev and I have our own separate tables. After dinner I either go for a walk or stay at home, reading, or we play a game of *vingt*. To bed at midnight but I usually read for an hour or more.

Yesterday I had a letter from Piotr Ivanovich in which he tells me of Auer's dirty trick in persuading Sauré and Kotek not to play my concerto. I was furious and with a great effort stopped myself from writing him a very rude letter.

Today is Christmas Eve here and I have just returned from St Peter's Cathedral where they had a special service with castratos singing. The day is cold and nasty. . . .

I kiss you, my dear boy, with all my love.

Yours

P. Tchaikovsky

[314] TO ANATOLI TCHAIKOVSKY   [Rome]
                                       19[–31 December] 1881

. . . I am having a queer correspondence with Kotek. He did not answer my letter, which I told you about in Kiev, but first went to Petersburg and only wrote after his return to tell me he could not play my concerto because Sauré was going to play it. I answered that, first of all, Sauré was not going to play it either, but that the whole question did not concern Sauré or the concerto at all *but* my belief in his moral integrity, and that contrary to my personal feelings, I was compelled to be very disappointed in him.

I had no answer to this letter for a long time. Then, at last, I got a very stupid one yesterday. First Kotek *explains* that he got the invitation to play it only a month before the concert and could not learn it in such a short time – he who had worked on it with me long ago – then he said, in the second half of his letter, that he could not possibly play an unknown concerto in a strange town when Sarasate was staying there. He added: 'It is like saying to someone – lend me a rouble otherwise I shall never forgive you!' To this stupid, even rude, letter I answered as he deserved! Yes! I am sorry to say that Kotek has failed me and shown his rather mean side.

As before, I correspond with Nadezhda Filaretovna once a week. She is enjoying the peace and quiet in Florence and is quite well again. Anatosha, I love and kiss you. I wonder if this letter will find you in Moscow?

Yours

P. Tchaikovsky

[315]   TO ANATOLI TCHAIKOVSKY   Rome
26 December
1881[–7 January 1882]

... I had a most interesting letter from Napravnik with all the details of the intrigues which led to his resignation. Absolutely disgusting. I am very sorry that Napravnik has left the Musical Society; for I do not for one moment believe that Davydov can be a good conductor. Meyerbeer's *The Northern Star* (in which Peter the Great is supposed to be in Finland), was on here and I went. The scenery looked like Switzerland, the people were dressed in Russian costumes, and Menshikov was selling hot pies. Funny and very silly.

Yurgenson writes that you are still paying court to Konshina. Is it true? Love and kisses to all the family.

I embrace you

P. Tchaikovsky

[316]   TO ANATOLI TCHAIKOVSKY   Rome
9–21 January 1882

Anatosha Golubchik!

For God's sake forgive me that this letter is not going to be very interesting. What is happening to me at the moment is what usually happens when I come to the end of a composition. I am finishing my trio and hope to get completely free of it tomorrow (Sunday) and take a long walk for relaxation. To this end I have been at work from 9.00 am to 4 pm, and so intensely that I cannot think properly any more. This excessive haste at the end of a composition always has a bad effect on it but I can't change my nature. As today is your day I did not want to miss it, and so that you would not worry I have forced myself to write. All is well with us. We are alone now, for all the Kondratievs have left. We missed them very much the first days, especially the charming Emma. What a delightful creature she is.

Modest has had a letter today from Alina Ivanovna's sister who lives in Algiers, imploring him to come and stay with them. As it will cost him hardly anything, and as the country is beautiful, Modest has decided to accept the invitation. Maybe I shall go with them; but, if not to Algiers, then we shall all go to Naples after the Carnival.

However, I cannot say anything for certain. I am completely engrossed in my trio, and attracted by this form of music which I have not tried before and is quite new to me. In a day or two shall start making a fair copy, and when it is ready, will send it to Moscow and you will ask Taneev to have it played. I am impatient to hear from Moscow about your stay in Kiev, although I know quite a lot from Nata's letters.

I kiss and embrace you

[no signature]

A. E. Bernard, owner and publisher of *The Novelist*, asked Tchaikovsky to write six pieces for his journal for a fee of 100 roubles each. Tchaikovsky found Yurgenson slow in answering his request that he should be permitted to do this. When he did write Yurgenson said that he wanted the pieces. (Op. 51; see Letter 326.)

[317]   TO ANATOLI TCHAIKOVSKY   Rome
                                        17–29 January 1882

I have become most diligent! My trio is finished, and am pleased with it (in my heart), and with my usual hurry am already making the fair copy. I want to finish it as quickly as possible, send it to Moscow, and find out what Taneev, Albrecht and others – all those whose opinion I value – have to say....

Nothing new here. Life is very monotonous, it could be very peaceful but for the news from Russia. I would love to accept Bernard's offer to earn 600 roubles without any effort but I fear to hurt Yurgenson's feelings. I wrote to him and said it could not possibly go against his interests. Am expecting his answer with impatience.

I kiss you with love.

Yours

P. Tchaikovsky

[318]   TO ANATOLI TCHAIKOVSKY   Rome
                                        22 January–3 February 1882

... I am now feeling wonderfully well, both mentally and physically. The reason, I think, is that the trio – which I am copying out at the moment – pleases me greatly. Later, maybe, I shall renounce it, and hate it as much as I hate most of my works. At the moment, however, I am proud of it, it satisfies me, and raises me in my own esteem. Lately I felt sure that I should not be able to compose any more and life without creative work is pretty pointless.

Here in Rome I have managed to arrange my affairs in such a way that nobody dares to invite me out, which means that I am absolutely free. But I must tell you about one curious visitor I had recently. The servant came in and told me that a Baron Schweinfurt wished to be received by me. I assured him that it must be a mistake. The servant leaves and I hear loud voices on the other side of the door. I open it and see a gentleman who looks very uncomfortable: 'Are you Mr Tchaikovsky?' he asks in French. 'I am!' – 'Are you a philanthropist?' he asks. I get confused and give him an answer: 'Yes . . . I mean no – I like philanthropy!' I mumble – quite like Kolia Peresleny. 'Oh! I know, you are the famous musician!' I get confused again and murmur something unintelligible. 'Allow me to come in,' he begs. After which he came in, said he had heard about the two brothers, the composer and the philanthropist, and wished to meet them. He made the acquaintance of Modest, and sat and sat, until, seeing that we were neither very pleased nor very hospitable, he left – with a pretty poor impression of Russian philanthropists and composers. . . .

I kiss you and embrace you, my dear.

Yours

P. Tchaikovsky

Anatoli had become engaged to Praskovia Konshina, daughter of a rich textile merchant in Moscow. She was both beautiful and charming. See Letters 321 and 322 for further particulars of the wedding. The projects discussed with Lentovsky in these letters came to nothing.

[319]   TO ANATOLI TCHAIKOVSKY   Rome
                                        7–19 February 1882

Tolia, Golubchik!

Just received your letter with the details of your engagement. I am so glad you are happy and, although I have never experienced anything like it, I think I understand what you are going through. We are all in need of special care and love which only a woman can satisfy. I sometimes get a mad desire to be petted by a woman's hands and sometimes when I meet an attractive woman, an older one, not too young, I wish I could put my head in her lap and passionately kiss her hands. I do not quite know how to express it.

When you are in a quieter mood – I mean after the wedding – read *Anna Karenina* which I have recently read with nearly fanatical enthusiasm. What you are now experiencing is so marvellously described in respect of Levin's marriage. . . .

I kiss you hard.

P. Tchaikovsky

A kalmyk was a member of a Siberian Mongolian tribe; the term was applied in general, however, to indicate someone of uncouth manners.

TO MODEST TCHAIKOVSKY

Warsaw
24 March 1882
8 in the morning

Just arrived in Warsaw. As the Moscow train will leave only at 3.00 pm I have taken a room at the Hôtel Europa and am going to start my ablutions. The journey from Vienna was not too long nor was it tiring. In spite of this I am tired; not physically, but my nerves were under a strain.

I have never been so disgusted before to have to return to my fatherland as I am now. Should this be a presentiment that I shall never be able to leave it again? The Russian porters seem to be rude kalmyks, the policemen – bears, the snub-nosed customs officers looked through my luggage with a sneer and then went to the refreshment room and nonchalantly took anything they fancied from the counter. They all made me want to do something nasty to them. Maybe, when I reach real Russia, this feeling will pass and the ability to enjoy the Russian atmosphere return. But at the moment it is repugnant. Have to travel another two days! Yes! Modia, I am ashamed to say I have lost my love for my fatherland and as I get nearer to it I have no tender feelings.

Tea has just been brought in and instead of the proper brown brew, a liquid the colour of ... came out of the teapot – disgusting! The *Golos* was brought in and as I glanced at this quintessence of Petersburgiana I felt frightened and sick! O, a hundred times sweeter Italy! You seem like a paradise to me (with the exception of Naples)! And how nice it is to think you are there. All the same, Modia, do not stay too long and remember that a journey is only pleasant when one has plenty of money. Yes! Also remember that if you travel by the express you will have *to stay the night in Vienna*; the train arrives from Italy at ten in the evening and only leaves for Russia the next morning at 11.00 am.

In Vienna I saw an excellent new production of the ballet *Der Spielmann*. There is a scene in the first act where all the rats of the town come from all directions, at the sound of an enchanted violin, and rush down into the river. A wonderful effect.

I kiss you, Modichka, and Kolia and Grisha. I often think of you. Kind regards to Mary [Kondratievna], Emma [Jenton] and Dina.

P. Tchaikovsky

TO MODEST TCHAIKOVSKY

Moscow
1 April 1882

... I am having a business meeting with Lentovsky, the agent, who wants me to write an opera for the new theatre that is being built. The subject will be either *Sadko*, the legend of the *Koromyslova Tower*, or Potekhin's *A lot of grief*. Which one is not yet decided.

Tomorrow the relations begin to arrive: Leva, Sasha, Tania, Vera, Korsakov, Malia, Niks, Kolia, Olga and many more. N. D. Kondratiev is here. I had dinner with him yesterday and went to the circus. I spend all my days in the society of merchants. Today dinner with P. M. Tretiakov.

I kiss you sweetly, Modichka, and Kolia, and Grisha.

P. Tchaikovsky

[322] TO MODEST TCHAIKOVSKY

Moscow
8 April 1882
between 2–3 at night

Modichka!

I am not writing anything about Tolia's wedding as you will know all about it from the hero and heroine of the solemn occasion. All I can say is that everything went off perfectly. I was very distressed by my official position as I had to sit at the dinner in view of everyone. But never mind, so long as it is going to be the dawn of Tolia's happy future! I continue to like Moscow. Sometimes, when it is a fine day, it seems so charming that I am ready to kiss the cobble-stones in the streets. But in spite of that, my life is very tiring. I am invited to dinner somewhere every day. I promise to come – sometimes through absentmindedness – both here and there on the same day, and feel bored everywhere unless I am with my nearest and dearest.

I have also collected a lot of new 'friends' – I mean Tolia's new relations. All these people are charming, but there are so many of them, and they all want me to come and see them, and that becomes rather complicated. No one realizes that you cannot visit hundreds of families in two weeks. Besides, so much work has accumulated that I cannot see an end to it. I shall go to Kamenka with indescribable delight. . . .

Have I told you that Lentovsky came to see me and that we are making plans for an opera he is commissioning? Nothing as yet certain but it will probably be *Sadko*. I expected him to come today to decide everything but, for some reason, he did not turn up. Kondratiev came and tried to persuade me to go with him to Peter but I am short of money and I do not really want to go. All I wish is to go to Kamenka as soon as possible and stop my disgusting life here. . . .

I kiss you hard, my Modichka! Embrace Kolia and Grisha.

Yours

P. Tchaikovsky

Kamenka
                                                                    19 May 1882

Modia, I am writing this late at night with undried tears in my eyes; do not
worry – nothing has really happened. It is only that I have finished reading
Bleak House, and I cried a little. First, because I am sorry for Lady Deadlock;
and secondly, because I was sorry to leave all these people I lived with for
two whole months (I started reading *Bleak House* on 20 March on leaving
Florence). Also thirdly, out of gratitude and kind thoughts to such a great
author as Dickens. In spite of a certain artificial way of ending his novel (this
is usually the case with him) I experienced so much pleasure from the first
to the last page that it would have been shirking my duty not to express my
deep gratitude to him on paper. And as in my diary I put only facts, not
thoughts or words, I am forced to begin my letter to you by putting down my
feelings. . . .

                                                                    21 May

. . . Modenka, I am writing bits of an opera, I mean a few scenes from
Mazeppa – those which attract me in any way. I am composing with an effort,
for, to be honest, it is impossible properly to compose a serious work like an
opera here. There is perpetual bustle and noise under my windows. My
dressing-room has been taken away from me and turned into a room for a
teacher, who is coming here in a day or two; besides, one is obliged to go
somewhere during working hours, either into the big house or the woods!
However, some of what I have done sounds good.

I kiss you hard and expect comforting news.

P. Tchaikovsky

Moscow
                                                                    15 August 1882
                                                                    2 at night

Dear Modia!

An hour ago I found your letter here at home, but the whole of my being was
in such an awful nervous state that I first had to calm down before I could
read it. Why this happens to me I do not understand. When I am asked why
I am so irritable and displeased, I start explaining but feel that somehow it
sounds all wrong. I have absolutely nothing to complain about. No one is
nasty to me; in fact, everybody is kind and respectful, and I cannot even say
that anyone bothers me. True – this morning, first Alexei Kisselev came to see
me, then Mikhail Klimenko (from Kamenka), then Vassily Ignatich. But none
of this is particularly awful. Then I went to see the Kondratievs whom I like
very much.

At a [Rimsky-] Korsakov concert I was at, everybody was angelically kind and pleasant, after which I had dinner at the Alexeevs where the food was perfect and the society charming. Tolia was there, and I played cards. I walked home and had some wine on the way.

Everything should have made me go to sleep with the feeling that a day had been happily spent, but, instead, I am suffering deeply and am more unhappy than the very least of miserable beggars. It is all because the proper life for me is in the country or abroad. Why so – God only knows, I do not; but I feel I am going out of my mind. I am sure that one day I will pass into the better world, because of this inexplicable, poisonous, torturing, awful sickness, which makes it impossible for me to stay for even one hour in our Russian Capitals without frightful anguish.

And, the more undefined it is, the less I know how to express my unreasonable sadness; the less I have a right to complain, the more I suffer. How often I conclude that all my pains and difficulties come from my extreme selfishness and egoism and from not being prepared to sacrifice anything for the sake of others, not even for the sake of my nearest and most beloved. But a consoling thought has just crossed my mind; that I would not be undergoing all these poisonous, nervous agonies of my own free will if I did not look upon it as my duty to bring pleasure not merely to myself but also to others.

However, what the devil! All I know is that although Kamenka is not very attractive and even horrid at times, I dream about my little corner there as of an indescribable bliss. Hope to leave the day after tomorrow, your letter has not consoled me, but it brought some peace. I feared misunderstanding and displeasure. I pray to God that you will be able to arrange for all of us a happy and peaceful life in Italy! Without you I cannot live there and if not there – where then?

Yours

P. Tchaikovsky

The relationship between Tchaikovsky and 'the Five' was never quite an easy one, despite the fact that from his early years Tchaikovsky had stood up for the group and campaigned to have their works played at concerts. In 1888 he was to write of his pride in being associated in a Russian Musical Society Concert with Rimsky-Korsakov (see Letter 504).

[325] TO MODEST TCHAIKOVSKY   Kamenka
                                                23 August 1882

Dear Modia!

After two days in Kiev – where every minute I felt the unending, wonderful happiness of being free, and far away from all the Moscow bustle – I arrived here the day before yesterday. . . . One of those who met me was Blumenfeld. On seeing him I made a very wry face. I came here first of all to work properly, and when I am at work every *Musicus* is in my way. As if on purpose, when I was not there nor was he, but he suddenly appeared, to spoil my pleasure, on the morning of my arrival. Well! It can't be helped! In spite of his presence I have already successfully composed the introduction to the Second Act.

Here I am human again; I live as a reasonable being ought to live, not like a log, which anyone can push about wherever they feel inclined, and bang, and hit, on its most sensitive parts. Before leaving Moscow I twice met Rimsky-Korsakov and his wife: *Ils m'ont comblé de* attentions and expressions of love and friendship. I firmly refused all their approaches and did not go to see them, nor have dinner with them at the Huberts, and am very pleased about it. Extraordinary how these 'mighty Five' always annoy me with their pretence of kindness; which, at the same time, is completely contrary to all their actions in respect of me.

It is wonderful how cosy I am in my little room and how happy I am, especially in the autumn. Only, please God, that there is good news from you, Tolia, Vera and that Blumenfeld should leave. I will then be happy to stay here for two months. I kiss you with all my love. Expecting a letter with impatience.

P. Tchaikovsky

Miss Eastwood, English governess to the Davydov boys, was well known to the translator of these letters.

[326] TO MODEST TCHAIKOVSKY   [Kamenka]
                                               30 August 1882

My dearest Modichka!

There is nothing extraordinary happening here. I lead such an orderly life that it would be impossible to say which day is which. In the mornings, tea, then a newspaper, and a chat with Miss Eastwood; then a walk round the disgusting 'big garden' and work until dinner time. After dinner another walk round the big garden and then I finish what I had no time to do in the morning. Afternoon tea at 4.00 pm. From 4.30 to 5.00 playing through what I composed in the morning. At 5.00 I go for a walk, usually towards Kossary. From 7.00–8.30 letter writing or reading, but unfortunately more letter writing as I have to correspond with different new people. I do go to the big house but not very often.

This life is very nice, only it is a pity that Kamenka is so disgusting and smelly, especially at the present moment when there is an impossible drought with strong winds and dust. It is a pity too, that for the sake of some money I accepted an order from the brothers Yurgenson to compose six piano pieces. This gets in the way of my inspiration. I have to force my music out of my head, both for the opera and the piano pieces and as a result of this perpetual effort I sleep badly, not peacefully – however, I am well as always. . . .

Yours

P. Tchaikovsky

On 14 September Tchaikovsky wrote to Mme von Meck saying how he had never before found it so difficult to compose a large scale work as *Mazeppa*. The act of composition, he said, had previously seemed entirely natural, but now it was burdensome and he feared the ebbing of his strength so that he would not be able to finish what he had set out on.

[327] TO MODEST TCHAIKOVSKY　　　　　　Kamenka
　　　　　　　　　　　　　　　　　　　　　　　10 September 1882

Modia!

It was nice reading your last letter. Although you complain that nothing is as yet ready at your place and I know what a long time the decorators take, I like to think that you are in your own little home. Actually the pleasantest form of existence is to live in Moscow in a good homely atmosphere. You will naturally retort – then why don't you do so?

Oh dear! In my case it is quite different. I have a painful love for Moscow, painful because there, more than anywhere else, I feel the inexorable passing of all that is earthly. Because I passed my best years and was very happy in Moscow, I love it best, but as all that made my life beautiful there is no more my visits are full of pain. I get the feeling that I am a visitor from another world! But you are settling in Moscow in the prime of your life and if you so desire you can become a perfectly happy person. . . .

　　　　　　　　　　　　　　　　　　　　　　　13 September

There was a short time here when under the strain of composing the opera and the piano pieces I did not feel very well. My head ached and I slept badly. Now the short pieces are ready, copied out, and sent to Yurgenson. The opera is finished and I have started the instrumentation, a job that is easier and more pleasant [than composing]. So I feel perfectly well and sleep as I have not slept for a long time. I have, in brief, given birth to a progeny and am now bringing it up.

P. Tchaikovsky

[328] TO MODEST TCHAIKOVSKY　　　　　　Kamenka
　　　　　　　　　　　　　　　　　　　　　　　18 September 1882

Modia!

You are so sweet writing as you do so often, when I, on my side, only send in return such short letters. I often wish for a heart to heart talk with you, but have been working so painfully and impatiently. I have given myself such a hard task (to write the three most important scenes of the opera and at the same time, six piano pieces which the brothers Yurgenson have commissioned), that I had practically no time to keep up my correspondence. Now, thank God, I have composed the six piano pieces and all I must do is to copy them out. I need them for the sake of money. As a result my nerves are in a bad state. So bad, for a time, that I had very painful nights.

13 September

I hoped to write a lot more, but will stop at two pages. I am flying full speed to the end of the first opera sketches, and the piano pieces are moving on. . . .

I want all my books to be bound properly and my library generally put in order. So will you, please, send me back the first volume of Shakespeare. Your money and books have arrived. . . .

I kiss you and Nikolai [Tchaikovsky].

Yours

P. Tchaikovsky

[329]   TO MODEST TCHAIKOVSKY   [Kamenka]
                                         20 September 1882

I am writing to you, Modichka, on a real autumn day. From early morning a fine rain, as fine as dust, has been falling, and the wind is howling. Last week some of the green vegetation was frozen; the rest has faded and turned yellow. The picture, in fact, is a rather sad one, but I am not at all upset. On the contrary I feel quite pleased. This is the only weather when I love Kamenka, for when it is fine I want to be somewhere else, far away. Your telegram about my health came just when I started to feel very well. Having finished both my undertakings I experienced a wonderful state of happiness, both mental and physical. I sleep well which makes me less irritable, and helps to suppress my irrational spasms of hate against everything and everybody. . . .

Have started the instrumentation of my opera. How well my introduction is going to sound (where Mazeppa is shown as furiously galloping away on horseback), I am sure that you will be pleased with it. The galloping music has been written exactly as you would have done it. Remind me, when we meet, to make you improvise on the theme of this introduction.

I have not yet thought about leaving, and shall stay as long as my patience lasts. . . .

Modia, tell Mary and Emma that I have dedicated a piano piece to each of them. Also tell Emma that I have received her charming letter and am very grateful, but beg to be allowed to answer later when I have had a proper rest after my tiring work. For the present I have decided to write only to you,

Tolia, Nadezhda Filaretovna and Alesha. For a time letter writing nearly drove me mad as I had so much correspondence to cope with. . . . I have decided to have all my books bound. I would very much like to get back the volume of Shakespeare that Kolia borrowed. Could you send it to me? . . .

How glad I am that you are working again on your *Benefactor*. I am sure that it will swim again and will be talked about. But, for God's sake finish your novel; in my opinion the novel has great qualities. . . .

P. Tchaikovsky

The Directors of the St Petersburg Opera having no dramatic soprano available required Tchaikovsky to rewrite the name part in *The Maid of Orleans* for mezzo-soprano. This, and some necessary rescoring, interrupted work on *Mazeppa* which the composer resumed with less energy than he had left off.

[330] TO ANATOLI TCHAIKOVSKY   Kamenka
                                                        3 October 1882

Anatosha, Golubchik!

Napravnik has insisted that I should make changes in the part of the Maid of Orleans. Through having transposed her part down I have to reorchestrate much of the music and all this has to be done as quickly as possible. I have, therefore, been tied to my desk from early morning to late at night and can only write a few words because I am so tired. This work bores me and makes me sick and I want to get rid of it as soon as possible. Am perfectly well. . . .

You are a funny boy. When you have nothing to complain about you start looking for trouble. Luckily I am so used to it that I only smiled when reading your letter. You have the same mania as Nikolai Vassilievich who is always perfectly well and always imagines that he is on the brink of the grave. Bless you! I embrace you with love.

P. Tchaikovsky

[331] TO MODEST TCHAIKOVSKY   Kamenka
                                                        1 October 1882

. . . Here I was orchestrating my opera and enjoying a rest after having finished composing it, my soul at ease and peace again, when suddenly, the necessity for these unhappy changes to *The Maid of Orleans* arose. I had a letter from Napravnik today, saying that I shall not only have to reorchestrate a lot of numbers but also rewrite a few; that means a mass of work, and boring work at that! To warm up a stale dinner which after sitting in the larder has started to go high – that is the right comparison for what I have to do. I am utterly disappointed in this *Maid* and am beginning to hate it as I do *Oprichnik* – but not quite so much. . . .

The weather is awful. To go for a walk one must be a hero! The wind was so keen today that there was a moment when I started crying, out of sheer anger with it. I will not be able to stay here for long, but would like to hold out at least for another month.

Recently I sent a huge letter, on three sheets, to – whom do you think? To Bishop Mikhail, Rector of the Kiev Theological Academy. I wanted to do so last year but did not have enough energy. Now it is done. The letter is to let him know how indecent it is to sing a kind of concert item instead of the pre-communion hymn. Last time I went to the Brotherhood Monastery I was deeply impressed, indeed shaken, by the beauty of the service, which cannot be compared with anything else. How disgusted I am with all the pretentious, affected singing, especially the concert-type stuff that dominates our contemporary church music.

4 October

Have no time to write at all today. Am up to my neck with *The Maid*. Sasha arrived three days ago. Everyone is well, thank God. The weather is horrid.

Good-bye. Write. I kiss you.

P.T.

[332] TO MODEST TCHAIKOVSKY   Kamenka
                                          25 October 1882

... Going to Moscow soon, but not before the beginning of November. Continue to write here until I let you know. Despite many tiresome aspects of my stay here I do not want to go away at all. As soon as the thought of leaving crosses my mind I put it away. I think it is that, however unattractive Kamenka is, it is a hundred times better to live even in a country place like this than to be a guest in any of our cities.

Judging by the article in the *Moscow News* my trio was not liked in Moscow. It is a pity that you haven't got Flerov's article about it. Nothing could be more silly. He says that my trio, in relation to Rubinstein is similar to Nemirovitch-Danchenko's reminiscences of General Skobelev. *Both are only memories. One variation is a memory of a trip to an Amusement Park out of town, another of a ball where we both went and so on. But, according to him, there is no proper sequence in the music, and so the work is not a success.*

Yours

P. Tchaikovsky

The von Meck brothers referred to below were Nikolai (father of the translator) and Alexander.

On 28 October Balakirev wrote suggesting that Tchaikovsky should write a symphonic poem on the subject of *Manfred*. He had tried this idea unsuccessfully on Berlioz in 1868 and now he supplied Tchaikovsky with his detailed programme. Anticipating that he might be asked, he said that magnificent though the subject was it did not harmonize with his own feelings, but that Tchaikovsky should 'fit it exactly'. Tchaikovsky did use the subject in 1885 (see Letter 394).

[333] TO MODEST TCHAIKOVSKY   Kamenka
                                             8 November 1882

Modichka!

I am still here in Kamenka. Actually I would like to leave but I know that everything in Moscow will be spoiled by my having to work to finish the first act, instead of, as I had hoped, being idle for a time. I shall be glad if your plan of my staying in Petersburg incognito can be arranged but I fear it will be impossible. I am a little tired of the letters I get from the brothers Meck; they both write, hoping for answers, and both are so nice and kind that it is impossible not to do so. Unfortunately writing letters becomes a real trial when I am in a hurry to finish some work.

At the moment I have a rather curious correspondence with Balakirev, which he started. He has become enthusiastic about the idea of my writing a large symphony on the subject of Manfred. I will show you the amusing letters this queer fellow writes. Kotek played my concerto in Moscow, but without much success it seems.

I kiss and embrace you.

P. Tchaikovsky

I am most curious about your Guitry.

[334] TO MODEST TCHAIKOVSKY   Moscow
                                             21 November 1882

I arrived here yesterday, my dear Modichka, without complications, but I was feeling ill, and I am still feeling poorly. . . . I am in the same room as before at Kokorev's [hotel]. I will stay here for about 10 days; first, to finish my First Act, and second, to be with Tolia for a few days at least and to see what is going on in general. Expect me, my Golubchik, in the second half of next week. Naturally I shall stay with you but if you don't want me to have miserable nights let me have a room as near as possible to you, otherwise I shall be afraid. You know very well that although I have never seen a ghost, I fear them more than anything in the world. Try to eat properly, Modia, and get fat for my arrival.

I embrace you and Kolia with all my strength. Regards to Grisha. Send one more letter here. My very kind regards to Kolia Meck.

Yours

P. Tchaikovsky

TO MODEST TCHAIKOVSKY

Moscow
8 December 1882

My dear Modichka!

I suppose you must be angry that I have not yet arrived. There were many reasons why I stayed here another week: (1) unfinished work, (2) a concert of Church Music on Friday when part of my *Vigil Service* will be sung and I want to be there, (3) the wish to hear Taneev's Overture at the Symphony Concert. Many people ask me to stay a little longer, and so on, and so on. Tolia too was another reason why I stayed longer. . . . Good-bye, my Golubchik. Do not forget that at least for three days I would like to stay incognito.

I kiss you.

P. Tchaikovsky

[336] TO LEV DAVYDOV

Petersburg
25 December 1882

My dear Levushka!

My bad health is keeping me longer in Petersburg. I have had to stay at home for several days and could not leave. As everybody thinks I have left and as I am not seeing anyone except for my nearest ones I am in consequence quite happy. The only complication is that time is being lost. . . . Please forgive me that I have not written to anyone and am not doing so. Generally speaking, I have completely lost all ability to write letters. During the last month I couldn't even force myself to write a few lines to Nadezhda Filaretovna. Oh dear! How much it goes against the grain to live in a capital! . . . Levushka! I want you to do something for me. Make Stepan look for my *yellow note-book* which I always carried about with me when I went for my walks in the summer. Nearly all my opera is in it and it is *absolutely indispensable to me.* Send it to Yurgenson, who will forward it to wherever I am going to be. I do not myself know where. Please, do this as soon as possible, for without the notebook my opera is lost. What a nuisance that Stepan did not put it in with my things, when he was packing.

I send you all my best wishes for the New Year. . .

Yours

P. Tchaikovsky

TO MODEST TCHAIKOVSKY   Berlin
                                                  30 December 1882
                                                  [–11 January 1883]

I hope that this little letter will still find you in Petersburg. Here, briefly is
what has been taking place. I adore Berlin when on my way out of Russia and
hate it on my way home. As usual, I arrived in absolute darkness. I drank tea,
ordered the stove to be lit, read the *Fremdenblatt*, and then dressed, and
wandered around for about three hours. Now I am back, and after a second
cup of tea will probably go to a museum. *Tristan and Isolde* is on at the
opera – lucky at last. I shall go, of course. Last night some movements of my
Suite were played at a concert.

It is nice being in a town where you are not quite unknown, and wonderful to
be able to go for walks without being afraid of meeting someone you know!
What luck that I am still able to enjoy the marvellous pleasure of being abroad.
I feared I would lose it as I grew older. I enjoy being abroad as much as I did
twenty years ago, when I came here for the first time. I am waiting for you,
Golubchik, with impatience. Remember, if Alexeev does not keep his promise,
all the money you need is enough to reach Paris. From there you will be my
responsibility.

Kiss Kolichka heartily.

P. Tchaikovsky

On 9 February Tchaikovsky had written to Yurgenson protesting that it was a mistake
to expect the Director of the Conservatoire to be a musician. He himself would
have liked Alexeev as Director with Albrecht as his second in command. If it would
help, he proposed, he would publish some works under Alexeev's name so that then
he could appear as a composer.

Saint-Saëns's *Henry VIII*, according to the papers, was doing well in Paris, a
circumstance that surprised Tchaikovsky. He wrote to Mme von Meck expressing his
surprise in view of what he knew of Saint-Saëns's other operas.

Having heard *Tristan* in Berlin, and having written to Mme von Meck of Wagner's
'negative merit', he found French enthusiasm for Wagner strange. A year later, on
27 February 1884, he was to revert to this, writing again to his patroness; 'There is
this passion for Wagner which has gone so far that they have become indifferent to
Berlioz, who a few years ago was the idol of the Paris concert public. All this is
something false, artificial, and devoid of serious foundations.'

[338] TO ANATOLI TCHAIKOVSKY   Paris
                                                  25 February[–9 March] 1883

. . . The opera is coming to its end, but so slowly that I sometimes lose hope
that it will ever be finished. . . .

I am most upset by the complications going on at the Conservatoire. What a pity that Alexeev obviously thinks it beneath him, or *no* help to his career to become a Director. How silly to imagine that a Director of a Conservatoire must be a musician. I find it more important that he should be a clever and active person who carries weight and has a good position. Alexeev would have made an ideal Director, but unfortunately he is aspiring to something higher.

Modia is more of a theatre-lover than I ever was at his age. I, on the contrary, have become rather indifferent and pass my evenings at home. Have not yet seen Saint-Saëns's new opera which has at last been put on this week. All Paris is talking about this performance. It was a great success. Saint-Saëns received 60,000 francs from his publisher. Although I feel and know that my *Mazeppa* is much better than Saint-Saëns's, it will not be produced anywhere but on the miserable Marinsky Theatre stage and I shall only get pennies for it.

How funny the French are. While Wagner was alive no one wanted to know him, and now all Paris is raving about him. All the concert programmes are full of his works and the excitement caused beggars description. One has to die to make Paris take notice. All the same, what a lovely city it is, and how big! Everyday I explore new, magnificent streets. To go for walks here is a great pleasure. . . .

I am sick of Paris food, have a longing for shtchy, borshch and Russian pirogs!

I kiss and embrace all three of you.

Special kiss for Pania.

Your

P. Tchaikovsky

Shtchy is cabbage soup with meat; borshch, soup with meat stock, mixed vegetables, tomatoes, and beetroot; pirogs, pie filled with cabbage or meat.

[339] TO MODEST TCHAIKOVSKY   [Paris]
                                                 7[–19] April 1883
                                                 Thursday

I think, Modichka, that I am going to write to you in the same way as I keep my diary. After seeing you off I went to the nearest café and wrote a letter to Nadezhda Filaretovna. From there I went to the Eden Concert where again I did not hear what I wanted to hear, but had a good laugh watching a stupid but extremely amusing play called *Les bottes de mon père*. After which, and having drunk two glasses of punch, I felt the urge to go for a walk and went off in the direction of the boulevards. . . . I only came home at 5 o'clock and then worked until 7.30.

Ungrateful member of mankind! I perpetually curse this work of mine, hope to have it finished, and am weighed down by it. But what would I do without it? The intense wish to return to Russia with a completely finished opera not only takes up all my time but also all my thoughts, and it is to this work (which I am sick of), that I must be grateful for living decently in such unfavourable circumstances! Had dinner at the Taverne de Londres – very good and cheap. . . .

I wanted to go to the Athénée but thought better of it. Decided to go home, read the *Bonheur des Dames*, and go early to bed.

You are now in Berlin. But still very far from Peter[sburg]! I will enjoy the thought on Saturday that you have arrived. Good-bye, many kisses to you and Kolia. I shall see you soon.

Yours

P.T.

Mme von Meck's secretary, W. A. Pachulsky, a Polish violinist of some talent but a composer of none, who was to marry Mme von Meck's daughter Julia, was something of a trial to Tchaikovsky. Mme von Meck believed that Pachulsky had a future as a composer; Tchaikovsky did not, but could only say so in veiled hints.

[340]   TO MODEST TCHAIKOVSKY   [Paris]
                                       9[–21] April 1883
                                       Saturday

Yesterday went like this. In the morning I worked in a bad humour because of the rain. I worked very long, because I was assailed by a passionate desire to finish the opera and sweeten my stay by doing so. I had dinner at the Européen and Alfred and Joseph both remembered you. Although I had a great wish to go to a theatre I decided that I must come to an end with Pachulsky and stayed all the evening at home, looking through his quite impossible musical nonsense. I upset my nerves and had no time to finish. Did not sleep all that well. Weather slightly better. Had lunch at the Boeuf à la mode, excellent and cheap. . . . Returned home at 4 o'clock and worked for two and a half hours and after writing to you I shall soon go to have dinner at the Diner de Paris. I ought to finish with Pachulsky tonight but I feel too tired and want some distraction.

All the papers are full of what happened on the boulevard yesterday. A man pulled out a revolver in a frenzy and started shooting into a crowd which was waiting for the bus at the Passage de l'Opéra. Three people were wounded. One of them, they say, is dying. The *Fils de Martial* at the Gymnase was very successful. Best of all was Sandrol who is very enthusiastically spoken of. I think of going to the Palais Royal tonight to see *Fond du Sac* or to the *Cabinet Piperlin*, or to the Summer Circus.

I kiss you and Kolia hard. While I am writing this you must already be in Peter and I am very happy at the thought.

Yours

P. Tchaikovsky

[341]   TO MODEST TCHAIKOVSKY   [Paris]
                                                 14–26 April 1883

Modichka!

I am writing this at a café on the Avenue Wagram. After dinner I had a longing to go either to our church or, at least, to be near it. I love this Service so much, and to hold the burning taper and to make tiny balls of the dripping wax after each gospel. At first I wish that the Service would go faster, and then I'm sorry it has come to an end and so on. But I was late, arriving when everybody was coming out of church, and I only heard Russian conversation. I love this day in Kamenka, especially when the weather is fine and I can watch the people coming out of church with their burning candles. . . .

I received two of your letters today and devoured them with the appetite of a shark. You made my tear glands shed several grains of salted liquid. You greatly exaggerate, Golubchik, my *soi-disant* kindness. Reading what you said about it I did not feel at all that you don't give me my due. On the contrary I do not deserve it all. My conscience is always troubling me because, what with my irritability, my habit of continual and uncalled for grumbling, and my getting angry without cause, I poison the lives of everyone around me. Even those whom I love most of all. The only excuse is that it must have a physical cause. Please, do not torture yourself by the thought that I am suffering and unhappy. I am so engrossed in my task of finishing the opera, that I could not care less where I am, as long as nothing gets in the way of my work. During the first days after you left I had several frightening moments, but now I feel better. What also makes me happy is the thought that you are with Kolia. I am quite ashamed about asking you to go and see Annette. Honestly, you should completely stop visiting people.

I forgot to tell you yesterday that two days ago I went to the Palais Royal. I was so delighted with the play *La Gifle*, which was excellently played. *Fond du sac* is very nice, and I am sorry you did not see it.

I kiss and embrace you.

P. Tchaikovsky

Last night there was a gas explosion at the Ambigu. Fourteen actors were hurt, some very badly. There was no performance.

Tchaikovsky received two commissions on account of the coronation of Alexander III: a *Solemn Coronation March* and a cantata, *Moscow*, to a libretto by A. N. Maikov.

[Paris]
18–30 April 1883
Monday 10.30 pm
Café Durand

The day before yesterday, Holy Saturday, after having written a letter to
I don't remember whom, I returned home through pouring rain at midnight
and found a telegram from General Richter waiting for me with the following
message:

> 'Votre cantate n'arrive pas, recherches n'abouttissent pas à la trouver, par
> quelle voie l'avez vous expédié, prener renseignements.'

You can imagine my despair. The cantata was sent three weeks ago and with
it the march and one act of the opera! Naturally, I thought everything was
lost. What was to be done? I rushed to the telegraph office at the Grand
Hotel to send telegrams to Richter and Osip Yurgenson, in whose name the
parcel was posted, and whom I asked to deliver everything personally to
Richter. Then I returned home and wrote an enormous and desperate letter
to Richter and that relieved my feelings somewhat.
Slept decently. At 7.00 in the morning, dear Anton, who had taken my
distress very much to heart, woke me up with another telegram from Richter:

> 'Partition trouvée à Moscou, pardon d'avoir causé inquiétude.'

Oof! What a relief and joy! But how the cantata got to Moscow I just don't
understand. Only later I remembered that P. Yurgenson had written to say
he wanted to make a copy of it. He is clearly to blame. . . .
Worked yesterday until 8 (!!!). Had a very late dinner, and as it was Easter
Sunday went to Sioud. Spent twenty francs without any pleasure.

I have an appetite only for dinners at the Diner Européen where I am at home.
The evening has become the most difficult time of the day for me.
I do not know what to do with myself as I have lost all desire to go to the
theatres; I even have an aversion to them. At last the weather today has
become more or less decent (though still not perfect). Again, as usual, I spent
the day quite pleasantly. I worked a lot but in the evening I was terribly
despondent. During the day I do not complain, think only of my work and
not much about the future; but in the evenings I start to worry, fret, and get
cross. Usually though when I am at home, in sight of my beloved bed and
anticipating a good night, I relax completely and sleep beautifully. The
mornings, thanks to your letters, are very pleasant.

Today the *Figaro* has come out with a large supplement, *Figaro Salon*, with
all the most important paintings. If I finish my work before the date of my
departure the Salon [Exhibition of pictures] will be a great source of pleasure.
What else can I say? There is nothing else worth mentioning. As to starting
to talk about what is occupying my thoughts, and what I think about when
I am not busy, here too, there is nothing new to say. You know very well the
nature of my thoughts.

Yesterday I read two more short stories by Maupassant and am completely enchanted by him. I did not like Sarah Bernhardt in a miming part. Brandukov has enjoyed great success.

That is all. Good-bye Golubchik! Continue to write often – it is a great consolation and joy for me.

P. Tchaikovsky

Guy de Maupassant's recently published *Mlle Fifi* gave especial pleasure to Tchaikovsky. While in Paris he visited the Salon several times, usually ending his visits complaining that there was too much to see. He complained also of 'the ordinary, vulgar French stuff' which he saw one night at the *Gymnase* in a play called *Le père de Martial*, in which Marais, Sandrock and Pasca starred. Of these only the first gave any sort of pleasure to Tchaikovsky.

343] TO MODEST TCHAIKOVSKY   Paris
                                     20 April [–2 May] 1883

This morning I was disappointed not having a letter from my dear Modichka, but after lunch I got two – no less – about the events of Good Friday and Saturday. You will never believe what a pleasure it is to get letters every day from you, especially in the morning. Yesterday – Tuesday – the weather was decent. I worked as usual, and so intensely, that I only left home at 1 o'clock. . . . Returning on foot very late, I worked until 8.30 and had dinner at the Russian Restaurant, but for some reason I felt slightly sick and scarcely ate at all.

At first I wanted to take a stroll and go home, but passing by the Vaudeville I suddenly thought, why not see the *Tête de linotte*. I went in and liked it. Very funny and talented, a farce, based on the usual theme of bourgeois adultery, but with new situations and treated with perspicacity. The scene on the stairs was most amusing. It was excellently acted. The charming Legault is particularly good and Mr Corbin (a very young actor, you remember in *Fedora* he played an attaché) is also good. There is nothing new. Do not be sorry for me, Modia, for thanks to my work I am quite all right, and only the evenings are tedious.

Oh, yes! I nearly forgot to tell you. I went to the Exhibition of Portraits at the Académie des Beaux Arts today. Very interesting and much to my taste. Am writing this at home. It is 7.15 now, and I am off to dinner. Then I want to go to the Hippodrome.

I kiss you both hard.

P. Tchaikovsky

While staying at Anatoli's dacha at Podushkino, near Moscow, Tchaikovsky was correcting the proofs of *Mazeppa*, and sketching the Second Suite (Op. 53). This work was completed in score on 13 October and was dedicated to Anatoli's wife. Tatiana Anatolievna, Anatoli's daughter, was born in 1883. She was variously known as 'Tota' or 'Tatochka'. She married a Baltic-German nobleman, Baron Ungernsternberg, by whom she had two daughters. After his death she married a Mr Warren-Cross and in her later life lived in the south of France.

[344] TO MODEST TCHAIKOVSKY

Podushkino
3 July 1883
12 midnight

It is extraordinary how badly I organize my time. I thought that all this summer I was going to live happily and have time to read, write letters, and go for walks. But, suddenly, I realized that from morning till night I torture myself with the thought that I have not time enough for all I want to do. That, clearly, is why I do not enjoy Podushkino as I should and as I expected. For example, I never find sufficient time to write letters, and have never written so few.

Proof corrections are killing me. Yurgenson is getting more and more slack with his publications, which are bad, and I often get angry with him, and am sorry that I have not given my works to a foreign publisher. Besides all this, in spite of having a rest from composition, I suddenly decided to write a Suite. However, I have no inspiration, and every day start something and then am disappointed. I begin to fear that I cannot compose any more, and am tortured by the thought that I force things, instead of waiting for inspiration, which results in perpetual dissatisfaction with myself.

And yet everything here is perfect for enjoyment. Excellent weather; the society of Tolia and Parasha; Tania who is getting sweeter every day; and last but not least Alesha, who is so marvellously sweet and attentive to all my wishes, that I find no words to say how much pleasure his presence gives me. However, I fear to spoil my sleep, and shall finish tomorrow.

4 July

I have now been in Podushkino, without leaving it, for two weeks, but tomorrow I go to Moscow to celebrate the birthday of Piotr Ivanovich. For God's sake, Modichka, do not be angry that I write so little and so unattractively. Somehow I can't write. Today I sat for several hours correcting and am quite exhausted. Please, if any letters from Elisaveta Mikhailovna arrive send them to me. I do not know anything about Tania. I haven't so much as a penny and as yet have no idea where to find money for my trip.

On the whole I have nothing much to report. Everything here is in order. Am most delighted with and full of enthusiasm for charming little Tania.

I kiss you lovingly and Kolichka.

P. Tchaikovsky

I have again missed a day set aside for writing to you. I was prevented by going to Moscow, whence Kondratiev was insistent with invitations to me to come. I passed a very boring evening there, and a bad night (no sleep, as I was eaten by flies, fleas, and mosquitos); the next day (I mean yesterday), I was very pleased to return to Podushkino. Guests pursue us here. Not a day passes without someone appearing; either Soldatenkov and wife, or Vintulov, or the Perfilievs with mother, or Kolia and Sasha von Meck, or Pania's relatives. Tomorrow her father is celebrating his Name Day here. They are expecting all the family, and an enormous dinner, etc. But I do not complain. When there are no visitors it is delightful.

The proof corrections are torturing me, Modichka, and I even suffer from insomnia. I have developed a sickening fear of mistakes and misprints in my works. All three sets of proof corrections I am doing myself, and with the greatest haste, to have them finished at the beginning of August so as to get away. Do not expect me before 10 August. I would like to go to Kamenka – I mean Verbovka – after staying with you. What do you think about it? I will have some money.

Everything as usual here. How mad I was to expect that I would be able to rest this summer. This correcting business is worse than hard labour. I read nothing but the *Archives* and *Old Times* etc. My plans to study English, play unknown works by Mozart and such like, have been postponed.

When will I be able to live a free life, for the benefit and the broadening of my limited knowledge and horizon? I envy you that you find time to read so much and so well, and it pleases me that you are writing your novel. Write, Modichka, as much as you can to finish it without fail. You are wrong not to send me your *Benefactor*. You cannot be your own judge. I would have given it here to competent critics to read, and I am sure they would have advised to publish it. I kiss you. Forgive that I do not write more. Deep in corrections.

Yours

P. Tchaikovsky

Tchaikovsky had expected money and not a diamond ring from the Czar in consideration of his services in connection with the Coronation. This was altogether a gloomy period. Tired with *Mazeppa*, angry with the Czar, distressed at his loss, he felt at the end of his tether when he realized how much he was being exploited by his publisher. In July of that year there was an earthquake on Ischia in which more than 3,000 people lost their lives.

Moscow
26 July 1883

My dear Modia!

A tragi-comedy story has developed over the Emperor's present to me. When
it arrived I was a little disappointed, for instead of the money I had hoped for
it was a ring with a large diamond. Afterwards, however, I was glad to have it
and wanted to keep it. But when I arrived in Moscow I decided to pawn it
for a short time, hoping that Yurgenson would find a way to sell it for a good
price later. The official pawn office gave 375 roubles for it. With my wallet in
my pocket I went off to Zverev's name-day dinner and was there all day. But
in the evening when I came back to Yurgenson's for the night my wallet had
disappeared. A search proved fruitless and I was left with nothing.

A frightful disappointment, but I console myself with the thought that it is
better to lose a wallet with a lot of money in it than be on the Isle of Ischia
during an earthquake, or even worse to know that one of your beloved ones
had been hurt there. Only one thing worries me; and that is, what sort of
impression this loss will make in Podushkino? Alesha, I know will be
inconsolable. Am off to Podushkino now.

I stayed two days in the country with Albrecht then came here yesterday,
and this morning am off to Podushkino until I leave for Grankino. How I shall
manage for money for the journey I do not know, but I will have to manage
somehow. It will seem strange to you that I have no special reason for giving
you the following bad news. This is what happened: as I had two hours free
before catching the train I went to see Yurgenson to kill time. He found
nothing better to do than to give me my cheque then.

You know I never dispute what I get from him and up till now have always
been satisfied with the amount. How great was my astonishment, then, when
I saw that he had paid me only 1,000 roubles for *Mazeppa*!!! I had 1,500 for
The Maid of Orleans. Since then four years have passed, I have saved at least
400 roubles for him by doing the piano score and proof corrections myself;
my costs have risen and suddenly he gives me such a miserable sum for my
work. I was disgusted and could say nothing, and to prevent myself from
being rude and also to keep face said I wanted to write to you, asked for
paper, and am writing.

Forgive me, Golubchik, that I had to vent my disappointment in a letter to
you. I must pour out my troubles, even if they are only financial ones, into
your brotherly heart. I simply cannot understand where my wallet vanished
to yesterday. Up till now I have never lost a large sum of money and just
cannot understand how it could have happened. . . .

Good-bye, my Golubchik, I embrace you with love.

Yours

P. Tchaikovsky

TO MODEST TCHAIKOVSKY   Podushkino
                                                         10 August 1883

... I have finished the proofs and when you pass through Moscow I shall give
you a copy of *Mazeppa*. Yesterday I was invited to a conference about the
production with the directors of the Bolshoi Theatre at 2 o'clock. The directors,
scenery and dress designers (including the artist Sokolov who knows you), the
conductor, the chorus-master, and others, were all there. The enthusiasm and
help which is forthcoming in respect of the production of my opera (without
any effort on my side), is beyond comprehension. I have been told that the
Petersburg directors have sent the scene-painter Bocharov to Little Russia
[Ukraine] ... to study the effects of the moon and other details needed for
staging *Mazeppa*. 'What does this dream mean?' Could it be that the Emperor
commanded that I must be helped? Yesterday everyone behaved as if I were
doing them a favour by giving them my opera.

Instead of resting I am deep in the composition of my Suite. What a beastly
nature I have. I just cannot live idle even for a few days.

Everything is lovely here. It is beginning to smell of autumn, the days are
beautiful, and there are heaps of mushrooms, more than even the oldest
inhabitants remember seeing before. Expecting a letter from you to know
where we are going to meet – here or in Verbovka. Recently I had such a
migraine that I thought I was going to die. But after falling into a deathlike
sleep, without undressing, I woke up quite recovered. My love to all.

Yours

P. Tchaikovsky

TO MODEST TCHAIKOVSKY   [Podushkino]
                                                         12 August 1883

... In my letter of yesterday to Kamenka, which I hope will be forwarded
to you, I told you about all the good fortune attending my opera. I have
finished the proofs and, 'full steam ahead', am writing a Suite for orchestra.
All the necessary steps have been taken for the ring to be returned to me but
I shall not be able to get it back from the pawn shop for three months. I have
long ago reconciled myself to the loss of the 400 roubles.

With Yurgenson I have dealt as follows: I wrote him a letter and said kindly,
but very firmly, that my opera is not worth 1,000 roubles but at least 10,000.
However, because of his limited capital, I shall not ask for this sum but insist
that he pays 2,000 roubles for the rights in the property, 300 for the piano
score, 100 for the proof correcting, total – 2,400. He answered at once to say
that he was in complete agreement. We have met several times since then and
our relationship seems to be as before. But I know that I cannot forget that
he wanted to take advantage of my irresponsibility, and that I have never

listened to the warning of all those people who said that he was exploiting me.

I am sorry and feel unhappy that I did not come to Grankino. Forgive me, Modichka, but circumstances are to blame. How I wish you could come soon.

I kiss both of you.

P. Tchaikovsky

Tchaikovsky wrote to Napravnik on 31 August expressing his displeasure at the way the singers had been chosen for *Mazeppa*. He asked for the production of *Mazeppa* to be postponed. On 5 September Napravnik wrote that the composer's wishes would be respected as far as possible, but, he asked somewhat ironically, 'Why do you think that the success of the opera depends almost exclusively on the performers.'

[349]   TO MODEST TCHAIKOVSKY   Verbovka
                                                 10 September 1883
Modichka!

I am completely in tune with the life of Verbovka and on the whole find it most agreeable.

                                                 12 September

Between ourselves Napravnik was very offended by my letter and answered rather sharply, but at the same time is trying hard to persuade me not to ask the direction to postpone the production. A new singer, who is soon to have her debut, is promised to take Maria's part, while the part of Orlik is being given to Stravinsky, who was my choice. At his request I have distributed the parts. He says the choruses have already been learned.

In Kiev I bought Glazounov's quartet and am pleasantly surprised. In spite of imitating [Rimsky-] Korsakov, in spite of an irritating habit of not developing his themes but confining himself to repeating it in a thousand different ways, in spite of neglecting the melody and chasing solely after harmonic curiosities, one senses real talent. The form is so fluent that I have a feeling his teacher must have helped. I advise you to buy a piano duet version of it and play it either with Alina or someone else. I have also bought *The Prisoner of the Caucasus* [*Kavkazski Plennik*]. This is very poor, feeble, childishly naïve, and it is extraordinary that a critic who fought against routine all his life has written a shamefully routine opera at the end of his career.

Work on my Suite, heaps of reading – literary and musical, sometimes a game of vingt, walks, chats with the girls and Nata; all this fills my life here delightfully. I am very happy. The only pity is that because of the drought nature is in a miserable way.

I kiss you and dear Nikolasha with all my love.

P. Tchaikovsky

Verbovka
19 September 1883

... I am happy here, and honestly Modichka, the nicest sort of life is in the country – the real country, far away from the capitals. The instrumentation of the Suite gives me great pleasure. I feel it will be charming. My walks are delightful, especially as these last few days the weather has been so perfect as to beggar description. Have plenty to read. In the evenings I look through and read the *Géographie universelle* of Reclus which Anna gives me, a part at a time. I have finished two of these. Plenty of interesting items. How wonderful a child's charm is. At first I had to force myself to like Rina but gradually I got used to her and now, less than two weeks later, I nearly adore her and find her quite nice looking, whereas at first she almost repelled me. ...

After which, good-bye, Modichka. I embrace you and Kolia from the bottom of my heart.

P. Tchaikovsky

Irina (Rina) the daughter of Vera Rimsky-Korsakov (née Davydova) and Admiral Rimsky-Korsakov, became Mrs Mishtov, and emigrated to the U.S.A.

To the end of the year the family letters concerned only family matters. The Suite was duly completed on 17 October, after which Tchaikovsky concentrated his attention on the *Sixteen Songs for Children* (Op. 54).

At the beginning of 1884 Tchaikovsky was looking forward to the production of *Mazeppa* both in Moscow and St Petersburg. He was pleased at the attitude of the new director of the Moscow Opera, Vsevoloisky, who admired Tchaikovsky's music. He was, however, less than pleased with the government officials who had turned down a request (backed by the theatre administration) for *Mazeppa* to be regarded as a four-act work and the composer paid accordingly. The officials decreed that it contained three acts and that the composer must, therefore, be paid according to precedent – by the exact number of acts. A second request, backed by the threat of withdrawal of the opera, brought a concession and the composer was informed that the royalties of 10% which he had previously asked for would be forthcoming.

The first performance of *Mazeppa* was in the Bolshoi Theatre, Moscow, on 3 February. Four days later the St Petersburg premiere took place. Fearing that the excitement would be too much Tchaikovsky did not go to this, but went abroad once more. Modest gave a good report of the performance in a telegram, but somewhat exaggerated the success of the work in order not to depress his brother.

Tchaikovsky had been in St Petersburg some weeks before when Anna Lvovna Davydova – his niece – married Nikolai (Kolia) Karlovich von Meck. (These were the parents of the translator.) Mme von Meck (mother of the bridegroom) did not attend the wedding.

Moscow
Monday
16 January 1884
11 o'clock pm

Just a few words to you, Modia, because I want to feel you near me. On my
return here I found a paper from the theatre office which upset me slightly.
I was informed that, according to the report made to the Minister of the
Imperial Court, my request, that I should be paid for three Acts of *Mazeppa*
what I should have been paid for four, was refused. 'His Excellency has given
orders that the petition shall not be entertained.' It was, in fact, on the advice
of the Administration here that I did put in my request, basing it on the
length of the opera, which – although only in three Acts – continues all the
evening, as one in four Acts, and which accordingly should be worth more.
With my everlasting habit of exaggerating everything I was terribly offended,
and wanted to withdraw the opera and have a row; but I was persuaded to
wait until the next morning and after a good night I cooled down. However, I
did write to Vsevoloisky [on 14 January, letter now in Klin Museum] protesting
at the despicable way in which I had been treated.

Rehearsals for *Mazeppa* began yesterday, and I have been at the theatre from
2–4 pm these last two days, accompanying the soloists. The singers know
their parts and show plenty of good will. Because I feel absolutely tired out
I realize that I will not be able to do this all over again and will probably not
go to Petersburg. But – not a word about it to anyone. Laroche's wife Ekaterina
Ivanovna has suddenly arrived with all her children and Laroche seems to be
quite pleased about it. *He has not been so much as once to the Conservatoire
and continues to sleep.* I am attacked by composers. This morning Simon played
his compositions, and after the rehearsal and until 6.30 pm Neitzel played his
opera. I am very tired and have decided, after dining at a pub, to go for a walk.
After that I'll go home and early to bed. Yesterday evening Grjymali gave a
party where quartets by Glazounov, Taneev and Davydov were played. The
last one I liked very much.

Mazeppa is to be given on the 29th but I doubt if it will be ready. Do not come
unless I telegraph. . . .

I kiss you hard.

P. Tchaikovsky

[Moscow]
20 January 1884

Modia!

Yesterday Bakhmetiev came to see Tolia with this answer. Both he and Yuriev
did want your *Benefactor* to be published, and wavered for a long time before
refusing.

Yuriev, on principle, does not publish dramas and comedies and less than a month ago he refused to publish Tchaev's *Shuisky* in *Russian Thoughts* although Tchaev is a friend of his. However Yuriev is very pleased by your articles and asks you to write monthly articles on artistic subjects without worrying that the paper comes out in Moscow. Bakhmetiev several times repeated that they seriously hope that you will and they will be grateful, for they are in need of such articles. Answer yes or no to Nikolai Nikolaievich Bakhmetiev of the editorial department of *Russian Thoughts*.

The opera will not be put on before the beginning of February.

I kiss you hard.

Please give the enclosed note to Nata[lia Plesskaia].

P.T.

[353] TO MODEST TCHAIKOVSKY   [Moscow]
                                                 24 January 1884

Modichka!

To your three questions I answer as follows. (1) I went to see Nikolai as promised, as soon as I returned from Petersburg, and at the appointed time; but he was out, and after waiting for more than an hour I returned home. (2) I have read *Mon frère Ives* on the way here. I give the author his due; he has great talent but I find the book sombre and even the happy solution of all the misfortunes did not help. It is sad, but original, new, and to the point. (3) I have already written about your *Benefactor* and the offer to write monthly articles.

The second orchestral rehearsal takes place today. Everything seems to be getting on quite well and I suffer from no disillusionment, as in the case of my earlier operas. Yesterday I saw Vera at Tolia's. I have just had an invitation from Petersburg to come at once to the rehearsals of *Mazeppa*. I answered that I can't and asked them to act as if I were not in Russia.

I kiss you with love.

Mazeppa will not be put on before the end of next week.

Yours

P.T.

[354] TO MODEST TCHAIKOVSKY   Berlin
                                                 7 February 1884

What a boring journey and how tiring! State of mind very dreary, especially the first day. I was sorry to leave all those whom I had to; solitude frightened me somewhat, and on the last day I was assailed by fears for *Mazeppa* in

Petersburg. Your telegram, that was waiting for me, was an act of great kindness. This morning I couldn't at first make up my mind where to go and then decided on Paris.

I want to know where Kolia and Anna von Meck are, and if they are in Italy I shall join them. For I feel that in the state I am in at present I should not be alone. The feeling of being abroad is not as strong as before. Oh! If only you or Alesha were with me. I want to go by sea from Naples to Odessa, and then on to Kamenka. Then in May to Paris, after which to Petersburg to fetch you. Well, we shall see! Write to Paris to the Hôtel Richepanse. I kiss and embrace you from the bottom of my soul.

Yours

P. Tchaikovsky

[355]   TO MODEST TCHAIKOVSKY   Paris
                                        13–25 February 1884

Modia!

I am not enjoying Paris very much. To tell the truth, not at all. The weather is bad, and there is no freedom, for the Golitzins have appropriated me and Massalitinov with them. Two days running I had to have dinner with them, then go to the theatre and visit all sorts of people. . . .

Let me tell you about the theatres, to which I have been three times. (1) At the Palais Royal where I saw *Ma Camarade*, with Daubray, Raymond, and Réjane, in the principal roles. A very amusing play but I was not in the humour to stay to the end and left early. Daubray as usual I found slightly antipathetic but he was good, and our Raymond above all criticism. Réjane so-so. (2) I expected more from *Manon Lescaut*. Very charming, well finished, but without one touching or impressive moment. The performance and scenery were as you can only find them in Paris. Golitzin and Massalitinov interfered all the time, by pointing to this and that, attracting my attention to the significant moments, and passing remarks on the music. What a lovely voice Heilbran has. As to the production it is not all that rich, but clever, and genuinely tasteful. I was envious. But Massenet himself was not up to the mark. He is beginning to get colourless, and boring, in spite of much effort and very fine work from beginning to end. As he dislikes dialogues the music never stops – not even for a minute – and in the end it gets tiring. Thanks to plenty of Talazak's deep notes and effective endings the success was enormous. (3) I went to the Comédie for the third time yesterday. They gave *Etourdi* (with Coquelin) and *Le Malade imaginaire* with a parade of the whole company. This gave me tremendous pleasure.

I was expecting your letter about *Mazeppa* with considerable, if secret, apprehension. At last, two days ago, I received and opened it, expecting it to be very disagreeable. But quite to the contrary. Thank you, my Golubchik

Modichka! Not much money! I wonder if I ought to go to Italy? I think I will, all the same. Shall let you know in time.

I kiss you and Kolia.

P. Tchaikovsky

[356] TO MODEST TCHAIKOVSKY Paris
18[–30] February 1884

Modichka!

I can imagine how difficult it was for you to lie about the *grand succès* of *Mazeppa* in Petersburg. All the same, it was a good thing you did. I could have been killed by the truth if I had not been partly prepared by some signs and hints in Emma's letter to Tania. I only found out everything from Yurgenson's letters (who was cruel enough not only to tell me the truth, but to *reproach* me for not going to Petersburg). I do not know how I lived through yesterday. The news was like a thunder-clap, and I suffered grievously all day as though some awful, irrevocable, enormous calamity had taken place. As usual there is a great deal of exaggeration, but – to be truthful – at my age, when it is difficult to hope for the future, every failure – even relative failure – appears as a shameful fiasco. And the shame is that if I had been a different person and had gone to Petersburg, I would have left crowned with laurels. Today I feel calmer but still cannot eat. How I needed you at my side yesterday and I still do today. I wished I could fly to you in Petersburg so much that it hurt.

Anton Rubinstein is here and I am terrified that, as is likely, he will find out that I am here too. Mostly I live as if on red-hot coals, maintaining my solitude at the expense of a great effort. I had many plans; to go to Spain for a little while, or London, or at least to Brussels, for some distraction. But it looks as if nothing will come out of it all. *La joie de vivre* is disgusting, tendentious, and affected, but there is something near to genius in the way Lazar is portrayed. Several times I was struck by the truth of some details, very familiar to me from experience but never before described by anyone.

Yours

P. Tchaikovsky

[357] TO MODEST TCHAIKOVSKY Paris
23 February 1884

Modichka!

How are you? Still a little in the dumps? As for me I am quite calm again and finishing my days in Paris quite nicely. The weather has been perfect for some time. I again went to the Comédie to see *Les maucroix* and *L'école des femmes*.

The first play is excessively vulgar, and I cannot understand how it got into that theatre. The second, on the other hand, with Got in the main part, delighted me. I also saw the new *jeune premier*, Lamary (whom you must remember), in it. He is very good looking, but not attractive as an actor – at least his voice is not. . . .

My plans are as follows: to stay in Kamenka until the lilies of the valley are out; to go to Moscow and Petersburg in May; to stay with Tolia in June, and the rest of the summer with you. . . . Have you finished your article for *Russian Thoughts*? Are you thinking about a comedy? Will you finish your novel? Send your answer to all this to Kamenka. . . .

I think I am going to write a symphony in Kamenka. Golubchik, I kiss and embrace you and Kolia. I will not see you for a long time!

Yours

P. Tchaikovsky

[358]   TO MODEST TCHAIKOVSKY   Moscow
                                                 the night from
                                                 24–25 March 1884

Modichka!

You will have a perfect right to be angry at my silence. I really had no time, for, from the very first day here, I started making alterations to *Mazeppa* and sat working from morning till night. I hope to finish in a day or two. I now live one floor higher, in a nice room, and – thanks to Alesha – comfortable and cosy. Moscow, this time, seems to me particularly dismal, and the weather is awful. Up to now one drives in sledges through impossible slush and deep holes. I go to see Tolia nearly every day, and have played vingt about four times. On the whole here too I am being torn to pieces but not as much as in Petersburg. I found Laroche in a state of final and complete decline. He never turns up at the Conservatoire and there is talk of dismissing him. What else can they do? As usual he never leaves me, but has become madly jealous and is easily offended.

I went to two concerts, neither of them without interest: (1) Shostakovsky concert where the overture by the critic Ivanov, who conducted, was played. Laroche and I tried hard not to laugh at the composition and his odd way of conducting it. (2) A concert by Ziloty, who has just returned from abroad, and is much talked about. He is being ranked with d'Albert but I find the latter much more wonderful.

Next week Tolia is joining Leva and they are going to have a look at an estate in Volinia. I have not quite decided whether to go with them or to stay here, where I have been asked to spend Holy Week and to greet Easter.

It is wonderful how clever Alesha is at making my life beautiful. Having arrived here I started to look for a house in the country and have had quite a few offers, but I suddenly realized that to buy property one needs money and I have none. So I stopped taking any further steps in this direction. Write, my Golubchik, to Kamenka. . . .

Good-bye, Golubchik, I kiss you both as I love you!

P. Tchaikovsky

Tchaikovsky also wrote to Taneev on 1 April. 'The production,' he observed, 'was really rich. The acting impressed everybody by its assurance, the ensemble was perfect and I swam in delight at Mozart's music. I must add that I did not know *The Magic Flute* very well, and for that reason loved it less than the other operas of Mozart, and am glad that thanks to this production this opera has become one of my favourites.'

[359] TO MODEST TCHAIKOVSKY   Moscow
                                                            1 April 1884

You will be astonished to see that I am still in Moscow, Modichka! I did not leave because they won't let me. Life here is impossibly tiresome, because as usual I am torn to shreds, and this has grown out of all proportion. I do nothing, read nothing, do not enjoy the spring as I should, lead a silly life, make enemies, and offend people by not going to see them. But this is not worth talking about! I must mention one event of interest: that is, the big musical evening at the Tretiakovs which was both official and festive. Then there were an evening at the Kapnists and the very successful performance at the Conservatoire. They produced *The Magic Flute* and it was excellent – a rich production.

I hope to leave on Wednesday this week. What a shame that I cannot pass this lovely springtime somewhere in the country! Yesterday there was an enthusiastic letter from Taneev who went off to commune with spring in complete isolation on the Maslov estate. How envious I felt!

I have a request to you, Modia! Go and find out what sort of dacha it is near the Mstinsky Bridge, that is mentioned . . . in this advertisement? Sounds attractive. Find out the price. But answer to Kamenka. Am off to the photographer Kanarsky to have a photograph taken. He pestered me so much that I couldn't refuse.

I embrace you and kiss you and Kolia hard.

P. Tchaikovsky

The cathedral square is in the middle of the Kremlin. There are to be found the Cathedral of the Dormition, the Cathedral of the Annunciation, and the Cathedral of St Saviour. The dedication of the first of these (in which the Czars were crowned) symbolizes the Orthodox doctrine that the Virgin Mary did not ascend into Heaven, but went peacefully to sleep and that Christ came to fetch her soul (hence the Feast of the Dormition, or 'falling asleep').

On Wednesday of Holy Week, according to tradition, the ceremony of anointing the chrism took place in the cathedral courtyard of the Kremlin. This was in public, on a high rostrum where there were huge cauldrons in which the oil was boiled before an assembly of bishops and then despatched to churches all over Russia. On 'Great' Thursday the Metropolitan and other bishops enacted the ceremony of the 'Washing of Feet'. On Good Friday the Shroud was brought out into the middle of the church, and in the evening of that day there was the service of Lamentation to commemorate the Entombment of Christ. The Shroud had a figure of Christ painted or embroidered on it, and also figures of the Virgin Mary and one or two of the Apostles. It was carried back into the altar before the midnight Easter service.

[360] TO MODEST TCHAIKOVSKY   Kamenka
                                                   12 April 1884

My dear Modichka!

I was greatly disappointed to find only one letter from you here. I expected to find quite a few. However, even this solitary specimen is very interesting. I am glad that the comedy is being written. I think there is no need to fear the impression that evil, depicted in strong colours in the first act, could make, so long as you do not accumulate evil as the play goes on. Write, for God's sake do write!

My last days in Moscow would have been very pleasant if it had not been for hundreds of roubles flying out of my wallet in different directions. I went to the Kremlin to watch the boiling of the oil of anointment, then to the Service at the Cathedral of the Dormition, to St Saviour's Cathedral for the short Vespers of Easter Day, and to many other church services. Everywhere I got a moving impression of beauty and grace; but unfortunately these feelings were always vitiated and sometimes almost entirely removed by the services being much too long, much too extended. This took the edge off the most sincere impulses. If our Orthodox Services need reform that is where a start must be made. One must not forget that in addition to people like the Pobedonoszevs and Shakhovskys there are simple people present, who must get weary listening to so much reading and singing. . . .

Good-bye for the present. Shall write again soon. I kiss you both from the bottom of my soul.

Yours

P. Tchaikovsky

Kamenka
                                                                18 April 1884

I had such a longing for you, my dear Modia, and wished so much to be on
the Fontanka on one of your 'thrones' with you and Kolia in the peace and
quiet of the after dinner hours. However, in spite of this sort of passing mood
I am, up till now, extremely pleased with my stay in Kamenka and have such
peace of mind and physical well being that could not be improved on. The
weather is foul, and one cannot describe one's fury at this cold, never-ending,
howling wind. The trees are still quite bare, and the violets are coming into
flower with difficulty; but little blue flowers which smell like the breath of a
baby's mouth have appeared. But it is still a long way from real spring.
However, it is warmer today and there is at last some hope of a change for
the better.

I have not yet started to work but out walking I make notes of a few ideas
that spring up. But they are a bit watery and insignificant, and on the whole
I am in a period in which I mistrust my creative powers. However, even if this
is true it does not worry me too much. I have done enough, and it is not
surprising that I have become a little stale. I have dinner and supper with
Leva, while for the rest of the time I go for walks, read, and study English
most zealously, and also visit the big house as well as others. I am very
pleased with the English paper Miss Eastwood told me to get. As to reading,
there is plenty of material available, for as well as the books purchased
previously and still unread, I have all the numbers of the *Russian Archives* and
Historical Annals so far published this year. In the evenings we play vingt, with
Flegont, Roman Efimovich [Derichenko], Sabaneev and others...

Modichka, I will send you one of the best Moscow photographs, when I get
them, meanwhile I can send a large boudoir one, but it is bad (there are better
ones). All the same I will send it to you. I kiss you, my Golubchik and also
Kolia.

P. Tchaikovsky

Am also sending a cabinet size one, not very good, will send some better ones
later.

At this time Tchaikovsky was assembling sketches for, he thought, a new symphonic
work. It turned out to be Suite No. 3 in G (Op. 55), completed on 19 July 1884 and
dedicated to the conductor Max von Erdmannsdörfer who gave the premiere in
Moscow on 19 January 1885 (see Letter 386).

  Having finished this (see Letter 365) he began the Concert Fantasy (Op. 56) for
piano and orchestra. This was played by Taneev, also in Moscow, on 22 February
1885 (see Letter 386).

TO PRASKOVIA VLADIMIROVNA TCHAIKOVSKAIA

Kamenka
20 April 1884

Pania-sweet, Pania-darling!

How are you my good little girl? How is it that neither you nor Tolia-Mila write to me? I am living very happily. Although it would be difficult to invent a more disgusting place than Kamenka, it is, in spite of all, a country place and this is enough in itself to make me feel well. I mention this so that you shall know that I am right when I say I want my own little nest. Seriously, I think about it more and more. Please, my dear children, if you hear of something, let me know and if it is near you go and have a look at it.

At first I found the weather here cold and irritating, with such an impossible wind that it stopped me from going out. But for the last three days it has been real spring weather, and I delight in it. From early morning I go off to the forest [Trostianka], stay there until dinner time, pick violets, admire the awakening of the little world of insects and birds, and enjoy nature in general. At the same time I am making sketches for a big symphonic work to come, and I return home for dinner, which we have together Leva and I, well pleased with myself. Then I read, play, write a little, drink tea, go for a walk and have supper at eight. After that there is always a game of vingt and I go to bed at 12.00 happy in the thought that on the morrow I shall not have to receive any guests or visit anyone.

Only one thing upsets me; that I am so far away from you, but when I buy an estate near Moscow I shall always be near you my dear ones! Somehow I feel that you will always live in Moscow. Anyway I shall come and see you there. Leva went yesterday to Elisavetgrad for the annual fair for two days. They are expecting Sasha back soon. The old Davydov ladies are flourishing. Am waiting for a letter with impatience. I embrace you in the strongest way and kiss Tania sweetly.

Yours

P. Tchaikovsky

TO MODEST TCHAIKOVSKY

Kamenka
22 April 1884

Here is a birthday present for which, I am sure, you will be grateful. I mean these autographs for your collection: In alphabetical order they are:

(I) Balakirev
(II) Bülow
(III) Davydov
(IV) Benjamin Godard
(V) Laub

(VI) Lavrovskaia

(VII) Napravnik

(VIII) Prince Odoevsky

(IX) Ostrovsky

(X) Pobedonoszev

(XI) Rimsky-Korsakov

(XII) Nikolai Rubinstein

(XIII) Anton Rubinstein

(XIV) Sadovsky

(XV) Stassov

(XVI) Taneev

(XVII) Lev Tolstoi

Busy, hence am not writing. Sasha is back. It has become warm, at last. I kiss and embrace you.

P. Tchaikovsky

The private word *besiguish*, used below, presumably derives from *besigue* (bezique), a once familiar game of cards.

[364] TO MODEST TCHAIKOVSKY   Kamenka
                                                      2 May 1884

Are you feeling better? I hope so. Your birthday was celebrated by all of us shivering with cold, and the wind was so awful that even I did not dare to go for a stroll after dinner but only walked up and down the room. Nothing out of the ordinary has happened lately. The lilies of the valley want to grow, but the cold is preventing them and they are coming out very slowly.

I am writing a Suite in a leisurely manner. A charming form but the word is disgusting; think, Modichka, of another one instead of this 'besiguish' word; the scherzo I have composed, and am now inventing the indispensable waltz-like movement. But it seems to me more and more that I have exhausted my powers and if I do not steal from others I do steal a lot from myself. Bobik is playing an important part in my life here. We are great friends and for the first time he is returning my feelings. At first he only accepted my love but now he seems to respond to it. And I really adore him more and more every day. What a wonderful example of the human race! He often comes in for a chat, but he respects the hours when I work – I mean in the mornings when I am writing.

I also work hard at my English and am sure that by the end of the summer, if I continue as I am doing now, I shall be able to read fluently. But it is still difficult for me to understand Miss Eastwood. Bobik, the Suite and English are the three great attractions of Kamenka. But how often I would like to be somewhere else – and what is queer, in Petersburg of all places! Of course you and Kolia are there but I shall see you soon in any case. However, this has nothing to do with it; but last year's life in Petersburg during the Coronation has left such a wonderfully beautiful memory that I am longing to be back again on the shores of the Neva, now, when the second part of the month of May is coming nearer. . . .

I kiss you with all my love.

P. Tchaikovsky

[365] TO MODEST TCHAIKOVSKY   Skabeevka
                                                 23 July 1884
                                                 Monday

Although this letter will only be sent on Wednesday I am writing today to satisfy my desire to talk to Modia. Prokonz has probably told you about our adventures. Up to Kochetovka (or whatever its name is), we travelled very comfortably. There I had supper and tea in the fresh air, in the middle of a small bee garden surrounded by sleeping bees. I read *Sappho* under the moon with the help of a lighted lantern and looked round apprehensively at the distant lightning. We left at 11.30 pm. Gradually the lightning flashes came nearer and at last right over our heads. The moon disappeared, and it became dark and fearsome, darker after every flash of lightning. It was a real 'sparrow's night'. Although all it amounted to was a sequence of mild thunderstorms, and it only really rained once, my sufferings were indescribable, and my nerves tense to the extreme.

As we drove on I was sure we wouldn't arrive in time. How angry I was with Shoffa who did not explain properly what to do and when to start, so as not to be late! What would I have done if I had listened to him and left about nine! ! ! The last six versts we drove *ventre-à-terre* and arrived a quarter of an hour after the train was due to leave. Fortunately though, it was late and we caught it.

A terrific thunderstorm came over here and I could only thank God that there had not been one like that during our drive. I would have gone mad with fear. The sight of this storm, as the sun rose with its rays shining through the stormy clouds, was so wonderful that, forgetting my fear, I stood at the door to watch. The rest of my journey was peaceful and comfortable (no change at Kharkov).

I slept a lot but had time to finish *Sappho* which I did not like. In my opinion if you think about it properly it is all disgustingly false, in spite of seeming realistic. Under the pretence of warning his sons against that sort of thing Daudet wrote a series of erotic scenes. . . . His sons, when they read it will certainly not look for a dull and vulgarly-colourless Ivenes but, if tempted will choose *Sappho* which is frightfully attractive to young men. It is a pity I do not know what your impression was when you read it. Laroche is enthusiastic and says that *Sappho* reminds him of Katerina Ivanovna who is extremely popular at the moment.

Alesha and I had a good journey but our luggage stayed behind in Kharkov. We arrived without it and God knows when we shall get it. Very awkward! The drive from the station was not too bad. Pania, Tolia and Laroche came to meet me. Both the surrounding country and Skabeevka are very attractive. I did not like the two rooms with balcony which were prepared for me, and moved to another one next door, that is smaller. It is cosy, and has a charming view. As soon as I arrived I had my things moved there in spite of Alesha's protests and am very glad. The bathing is perfect. I found that Pania has grown fatter. Tolia, as usual, felt unwell towards evening, had a headache, a bad throat and a temperature. It is extraordinary how he manages to be ill so often. At first I became worried, as I am very afraid of all throat complaints, but he is better today. Yesterday, on the day of arrival, I went for two long walks with everybody. Today Laroche and I walked all the morning. I was very glad to see him. His state of mind is fair. It will be difficult to work here, if at all. First of all Laroche will be in the way and there is no piano, just as I had planned to work on a piano piece.

I very often fly in my thoughts to Grankino. Of course one cannot compare how much nicer, and how much more picturesque it is here, but I cannot really say why I like Grankino so very much. I kiss you and Kolia. My kind regards to Nikolai Nikolaievich, Nara, Franz but not to Shoffa; I am angry with him.

Good-bye Modichka, my dear.

Shall go to Moscow very soon.

P. Tchaikovsky

[366] TO MODEST TCHAIKOVSKY   Skabeevka
                                                26 July 1884

How different is nature here from what it is in the south; so very different that it still seems like a dream. Leaving aside the matter of picturesqueness, the air here is sweeter and the vegetation, if not richer, much more lush. I think of you all the time and am sorry you are not here. How you would have enjoyed it, Modichka! Just think! The woods are still full of wild strawberries – and what strawberries! – ripe, juicy, and sweet-scented. And there are masses of mushrooms. As for the walks, each one is better than the last. I find Skabeevka much more attractive than Podushkino. The weather, they say, is bad for the time of year, but so far as I am concerned it adds to the charm of the place. I did not like the two rooms prepared for me and moved into the one you slept in. What a view out of the window, and how charming and cosy it is! After the vastness and luxury of Grankino the furnishings are very shabby but I am quite content because of the view.

As yet I have not started to work, and must first go to Moscow. In any case I do not intend to force myself too much. From 10.30–12.30 in the mornings Laroche dictates his article on Mozart to me. I may be wrong, but to my horror, I find his talent and imagination fading. All he has so far dictated to me is empty-sounding chatter, which I would have found very colourless if I had read it in a newspaper. Up till now, however, he has been very charming, and amusing. . . .

Modichka, forgive me for being enthusiastic over Skabeevka as if out of spite for Grankino. I love Grankino and would like to spend part of the summer there, but the north is so much better than the Ukraine even though the rye is still standing here whereas there the harvest has by now been forgotten. It may happen that after Tolia and Pania have left for the Crimea, on 25 August, I shall stay here for another month. I hope that you got my first letter on Sunday and get this one on Thursday. A sweet kiss and hearty embrace. Write your drama in the belief that it will be excellent, always provided you make the end really good. I am burning to know how you have done the end.

I kiss Kolichka. Kind regards to Nikolai Nikolaievich, Nara, and Franz.

P. Tchaikovsky

[367] TO MODEST TCHAIKOVSKY   Skabeevka
                                                                6 August 1884

Modia!

Your yesterday's letter has irritated and upset me. I wanted to write about it and discuss it at once but a thousand versts separate us, and besides, the post does not go from here every day. First of all, your disappointment in your own play and your desire to tear it up does not astonish me at all. I know that feeling very well and there is no composer or writer who has not had a similar experience; only ordinary, untalented people never lose faith in their own capacities. Your disillusionment is temporary and any occurrence like the one that caused it may lead you to the other extreme, then back again, and so you may go on from one extreme to the other; this is the order of things. But what worries me is that you have destroyed the fourth Act.

I cannot say how I will like your changes, but I fear that by ending your tragedy in the third Act you have shortened the end too much; for the former one was magnificent, very impressive. I remember how, listening to it, I was all tense and then, at the end, how I relaxed and had several moments of great and sweet joy at the wonderfully touching final scene with the children. You lose a wonderful finale by leaving that out. How is it that you have thought out the whole play so meticulously except for the end?

I think that the fourth Act is indispensable and yesterday it came into my mind that it should be completely different. You ought to stop thinking about it for a time. Copy out the first three Acts and then quietly think of something quite new. Never mind missing Strepetova's Benefit. It does not matter for it is she who will have the part anyway. Could you set the action of the fourth Act in another place? Could it, perhaps, take place later, several months after the other three? Liza, completely defeated by the degrading circumstances, accepts all the filth against which she has been fighting, purely for the sake of being with the children. They could all find themselves in the town where Igor forces them to live. One could even add a few casual characters; you could, for instance, write in a drunken party at Igor's house. The scene between Pasha and Ivanov could take place in this Act. Pasha tells Ivanov how Liza has changed; after this a love scene between them. Then the aunt comes in and tells them what Zinka is up to now. Then come the children and while talking to them Liza suddenly realizes that, under the father's baneful influence, they are becoming strangers to her. Here, hate surges up in her with tremendous force and violent energy, and it can only end in death. As soon as the children have gone, Igor appears, delighted at Zinka's 'tricks' (as in your fourth Act). A short fearful scene follows and Liza kills Igor.

Here I have returned to your first version, I think that she has to kill him. However, maybe you are right and it is he who has to kill her. I am not quite sure which is better. But what I am absolutely certain of is, that there must be a fourth Act. I am not sure that all I suggest for the fourth Act will please you but this is not important. What I want you to understand is, that you must leave the excellent third Act as it is and write a completely new fourth Act.

I advise you to write to Strepetova telling her she need not worry herself about waiting for the play for her Benefit and put off writing the fourth Act, even for quite a long time. *Do not hurry*, the excellent first three Acts are worth being crowned properly.

I am in haste to finish this letter. Let me know if you are coming straight here or first to Moscow for a good time.

I kiss you and embrace you, my dear Modichka. Have no doubts and trust me. Your play will be magnificent, provided it has the proper ending.

P. Tchaikovsky

[368]   TO MODEST TCHAIKOVSKY   Skabeevka
                                                   1 September 1884

Modichka!

Forgive for not writing, but I had all kinds of business to attend to. Taneev is going to play my concerto at one of the first concerts of the R.M.S. and I am working hard. I went to meet Bob and Mitia and this took up a whole day. Yesterday I saw our people off. Poor Anatoli was almost in despair when he left as if only sorrow was in store for him, and Pania was upset too and regretted having planned this trip to the Crimea. I am off to Moscow with

Laroche where I shall stay for a couple of days and then on Monday I will settle in Pleshcheevo.

The evening after you left we were with Taneev who played us his symphony which I liked but not all that much. Stayed the night at Laroche's. He had an advance of 100 roubles from me but spent it so energetically that scarcely anything is left. The article was not even touched these last days. The weather is magnificent and I am sorry to leave. I cannot say when, but I must go to Petersburg soon. I must, however, first get used to the life in Pleshcheevo. I kiss and embrace you and am waiting for news with impatience.

P. Tchaikovsky

Mme von Meck's estate, Pleshcheevo, near Podolsk and not far from Moscow, later belonged to her daughter Mme Pachulsky. Taneev's Third Symphony, in D flat, dedicated to Arensky, was composed in 1884 and first played at a Russian Music Society Concert in Moscow on 26 January 1885. The composer conducted.

[369] TO MODEST TCHAIKOVSKY   Pleshcheevo
                                                 4 September 1884

My dear Modichka!

Yesterday, after two days in town, I was quite in the mood to appreciate the country and solitude. Here, as if it were on purpose, I am at last in Pleshcheevo. I was met in Podolsk by Pachulsky with great ceremony, in a landau driven by a magnificent grey troika, and taken to Pleshcheevo where Alesha was already waiting for me. Pachulsky spent the whole of yesterday with me, and today I am getting acquainted with the house and park. Tomorrow I will settle down and start working properly.

The house is large and spacious, and furnished in the von Meck style, which is already known to you. My bedroom is very cosy, as also is the study; as to the other rooms, they are much too rich, but I will get used to them! No servants besides Alesha! Very pleasant for me and will do him good to do a little more work than usual. The cook – Dimitri – as you know is Tolia's! The park is beautiful and very unusual as it runs in a narrow strip all along the banks of the river Pakhra. But what one misses here are distant vistas, wide horizons. It is too enclosed on all sides – not that it really matters at this time of the year. I had time today to walk to Podolsk and back.

I am glad about the new scene. I feel it is well thought out. Poor boy, I can imagine how sick you were to start working again on a finished play. I think I will come to Petersburg during the month. I kiss you, my Golubchik and also Kolia.

Your

P. Tchaikovsky

It is impossible to describe how thoughtful Nadezhda Filaretovna is.

Pleshcheevo
7 September 1884

My dear Modia!

I understand perfectly your present state of mind and greatly sympathize. As long as you have not got the play off your chest you will not have any peace. Although I am certain that the play's future will be a brilliant one, until this happens you will have to go through many ups and downs between fear and doubt and back to assurance of success. I advise you to develop a philosophic, calm attitude to it all. Remember that this play is not the *sole interest* in your life and even if here and there you will encounter hostility – spit on it – sooner or later you are bound to succeed.

11 September

Am getting more and more used to Pleshcheevo and how I shall hate to be forced to take trips to Moscow now and again. Not later than the 15th I must go and take my work there and meet Taneev (my concerto). Not that I shall not be glad to see Moscow, but I have no desire to move. . . . Nadezhda Filaretovna continues to look after me. Yesterday she sent me a magnificent harmonium. I think I have written before that I am studying *Parsifal*. Oh, God! – How exhausting and, in spite of it being the masterpiece of a genius, what falsehood, lies and *nonsens* [sic], all this prodigious thing is.

From 7.00 to 8.30 I read. You will wonder how it is that I am reading *Wilhelm Meister* for the first time in my life. It was a *révélation*, I always thought it would be boring. But, good gracious! How charming it is, and how glad I am I have come across it.

I only get the *Moscow News* here and am very glad not to know anything about Petersburg. We should both have been worried as we are going to appear publicly on the stage there at the same time. But *Lizaveta Nikolaevna* worries me much more than my *Onegin*. Please, be a philosopher, and prepare yourself for success only after a multitude of petty irritations inevitable in such cases.

I kiss you as hard as I can.

Yours

P. Tchaikovsky

Pleshcheevo
20 September 1884

My own dear Modinka!

I do not expect you to write often and much, as I fully understand that you are too busy. However, as one worry – the comedy – is now at an end, I am sure the second one too will disappear.

Here the weather has changed at last and today is so lovely that I am sorry I have no one to share it with. Went to Moscow for two days; primarily to take the proofs and to see Taneev who has started to study the score. Also to celebrate Sophia Ivanovna's Name Day. On the next day was at the Conservatoire where all our chaps came in a body to hear Pabst's *Fantasia* on *Mazeppa*. It is quite effective. Then we had supper together, but I cannot say why I got such an 'attack of the dumps' that back home I shed torrents of tears, after which I slept beautifully. On the next day I returned to Pleshcheevo with great pleasure, taking Laroche with me. He only stayed the night and early next morning – at 4 o'clock – he left by the first train so as not to miss his classes (just fancy!).

Up till now, as at the beginning of last year, Laroche does not miss his work at the Conservatoire, but otherwise he *does nothing at all*. He neither finishes his article nor the promised translation of Hanslick. He took an advance of 300 roubles from the Conservatoire and spent it in no time. However, he at least had a new suit made.

I have written to Napravnik to find out when they will summon me to Petersburg. If in the middle, or even at the beginning of October. It makes no sense going there before. I am insistently invited to Kamenka. I do and, at the same time, do not want to go. For all I know I shall not. . . . Working hard. Continue to be enthusiastic over Dickens and Goethe. Play a lot.

I kiss and embrace you.

P. Tchaikovsky

Laroche had begun a translation of Eduard Hanslick's famous *Vom Musikalisch-Schönen* (Leipzig, 1854) in 1879, but working on it only spasmodically did not finish it until 1889. The first professional performance of *Eugene Onegin*, conducted by Napravnik, took place in St Petersburg on 19 October, the composer being recalled by the audience many times and being presented with a laurel wreath. Thus began the great popularity which the work has ever since enjoyed.

[372] TO MODEST TCHAIKOVSKY   Pleshcheevo
                                                        25 September 1884

How quickly time flies! Before one has time to realize it a month will have passed since I came here. I am getting more and more used to solitude, enjoy it more than ever, and come to the conclusion that to end my life in the country, as I wish, would be the wisest and best thing I could do. I have no desire to go to Moscow, on the contrary I do not want to move. All the same the knowledge that a large and much loved city is near, is very pleasant. The weather lately has been ideal.

Got your letter today. Although you say you have become indifferent to the fate of *Lizaveta Nikolaevna*, I know that actually this is not the case! Authorship is the source of great and rare joys, and at the same time a cause of thousands of large and small disappointments. If you have acquired a philosophical armour against them, so much the better. As to joy, it will come, for whatever the critics will say I am sure the play is going to be a sensation.

Although Apukhtin and Meshchersky are authors I do not look upon them as authorities, as to Lelia he does not understand anything about drama. Pleshcheev's remarks carry weight, but to judge a play properly it must be seen on the stage. We shall see what he says after it is produced. I wish Strepetova would arrive and everything could be started. We will discuss the matter of teaching the deaf and dumb when we meet. It is not possible to say anything definite without discussing it from every angle. I think you can manage both. I am in favour of both activities and if you should be offered an independent position as an educationist, you should definitely think about it. Your future must be made secure. On the other hand it is desirable that you do not give up literary work, for you may go far. However, we shall see.

I had a letter from Napravnik saying that *Onegin* will probably be on about 20 October. It means we shall see each other soon. What am I going to do after that? No one comes to see me. I only see Alesha and the parrot (I love this delightful creature), and do not wish it otherwise.

I kiss and embrace you.

Yours

P. Tchaikovsky

[373] TO ANATOLI TCHAIKOVSKY   St Petersburg
25 October 1884

Tolichka, Golubchik!

Anna and Kolia will tell you and Pania all about why and how. I will only explain briefly why I did not go to Moscow (it is 3.00 am now), I found out that Kotek really has T.B., and that he is expecting me with great impatience. So long as I have not seen him and do not know how much he is a candidate for the other world I cannot be happy. So I have decided to go straight from here to Switzerland – to Davos – where Kotek now is. I will return not later than the beginning of December, spend the Christmas holidays with you and what will happen after that I don't know. Please, do not complain that I am not keeping my promise. But poor Kotek is absolutely alone and must soon die! It is impossible not to go.

Eugene Onegin is a success, the returns are magnificent.

On the whole Petersburg has brought me much happiness and the sweet knowledge of real success, but I am very tired of this life full of bustle, and it will do me good to travel.

I kiss you innumerable times, and Panichka, and my sweet Taniusha.

Good-bye,

P. Tchaikovsky

Address your letters and telegrams to Schweiz (or Suisse), Graubünden, Davos-Platz, Kurhaus Holzboer.

[374] TO PRASKOVIA VLADIMIROVNA TCHAIKOVSKAIA
Berlin
3–15 November 1884

My dearest dove Panichka!

I was so busy in Petersburg that I did not find a minute to write a farewell letter to you and Tolia. I was going to leave on the 30th but the day before was told at the theatre that the Emperor intended to be at the fourth performance of *Onegin* and I was obliged to stay for another two days. But the Emperor did not come, and no one knows why. I am sorry he didn't, but *Onegin* has generally made a very good impression in Petersburg. I never expected that this opera would be liked so much by the masses. We shall, however, see how things get on; it is better not to rejoice too soon. In any case, to my heart's great delight, the first four performances were brilliant, and I feel very happy.

It is nice to rest in solitude, where no one takes any notice of you, and at the same time to have a heart full of happy thoughts about the opera I love more than anything I have ever composed. I shall stay here in Berlin for two days to see the performance of Weber's *Oberon* which I have never heard. The journey passed most pleasantly, for I was so comfortable – in my little compartment up to the frontier, and in a large one from there to here – that I did not notice how the time passed. The weather is good. I am back from a long walk and have started writing letters; a multitude of them, so do not be surprised that this one is so short.

A letter from Kotek was waiting for me here, not a bad one and judging by his handwriting he cannot feel as weak as they said he was. Shall write at once from Switzerland. Am going via Munich where I want to stay for two days and will only reach Kotek in five days' time. Back in Moscow not later than 10 December. I embrace you, Tolichka and Taniusha.

I kiss your hands.

Yours

P. Tchaikovsky

7 November 1884

I can't be bothered to unpack and get out my own paper but this piece is so huge that I doubt if I will get to the end of it. Arrived here today. I travelled very comfortably, alone in a sleeping car; but I suffered from the cold, in Berlin on the last day, on the journey, and here. The winter has come; there is frost; everything is covered with snow, which slightly thaws by day and makes an impossible slush.

I stayed so long in Berlin because I wanted to compose the *Hymn of the Cherubim* for the Emperor and the entre-acte for the Samarin performance. The latter is done and posted. The *Cherubic Hymns* are also ready, two of them, but not copied, and I wrote Obolensky a long letter asking him to explain to the Czar why I have not yet carried out his wishes. Time in Berlin went pleasantly, and I saw *Oberon*. I have always been told that it is boring but I enjoyed it very much. In some places the music is charming; although the plot is silly. It is a bit like *The Magic Flute*, and quite amusing; and in the scene where the whole corps de ballet falls on the ground in convulsions, at the sound of an enchanted horn, I laughed like a madman. *Oberon*'s music is delightful, and wherever he appears the music is inspired and poetic. What I like in Berlin is that everything starts at 7.00 pm. There are hardly any intervals, and everything was finished by 9.30.

One evening in Berlin I met an acquaintance (Barzevich) in a *Bier Halle* and begged him not to mention me to Anton Rubinstein (who prepares some horrid stuff of his own for an extraordinary concert), and also not to Klindworth. Went to Bilse's and listened to the Andante of my Quartet. Why always the Andante? They do not seem to want to know anything else! On the day I left I saw that my Andante would be played again at another concert. Every day at dinner I was struck by the enormous quantities of food the Germans devour, much more than the Russians. I find all these dinner-times very congenial, for one can keep silent and no one tries to talk.

As usual I have had no luck with the theatres. Yesterday there was a performance of Gluck's *Armida*, but today it is *Carmen* which obtrudes everywhere. Tomorrow *Posse mit Gesang*, whatever that might be and also tomorrow *Die Meistersinger*. Alas! I shall not be able to stay until then, as I have already sent a telegram to Kotek saying I will be there on Friday.

Today I had time to go to the National Museum and tomorrow I want to go to both *pinacothèques*. Good-bye, my Golubchik, I kiss all three of you. I think that when Bob leaves, you will miss him very much. On my journey I read *Le petit Bob*; quite nice.

Write, my dear soul.

P. Tchaikovsky

Davos
                                                    12–24 November 1884

I arrived here at last at four o'clock after a complicated journey. After Munich
I stayed a night at Lindau and another at Landwart station in Switzerland,
where the railway ends. From there I had an eight hour drive. In Landwart I
was obliged to sleep in a rather miserable little room, but it was clean. From
there you usually go by coach to Davos but fearing the close proximity of all
the people in the cramped space of a coach I hired a carriage and travelled
alone. The higher we went up into the mountains the more severe both nature
and the cold became. I suffered badly from the cold, especially in my feet.

Driving up to Davos I imagined it to be a wilderness and feared that I would
not be able to get either cigarettes or cigars. But I found that at this great
height there is a row of first class hotels, and shops where you can get
whatever you like. They have their own newspaper, theatre (where I went
yesterday with Kotek); and as to cigarettes and cigars there are plenty. All
this makes a fantastic impression and I still feel as though in a dream. When
I arrived at the main hotel, where Kotek lives, he was out. He expected me on
the coach later and had gone to look for a room for me.

For one night I had the room of a man who had gone away. At last Kotek
appeared. I was afraid that I would see only a shadow of his former self and
imagine my joy when I saw him looking much fatter, with a clear
complexion, and seeming perfectly well. But this is only on the surface. When
he started talking I understood how bad his lungs are. Instead of a voice he
has a hoarse croak and an incessant heavy cough. . . .

The place is crowded, and all the hotels are full. I got a poor little room far
away from the Sanatorium. In spite of 5° (Centigrade) of frost all the patients
are out all day. Many are dressed quite lightly and go about without coats,
tobogganing (Russian style), skating, and so on. The whole cure consists of
breathing the pure but rarified air which is easy for the sick to breathe. About
200 people have their meals in the Sanatorium dining-room and the food is
excellent. They say that healthy people feel suffocated and cannot stand the
rarified air at all but up till now I feel perfectly well. But, in spite of the scenery
being so grand and magnificent, it is sad and mournful here. My heart
contracts from sorrow, and all I want is to leave as soon as possible. Maybe
this feeling will pass after a time.

I tactfully told Kotek that I am staying only for a few days, so if I stay a whole
week, he will be very pleased. I am terribly sorry for him. He is tortured by
the thought that he will not be able to go back to Berlin next year and work.
However, he is not lonely, for there are plenty of nice people around, and
some of them Russian. He knows everybody, though not intimately, and my
staying with him for long would be too much of a sacrifice; so I am going to
leave as soon as I can. It is extraordinary that a whole settlement of
consumptive people live in a real severe Russian winter! But Kotek says that
out of a hundred people at least sixty get perfectly well again.

Good-bye for the present, Golubchik. I am glad you are pleased with your
new home. . . .

Kotek sends his best love.

P. Tchaikovsky

[377] TO MODEST TCHAIKOVSKY   Zürich
                                       18–30 November 1884

Modichka!

Last night I arrived here to have a rest and I go on to Paris today. I decided
to go to Paris now as I am beginning to doubt if I shall go abroad again in
the spring, more probably to Kamenka or another place in the country, to
work and to put some money by. I left Davos with the pleasant feeling that I
had done right in going to see Kotek. You would not believe how much better
and happier he feels. As to his health, my first impression was misleading. He
is a very sick man . . . I did all I could for him. I visited the doctor, secretly,
and begged him if he finds Davos no good for Kotek to send him to the Riviera.
I left Kotek some more money and, having done what I could both spiritually
and materially, I left Davos knowing that I had done my duty as a friend.
Life in Davos is typical of hotel and restaurant life. I met a multitude
of people, even became quite friendly with some of Kotek's friends. A German,
very nice chap, left a most pleasant memory of himself. Was invited to a tea
party by Radecky who played his works to me; then to a tea party given by
a Russian lady – Gulak-Artemovsky – a very stupid and empty-headed woman
whose son is a school friend of Bob's and very nice. The frost was fierce all
the time and my room so cold that I even got awful chilblains on my left hand.
On the way back I was driven first in a sledge and then in an ordinary coach,
alone, and enjoyed the wild beauty of the mountain road.

Had a curious letter from Stassov today, will tell you about it when I see you.
From Paris I shall go to Petersburg for a few days and must be in Moscow
on 10 December. How are you getting on, Golubchik? Shall stay in Paris not
less than ten days, will you have time to write?

P. Tchaikovsky

Stassov asked Tchaikovsky to present the Public Library with some of his original
manuscripts. While in Paris, Tchaikovsky composed the five songs of Op. 57 and
three *Cherubic hymns* (Nine Liturgical Choruses, a cappella). (See Letters 380, 391.)
Work in the liturgical field was undertaken at the request of the Czar.

TO MODEST TCHAIKOVSKY   Paris
                                              21 November 1884

Modichka!

Paris is as charming as ever and as before I feel at home in it.

Having a wonderful time. Have ordered a mass of linen at Tremblet's and two
new suits at Nicholas's. I am slightly ashamed of being extravagant but,
honestly, I was beginning to look shabby.

I dined at expensive restaurants and passed both evenings at the theatre. First
at the Gymnase, where the play, *La Ronde du commissaire*, was not very good,
but thanks to Landrol and St Germain I enjoyed it. Yesterday I went to the
Grand Opera for an excellent performance of *Hamlet*. I like the first three
acts very much. Lasalle and our sweet Isaac were perfect. Tomorrow I shall
go to the Comédie Francaise to see *Le Gendre de Monsieur Poirier* and *Les
Jeux de l'amour et du hasard*. For the most part the theatres have plenty of
interesting plays and I will have to go nearly every night despite its being
tiring.

The weather is awful – warm and rainy. Will stay another week. How I love
dear Paris!

I kiss and embrace you!

I shall probably receive today the letters forwarded from Davos including one
from you.

P. Tchaikovsky

[379] TO MODEST TCHAIKOVSKY   Paris
                                              30 November–
                                              12 December 1884

My dear Modia!

After deliberating and worrying I have at last decided to put off my journey to
Petersburg and go straight to Moscow a week before the performance of the
concerto, to clear up some doubtful points. I must also correct the proofs of
the Suite. So, if I leave for Petersburg the day after tomorrow (cannot go
earlier as my linen and suits will not be ready), I could stay in Petersburg not
more than two days. In this short time I would have to be at the opera, as
promised, and at the revival of *The Maid of Orleans*. I would also have to see
Balakirev and [Rimsky-] Korsakov without fail and the Kondratievs, Sasha,
Vera etc. etc. . . . I have decided, therefore, to go to Petersburg after Moscow
and time it so that I will be able to see your comedy. I think I am wise to
have decided it this way as it will cost less money and time.

But I am worried that somebody is sure to be angry with me. However, the
only people who matter are you, Kolia, and Bob. The others are not so
important. In any case we shall see each other soon. Who knows, maybe you

will have to come to Moscow about *Lizaveta Nikolaevna* before I go to
Petersburg. And so, Modia, do not be angry and write at once to Moscow, so
that I shall know how things are. I am absolutely in the dark. . . . Stopped
going to the theatres. Have suddenly developed a disgust for them and rejoice
like a child that I need not go.

I kiss you hard.

Yours

P. Tchaikovsky

[380] TO MODEST TCHAIKOVSKY Paris
3–15 December 1884

I have no words to describe how sad and weary I have been these last days,
dear Modichka, although there is no good reason. It is probably a longing for
my own country, and for a home of my own, but this cannot be satisfied by
my going back to Russia tomorrow, as I have no proper home there. Foreign
countries make me sick, Paris has ceased to attract me, and I cannot understand
how I managed to stay in Paris for five months two years ago. It is not the
absence of work that bores me; I have had time here to plan all the changes
in *Vakula*, to write three songs and one hymn.

No! If I had only written more clearly about my stay here, if I had asked you
to write, then I would have known what you and all the others are doing. My
not knowing anything about you all makes me even more depressed. All this
will fly away, of course, but I simply must have a *home of my own*. If it is to
be Kamenka, let it be Kamenka, if Moscow, then Moscow: it is beginning to be
absurd to be leading the life of a wandering star.

Yesterday and the day before I saw young Jedrinsky and was awfully glad to
pass the time with him. We had dinner together at Bignon's. Quite
often during the last few days I went to see the Béliards and stayed to chat
for hours. So I am in need of a certain amount of human society. This worries
me. It means that to live completely alone in the country would not suit me.
Where should my home be then? When shall I see you? I do need a heart to
heart talk with you. If it were not that I find it impossible to stay incognito
in Petersburg, I would come with pleasure for a few days. But just the thought
of running round to see my musical acquaintances makes me shiver. I kiss you,
good-bye.

P. Tchaikovsky

Maybe I can manage to come for a day or two to Petersburg between the
Concerto and the Suite. Write to Moscow.

Moscow
18 December 1884
in the evening

Modichka!

Tolia does not advise going to Fedotova who has not responded in the proper
way at all to the honour we are doing her. Should I go to Ermolova or wait
for you? Let me know when and if you are coming? I strongly advise you to
come here. On Thursday I have been invited to a rehearsal to hear some new
singers and will have a chance of speaking with Pchelnikov (who is at the head
of the theatres here), about *Lizaveta Nikolaevna*, and on Friday evening I will
be playing *vingt* at Pchelnikov's and you may be certain that I shall talk to him
about your play. If you wish, I will also go and see Ermolova. I feel that
Suvorin's article has upset you, it has me, very much, and all day today you
were in my thoughts. I know that this doesn't really mean anything and that
sooner or later, you will be recognized but I understand perfectly how disgusting
such unfairness is and how it must have affected you. How filthy these
newspapers are! Come, Golubchik! I kiss and embrace you a thousand times.

Yours

P. Tchaikovsky

Modest's play *Lizaveta Nikolaevna* was played for the first time at the Alexandrinsky
Theatre, St Petersburg, on 11 December, and criticized by A. S. Suvorin in the *Novoe
Vremia* (*New Times*), 1884, Nos. 3159, 3164.

Piotr's Diary for 1885 (and most of his other diaries) were destroyed by their
author. Fragments were published – in the opinion of the translator of these Letters
inadvisedly – in 1923. News of Kotek's death had come in a telegram on 24 December.

[Moscow]
1 January 1885

My dear Modichka!

I have not written my diary for a whole week. This will give you some clear
idea of my abnormal state of mind and make you understand why I have not
written to you either. The reasons are: first of all, Kotek's death; then the
unending hours of proof correcting; then a perpetual fight against invitations.
All this prevents me from chatting to you in my letters and even with myself
in my diary. I am perfectly well. Shall be in Petersburg about the 10th, and so
we will see each other soon. I will definitely know everything about the chances
of *Lizaveta Nikolaevna* in Moscow after the holidays. I kiss and embrace you,
good-bye, my Golubchik! I have so much to tell you about! A kiss to Kolichka!

Yours

P. Tchaikovsky

Moscow
29 January 1885

Modichka!

Only a few words this time. I have lately been full of the idea of either buying
or renting something. Today, alas, all my hopes have been destroyed. Tolia,
Pania, Laroche, Alesha, Stepan and I went to see an estate – a house in
Zvenigorod which I thought would be ideal in every respect. But what a bitter
disappointment; this house could not possibly satisfy me. I was so upset that
I decided to stop doing anything to realize my dream and simply go abroad
to work on my *Vakula*, which means that we shall see each other soon as I
have to go to Petersburg first. I am glad that Lent is coming and that you will
not think about *Lizaveta Nikolaevna*. Believe me your time will come, as mine
has. Success never comes at once.

I kiss you as hard as I can.

Yours

P. Tchaikovsky

Maidanovo, a village near Klin in the Moscow district, gave its name to the
estate and house belonging to N. V. Novikova (Novichikha) (see Letters 387, 456).

Tchaikovsky rented a house, which stood in a park and beside a river, and lived
there until 1887. In May 1890 he returned for another year. The house no longer exists.
There was, as the following letter shows, no difficulty in those days about servants.
The *moujik* (man, peasant) referred to attended to the stoves and was a general
handyman.

During February and March Tchaikovsky was busy with alterations to *Vakula*,
which was re-named *Cherevichky*. (See Modest's biography, pp. 58–9.)

On 11 February he had been elected a Director of the Russian Music Society
(Moscow branch), to which reference is made in Letter 386 (see also Letter 556).

Cherevichky signified a kind of high-heeled boot worn by women in the Ukraine.
This opera is also known, after its heroine, as *Oksana's Caprices*.

Maidanovo
14 February 1885
7 in the evening

Modia!

Arrived safely. First impression – disillusionment. What seemed to Alesha
luxurious and magnificent looked to me tasteless, rather shabby, multi-coloured,
and a bit dirty. I decided immediately, and quite firmly, that Maidanovo was
not to be my permanent home. But to stay here a year or, at least, to the
beginning of next winter, is quite possible; and in summer it will be delightful.

We are, for the time being, occupying four rooms, one of which, the sitting-
room, is so frightfully cold that it cannot really be counted. The other rooms are

also cold, but besides the stoves they all have open fire places and, anyway, the end of the winter is not far off. The rooms are quite cosy but the medley of colours annoys me. The house is large and there will be plenty of room for all of us in summer.

The surrounding countryside is charming, and you will be quite satisfied. I quickly got used to the unattractive furniture, having decided that I shall not stay permanently. On the other hand the lovely view out of the window, the peace and quiet, the feeling that I am in my own home, make me happy and I have been in a good humour all day.

The cook is good and cheap. The other servant at present is the 'loujik' (Alesha's sister's husband), and tomorrow the washerwoman comes. After dinner I walked to Klin along the river (delightful walk), had tea at four o'clock, and wrote a long letter to von Bülow. Am writing to you and Tolia, will have my supper, play, read and then to bed. . . .

In spite of a certain feeling of disappointment I am happy, pleased, content and at peace. This is also just the thing for Nikolai Dmitrievich, and I shall write to him tomorrow. Meanwhile, I kiss and embrace you with love.

Yours

P. Tchaikovsky

[385] TO MODEST TCHAIKOVSKY
Maidanovo
17 February 1885

I was obliged to meet my landlady. She is a woman about fifty, most ladylike, who seems to know everybody: Sasha Karzova with whom she was at school, and Annette, and Mary Kondratiev, and N. D. Kondratiev and Liszt and Rubinstein and George Sand, and Alexandre Dumas fils, whom she calls her friend. She was very rich once upon a time, but now she lives only on the rent from Maidanovo. I went to see her on business twice. As soon as I appeared for the first time she said she would keep me for a game of piquet. I answered that I did not play; but then I felt sorry for her and promised to come one day in order to learn it. I continue to be perfectly well, have got used to the rooms, and am getting acclimatized. The weather is wonderful and the beauty of the Russian winter landscape has never been as enchanting as it has been these last few days. Am very pleased with Alesha. In general all is well.

19 February

Newspapers and journals are arriving and embellish my life. I read a lot, study English with pleasure, my work is getting on perfectly; I eat, go for walks, sleep when I like and for as long as I like, in a word, I am living. Only I had better not boast about my delightful solitude in case you get jealous. I am reading the novel *Theatrical Marshes* with great, if unexpected interest. All live characters from back stage.

I embrace and kiss you. After tomorrow I am going for two days to Moscow.

P. Tchaikovsky

[386] TO MODEST TCHAIKOVSKY   Maidanovo
                                                25 February 1885

I have just returned from Moscow where I spent four, not very nice, days. Was present at two committee meetings of the Musical Society as a director. Heard my Fantasia beautifully played by Taneev and orchestra and am very pleased with it. It had more success than the Suite (in Moscow). Stayed much at home, at Tolia's. Tania is getting more charming and sweet every day, she is absolutely adorable. She can say everything. For example, on the day I arrived she said: 'Uncle Piotr is coming and he will say "Tata has scented herself, fluffed herself out!"' and she asks her father: 'Papa where do you come from?'

I like returning to Maidanovo but it could never be my real home. Modichka, if Guitry's Benefit is to be on the 9th I definitely shall not be able to come as Rubinstein's Memorial Concert takes place on the 10th and I must be present. As it is too late to send this today I will add a little more tomorrow.

No, I shall not have time. I kiss you—

P. Tchaikovsky

[387] TO MODEST TCHAIKOVSKY   Maidanovo
                                                4 March 1885

... All last week a furious snow storm raged without ceasing, but in spite of it I went out for walks. Sometimes it was a great effort, and how nice it was to return home. Once I also went to see Novikova. What a chatterbox! And how boring I find it with her as my neighbour, as I feel I must visit her now and again. I think, though, that she has realized by now that it is to her benefit if she does not expect me to come too often.

My work is not getting on very fast but how pleased I am with it! How pleasant it is to know that *Vakula* is going to surface out of the river of oblivion once more. Modichka, I wish you would find a new name for the opera. I do not want either *Kuznec Vakula* [*Blacksmith Vakula*] or *Notch pod Rojdestvo* [*Christmas Eve*] or *Zarizyny Bashmachky* [*The Empress's Shoes*]. It must be something different. How are you? What about coming here for a rest, for a day or two? I would be pleased. I wonder if I should go to Petersburg instead of Moscow for Easter? Which is better? If you decide to come here to practise your devotions over Easter I would not go anywhere. On Saturday I am going to Moscow for a Memorial Service for N. Rubinstein.

At the moment I am reading the *European News* and the *Historical Annals*

and the life of Josephine (frightfully interesting), and Byron and Shakespeare.
I play every night. Have played through Salvayre's *Richard III*, but did not
like it much.

P. Tchaikovsky

Erdmannsdörfer conducted a Memorial Concert for N. Rubinstein on 11 March. The
programme included Mozart's Masonic Funeral Music, and excerpts from Berlioz's
Childhood of Christ and Liszt's 'Dante' Symphony. In revised form *Vakula* was re-
named *Cherevichky* (see p. 327).

[388]   TO MODEST TCHAIKOVSKY   Moscow
                                                   13 March 1885

Modichka!

Am writing from Moscow in such a scurry that you must not be surprised that
the letter will be brief. I came here just for one day for the Rubinstein
Memorial Service and got stuck for five days. And all because of a
misunderstanding. Tolia told the Kapnist woman that I would love to see a
repeat of the performance at their place. For some reason she decided that
I should stay here a whole week, collected all the actors, and declared that she
would never forgive me if I did not stay. So here I am, without anything to do
or any pleasure.

We had a service for Nikolai Grigorievich in church, then there was a concert
in his memory at which Liszt's 'Hell' [*Dante* Symphony] was beautifully
performed (you remember we heard it together in Rome). Also one at the
Conservatoire and two dinners in his memory at the Hermitage. Yesterday
I had dinner with Laroche, and am going home tomorrow. I just cannot wait
for the moment when I shall be alone, and at home again. There must be a
letter waiting for me there. If an answer is needed I will write again tomorrow.

I have decided to spend Easter here and do not know when I will be in
Petersburg.

I kiss and embrace you.

P. Tchaikovsky

[389]   TO MODEST TCHAIKOVSKY   [Maidanovo]
                                                   15 March 1885

Modichka!

After thinking things over I have decided that I must work hard to finish
Vakula in time; I shall not go to Moscow and shall not invite you to come here
either. Instead I will come for Guitry's Benefit. Get a room ready for me! How
glad I am to be home again!!! I shall probably go to Moscow on Saturday of
Holy Week and return on Easter Monday. Will be in Petersburg on 30 March

for certain. Besides Guitry I must see Polonsky to discuss the changes I made in the libretto. As the music for *Vakula* will be ready by then it will be possible to have a few free days with you. All the same, I beg you not to tell anyone I am coming.

Must go to the Post Office, no more time to write. Please forgive the short letter. I embrace you.

Yours

P. Tchaikovsky

[390] TO MODEST TCHAIKOVSKY   Moscow
                                                      8 April 1885

Modichka!

Forgive me for my long silence. I am in a hurry to stop you from letting Guitry visit me either in Moscow or Maidanovo. I am afraid of it. I am also writing to him and warn you that that letter will be a pack of lies, which runs as follows: I have, I shall say, to go at once to the South of Russia for family reasons and was thinking of going in May, but as in May I shall have to be in Odessa for the production of *Mazeppa* (this is true, but I am not really going), I am compelled to go to the country now. So, please, remember that is how you must lie to him.

I stayed three days in the country but had to come back for Konshin's wedding which, being a Konshin one, was celebrated with great pomp. Staying here today on business. I shall have dinner with Altany who warned me he had important things to discuss. I have a feeling that they want to cheat me over *Vakula*. Going back to Maidanovo tomorrow. I kiss you. Forgive the short letter.

P. Tchaikovsky

Earlier in the year Modest had spoken to his brother of Shpajinsky's *Charodeika* (*The Enchantress*). Tchaikovsky read the play and conferred several times with the author. He began work on the music in September 1885 but the sketches were not finished until 18 October, 1886, and the score on 6 May, 1887.

Tchaikovsky went to Smolensk for the unveiling of the Glinka Memorial but, terrified by the number of his acquaintances assembled there, ran away.

At this time he was beginning the sketches for *Manfred*, a subject which had been proposed by Balakirev (see Letter 333) in 1882. The character of the hero of the poem obsessed Tchaikovsky. He wrote to Mme von Meck in August saying that he had 'temporarily turned into a kind of Manfred', and to his brother Nikolai explaining how upset he had become as a result of working on this idea. On 13 September he wrote to Balakirev hoping that he would be pleased with the work – which was dedicated to Balakirev – and adding that he had 'never . . . made such an effort and never been so tired'. (See Letter 415.)

Maidanovo
15 April 1885

My dear Modichka!

Do you know that my correspondence is growing out of all proportions? It 'grows not by the day but by the hour'! Soon it will come to such a pitch that all my time will be taken up by letter writing, boring answers to people I don't know, with no time to write to my nearest ones. I wrote seven letters yesterday!!! This will be the fifth (sorry, the sixth) this morning, which is the best time for work.

I am at the moment writing all sorts of varied church music, and have done a trio to be sung at the Presanctified Liturgy. On the 22nd Shpajinsky will bring me the first act of *Charodeika*. I had a long letter from Pavlovskaia imploring me not to write an opera on this subject. I know you are also against it. But neither of you know to what extent the libretto will be different (from the play), and how the characters and situations will change. The heroine is not the same at all. In the play the last act is bad, but in my opera it will be magnificent. The whole audience will shed tears when this same Pavlovskaia is about to die.

The spring is slow in asserting itself but it comes gradually. Yesterday we had a thunderstorm. Very little snow is left, and only in holes and ditches. Yesterday I had visitors all day long: Yurgenson, Kashkin, Laroche. You can't imagine how much wine they mopped up – particularly Kashkin. As I had been long enough in solitude and at work before they came, I enjoyed a day of fun, drink, and idleness. All three of them liked Maidanovo. I am sure you will like it too.

The country hereabouts is charming, but the fact of all these dachas and 'dachniki' [summer residents] being so near is killing me! One of these dachas, next door to us, too, has already been taken. I do not look forward to the month of May as I shall have to attend the Conservatoire examinations, and – on the 20th – the unveiling of a monument to Glinka in Smolensk. Ugh! How I do not want to! After all this, I kiss and embrace you and Kolichka. It could happen though that I shall come to Petersburg at the end of April.

Yours

P. Tchaikovsky

Maidanovo
26 April 1885

Modichka!

I have just returned from Moscow where I stayed a whole week. Here I found a mass of letters requiring answers, so do not expect a long one yourself. Everything has been decided about *Cherevichky* in a marvellous manner. Nice Vsevoloisky has ordered luxurious stage arrangements for *Cherevichky*, and

I was present at the meeting where it was discussed. Valz, the designer, is being sent to Zarskoie Selo to copy the Amber Drawing-room and a particular salon in the Palace. I am terribly pleased.

The 'good time' in Moscow was terrific and money went like mad. Yesterday my forty-fifth birthday was celebrated with a dinner at Tolia's and supper at the Conservatoire. Meanwhile Alesha was arranging my new rooms in Maidanovo. Not bad – but all the same, Maidanovo does not entirely satisfy me. Your room is ready too, but both the room and the balcony face north and you will not have much sun. On the other hand they will be cool in summer. I am so glad that you are going to stay with me. Kolia's room is also ready (it is already called 'Kolia's Room') next to yours, but quite separate. Maybe that Laroche will stay in it before Kolia, or perhaps after him, as their plan to go to England is not coming off.

Shall probably come to Petersburg in May, but cannot say when exactly.

I kiss and embrace you.

Yours

P. Tchaikovsky

[393]   TO MODEST TCHAIKOVSKY   Maidanovo
                                                 20 September 1885

Modia!

Last night I returned home; the weather was awful (unceasing snow with rain), which made me the more happy to find myself in my nice cosy house, all bright and warm. Alesha has arranged everything, or nearly everything very well. Only the bedroom and dressing-room are not quite to my liking, and as I am not good in making things comfortable I do not quite know how to improve them. In the dining-room, during supper, I was welcomed by a mouse which twice ran past under my very nose. But even the mouse did not worry me, so comfortable and pleasant it is here. Oh dear!

Why am I saying all this? You understand it all anyway and probably feel envious. I feel slightly ashamed to be enjoying solitude when you are in all that bustle. . . . Just think, I have not yet finished *Manfred*, and it will take me a few more days to do so. During my hectic days in Moscow I tried to see Pchelnikov but did not find him at home. Next time – I mean next week – I shall have an opportunity to talk to him about *Lizaveta Nikolaevna*. Am writing several letters at the same time, so forgive me if this has been written anyhow.

I kiss and embrace all three of you.

Yours

P. Tchaikovsky

Maidanovo
27 September 1885

My dear Modia!

I have grown so used to my environment that it seems to me that I have always lived here. I continue to be content and happy, and everybody around me also seems pleased. . . . I have at last finished *Manfred* and started to work at once on *Charodeika*. Did I give you the libretto of the first act to read? It is marvellous. I read a lot and play a lot, and have played through Soloviev's [opera] *Cordelia* which Bessel sent me. Very bad. It is ridiculous to compare it with [Napravnik's] *Harold*.

Laroche stayed for two days. He suffers from insomnia, is terribly nervous, and absent-minded, but now and again he has bouts of high spirits. When he was here a very much revered holy statue was brought to Maidanovo. It was brought to my house and after the short service which was held outside, at the door, we had, as is the custom, to crawl under it. Laroche did not know how to behave and looked awfully funny. This holy figure, a very ancient wooden statue of St Nicholas, is from the Volokolamsk Monastery. Its having been brought here to Maidanovo is looked on by the people as a great honour.

The weather is not kind to me. Either it pours or the wind is bitter. There has been only one fine day. I have decided to write the opera little by little, for two hours only each morning. I want to stop tiring myself out and am going to damp down my composer's zeal.

I honestly think it would be better for you to switch over to the *Northern News*, actually *Russian Thought* is not your type of writing. In your place I would make the change without compunction.

I kiss you sweetly, also Bob and Nikolushka. Good-bye my Golubchik.

Yours

P. Tchaikovsky

Maidanovo
6 October 1885

My dear Modia!

I have just returned from Moscow, and am obliged to write a multitude of letters, so there are no more than a few words for you. I went to Moscow on business about the directorship of the Musical Society, and talked to Pchelnikov about *Lizaveta Nikolaevna*. He could not say if the play was going to be put on soon but thought that they have decided to produce it. He also told me, privately, that Ermolova was going to have her Benefit and suggested asking her if she would agree to choose *Lizaveta Nikolaevna* for it. But he added that Ostrovsky was writing something specially for her.

The question now is, what is to be done? I find it awkward to ask Ermolova without first talking to Fedotova. Pchelnikov obviously does not know anything about the repertoire of the Malyi Theatre and does not interfere with it; so I think we should ask Fedotova what she thinks about it, and only if she refuses, turn to Ermolova. . .

Shameless Zola! Last week I came across his *Germinal*. I started reading and was carried away, finishing it very late at night. I got so excited that I could not stop my heart from thumping, which prevented me from sleeping, and in the morning I felt quite ill. Now I think of this novel as an awful nightmare. . . .

Yours

P. Tchaikovsky

Laroche had a brilliant article in the *Russian Annals* and since then has been perfectly well and started sleeping again.

Zola's *Germinal* had only just been published. Laroche's article, 'A new Russian opera' – i.e. Rimsky-Korsakov's *The Snow Maiden* (after Ostrovsky), appeared in the *Russian Annals*, October 1885.

At this time Tchaikovsky's relationship with his publisher was more than usually uneasy.

[396]   TO MODEST TCHAIKOVSKY   Maidanovo
                                                 9 October 1885

Modia!

Got your letter. I shall certainly go and see Fedotova and, if necessary, Ermolova. But I am in the kind of predicament I have not experienced for a long time. I have absolutely no money, and shall not be able to move before next week. Nadezhda Filaretovna, who usually sends me my 'budgetary' sum two weeks before the appointed date and which I expected on the 15th, is late this time and I only got a letter from her eight days ago asking where I wanted the money to be sent. I answered at once but it will be a few days before I get the positive result. At the same time my money relationship with Yurgenson is rather complicated, and after an unpleasant scene we had I have decided not to ask for so much as a penny for the time being. I borrowed all I could from Alesha and have spent it. It got so bad that in Moscow I was going to beg Kolia Peresleny to pawn my watch for me but, fortunately, the Huberts lent me some money. In a word, the crisis, though short is quite intense. It will end in two or three days when I get my allowance.

All this is to stop you from grumbling that I am not going to Moscow at once. But rest assured, all I can do will be done. . . . A pity that your new comedy is not finished. It would be nice if you could have it ready for the end of the season. . . .

My opera is getting on, and at least half of the first act is written. But I feel that I am forcing myself too much. Today I got so tired after working on a difficult passage, and I was so upset about a letter I got from Levenson (who wrote that the baby died of suffocation – caused by a faulty rubber teat – when the mother was out of the room) I even cried a little. This has given me a headache and as you can see, prevents me from putting even two sentences together properly.

I kiss and embrace you.

P. Tchaikovsky

All the same, I am happy here.

[397]   TO MODEST TCHAIKOVSKY   Maidanovo
                                                  17 October 1885

... The death of the nice, kind Kross has made me very sad. I know that his wife loved him deeply – she must be quite stunned by grief. My work is getting on wonderfully fast. If it were not for my journey to Kamenka the whole of the first Act could be ready for 1 November. I think it is quite good.

I have just read Korolenko's stories in the *Northern Annals*, and judging by what you said I expected something quite out of the ordinary. But, honestly, do not find it so. The language in the *Oubivez* [*The Killer*] is very good but the plot itself is not new and reminds me very much of Turgeniev – or someone else. Generally speaking your praised *Northern Annals* did not impress me as much as I expected. First of all there was a most amusingly vague article by the editors, full of philosophical terminology. What do they want all these 'intuitions' and such-like frightening words for? Second, there are two poems next to each other – one by Polonsky, the other by Merejkovsky – which are quite sweet, but both begin with the author apologizing for the fact that his Muse had 'flown away'. Third, one finds silly, idle talk by Liszt. And the paper is grey and dirty-looking. No, out of all these mildly liberal papers the best is the *European News*. The last issue is magnificent.

With the greatest reluctance I shall leave my adored home for a long time.

Write to Kamenka a few times. I embrace all of you.

Yours

P. Tchaikovsky

Shall let you know from Moscow about my meetings with the leading ladies of the Malyi Theatre.

The first number of the *Northern Annals* had appeared in September. The poems about the fleeting Muse were by J. P. Polonsky and S. Y. Nadson respectively. D. S. Merjkovsky's poem (like Nadson's, without a title) was on another theme. G.

Korolenko's 'Sketches of a Siberian tourist' and letters of Liszt and George Sand were also published in this first issue (Cf. Letter 402).

The first of the Russian Musical Society Concerts, conducted by Erdmannsdörfer, took place on 19 October. The programme comprised Tchaikovsky's *Coronation March*, B. Godard's Second Violin Concerto (the 'Romantic'), a Bach Suite, and Beethoven's Eighth Symphony.

[398] TO MODEST TCHAIKOVSKY

Moscow
24 October 1885

Modinka!

I went to see Fedotova on Monday but she was out at a rehearsal. The same evening I went to the Malyi Theatre, where they were playing *Richard III* and Fedotova was in it. During an interval I asked her son when I could see her. He said that she is busy with [N. E.] Vilde's new play and is at the theatre the whole day. She can only see people at dinner time when she is not acting. But it so happened that she was on the stage every night. Not knowing what to do I went to see Shpajynsky who is a close friend of Fedotova. He said:

> 'Leave her alone, she is so engrossed in her new play that until after the first night she will not think of anything else. Better let me talk it over with her and by the time you are back I will have everything clear and will arrange a meeting for you.'

When I told Shpajynsky that Fedotova insisted that you ought to change the end and that you were afraid it would spoil the play, he offered to read the play himself, and to give his advice. It will, he points out, be easier for him to decide, as an outsider, what is wrong with your play. I have ordered a copy from Rassokhin's. For God's sake do not be angry and think that I did not want to keep my word but circumstances were against my meeting Fedotikha. This worries me very much.

After I come back, with Shpajynsky's help, I will do all I can to ensure that *Lizaveta Nikolaevna* is produced as soon as possible.

Completely exhausted from my life in Moscow. Off to Kamenka tomorrow.

Yours

P. Tchaikovsky

[399] TO PRASKOVIA VLADIMIROVNA TCHAIKOVSKAIA

Kharkov
27 October 1885

Pania my dearest!

I have not written to you for two weeks! The reason is that Moscow where

I stayed for about a week was in such an impossible state of turmoil that I just could not write.

I arrived on the day of the first of the Musical Society concerts, but somehow it was dull and gloomy. They started with my *Coronation March*. Kolia Peresleny has probably told you of my failure. I imagined that I would have an ovation, but instead, not even *one* voice tried to shout my name. Then the usual kind of days followed, with house to house visiting of friends, and leading a dissipated life without end. How I longed for my Maidanovo solitude!!! It did not prevent me from working hard with A. Hubert who is helping me with the piano score of *Manfred*. Everyone I met asked and wanted to know all about you. You were missed by many of the audience – including myself – at the Musical Society concerts. . . .

You will certainly want to know what the devil I am doing in Kharkov and why I came here. To have a rest from people. I was exhausted in Moscow by running round all day from one of my fellow-men to another. I go to Kamenka tomorrow and will write from there. Arrived here last night, got a box at the theatre, and listened to a concert given by the well-known singer Motté. It was great fun hearing several of my compositions, knowing that not a soul in the theatre realized I was in the audience. I have seen many acquaintances, and have written a multitude of letters. I did very well to remain here and am enjoying my rest.

I kiss the hands of my dear Panichka, and also beg you to give a hug to the Public Prosecutor [i.e. Anatoli] and Tatussia.

Yours

P. Tchaikovsky

In September Tchaikovsky had composed *The pure bright flame of truth* (the words were his own invention) for chorus and orchestra, and a March, for the Jubilee of the St Petersburg Imperial School of Law, of which he was an alumnus.

At this time Alexandra Davydova was celebrating her silver wedding. Her mother-in-law, Alexandra Ivanovna, widow of the Decembrist, was now eighty-three. Despite his report on her state of health she was to outlive Tchaikovsky by two years.

[400] TO PRASKOVIA VLADIMIROVNA TCHAIKOVSKAIA
Kamenka
4 November 1885

My dearest soul Paniusha!

I have already been here, in Kamenka, for a few days. Having found everyone well, I pass the time quite pleasantly, but am not upset not to be a permanent resident. There are many reasons why life in Kamenka would be impossible for me. However, I do not wish to go into details now – better leave it until I see you in Tiflis. Just think, my dear soul, I am working even here.

The Committee which is organizing the Jubilee Festival of our School of Law begged me to compose a march. I cannot refuse and, in spite of an absolute aversion, I have been sitting motionless over this march for several days. The silver wedding celebrations take place on the day after tomorrow. Besides the Korsakovs, the von Mecks, and myself, there is no one here. Our present has arrived and I like it very much, but Anna and Tania are extremely critical. Alexei arrived, packed all my books and things, and they are on the way to Maidanovo.

My rooms are empty and look sad. Oh, Lord! How glad I am that I have my own little home now. Alexandra Ivanovna, dear old lady, is well, but has grown much weaker and it makes one sad to see how mournful she looks. The poor old lady does not want to die. I am very glad to see her again for I have a presentiment that it is for the last time. I shall leave on the day after the celebrations, which I will describe to you on the following day. You say that the Georgian Military Road is a risk in spring, but here I have been told it is nothing of the sort. Anyway I think I shall go by steamer. My God! How glad I shall be to see you! I am not asking for a portrait of you, I insist on having one. You promised it, you know. . . .

P. Tchaikovsky

[401] TO MODEST TCHAIKOVSKY [Moscow]
17 November 1885
Sunday
10 in the morning

At last, yesterday, I saw Fedotova. How difficult it is to catch her in winter. I had to walk up and down in front of her house waiting for her to return from the [Imperial] School [of Drama], otherwise I would not have seen her. She was very kind, but asked if you had changed the end. I answered in the negative to which she retorted that, in spite of the first two excellent Acts, she could not play the part. She added that she understood perfectly that it is difficult for you to change the end and she advises you to start on a new play as soon as possible. Now, what is to be done? You must forgive me but I have absolutely no desire to go to Ermolova. It would look like us needing her only now that the other one has refused. Modenka! Be so kind as to come here yourself!

If you have no money I can send you some, but it would be much better if you went to see Ermolova personally, and read the play to her, and so on. I must also add that when I last saw Fedotikha on the stage I thought her quite bad whereas Ermolova, on the other hand, delighted me in [Shpajinsky's] *A Simple Story*.

If you won't come I will go and see Ermolova in a fortnight's time when I return from Maidanovo. Today, after having seen Fedotikha only yesterday, I don't feel like going to Ermolova. How can I say to her, 'Glikeria has refused, so please will you play?' I think you should come here yourself. Come straight to Maidanovo, stay a day with me, then go to Moscow to see whom you must see, come back to Maidanovo, and then go home.

Tomorrow, at last, I am going home. Oh God! How tired I am and wish for peace!

I kiss and embrace you.

P. Tchaikovsky

Answer at once.

It is all my fault; I ought not to have advised you to ask Fedotikha.

---

[402]   TO MODEST TCHAIKOVSKY   Maidanovo
                                       19 November 1885

My dear Modia!

Did you get my little letter about my visit to Fedotova? I hope so. If not then you should know that this important person has refused to play the title role in *Lizaveta Nikolaevna* unless you change the end. As to any discussion with Ermolova I think you ought to come and conduct it yourself. And at the same time visit me in Maidanovo.

I was very glad indeed to come back home. All my belongings from Kamenka have arrived; the books are on the shelves; the pictures on the walls; and it looks cosier than ever, but – *cold*. Novichikha apparently lied when she assured me that the house was warm; it is quite the reverse. About the last days I spent in Kamenka, I can only say that I was glad that I did not live and was not going to live there any more. . . . But I shall not write about it, for there is too much to say. I had many dull hours in Moscow but also some very pleasant ones. Ziloty's concert, the Musical Society concert (with none of my works), and the quartet evening gave me enormous pleasure – probably because it is a long time since I have heard good music by other people. No news about my opera. They have not yet started to rehearse *Cordelia* and I am almost certain that my work will not be done this season. . . .

What do you think of the chorus of praise in the Petersburg Press about *Cordelia*. Quite odd! [Cf. Letter 394.]

Good-bye my Golubchik, write or come.

P. Tchaikovsky

I am very glad you are going to write for the *Northern Annals* – nice periodical.

[Maidanovo]
21 November 1885

Modenka!

I do not like your letter to Ermolova. It is too much of a *Padam do nog* [I fall at your feet]. From what I have heard of her she would not like it either. Besides in cases like this you must simply ask, will she take the part or not, and not pretend that the letter has been written purely to show your respect and appreciation. Also, it is wrong to write to an actress who is nearly forty about her 'youth', she might think it a mockery. In one word – 'Sorry'; but I decided to write another letter, sent it, and here is the copy. Your letter is so worded that it does not call for an answer. You do not ask for one, only saying that you want to tell her that you look upon her as an ideal.

I wrote asking her to do certain things and to let me know; and if she does not, then I shall write again. If I get a positive answer I will go and see her. I hope you will excuse me for my decisive action but it is for your good.

You want to know when I shall be in Petersburg. For the holidays; I will stay with you all through Christmas.

Meanwhile I kiss and embrace all three of you.

P. Tchaikovsky

I have told Yurgenson to order a copy of *Lizaveta Nikolaevna* for Ermolova from the Rassokhin bookshop.

Maidanovo
4 December 1885

My dove Pania!

Quite definitely letters must get lost in the post, otherwise I can't understand why I get news from you so rarely. Probably mine do not reach you either.

I have just got back from Moscow, as exhausted as usual. On Saturday the 30th there was a concert, at which my Suite [No. 3] was played. I miss you and Tolia most at the concerts of the Musical Society. After the concert I stayed in Moscow for three days in a whirlwind. An important decision was being made concerning the invitation to Erdmannsdörfer to come over here for three years. I was given the task of persuading the capricious German. Somehow I managed it, but did not enjoy the job. My opera is obviously not going to be performed. Soloviev's *Cordelia* is not yet ready, because Altany is ill, and this means it will not be on before January at the earliest. So one can 'wave one's hand in farewell' to *Cherevichky*. . . .

The Huberts are as usual. This time I stayed with Yurgenson, and not at a

hotel. My room is ready, and a very cosy little 'cabin' it is. . . . On Saturday
the 7th I am expecting friends: Hubert, S. Yurgenson, Sasha Gudim and
Kashkin. I kiss your hands, my Golubushka!

Yours

P. Tchaikovsky

On 6 December Modest informed his brother of von Bülow's request that Piotr
should come to St Petersburg to hear his interpretation of the Suite. (Hans von
Bülow had recently resigned his appointment as music director at Meiningen.) Modest
attended the School of Law Jubilee and was able to report: 'Your chorus, called by
everybody a cantata, was not performed very well but it was an enormous success.
Many people asked to be remembered to you – especially all your former college
friends, and the March – repeated at the dinner – was loudly applauded.'

[405] TO MODEST TCHAIKOVSKY   [Maidanovo]
                                      9 December 1885

Modenka!

Forgive me that I also write little and rarely. We shall see each other soon
and then talk everything over. Ermolova has not yet answered, and I do not
understand why. A week ago I was in Moscow, and will go there again on the
14th (I'm not going to Petersburg for the Suite), for a quartet concert
(Davydov and Co) and, most important, to find out what is decided about
Cherevichky. Altany is ill and will be probably ill for some time; *Cordelia* has
not yet been rehearsed and I want to make a heroic attempt to have my
Cherevichky produced immediately. I am being persuaded to conduct myself –
maybe I will try.

But in any case I will spend all the holidays in Petersburg. How glad I am I did
not come for the Jubilee. Just the thought that Lyshin shone, and was the
foremost figure there, would have been equivalent to a slap in the face for me.
Am busy on the *Manfred* proofs. The more I think, the more I come to the
conclusion that it is my best work. *Charodeika* is at a standstill for the present,
but the first Act is complete. The libretto is wonderful.

I feel perfectly happy here, especially as Novichikha is away – she has been
in Moscow the last two months. However, her son is here, though I have not
seen him yet. Expect me on the 23rd. I will be obliged to chuck you out of your
room again; would it not be better for me to live at a hotel? Be honest about
it. I would like it with you but it is not bad at a hotel either.

I embrace you.

P. Tchaikovsky

TO PRASKOVIA VLADIMIROVNA TCHAIKOVSKAIA

Maidanovo
11 December 1885

Pania, dearest!

Your long letter has worried me. I wish I could fly to you and have a long
talk. Alas! It will be impossible before the spring. Here everything is as before;
quiet, very pleasant, and a great relief without Novichikha. I cannot stand her
any more, and it is much better when she is away. On Sunday I had guests:
the Huberts, S. Yurgenson and Kashkin. Sasha Goudim promised to come but,
as usual, did not turn up. It was very jolly and my guests were pleased both
with me and the dinner. The cook, Vassily, improves every day and he
distinguished himself for my guests.

I am exceedingly worried about the fate of *Cherevichky*; Altany is ill, and I
went to see him ten days ago and doubt if he will be able to leave his house
this season. He is covered with eczema practically from head to toe. Meanwhile
Cordelia has got to be staged, and before *Cherevichky*. I made a heroic
decision, and wrote to Pchelnikov saying that I was ready to rehearse the
opera personally and to conduct the first three performances, if they will
allow me to do it at once. Where did this brave decision come from? I feel
that in my present condition – of health and nerves – I can do it. I begged
Pchelnikov to talk it over with Altany, and let me know. No answer
yet. On Saturday, without fail, I shall have lunch with *Papasha*; then I shall
have to dine with Yasha the nuisance, who takes it very amiss if I don't see
him.

For the Christmas holidays I shall go to Petersburg.

So, my dear soul, write to me there...

P. Tchaikovsky

TO PRASKOVIA VLADIMIROVNA TCHAIKOVSKAIA

Maidanovo
22 December 1885

My Golobushka Panichka!

I stayed a whole week in Moscow and returned home so tired that even now, on
my second day back, I still can't get over it. A mad week! On Saturday the
14th, a concert; Sunday, lunch at your delightful Papasha's; then the quartet,
with the eminent lady violinist Arma Zenkra; Monday, dinner with Sergei
Mikhailovich; Tuesday, the Petersburg quartet (Auer, Davydov and Co.);
Wednesday, dinner with our new professor, Safonov; Thursday, second evening
of the Petersburg Quartet; Friday, a 'high society' musical evening at Elena
Andreevna's with the aristocracy; Saturday, a popular musical matinée at the
Conservatoire, for the Petersburg guests; and in between, proofs, numerous
visits, meetings with relatives, seeing them off. In a nutshell – I nearly went
mad.

The Tretiakov evening yesterday was particularly dull. At tea-time I was put between two important ladies, and for a whole hour had to keep up a most insipid conversation.

How miserably boring.

I also did all I could for my opera, even offering to conduct it, but at the moment the directorship of the Moscow theatres is changing hands and I could not get a definite reply. It is obvious that the performance of the opera will not take place this season. I lived at Yurgenson's where I was very comfortable. I hoped to go to Peter[sburg] for the holidays but the *Manfred* proofs are not finished and I shall have to stay here until the 28th. I will have guests on the second day of Christmas. The snow is so deep that it is difficult to go for walks.

I wish you very pleasant holidays and a happy New Year. Shall think of you all the time. . . . I kiss your dear hands. Tolia and Tania I also kiss.

Yours

P. Tchaikovsky

[408]   TO ANATOLI TCHAIKOVSKY   Maidanovo
                                                   13 January 1886

My Golubchik Anatosha!

I am full of shame! First of all, for not writing to you for so long, and secondly, for not sending the money. Please, forgive me! I had two such exhausting weeks in Petersburg that I did not write so much as one line to anyone. As to the money, I hoped to get it for nine performances of *Onegin*, but in spite of all my efforts it will not be paid before next week. I have seen to it that as soon as this is done Osip Yurgenson, who has your address, will send you 300 roubles.

I did not bring back many happy impressions from Peter, for they have not been particularly nice to me there this season. Despite the wishes of the people who crowd the theatre every time *Onegin* is performed, it is put on very rarely – not even once during the past month and a half. As to *Mazeppa*, it has not been on at all. In Moscow *Cherevichky* has been put off until next year.

As a result of all this my finances are rather shaken and I shall not now get even half of what I expected. In Petersburg *Manfred* is also not going to be played. This hurts my pride. As to the life in Petersburg I will not describe it – the usual mad bustle and crowds. After the first three days there I felt so ill that Modest fetched Bertenson. It was nothing much but I have been advised to go to Vichy.

My plans are now firmly decided as follows, if nothing happens out of the ordinary. In the middle of March I am coming straight to Tiflis to stay a week or two with you. Then I will sail from Batum, by way of Constantinople, and Italy, to Vichy. After recuperating there I shall return to Maidanovo, work all the summer on *Charodeika* to have it ready for the autumn, where I shall be able to visit you again. Could you, Golubchik, find out about boats which go from Batum to Constantinople. We shall see each other in two months time!!! How wonderful! I miss you frightfully. . . . How happy I am to be back home again. I love my little house more and more. I kiss and embrace you a thousand times my dearest ones!

Yours

P. Tchaikovsky

Shall be writing regularly every week now.

One of the most charming and kind of Tchaikovsky's actions was the institution of a village school in Klin. He supported this for the rest of his life. Later that year Tchaikovsky wrote a long letter to A. S. Arensky concerning the Suite referred to in Letter 410.

[409] TO PRASKOVIA VLADIMIROVNA TCHAIKOVSKAIA
Maidanovo
23 January 1886

My Golubushka Panichka!

Since I wrote to Tolia last week I had to sit at home, for the weather was so bad that even I did not dare to leave the house and was obliged to walk round the rooms instead. The wind howled insufferably, the shutters rattled, and if my study did not have an enclosed gallery outside, the noise would have put my nerves completely on edge. However, the weather today is so lovely that after a long walk I have made peace with my dear cosy corner.

I have been working with great energy, and am finishing the second Act of the opera. I worked a bit too hard, and my nerves started worrying me. Last night I did not feel well at all. Tomorrow I am off to Moscow again to a concert of the Musical Society, then to the fourth Rubinstein concert, then a Directors' meeting etc.

On Monday the 20th the little school, which was started on my initiative, was opened. We have 28 boys and girls. I was at the opening and today attended all the morning lessons. The teaching method of the priest and the deacon is a bit queer but they put all their love and goodwill into it. The school is so organized that Novichikha and I share the expenses but as her money matters are in an awful state there is no doubt that Novichikha will not pay at all, and it is clear that I shall have to finance the school alone. . . .

Panichka, I hope to leave for Tiflis on 12 March. Let me know if there is any risk this year in taking the Georgian Military route. I kiss your little hands.

I kiss the Public Prosecutor, and his daughter, and send my regards to Kolia, Niana, Stepan, Misha.

P. Tchaikovsky

[410] TO MODEST TCHAIKOVSKY   Moscow
                                                28 January 1886

Forgive me, Modichka, for not writing. I have been here for several days, and so just can't write properly. I am going back to Maidanovo tomorrow, but not for long. Decency compels me to be present at Rubinstein's concerts and I fear that I shall have to come back here next Tuesday. Nothing out of the ordinary to report about Moscow and myself. I went to the Musical Society concert on Saturday, and heard Arensky's Suite – very talented. Yesterday I dined with Anton Rubinstein at the Huberts, and today shall hear him play. *Manfred* will be played on the anniversary of the death of Nikolai Grigorievich. You must come. I also hope to see you in Maidanovo at Shrovetide. Do you know, having read the article about [Gounod's] *Sappho* I nearly went off to Petersburg for a day on Sunday. Alas! impossible, and also no money.

I kiss and embrace you.

P. Tchaikovsky

Surely a quiet time has at last started for you!

[411] TO MODEST TCHAIKOVSKY   Maidanovo
                                                30 January 1886

To add to my short letter from Moscow I am writing now from Maidanovo. I went to the Schumann concert. Rubinstein has never pleased me more than this time. As I noticed that he was touched by my being present for the fourth time and as he is now especially kind and sweet to me, I feel it my duty to be present at all his concerts and at the festival in his honour on 10 [February], as also at all the other dinners and suppers given in his honour. A life full of bustle.

Manfred will be played on 11 March, on the anniversary of N. Rubinstein's death. You simply *must* come. Tell me honestly, Modichka, what you prefer: (1) for me to come to Petersburg for Shrovetide (I very much want to see *Sappho* and generally to go to the Petersburg theatres), after which you could come here for 11 March; or (2) that, according to our plan, you come here for Shrovetide. Please give me your honest answer. I do not mind which way you decide. But I want to come to Petersburg before I leave for the Caucasus.

I kiss, and embrace you, and wait for an answer.

Yours

P. Tchaikovsky

Maidanovo
31 January 1886

Well, my soul Panechka, now I have the right to reproach you for not writing.
But, I am not in the least annoyed. What I want to know is that you are all
well. I spent a few days in Moscow. I had planned on Sunday to have lunch
with Papasha, but Yasha warned me that Papasha was going to have lunch
with them and invited me. I must mention that Papasha is displeased with
Tolia. Tell him that he simply must write to him and as kindly and sweetly as
possible. On the same day Papasha gave a dinner which I did not attend, and
only went afterwards for tea.

The Alexeevs, Vera Nikolaevna and Pavel Mikhailovitch, Yasha with Nadezhda
Mikhailovna [Hartung] etc. were there. I chatted a lot with Alexandra
Vladimirovna and passed the evening very pleasantly. On the next day a big
dinner was given at the Huberts for Anton Rubinstein, and on the next day his
concert and supper. Anton Grigorievitch was exceptionally nice to me this time
and I suppose I shall have to go to all his concerts. Which means that I
shall have to go to Moscow every week. It can't be helped! . . .

I live in Moscow at Yurgenson's and this time was not quite happy to take
advantage of his hospitality. The fact is, we had a rather serious
misunderstanding (completely his fault). I'll tell you all about it in Tiflis.
Although we have cleared it up, and he is being extremely attentive and kind,
I do not feel properly at ease with him. *Manfred* will be played on the 11th
and on the 12th I want to leave for Tiflis. I am a bit frightened of avalanches
(on the road), but hope all will be well. Meanwhile I kiss your dear hands,
eyes, and brow. I hug Tolia. Met the deacon's wife today who made me promise
that I shall not forget to send you her kind regards.

Yours

P. Tchaikovsky

My school here is getting on very well.

On 3 February Tchaikovsky wrote in his diary: 'Received cheque from Yurgenson.
I got so worried and upset that I could not work . . . wrote a letter to Yurgenson
after supper concerning the allowance, but will send it later.' The publishing
situation had become more complex as Felix Mackar of Paris had taken over the
promotion and issue of Tchaikovsky's works in France.
   On 30 January Tchaikovsky wrote to Shpajinsky about *Charodeika*: 'The third act
is the culmination of the drama. Here the musician has to be at the very height of
his capacities, intense to the very limit. This intensity, this stress, must be felt by
the audience; there must be a feeling that a frightful catastrophe is inevitable. The
Fourth Act is to be the catastrophe itself, after which the listener will leave the
theatre shaken but also reconciled and satisfied. After the magnificent, frightening
and passionate two scenes of the Third Act I feel that I am only able to compose one

more good Act. I shall never find enough colours nor enough inspiration to illustrate in music such strong dramatic situations as you have in the last two acts of the drama in two acts of opera. In a play you can keep up the interest of the audience by the brilliance of the language, and by the clever addition of episodes which have no direct connection with the action of the play. In an opera (where this is only partly possible) a concise and fast action is indispensable, otherwise the composer will not have the strength to compose, or the audience enough patience to listen to it all.

My misfortune is that I do not find enough arguments to convince you. I have come to the conclusion that it is absolutely imperative to limit the opera to four Acts, not through reasoning but through unfailing musical instinct.'

On 1 February Modest wrote to his brother: '*Lizaveta Nikolaevna*, I think, has died on the stage here. The play was on this week as substitute for another play (not for the first time has it been shown in this way) and the theatre was nearly empty. My author's pride did not suffer; it seems to me that it has been badly presented on purpose during the whole of this season, but it is a pity that I shall not get any money.'

[413]   TO MODEST TCHAIKOVSKY   Maidanovo
                                                 6 February 1886

Modinka!

How exacting these Rubinstein concerts are; not the concerts themselves which give me great pleasure (I never liked him better as a pianist), but all the awful other things connected with them, such as the official dinners! Having to go to Moscow for at least three days a week etc. does not make me at all happy! Yesterday the Tretiakovs gave a big dinner, at which I sat between two ladies. Oh God! It was awful! Laroche behaves in a silly way. He sulks, making a great to-do about his attentions and 'non-attentions' to Rubinstein, and imagines that Rubinstein takes notice of them, whereas the latter could not care less.

I think, Modia, that I shall postpone my journey to Petersburg from Shrovetide to the first week in Lent. You see, on Monday the 16th I have to be at the dinner in honour of Rubinstein at Taneev's house, at a concert on the 17th, and shall not be able to leave before the 18th. I will have to do it this way as I would like to come and see you in Peter when all is quiet.

Two Acts of *Charodeika* are ready and I am as much in love with them as I am usually in love with any new offspring of mine. But while composing it I came to the conclusion that it is impossible to have five Acts as it was first planned. After the third Act – i.e. the scene of the Kuma with the Prince and his son where the drama has reached its highest point and is on the brink of catastrophe – it is impossible to drag on for two more huge Acts. I mean, you cannot do it in an opera. I will never have enough strength to write so much music and the audience will not have enough patience to listen to it. So I have written to Shpajinsky (who has left the country), that, whether he likes it or not, instead of the fourth and fifth Acts, he has to invent a completely new ending, quite different from the one in the play; I do not know what he will say.

You are perfectly right (although I do not quite believe you, as I know from experience how painfully hurt personal pride can be), to accept with philosophical indifference what is being done to your poor *Lizaveta Nikolaevna*. But your hour will come, I have never doubted it. One has to suffer much sorrow and many rebuffs before one is rewarded according to one's deserts. We still have frosts but the sun is beginning to get warm; the trees are covered with hoar frost and the winter countryside is so beautiful that one simply can't describe it. . .

And now, good-bye, but not for long.

Yours

P. Tchaikovsky

[414] TO MODEST TCHAIKOVSKY   Maidanovo
                                 13 February 1886

Modia!

The Week of Shrovetide is planned as follows: on Monday I must go to a big dinner in honour of Rubinstein at Taneev's house, and in the evening to a concert of church music at the Conservatoire organized by me. (Besides my own new church compositions, music by [Rimsky-] Korsakov, Azeev and others will be played.) This concert has become quite an event; Anton Rubinstein will be present, three bishops are coming, as well as many other important people. Tuesday, Rubinstein's concert which he begs me to attend. Wednesday, the farewell *dîner monstre* at the Tretiakovs in Rubinstein's honour. So I shall not be able to leave before Thursday either for home or for Peter[sburg].

I am not quite sure what I want to do; to go straight to Peter[sburg] or, first, to stay a few days at home. Perhaps you would like to pass the last days of Shrove Week with me here? As to *Manfred* on the 11th you can come again (with help from me), and as I am going to leave for the Caucasus on the 12th you will then see me off. I would like you to come to my little house in winter. . . . Think it over and answer. I embrace and kiss you.

Yours

P. Tchaikovsky

At Rubinstein's last 'Historical Concert' Tchaikovsky's *Russian Scherzo* (Op. 1) and *Romance* (Op. 5) were played. On 11 March *Manfred* (see Letter 333, and p. 326) was given its first performance, at a concert in memory of N. Rubinstein. Tchaikovsky was well pleased with its reception and considered that it was his best work.

TO PRASKOVIA VLADIMIROVNA TCHAIKOVSKAIA

Maidanovo
13 March 1886

Panichka my dearest!

After ten days in Moscow I returned to Maidanovo yesterday. On the day the Grand Duke came for a concert of the Conservatoire pupils I caught a bad chill, was ill a whole week, and had to stay at home five days. Then, taking all possible care, I went for three consecutive days to the rehearsals of *Manfred*, which was played on 11 March. It was excellently performed, but it seemed to me that the audience did not understand it very well and in spite of the ovation at the end, which was more on account of my previous successes, it was only moderately successful.

Now I must rest for a week, put all my business in order before leaving, and get everything ready. I shall leave for Kharkov about the 20th – then to Taganrog (where I shall stay with Ippolit for two days), so that – still in March – I will arrive in the 'famous' Kuckas', at the famous Solovzov house, and join the most famous beauty Panichka! I shan't go to Petersburg. Modest came to hear *Manfred*, then went with me to Maidanovo yesterday, where he will be staying two days....

I shall not write to you from now on, only send telegrams. How lovely it will be to meet in Mzkhet, my dear Panichka. Your Papasha has gone abroad.

I kiss and embrace you.

P. Tchaikovsky

TO MODEST TCHAIKOVSKY

Vladikavkaz
29 March 1886

Modichka!

Here, in short, is everything that has happened since I left Peter[sburg]. I had one day in Maidanovo, and left on Friday, mourned by Arisha whose tears touched me very much. In Moscow I was busy getting a passport, rushing around, and saying good-bye to everybody. I left on the 23rd, arrived in Taganrog on the 25th, and was met by Ippolit and Sonia. They live very comfortably – one could say luxuriously, and the old lady who lives with them is sweet. Also I must say that I like Sonia better every time I see her. I stayed with them for a day-and-a-half. Ippolit took me on a short cruise on his ship and then for a drive through the town. The Palace where the Emperor Alexander I died interested me very much; this is a page out of my favourite issue of the *Russian Archives*. How Kolia would have enjoyed himself, and I thought of him there. The rest of the time we ate, played vingt and listened to the orchestrion, a very good one. Ippolit is his old self, kind, sweet, pleasant, but as before if not more so, like a volcano ready to erupt any minute. Especially noticeable during a game of vingt.

On the morning of the 27th I left. The road to Rostov (along the sea and the arm of the river Don), and the town itself I liked very much. From Rostov to Vladikavkaz the road runs along the characteristic unending steppe, and the nearer you come to the Caucasus the more it reminds you of Mohammed and the East. At the stations you see very few Russian faces among the eastern people. Their faces are often beautiful, but a bit frightening. Elbrus is seen long before the 'Mineral Springs' station from where the real Caucasus begins. Here the road goes along with the mountains in view all the time.

We arrived at four in the afternoon and I hoped to leave at once but I shall not be able to get a carriage and horses before tomorrow. In the end I was forced to wait for nearly two days. It did not matter, for the weather is fine and clear. Kazbek can be seen in all its glory and the little town itself is charming and lively, but – Oh my God! – how awful the hotel is! ! ! In spite of its being the very best one.

Good-bye! I kiss you, give Kolia my letters to read. I embrace you both.

P. Tchaikovsky

The orchestrion, mentioned above, was a kind of music-box that imitated orchestral sounds. There had been such an instrument in the Tchaikovsky house when Piotr was a child, and it was this – with its excerpts from *Don Giovanni* – that gave him his first love for the music of Mozart.

The Georgian Military Road to Tiflis crosses the Caucasian Mountains; its highest point is the Kresstovsky Pass.

[417] TO MODEST TCHAIKOVSKY   Tiflis
                                                  1 April 1886

On Sunday the 30th the carriage, harnessed by four horses, came to fetch me, and after getting in we started on our journey, accompanied by a guard whose special task it is to look after the needs and comforts of the traveller. The whole of the previous night I could not sleep because of the horrid bed and the fleas (it makes me sick to remember the so-called 'best hotel'), and expected that the beauties of the Georgian Military Road would make very little impression on a tired man irritable from lack of sleep. But the road is so wonderfully grand, so imposing and beautiful, that I never thought of sleep all day. The variety of impressions is so great that interest does not slacken for one single minute.

At first you drive towards the high mountains getting the impression that they are quite near and yet the road winds on and on. Then, at last, the valley of the river Terek starts getting narrower, and then finally you climb up to the snows. Just before I came a terrific avalanche occurred; this has been all but cleared away by hundreds of fierce-looking natives of the place. We drove through walls of everlasting snow which grew higher and higher. I had to put my fur coat on.

At 6 o'clock in the evening we came down into the valley of the river Aragva and passed the night at the road station at Mzhet. I was given the Imperial rooms. After the disgusting Vladikavkaz hotel it was nice to be in those beautifully clean rooms, with comfortable beds, with a dinner-table properly laid, and so on. I had dinner, strolled along the balcony in the moonlight and went to bed at nine.

We continued our journey early in the morning. From here it started smelling of the south; ploughed mountain slopes, little 'auls' [small Caucasian villages set on the slopes of the mountain], and other settlements came into view. The descent is a terrifically sharp slope, especially where there are bends. Just before the station at Dushet a panorama opens up before you, that is so magnificently beautiful that one would like to cry out from pure ecstasy. The further you drive the more you feel the south. At last we passed by the old town of Mzhet (where there are ruins of a castle and the famous cathedral), and about 4.30 we were in Tiflis. Tolia and Pania were not at home; expecting me later, they had gone to Mzhet to meet me. They didn't get back till 8 o'clock. By then I had had time to wash, change and take a stroll through the town.

The town is wonderfully picturesque; the trees are not all out but the fruit trees are in full bloom. The gardens (as in Rome, full of evergreens) are masses of flowers, and it is very warm. It is, in short, a real spring, as it was in Naples when we left it four years ago. The main streets are full of people, the shops luxurious, reminding one of Europe. On the other hand when I went to the native quarters, the 'Maiden', I found myself in quite new surroundings; where, as in Venice, the streets are exceedingly narrow. Along both sides is an endless row of little shops and workshops where the local inhabitants (Georgians), sitting with their legs crossed, work in full view of passers-by. There are also bakeries and food shops, where all sorts of things are baked and fried. Very attractive and unusual. . . .

The first evening we had dinner after 9 o'clock (because of their trip to Mzhet), and chatted; Kolia Peresleny was present and very amusing. On the whole my first impression of Tiflis is delightful. Going to have dinner now and tonight we are going to the famous [thermal] baths.

I kiss you both and embrace you. Many kisses to Bobik when you see him.

Yours

P. Tchaikovsky

[418]　TO MODEST TCHAIKOVSKY　　　　　　　　Tiflis
　　　　　　　　　　　　　　　　　　　　　　　　9 April 1886

A week has passed since I arrived here and it seems to me that I have been here all my life. I have seen and done many interesting things. I went to the Baths and, horror-struck watched two strong fellows pulling at Kolia Peresleny's and Tolia's bones. I also went up to St David's Monastery where Griboiedov is buried, and from where there is a beautiful view down to Tiflis. In a restaurant on the banks of the Kura I had dinner with a large crowd of people and listened to the interesting local singers and songs and watched them dance their Lezginka [Georgian dance]. I made the acquaintance of the local musicians who very kindly showed their pleasure and appreciation.

I was at a concert of the Musical Society, the circus, a wonderful service in the Sion Cathedral (the Exarch officiated), and twice to the Armenian Church which is full of curious things. I played vingt several times, and went for many delightful walks. All of which means that time passes very pleasantly; but unfortunately not at all productively, as I do not find a moment for work although I would like to get on with *Charodeika*.

Of the musicians I like Ippolitov-Ivanov and [G. O.] Korganov best – the latter is the brother of the vulgar Petersburg chap, but infinitely more interesting and sympathetic. I very much like Tolia's and Pania's friends and acquaintances. Kolia Peresleny comes to dinner every day. He works efficiently but as usual leads a rather disorderly life. However, also as usual, he is very pleasant.

I will leave on the 26th. It is impossible to go earlier and I would not want to anyway, as I am enjoying my stay here so much. After this letter, write once more here and then to Naples, Hôtel des Etrangers.

A kiss for you and Kolia.

Christ is risen!

Yours

P. Tchaikovsky

How absolutely sweet Tania has become – delightful.

[419] TO MODEST TCHAIKOVSKY   Tiflis
                                                17 April 1886

Well! Modia my dear, I do not know where to begin. I have so many different impressions to talk about but have neither time enough nor proper words to describe everything. The last days of Holy Week I mostly spent in visiting churches – Russian, Armenian, Georgian. The Archbishop, Exarch Paul, is a very sympathetic man. For the Easter night service we went to the Sion Cathedral. It was very grand, beautiful, and not crowded.

From then on there was an unending series of parties, both at home and at the houses of friends. At the Gontcharovs, rehearsals of a play – *Night in Sorrento* – in which Pania, Tolia, and Kolia Peresleny take part, are being held. I am to accompany Tolia's singing from behind the scenes. Yesterday there was a Charity Ball at which I saw the whole of Tiflis Society. Pania was the hostess and the belle of the ball. They danced the Lezgian dance, which is delightful to watch, as well as others. On Saturday a big musical celebration is being given in my honour. It is not at all to my taste but it is impossible to get out of it.

I take long walks here as there are plenty of lovely places around, and have studied Tiflis much better than Tolia and Kolia Peresleny who live here. In the musical world I very much like the singer Zarudnaia. Shall hear *Mazeppa* soon. Have been told she and Lodi are excellent in this opera.

I am pleased you are going to Grankino and would love to come and stay with you for a few days but – how can we manage it? Are you sure you cannot stay in Maidanovo for a few days? Am leaving in about a week's time. Shall not be able to go to Vichy.

I kiss and embrace you.

Yours

P. Tchaikovsky

[420]   TO MODEST TCHAIKOVSKY   Tiflis
                                                          23 April 1886

Modichka!

I am passing the last days of my stay in Tiflis. If it had not been for visits and Society life (like for example, taking part in a play at the Gontcharovs as an accompanist and going there every day), this month would have been one of the happiest of my life. Have I told you about the solemn performance in my honour on the 19th? It was very imposing.

At 8 o'clock Pania and I entered the directors' box; the whole theatre, all the audience, rose, and after long applause the presentations began – such as of a silver wreath and a mass of others – and a committee member of the Musical Society made a speech. Then there was a concert entirely of my works. The applause was never-ending and I had to appear again and again. After the concert a subscription supper and more speeches. I have never experienced anything like it before. A most tiring evening but very nice to remember.

Am leaving in three days. Because of cholera in Italy the boats of the Messagerie Maritime do not put in at Naples for the time being, and my plan to visit Italy is off. I must go straight to Marseilles from Constantinople. Rather awkward, as I do not know what address to give you. I still do not know if I shall have enough time to go to Vichy. It is most likely that I shall go straight from Marseilles to Paris and you had better address your letters to the Hotel Richepanse. If, after all, I decide to go to Vichy I shall ask Mme Béliard to forward them there.

Yesterday Pania was so infinitely sweet that even now I am ready to cry when

I think of it. During lunch she started talking about my leaving them soon, and then she suddenly burst into such a flood of tears that I myself was so moved that I too was on the verge of them. Dear God! All one's life one gets separated from someone and suffers from the frightening thought of uncertainty about what could happen after the parting. I am very upset at leaving them and now my stomach is getting disturbed at the thought. This uncertainty is horrid.

I went to the opera here twice, and the performance and stage sets are very decent. *Mazeppa* is going to be put on for my birthday. On the morning of that day I am giving lunch to all the leading members of the Musical Society: what a lot of new friends I have found here! ...

Kolia Peresleny has been leading a very fast life all through the holidays. Now, however, he is working steadily again. In the play at the Gontcharovs he is taking part, with Pania (she speaks in rather a low key but acts quite nicely), and Tolia, whom I accompany in the song 'Evening in Sorrento'.

Good-bye, my Golubchik! I wonder when I shall get a letter from you now. Be well. I kiss Kolia and everybody else.

Yours

P. Tchaikovsky

[421] TO MODEST TCHAIKOVSKY   At sea
                                               [Batum–Constantinople]
                                               1 May 1886

Dear Modichka!

I am writing in a cabin of the steamer *Arménie*, which belongs to the Paquet Company. Everybody in Tiflis for some reason advised me to take this boat but I am sorry I did, for in Batum I saw the Messagerie Company steamer, which leaves tomorrow and which looked much better and larger. However, the weather is so beautiful, and the scenery is so lovely that it does not matter which boat it is, as long as I have a cabin to myself, and I have. Alesha is travelling second class. He says it is not as comfortable as with the Messagerie but the company is friendly and he is quite content. There are not many of us in the First Class. The Batum Turkish Consul with two wives, who hide all the time, a good-looking Italian merchant's wife with three pretty daughters, and me – that's all. The captain – a very nice man – has his meals with us. But the conversation is uninteresting, which is a pity, for it spoils the excellent food.

And now all the details of my departure. We started from Tiflis on the morning of the 29th (by 'we' I mean Tolia, Pania, Kolia P. and I). I was seen off by a multitude of people. We journeyed all day, most agreeably – the pass over Suram is beautiful. At 11 o'clock at night we arrived to find, to our horror, that all the hotels were full. We begged for rooms everywhere and, at last, out of kindness, were allowed into the Hotel Imperial where we passed the night as best we could. Batum is wonderfully situated. First there are magnificent wooded mountains, then, at the back, snow-covered peaks. The sea is deep blue, and the vegetation nearly tropical. The day passed painfully, for we were all afraid of the coming separation. Pania, who had already started to weep a few days ago, now behaved as if I were under sentence of death. To add to all this, Tolia suddenly got angry with Alexei and nearly beat him up. The last three hours we sat on the steamer in a most tortured state of mind.

At last we said good-bye. They were rowed back on shore. After that we waved our handkerchiefs to each other for a long time and then, at 8 o'clock, the steamer left.

It took me a good two hours to comfort Alexei who had been insulted by Tolia for no reason at all. I went to bed in despair but, as usual, slept like the dead, and when I woke up, I got up, dressed and came on deck; we were coming up to Trapezund and the morning was glorious. Trapezund itself is beautifully situated and is fairy-like. Alesha and I went into the town which is large and quite oriental, the people seem very nice. . . . Now, after a magnificent sunset we are off again, the sea is calm.

2 May

This morning we stopped for about three hours and again the weather continues perfect. On the whole the voyage could not be better but several times during the day I had attacks of terrible depression. These did not leave me at all, except at lunch and dinner, and then thanks to the wine. Thank goodness Alesha is with me, his presence is a great boon. You would have been mad with delight if you could have seen the sunset.

Today I felt happier and the wonderful sea and the sight of the mountainous shores brought more and more pleasure.

Tomorrow morning about 12 o'clock we arrive in Constantinople where we stay only six hours. I shall only have enough time to go and see St Sophia and then on again.

I kiss and embrace you, please, write to: Paris, 14 Rue Richepanse. Do write.

Yours

P. Tchaikovsky

[422] TO MODEST TCHAIKOVSKY   The Archipelago
                                            [Constantinople–Marseilles]
                                            6 May 1886

Stayed twenty-four hours in Constantinople. The Bosphorus not only did not surpass what I expected to see but was completely different from what I imagined. I could not find a room in a hotel and had to content myself with a dirty little room, with bugs, in a boarding house. On the day I arrived I did not go to see anything in particular, but just wandered round the town and the Pera. The whole of the next day, until five, was spent in seeing the sights with a guide. The dogs and St Sophia are much the strongest impression. The dogs so disgusted me that I have lost at least half my love for the whole species. On the whole the inner city of Constantinople is interesting but it does not attract me. Returned on board at 5 o'clock. New passengers have come on board but I still have my own little cabin. I was glad to be back in it. In the evening the sea (which had become a little rough), under the full moon, and thanks to my being quite alone on deck, was so enchanting that I decided to go somewhere by steamer every year.

Today (6 May) the sea got quite rough, and many passengers are ill. I am perfectly well although there was just one moment when I thought I would be sick. Had an excellent dinner. At intervals I am either in raptures over the beauties of the angry sea (not very angry really), or feel depressed, but that is not for long. By the expression on the faces of the captain and other seasoned passengers, I see that this sort of rough sea is nothing much! Alesha too, is quite well. I have become acquainted with all the passengers and have made friends with a Turkish officer. Am slightly frightened of the captain, a good-looking fine fellow of about forty and I get in a panic when he has a tête-à-tête with me. I stop being Petia and start talking nonsense.

7 May

In the night we passed the squadron which is blockading Piraeus. Some of the ships are lit by electricity. Two mine-carriers followed us for a long time. By the morning the wind went down and the sea was calm again. At 11 am we were practically a few steps away from the sheer St Angel rock. In the middle of the rock stands a little cell built for a hermit who, when he hears the boat's siren, comes out holding a flag and blesses the travellers. When we sailed past he was working on his plot of land. A charming day. The sunset beautiful.

8 May

The sea today is like a mirror. Up till now luck has followed me, nothing could be better than this trip. Naturally there are boring moments especially as everybody wants to talk about music. An Englishman, who all the time keeps on asking if I like this or that song, by Tosti, Denza, etc., is a special bore. There is also a Frenchman who has invented a new fortepiano which has separate keys not only for the sharps and flats but also for the double sharps and flats. He will not stop talking about his invention and makes one read endless treatises about it. We are now sailing in sight of Sicily and the heel of the Italian 'boot'. Etna is slightly smoking but on the left of it there is a huge pillar of smoke and fire which is intriguing all the passengers. The captain does not understand at all what it could mean and seems slightly worried. So I too am a bit afraid.

9 May

The smoke and flames seen yesterday were from a huge eruption of a new crater at the foot of Etna. As we came near, the sight became more and more grandiose and imposing. I scarcely slept at all for, about 2 o'clock, Alesha woke me up to see the eruption from quite near, and at 5.00 the captain woke me up to look at the sunrise, and Messina and Etna from the other side. The captain thinks there must be a great and terrifying catastrophe somewhere near Catania. Stromboli, which we passed, is also erupting. We shall know all about it in Marseilles. Another two days at sea. Today it is calm again; I could not have imagined a more agreeable, fortunate, and interesting voyage. Have got so accustomed to being on a steamer that it seems to have always been so. Have lost all fear of the captain. A very nice man.

10 May

It was most interesting to pass through the so-called Bouches de St Boniface, i.e. the Straits between Corsica and Sardinia. Sardinia reminded me of a moon landscape I saw in a book by Flammarion. It is a conglomeration of endless and most complex rock designs, with no vegetation at all. Corsica is monumental and picturesque. The channel is only possible when the weather is fine, as there are many underwater rocks. A French ship, *La Lémillante*, was broken to pieces here in 1856 and on the Corsican shore there is a chapel in memory of those who were lost. From there we turned to the open sea. It was a wonderful starry night.

11 May

Last day on board. Are getting ready to land.

in the evening

Arrived. Marseilles is a beautiful town. The hotel is magnificent.

I kiss and embrace you.

P. Tchaikovsky

[423]   TO MODEST TCHAIKOVSKY   Paris
                                                16 May 1886

Modia dear!

I arrived in Paris today so tired that it will be only one little page; I had to stay in Marseilles for three days because so much linen had collected that they said it would not be ready for three days. We had a good journey, with a compartment all to ourselves; the Béliards met us with kindness and enthusiasm. I have my old room, Alesha the one next to me which you once had. Everything in the rooms is as before; the whole of Paris makes me feel that I left it only yesterday. I feel no pleasure at all at the thought that I am in Paris; on the contrary, some apprehension – at having to do business with Mackar and pay visits to musical celebrities. . . .

Today and tomorrow I shall indulge in not appearing at Mackar's, and will start my social life on Monday.

18 May

... Am terrified at the inevitable meeting with Mackar and *tutti quanti*. I am sending Alesha back next week. He is bored, and longs to get home, and I do not need him at all.

Went to the Variétés (*Fiacre 117*), and to the Châtelet with Alesha (*Aventures de M de Grati*). Weather glorious. Paris delightful but I would give anything to be able to go home at once, perhaps also to Petersburg to see you! Alas! I am forced to stay here at least another three weeks. What a pity that you and Kolia will not be in Maidanovo and I cannot come to Grankino. Please write again. I kiss and embrace you.

P. Tchaikovsky

As far back as 1875 Tchaikovsky had attacked pseudo-folk music, particularly condemning Slaviansky whose principal aim was to please the 'Zamoskvorezk' public, dominated by the textile millionaires who lived across the Moscow river in Zamoskvorezk, a quiet, residential suburb, with wide streets, private houses, and gardens. The so-called 'Russian Serenade' was a popular waltz of Shilovsky, popular in cafés, parks, theatres, and other places of entertainment. In 1889 Tchaikovsky was annoyed at the way Slaviansky was fêted every time he played this piece.

[424]   TO MODEST TCHAIKOVSKY   Paris
                                                       25 May 1886

Modichka!

Life here has greatly changed since my last letter to you. After a supreme effort to suppress my reluctance and a painful feeling of boredom I decided to see Mackar, since when a life full of visits, dinners, restaurant and theatre parties, etc., began. The most frightening item, visiting musical notabilities, is still to come. But there are also pleasant interludes, as when Brandukov talked me into going to the Bouffes to see the operetta *Josephine vendue par ses soeurs*. I was not very keen to go, but it happened to be the most charming and amusing theatrical performance I had seen for a long time. Tomorrow I am going with a lot of people to see Sardou's *Patrie*.

Today I went to Longchamps and watched the Grand Prix. On the whole this is a most boring spectacle and the jostling crowds are quite disgusting. It is only at the very last moment, when the question as to which is going to be first is decided, that there is any real interest. On this occasion an English horse came first, taking the lead from the French one at the very last minute. The rain, which has been coming down without stopping since last night, was pouring during the whole race. I returned covered in mud. ...

Last night heard part of a Slaviansky concert at the Trocadero. Some of the things are not badly sung but when, under the name of *Sérénade Russe*, the whole chorus started singing 'The little tiger' I ran away.

At present I am reading a large work by Melchior de Vogue called *Le Roman Russe*. Try and get this excellent book. How clever he is! What an excellent definition of Zola and Zolaisms I found in it.

How I envy this letter, it is going to Grankino. I do wish I could be there.

I kiss you.

P. Tchaikovsky

Have sent Alesha back to Russia, he has probably reached Maidanovo by now.

[425]   TO MODEST TCHAIKOVSKY   Paris
                                                        27 May 1886

My very dear Modinka!

Two days ago I sent you a letter addressed straight to Constantinople without putting Novo-Nikolsky station on the envelope. I hope it will reach you.

For the last four days it has been raining incessantly. The air is so damp that when I creep into a completely humid bed my memories go back to the dachas around Petersburg at the beginning of June, I have an awful cold in the head and, in general, this sort of weather affects the nerves. In spite of it I went to the Race Course three days ago to see the Grand Prix. Yesterday Brandukov, Marsick and his wife, and I had dinner with the Mayor (I gave the dinner which cost 90 francs). Then we all went to Porte St Martin where Marsick had a free box. At last I have seen *Patrie*, and the stage sets are wonderful. Such exquisite and precise sets can never be found in our theatres no matter how much money is spent. You are, in imagination, transported back to a medieval town and real medieval life. The play is very impressive, but painful, and heavy. A lot of shooting. Every other minute I shuddered and was in such a state of nerves that my companions wondered at my involuntary movements and convulsive jerks. Of the actors I liked Mme Teissondier but best of all our dear attractive Marais. A few days ago I went to Slaviansky's concert. A Charlatan! However, his appearance on the stage was most effective.

Ah! Modinka, if you only knew how I count the days and hours which bring me nearer to my departure from here! I sometimes think that I shall never go abroad again. Brandukov and I are nearly inseparable. He is very charming....

I kiss and embrace you.

P. Tchaikovsky

Paris
1–13 June 1886

Honestly Panichka, who should I be angry with? All of you? Or the post? Or someone else? It is already June and I have not yet had even one word from you. What does it mean? I am still in Paris, leading a rather unpleasant and busy life. As I have to pay calls, receive visitors, have consultations with my publishers, etc., I can write but seldom. Some of my new acquaintances are pleasant, but others are impossible and boring.

Yesterday I had lunch with the old lady Viardot[-Garcia]. I am absolutely enchanted by this charming and interesting woman. In spite of her seventy years she behaves like a woman of forty, is amusing, pleasant, and active, and she knew how to put me at my ease.

There are a few boring Russians but I like Brandukov, who is with me all the time, very much. The weather is vile, cold, rainy, irritating. Do not go to the theatres very often. This week I shall have to dine out and the thought that it will be impossible even to pass one evening comfortably, upsets me to the limit. But what is to be done? It is a must!!

P. Tchaikovsky

[Paris]
1–13 June 1886

Dear Modinka,

Forgive me if my next letters are short and not particularly interesting. I have scarcely any time for writing. Acquaintances get more numerous every day and my stay here more tedious and difficult. But there are quite nice moments. For instance, yesterday, very reluctantly, I went to lunch with an old lady, Mme Viardot[-Garcia], but she happened to be so charming, and so sweet and motherly, that during the hour I stayed with her I kissed her hand at least ten times and will go again tomorrow with the greatest of pleasure to have dinner with her.

Just fancy, I had to appoint official reception hours at home three times a week. Yesterday I had a reception for the first time from 4.00–6.00 pm. It was a real torture. However, the most frightening guests came at another time, for example Colonne, Lamoureux, Ambroise Thomas, the latter inviting me to a very interesting examination at the Conservatoire. Brandukov is with me nearly all the time, and is very useful and kind. Remind me to tell you, when we see each other, what takes place in the evenings on the Champs Elysées, near the Café chantant, and what amusing things happen there. . . .

Oh dear! If only I could be in Maidanovo! Alesha already writes from there.

The weather here is awful. Today it is as cold as in November, the rain does not stop.

I kiss and embrace you. Be more energetic about writing your comedy. I kiss Kolia with love.

P. Tchaikovsky

[428] TO MODEST TCHAIKOVSKY   Paris
                                                          11–23 June 1886

Modia!

My relationships with all sorts of new acquaintances have become so complicated and numerous that I did not know *où donner de la tête*.
I got to know so many people. Guitry came and we had dinner with him and Angèle [his wife] at a restaurant. Yesterday at A. Thomas's invitation I went to the Conservatoire to be present at the examinations. He is a very nice, kind, old man. One Mme Bohomoletz, a rich Russian lady, gave a dinner in my honour in the evening, where my quartet was played (Marsick, Brandukov), and my songs were sung.

Did I tell you that M. Detroyat, the author, is nagging me about a libretto on a Russian subject? And if it had not been for kind, delightful Guitry, I should not have managed to get rid of him. Léo Delibes came to see me first, this touched me greatly! In general it seems that I am not so unknown in Paris as I thought. I am tired to exhaustion and sometimes I feel stunned and do not understand or know anything. . . .

P. Tchaikovsky

While working on his libretto for *Charodeika* Shpajinsky was in deep domestic turmoil. Tchaikovsky was entrusted with Mme Shpajinskaia's confidences, and, as his letters to her and also to Taneev indicated, he was on her side in respect of the marital problems.

As always Tchaikovsky was alert to new books and acquired Paul Bourget's *Un crime d'amour* (1886). Soon after writing the following letter he went on to read Tolstoi's *The death of Ivan Illich*. On 18 July he wrote in his Diary: 'I am more than ever certain that Tolstoi is the greatest author who ever lived, Just he alone can suffice for the Russians not to hang their heads when they are confronted with everything Europe has given to mankind.'

[429] TO MODEST TCHAIKOVSKY   Maidanovo
                                                          25 June 1886

. . . You say that what you have already written of your comedy does not give you any satisfaction or pleasure. I feel the same about *Charodeika*. I compose but do not feel that rapture which sometimes moves the heart of the creative artist. But this does not mean anything. I know from experience that it is not always that which pours out of a storm of inspiration that is good but, on the contrary, that which is the result of a great effort. Went to see Shpajinsky and got from him a perfect Fourth Act for the libretto.

Oh dear! what an awful family drama is going on in this playwright's home, and what an excellent subject it would make for a play or a novel. But it is too complicated to describe in a letter. I will tell you about it when we meet. I am beginning to know Shpajinsky better and better as a man. He has fallen in my esteem (as a man not an author), as his wife is growing in it every day. A wonderful and deeply unhappy woman.

I read the *Crime d'amour* at sea, on the boat, and also liked it. It seems to me that it has been influenced by Turgeniev or even Tolstoi. Bourget is much nearer to them than Zola. I reread [Gontcharov's] *Oblomov* not long ago in Pleshcheevo. . . .

P. Tchaikovsky

[430] TO MODEST TCHAIKOVSKY   Maidanovo
                                                6 August 1886

Modia dear!

This, I think will be my last letter to you, for after you get it, I shall be leaving. Brother Kolia passed here and begged me to come to Ukolovo about the 15th. I would like very much to do so and probably will go, depending on my work. I have got over all the reasons for worrying, am perfectly well again, and work is getting on nicely. I should not like to interrupt it. But in any case, when you arrive in Ukolovo find out by telegraph if I am coming to fetch you or will wait for you here. We cannot miss each other.

I have stopped being moody, get a great satisfaction from my walks, am again full of the charm of each little blade of grass, and solitude does not worry me in the least. Which does not prevent my expecting you with great pleasure in Maidanovo. I hope the weather will get better; it has done nothing but rain so far. There were a few fine days but yesterday and today it is pouring again. . . .

I think of putting you in the room upstairs and Kolia downstairs. However just as you like best. Expecting a definite communication about your arrival.

I embrace you.

P. Tchaikovsky

Between 19 August and 18 September the songs belonging to Op. 60, dedicated to the Czarina, were written.

TO ANATOLI TCHAIKOVSKY   Maidanovo
                                        30 August 1886

Dear friend Tolia!

Pania, I think is still in Tiflis, hence I am addressing this to you. But, please,
do write me back a few words, for I have news from you so rarely. Modest is
here since the 16th; Kolia also stayed here nearly two weeks and has left now.
Their visits have given me great pleasure. Modest has written a comedy, an
adaptation of Potekhin's novel [*The ailing one*], at the author's request, which
I think is excellent.

I have been working hard lately, and have finished my opera. But as the paper
I ordered is not yet ready I have not started the instrumentation, but, instead,
have written ten songs. As far back as the spring the Grand Duke Konstantin
Konstantinovich told me that the Empress wished me to dedicate something
to her, which I have now done. My plans concerning . . . are not yet decided.
I shall probably stay in Maidanovo until *Cherevichky* is produced, and then –
as God wills. They insist that I conduct the first performance myself. I would
like to – very much – but fear that I may not be able. I'll try at a rehearsal
to see if I can force myself. I would love to go to the Caucasus but do not
know when and how I could make the trip. I simply must do the
instrumentation of the opera, which I am very pleased with, during this
winter.

A few days ago I was in Moscow with Modest, and met Lodi and his wife at
the hotel. I was glad to see him, as it reminded me of Tiflis. Modia is leaving
tomorrow and on 1 September will go to a celebration of Yurgenson's 25
years, at the Conservatoire. The weather now is heavenly; all the summer
residents – the dacha people – have left; and Novichikha is not here either;
so it has become very pleasant. Do write me a few words, Golubchik. Modia
wants me to pass on his kisses and regards. . . .

Please, send me a copy of the group. I must have one.

P. Tchaikovsky

Zai and Bull, former dining companions named below, are presumed to have been
dogs.

  Petrovsk-Rasumovsk was formerly an Imperial hunting palace. It is surrounded
by a magnificent park and is now the Institute of Biology and Natural History. The
Sinodalny foundation maintained the choir (and choir school) which sang in the
Cathedral of the Dormition and on great occasions in all the Kremlin cathedrals
(see pp. 302–3).

  Lentovsky's Hermitage was a pleasure garden, with restaurant, named after the
Moscow actor and producer Mikhail Valentinovich Lentovsky (1846–1906).

[Maidanovo]
3 September 1886
7 o'clock a.m.

Modinka!

It seemed so empty and sad after you left; today especially, when I returned from Moscow the house felt lonely. I am writing exactly at the same time as when we five (including Zai and Bull) sat at supper in my study. Very sad. But this feeling will gradually fade away. The day after you left I went up to Moscow. I had lunch at the station. From there I went straight to the Conservatoire for the service, the reading of the report, and also a speech by Kashkin in honour of Liszt. The weather was so lovely that, not waiting for the end of all the celebrations, I went off to the Butyrsky Gates, took a seat in the steam tram (delightful thing), and found myself in Petrovsk-Rasumovsk. You cannot imagine how charming it is.

I experienced that great silent rapture, which comes when the soul completely responds to the impressions, and appreciation, of the beauties of nature. I cannot remember having enjoyed myself like that for ever so long. No one disturbed my solitude in this wonderful park which gradually turns into a forest. And what a forest!

Later there was a dinner at the Hermitage in honour of Yurgenson. Unending speeches and actually – boring in the extreme. After which, went to Lentovsky's Hermitage and then had supper at an inn. The whole of the next day too I was in Moscow. There was a meeting of the Committee of which I am a member at the Sinodalny Office and I was also present at the meeting of the Choral Society. Later at Yurgenson's, Catoire's quartet was played, with Taneev and Hubert. Taneev and I (especially Taneev), think he is very talented.

Wishing to repeat yesterday's ecstasy I went to the forest between the Park and Petrovsk-Rasumovsk once more. I enjoyed it, but not so much as yesterday. I did not have any dinner at all that day, and in the evening was in a box with the Huberts and Sasha Gudim at a performance of *Russlan and Ludmilla*. . . . Today I arrived by the morning train in time for dinner. Tomorrow shall start copying out the songs.

I kiss and embrace you.

P. Tchaikovsky

On 7 September Modest complained that Nadezhda Vassilieva insisted on changes in his comedy, *At the wall* (based on Potekhin, see Letter 431); 'She said she was very pleased, gave some good advice but already, in her attitude, I faced the same lack of understanding of the essence of what I wanted to say that I shall also have to face with an audience.'

Regarding A. Rubinstein's *The Demon* (1875) Tchaikovsky thought this his best work, as he wrote to Mme von Meck on 23 September 1886. B. A. Fietinghof-Shell was the composer of the opera *Tamara* to which reference is made below.

On 15 September Modest wrote that Potekhin was now being awkward over the play. 'He likes the middle but insists on changing the first and the last Act. I answered by refusing, as I have no wish to turn this work into an artistic problem. . . . Anyway this failure has shocked me and brought several nasty hours of suffering to my author's pride.'

[433] TO MODEST TCHAIKOVSKY   [Maidanovo]
                                                9 September 1886

Modia Golubchik!

I should start by grumbling at the weather but I presume it is as bad where you are. Actually I a-d-o-r-e bad weather and never feel as well and full of energy as during the autumn gloom. However, the wind is my everlasting enemy. As long as it does not blow I do not mind. . . . To make it a dozen I have written two more songs. They are all copied out and sent off to Yurgenson. For the last songs [Op. 60] I chose the words from Khomiakov. What a poet he was, and how charming are the two poems I used. They are so lovely and original that I am sure my music is better than in all the other ten.

I advise you not to change anything in the first three Acts – nor take into account Vassilieva's comments. She has been on the stage for many years, and the routine of the Russian theatre has taken deep root in her being. In your play a clever actor, in spite of having been spoilt by the vulgar repertoire, will sense at once something disturbing. But if you notice that Vassilieva does not understand the part and is not enthusiastic about it, do not give it to her. [V. N.] Davydov is the one who will understand better than anyone. In general take his advice and do not despise the Korsh Theatre [a private institution].

I have played through Fietinghof's opera. How very poor. He may have more talent than Soloviev but the latter has more of a composer's technique. Fietinghof's dilettantism is awful. He is a small child, not a mature artist. Honestly it is a shame that they perform such operas on the stage of the Imperial theatres.

What a good service the directors have done to Rubinstein. His *Demon* now seems brilliant in comparison with Shell's. But, to be honest, the best operas are composed by P. I. Tchaikovsky and of all his operas the very best is *Charodeika*. Every page is a precious pearl. So it seems to me at this moment, but I am sure that Fietinghof thinks that his *Tamara* is much better, and God only knows which of us is really right. . . .

I kiss you and embrace you.

P. Tchaikovsky

[434] TO MODEST TCHAIKOVSKY   Maidanovo
                                                18 September 1886

Today I returned from Moscow where I stayed five days. There has been plenty of activity – eating and drinking too much, sleepless nights and so on. I saw a very good production of *Don Juan*. Yesterday we celebrated Sophia Ivanovna Yurgenson's Saint's Day. Oh yes! I forgot to tell you: On 13 September, standing with the Sinodalny Choir in the Cathedral of the Dormition I attended a three hour vigil service, sung according to the Dormition Statutes. This is a magnificent service. It reminded me of late Nikolai Lvovich with whom eight years ago I was in the same church at the same service. The next day I again went to hear the Liturgy. All the same I am more than delighted that my stay in Moscow has come to an end and that I am home again.

I saw Laroche; he has not changed much physically or otherwise, and is as usual. . . .

Before leaving Moscow I played through the whole of *Charodeika*. To my horror I found that each of the four Acts lasts for an hour; the first one even longer. It is clear that they must be drastically cut down – most annoying. Shpajinsky is away and without him I do not know what, and where, to leave out. . . .

In answer to my letter that the songs for the Empress were ready, I had a charming letter from Konstantin Konstantinovich, who also sent me a book of his own poems. What a pity I did not have them earlier. What could have been nicer than to set some of his words and dedicate them to the Empress. Some of the poems are very sweet.

Modinka, I do not quite understand why you protest against Potekhin's wishes. He is the author of the novel and once having agreed to do this job for him you should give way to his demands. It will not take you long to do it and in general it would be a good thing to please him. Did I not change whole Acts more or less, according to what Napravnik indicated? It is, of course, annoying that he did not approve of everything from the first but I see nothing detrimental to your pride in his doing so.

I shall be in Petersburg at the very end of September and will have some money then, or, at the very beginning of October. Starting the instrumentation of the first act tomorrow. . . .

P. Tchaikovsky

[435] TO PRASKOVIA VLADIMIROVNA TCHAIKOVSKAIA
                                        Maidanovo
                                        18 September 1886

My Golubushka Pania!

Dear me, how rarely you write! Why are you angry with me? Well, as God wills! However, do not force yourself, write when you feel like it. I was in Moscow five days; have just returned. I did not see any member of your family. Again I stayed with the Yurgensons and felt uncomfortable, but dared not refuse kind Sophia Nikolaievna the pleasure of having me for a guest. . . .
My opera, so they say, is going to be given in November, and everybody wants

me to conduct. I want very much to do so but am a little afraid, even more than a little. I shall decide at the rehearsals if I can manage to triumph over my frightful shyness. Modest is not like you and Tolia, he writes very often. Some people of authority are delighted with his new comedy. But as usual he complains of the toing and froing and exhaustion of life in a capital. The weather is bad but I feel happy and content when I can be at home in Maidanovo. Now that all the summer residents have left, and Novichikha is away in Moscow, I love Maidanovo again. Everybody asks how you are; they all love and remember you. . . .

I kiss and embrace you.

P. Tchaikovsky

The Russian Musical Society was beginning to feel the results of the competition offered by the Philharmonic Society founded by P. A. Shostakovsky. Napravnik's *Harold* was founded on a German play by E. von Wildenbruch.

[436] TO MODEST TCHAIKOVSKY   Moscow
                                           29 September 1886

Dear Modia!

I am again in Moscow, where I had to go to fetch some money and to decide Laroche's fate. He has stretched Taneev's patience to the limit by never appearing for his classes. We have all decided to give him a year's leave, so that his leaving the Conservatoire would not look like a complete dismissal. He was very much afraid to be chucked out and we didn't want to upset him. I go to Maidanovo today and on Saturday, 4 October, have to return for a very important directors' meeting concerning our situation. This year we have one third less members in the Musical Society, which is very upsetting. Besides that, also on the 4th, Karlusha Albrecht will be fifty years old and the directors and professors of the Conservatoire are giving a big dinner in his honour.

I shall return home on Sunday and arrive in Petersburg on the 14th for the first performance of *Harold*. Napravnik has written saying he would very much like me to come and I definitely will. But, as I am nearly positive that the opera will be put off, I will not come to Petersburg before the 14th, so as not to stay too long. I must be at home and do some work. . . . Am in a great hurry, so no more for now. I kiss you hard. Please, forgive that the money will be late.

P. Tchaikovsky

TO MODEST TCHAIKOVSKY   Maidanovo
7 October 1886

Modinka!

Forgive me, but this will be very short. I have a splitting headache from intense work, but do not want to put off my letter as I have not written for a long time. At the same time I am writing to Napravnik asking him to book a box for us for the performance of *Harold*, so do not worry about a seat. I think of taking Anna Merkling with us.

The title, *At the wall*, I do not like. I do not understand what it means, *Au près du mur?* I suppose?

Laroche is staying here, and I am very pleased that he is. He is writing hard, which I did not expect, as he had gone as far as to be thrown out of the Conservatoire under the pretence of a year's leave.

I am forcing myself to work as much as possible to make up for the time lost in Moscow. I had to go there again, and these journeys take up all my time, money, and health.

And so, *au revoir*, Golubchik. If I stay alive and well, shall arrive in Petersburg on the 14th on the [slow] mail-train.

I embrace you.

P. Tchaikovsky

TO MODEST TCHAIKOVSKY   [Maidanovo]
10 October 1886

I fear you will be angry with me, Modichka, but I have again put my journey off for a few days. A telegram from Napravnik said that *Harold* has been postponed for two weeks. If I had come on the 14th I should not have been able to wait for the first night, and I am rather curious to hear this opera which sounds very glum when one plays it. Whereas, if I start on Friday and arrive on Saturday the 18th I shall see Bob at your flat thus saving me the trouble of visiting him at the college, which I have no desire to do. Also at that time I hope to stay on until *Harold* is produced. As to coming twice it is expensive and tiring. And so on Saturday the 18th I shall arrive (either by the slow mail-train or by the fast one). On that day I would like to have dinner at your place with Bob, then go either to the Circus or the theatre.

Laroche left yesterday after staying for five days. I was very pleased to have him. But it is sad that, with all my efforts and writing from his dictation, I only got a few pages out of him. My work is moving with difficulty. I get easily frightfully tired and my head often aches from the effort. (You know my 'nail' at a certain point of my head.) I think it will do me good to take a trip to Petersburg. The weather today is heavenly.

I kiss, I embrace you.

Yours

P. Tchaikovsky

[439] TO PRASKOVIA VLADIMIROVNA TCHAIKOVSKAIA

Petersburg
4 November 1886

Dearest Panichka!

I can imagine how angry you must be, I deserve it for I have not written for nearly a month. I have been here about three weeks, and – as is usual in Petersburg – am leading such a mad life that it is physically impossible to write letters. But I am not sorry I came. It has been good for business, and for the future of my opera *Charodeika*. Everybody here seems ready to help. Obviously my music is being appreciated more and more. All this is very nice but, my God, how tired I am and how I wish to be back in Maidanovo! I am living very comfortably at Modest's. They have the same flat but it has been partly rebuilt and I now have my own room.

These last three days I have not been well and shall stay at home today with a bad cold. I suffered all day yesterday from a frightful pain in my cheek. Hope to leave for Maidanovo after tomorrow but not for very long as the *Cherevichky* rehearsals will be starting nearly at once. Shall have to work hard on my opera in Maidanovo. . . .

P. Tchaikovsky

Tchaikovsky refers to himself in the next letter as 'Petia Mila' ('Peter Darling'). Either this was a relic of childhood, or an ironical self-allusion.

The ballet *Undina*, referred to in the following letters, was not written. Tchaikovsky's next ballet was *Sleeping Beauty* (1889) (see pp. 406/412).

[440] TO PRASKOVIA VLADIMIROVNA TCHAIKOVSKAIA

Maidanovo
10 November 1886

My Golubushka Pania!

At last – from this morning – I am in Maidanovo, and infinitely happy, especially as I have been informed that the rehearsals of *Cherevichky* will not start before the end of November. This means I can stay here and work for nearly two whole weeks. In spite of my journey to Petersburg I was not, in the end, able to wait for the first performance of Napravnik's opera, which was the reason I went there in the first place. The last three days of my stay I got into such a state of nerves that I feared I would go mad if I did not leave at once. But, to be just, I must say that 'Petia Mila' was greatly feted in Petersburg and there were many moments most rewarding to his artistic pride. . . .

You have probably read in the papers what a tremendous success A. V. Panaeva-Karzeva had in the Mamontov opera. I shall have to work hard all this winter and next summer. The opera *Charodeika* must be ready for Lent, as I have promised, and after that I will start composing the music for the ballet *Undina*. That will bring me good money, not less than 5,000 roubles.

Too many letters to write, so I kiss and embrace all three of you.

Yours

P. Tchaikovsky

[441]   TO MODEST TCHAIKOVSKY   [Maidanovo]
                                                 14 November 1886

My dear Modia!

No luck this time in Maidanovo. I hoped to find peace and absolute contentment here, instead of which, from the very first working day the same headache that I had in Petersburg a month ago returned. . . . Tomorrow I shall start my work again but slowly and without in any way forcing myself. All this is only nerves, and not serious but don't you think that after *Charodeika* I should have a rest and not start on a ballet until next season. It is wiser to rest in summer and build up one's strength. All the same continue to compile the scenario for *Undina*.

And yet how delightful it is here. True, the weather is grey but windless, excellent for walks and, most important, (there is) this heavenly quiet. . . .

Tomorrow there will be a concert of the R.M.S., but I have decided not to go. Partly because of not feeling very well, and partly from an antipathy to Moscow which I have been feeling of late. How curious!

I would like to know how *Harold* went. Pavlovskaia sent me a telegram saying that there was something of a furore after the third and fourth Act.

I kiss and embrace you and Kolichka.

Yours

P. Tchaikovsky

Modinka!

The first page of my letter was written this morning when I had not yet recovered from a feverish night. Now I am well again, have had a good dinner, and feel so full of energy that I am not frightened any more for *Undina*. So forget everything I said about being afraid that I was not going to be able to compose. I am writing the scenario, talking things over with Petitpas and Vsevoloisky, and *Undina* attracts me so much that I think I shall have the music written without difficulty by December – this is not an opera – so long as I keep well. At the moment I feel perfectly well. My head does not ache at all, although I had to write a multitude of letters. I am writing in my room. In front of me is the garden with trees that have shed their leaves, with snow that fell in the night, and a frozen pond. The sunset is colouring everything in a reddish light. Wonderful!

I kiss you.
[No signature]

[442] TO MODEST TCHAIKOVSKY   [Moscow]
                                                19 November 1886

Modichka!

Am sending you the 30 roubles I owe you and your monthly allowance of 100. I am in Moscow where there has been a rehearsal since this morning. Since my last letter I have had an attack of awful diarrhoea and a raging headache. I nearly sent for the doctor. I thought some fiendish illness had started. Suddenly a telegram arrived saying that I must attend a rehearsal. I sent back word that there was no question of a rehearsal, and that I could not come. But half an hour later, in spite of having absolutely no desire to go, I suddenly felt perfectly well and now it seems as if this sickness which has poisoned my life for the last ten days has never been. The diarrhoea disappeared, and my appetite is magnificent. Is that not a most curious pathological fact? It could only happen to me. Now there will be rehearsals every day.

They say that the opera will be played on 15 December, but I doubt it. I very much hope you and Kolia will come. As yet I have not decided whether I shall conduct it myself. Sometimes I want to, then I don't. Because of the illness which plagued me in Maidanovo I had a thousand thoughts and plans to leave everything and go away. . . . Now, of course, nothing will be altered. I shall get *Cherevichky* into production and then come to Peter[sburg] for Christmas.

I kiss, I embrace you.

Yours

P. Tchaikovsky

[443] TO MODEST TCHAIKOVSKY   Moscow
                                                26 November 1886

First, I am perfectly well and in spite of tiring rehearsals (still only with piano),

working till late at night, all sorts of suppers, and so on, I feel
wonderfully well; and all my Maidanovo aches and pains have vanished.
Second, I am very comfortable in my hotel. I have managed things so cleverly
that the time spent on *Charodeika* is not lost, and I compose at least three
hours a day. The First Act is already being printed. Alexei is here with me.
My antipathy to Moscow which had become very strong is now much weaker.
Laroche seems to me to be in a very bad state, and he even tries to avoid
me. Your novel is at the publishers of the *Russian Annals*. *Cordelia* is an awful
flop. I went to the third performance, the theatre was half empty. But do not
mention it to anyone, if you do not want Korsov to poison or (otherwise) kill
me. He has gone absolutely mad because of his failure. Forgive me for writing
only a few lines. I kiss and embrace you.

P.T.

Kolichka and Bob I kiss with love.

On the fiftieth anniversary of the first night of Glinka's *A Life for the Czar* a special
performance was given in Moscow. On 4 December Tchaikovsky wrote to Mme
Shpajinskaia: 'At the jubilee performance I presented Glinka with a wreath. Kashperov
[see Letter 35] insisted on carrying it with me. I definitely refused. However, he
managed it so that the stage director made us appear together. This upset everybody
and the papers mentioned his effrontery. At that he got very offended and sent me
(25 roubles) half the price of the wreath. I sent them back. He got even angrier and
Shpajinsky came to see me to find a way to close the incident. I suggested that the
money should go into the fund for poor Conservatoire pupils. And that was the
end of it. I suppose Kashperov should be pitied, for he meets with a negative attitude
from people all around him. But if he would stop being so arrogant and tactless he
would not be so despised and would have a happier existence.'

[444] TO MODEST TCHAIKOVSKY   Moscow
                                                        4 December 1886

Today, Modinka, a most significant event in my life has taken place. I conducted
the first orchestral rehearsal and in such a way that everyone was staggered;
for they all expected me to disgrace myself. I will not tell you all the torture
I suffered when, a few days ago, Altany arranged the rehearsal. The nearer the
dreaded time, the more I suffered, and many times I wanted to refuse. But in
the end – with great difficulty – I forced myself to go. When I went I was
greeted with enthusiasm by the orchestra, bravely made a speech, and – most
bravely – started waving my baton. Now I know that *I can conduct* and will
probably not be at all scared at the performance. But it will not take place in
the very near future, probably not before January, between the 10th and
the 15th. I shall conduct all the rehearsals, then go to Maidanovo for the
holidays (where I expect you with Kolia), or I will come to Petersburg myself
so that we shall see each other before the first night. Many of the rehearsals

were with piano accompaniment. All my free time I work on *Charodeika*. And I also go everywhere. Lately, on account of Arma Zenkra, I have had to attend a good number of receptions, and suppers, and lead a dissipated life.

I see Panaeva and George now and then. I heard her in *A Life for the Czar* when she sang beautifully, but she has no self-assurance as an actress. (Do not mention it to anybody.) Tomorrow I shall hear her in *Aida*. At the Glinka celebration the directors unexpectedly made me and Kashperov present a wreath to Glinka for which I had to pay 50 roubles. I scarcely see Laroche. My God! How unhappy I was this morning and how happy I feel now. I am perfectly well but work often makes me tired. I will soon have an answer about your novel, and I will see that it is published. I kiss you.

P. Tchaikovsky

You too, do not send me much news.

[445] TO PRASKOVIA VLADIMIROVNA TCHAIKOVSKAIA
                                              [Moscow]
                                              15 December 1886

How often I think of you, Panichka!

How often I have a crazy wish to find myself with you in Tiflis. But I still do not find enough time to write proper letters. *Cherevichky* is being rehearsed every day but will not be put on before 15 January. This is an awkward time for a new opera, and it would have been better if it could have had more rehearsal. I conducted four rehearsals, with orchestra, myself. At the first I nearly died of fright. Now with every rehearsal I am getting better, and today I was quite composed when I waved my baton. I go back to the country for the holidays, then I shall be here again from 7 January. In all probability the opera will be staged at last in a month's time. . . .

Everybody is hurt at your not writing. I too am forgotten. You have not got to produce an opera, so surely your time is your own. I suppose you have become quite indifferent to me, which ought to have been expected.

I kiss you all lovingly.

P. Tchaikovsky

[446] TO ANATOLI TCHAIKOVSKY   [Maidanovo]
                                              26 December 1886

Well! I have already conducted seven rehearsals of *Cherevichky* and am becoming more sure of myself with each one. I cannot say what it will be like with an audience. I was more afraid of the performers than of the public, but now I have got quite used to them. All the same these rehearsals have absorbed so much of my nervous energy that I could not do anything else. As it was important to work on my *Charodeika*, I have been in no fit state to write letters, so do not be angry at my long silence. Every time I get a letter from you I long to fly to you. I miss you, and the Caucasus has captivated my heart. As soon as I get rid of *Charodeika* I shall come to you at once; it is difficult to say exactly when, but I hope earlier than you expect. Have you heard that Vera Tretiakova is engaged to Ziloty? On the day before I left I went to a dinner in their honour. . . .

Look here! Do please ask me in every letter to come as soon as possible, for this will compel me to come to a definite decision. I kiss and embrace all three of you with love.

The first performance of *Cherevichky* is planned for 15 January.

P. Tchaikovsky

The leading parts for *Cherevichky* at the first performance on 19 January 1887 were as follows: Vakula, the blacksmith – Oussatov; The Devil – Korsov; Pan Golova, the Major – Strelezky; Choob, a rich peasant – Matchinsky; The Prince – Khokhlov; Master of Ceremonies – Vassilievsky; Oksana – Klimentova; Solokha (the merry widow) – Sviatlovskaia.

[447] TO PRASKOVIA VLADIMIROVNA TCHAIKOVSKAIA
[Moscow]
[21–22 January 1887]

Here is a short report on the first night. The dress rehearsal took place two days before. During the rehearsals I became so assured in my conducting that I was quite calm at the last rehearsal and hoped all would be well on the first night. But on the night before I began to feel ill and on the morning of the 19th I woke up so ill that I wondered if it would not be better to cry off.

I do not know how I lived through the day, for I suffered agonies. Towards the appointed hour I appeared in a dazed condition, and when the hour of doom struck I walked to the orchestra like an automaton. Then terrific applause broke out, and wreaths and flowers were showered on me from the stage. I felt better at once. Bravely I started the introduction, and with every minute felt more at ease. For the second Act I came out as calm as an Altany who has conducted all his life. Presentations, wreaths, curtain-calls, etc., ovations – more than enough. Just imagine, Panichka! Everybody is of the unanimous opinion that I am a conductor of talent. If this is true, then it is strange that all my life I have been wrong in imagining myself to be hopeless in this respect. Anyway everything went quite splendidly, and I was very pleased with the performance.

Unfortunately Krutikova (a magnificent Solokha), fell ill the day before the dress rehearsal and her part was sung by Sviatlovskaia, a good singer but certainly not the actress for this part. Of the others, Klimentova, Korsov and

Oussatov were best. Of the members of our family Modest, brother Kolia and Niks Litke were present. I shall conduct twice more.

I kiss and embrace you.

Yours

P. Tchaikovsky

[448] TO MODEST TCHAIKOVSKY

[Moscow]
22 January 1887
8 o'clock a.m.

After you left, dear Modichka, I went home and by 6 o'clock was already at the Hermitage. I had dinner with Kolia and Laroche, and Laroche stayed with me all the evening after Kolia left. I went early to bed and slept well. Had a sad day yesterday. Wanted to work but somehow could not. Oh, what an impossible institution the post is! ! ! I have a mass of letters on my conscience and today I tried in vain to cope with them, but have still not finished. Today I was busy clearing up the matter of the offence given by the Musical Society to the artistes of the Bolshoi Theatre. Scandal, ambition, pettiness, and unwarrantable conceit of artistes – that is what I have been up to my neck in all day. Yesterday Bob's telegram gave me an exquisite sense of comfort. Was it really on his own impulse? If so, I am infinitely gratified and flattered. Then the *Novoe Vremia* arrived, and I got all the details. Much later your telegram came. In the evening I went to d'Albert's concert. . . .

Although I seem to be living these two days in a nightmare I am perfectly well. The public is thronging to *Cherevichky*. After tomorrow I will let you know all about the second performance.

I kiss and embrace you all three I mean you, Bob and Kolichka.

Yours

P. Tchaikovsky

[449] TO MODEST TCHAIKOVSKY

Moscow
26 January 1887

Dear Modia!

The second performance of *Cherevichky* went more smoothly than the first. Krutikova was not at her best, but all the same she is better than Sviatlovskaia. At first the audience was somewhat cool, but it warmed up gradually and finally there was more than enough of noise and shouts. I found it more difficult to conduct on this occasion, and now and again I had the feeling that in another minute I would have no more strength to wave my baton. No one, however, noticed it. I explain it by being overtired after all that has happened to me lately. It is time to leave, and how! My heart aches, and stops beating

at the happy thought that soon I shall be alone in the country again. . . .
I tried to work, at least a little, on *Charodeika*, but have not done much.
Heard d'Albert twice. Magnificent pianist. . . .

Have to go to a rehearsal. As Khokhlov is away the part of the Prince must
be rehearsed with Borisov. No time to write any more.

I embrace you.

P. Tchaikovsky

[450] TO MODEST TCHAIKOVSKY   Maidanovo
                                                  29 January 1887

Today I returned to Maidanovo, my dear Modia, and am happy to be back
after all that has been happening in Moscow. The third performance was
a success. As at the first two I was terrified at the beginning, but soon became
quite calm, and seemed to have even more assurance than before. I am not a
bit surprised that as yet there is more curiosity about the opera than genuine
enthusiasm for it. At first the audience seems uncertain and responds coldly;
but the longer the work goes on the more interested the audience becomes,
and the Fourth Act is always greeted enthusiastically. I think that *Cherevichky*
will like *Onegin* be appreciated gradually by the public and loved in the end.
My own love for it makes me certain that one day it will be loved by everybody
else.

I received an invitation from the Petersburg Philharmonic Society to conduct
a concert of my works during Lent. Do you know, I think I am going to accept
it! If I have not made a fool of myself in an opera you can be sure I shall not
do so at a concert. . . .

All the Moscow wreaths have been hung round the walls and decorate my
rooms very nicely. This must be my fifteenth letter today, so forgive if it is
short.

I kiss all of you very hard.

Yours

P. Tchaikovsky

Yurgenson is sending you an autograph of d'Albert.

[451] TO MODEST TCHAIKOVSKY   [Maidanovo]
                                                  12 February 1887

I am sorry, Modinka, that you and the boys did not come. The weather is
beautiful and I am sure we would have all enjoyed ourselves, though, as a
matter of fact, I do not enjoy the weather very much. I am working so hard
that I have a headache every day and all I think about is: shall I finish it?

Will I have enough time? Oh, God! how much I still have to do! and so on. . . .

I have decided to conduct the concert of the Philharmonic Society. I will arrive, God willing, on Monday for the two weeks of Lent and will stay with you for two weeks. Naturally I am scared but all the same I have a great desire to wave the baton a bit. Now, *au revoir*, but not for long. Sorry to have written so little. I kiss you.

P. Tchaikovsky

[452] TO PRASKOVIA VLADIMIROVNA TCHAIKOVSKAIA

Petersburg
27 February 1887

My dove, my sweetest Pania!

Oh dear! How rarely I write, more rarely even than you! But the whole of this winter has been such a mad rush that it has been impossible to keep up a proper correspondence! Now I am in Peter[sburg] to conduct a big concert of my works. I am very nervous, and very frightened, and I am also invited out and pulled this way and that by all sorts of people all the time. Everything, in fact, is as usual!

What I would like to tell you is something definite about when I shall be able to come and see you. I thought at first that I would like to come in spring – as I did last year – because I want to see you as soon as possible and repeat the lovely times I had. But now I think I ought to come later and spend the whole summer with you. In any case I am not going to stay in Maidanovo, and have let my house for the summer to N. Mamontov for 300 roubles. So it is altogether best that I should stay the summer with you. However, I would like to stay in Kamenka for a time. Also, I ought to go to Paris and – what is most important – finish my work before the summer.

So here I am, indecisive as ever, not knowing what to do. I think, though, that when my concert has taken place and I have calmed down I shall be able to plan properly. In any case I shall be with you for the most of the summer at least. This, providing I am still alive, is definitely decided. . . .

Oh, Panichka, how frightening! The first rehearsal is tomorrow and at the mere thought of it my tummy starts aching. Shall send a telegram after the concert. I embrace you and kiss you hard. I miss you, my dear and my dearest Tolia and Tatussia. Here all is well.

P. Tchaikovsky

On 5 March Tchaikovsky conducted a Philharmonic concert in St Petersburg, the programme was entirely of his works, comprising the Second Suite (first time in St Petersburg), vocal and instrumental excerpts from *Charodeika*, two movements from the Serenade for Strings, *Francesca da Rimini*, the *1812* Overture, and some songs. Tchaikovsky was well received and was regarded as a good conductor. He described his feelings to Mme von Meck in his letter of 10 March as follows: 'The night before was torture. I slept badly and came to the rehearsal quite ill. But as soon as I went up to the rostrum, took up the baton, and was met by the enthusiasm of the players, all fear left me and I was told I did my work very well. At the next rehearsal I was completely sure of myself. Before appearing at the concert I was naturally very nervous but this was not fear; rather was it a feeling of that deep artistic elation a composer experiences when he directs a first-class orchestra playing his works with great love. It is so deep and so extraordinary that it would be impossible to put it into words, and if my efforts to conduct were the result of an awful struggle with myself and, maybe, cost me a few years of my life I am not a bit sorry. I have experienced moments of absolute happiness and felicity.'

[453] TO PRASKOVIA VLADIMIROVNA TCHAIKOVSKAIA

Maidanovo, near Klin
12 March 1887

My dove Pania!

You have the right to be angry with me for not writing – but this is a year in which I cannot write. I have returned to Maidanovo after an absence of three weeks. My concert, as you probably know from the papers, was a great success, and I conducted with real assurance. Can you believe it? Do you remember how ill I used to feel when a work of mine was to be played. And now, I myself conducted a whole concert and, except for the first moment, did not feel a bit nervous. It is a pity you could not see me. I hope that, all being well, you will be able to see me next season.

My life in Petersburg was, naturally, impossible, and I cannot say how happy I am to be at home. The last days were particularly bad. I was very glad to meet [Ippolitov-]Ivanov and Zarudnaia at the concert. I met them again several times and one evening at Pavlovskaia's house Varvara Mikhailovna sang and everybody thought her very good. They want to pay me a visit on their way back. I am not very pleased about it, but it cannot be helped. . . . Now I must get back to work properly, and it is difficult to say when it will be possible for me to leave. But, without fail, I shall spend the summer with you. It would be that if I have time to finish the proofs before Easter then I shall come at once.

Do not forget that Modest and Kolia also want to be with you for the summer; so take a large dacha for all of us. Naturally, Modest and I will pay our share, and I want to stay with you in Borjom – but not as your guest, else I should feel embarrassed. I miss you terribly and my heart yearns for you all the time. . .

My dear soul! I kiss your hands. Embrace Tolia and Tata. Keep well, my dears.

Yours

P. Tchaikovsky

Maidanovo
15 March 1887

As soon as I arrived I got down to work, and as usual too hard – to the point
of exhaustion. Yesterday morning Ivanov and Zarudnaia came! How I hated
them for the first few moments! It meant that I would have to be idle all day.
But gradually their great charm (especially hers) completely conquered me,
and when they were leaving I was on the verge of asking them to stay a little
longer. She also sang – charmingly. I like *Ruth* more and more. I think
Ippolitov-Ivanov will go very far for he has an individuality of his own, and
this trait of personality is very attractive.

The weather is still wintery and during my absence a lot of snow has fallen.
But one gets a bit of warmth from the sun during the day and walking is very
pleasant. I was going to tell you before leaving, and did not, that you ought to
write a new comedy – a simple one without any extraordinary complications
in the plot. One has to give in and conform to the fashions of the day. One
must have had enormous success before that, to be able to produce your last
play, which I still think very good. Let me know if a new play has germinated
yet.

Do not forget to give Nazar my portrait. Has Nara one, I am not sure, if not
and she wants one I shall send one to her.

P. Tchaikovsky

Nazar (Litrov) was Modest's servant (see p. 428), and Nara was Nikolai (Kolia)
Tchaikovsky's nanny (see Letter 365).
   Ippolitov-Ivanov's first opera, *Ruth* (Tiflis, 1887), was dedicated to Tchaikovsky,
who had taken a great interest in it throughout the course of its composition. On
7 July 1886, on returning from Tiflis, he wrote: 'I am quite sure that the music of
your opera will be very successful, poetical and touching, but do all you can to make
the plot interesting and attractive. I do not mean a piling up of effects. But what
takes place on the stage must be affecting and attract the warm interest of the
audience.' On 20 July 1887 he wrote again: 'From the musical point of view it is
absolutely charming, and what pleases me is that it has its own musical character –
a pledge of an excellent future as a composer. . . . Naturally *Ruth* has a few faults,
but how can it be otherwise with a first opera!' Tchaikovsky did his best to have
the opera produced and to have excerpts given concert performance.

Maidanovo
23 March 1887

I went to Moscow for two days, and was at the twelfth and last concert of the
Musical Society. At the Italian Opera I heard a lovely singer named Russel and
I attended a meeting of directors, etc. Yesterday, Sunday, I was going to have
dinner and pass the evening with the von Mecks, but on arriving home at

5.30, to change, I found a telegram waiting for me: 'Broke my arm, please come. Laroche.' You can imagine what I felt. I went at once and that is what I found.

The previous day Laroche and Katerina Ivanovna were with me at the opera. After the theatre Kashkin and Albrecht joined us and we had supper together and enjoyed ourselves until 3.00 am. Then Laroche and Katerina Ivanovna went along an awful road to the park and called at the Yar. On their way back, at 6.00 in the morning, just before they came up to the Triumphal Gates the driver capsized the sledge and poor Mania broke his arm. He has been properly attended to, and his arm is in a plaster cast. I stayed with him all the evening. He is not suffering very much but is lying quite still and he looks feverish. The plaster cast makes him look a bit funny – like the statue of the Commandatore. There is nothing really very terrible about it, but the bone is broken along the whole length of the arm, and he says he can hear it cracking when he moves.

He is being looked after perfectly. Yesterday, for the first time I really liked Ekaterina Ivanovna. All the best of her womanly qualities came to the surface. His mother, his daughters, his friends, all crowded around him. Laroche was even quite jolly.

I kiss and embrace you.

P. Tchaikovsky

[456] TO MODEST TCHAIKOVSKY   [Maidanovo]
                                             20 April 1887

I am still here, working frantically, and I still can't get to the end of the Fourth Act. I shall probably have to work for another four or five days. Novichikha is back – the same as usual – and has sold a forest and acquired some money. Although I am quite content here both Kamenka and Tiflis are urging me to come as soon as I can, which irritates me and makes me feel rushed. Are you thinking about a new play? Have you got a plan? Yesterday, reading *Novoe Vremia*, I was quite bowled over by a short story by Chekhov. Don't you think he has great talent? I am not writing any letters; I do not see anyone; and I am so deeply wrapped up in *Charodeika* that I feel I am one of the characters in it.

I kiss you and Kolia. I understand Kolia is going to have his examinations very soon.

Yours

P. Tchaikovsky

The story of Chekhov mentioned above was 'The villagers'. Work on *Charodeika* was completed at the beginning of May. A visit to Kondratiev in St Petersburg distressed him, for it was clear that his old friend was a dying man. In July Tchaikovsky broke off from his holiday in the Caucasus which he had planned to spend with Anatoli and his wife in order to be at the bedside of Kondratiev in Aachen. He spent six weeks here, interrupted only by a one day visit to Paris. By the beginning of September he was back in Maidanovo, where he studied Schumann's *Genoveva* and looked around for another house in the neighbourhood.

[457] TO PRASKOVIA VLADIMIROVNA TCHAIKOVSKY

Batum
6 July 1887

Panichka!

My God! Can it be true that I have left Borjom and all of you? Is it possible that I am really compelled to sweat and fry in the town of Aachen? I do not know why, but, during my last days in Borjom I did not realize the full bitterness of the impending change. I only understood it properly for the first time yesterday towards evening. A fearful sadness overwhelmed me and I felt a sharp pang of sorrow for Borjom and all of you. . . .

Just fancy, I travelled in a private carriage. Some big shot of the railway was travelling to a station beyond Suram where the carriage was going to be left, but when he discovered that I was such an important person he begged me to continue on in his delightful *wagon-salon* and I made the journey all alone right to Batum, where I took rooms at the Hotel Imperial. I had vivid memories of our stay here last year! The same rooms, the same faces. . . . This morning I went to get my tickets for the boat then walked in the impossible heat. Now shall go for a swim, have lunch, and go on board at 3.30.

Stay well, my Golubchiks, my dears, my sweet ones. Will write from Odessa. The Hotel porter promised that he would arrange for me to travel alone in a three berths cabin. I kiss and embrace all four of you thousands of times.

Yours

P. Tchaikovsky

[458] TO MODEST TCHAIKOVSKY

on the steamer *Vladimir*
[Batum–Sebastopol]
8 July 1887

Modia!

This is addressed to you but is written to all of you and will be sent from Odessa. So that you will not feel hurt, or fight for the honour of getting letters from me, I shall send them in turn to Pania, you and Kolia, but not Tolia as he is not always in Borjom.

Yesterday I wandered through Batum all the morning. Compared with last year it seems more drab. The merchants look glumly out of their shops; the streets are empty; and the garden by the sea looks very much overgrown. I had a swim in the sea with Alexei, and after lunch went for another stroll, had coffee in a Turkish Coffee House, and read the papers. Went on board after 3 o'clock. The name of the boat is *Vladimir*. I have a three-berth cabin to myself and have been promised to be alone until Odessa. The dinner was at 6 o'clock – tasty, but a bit heavy. There were about 15 people in the dining saloon. The women: an Armenian matron with three long-nosed daughters. The men, all in suits of Chinese silk, eat off their knives, and are not at all nice. It seems they are all travelling free. I stayed on deck until 10.30 and admired the night – full of stars; then I went to bed and slept until 7 o'clock. I slept so well that I did not hear us arrive at and leave Sukhum. The weather was heavenly. The sunset, the like of which I had not seen for a long time, gave me indescribable delight.

It is 10 o'clock in the morning now. I am longing for lunch and dying of hunger.

9 July

Last night we came to Kerch, where we stayed the whole night as we were taking on coal. To prevent coal dust from getting into the cabins all the windows were closed, which made it so hot that all night I suffered all over from an itch like a nettle rash. It is 10 o'clock in the morning and we are still here. A little steamer brought some more passengers; but we shall not be able to see Kerch. Off at last. I go on not knowing anyone. Frightfully hot and a bit boring.

10 July

Arrived at Sebastopol. Sealing my letter and taking it myself to be posted. Weather lovely.

P. Tchaikovsky

The first performance of *Charodeika*, with Fyodor Stravinsky again in a leading part, took place at the Marinsky Theatre, St Petersburg, on 20 October. Tchaikovsky, who did not mention this in letters to his brother, conducted and was given an ovation, but with subsequent performances interest waned and the critics complained as they had done before, in respect of other of his operas, that there was a lack of dramatic power. The performances in Tiflis from 14 December (see Letter 461) were more successful. The opera was played six times to full houses, but quickly dropped into relative oblivion.

On the other hand the first concert conducted by Tchaikovsky in Moscow, on 14 November, was a great success. The programme was exclusively of his works, comprising *Mozartiana* (Suite No. 4, Op. 61, first performance), *Francesca da Rimini*, the Concert Fantasy for piano and orchestra (Taneev being the soloist), excerpts from *Charodeika*, and some songs sung by A. Skompskaia. The next day the same programme was repeated at an afternoon performance for a popular audience admitted at cheap rates. This was also most successful.

Mozartiana was played at a Russian Musical Society Concert in St Petersburg, conducted by the composer, on 12 December.

The tour described in the following pages was the first such tour undertaken by Tchaikovsky, and it was largely instrumental in establishing his reputation abroad. This was achieved by a kind of dialectical process. The French said that Tchaikovsky was too German for their taste, the Germans that he was too French. Both sets of critics agreed that there was a distinctive Russian quality in the music. Audiences, however, were unimpressed by critical notices and showed an alarming tendency sometimes to like music for no other reason than it seemed to possess a particularly personal cathartic character. Autobiographical notes on this tour are available in Modest's biography of his brother.

[459] TO MODEST TCHAIKOVSKY   [Moscow]
                                                 15 November 1887

Modia!

The whole week was taken up by rehearsals, of which there were four, by visits to Pania who is very ill, and by the general spate of activity. Pania has typhus. Yesterday's concert was extremely pleasant and the audience very enthusiastic. I was given a number of expensive presents and a mass of bouquets. What was bad was that I did not enjoy myself as much as in Petersburg on 5 March. My heart thumped, I was out of breath, and in general, something somewhere was wrong. This afternoon there is a repetition of the same concert. I am sorry that I agreed to conduct it, since I am frightfully tired.

I am not going to Tiflis but, instead, shall stay in Maidanovo for three weeks from Tuesday – that is, the day after tomorrow. I am telling you, as a secret, that I'm not going to conduct in Petersburg on the 26th as I have been invited to conduct at the Leipzig Gewandhaus on the same date. This is so important that I must give up Petersburg. However, we shall see.

I am so tired that I cannot write any more. . . . I kiss and embrace you, Kolia, and Bob.

P. Tchaikovsky

[460] TO MODEST TCHAIKOVSKY   Maidanovo
                                                 19 November 1887

Modia!

On the morning I wrote to you last I felt so rotten that I thought I would have to refuse to conduct. But, with an effort, I went to the hall. When I got there I had a fit of hysteria, after which I mounted the rostrum and felt that I was conducting better than ever. I have never before had such a triumph and met such enthusiasm. The audience, who had tickets at reduced prices, behaved quietly, listened attentively, and were very nice. I stayed all next day with

Pania who is worse. When I left I was very worried indeed. Maidanovo looks completely dismantled.

In anticipation of my trip to Tiflis Alexei has packed up and put everything away. I live as if I were camping, but am nevertheless pleased to be here. I have acquired a new complaint, a sort of shortness of breath which bothers me a lot in the mornings. I think it must be nerves, as the rest of my body is in perfect working order. I promised Auer that I would conduct *Mozartiana* at the third concert instead of the fourth, as I have been invited to conduct at the Gewandhaus on the 23rd and would not like to miss the opportunity. So I think we shall see each other earlier than I thought.

I kiss and embrace you.

Yours

P. Tchaikovsky

[461]   TO ANATOLI TCHAIKOVSKY   Berlin
                                                   17–29 December 1887
My dear Tolia!

I arrived in Berlin this morning, having stayed a week in Petersburg when I successfully took part in a Musical Society Concert. I was very unhappy all the time I was in Peter because I was going abroad. Who knows, it may all turn out well. In any case, if I find it impossible to go on wandering through Germany. Nothing can stop me from leaving everything to return home. This thought is a great consolation. Up till now I have not seen anyone. Tomorrow I'll let my agent know that I am here and will probably leave for Leipzig, where the first rehearsal will take place, on 21 December (2 January). Will write to you a little bit at a time as there will be so much rushing about that it will be difficult to find real time for correspondence.

My health, thank God, is perfect. I have just had a telegram from Tiflis saying that *Charodeika* went off well. Very happy. Please, thank all the theatre people for me. Dear God, how I would prefer to be in Tiflis now instead of Berlin!!! Pania will surely have returned by the time this letter reaches you.

I kiss and embrace you all. You may expect a letter from Leipzig.

Yours

P. Tchaikovsky

[462]   TO MODEST TCHAIKOVSKY   Berlin
                                                   18–30 December 1887

Thanks to interesting reading matter, the journey was quite pleasant, except for the evenings when gloom set in. . .

Nearing Berlin I was very much afraid that [D. A.] Friedrich would meet me; thank God, however, he didn't. I ordered tea at the hotel and read in the *Fremdenblatt* that I was in Berlin, that my friends and admirers (!!!!) are giving a lunch in my honour at 1 o'clock on the 30th, and that (*man bittet*) everyone not to be late!!!! My fury and horror are inexpressible – I would gladly have killed Friedrich if he had been present. I dozed until eleven, and then went to the Galleries, to a café to have lunch, and to a museum. At every step I was in fear of running into Friedrich or any one of 'my friends and admirers!'

The winter here is very much like in Petersburg and quite a few men drive about in sledges of the most fantastic shapes. In the museum, looking at Murillo's *St Antonio*, I thought of you, and in general had a great feeling of pleasure. It would have been perfect in the dining-room (where I find the table-d'hôte menu represents the best form of cooking in the world), if it had not been for the proprietor who started talking about Russia, politics, and so on. After dinner I went for a long walk without galoshes or overcoat, and felt absolutely frozen, not being used to this foreign fashion of not being warmly wrapped up. I went back to the hotel having bought a lot of books, which included Daudet's *Trente ans à Paris*. I fell into a state of sorrow, anguish, and even despair. Several times I thought of leaving everything and going back home. Honestly, this sort of life is not for me, especially in my old age!

I wrote to Friedrich and told him to appear tomorrow at 10 o'clock. Then, as usual, I had a cry and felt better. Having asked for a lamp, I drank tea and read with pleasure, but shuddering ever so often at the thought of Friedrich, I imagined that this villain was coming with the sole desire to torture me. When he turned up he happened to be not in the least unpleasant. *I* at once declared that I did not want to see anyone or go anywhere today. I got rid of him politely, went to the Passage (Galleries) to have some lunch and to read the *Novoe Vremia*, then took a walk through the Tiergarten (masses of people driving sledges, some with Russian harnesses). At 7.00 pm Friedrich is coming to take me to a concert where they are performing Berlioz's *Requiem*, and where I shall meet several people I need (to see). Tomorrow am off to Leipzig at 3 o'clock.

What will happen next I cannot say but for the present, no joy!

I kiss and embrace you.

P. Tchaikovsky

[463] TO MODEST TCHAIKOVSKY   Leipzig
                                     21 December 1887–
                                     2 January 1888

Modia!

It is very difficult to describe in full all I have felt, and shall feel in the near future. In Berlin I went to a big concert where Berlioz's *Requiem* was performed, with Szarwenka conducting. Here my Friedrich showed himself to be as nasty and mean as Bessel, and I started hating him with all the power of my being. He involved himself in so much intrigue that I almost quarrelled with the Philharmonic Society by seriously hurting the feelings of their Director. It would take too long and be too boring to describe (in detail). I made the acquaintance of Szarwenka and a mass of other people and unexpectedly ran into Artôt. After that Friedrich annoyed me by sticking to me all the evening. Next day I went to see Bock (everybody wonders why I have Friedrich following me like a shadow), and left at 3 o'clock for Leipzig – luckily without Friedrich.

I was met by Brodsky, Ziloty and two fans. The hotel is lovely. I had supper with Brodsky, and there was a Christmas tree. His wife and sister-in-law are two charming Russian women and I was on the verge of tears. The next morning I went for a walk (New Year's day here), then went with Ziloty to dine with Brodsky. He was rehearsing Brahms's new trio, and Brahms himself played the piano. He is a red-faced little man, with a large paunch. He behaved kindly to me. Then we had dinner. Brahms is a terrific drunkard. Grieg, who is most charming, was also there.

In the evening I went to the Gewandhaus where Joachim and Grussmann played the new Brahms Double Concerto and Brahms conducted. I sat in the Directors' box and met so many people that it is impossible to name them all. The Directors told me that my rehearsal was to take place the next day. I just cannot describe my sufferings on that evening and, indeed, during the whole time. If it had not been for Brodsky and Ziloty I would have been ready to die. The night was awful!

The rehearsal took place this morning. Reinecke presented me to the orchestra, and I made a short speech in German. The rehearsal was excellent, and the orchestra above praise. Yesterday and today I saw Brahms several times (he came to the rehearsal). We are shy of each other, but he tries his best to be pleasant. Grieg is charming. Friedrich arrived yesterday and annoys me frightfully. How I hate him! Had dinner with Ziloty. At the quartet concert in the evening. Brahms's new trio is boring. Supper. Disgustingly tired. I kiss you.

P. Tchaikovsky

One cannot describe how luxurious the Gewandhaus Hall is. It is the most wonderful hall I have ever seen in my life. Forgot to say that I met Davydov (K.Y.) in Berlin, and was immensely glad to see him.

[464] TO ANATOLI, AND PRASKOVIA TCHAIKOVSKAIA
                                          Leipzig
                                          21 December 1887–
                                          2 January 1888

My good Tolia, and Panichka, my dear!

This is my third day in Leipzig. So much has happened that I cannot describe it all. I will try to write as often as possible, but only short letters, as I have not much free time. Today was my first rehearsal at the Gewandhaus. I was dreadfully worried about it all last evening, all through the night, and this morning, but everything went quite well.

I have met an immense number of people here, of whom the most notable are Brahms and Grieg. Brahms is a bon viveur with whom I had a lot to drink at Brodsky's house. Grieg is an extremely likable man of my age. I am being pestered and followed everywhere – as if by a shadow – by Friedrich, my agent, who is in charge of my itinerary. I am forever in a state of deep dejection, but luckily two of my close friends, i.e. Brodsky (with his charming wife and sister-in-law), and Ziloty, are here. I can open my heart to them. Vera Ziloty has greatly changed; she looks older but very happy, and the child is sweet. The last rehearsal, with an audience is the day after tomorrow and the concert on Thursday the 5th (on 24 December according to our calendar).

You can't imagine how luxurious and wonderful the Gewandhaus is. The orchestra is above praise. Reinecke introduced me to the orchestra at the rehearsal, and I made a speech in German. I shall go from here to Berlin, where I have to talk things over with the Philharmonic Society, and then on to Hamburg. As yet I have not anything definite about Copenhagen. In Berlin on 8 February (new style). Leipzig is a large, beautiful town. The frost is bitter. . . .

Going to bed. Dear Lord, how I wish I was in Tiflis now. I will write after the concert. I kiss you heartily.

P. Tchaikovsky

At the concert on 5 January (western style) the First Suite was played, and next day at a chamber music concert arranged by the *Lisztverein* the Piano Trio, the First String Quartet, and arrangements of Pieces from *Eugene Onegin* were performed. Tchaikovsky sat with the Griegs.

While in Hamburg Tchaikovsky had a telegram from I. A. Vsevoloisky informing him of the award of a life pension of 3000 roubles by the Czar.

[465] TO ANATOLI TCHAIKOVSKY   [Berlin]
                                  28 December 1887–
                                  9 January 1888

Tolia!

I do not remember when I last wrote from Leipzig! I think it was after the first rehearsal. The next one, which was most successful, was public – with tickets. Next day – the concert. I shall not repeat all the fears, excitement, nerves, and longing to run away that I endured. However, I had an excellent reception and was twice recalled. In Leipzig this is regarded as a signal honour.

After each piece, especially after the first, they applauded energetically. After the concert I had an evening at Reinecke's, and then had to go to one arranged by Russian students. Returned home very late. Next day there was a 'Tchaikovsky Feier' in the *Lisztverein*. My trio, quartet and some short pieces were played. Their reception was enthusiastic, with bouquets being presented amid great applause. Then there was a tremendous lot of eating and drinking. Next day I arrived in Berlin.

Here Brodsky and I are inseparable. Two days ago he played at the von Bülow Concert. Yesterday I had a conference with the directors about my concert. The programme has been very well chosen. I also had a long talk with the Wolff agency, who promised to set me free from the continual persecution of Friedrich, the agent whom I mentioned to you in Moscow. He is a fool and a blackguard. In Leipzig I had great moral support and sympathy from Brodsky, his wife, Ziloty and Vera. In Leipzig I have also a number of fanatical – musically speaking – friends. I became particularly friendly with Grieg and his wife, who are charming people.

Late tonight I will be going to Hamburg with Brodsky, and will be there tomorrow for the von Bülow concert. My rehearsal there will be on the 5th (17th). In between I want to hide in Lübeck to have a rest in solitude, (and to recover) from this impossible nervous exhaustion. Write to Berlin: (37, Leipzigerstrasse, Bote & Bock).

I kiss with all my heart you, Pania and Tata.

Yours

P. Tchaikovsky

[466] TO MODEST TCHAIKOVSKY   Lübeck–Hamburg
                                                30 December 1887–
                                                11 January 1888

My God! What happiness! And how well I feel at finding myself in a lovely hotel in a strange town, looking forward to five days of solitude and perfect peace. I left Berlin in the evening of the day before yesterday and arrived in Hamburg at 6.00 in the morning. At 10.00 am there was a rehearsal of the von Bülow Concert in which Brodsky takes part. Von Bülow was very pleased to see me. He has changed, looks older, softer, and has become more kind and more serene. After the rehearsal I had lunch with Brodsky at one of the famous Hamburg Clubs. Then I went to see Rater and Berndt and have definitely decided upon the programme of the concert, rehearsals, etc. Von Bülow conducted like a genius, especially the 'Eroica'.

I arrived here today and am in a very pleasant mood. What bliss to be silent! What delight to know no one will come and drag you somewhere! Tomorrow I shall work preparing pieces that I do not know but which I will conduct in Hamburg and Berlin.

At last our January has come. It is now possible to reckon that there are only four more months before I return to Russia. I am living here very pleasantly and in spite of greeting the New Year quite by myself I do not feel lonely or upset. That shows how much I needed freedom and quiet. The weather is heavenly, and there are plenty of fine walks in Lübeck. I work in the mornings and go out for a stroll before dinner, which is at 1.15, and do not talk to anyone. I just watch actors and actresses who have a good time here. Go for a walk again – work. Two days ago I whiled away the time at the [Turkish] Baths and had supper in my room.

Last night I went to the theatre for *Othello*. Barnai came for one performance and was good – at some points absolutely wonderful. But what a torturing play. Iago is more than disgusting – there cannot really be such people. The sets are bad. Desdemona not quite hopeless; Iago awful; Rodrigo wonderfully sympathetic; Cassio really funny. I had supper at home, read Muravlin's novel *Next to Money* (full of talent: I liked especially the portrayal of the author's feelings when his works are being discussed in public), and went to bed early. Today the weather is heavenly again. In short, a delightful episode in my present life.

Last night something disagreeable happened which has spoiled my stay in Lübeck. In the evening I went to the Opera House, where *L'Africaine* was on. In spite of a small orchestra and small chorus it was not at all bad. Naturally the production had a few comic provincialisms, but on the whole it went quite smoothly. Then, as I came out for the interval an unamiable person came up to me and said: 'Allow me to introduce myself. I am Ogarev. I also studied at the School of Law, and am also a composer, and my opera was performed in Sshwerin. Allow me to present to you the Musikdirektor Stiehl, and this Herr Direktor is. . . !' and it went on, and on, and on. I was dragged away to drink beer – they wanted to take me to a club – with Ogarev never stopping talking about his opera. . . . My God! How awful it was! They saw me to my hotel, where I insisted that I was not well and that I was leaving the next day.

Apparently the son of the hotel proprietor is a music-lover and I had noticed before that he pointed at me in the dining-room. He gave me away today, so I instructed the porter to tell everybody that I had left, and I kept to my room all day, except for creeping out secretly for a walk. I heard about the pension, and what a great boon this is I shall realize tomorrow. Today I tortured myself over a thank-you letter which I wrote with immense effort. Yesterday homesickness for all my nearest and dearest and my homeland came back once more – hence utter despair. Drank all day! Read *Pierre et Jean*, Maupassant's new novel. First time this author made me cry.

Rehearsals yesterday and today. Shall not describe all the fears and excitement.

The musicians are most sympathetic. The sadness gone but all I think of is – when will it all end?

You write you are in the dumps! Could it be because you are not doing what you ought to be doing? In my opinion you must write for the theatre. Put Shakespeare away for a time and write a good new play with an interesting plot, but be practical and do not make it too complicated to be produced. Please – do think about it, Modichka! As soon as you have a job that enables you to be a writer all your gloomy thoughts will disperse. Bob's letters and telegrams arrive most punctually.

Will write again tomorrow after the public rehearsal and concert. I kiss and embrace you. Have sent Shapiro a little note. Kiss everybody especially Kolia, and Bob.

P. Tchaikovsky

Modest's depression was caused by his attempt to translate Shakespeare's *Richard III*.
    In Hamburg, Tchaikovsky had to endure a certain amount of patronizing approval. He would, it was suggested, be better if he could abjure his noisy and provincial habits of musical speech, and learn how most effectively to compose by prolonged study of German music. Theodor Ave-Lallemant, President of the Hamburg Philharmonic Society, was among the most vociferous of well-intentioned critics. Tchaikovsky dedicated to him the Fifth Symphony! On 8–20 January he conducted the Serenade for Strings, the first Piano Concerto (soloist Sapelnikov) and the Theme and Variations from the third Suite.

[467] TO ANATOLI, AND PRASKOVIA TCHAIKOVSKAIA
                                              [Hamburg]
                                              8–20 January 1888

I have already been here for some days, and am constantly alternating between boredom, distress, worry and fear, and the exact opposite frame of mind; but the latter is rarer than the former. I had three rehearsals, and found the players most sympathetic, with many quite enthusiastic. The orchestra is not so good as that in Leipzig. I met a multitude of people, and paid many visits. Yesterday there was a big dinner – in evening dress – after the last rehearsal and I even had to make a speech in German. After tonight's concert there will be another festive dinner for which evening dress again is required, at the house of the Director of the Philharmonic Society, and I shall have to make another speech in German. Having to speak German all the time is an awful bore. My great consolation is the pianist Sapelnikov, Menter's pupil, who is playing my concerto tonight. My soul gets a rest with him. All this life will probably seem like an awful nightmare later on.

I have heard that you have been made a general. My heartfelt congratulations, your Excellency! I would give anything to find myself in Tiflis, now, so as to have a nice day with you. I shall finish this tomorrow, to be able to tell you about the concert.

10–22 January

The concert was a success, and the audience received me very well. The following works of mine were played: (1) Serenade for Strings. (2) Piano Concerto (Sapelnikov played marvellously). (3) Variations from the third Suite. After which there was a big reception at Bernut's – the Director's – house. About a hundred people were present. I made a speech in German, which I learned in advance and it created quite a stir. After this I went to celebrate at a restaurant. The whole day yesterday I either had visitors or went to see people in town. In the evening there was another celebration in my honour at the *Tonkünstlerverein*. Only works of mine were played. After that we went on drinking until four in the morning – quite indescribable. I am in a fog! Off to Berlin today. There are articles – large ones, small ones, some with a biography and analysis of the works – in the papers. Naturally there are also some curious ones, but with sympathy showing between the lines.

My dear ones, I kiss you with love.

P. Tchaikovsky

[468]   TO MODEST TCHAIKOVSKY   Hamburg
                                                 10–22 January 1888

The concert took place the day before yesterday but it is only now that I find time to write. All went well. When I appeared the orchestra gave me an ovation; so did the audience (something that did not happen in Leipzig). I conducted calmly and with assurance, but towards the end I felt so tired that I feared I should not be able to stand any more. The applause was terrific. Sapelnikov played excellently and enjoyed great success. After the concert there was a big reception at Bernut's, with about a hundred men in dress suits and the women in ball dresses. After Bernut made a speech I followed with one in German that I had prepared beforehand. It went down very well. Then they took me off to a drinking-party.

Yesterday was awful – I was torn to shreds by everybody and in the end was completely worn out. In the evening there was a celebration in my honour at the 'Tonkünstlerverein' at which only works of mine were played. The press has been very kind. I am sending you two articles, which you can get someone to translate for you.

After this there was a great deal of drinking, with crowds of musicians, critics, and music-lovers, who were delightful and entirely charming to me. I feel as if in a fog. Today I go to Berlin. Von Bülow is very kind.

I kiss and embrace you.

(signature lost)

Magdeburg
12–24 January 1888

Modia, Golubchik!

I am happy again that I can have time to breathe freely and collect my thoughts.
The last days in Hamburg and the day in Berlin were awful. In Berlin I heard
works by Richard Strauss, the new German genius. Von Bülow fusses over him
as he did over Brahms and others. In my opinion there has never yet been
anyone of less talent and so full of pretension. All day yesterday I was running
about everywhere like a madman. What a shame, every day I get invitations
to conduct my works in many centres of music and cannot accept them. Have
I told you that everything has been arranged in the best possible way in
Paris? I will not give a concert of my own, but Colonne has invited me to take
part on 11 and 18 March at the Châtelet, i.e. on these dates he will let me
have half the programme.

Magdeburg is a lovely town, even magnificent. The hotel, as usual, is excellent.
Tonight I am going to the opera. On the advice of von Bülow, Wolff, and
others, the programme of the concert has been changed. They all insist I must
not play *Francesca*, and they are probably right. I have learnt a lot in these
last months, and understood a lot that I did not understand before. Only it
would take too long to write about.

The needs of the German symphony public are quite different from ours.
I understand now why they deify Brahms, although my opinion of him has not
changed at all. If I had known all this before I might have even composed
differently. Remind me to tell you, when I am back, about my meeting with
the dear old Ave-Lallemant which deeply touched me. Sapelnikov made a
sensation in Hamburg. I took him to Berlin with me and have now sent him
off to Dresden; then we shall meet in Berlin, where he will play at two great
dinner receptions by Wolff and Bock. Perhaps this will help him. He is really
very gifted, and also a most charming and kind young man. I have been
writing letters all day, am very tired, and will finish this later. Friedrich has
started again to bombard me with letters. He is not only mad but a son of a
bitch. I shall be obliged to get rid of him by paying him off.

Leipzig
15–27 January

It's a month now since I left. Up till now I have only seen Brodsky and Ziloty.
Yesterday I had an invitation for the Directors' box at the Gewandhaus, but
preferred to stay at home as I had to have a good night's rest; for the day
before I passed a horrid night on account of the muddle with letters and
telegrams from Colonne. It upset me very much. Now everything is in order.
Sorry but I forgot to send you a note for Shapiro. Am sending it now.

I kiss and embrace you.

P. Tchaikovsky

Modest had asked for a note from his brother to Shapiro the photographer, so that members of the family could have a discount when buying photographs of Piotr.

TO MODEST TCHAIKOVSKY   Leipzig
20 January–1 February 1888

How can I describe all my experiences? A perpetual change from gloom and awful hours back to moments of delight. I hoped to pass a few quiet days, but instead I lead a life of dissipation and all my days are full of dinners, visits, concerts, theatres, supper-parties, and so on. My consolations are Ziloty, Brodsky (quite in love with his wife and sister-in-law), and Grieg and his wife (charming people). But every day here I have found, and find, other new and delightful acquaintances. I keep Sapelnikov with me for the time being. I have introduced him to many people in the musical world and he creates a sensation wherever he plays. His is a great talent. I come to this conclusion more and more. I have learned really to love him – there could not be a kinder and nicer boy. By the way here is an autographed photo of Menter he received for you yesterday. She loves him and by the amusing tone of the letter one can judge how she feels.

So far as music is concerned, I heard a new opera by Weber here. I mean an opera which he left unfinished – only in sketches – and which has only now been completed, arranged, and orchestrated. The music is sweet, the subject silly (it is called *Die drei Pintos*). I was at a chamber music concert where they played a quartet by a wonderfully gifted Italian composer Ferruccio Busoni. We very quickly became friends. I enjoyed Grieg's Sonata at one of Brodsky's musical evenings. Grieg and his wife are extremely interesting, original, and unusual. I find Grieg immensely talented. I had dinner with the Griegs at Brodsky's today. In the evening there is a special concert to collect funds for a memorial to Mendelssohn.

Tomorrow the public rehearsal of the Gewandhaus Concert (in the programme – Rubinstein's Symphony), takes place, after which I give a dinner to my friends at the famous local restaurant and leave for Berlin at 5.00 p.m. Expect a letter from Berlin. Anyway, you will know everything from Sapelnikov. Please, be specially kind to him and ask him to play. You will be astonished.

Concerning money, shall give an order by telegram. Oh God! How tired I am. I kiss, embrace you, Kolia, and Bob.

P. Tchaikovsky

TO MODEST TCHAIKOVSKY   Berlin
23 January–4 February 1888

Golubchik, Modia!

This is my third day here, but have had absolutely no time to write. The first
rehearsal was on the day after my arrival. The musicians received me not only
well, but even enthusiastically. My conducting improves with every performance.
A big dinner in evening dress and ball dresses took place on the same day at
the Wolffs.

The dinner was at my suggestion to enable Sapelnikov to be heard by all the
people who count in music. There were also critics present. Sapelnikov caused
a sensation. He and I have been inseparable for the last three weeks, and he
has become as dear to me as the very nearest of my relatives. I have never
loved anyone so much since Kotek. A more sympathetic, soft, sweet, tactful,
and noble person one cannot imagine. Please, when he returns do not only
receive him politely, but introduce him to Sasha, Kolia, Bob and all the other
members of the family. I (and not only I) look upon him as the pianist of
genius of the future.

Yesterday there was another official dinner at Wolff's. Artôt was there, and I
was infinitely glad to see her. We instantly renewed our friendship without one
word about the past. Her husband, Padilla, nearly suffocated me in his
embrace. She is giving a dinner on the day after tomorrow. The old dear is as
charming as she was 20 years ago. I had a whole row of fights with Friedrich.
He is nothing less than a blackmailer. With Wolff's help I got rid of him for
500 marks. His blackmail did not frighten me in the least, as I was in the
right, but I would not have been sorry to throw out a thousand to get rid of
the scoundrel. Besides, he is not only a blackmailer but also quite mad. Think
of me on Wednesday, 27 January–8 February; it's the day of the concert.
I have got to know thousands of people. No peace. In the mornings I feel
frightfully unhappy but gradually in all the bustle I forget sorrow and
unhappiness. How tired I am! Vassia Sapelnikov is a great consolation.

I kiss you.

P. Tchaikovsky

TO PRASKOVIA VLADIMIROVNA TCHAIKOVSKAIA
Leipzig
30 January–11 February 1888

My dove, Pania!

You could have written at least a word. If only you knew how I need letters.
I heard from Modest that Tata has been ill, about which I had no idea. Thank
God, he writes, she is better now. My concert in Berlin was brilliant, and the
audience enraptured – maybe there were many Russians present. I stayed a

week in Berlin where there were dinners and suppers without end. Not a moment's peace. I marvel at my own endurance. The programme of the concert was:

(1) *Romeo* overture.
(2) Piano Concerto – Ziloty played very well.
(3) *Introduction and Fugue* from the first Suite.
(4) *Andante* from the Quartet.
(5) Songs, sung by Mme Friede.
(6) '1812' Overture.

I came here having promised to be present at a concert which the *Lisztverein* wanted to give in my honour, but it did not take place; instead, at my request, they gave Wagner's *Meistersinger*, which I had never heard. At 8 o'clock this morning I was woken up by the sounds of 'God protect the Czar', which came from outside my window. It was a serenade in my honour. They played for more than an hour, and all the hotel guests came out to listen and to stare at me.

Tomorrow morning I go to Prague, where a series of celebrations will take place. The concert will be next Sunday, 7–19 February. From there to Paris, where the concerts will be on 4–11 March (new style). Write to Paris, 14, Rue Richepanse.

Frightfully tired. Good-bye, my dears until we meet. I would like to travel back by sea. I kiss you.

P. Tchaikovsky

On 15 April 1882 Tchaikovsky had written to A. S. Suvorin: 'It is not important that European audiences applauded me but that all Russian music and Russian art were received with enthusiasm in my person. The Russians ought to know that a Russian musician has held the banner of our art high in the big European centres.'

Tchaikovsky felt that his foreign travels were in the nature of diplomatic missions, and he was inspired by intensely patriotic feelings. Speaking in Prague, in Czech, he said: 'I must state, without being too humble, that all these honours bestowed on me greatly surpass my merits. They would have completely crushed me had I not known how to differentiate between the sympathy extended to me personally and that, of a much higher kind, shown through me to something greatly more significant and superior than myself. Believe me, a neighbouring, brotherly country will know how properly to reply to that part of your hospitality which has been shown through me but not to me personally.'

On 7 February the concert at the Rudolfinum (the principal concert hall in Prague), conducted by Tchaikovsky, included *Romeo and Juliet*, First Piano Concerto (soloist, A. Ziloty), 'Elegy' third Suite, Violin Concerto (soloist K. Galir), *1812* Overture.

At the second concert in the National Theatre the programme was: Serenade for Strings. 'Theme and Variations', third Suite, piano solos (played by Ziloty), *1812* Overture, Swan Lake, Act II.

I have positively no time to write, and yet everything that is happening here
is so interesting. After Vassia left (I really adore him), I stayed the night in
Berlin and travelled to Leipzig in the morning. In the evening went to the
Opera House to hear the *Meistersinger*. Very interesting. The day after, dinner
at the Brodsky's, with the Griegs, and an evening in the same company at
Ziloty's.

On Sunday the 12th I left for Prague with Ziloty. At the frontier I already felt
the coming celebrations. The chief of the guards asked if I was Tchaikovsky,
and when I said I was he became most deferential. In Kralupa (the last station
before Prague), a delegation and a whole crowd were awaiting us and
accompanied us to Prague. At the station in Prague crowds of people, another
delegation, children with flowers, two speeches: one in Russian, another,
long one, in Czech. I responded, and walked to a carriage through a thick wall
of people all shouting 'Slava!' ('Hail!'). At the hotel I was given a magnificent
apartment. In the evening *Otello* at the Opera House; a mass of new
acquaintances and more welcomes. Rieger and his daughter spoke Russian to
me. After the opera, supper at my hotel.

Yesterday morning a visit from Dvořák who stayed over two hours. A tour
round the town and a look at some of the important sights, accompanied by
the director of the museum and the Russian priest (who asks to give his
kindest regards to Sasha and Nata). Supper at Valechka's (prominent bookseller
and Russophile). A ball in the best hall of the town, where I sat in a box and
everybody looked at me. Today a Service in our Russian Church at 10.30, a
visit to the Students' Club; dinner at Dvořák's; another drive through the town
with the Museum director (he speaks very good Russian); and a big evening
reception in my honour at the Umelecka Beseda. All this is very nice, very
complimentary, but you can imagine how tired I get and how I suffer. I am in
a fog, and the only thing that keeps me going is the dawn of freedom which
I begin to see on the horizon and also Sasha Ziloty who does not leave me for
a minute.

It seems that my stay here makes sense, not so much because I am a *good*
composer but because I am a *Russian* composer. Am sending cuttings from the
papers. Good-bye, Modinka, be pleased for my sake but also be sorry for me.
Kind regards and kisses to everybody. What about Vassia? Did you like him?
The most charming monster who ever lived on this Earth. Shall write about
all that takes place bit by bit.

P. Tchaikovsky

[474]   TO MODEST TCHAIKOVSKY   Prague
                                                  10–22 February 1888

Golubchik, Modia!

To write was impossible. My stay in Prague is quite an epic. I think some
mention of it will be made in the papers and you will soon read about it; if
not, you'll have to wait till I return and tell you everything. I should never
have thought anything like it possible. The second concert took place yesterday,
and after it they put on the second act of *Swan Lake,* which was beautifully
staged. My success was absolutely terrific. During my ten days' stay I made a
multitude of speeches, and at a big banquet on the day of my concert a speech
in Czech.

On the whole the Czechs are very nice and some of those who have been with
me everywhere I have learned to love. Charming Ziloty was with me all the
time, looking after me like a nanny, and several times he saved me from
complete exhaustion. P. Yurgenson also came.here and stayed for five days.
I was very glad to see him. They both left an hour ago and I am leaving for
Paris tonight. It is impossible to describe how tired I am; one can only wonder
how I could have stood up to it all without ruining my health. Of course, there
were also many delightful moments, and I could never dream of having such
success in Russia.

I have made friends with Dvořák and all the other composers. I must also add
that the Czechs are great chaps – the open way in which they showed their
sympathy for Russia in connection with my visit was wonderful. Please write
to Paris, 14 Rue Richepanse. I am sending you three of my portraits from the
papers. As to the papers, it is impossible to send them all; for the last ten
days they have been absolutely overflowing. I embrace you.

P. Tchaikovsky

Tchaikovsky looked apprehensively on a visit to Paris, where for the time being
political considerations decreed that all things Russian should be praised. On 14/26
February he wrote to Mme Shpajinskaia from Paris: 'Endless fears and worries await
me here. It seems that in Paris also they intend to receive me not only as Piotr Illich
but as a Russian and will give me a very warm reception.'

[475]   TO ANATOLI AND PRASKOVIA   Prague
                                                  10–22 February 1888

My Golubchik Tolia and Pania!

During the ten days I was here, it was absolutely impossible to write. I am
putting everything down in my diary and shall be able to tell you all about
what happened later, but to write now – that is out of the question. I was
received here as a representative of Russia. The reception on the day of my

arrival was very grand. From then on my stay was a series of festivals, receptions, sight-seeing tours – taking in the museums, etc. – serenades, rehearsals, concerts and so on. I met many Czechs who could speak Russian. From morning till night I have been spoiled, fêted, taken about everywhere and pampered. After yesterday's concert at the theatre they gave an excellent performance of the second act of *Swan Lake*. I not only became an orator, making speeches at all the festivities given in my honour, but at a big banquet gave a long speech in Czech to the great joy of all who were there.

It is impossible to describe everything in a short letter. I am absolutely worn out and wonder where I get the strength to stand it all. Today I am off to Paris. Ziloty was with me all the time, and P. Yurgenson arrived two days before the concert. They both have just left. And I am writing letters which have accumulated to such extent that although I have so much to say there can only be a short page for each. I hope that I will see you in the near future. Oh Lord! When will peace come at last! ! ! ! All the same I must be honest and state that I experienced many lovely moments in Prague.

I kiss and embrace you.

P. Tchaikovsky

[476]　TO ANATOLI TCHAIKOVSKY　　　[Paris]
　　　　　　　　　　　　　　　　　　19 February–2 March 1888

Golubchik Tolia!

Forgive me that I have not written at once from Paris, but my life is even more hectic here than in Prague. Not one day passes without invitations to dinners, evening parties, etc. I never get out of my dress suit and in addition to all this there are rehearsals, visits, receptions – all of which makes it impossible to keep up a proper correspondence with anyone. I cannot say that it is a burden, for I am being received with very much warmth and everyone is making a fuss of me. The papers are full of news about me; some have long articles in which truth and fiction intermingle, my appearance is described and so on.

On Tuesday the 16–28th the big concert took place at Mme Bernadaky's luxurious home! I conducted the orchestra, the audience of about 300 was a selected one, the best artists and singers took part, only works of mine were played, and the whole affair was immensely successful. New acquaintances are too numerous to be counted. The orchestra played wonderfully at the rehearsals; the players applauded me when I appeared; so, there is no more that could be said about the courtesy of the Parisians. All the same, I naturally dream about the possibility of running away back home. On the 10–22 I shall be in London, but I fear that I will have to come back to Paris as they are planning to have two or three more concerts for me to conduct – which I was weak enough to promise to do.

How much sweeter I am than you and Pania; in spite of all my fears and worries I have found time to write. But from you – not a sound. Please, write and as often as possible; however I still hope to see you soon. I kiss you, hard!!!

P. Tchaikovsky

TO MODEST TCHAIKOVSKY   Paris
                                                        8 March 1888

You wonder Modia, why I am silent. But you cannot imagine what a dog's life I lead. Even if you multiply the Petersburg bustle a hundred times it will not come anywhere near what it is here. It is absolute madness, and I do not know why I am still well and hearty. It is impossible to write. Today, pretending that I was unwell, I refused a dinner and evening out (at Kotzebue's, Counsellor at the Embassy), and decided to pass at least one evening in solitude. Hence, my letter to you.

The concert was a great success, and I had an enthusiastic reception, but I must say that the choice of the music was not entirely successful. The poor Frenchmen had to make an awful effort to applaud the piano Fantasia. What they really liked was the *Serenade* and the *Finale* of the third Suite. *Francesca* will be played at the next concert. Today's rehearsal was a difficult one. Since I have written there have been numerous receptions, dinners, etc. The Ambassador, Morenheim, gave a big dinner and reception, and there was also a reception at the Russian Club, while Colonne had a big evening in my honour. Yesterday there was an enormous crowd of people at Diémer's, who is very rich and entertains lavishly.

Today I went to Mme Adam's reception. Everybody praises and honours me very sincerely. Gounod loudly demonstrated his admiration at the concert, and all the young musicians are also very friendly. I have met practically everybody; Delibes is the nicest of the lot. The papers are very occupied with me, and I had a series of interviews with various journalists. One of them wrote a specially nice article about me in the *Temps*. Next Wednesday there will be a big reception given by the *Figaro*. I had a conference about it with Mognard, who wants to do it *en grand*. In brief, I cannot complain about lack of fame. I meet the Bernadakys – extremely charming and attractive people – more often than anyone else. I dined twice with the Princess Ourussova, and Widor gave me a huge lunch. So much has happened, in fact, that it would be impossible to describe it all. I return to the hotel completely exhausted and flop down to sleep like a log. I have been to the theatre only once, and then did not stay to the end. All my evenings are full up, which is very disappointing.

As to money, very bad. All the same, take as much money as you need from Ossip Ivanovich; I will write to him at once. As I have already spent a lot and shall have to spend more I am getting very interested in my pension. Could you find out what the formalities are to get it? It is most amusing that Colonne, playing upon the sympathy of the French for everything Russian, is making an enormous amount of money, while I get nothing. I am advised to give a concert of my own, but I do not dare.

Unfortunately 'the dawn of freedom' is not very near. On the initiative of Mme Adam's Franco-Russian Society they want to give a festival at the Trocadero in aid of it, with me conducting. If the festival does take place I'll have to stay here for God knows how long after my return from London. However, if I get too tired I'll run away. . . .

Please, write, you cannot imagine what a joy letters are.

I embrace and kiss you.

P. Tchaikovsky

[478]   TO MODEST TCHAIKOVSKY   Paris
                                                 1–13 March 1888

Modia!

It is quite impossible to write, but I will do so more fully after London. As yet I have not decided where to go after all this. My God! How tired and sick of it all I am. The second concert was a *great* success, especially *Francesca*. Am sending all the posters, they will interest you. From now on, until London, I have not a moment free. Am going mad.

Good-bye, I kiss you.

P. Tchaikovsky

Am also sending an autograph of Mme Adam.

[479]   TO ANATOLI TCHAIKOVSKY   Hanover
                                                 5–17 March 1888

Really, Tolia, you and Pania astonish me; not even a line from you! I gave you my address. After my last letter (I think from Berlin), I went to Geneva to a festival of my works. The orchestra was very bad and it was with difficulty that I managed to make them play decently. But I had a huge success. Then I went to Hamburg. God! How tired I am of all this travelling. In Hamburg everything went along fine and the new [*Manfred*] symphony was also a great success.

All this is perfect and pleases me greatly at the moment; but, as soon as there are no rehearsals I fall into an awful state of despondency and boredom. What worries me more than anything is that time is being lost and it is time that I value more and more. Now there is only one concert in London left, which I could miss, were it not for Sapelnikov, who will lose the opportunity to play in London if I do. Yesterday I was in complete despair at the thought that I still have a whole month of torture and boredom in front of me.

From London I shall fly straight to you. But I must know something about you first. Supposing Pania has decided to go to Moscow for the summer? And you go away on leave? Then why should I kill two weeks of my time on a journey? For God's sake send at least a telegram.

I kiss and embrace you.

Yours

P. Tchaikovsky

[480] TO MODEST TCHAIKOVSKY   London
                                                8–20 March 1888

Modia!

Last night I left Paris in a frightful snowstorm, and arrived two hours later at Calais. The crossing was awful! ! ! I was the only one who was not sick. I am quite certain now that I do not get seasick. I got to London at midnight instead of 7.00 pm and there is deep snow everywhere as with us in January. I have not seen anyone. There is a rehearsal tomorrow, another on the day after, with the concert in the evening, and on Friday the 11–23 I am leaving more or less straight away for Tiflis.

You will understand that I cannot go to Petersburg now, I will be torn to pieces there just as in Moscow. Tolia is begging me to come to Tiflis and I do want to go, very much, but I do not yet know which way. I would like to go through Italy and by sea from Naples, but am afraid of the March storms.

In any case it will not be by way of Paris, where I do not dare to show myself for fear of all those people who want me to give concerts for them, and who will tear me to pieces. It was a great effort to get out of Paris. If I had stayed there one more day I would have gone mad; for I was being tortured so much. Write to Tiflis.

I kiss and embrace you.

P. Tchaikovsky

[481] TO MODEST TCHAIKOVSKY   [London]
                                                [12–]24 March 1888

My Golubchik Modia!

I am writing a longer letter to Sasha, so all I will say is: that London is very sad and glum; that the concert was a brilliant success; that all the papers say so; that I wanted to leave yesterday but felt very unwell; that I am perfectly well again and am leaving straight for Tiflis tonight. I travel overland, with a stop either in Vienna or Berlin (have not decided which). No words to express how happy I am that all has come to an end and that I may go home;

I would like to be in Petersburg for Easter but this has not been decided yet.
I want to go to Taganrog on my way to see Ippolit.

Good-bye! Farewell! I embrace you and kiss you.

Yours

P. Tchaikovsky

The concert in London on 10–22 March included the Serenade for Strings and the
'Theme and Variations' from the third Suite.

[482] TO MODEST TCHAIKOVSKY   Vienna
                                                15–27 March 1888

Golubchik Modia!

I left London still somewhat ill but I completely recovered during the journey.
Vienna is as boring and nasty as usual. What a long way I have before me.
I leave tomorrow morning (I have to stay to get all my linen laundered), for
Volochisk. On Saturday, 19 March, I will be in Kharkov (no other way), where
I shall have a day's rest; on Monday, Taganrog, where I shall stay two or
three days; from there to Rostov and Vladikavkaz; and provided that nothing
prevents me, shall even then only reach Tiflis on Sunday, 27 March. Nearly
two weeks before I get there!!! On the other hand I am a little apprehensive
about going by sea, and also I do not want to miss Ippolit whom I have been
misleading for more than a year. Besides, it would take even longer.
I am perfectly well. For God's sake write to Tiflis.

I kiss and embrace you.

Yours

P. Tchaikovsky

[483] TO MODEST TCHAIKOVSKY   Taganrog
                                                22 March 1888

Modia!

At last two days ago I arrived in Taganrog, after a never-ending journey with
six nights on the trains. True – I had a rest in Vienna, but all the same the
journey was very tiring. As if on purpose, the weather is glorious and I ought
to have gone by sea without any fear of the March storms. Even now if it were
not for the desire to get to Tiflis more quickly I have a great longing to take
a boat to Kerch and Batum. But, alas! This would mean losing a whole week
of my time, and I am passionately eager to get home and settle in the country.

Exactly where 'home' is going to be I still do not know but hope to get letters in Tiflis from Alexei which will give me the news.

I need not say how pleased Ippolit and Sonia were and how happy I felt with them. Unfortunately all sorts of people insisted on meeting me here too; but this is nothing in comparison with Paris! The house they live in is charming, with a lovely view on to the sea. I have been here for two days and am leaving tomorrow morning. Am perfectly well but slightly tired. Read a multitude of novels on the way; including several by [A. K. Sheller-]Mikhailov which I find very good and do not understand why he isn't more famous. All the foreign countries seem like a dream. I still cannot get over it.

Write, Golubchik, to Tiflis. Am being called to lunch. I embrace and kiss you. A thousand sweet thoughts to Kolia and Bob.

P. Tchaikovsky

Tchaikovsky rented a large house at Frolovskoie, a village some 5 miles from Klin. He lived here from April 1888 until September 1889 and again from May 1890 – May 1891. The house was destroyed by fire during the Second World War. The Taneev estate was nearby (see Letter 485). The newspapers as already stated were not enthusiastic about *Charodeika*, but the composer was not disposed to mistrust his own opinion. On 24 April he wrote to Mme Shpajinskaia: 'If I am not wrong it seems that Ippolit Vassilievich wants me to make changes in *Charodeika*, which I don't want to do at all. The more we tear this unfortunate opera to pieces the worse it will become. Besides I cannot warm up my feelings any more and compose something decent on the same words. I find *Charodeika* an opera which has been properly and seriously written and if the public does not like it, so much the worse for the public. . . .' At this time Tchaikovsky was thinking about a new libretto Shpajinsky was preparing from *The Captain's Daughter* (Pushkin). Again he wrote to Mme Shpajinskaia on 9 May: 'On reading the book over again I did not find any characters asking to be put to music, and the heroine especially is too colourless. What attracted me probably when we talked about it was the setting in the last century and the *contrast* between the gentry in European dress and Pugachev with his wild band. But a contrast is not enough for an operatic subject. It needs live people and affecting circumstances. I fear the Censor, however kind, would find it difficult to pass an interpretation on the stage that made the audience leave the theatre absolutely enraptured by Pugachev.' The subject was dropped and Tchaikovsky passed on to the composition of the Fifth Symphony.

On 2 May he was for the second time presented to the Czar, but did not find the occasion very rewarding. The Czar this time appeared to lack the warmth he had evinced previously.

[484] TO MODEST TCHAIKOVSKY   Tiflis
                                                   28 March 1888

I arrived here with my face absolutely burned by the sun, for, beginning at Dushet, the heat has been impossible. It has been like that for some time.

Everything is green, and the fruit trees have finished blossoming. Found Tolia, Pania and Tania absolutely well. The house is charming, especially the view. I like it in Tiflis very much but shall not stay here for long, for my craving to be 'at home' is too great. Frolovskoie, which Alesha has taken, I know perfectly well. It is a most picturesque place and you have seen it a hundred times when passing in the train from Klin to Moscow, on the woody slopes on the left, just after Klin.

I am angry about the pension granted to me because I can only get it on personal application. Anyway, I shall send an official power of attorney to Ossip Yurgenson as I do not want to go to Petersburg myself; I am afraid of it, however much I should like to see you, Bob, Kolia and the rest. What is more than likely is that I shall come and see you in May. There will be concerts during Easter week, and as Taffanel and Diémer are coming from Paris I would have to cope with them, and honestly, at this moment I am definitely not in the mood to see anyone but my own people.

I am very glad you want to write a drama but it would be better to write a comedy; more appropriate to the capacities of our actors. It is a pity you have lost so much time on the libretto for Klenovsky. Forgive me, Modia, but I am not a bit sorry that I have decided not to write *The Queen of Spades*; after the failure of *Charodeika* I was, out of revenge, ready to pounce on any subject and angry that I was not composing anything. However, all this has passed; during the summer I am going to write a symphony, and will compose an opera only if the subject attracts me really. *The Queen of Spades* does not impress me and I could only write something insignificant on that subject.

Thank God that Sasha is better and Sapelnikov out of danger, but I am waiting with impatience for your next letter to know if Sasha's gallstone has come through. I have not seen Sasha for more than two years. Want to see you all at Easter very much but, you cannot imagine how frightful Petersburg seems to me, still full of the winter season bustle. Unless I try to come incognito for a day or two! But my God! I have been travelling so much all this last year that I am sick of railways and do want to settle in my own home at last. It will all be decided in a few days' time. In any case I am staying here until the first half of the sixth week in Lent and shall be in Moscow – I mean in Frolovskoie – at the end of April.

What have you decided about summer? Is Kolia going to Borjom? Where will you be?

Good-bye, Golubchik, Modia!

How tired I am and how I only want to work, only work, and only the knowledge of doing something positive can bring me peace and health: 'put me back on my own plate' [Russian proverb].

I kiss you all.

P. Tchaikovsky

TO ANATOLI TCHAIKOVSKY   Frolovskoie
                                             25 April 1888

My Golubchik Tolia!

Two days ago, in the evening on Holy Saturday, I arrived here at dinner time.
Alexei has arranged my new abode delightfully. It is not as select as the one
in Maidanovo, perhaps, but the rooms are large and high and the furniture is
antique and charming, which gives a romantic atmosphere to the whole house.
The house stands on a hill and the view is lovely, but not out of the windows
(except for the dining-room). You need to step out of the house to see it. The
garden is very nice, and what is even nicer is that you can step out of the garden
right into the woods and roam there all day. No trace of any dacha inhabitants.
In a word – I am very pleased with my new home.

Alexei's wife is pretty and sweet, something you could not judge from the
photograph and her appearance is particularly enhanced by her wonderful
teeth. I still have a slight cold which showed itself two days ago. In spite of
that, however, I went at night to the Easter Service at our church, which is
rich and beautiful. Yesterday, just as I had decided to rest and put my papers
in order, Taneev turned up and stayed the whole day. I like Taneev very much
but would have preferred his visit some other day. Today, after a good night,
I feel much better despite the weather changing suddenly, after it had been
as hot as in July. . . .

I shall stay at home for another three days to put my papers, music, and books,
in order; and then I shall go to Petersburg where, it seems, they are impatiently
expecting me. . . . It is a pity you live so far away and we can't see each other
more often. All the same I may take a trip to Tiflis in late autumn. Please, tell
Pania – the heartless one – to write more often.

I embrace you, her and Tania. Think of you all the time. Kind regards to
Kokodeks.

Good-bye, dear people.

Yours

P. Tchaikovsky

TO MODEST TCHAIKOVSKY   Klin
                                             15 May 1888

I am writing to you Golubchik Modia, and am quite ill, although better today.
It is all Alexei's fault because he will not heat the stoves, in spite of the
frightful cold in the house which brought on a chill. I was quite ill yesterday
but feel better today, thanks to having taken measures to deal with it, and
also to the unexpected arrival of dear Hubert. How important any distraction
is when one's nerves are on edge! When he appeared I was in bed, slightly
feverish, and after chatting to him for two hours I felt infinitely better!

I am completely in love with Frolovskoie, where, compared to Maidanovo, all the surrounding country seems a heavenly paradise. Really, it is so lovely that in the mornings I often decide to go out for half an hour, but I get so enthralled that sometimes I only return two hours later. Woods all around, and in some places, real, mysterious, pine forest. Alas! A lot of it is being cut down. In the evenings, at sunset, I wander about the open spaces where the view is wonderful. All would be perfect, in fact, but for the rain and cold. Last night it just poured. As yet I have not started to compose, as I had some proofs to correct. To be honest, I have not yet felt the desire to create anything. What does it mean? Surely not that I am finished? No ideas, no moods at all! But I still hope that, little by little, material for a symphony will come.

Today we were going to sow seeds and plant flowers in the beds in front of the house. I was looking forward to this very much but, alas, it never stopped raining. However, by the time you come everything will be planted. Am very upset about the news that Bob has failed.

Am going to stay here all this week and then at the beginning of the next one go to Moscow.

I embrace and kiss you! Write about Kolia's and Bob's next examinations.

Yours

P. Tchaikovsky

[487] TO MODEST TCHAIKOVSKY   Frolovskoie
                                                17 June 1888

At last it looks like summer! It has been absolutely awful up to now and I did not feel at all well. But in spite of this the work kept moving on. Nearly all the sketches for the symphony are ready and at the beginning of next week I will start orchestrating it. It is understandable that in this awful weather I did not feel very happy. Even I felt the need for human society and last Sunday I went to Maidanovo where I spent the whole day. Everything there looked sad and forsaken, and nowhere did I feel more sorrow and grief about N. D. Kondratiev's disappearance from this world than on his favourite walk; three years have flown past since then. I had dinner with Novichikha. (She, at least, has not changed; I even enjoyed her this time.) Played vingt with her and in the evening went to see Simon who occupies the big house. No one else is staying there and Simon took the house only because she let him have it very cheap. . . .

The flowers here are in an awful state, only the sweet peas are still holding out. The mignonette has turned yellow and red as in autumn. The heliotrope has shrivelled and turned black. Only the lupins are still showing much sign of life; as to all the others they have appeared out of the earth but do not grow at all. I was astonished at the lush and thick vegetation in Maidanovo compared with Frolovskoie. Here it looks bald and everything grows badly. However, I continue to be delighted with the walks as much as the weather permits. The hen that was broody when you were here has produced ten chicks. Quite unexpectedly Rater came and stayed a whole day. You can imagine my having to talk German all the time. Actually he is a nice old boy.

And now! I expect news from Borjom, it is quite time to get some. I embrace you Golubchik, Modia! Also Kolia! Volodia too. Dear God, how I wish I could be in Borjom!!!

P.T.

Tchaikovsky's Name Day was June 29.

Modest had started to translate A. D. Oulibishev's *Mozart* (1843) from the French. The first volume, with annotations by Laroche, was published in 1890; the second, also translated by Modest, a year later; the third, translated by Zinaida Laroche, in 1892. (See Letter 560.)

The actor Guitry requested a short orchestral piece for a charity performance of *Hamlet* in which he was taking part, and this – written during the summer of 1888 and orchestrated between 14 September and 7 October – developed into an independent composition. It was dedicated to E. Grieg. Tchaikovsky composed incidental music for *Hamlet* (Op. 67 b) for Guitry's Benefit in 1891 (see Letters 557/578).

[488] TO MODEST TCHAIKOVSKY   Moscow
                                      26 June 1888
Modia, my Golubchik!

I have now been in Moscow for three days on business. Alexei, who has arrived to do some shopping for 29 June, brought me a letter from you. You ask me to fix a price for your work and to seek an advance of 200 roubles for you from Yurgenson. It is Sunday today and Yurgenson has gone to see Pechkovskaia at her dacha. He is coming to see me in Frolovskoie on the day after tomorrow and I shall tell him you would like money in advance. As to the fee, I had already talked it over with Piotr Ivanovich before I got your letter. He told me that the normal rate for a translation from the French is 20 roubles a sheet but because of the special subject of the work, and our name, you must get much more.

In the first volume there will probably be about ten sheets (not printed as large as in the original). If we count on forty roubles a sheet it will bring you 400 roubles, maybe more. I shall definitely fix the price after the proofs are ready. In any case this work must bring you a good sum of money. I would like you to send what you have already done to Yurgenson at once, especially as I shall have to edit your translation since everything concerning music must be done carefully. Also, it is awkward to ask for money when no work has been done yet. On the 28th I shall tell Piotr Ivanovich that the first volume is nearly finished, that you are sending it to him and will, at the same time, explain about the 200 roubles.

Now a few words about myself. Am here on business concerning a great feast which I am planning for the 29th. The Symphony and *Hamlet* overture are ready and will be orchestrated after the 29th. Nazar stayed at my house for about five days and seemed pleased and happy.

And now, good-bye, Golubchik. Am off to lunch with Konshin and at 4 o'clock back to the country.

Yours

P. Tchaikovsky

[489] TO ANATOLI TCHAIKOVSKY   Frolovskoie
                                                      1 July 1888

... Working well. I have finished both the Symphony and the *Hamlet* Overture, and have started the orchestration. Thanks to having finished two large compositions I am in an excellent mood. I was beginning to fear that I was completely at an end, for, at first, it was so difficult to work. All sorts of concert tours are offered to me for the winter, one even in America. I cannot say yet if it will come off. The American offer is superb, but I shall only believe in it when I get an advance. Tolia! I will be a blackguard if I do not visit you in the autumn; I do want to so much! Anyway, I am a beast I have not wished you a happy Saint's Day! At this moment a terrific storm is making a hell of a racket as I am writing and I am getting more and more frightened. I kiss you hard. Write!

Yours

P. Tchaikovsky

[490] TO ANATOLI TCHAIKOVSKY   [Frolovskoie]
                                                      12 July 1888

Forgive me, Golubchik Tolia, that I am writing on a postcard. Returned just now from Peter and found twenty letters waiting for me all of which have to be answered. I do not understand why you complain that I do not write – quite obviously letters get lost in the post. I went to Peter for a change and to keep my promise to Laub to hear his orchestra in Pavlovsk. Now I am going to orchestrate my symphony and stay here without going anywhere for a long time.

I passed the time in Petersburg very pleasantly, going to Zarskoe Selo, Pavlovsk, and – for one whole day – to Petergoff. Before that I was in Moscow to celebrate P. I. Yurgenson's birthday. On the whole I have not worked very hard of late. Forgive for not sending a telegram in reply on the 29th, but I hoped you would get my letter on that date. Shall write more fully soon.

How queerly you address your letters. All you need is Klin, District of Moscow.

I kiss you.

P. Tchaikovsky

[491] TO ANATOLI TCHAIKOVSKY   [Frolovskoie]
                                                  25 July 1888

Tolichka, Golubchik,

Don't be angry because I only write short letters. After working I am too tired
to write long ones. I simply must finish my symphony and the *Hamlet* Overture
during the summer, and orchestrate Laroche's overture, which I promised to
do long ago. He and his wife are staying with me, their circumstances are
awful. Plevako has so implicated them that they have neither the money to
get clear nor any hope of doing so. However, they have not lost heart.

The weather has been lovely for ten days and I enjoyed it immensely, but now
the everlasting rain has started again. I dream of coming to see you in the
autumn. Am expecting Modest and Kolia. Everything is in order, thank God!
Have a change in the house. The cook Vassily left of his own accord and a
new one has been engaged with whom I am very pleased.

I kiss you. Not a word from Pania.

Yours

P. Tchaikovsky

[492] TO PRASKOVIA VLADIMIROVNA TCHAIKOVSKAIA
                                          Frolovskoie, near Klin
                                          1 August 1888

My dove Pania!

I was so glad to get your letter. What is that silly idea you have got to read
Schopenhauer? The most useless and meaningless occupation. Such a nasty
philosophy! What has come into your head to climb into spheres quite indecent
for you women to look into. As for your dismal mood, my dear Panichka! The
best cure is – occupation. I invite you to find some work for yourself, for
example embroider an enormous carpet for your brother Piotr Illich. Having
read your letter I had a great desire to see you, scold you, pet you, and I
have sworn to myself to go to Tiflis in the autumn. You are angry that I do
not write, but honestly, dearest, it is impossible both to work and to write
letters.

The Laroches are staying with me. They are in an awful fix and I cannot think
how they will be able to get out of the impossible situation they are in – not
a penny, not enough to eat sometimes. However, they bear it well. We pass

the time very happily. They do not disturb me in the least; we meet only at meals, and read together in the evenings. What a silly girl you are for not sending me your address. I am addressing this to Tolia and if you have kept it secret from him that you are reading Schopenhauer you will be the only one to blame. Shall send this to Tionety. I kiss you frightfully hard.

I love my sweet Pania.

P. Tchaikovsky

Tchaikovsky thought well of an overture of Laroche and turned aside from his own interests – the Fifth Symphony now being complete – to orchestrate it. On 14 September he wrote to Mme von Meck: 'The work is extremely talented and proves how much music has been lost because this man of genius suffers from a sickness of will which completely paralyses his creative work.' Tchaikovsky was reading the libretto of the *Sleeping Beauty* (from Perrault, by M. Petitpas and I. Vsevolojsky) although he was not to commence work on the ballet until December.

[493]   TO MODEST TCHAIKOVSKY   Moscow
                                                     22 August 1888

Golubchik Modia!

I have not written for a long time, first because of not feeling well and also because I was working beyond my strength to finish Laroche's overture. I have not finished it, but I have done quite a lot. I felt very sad to be leaving Frolovskoie. On Saturday evening we all left together from Klin. . . . Yesterday, I spent the whole day with Zet, and we had lunch and dinner together. On 18 September there is going to be a concert in Petersburg in aid of the flood victims in Sweden and I shall conduct, so I shall be in Peter about 10 September.

Have just seen Hubert. He is very ill. He has typhoid fever or something like it. He has been ill all the summer and now Alexandra Ivanovna has not slept for two weeks. They let me see him only for a minute. He is most terribly changed and I am very sad about it. Am going to Kamenka tomorrow. What a pity that I shall not find Bob there – we shall probably pass each other on the way.

Yours

Tchaikovsky

The Manege, a large building in Moscow outside the Kremlin, was originally intended for horse shows, dog shows, military parades, and so on. Popular concerts were given there, and it is clear that Tchaikovsky doubted that in that setting his music would draw an audience.

Tchaikovsky liked to show off his knowledge of the English language and 'great attractions', therefore, was written in English.

Modest was writing a libretto for *The Queen of Spades* for N. S. Klenovsky.

406

TO MODEST TCHAIKOVSKY   Frolovskoie
7 September 1888

My dear Modia!

Why haven't you written for so long? Our meeting in September will not take place either, for there won't be a concert or if so then it will be without me. To be honest I am very glad, but am sorry that I shall not see you, Bob, Kolia, and the rest, soon. This concert doesn't attract me at all. Either one needs to make a lot of money – which makes it silly to (try to) interest the audience at the Manege with my symphonies, and it would be better to have Figner and such like 'great attractions', which have nothing to do with my symphonies – or Zet wishes me to show off as a composer-conductor. In this case, however, it must not be in September in any empty Manege, but later and something quite different.

I cannot say how I enjoy being here. I cannot understand how I could live and work for so long in the perpetual turmoil of Kamenka. Either you have to go to the big house, or receive somebody, in addition to which there is the everlasting singing of the washerwomen and the soldiers – extraordinary! During my absence a new fireplace has been put in the hall and the windows have new frames, which make the room look much more attractive. I am working hard at Laroche's overture – very difficult but it will be quite brilliant. Imagine my joy – my new symphony, according to all my friends, has caused a sensation, and Taneev (this is most important) is completely enthusiastic. And I imagined that it was no good at all, and was afraid that they might be trying to keep from me that I had composed something too awful for words.

Had dinner in Moscow with the Laroches. They had a stroke of luck! Plevako has suddenly sent them 3,000 roubles and their mother 1,500! They gave a magnificent dinner. Am sending you 100 roubles for September.

P. Tchaikovsky

TO MODEST TCHAIKOVSKY   Moscow
19 September 1888

Modia!

Just a few words. I am in Moscow on business but, what is more important, because Hubert is dying. It is quite hopeless. Dropsy of the brain, with complete loss of mental and physical powers, and death is expected any minute. Poor Alexandra Ivanovna is in absolute despair. All this is very sad.

The Laroches are blooming. You ask about Oulibishev. In October Laroche will stay with me and write the notes and Preface which I promised Yurgenson to have ready by November. I shall not be in Petersburg before the end of next month. I shall arrive just before the concert which is to be on 5 November.

The programme will consist of my three summer works; the symphony, *Hamlet* and Laroche's overture. The symphony is making a stir in the musical world.

Yours

P. Tchaikovsky

I shall probably leave tomorrow for Frolovskoie, if by then poor Hubert is not dead. It is difficult for me to stand it all.

[496] TO MODEST TCHAIKOVSKY   [Frolovskoie]
                                              27 September 1888

I passed two weeks at home getting bad news about Hubert every day. Have just received a telegram from A. I. Hubert: 'Only a few hours left.' Going to Moscow and shall stay there until it is all over. How hard it is for me. Worked hard. *Hamlet* is nearly ready. Went to Spasskoie to see the von Wiesens. The countryside is beautiful after Shchapovo and I liked Spasskoie very much. At home all is ready for winter and is warm and comfortable.

I hope all is well with you. I kiss you, Kolia, Bob.

P. Tchaikovsky

[497] TO ANATOLI TCHAIKOVSKY   Frolovskoie
                                            1 October 1888

Golubchik Tolia!

I have just returned from Moscow. We have buried poor Hubert about whose death you have heard. Thank God he died, for had he lived he would have had to exist as a senile idiot. He died without suffering, and without regaining consciousness, so that he could not have experienced the fear of death. Alexandra Ivanovna is deeply unhappy and you cannot look at her without tears, but in such cases time is the only healer and I hope she will be able to stand up to this awful blow. . . .

You wonder why I did not come to Petersburg on 18 September. For the simple reason that the concert did not take place. Now I have decided to stay here the whole of October and be in Petersburg about 1 November. My concert will take place there on 5 November, and on the 12th I am going to take part in a concert of the Musical Society. Then I shall have to go to Prague for the production of *Onegin*. As to December, I hope to be at home in Russia.

Take all this into account so as to plan your arrival in such a way as to see me either in Moscow or Petersburg. Why does Ivanov not let me know about the concert in Tiflis? I think it could possibly be in the spring. I can imagine what celebrations are taking place now that the Emperor is staying in Tiflis. Have written a mass of business letters, am tired and shall not write any more.

I kiss you all hard. Laroche sends his kisses and regards.

Yours

P. Tchaikovsky

[498]   TO MODEST TCHAIKOVSKY   [Frolovskoie]
                                                         16 October 1888

Hoping that you will, perhaps, come here next week with Sapelnikov I am not writing a long answer. I will talk with you about Klenovsky. It is a pity you have lost so much time over this idiot. I do not have his address but will get it. Saw him at Hubert's funeral. He told me he was moving to Paris (!!!) and is going to give Russian concerts there (!!!) I will get his address. You did not mention in your last letter if you got the 100 roubles I sent you from Klin. If you decide to come, let me know.

I kiss you.

Yours

P. Tchaikovsky

[499]   TO PRASKOVIA VLADIMIROVNA TCHAIKOVSKAIA
                                                         Frolovskoie
                                                         16 October 1888

My Golubka Pania!

I received your letter last week, but am answering it only now as I had to go to Moscow on business. Am pleased to hear that Pania shone at the receptions during the visit of the Czar. My life in the country is coming to an end; soon I shall have to start my wanderings again. Must be in Petersburg about 1 November, where I will stay until the 12th and on the next day I am travelling to Prague for the production of *Onegin*. After that I do not know myself where and how I am going; I have plenty of invitations abroad, but my agent, Zet, has not told me yet exactly where I must go. So I can't answer your question about when and if I am coming to Tiflis. All I can say is that I want to visit Tiflis, very badly and cannot imagine how I can live even a few months without seeing you.

Poor Alexandra Ivanovna Hubert still cannot get over the loss of her dear Tonichka, and I myself have not yet got used to the idea that our delightful and kind friend is no more in this world. Except for Vera Ziloty I have not seen any of your relatives. I will definitely go and see Papasha when next I am in Moscow. When we meet I'll tell you about the scene I had with S. M.

Tretiakov. We shouted at each other in the most awful way (I had had a few drinks). Next day we made it up and I am sorry I shouted so stupidly – but actually I was absolutely right.

All my work is quite finished and I am preparing myself for my conducting. My house, ready for the winter, has become charming and cosy. Ask Tebenkov diplomatically about the carpet – you know what I mean! I feel ashamed to remind him about a present but it is not a present I want only the opportunity to buy cheaper.

After which, besides effusions of love, I shall not write any more. Please, embrace Tolia and Tatochka, and kiss Kokodeks for me. I kiss your hands.

P. Tchaikovsky

[500]   TO ANATOLI TCHAIKOVSKY   Frolovskoie
                                              17 October 1888

Golubchik Tolia!

All I know about my plans in detail is that: on 30 October I am going to Petersburg. On the 5th and 12th I am conducting there at Philharmonic and Musical Society concerts. On the 13th I go to Prague where they are expecting me for the last rehearsal and first performance of *Onegin*. There will also be two Benefit concerts for me in Prague. From there I shall in all probability be invited to Vienna and to other places as well. But it could be that after Prague I shall return home and go abroad again in January. When I shall come to see you I do not know but I will, for sure, as I have a great wish even now to come to Tiflis. All this will be decided in the very near future and then I shall let you know. So if you came to Petersburg between 1 and 12 November you would find me there. It would be very nice to meet but not worth while making the journey just for this alone. If you need to come on business then it would be worth it.

Recently I went to Moscow and saw A. Hubert. On my advice she has made a great effort and has started giving lessons, which has a wonderfully beneficial effect on her. After all, there is nothing worse than letting grief take too much of a hold on you; work is the only cure to take your mind off it. It will, I am sure, get better gradually and in time she will be all right. I still cannot get over the death of our kind old boy. He was indeed the kindest of men. What a difference to Laroche! How utterly selfish and devoid of real kindness he is. This I have written because 'of a little cat which has been running between us lately' [i.e. misunderstanding]; but it would take too long to explain.

It will be sad to leave my little home now that it has become so very nice, cosy and peaceful. The day after tomorrow I am going to Moscow for the Musical Society concert. Then back here for a short time, and then I shall leave on the 30th. All my Moscow friends are in raptures over my symphony, but how the public and the Petersburg musical world will receive it, God only knows.

I embrace you, Pania, Tata. How I long to see you and how far away you are! I wish and at the same time do not wish you to leave Tiflis.

Yours

P. Tchaikovsky

[501] TO ANATOLI TCHAIKOVSKY   Frolovskoie
                                            27 October 1888

Just returned from Moscow, where I went to the first Symphony Concert as well as a special one organized by Ziloty. The Society has lost another hundred members. Modest came for two days and we went to Moscow together. On the day after tomorrow I am going to Petersburg, and then to Prague. Until the 13th write to me at Petersburg and then at the Hôtel de Saxe, Prague. Shall be back in Moscow in December where I am conducting at the Musical Society on the 10th. What will happen next I do not know.

I embrace you all.

Yours

P. Tchaikovsky

Sorry that this is so short.

This was an intensely active period. On 5 November Tchaikovsky conducted the premiere of the Fifth Symphony and the Second Piano Concerto (soloist Sapelnikov), and Laroche's overture in St Petersburg; on 12 November he conducted another performance of the symphony as well as *Hamlet* in St Petersburg; there were performances of the symphony and the Second Piano Concerto, and also of *Eugene Onegin*, to direct in Prague. The critics doubted that the Fifth Symphony was of the quality of, for instance, the Second and the Fourth, and depressed by the death of his niece Vera, Tchaikovsky relapsed into an introspective and gloomy mood.

[502] TO ANATOLI TCHAIKOVSKY   [Petersburg]
                                            13 November 1888

Tolia, forgive me! It has been impossible to write. You probably know from the papers that everything here is in order. Off to Prague now. Will be in Moscow on 6 December; write there. If you come in January we shall probably see each other. Feel very well. Had an enthusiastic reception yesterday at the Musical Society and now – at this very moment – I have to leave.

I kiss you, embrace you, good-bye!

P. Tchaikovsky

TO PRASKOVIA VLADIMIROVNA TCHAIKOVSKAIA

Vienna
26 November–8 December 1888

My Golubushka Pania!

I am on the way from Prague to Petersburg. I wanted to go to Moscow first,
but read in the papers about the death of Vera Rimsky-Korsakov
and want to go to Petersburg to find out how it all happened, and how my
poor Sasha is bearing it. I was in Prague for eleven days, when I conducted
a concert and my opera. The opera was a success, the sets were very good,
and also the singers, while Tatiana was better than I could have dreamt. The
applause was terrific and I think the opera pleased everybody. Between
ourselves, I am bringing plenty of laurels with me but very little of the
'despicable metal'. I never know how to manage the business side of things!

Although Vera's death was not unexpected it gave me a great shock. I cannot
think of Sasha and Leva without horror. What a fiend is death when, without
pity, it cuts down the life of a young and sweet being!

I am going to Peter now, then home for two or three days; on the 10th I have
a concert in Moscow and on the 17th I have promised to conduct in Petersburg.
That is why I should like to stay in the country for a whole month to compose
my ballet which I promised to the Directors of the Petersburg Opera. After
that another trip abroad, and in the spring I hope to travel by sea to you in
Tiflis.

I kiss you all very hard, my dears! Forgive me for not writing more often.
Honestly, it is impossible.

P. Tchaikovsky

Each Russian county, in Czarist times, had a Governor and a Vice-Governor,
appointed by the central government. Anatoli was now advanced to the latter office.
   On 17 December Tchaikovsky conducted *The Tempest* at the fourth of the Russian
Symphony Concerts organized by M. P. Belaiev, a timber merchant with keen musical
interests who founded a publishing house in 1885 for the propagation of Russian
music. Throughout this period Tchaikovsky was busy with *The Sleeping Beauty*,
the first four scenes of which were taken to St Petersburg, and a second European tour.

TO ANATOLI TCHAIKOVSKY

Petersburg
19 December 1888

Tolia Golubchik!

I congratulate you on your appointment to the position of Vice-Governor. I did
not expect it to happen so soon and was quite staggered by the news of it in
the papers. I am glad, but also sorry you have left your proper occupation. . . .

On Saturday I took part in a 'Russian' Symphony Concert. I am very glad that I could prove, in public, that I do not belong to any particular party, and look upon it as an honour to be there when Rimsky-Korsakov is the most important person. I contemplate being here for Christmas and leaving for the country on the 26th. I shall stay there, without moving, until my journey abroad at the end of January. In my thoughts I have decided to pay you a visit in April, travelling back from London to Batum by sea.

I kiss and embrace you.

P. Tchaikovsky

[505]   TO ANATOLI TCHAIKOVSKY   Frolovskoie
                                                        5 January 1889

Anatosha Golubchik!

I am leaving Petersburg on 20 January, from there abroad on the next day, where I have a whole series of concerts. The last one, as last year, will be in April, on the 8th, new style. On the very next day, God willing, if still alive and well, I will go straight to you in Tiflis – but this time by sea from Marseilles. In any case I will be with you either for, or about Easter. You can count on it for I have quite made up my mind. You can't think how happy the thought that I shall join you in Tiflis makes me. I miss you all very much and love Tiflis. Am working on a ballet from morning till night and have nothing to write about. I am very, very, very glad that you are no more at the Ministry of Justice. It is really excellent!

I kiss and embrace you.

P. Tchaikovsky

[506]   TO MODEST TCHAIKOVSKY   Frolovskoie
                                                        9 January 1889

Modia!

I have not written to anybody, for I am too deep in the composition of my ballet and have no time for anything else. If I do not finish at least two-thirds of it before my journey it will not be ready for next season. The work is bubbling over and I get very tired, but it cannot be helped. Anyway we shall see each other soon. I am leaving here on the 19th and shall stay two days in Petersburg. On the 22nd I must leave for abroad to be in time for the rehearsals for the Cologne Concert. I would like to meet Guitry at least once, in Petersburg. Tell Vassia I received his letter but cannot answer today. All is well here. I embrace you. Do not expect any letters.

Kisses for Kolia and Bob.

P. Tchaikovsky

TO MODEST TCHAIKOVSKY   Cologne
                                         30 January–11 February 1889

30 January! How awful, another two months!! All I think about from morning
till night is for time to pass more quickly and to live until 8 April (new style).
I am bored to death – to the point of madness. Perhaps it will pass. I stayed
two days in Berlin, and am here for the second day. The first rehearsal was
today. All went well; the orchestra is first class and the three hours I spent
with it were very pleasant, except for the initial moment of shyness and fear.

But as soon as I returned to the hotel the same sense of misery, and a desire
for 8 April, came back once more. If it had not been for Vassia I would certainly
not have had the strength to put up with it till then and would have left for
home about ten days after the Berlin concert. But the thought of Vassia keeps
me back. Were I rich I would send for him. Anyway, it may all pass again.

The concert is tomorrow, and the next day I go to Frankfurt. Two days later
to Dresden, and from Dresden to Leipzig for two days to meet Brodsky, then
to Berlin and Hamburg. After which – eight days of rest. I look forward to
them and hope to stay near Geneva and work. Then on to Paris where I shall
await Vassia's arrival with pleasure.

I kiss you Modia! Last night I saw Bob in a very romantic dream, and I have
been thinking of him all day today. I kiss Kolichka heartily.

P. Tchaikovsky

[508] **TO ANATOLI TCHAIKOVSKY**   Frankfurt
                                         2–14 February 1889

I left Petersburg eight days ago, and stayed in Berlin for two days. My first
concert was in Cologne, two days ago, and a great success. After the third
Suite the orchestra played a beautiful, triumphant salute for me. Today I had
the first rehearsal for the Frankfurt concert, which takes place tomorrow.
Dresden the day after tomorrow . . . to write is impossible. Mood bad; am
bored to death and all I think of is that everything will be at an end on the
8th of April and I can go straight to Tiflis into your arms. I embrace you all
three to suffocation.

P. Tchaikovsky

[509] **TO MODEST TCHAIKOVSKY**   [Frankfurt]
                                         2–14 February 1889

Modia!

No time for letter writing. Shall only send short news. Great success in Cologne.
The musicians played a three-fold salute in my honour after the third Suite.

The rehearsal for the Frankfurt concert took place today. Am frightfully bored and unhappy. The worst thing is that one cannot be alone at all and everlasting exhaustion reaches the point of absolute numbness. Tomorrow another rehearsal and concert. After tomorrow in Dresden. Am sending an article which appeared in Cologne, in the *Kölnische Zeitung*, on the day of the concert. Show it to Zet and give him my regards. I kiss and embrace everybody.

P. Tchaikovsky

The Fourth Symphony and the First Piano Concerto (soloist E. Sauer) proved taxing exercises for the Dresden orchestra. Tchaikovsky's chief pleasure in the Saxon capital was revisiting the *Gemäldegallerie*, whose most famous exhibit is Raphael's 'Sistine Chapel Madonna'. After the concert Sauer entertained a small party to dinner. Some days later a concert notice from the *Neues Dresdner Tageblatt* (from which extracts appeared in the *Moscow News*, 1889, no. 62) was forwarded to Tchaikovsky (see Letter 511).

[510] TO MODEST TCHAIKOVSKY　　　　　　　Dresden
　　　　　　　　　　　　　　　　　　　　　　　　8–20 February 1889

Thank you for your letters, dear Modia. You would not believe how pleasant letters are, for I continue to be terribly bored. I am not pleased with Dresden. I expected a first-class orchestra similar to those in Cologne and Frankfurt but I was greatly mistaken. The orchestra is small and indifferent and by the end of the three rehearsals I was quite exhausted. The concert will be in two hours time and I am leaving space at the end of this letter to tell you how it went off. I send cuttings, which I received today, from the Frankfurt papers. Today I also went to see the Madonna. Both she and the Gallery made a much stronger impression than before.

I am beginning to wonder if I should not leave everything and go home; I would if it had not been for Sapelnikov who would probably not go to London without me. Going to Berlin tomorrow. Was very nervous and conducted badly. The audience did not like the first part of the symphony, but liked the *Andante* better and the *Scherzo* even more, and after the concert there was a supper with speeches. Mood awful.

[no signature]

[511] TO MODEST TCHAIKOVSKY　　　　　　　Berlin
　　　　　　　　　　　　　　　　　　　　　　　　15–27 February 1889

Golubchik Modia!

The Berlin Concert took place last night. I played only two works – The *Serenade for Strings* and *Francesca*. Actually *Francesca* did not have the effect

I expected, in spite of it being played so wonderfully that the performance alone ought to have been enough to delight the audience. I heard, quite clearly, two or three whistles. The Waltz from the *Serenade* was a special success. It seems to me that since Aachen I have never had such tedious and boring days. I am very unhappy, and – quite honestly – in my thoughts I often blame Vassia for having to sit here and worry.

If it had not been for the London Concert with Vassia I would go from Berlin straight to the Caucasus, but yesterday I had a letter from him in which he writes that he is so excited and happy about going to London that I haven't the courage to disappoint him. I lead the same life in Berlin as in Petersburg; I mean I am at someone or other's house every day, and this is what I can't stand.

The only consolation is Artôt, who is always invited wherever I have to go and whom I love very much. At this moment I go to lunch with the Ambassador, and in the evening will go to Klindworth's. He is giving a musical *Soirée* in my honour at which only works of mine will be played. Tomorrow I am going to Leipzig to see Brodsky, and from there straight to Geneva. After the Geneva Concert I would like to stay in Vevey for about two weeks and compose the Fourth Act of the ballet.

For the present, continue to write to Wolff. Thank you, dear Modia, for writing so often. Yesterday there was a charming letter from Kolia, which I will answer from Leipzig. Here is an article which I have just received from Dresden.

Hartmann is a very well-known author.

I kiss and embrace you.

P. Tchaikovsky

[512]   TO ANATOLI TCHAIKOVSKY   Geneva
                                      20 February–4 March 1889

My dearest Tolia and Pania!

It is quite frightful to think how far away from you I am, and how long this letter will take to reach you. I write to you as rarely during my travels as I do to anyone else, but honestly it cannot be otherwise. All my time has been full of rehearsals, concerts, and travelling. I reached Geneva yesterday, and will stay five days and then leave. Everywhere where I made an appearance I enjoyed great success, so I must not complain. But my state of mind has been awful, and what made it worse was that I could never be alone. Either I had to go somewhere or people came to see me; or if alone I was utterly exhausted. However, I am perfectly well, and think that, on the whole, these tours are good for my health.

I have only one wish; that all this should finish as soon as possible, and I count the days to the end. Several times I felt so miserable that I was ready to leave

everything and join you; but if I did my protégé Sapelnikov could not then
go to London, and then I persuade myself that I am suffering all this agony
for the glory of Russian music. At the same time I am extending my reputation
as a composer. Why no word either from you or Pania? I did send you my
address (19 am Karlsbad, W. Berlin, Hermann Wolff für P. Tchaikovsky).

From here I go to Hamburg. Then Paris and from Paris to London, where my
concert will be on 27 March–8 April. On the very next day I travel to Tiflis,
either overland or by sea, and I shall stay with you there for three or four
weeks. I kiss you, my Golubchik!

A great pity that I will be late for Easter week. I embrace you. Do not address
to Wolff after all. Write to: Paris Rue Richepanse 14.

P. Tchaikovsky

The Geneva concert included the Serenade for Strings, the first Suite, and 'Don
Juan's Serenade' (Op. 38, no. 1). Tchaikovsky's annoyance that the Russian papers
ignored his foreign successes was principally on account of their apparent failure in
patriotic duty. He contrasted the treatment accorded to a German opera company
currently performing Wagner in St Petersburg (see Letter 515).

At Hamburg on 3–15 March Fifth Symphony (dedicated to Ave-Lallemant – see
pp. 386, 388) was played for the first time.

[513]   TO MODEST TCHAIKOVSKY   Hamburg
                                     28 February–12 March 1889

Dear Modia!

I have not written for a long time, but you probably read my letter to Bobik.
In spite of a poor orchestra the Geneva Concert was an immense success. The
Theatre was filled to overflowing, I was presented with a gilded wreath from
the Russian colony, and all was as it should be. I left the next day, and was a
bit sorry to do so as the weather was lovely – real spring. I am here since
yesterday evening, and the first rehearsal took place today.

Brahms stayed an extra day to hear my symphony and was very kind. We had
lunch together after the rehearsal and quite a few drinks. He is very
sympathetic and I like his honesty and open-mindedness. Neither he nor the
players liked the Finale, which I also think rather horrible.

I will not say anything about my boredom, sadness, and despondency; it is still
the same. All the time I count the days and hours until I am free. My letter to
Bob crossed with his, as I wrote to him on the same day he had written to
me. This time his letter is charming, not at all a letter to an old uncle one
should please.

I am very glad that you have started to write a play. What a pity about poor

Mania!!!! The concert in London will be not on the 8th as I thought but on the 11th.

Going from here straight to Paris. Hope not to feel so bored there. So, write to Rue Richepanse 14.

I kiss you and embrace Kolia.

P. Tchaikovsky

What a shame that the Russian papers do not mention my concerts at all.

[514]   TO MODEST TCHAIKOVSKY   Hanover
                                                        5–17 March 1889

I do not remember, Modia, if I wrote from Hamburg. Did I tell you that Brahms stayed an extra day to hear my symphony and sat through the whole of the rehearsal? Also that we had a good time with him afterwards and that he liked the symphony (but not all of it), etc. etc? There were three more rehearsals after the first – the fourth with audience and tickets. The players by degrees came to appreciate the symphony more and more, and at the last rehearsal they gave me an ovation. The concert was also a success. Best of all – I have stopped disliking the symphony. I love it again. Two days before the concert I was at Laub's Benefit (the one who plays in Pavlovsk) and after the two opening movements of the *Serenade* the audience gave me an ovation and the players one all of their own.

All this is very nice and fills my thoughts for the time being, but as soon as there are no rehearsals and no concerts I start getting into the usual state of gloom and boredom. Yesterday when I woke up I was in utter despair. All I had left was one concert in London in nearly a month's time. How to kill time? Go to Switzerland? It would be too far, and it is not worth while settling in some pleasant place only for a short time. To Paris? But I have a horror of repeating the life I led there last year, and I don't want to stay there for long. Nice? That is also a long way off, and somehow I don't want to go. So in the end I have decided to stay for two or three days in Hanover and return to a normal state of mind.

Here I will write a mass of letters that are weighing me down and then move on. Maybe on the way I shall stop off in Aachen. I would again like to see the town where I was so happy and cry over the loss of Nikolai Dimitrievich. But perhaps, after all, I shall go straight to Paris. There the life of the town might kill my boredom. How much time gets lost!!!

Please embrace poor Mania for me. I kiss you and Kolia.

Yours

P. Tchaikovsky

418

TO VLADIMIR DAVYDOV   Hanover
                                                 5–17 March 1889

Bob!

You will probably wonder why I am writing from Hanover. Quite simply, I had
to write about 25 letters and have some solitude, and this is only possible in
a town like Hanover where not even the stray dogs know me. Since I wrote to
you last the Hamburg concert has taken place and again I must boast of a
great success. The Fifth Symphony was beautifully played and I have started
to love it again – I was beginning to develop an exaggerated negative opinion
about it. Unfortunately, according to my correspondents, Russian papers in
the Capitals continue to ignore me and apart from my nearest friends no one
is interested in my successes.

On the other hand all the papers here are full of telegrams about the reception
of Wagner's operas in Peter[sburg]. I am not, of course, a Wagner; but I would,
all the same, like them to know at home how well the Germans are receiving
me. What do you think of the Tetralogy? I feel that we too shall soon have our
own Wagnerians. I hate that species. Bored through a whole evening but
suddenly struck by an impressive moment they will imagine that they have
understood Wagner; and will boast about their fine appreciation, deluding both
themselves and others. I do not think that Russians can like Wagner the
composer of the Tetralogy (I do not mean the composer of Lohengrin).

These German Gods with their Valhalla quarrels and scandals, and the
impossibly drawn-out dramatic nonsense, must seem merely ridiculous to the
French, the Italians and the Russians. As to the music, where wonderful
symphonic episodes do not save the ugliness and artificiality of the vocal side
of these musical horrors, it must make you glum. But, just as in France and
Italy, we shall also have our filthy breed of Wagnerites.

If all this attack on Wagner astonishes you I must tell you that I praise
Wagner's creative genius very highly but I hate Wagnerism and cannot stop
myself from having an aversion to his present manner...

[no signature]

TO MODEST TCHAIKOVSKY   Paris
                                                 21 March–2 April 1889

Dear Modia!

You would like to know something about Sapelnikov. He is completely in love
with Paris. I have decided that after London he must come back here and stay
for about four weeks under the tutelage of Brandukov. Even if he does not
manage to play at a big concert he can make plenty of useful acquaintances.
Yesterday we had dinner at Mme Bernadaki who is delighted with him and is
going to give a splendid musical evening for him. As she is on the best of terms

with all the newspaper people this will be very important for Sapelnikov. Brandukov, also, will introduce him to many people. I have arranged for him to practise every day at Erard's. Yesterday I took Diemer to hear Vassia and he was struck by his wonderful technique. On Friday Vassia is playing at a dinner we are having at Colonne's. In general I will do everything I can for Sapelnikov.

My nice Paris life is at an end. Now everything is as it was last year. Every day – dinners, evening concerts etc., and a dress suit every night as from 7 o'clock. The variations from the third Suite were very successful at Colonne's on Sunday. Did I let you know that from London I am going to Tiflis via Batum. I don't think you need write any more as I don't think your letter will find me anywhere.

I am leaving London at 8.00 am on Friday, 31 March–12 April, and shall travel by the fastest train non-stop to Marseilles – from where, on Saturday, a boat leaves for the East. I will probably be in Tiflis during Easter Week. Please write there. . . .

Yours

P. Tchaikovsky

Please let me know what your summer plans are. Frolovskoie is at your service.

[517] TO MODEST TCHAIKOVSKY   Paris
                                             26 March–7 April 1889

Modia!

Last night Sapelnikov played at Colonne's house and made a great impression. After the Chopin Polonaise Colonne came up to me and said he is going to invite Sapelnikov and do, as he said, *les choses en grand*. Charles Darcours, the critic of the *Figaro*, was also present, and quite enchanted. Altogether Vassia has made a tremendous hit. I am sending him to Paris for three weeks, from London, where – under Brandukov's mentorship – he will meet all the people who matter in music. It is a pity that the concert season is at an end; otherwise Colonne would have given him an engagement at once. Anyway, yesterday's evening was very important for Vassia, and Colonne has told him he will have him next year. Vassia behaves perfectly. Every morning he goes off to Erard's and works there all day. We sometimes have dinner together. Two days ago I gave a dinner for Mackar and other French friends and Vassia was also there.

Have you read about me in the *Figaro* (Wednesday, 3 April)? I have been very worried not to have had any letters from you. . . . In a week's time I shall be at sea. Please, write to Tiflis. Will write again before I leave.

P. Tchaikovsky

Tell Menter about Vassia.

On 3 April the Paris *Figaro* contained an appreciation of the Colonne concert, in which it was written: 'The theme [of the third Suite] is simple, even naïve, but the variations are marvellous in their diversity, brilliance, and colour. The triumphant finale electrified the whole audience. . . . This Russian music is full of sincerity and characteristic taste. It is impossible to copy these qualities.'

Tchaikovsky had first toyed with the idea of composing an opera for the French theatre in 1886, but despite the resurrection of the idea in 1889 (proposed libretto by L. Gallet and P.-L. Detroyat) nothing came of it. Vassily Sapelnikov, Tchaikovsky's protégé, was unprepossessing in appearance; hence, unkindly, he was referred to by his mentor as an 'ape'.

[518]   TO VLADIMIR DAVYDOV   London
                                       29 March–10 April 1889

Bob!

I got your letter a long time ago in Paris. But to write from Paris was absolutely out of the question, especially during the last days of my stay there. Here I scarcely know anyone (and do not want to either, as I am much too tired of acquaintances) and today, after the rehearsal, I am completely free.
First, I must tell you what a London fog is like. Last year too I had the pleasure of enjoying it every day, but what happened today I would never have thought possible. When I went to the rehearsal in the morning it was foggy as it sometimes is in Petersburg; but when Sapelnikov and I left St James's Hall at 12.30 pm it was pitch dark – just like at 8 o'clock on a moonless autumn night in Petersburg. It made a very strong impression on both of us. Even without fog I find London very antipathetic. (But for God's sake don't mention this to Miss Eastwood.) And now I have the feeling that I am sitting in a dismal underground dungeon – 4.00 pm it is getting somewhat brighter. The extraordinary thing is that this happens in the middle of April; even the Londoners themselves are surprised.

The pleasure of being in Paris was spoiled by having every day to mix with the social set; but what a lovely, jolly, dear town it is compared to London. On the day after tomorrow (Friday 31 March–12 April), I go from here to Marseilles, and on Saturday (1–13 April), by steamer straight to Batum. When you get this letter I shall be at sea. The voyage by sea is very attractive but a bit too long. I shall have no news from Russia for two weeks!!! Dear Bobik! How happy I shall be when eventually I get back home to Frolovskoie.

Sapelnikov has not yet played, and I expect him to make a sensation at the rehearsal tomorrow. In Paris, where he played in private houses, he was immensely successful, and he has very important engagements for next year. I have a feeling that in a year or two Mr Sapelnikov will be very famous and look down upon us all. . . .

The future celebrity suffered cruelly from sea-sickness between Dover and

Calais, whereas I, as usual, did not feel sick at all (it was not very rough anyway).

I am very happy that this ape is with me. Since he joined me in Paris my unhappiness came to an end. . . . On the eve of our departure Viardot gave an evening, at which an opera which she had composed on a libretto from Turgeniev was presented. Her two daughters and some pupils sang, and one of them danced a Russian dance to the great delight of the audience. I saw the famous Eiffel Tower from quite near. A grandiose thing! Colonne conducted my orchestral variations beautifully at his last concert and they were a big success. I had great pleasure in hearing Berlioz's best work, *La Damnation de Faust*, which is never played in Russia. How I love this fine piece of music, and how I wish you could know it! I also liked Lalo's opera *Le Roi d'Ys* very much. Tell Modia to try and get it. It has been decided that I am to compose a French opera, *La courtisane*. I have made the acquaintance of a multitude of young French composers, who are all terrific Wagnerites, just like – Bob. But this Wagnerism does not suit the French! It has all turned into a game which insists on being taken seriously.

This, more or less, is all of interest that I can report. Just one more item: I adore Bob and am delighted that he has written two such charming letters.

I embrace you, my joy!

Yours

P. Tchaikovsky

Kisses and kind regards to everybody.
If you can, show this letter to Modia – I doubt if I shall have time to write to him!

[519] TO MODEST TCHAIKOVSKY   Constantinople
                                                  8 April 1889

My dear Modia!

Vassia must have told you about London. I went from London to Marseilles with terrific speed. In Paris, at the railway station, I met Kolia Rimsky-Korsakov (he wept when he saw me and I was very touched) and I travelled in the same train with the Bazilevskys. I spent only a few hours in Marseilles, from where we sailed exactly a week ago.

The steamer is very good, and the food excellent. The sea was really rough at times, and between Siros and Smyrna we had a bad storm which – even now – I can't think about without horror. They say such storms often happen there. Two Russians were on board with me: a fourteen-year-old boy – Sklifosovsky (the son of the well-known surgeon) and his tutor, Germanovich – a student at Moscow University. They are both charming young fellows and

I became very friendly with them. But from here we are going our different ways: I to Batum and they to Odessa. We arrived here yesterday at 4 o'clock, and wandered about the town together all the evening, and spent the night on board. I shall miss them very much. The captain, his second-in-command, and the whole staff are very nice.

On the whole, in spite of the rough sea, I am very pleased with my journey, only it takes too long. I shall not get to Tiflis before Thursday of Easter Week.

Sent you a telegram yesterday. I embrace you.

P. Tchaikovsky

At this very moment I am off to the town with my friends. Leaving tomorrow for Batum at 7.00 am on Easter Day.

[520] TO ANATOLI TCHAIKOVSKY   Moscow
                                               12 May 1889

Golubchik, Tolia!

Together with this letter you will get 600 roubles. I thank you! I have now been in Moscow for six days. The journey bored me to death and I was glad when I got here.

Straight from the railway station, more or less, I found myself at a Conservatoire performance in the Malyi Theatre, where everybody was pleased to see me. Since then, every day, I have been at committee meetings of the Musical Society, with a lot of business to discuss. The Conservatoire experienced a *coup d'état*: Taneev resigned the directorship and Safonov agreed to take it only on condition that Albrecht was relieved of his post of Inspector. The fact is that Karlusha has become completely impossible and has antagonized absolutely everybody. I stood up for him as long as I could, and in the end said that I should give up my directorship if he had to leave. After a long conference it was decided that I must persuade Karlusha to resign, and that we must keep up decorum by not letting anyone outside the Board know that he was forced to go.

All this Conservatoire business has tired me exceedingly, and I long to get home into the country. Unfortunately I must go to Petersburg first. I am going there tomorrow. From now on please address your letters to Klin. Did the Shah of Persia present you with a Persian Order? How are you, my dears? I embrace all of you. I have a very pleasant memory of my stay in Tiflis. Be sweet and write.

Yours

P. Tchaikovsky

The weather here is heavenly.

TO ANATOLI TCHAIKOVSKY   Frolovskoie
12 July 1889

Tolia, Golubchik!

The news is that I have taken an apartment in Moscow and decided to try
and live in town. To tell the truth I need some distraction in the evenings, and
in winter all I can do here is read – which is one more occupation for the mind
and brings with it those nasty headaches. I have taken a little house in Shtatny
Lane, off the Ostojenka road, very cosy and sweet. It costs 850 roubles per
annum. As well as Modest, Laroche is also staying here, and time passes very
pleasantly. We all work, meet at meal-times, and in the evenings read, or – if
an unexpected guest comes – we play vingt. My work is getting on quietly.
I cannot now work as fast as I could before, not because I haven't the strength,
but because I have become more exacting than I used to be.

Modest is writing a comedy [*The Symphony*]. The first Act is ready but he has
not yet read it to us.

I kiss you.

P. Tchaikovsky

[522] TO ANATOLI TCHAIKOVSKY   Frolovskoie
31 July 1889

Tolia, Golubchik!

Forgive me for not writing very often. My work makes me so tired and is not
yet finished. There is nothing much to say. Kashkin has enlarged the circle of
my guests by coming to see me. It is two months since I received any money
from anywhere and I live on what I borrow from Alexei. Yurgenson has
disappeared somewhere; so far that I do not know how to reach him. Naturally,
thanks to Alexei being very careful, I am not in need of anything, but if I
suddenly wanted to go somewhere it would be impossible . . . nor have my
guests a penny between them. I am mentioning it as a curious phenomenon.
Here are three gentlemen living comfortably on their valet's money! This,
of course, will not last long. . . .

Pania has not yet written from Kislovodsk. After which I kiss and embrace
you. I can imagine how sick you are of the heat and the solitude.

I embrace you.

P. Tchaikovsky

[523] TO ANATOLI TCHAIKOVSKY   Frolovskoie
21 August 1889

Am off to bed now as I have to get up early tomorrow. I am going to Kamenka for a week – purely for a change. I am very tired but finished my work a few days ago. Very pleased. On the whole this summer passed quite pleasantly, with fine weather and pleasant company. Zassiadko wrote to Modest in detail about his meetings with you. Shall return here at the beginning of September. Write to this address. Will be sure to write from Kamenka. If only Tiflis was nearer to Kamenka! But at the beginning of September I must be in Moscow.

I embrace you.

P. Tchaikovsky

Kamenka was made lively at this time by the youngest of the Davydov girls, Natalia (Tasia), and the birth of Irina (Rina) Rimsky-Korsakova, the first child of Vera (née Davydov) and Nikolai Rimsky-Korsakov.

During this year A. Rubinstein celebrated his jubilee as a concert pianist and Tchaikovsky was a member of the committee which was set up to organize appropriate celebrations. He conducted the jubilee concerts and composed a *Greeting to Anton Rubinstein* (words by Y. P. Polonsky) for unaccompanied chorus and an Impromptu in A flat for piano also dedicated to Rubinstein.

The honours accorded to Rubinstein prompted some people to attack musical education and the teaching of the Conservatoire. Places like this, it was argued, encouraged young men to evade military service and young women to suffer nervous disorders. Laroche attacked the *Novoe Vremia* in the *Moscovskie Vedomosty* (*Moscow Gazette*) 1889, No. 207. On 6 and 18 November he replied to the scurrilous personal attacks by Prince Vladimir Meshchersky in *Grazhdanin* (*The Citizen*). Meshchersky, cynical, corrupt, and viciously reactionary, was a close friend and adviser to the Czar, to whom he wrote in ingratiating terms and by whom he was addressed as an intimate. He had also been a friend of Tchaikovsky when both were students. *Grazhdanin* was subsidized out of State funds and was intended to aid the implementation of a hard line policy. (See Letter 527)

[524]   TO ANATOLI TCHAIKOVSKY   Kamenka
                                                        31 August 1889

Dear friend Tolia!

I have been here for a whole week and am very pleased with my visit, and shall stay until the day after tomorrow (2 September) and then go to Kopylovo, just for a day, to see Anna. Then to Moscow. A very busy time lies before me. On 10 September a rehearsal of the new production of *Onegin* in Moscow. Then, preparations for the concerts and the concerts themselves. In November, conducting at the Rubinstein Festival. Then Moscow again, and later, maybe, a journey abroad. I hope that you will have returned to Petersburg in time for the Rubinstein celebrations.

Life here is very noisy; first Tassia's Name Day, then Rina's birthday, and a drive either to Verbovka or to the forest; then meeting new arrivals, and next seeing them off – I am astonished that I could ever consider living here permanently! I could not possibly do so any more; but to come and stay for a short time in Kamenka is very pleasant. . . .

Quite impossible even to think of work – but that is good; it is a great pleasure for me to do absolutely nothing.

And now my poor sufferer (I call you sufferer because I hear you have a terrific heat-wave in Tiflis), I kiss and embrace you. My written kisses to Pania and Tania.

Yours

P. Tchaikovsky

[525]   TO MODEST TCHAIKOVSKY   Moscow
                                              13 September 1889

How absolutely silly! I arrived here on an invitation to come on Sunday, but found Khokhlov ill, and no rehearsals; so for the fourth day I am sitting here idly, fruitlessly. Just when the weather has become lovely! What a shame not to be in the country. I fear I am being a fool to move into town. Moscow makes me sad and gloomy. Everything here irritates me, beginning with hundreds of beggars who poison the pleasure of my walks and finishing with the smells that fill the Moscow streets.

All the same I spent two pleasant evenings at the theatre: at the Malyi Theatre where I saw a first-rate production of *Tatiana Riepina*; and at the Bolshoi, where *The Magic Flute* was beautifully sung and staged. In the *Riepina* it was not so much Ermolova who impressed me – she was really good only at the end – but all the actors in the secondary parts. Pravdin was particularly good as the Jewish banker.

Tell Mania that since his disappearance from Moscow I have become much lonelier than I have been during recent years, and that I miss him frightfully. No, next year I will definitely move to Petersburg.

Well! Good-bye, dear Modia, nothing more to write about. I embrace you.

P. Tchaikovsky

Onegin will be given on Monday the 18th; but if not I shall leave for Petersburg anyway on the 19th, in which case the opera will be postponed until I return. Shall be with you for certain on Wednesday the 20th.

Poor Fitzenhagen is dying.

TO ANATOLI TCHAIKOVSKY   [Moscow]
                                         Pretchistenka
                                         Troizky Pereoulok No 6
                                         1 October 1889

Golubchik Tolia!

I am just back from Petersburg to my delightful, but much too miniature,
apartment. I had so much to do in Petersburg that it was impossible to write.
I had rehearsals of the ballet every day, which, I must say, I attended with
great pleasure. In addition to this I was also busy at the Rubinstein Committee.
Both in Petersburg and here the weather is just like summer and my heart aches
for the country where I do not live any more....

I lied to you in my last letter. I shall stay here the whole of October; and the
whole of November and probably the first half of December in Petersburg. Now
I have to prepare myself for the special Rubinstein concert which means work
on the scores and I will write only very short letters to you and Pania. Anyway
it is not long now until we meet again. I embrace both of you. Heaps of kisses
to Tata.

Yours

P. Tchaikovsky

Tchaikovsky was much interested in the writings of the young Chekhov and was
delighted when he received a copy of a volume of short stories, *Sombre people*, with
the inscription, 'To Piotr Illich Tchaikovsky from a future librettist'; the aspiration
expressed in the inscription was not to be fulfilled.

[527] TO MODEST TCHAIKOVSKY   [Moscow]
                                        16 October 1889

I am sending you, dear Modia, yesterday's *Grazhdanin*, in which I read the
'Diary' and wondered which was worse, Meshchersky's meanness or his idiocy.
Show this to Laroche, who ought to write an article in reply to all the attacks
on Rubinstein in the *Moscovskie Vedomosty*. What an excellent opportunity
for Laroche, with his sharp humour, to retort – in a short article – to this
son-of-a-bitch, Meshchersky! Especially as Petrovsky would be delighted. Don't
let him say it is not worth while. It is decidedly worth while. Meshchersky
hates to be attacked in the conservative press. It would also teach Suvorin a
lesson. The article in the *Grazhdanin* I read yesterday in the train on my way
to Ziloty's, where I passed the whole day.

Do not wonder why I do not answer any letters. I positively have no time
and have completely renounced all letter writing....

Just fancy, Chekhov has written saying he wants to dedicate his new volume of short stories to me. I went to see him to thank him. I am awfully proud and pleased.

Heaps of work, and cannot complain about too many visitors. Up till now I have managed to protect my freedom. In two weeks' time I shall be in Petersburg. Our concert season, for which plenty of tickets have been sold, is going to be brilliant. Rimsky-Korsakov is arriving tomorrow. Very pleased with my lodgings and the cook. Chekhov is very interested in your play.

P. Tchaikovsky

In December Tchaikovsky conducted a concert in Moscow for the benefit of the dependants of musicians and the *Pezzo capriccioso* for cello and orchestra (Op. 62) received its first performance. Tchaikovsky also conducted Beethoven's Ninth Symphony. In St Petersburg he discussed the preparations for the forthcoming premiere of *The Sleeping Beauty*, also a project for an opera based on Pushkin's *The Queen of Spades*. On 2 January, 1890, the dress rehearsal of the new ballet took place in the presence of the Czar and his courtiers and other notables. The Czar showed no great interest in *The Sleeping Beauty*. What was worse neither did the public on the first night, on 3 January. In due course, the enormous expense incurred by this lavish production proved justified and posterity was to overturn the opinion of the first audiences.

Immediately after the performances Tchaikovsky decided to go abroad. In Florence he thought he could work on *The Queen of Spades*, for which Modest had prepared the libretto. His own servant, Alexei Sofronov, could not travel with him on account of the grave illness of his wife, so his companion was Modest's servant Nazar (see Letter 454).

Nazar kept a diary in which he wrote his impressions of his temporary employer and also of Florence (see Letter 531). Nazar was no scholar nor was his diary a literary chef d'oeuvre. In writing of his master he used the third person plural. His entry for 29 January runs somewhat as follows: 'P.T. is in a good mood today. Yesterday they [i.e. he] began another scene and as I see it it is going well. They praise Modest Illich for the libretto. Every time before the end of work I come into the room and say it is time to dine or to have supper. I do not know, maybe I interrupt, but no displeasure is shown. If I had noticed, of course, I would not go in; it is a riddle. P.I. perhaps thinks that I come in through boredom, that at this time they are free and make a kind and good-natured face. But no, I am not now bored at all. I come in to distract them, and if I did not do it they would think I am displeased with something; but all the same, up till now all is good, thank God. At 7 o'clock I came in. P.I. had not yet finished. I said "It is time to finish". They answered, but continued to draw hooks [notes]. "Yes", I say, "it is soon seven". "This minute", they replied and made one more hook and banged the lid of the piano. I stand. They took out their watch and open it. "It is only twenty to – I can work another ten minutes". I said something and they – "Please, allow me just ten minutes". I went out. In ten minutes they came to me. "Well, I have finished" and started asking me what I did (I was writing when they came in, I closed the copy-book) and we went into his room and I stand at the table. Started talking about

with him and very glad he is with me, for if it had not been for his presence the gnawing feeling of sadness would have been much greater.

Now about work. I started with great zest and have done quite a lot. If it goes on like that I shall have to ask you to send me the next Acts. You did the libretto very well but for one thing – it is too verbose. Please be as short and laconic as possible. I have left out a few things. For instance, everything Hermann says to the Count in the little verses after he has told him of his love. I mean, after the words 'I am ill, I am in love' I have left out all that comes after the chorus. He has so much more to sing after that. The words are sometimes quite good, sometimes a bit harsh and sometimes no good at all. But on the whole the libretto is excellent and one can see that you appreciate music and its requirements, which is so important for a librettist.

I had your letter this morning and was very upset about Sapelnikov. I sent him a telegram immediately and have already got an answer. For God's sake explain why he did not have any success. Please, write more often. The weather has been frightfully cold, but it is warmer today.

I embrace and kiss you.

P. Tchaikovsky

[531] TO MODEST TCHAIKOVSKY   [Florence]
                                      25 January 1890

Dear Modia!

I am in a hurry to answer your letter in which you offer to come here. Thank you for taking my complaints about my melancholy so much to heart. At first I felt really tortured, but now everything is different, and although I have no particular pleasure in staying in Florence my former sadness has altogether gone. My work is going on – and going on well – and that has completely changed my morale. I must finish the opera by the spring. You ask if the setting which surrounds me answers the requirements for successful work. Yes, I would say, perfectly. Nothing, and no one disturbs me; I have plenty of entertainment in the evenings, pleasant walks, and everything I need for work. And there is no strain on my health. I don't care at all where I am so long as I can work well and in peace.

In Russia I have no real home at the moment, and even if I still had Frolovskoie it would be too near both to Moscow and to Petersburg. It is lucky that distance lessens my interest in musical affairs in Moscow which I take too much to heart. I cannot say Florence is bliss, but I have found here all I need for satisfactory work. Naturally I would be very happy to have the companionship of someone near to me, but at this moment it is not indispensable. If I had plenty of money I would have taken advantage of my solitude as a good reason for giving you an opportunity to come to Italy. But money is very short. I have written to Gerke asking him to get me a subsidy from the Fund for

Musicians – as a loan, of course. The Laroches are always promising to pay me back for my help to Mania, now they are rich. It would be much better if they gave you enough money to travel to Italy and came with you. It would be lovely.

Nothing special has happened. The weather is warmer and I had a lovely walk today. Nazar seems sincerely pleased to be here. I would like to peep into his diary, in which he writes every day. I have, in my work, come to the 'Ballad'. It is quite a lot for seven days. I think it is coming on well. Don't be late with the next Acts. I think I am nearly ready with the whole first Act, i.e. the first two Scenes. Am very worried to be without news from Alesha – I fear that Feklusha is dead.

I kiss you.

P. Tchaikovsky

Tchaikovsky had by now finished Tomsky's ballad (Act I, scene 1, no. 5).

On 23 January Laroche wrote: 'You and your Vsevoloisky are wrong to insist on the tragic scene on the embankment with the view on the Petropavslovsk Fortress. Please do not sacrifice the uniformity (or fluidity) of the drama for the sake of a pretty setting. Wagner is right when he is against the effect which is no more than "Wirkung ohne Ursache". There are plenty of sad and pathetic moments in *The Queen of Spades* and the scene on the embankment only increases the sad element which is so often your enemy.'

[532]   TO MODEST TCHAIKOVSKY   Florence
                                            2–14 February 1890

Modia!

I sent you a telegram about the fourth Scene of the Second Act today, but by mistake called it 'the second Scene' – the second Scene of the Second Act. I hope you understood. The Scene is very well made from the point of view of music and I am very pleased with you as librettist. Only remember to be brief, and beware of long-windedness. This little sin is actually worse in the preceding Scene. I have been thinking a lot about the Scene on the embankment. You and Laroche are absolutely against it but – in spite of wishing to have as few of them as possible I fear that without this Scene the whole Third Act will be without women – and this is boring. Besides, the audience must know what happened to Liza. One cannot finish her part in the fourth Scene. I would be very grateful if you talked it over with Vsevoloisky and other people in the theatre, to decide once and for all – yes or no. I am at the end of the second Scene; as soon as you send me the third (the ball) I shall start on it. If the work continues to go as it has up till now, I can hope to finish it on time. Whether it is good or bad, I don't know. Sometimes I am very pleased, sometimes not, but I am no judge.

The time will soon come when, except for the libretto, I shall have nothing else to write about, for my life is so set in its groove, and one day is so much like the next, that there is no variety at all. The hotel, which was nearly empty when I arrived, is beginning to fill up. Palen (the former Minister) is here with his family and has a table next to mine. I continue to ignore Florence; I mean, I do not visit any museums or churches – only cafés after dinner. I mostly go for walks on the Viale dei Colli. Where did you and Kolia live in 1882, after I left? I do not remember. Yesterday, along the Lungarno, carriages drove by with masked figures, masses of people in masks walked by, and crowds passed under our windows. A poor parody of the Roman Carnival!

The weather is still very cold, but clear, and in the afternoon on Lungarno the sun is intense and quite hot. Nazar has made many friends and is very happy.

I kiss and embrace you. Ask Kolia to write.

P. Tchaikovsky

[533] TO MODEST TCHAIKOVSKY   Florence
                                           6–18 February 1890

Modia!

You are late with the Russian song! I have composed my own long ago and am not a bit sorry. Although the words are rather silly they are not at all bad with the music. I have long ago finished the second Scene and am writing the fourth which – I don't know why – I find very difficult. Perhaps because I am upset and am the involuntary cause of Nazar being upset too.

Yesterday morning he did not walk but crawled into my room. Apparently the evening before, back from the circus, he slipped on the stairs and hurt his leg very badly. I got very frightened, especially as when I suggested sending for a doctor he did not object – it meant it was serious. I sent for a doctor who took a long time in coming and seeing that Nazar could not walk at all I was certain the leg was broken. But after a proper examination the doctor said there was no fracture, and ordered compresses with *aqua vegetale* and absolutely no movement. So poor Nazar has been in bed for two days. The greater pity as today is *Mardi gras* and there has been quite a Roman-like battle of flowers – and flour – and in general Florence looks animated and jolly. However do not worry; nothing too serious has happened. The doctor has been again and confirmed that there are no bones broken and all that is needed is to keep still. Today Nazar is even allowed to get up a little. He can't complain of loneliness either, for he now has three Russian friends who come to see him and pamper him. On the whole he is very popular here – the landlord, the secretary, the landlord's son, and all the staff, like him very much and come during the day to keep him company. The real pity is that he is otherwise quite well and it must be boring for a healthy man to stay in bed.

Now I am not worried any more but yesterday was awful. Besides, I was jerked out of my orderly existence by Count Palen who unexpectedly came up to me in the dining-room, presented himself, chatted and then presented me to his wife and daughters. They are all very charming but you know what sort of burden this is to me. All I can say is that yesterday was an unlucky day.

Today, for the first time, I felt real delight at being in Italy. Up to now I have been completely indifferent, even antagonistic, to it. But the weather today is so heavenly! I was so glad to find a few violets in Cascino that my heart melted, and I gave praise to this lovely country for its climate. However this delight is not nearly so strong as that which even a bad spring at home brings. Here everything seems to be at the wrong time – not as it ought to be. All the same I enjoy it. I have found a way to go for walks in Cascino so as to be in absolute solitude as near as makes no odds. I do not know if the spring has really come but, judging by the multitude of wild flowers, I think so. Can you imagine, I have found – not in Cascino itself but near it – a blue flower which appears in Kamenka in April; the one that smells like the breath of a small child – you know which one! I was so very glad to see it.

Let us talk about *The Queen of Spades*. What can be done so that poor Figner does not have too large a part? Seven Scenes and he has to be on the stage all the time! Just think! Discuss it with Vsevoloisky. For this reason alone it could be better to leave out the Scene on the embankment. I get frightened when I think of all I have already composed for him and how much I still have to write. I fear the poor fellow will not find enough strength to do it. Not only Figner, but any other singer will begin to be afraid, and to tremble at the thought of being on the stage, and singing, all the time. What about the Scene at the Ball – has he a lot to sing in that too? I await it with impatience. For God's sake, Modia, don't lose any time, for I am afraid to be left without a text; I want to finish the fourth Scene in a week's time. Sometimes composing comes easy, sometimes it needs great effort. Actually it does not matter, the effort, maybe, comes from the desire to compose as well as possible and not to be content with the first idea that comes into one's head.

Tired. Nazar sends his regards and will write tomorrow. I went to see him today, and he feels very well and is very happy. Why doesn't Kolia write?

I embrace you.

P. Tchaikovsky

On 8 February Modest wrote 'About the scene on the river – I am beginning to like it. No need to ask Vsevoloisky, I am sure he will be for it. Figner too is for it, but begged for his part to be as short as possible to save his energy for the last scene where he asks to add the Brindisi after the second card, before the appearance of the Queen of Spades. I like this idea.' Regarding the Interlude Modest offered as alternatives an allegory by Derjavin and a pastoral *The Faithful Shepherdess* by Karabanov. Modest preferred the former, Laroche the latter but suggested shortening it.

In the middle of work on the opera Tchaikovsky had word of Antonina Ivanovna from Yurgenson. What he heard is not known, but it distressed him for a day, after which he resumed work. Six years later the unfortunate Antonina was admitted to an asylum for the insane.

Nazar's diary for 11 and 13 February reads: 'I am not at all bored but fear that P.I. does not like [it]. A doctor comes, and a masseur, and always disturb him, and this Piotr Illich hates though does not show it. But I know for sure it is very disagreeable to him.' 'P.I. went for a walk and brought flowers for three vases which I filled but could not place them on the table. That is the sort of servant I am to P.I. at the present moment. It seems to me they are now sorry that they took me. Of course it is my surmise but one could think it so. It is ten days now and I am still limping on four legs. P.I. always teases me that I am a four-legged one, and especially when I want to serve something. "What about it four-legged one, crawling again?" and, of course, they themselves take what I ought to be serving, such is my position.'

[534] TO MODEST TCHAIKOVSKY   [Florence]
                                           13–25 February 1890

As I have reported through a letter to Kolia, I have got the third Scene. It arrived – just in time – as I was finishing the fourth. I started with the Interlude as it was the most difficult part. I chose the pastoral. Your letter today includes Laroche's advice, but too late as the Interlude has been written. I think it is quite in the style of the times and is short and interesting. At the end there must be a chorus and I have written the words. If you like you can change them so long as you keep to the rhythm. In accordance with Vsevoloisky's wish Cupid and Hymen will crown the couple and the followers dance. Then, instead of a march, a chorus, which I mentioned before, with the music a repetition of the former chorus. As the chorus is on stage it would be queer if it did not sing at the end; so this is how I have done it. I wonder how you will do the 'Brindisi'? But I find it difficult to imagine mad Hermann saying something like this:

All the same, try to please him. We must please everyone, to make them try very hard. When I come to the place, in the third Scene, where the prince talks of his love for Liza, I might have to add a bit, to make the part of the

435

prince more important. If so, I will write the words and, again, you can edit them. The Interlude is finished (it is 11.30 am now) and about 3.00 pm I shall start the third Scene proper. If by then I haven't got anything from you I may go somewhere for three days to distract my thoughts for, as a matter of fact, I continue to be bored. Apart from pleasant moments during my walks (although the weather has become worse), as soon as I am not working, or walking, or eating and drinking, boredom and a curious antipathy to Florence set in at once. However, I am afraid to move as it would be difficult to find better working conditions. I am wonderfully comfortable here.

Poor Nazar still cannot walk properly, nor leave the hotel. Now a masseur comes to him. The doctor who looks after him is a delightful old boy. He says that the torn ligament will take a few more days to heal. Nazar is not bored at all but because of his delicacy he worries that I spend money on his cure. On the other hand I get angry that he doesn't believe that I'm not sorry to spend it. I must say the more I know him the more I love him. What a good fellow he is.

Well, Modia, if God wills it that I finish the opera it will be *chic*, the fourth Scene, I'm sure, will make a stupendous impression.

I embrace you.

Yours

P. Tchaikovsky

On 20 February Nazar wrote: 'P.I. started a letter to Modest Illich where they promised to give my regards [lit. "my bows"]. P.I. says that with this scene they had to work properly although it is so small. They say, a rather difficult scene is 5 [Act III] ghost to Hermann, how the Spade Lady appears to him [Scene 7] and burial service singing. P.I. asked if I could do it quicker. I said to that "Without any doubt quicker".'

[535]   TO MODEST TCHAIKOVSKY   [Florence]
                                        20 February–4 March 1890

Dear Modia!

I do not know what you will say but I have completely changed the end of the fourth Scene; for, in the way you have done it, it is not really effective and has no ending. Also, it is funny to finish with a polonaise; better to start with one. I find that it won't do for the guests to leave the stage twice. After the fireworks the guests must gradually return to the stage at the moment when Chekalinsky and Surin are pursuing Hermann. Before the Interlude I added these words for the Master of Ceremonies after the first ones: 'The host requests the honoured guests to listen to a Pastoral which is entitled – "The true feelings of a shepherdess".'

436

The guests take their seats and then the Interlude begins. After the Interlude all remain on the stage. Some sit, some walk about, and talk. The meeting between Hermann and the Countess and the conversation with Liza takes place at the front of the stage. After Hermann's words: 'Now not I . . . but fate itself' etc. the Master of Ceremonies, looking worried, runs in once more and says in a hurry:

Master of Ceremonies:
Her Majesty has just this very minute graciously consented to appear.
Chorus of Guests: (with joyful anticipation)
Her Majesty! . . . The Empress!
What happiness! Her Majesty is coming. . . .
The greatest honour to the host. . . .
What a great honour! . . . What a joy – to be able to look on our dear Mother.
Is that the French Ambassador with her? It could be!
No – he has gone. . . . The Prussian Prince?
No, His Serene Highness is sure to come.
There she is!
The Master of Ceremonies: (to the choir)
Now sing: 'All hail to them.'
Chorus of Guests:
There she comes!
Well! This truly is a Festival!
(The Master of Ceremonies makes a sign to the choir to begin. Meanwhile the guests have placed themselves so that the Empress has a free entry)
Choir and chorus of Guests together:
Hail to you Catherine!
Hail our Mother, gentle, kind!
Vivat, vivat, vivat!
(Pages, in pairs, appear through the middle door. Everybody turns that way. The ladies curtsey low. The men bow low according to proper court etiquette when it seems that the Empress is about to enter.)

Curtain

I do not insist on the exact words, but I do insist on the scene. I have composed it in that way and would not like to change it. I think it will be a most effective ending.
Here are the words of the prince (I think that Yakovlev will sing the Prince, and Chernov the part of Tomsky, or even Melnikov – if they do not think he is too old for the part)

The Prince's Aria
I truly love you, my love is immense.
Without you love has lost all sense;
The greatest deed of strength and valour
For your sake I wish to achieve.
But freedom of your heart I would not
In any way try to impede.

To please you I would gladly leave you
And damp the fire of my thoughts.
Not only be a loving husband,
Or servant, needed now and then,
I wish to be your friend forever
And true consoler to the end.
Alas! Now I see and sense
My dreams have taken me too far,
How little trust you have in me –
A stranger to you and so distant.
Oh what a torture is this separation!
My soul is with you in your pain,
My sorrow is the same as yours,
My tears I mingle with your tears.
Liza
You are a kind and honest man
A real friend. . . . Shall tell you all tomorrow (She leaves)

The verses are not bad when sung, but I fear that sometimes they do not make sense. One does not always understand that the Prince is ready to sacrifice everything for her sake. Change them as you like, to make more sense, but do not change the rhythm and form, as I have already composed the music.

I finished the fourth Scene yesterday and did not know what I was going to do today when – just in time – your letter arrived with scene five. I started work at once. For God's sake do not keep me waiting; the sooner I finish the composition and the quicker I send the piano score off the better.

What do you think? Does it matter if Liza turns to the night, in April, and says to it: 'It is as dark as you?' Are there dark nights in St Petersburg in April? The cold here is awful – just at this moment Nazar is using the bellows to blow the fire up. He still limps, his leg is getting better, but only very gradually.

If you only knew how boring and disgusting Florence is!

I embrace you. I hope that Kolia is well. Kiss him and Bob.

Yours

P. Tchaikovsky

Talk to Vsevoloisky about my ending to the fourth Scene.

[536] TO MODEST TCHAIKOVSKY   [Florence]
                                      21 February–5 March 1890

Modia!

As soon as March comes, please go to see O. I. Yurgenson and ask him to give you my pension for two months. Take 100 roubles (or 200 if you need them) and send the rest here by telegraph. It is very simply done, and you can give it to Nara to do. I started on the fifth Scene, not from the beginning, but from the knock at the window; and it is finished. You write in the libretto, 'From back stage one hears funeral singing', but you did not send the words. The words are indispensable and must be a free adaptation of the words from the *Panikhida*, the Funeral Service. I do not need the tunes but need a hint. You say, 'I am sending them!' but have not done so. I must have these words now, otherwise shall have to invent them myself.

P.T.

[537]   TO NIKOLAI TCHAIKOVSKY   Florence
                                         22 February–6 March 1890
                                         Hôtel Washington

Dear friend Nikolasha!

I must say this about the Pension Modgio: first, that you paid so little because it was summer; and second, it is very difficult to get completely separate accommodation in these boarding houses, and live without hearing some English Misses practising on the piano, or singing scales, and horrid sentimental songs. Third, judging by its cheapness, it cannot be on the sunny side, which in winter is indispensable since the sun takes the place of stoves here and without which it gets so cold that no open fire burning all day could save you. I, on the other hand, have a separate apartment, a whole floor of a narrow house with only three windows which face the Arno and the south – absolutely no neighbours, and absolutely no sounds as the walls are thick. This is most important for me. Truly I pay quite a lot (30 francs a day for my 3 rooms, Nazar's large room, food, lamps, and fuel) but this is a whole flat. I doubt that one could find one with full board and lodging like this in Petersburg.

I am working very hard and I think that *The Queen of Spades* will be an interesting opera. A bit too frightening, sometimes so frightening that I am glad Nazar is near me. My days are very regular and monotonous. Several acquaintances tried to see me and I had to chat to one family (Palen the former Minister) but they have left now and I was so distant with the others that they have left me in peace. I work from 9.00–12.30 and then from 4.00–7.00; 6½ hours in all. This does not sound very much but as I work very much like a pedant, and never break the order of my work – not even for a second – it is moving along fast, and I know – as long as I stay well – that I shall finish the opera on time. Between working hours I go for a walk and have lunch, but in the evening I feel bored although I have plenty of books. I feel better now, but at first I was ready to cry I was so homesick. Apparently I am much more attached to my dear Fatherland than I thought; the delights of climate and nature here rarely have much attraction for me. Probably because I am too deeply engrossed in my work. The cold has been awful.

People say that they do not remember such a long cold spell. I am glad that you and Olia are pleased with the portrait. As soon as I see you I shall make a proper presentation.

I kiss you both heartily and also my dear Golubchik George.

Yours

P. Tchaikovsky

Tchaikovsky had numerous letters from Modest concerning details in the libretto. Absorbed in the mystery of the story, he also found its terrors affecting his own moods. The fourth scene of Act II in which the Countess – having failed to name the cards for Hermann – dies of fright, especially haunted him. 'I am,' he wrote to Anna Merkling, 'still under the impress of this terror.'

The following lines were written on 23 February. The composer wrote in his diary: 'Tortured myself all the morning writing the words for Liza's arioso. [See pages 443f.] I am definitely no poet.'

[538] TO MODEST TCHAIKOVSKY   Florence
                                      25 February–9 March 1890

You ask for additions and changes. There are not so many other than those
I have already sent:
(1) Scene I
In the chorus of the governesses I did not like the third line not rhyming with
the first – and the fourth with the second.
Anyway, never mind about the third line – but it would be better if it did.
(2) Correct the words of the Boy Commander in the light of what you
discovered from the Military Statutes; I have written them down as you sent
them. After the boys leave I added words for the women's chorus:
Chorus of Nurses, Governesses etc.
How wonderful are our soldiers,
In truth they'll terrify
              a fiend. . . .
(3) For the sake of rhyme you have made Surin use a word I do not like, I have
used the former version:
Surin
If only to win, once!
Chekalinsky
Has Hermann been?
Surin
Yes, and from eight as usual etc.
(4) Have eliminated Hermann's following words in the same scene:
I roam just like a madman . . . etc.
until Tomsky asks:
'Hermann, is that you?' etc.

(5) The young men's words are unrhymed but I need rhymes here, I changed as follows:

Sun and sky and firmament
Songs of nightingales
Fresh and flaming blushes
On the cheeks of maids!
It is spring that grants them
And with it young love
Voluptuously arouses
Fresh and youthful blood.

(Now I definitely do not know why I changed the second couplet, I see you have also rhymed it. You can leave it, if you like, as you have done it, it does not matter.)

(6) The last of Hermann's monologue during the storm I have shortened – after the line: 'Thunder and hurricane in comparison are naught.' He goes straight over to the words: 'As long as I am alive' etc.

In the second scene:

(1) The solo after the duet is sung not by Liza but by Pauline. This I have done to enhance Pauline's part and also for a contralto to be heard which will bring Liza's soprano singing more to the fore after it. Consequently not Pauline but Liza says:

Liza
Sing Pauline, please alone . . .
Pauline
Alone . . . what must I sing?
Friends
Please, do . . . etc.
Pauline
I will sing you . . . etc.
After the song Pauline says:
Pauline
Why have I sung this mournful song
So tearful and so sad, I wonder why,
As you look sad without it, tell me Liza!
On such a day. . . .

(2) After Liza's words:
Oh God, Almighty God!
in the third scene I have added before Hermann's words:
Oh! Let me die and bless you to the last. . . .
the following ones:
These are my last, my only mortal hours
I have been told today about my sentence
To someone else, oh cruel one
Your heart you have entrusted.

Note: As in many cases in your libretto where it is poetry but written like prose these words must be prose although there is rhythm in them. In the very last version see to it that only proper poetry should be published as such. For instance I like the way you changed Hermann's words in the most important scene with the old lady. The Pushkin text is scarcely altered but has rhythm; it must be printed in prose. In this same scene I have slightly changed Hermann's words as here they must rhyme properly.

Hermann
Oh, let me die with blessings on my lips
Not any curses,
How can I live one day when you a stranger
Have now become.
My life was yours, only one feeling
And just one thought
Had hold of me. I have to perish
But must before, with her . . . and so on

However leave it as you have done it, it does not matter if the piano score does not quite coincide with the libretto.
Also about the second Scene. You too often have 'Oh! Righteous God!' Could you change that? I have in one place changed it to 'Oh God! Oh God!'

(3) Oh yes, I have forgotten to give you the Russian song Pauline and the other young ladies sing.

Pauline
Come my own sweet Mashenka, make us merry
Come and dance,
Ai luly, luly, make us merry
Come and dance!
Lift your dainty hands up your sides
Lift them up.
Ai luly, luly, up your sides
Lift them up.
And your dainty feet do not stop
Let them dance.
Ai luly, luly, do not stop
Let them dance,
If your mother asks: 'Are you happy?'
Say of course:
Ai luly, luly, I am happy,
Yes, of course!
And to Tatia's question, did you,
Drink until dawn?
Ai luly, luly,
Yes, I drank until dawn!
If the young man blames you, tell him:
Go, go away!
Ai luly, luly, tell him
Go! Go away!

442

3rd Act

(1) Scene 2 *The Prince*
How sad you are my very dearest,
What sorrow is afflicting you
Trust it to me.

Liza
No, later Prince,
Another time, tomorrow . . . I implore you

The Prince
Please, wait for just another moment,
I must, I have to tell you. . . .

(then comes the arioso the words of which I have sent before)
(2) The end, as I did it, I have also sent you. Please, leave it so.
(3) In the Pastoral in Milovzor's words I have written:
To my own heart I listened
Agreed to love that one etc.
I do not understand where the 'you' comes in, who is 'you'?
Then I have added the last chorus:

How bright the sun is shining
The Zephyrs have flown by.
Have a good time Prilepa
With this so charming boy.
The end of all the sadness
The bride and bridegroom
Are worthy of our praises.
Oh, love, let them be one.

Scene 5
All the advice and comments which you and Laroche have sent always come too late. For example, you advised not to use the prayer: 'With the saints rest in peace', I have done so already and used something else. Vsevoloisky asked, through you, that the Countess should appear twice – again I did it before he mentioned it. Hermann, who, as you put it, sat down and hid his face in his hands, lifts it, but does not move as he has not yet seen the apparition when the audience sees it. He listens – another knock – here he rises and sees her, but in another place.

Sixth Scene
(1) I have written the arioso for Liza where you suggested. The words were written to a music already composed and are not very good:

I am exhausted, so tired I
All day and night
Only of him
Thoughts full of torture
Are in my mind.

Life had such bright days in store for me
Then came a cloud
And lightning struck
All that I loved in the world
Happiness, luck, are completely gone.

And these are all the changes. When you will see Vsevoloisky tell him that
in the sixth scene, if he wants the clock to chime the hymn *Kol Slaven* it will
have to be ordered. I do not insist upon the chiming but have composed so that
there is enough space for it. But I think this would be too factual and I fear
that it will clash with my tonality before and after it. Would not an ordinary
bell be better ringing twelve times? Also tell him that (and do not forget) at
the beginning of the second scene not a harp but a clavecin, i.e. a fortepiano is
going to play the accompaniment. I have written it that way. First of all it
is more appropriate to the time of action and secondly it will not remind one
of *Onegin*. So, one must order a mock Louis XVI fortepiano. It can at the same
time be played in the orchestra on an ordinary upright piano. But it would be
much better if it is a real instrument of the epoch and a real pianist
accompanying on the stage.

Oh! I am tired. No composing today.

I kiss you. 11 at night.

P. Tchaikovsky

The hymn *Kol Slaven* (*Hail to Thee, God of Zion*) was the hymn of the Russian
Order of St John, the Templars. On 17 February Modest urged that the libretto
should be exactly ordered so that he could present it to the theatre administrators
for work on the scene painting to be started in earnest. Modest reported that
Sapelnikov had enjoyed a considerable success in Paris.

[539]   TO MODEST TCHAIKOVSKY   [Florence]
                                        26 February–10 March 1890

Dear Modia!

I did not tell you yesterday when I am returning, nor what I intend to do. As
soon as I have finished the rough draft of the opera I shall start on a complete
piano score. In order to do this, which will be boring but easy, I want to move
to another town, but not to go home. I will return home only when I have
finished the piano score. Where I will go I have not yet decided; now that
I cannot evade the Palens, because Nazar is somewhat in love with their valet
Karl, Rome will be ruined for me. They are kind but rather frightful people!
They insist that I should play *The Queen of Spades* to them!! In any case I will
go somewhere south – probably to Naples. I have been in a great turmoil
today. I had a letter from Artôt saying that Capoul has written a magnificent

libretto on Russian life and that the music must be composed by no one but me, and that he is coming here to discuss it! ! ! ? ? ? I sent a long telegram straight back, saying that I cannot write the opera and that I leave for Russia tonight. Then I had to write a long letter to her.

Have finished the sixth scene and started to compose the Introduction – Overture. If the seventh scene does not arrive tomorrow I will be very upset. I hate interrupting this first rough work. It seems to me that the sixth scene has come out quite well and I am very glad that I have written it. There would be no proper ending without it. It is only from you that I have found out about Sapelnikov – the ungrateful wretch. I expected a telegram on the 23rd, was worried, and decided that he had disgraced himself! He could at least have written a few words. Disgusting!

I kiss and embrace you.

P. Tchaikovsky

I do not know if you have heard that Feklusha died on 18 February. I think Nazar wrote to you about it.

I fear the seventh scene will not arrive tomorrow. What am I going to do? But I must say you have been sending the libretto very punctually – thank you!

On 27 February Nazar wrote: 'Modest Illich have sent the 7th scene. When I returned after coffee P.I. were reading the scene that was sent and say, "This scene is more than all the former", and showed that they had already composed the first page. I also looked at the half page – lines and hooks were made. I asked if they will finish it this week; but Piotr Illich said, "I do not think so. . .". At 6½ P.I. finished their occupation. When I came in one could guess by the happy face of P.I. that it went well with them. "If", they said "it will go like this I will finish by Sunday." P.I. told how by absentmindedness they lit the candles on the piano and after a time noticed that their head or in their head – it did not match the hands. For sure at that moment in the head swirled a swarm of musical notes and they caught them, and let them out, and put some together, and at the time hands also wanted work so they unconsciously lit the candles during the bright day.'

[540]   TO MODEST TCHAIKOVSKY   Florence
                                      27 February–11 March 1890

Received the seventh scene. Excellently done. Brindisi needs one more couplet. I will try to do it myself, but will you also try to add one and send it to me.

Thank you Modia! My deepest gratitude for the quality of the libretto and your rare punctuality. How wonderful – I only finished the sixth scene yesterday when I had the seventh here this morning.

I embrace you.

P. Tchaikovsky

Roujé – the term referred below to Modest – should have been *router* (to play with three cards in a deal and to continue only if one of them has been a winning one).

On 23 February Modest wrote: 'The words of the chorus in this scene worried me. I think you will have to change them. Having women in the chorus is up to you. It would be more lifelike if there were none, but I do not see why there cannot be any whores in a gambling house. One can allow for it in the beauty of the sound. In Hermann's last aria I at first wanted to have two couplets; if you agree, send a telegram.'

[541]   TO MODEST TCHAIKOVSKY   Florence
                                                  2–14 March 1890

Most probably my very short letter has reached you; I will not say again that I am as pleased with the seventh as with all the other scenes. But I must have a second couplet for the Brindisi. I did not telegraph, however, as it will not hold me back at all. The second couplet must have the same rhythm as the first and begin with the words: 'Your turn today, and mine tomorrow,' – the words must be kept. In the special terminology of the Gaming House I do not understand what Surin means when he says: 'I stake on roujé!' What is 'roujé'?

In the Gamblers' song one ought to get the beginning of it, only I do not know from where. Apukhtin is sure to know. I remember only the three first lines:
'Or where are the green Islands
Where the simple grasses grow?
Brothers,'

But this is not important.

Oh yes! I have forgotten to ask you to make a continuation of 'Hail to you, Catherine', after the words 'Our most gracious Mother'. I need about two more lines. How could you imagine that I would allow women in the last scene? It is quite impossible and would be unnatural. Besides only whores could be present there and you want a whole chorus (of them) . . . a bit too much!

Why did you think I would change the words of the chorus? Not at all. I only added a word here and there for musical reasons; but this is a triviality.

When this letter reaches you I will be in Rome, where I have made up my mind to do the piano score. Shall telegraph my address. Yesterday morning I received 810 francs by Mr Konradi's order. I am waiting for an explanation, but my guess is that it is Kolia who sent the money as an advance on my pension.

The weather is summery but I still do not like Florence and except for my rooms, and lonely parts of Cascino, everything else makes me sick. I have also lately developed a distaste for the hotel fare, and am tired of its everlasting monotony. I embrace you and Kolia. Thank him for me. Next time I shall write to Kolia. Nazar sends his regards.

[no signature]

[Florence]
                                                    3 March 1890

I wanted to write to Kolia but will do so tomorrow, as I have a lot to tell you.
I finished the opera three hours ago and sent Nazar off at once, with a
telegram to you. I had a letter from you today and you sound worried about
some points in the libretto. You probably resent that I have altered some of
your rhymes, Modinka, and I understand very well how you feel. Either one
must be a complete author or not at all. But, first of all, we live at a distance
of a thousand kilometres from each other and it is impossible to discuss
things properly. Secondly, I have changed and added so very little. Thirdly,
you may change my rhymes as much as you like.

I am very glad that you like the idea of ending the third scene with the
appearance of the Empress.

The text of the funeral choir is as follows: (I forgot to send it with the other
changes.)

Chorus (back stage)
(1) 'I pray to God that he hears my sorrow, for my soul is full of evil and
I fear the bondage of hell. Oh! look down, my Lord, upon the sufferings of
your slave!'
(2) 'Give her life everlasting.'
I think that it is not worth while placing any of the words of the choruses in
the published libretto – or just put in the opening, as the words 'Give her
life everlasting' come at the end of the scene from a distance from where the
audience will not hear them. In any case the real words, in Slavonic, cannot
be used; either the censorship will not allow it or, if it will pass them, then
someone – full of the spirit of Pobedonostev – may attack them [see p. 454].

Melnikov must sing Tomsky (if they must have a substitute, then Chernov).
I quite agree that Tomsky is a bit old, about forty, which does not make it
necessary to change anything in the words. All they have to do is for Melnikov
to make himself look twenty years younger, and Chernov can make himself
look ten years older. I do not think there is any need to change April on
account of Liza's soliloquy to the night. But if one has to make a change, then
to the autumn with the first scene taking place in September. Isn't the
beginning of the night in April still dark? Is it worth while worrying about
an unimportant detail. However, as you wish; but remember that in the first
chorus scene there is a hint of a nightingale singing, and that will be very
difficult to eliminate.

Modia, I have completely forgotten to send the words of Grétry's *Ariette* which
the Countess sings in the fourth scene. They must be put into the published
libretto.
Scene 4
The Countess in her room:
(Her monologue ends with the words: 'The king heard me. I see it all quite
vividly. . . .')

She sings: Je crains de lui parler la nuit,
J'écoute trop tout ce qu'il dit.
Il me dit: 'Je vous aime'
Et je sens malgré moi
Mon coeur qui bat, qui bat,
Je ne sais pas pourquoi!
(She stops singing, looks around as if coming to her senses)
'Why are you standing here? Get out!'
(The maids and companions leave on tiptoe. The Countess goes gradually to sleep, singing the same again.)

I think I have nothing more to say about the libretto. Today I have written the Brindisi (planned earlier) and finished the introduction. I composed the end of the opera yesterday, before dinner, and when I got to the death of Hermann and the concluding chorus, I was so sorry for Hermann that I began to sob. This continued for some time and turned into a light bout of hysteria, of the most pleasant kind – I mean it was terribly sweet to cry that way. Later I understood why (as I had never sobbed over the fate of a hero of mine before I tried to understand the reason for it). It appears that Hermann was not just a subject about which to compose this or that music, but a real living person whom I liked; and as I like Figner very much, and imagined Hermann to be Figner, I took the most personal interest in his fate. I hope and believe that this warm interest in the hero of the opera had a good influence on the music. At the moment it seems to me that *The Queen of Spades* is really good. We shall see what will happen later.

I am leaving for Rome in two days' time. I have written to several of the hotels there stating the conditions on which I would agree to stay. As soon as I get answers I shall decide where I am going to live, and then leave at once. I will not even dream of coming back to Russia before finishing the piano score. Although I have for quite a long time now had the longing to go back, especially to Frolovskoie. My poor Alesha! I kiss and embrace you and Kolia.

P. Tchaikovsky

It is quite like summer here.

Have forgotten to say the most important thing. Shall not, for anything in the world, go to the Consul to have my papers witnessed. Instead I will receive the pension in May when I am back, and have written to P. Yurgenson asking him to send 500 roubles to Osip Ivanovich (he will let you know when he gets the money). Please return what I owe to Kolia (I am very touched by his kind desire to help), and do what you like with the rest. Better take the whole 200, I am sure you need it.

I am in need of money but in the summer my finances will improve and also, at the present moment, I do not care. I am sure to manage somehow. What is most important is, that the opera is now finished!

Nazar scarcely limps any more. He is well and happy. Understands quite a lot of Italian. Och! How tired I am.

P.T.

Tell Bob that I have finished the opera and also let Vsevoloisky know.

Modest wrote on 9 March: 'The news that you have finished the opera makes every one gasp with astonishment. It is real magic! Also, all the scenery has been ordered and the first performance is to be on 5 December. . . . I assure you that your changes in the text have not offended me. I am very particular about the scenario but I liked your changes. However, some of them I did not understand since I did not know the music. As to the rhymes, there were some awkward ones, but mine have probably seemed the same to you. I am very proud to know that you like my libretto. . . . This collaboration will always be one of my happiest memories.'

Tchaikovsky wrote in his diary on 2 March: 'Cried bitterly when Hermann expired. Either I am very tired or it is really good.' Twelve years earlier he had wept when he finished the execution scene in *The Maid of Orleans*, though this he seemed to have forgotten.

Nazar had his version of the end of *The Queen of Spades*, also writing on 2 March: 'At 7 o'clock P.T. finished their work. During their ablutions they told me how they had finished the opera. Lately they tell me everything they do. True there is no one else. "Well, Nazar", they addressed me and started telling me how they finished Hermann's last words and how Hermann killed himself. P.I. said that they cried all the evening – their eyes were indeed at that time quite red – they themselves were quite exhausted, tired, and in spite of this exhaustion it seemed that they still wanted to cry. . . . I love these sort of tears and I think so does everyone who experienced them. It is the same with Piotr Ilyich. They were sorry for poor Hermann, that made them rather sad. When P.I. played the "death of Hermann" composed by them then the tears flowed out which had filled their soul while composing. . . . It was worthwhile to me to notice P.I.'s tears. If God wills P.I. will finish so well and it will be possible to see and hear this opera on the stage then, after P. Illich's example, many will shed tears.'

[543]   TO MODEST TCHAIKOVSKY   [Florence]
                                              5–17 March 1890

I have received answers from the Rome hotels saying that they are full up and cannot give me the accommodation I asked for. After thinking it over I have decided that, not being able to get anything better than what I have here, I will stay on and work hard without losing any time looking for something else. It is very boring and monotonous here but one could not find better conditions for work. I did not come here to travel but to write; so I am staying here until I have finished the piano score. I feared that Nazar would be upset, but not at all. He is wonderfully adaptable. Am working full speed on the piano score. Have just written a long business letter to Moscow and am very tired. Shall write to Kolia tomorrow.

I kiss and embrace you.

P. Tchaikovsky

[544] TO MODEST TCHAIKOVSKY   [Florence]
                                                9–21 March 1890

I do not quite agree with you that one must make two acts out of the two first scenes. A long first act does not mean anything as long as the interval before the second scene is short. It is wrong when the next two acts are too long. In my *Klavierauszug* the opera will be divided into three acts. The Marinsky Theatre will not exist forever; some day a new theatre will be built with all sorts of improvements, and then, believe me, it will be much better (as is the case in Vienna and Paris) to have several changes, even if the sets are complicated in the first and second scenes. I have written it so that the first scene ends and the second one begins as another scene, not a new act. That is the difference! It will not do to spoil the audience at the beginning and make them sit through long intervals between scenes later. No leave it as it is. Now, even if my opera written in three, will be given in four acts I will not mind. *Don Juan* was written in two acts, and has been divided into four in Petersburg.

The first two acts or scenes I am sending to Yurgenson tomorrow to be printed, so as not to lose any time. Which means that, not later than in May, all the singers will have printed parts and Figner will get his before leaving. . . . Will not write any more, am very tired. The weather is horrid, rain all this week and awfully cold.

I embrace you.

Yours

P. Tchaikovsky

[545] TO MODEST TCHAIKOVSKY   [Florence]
                                                14–26 March 1890

I have not been at all well these last few days. The same thing as I had in Rome before: fever, a continual feeling of sickness, drowsiness, no appetite, and no strength. Now, at last, I feel better but still very weak. I did not stop working, but the work went badly. How lucky it was that this illness didn't happen when I was writing the opera. I have already sent the first Act to Moscow to be engraved. Tell my correspondents Emma and Annette that I cannot write letters at the moment. During my illness my antipathy to Florence has developed into fierce hatred. All the same I shall not leave before finishing the piano score. I embrace you. Forgive for writing so little but a lot of letters to be answered have accumulated.

The weather is awful.

P.T.

[546]   TO MODEST TCHAIKOVSKY   Florence
                                            18–30 March 1890

My dear Modia!

After my last letter I felt worse again and for a few days could scarcely drag my feet about. A curious illness – could it be influenza? But yesterday I suddenly felt much better, and today I am nearly well again. This illness was not serious but it lasted longer because of the nervous strain. However, I was up and working all the time. Shall definitely leave and give myself a rest in a week's time. Next letter will be longer.

I kiss you.

Yours

P. Tchaikovsky

Weather glorious.

[547]   TO MODEST TCHAIKOVSKY   [Florence]
                                            19–31 March 1890

Exactly two months ago I started to compose the opera! Today the piano score of the second Act is nearly finished. Only one left! This work is the worst and most severe strain on my nerves. I wrote the opera in complete oblivion of all else, with real enjoyment and I shall certainly orchestrate it with great pleasure. But writing it all out is awful, for you are always having to spoil what has already been written for orchestra.

I think that my illness was partly the result of nervous strain. For two weeks I was ill, did not eat anything, and felt frightfully weak, and – according to Nazar – have become much thinner. And I was in an awful humour. Is it because the weather has become fine, or because the most difficult and boring part of my work is finished, but since yesterday I feel quite well again. Your telegram arrived exactly at the time when I recovered. I shall have to suffer tedium over the third act for another week and then I want to try and orchestrate, if not the whole act, at least the first scene. I would not like to return to Russia without bringing at least part of the full score. Only when some of it is ready will I believe that the opera really exists.

Modia, either I am making an unpardonable mistake, or *The Queen of Spades* is going to be my *chef-d'oeuvre*. In some parts of it, for instance in the fourth scene, which I was scoring today, I experienced such terrific fear, horror, and violent alarm that surely the audience will have to share that experience.

The Bazilevskys are here. I received them very coldly; my misanthropy is awful. However, last night they came for tea and by my courtesy I hope to have eliminated the impression of my cold reception. Tomorrow they are having lunch with me. Remember that my 50th birthday is on 25 April and I am definitely going to celebrate it in Petersburg. I shall not write to anyone until I leave, except to you, Yurgenson and Anatoli. Not later than a month tomorrow, on the 20th, I shall be in Petersburg.

I embrace you.

Yours

P. Tchaikovsky

Thank you for worrying about the libretto. Poor you! It must have been boring writing it out again but it is nothing compared with the piano score.

P.S. Dear Modia! Forgot to tell you that the second couplet of the Brindisi is excellent. I wrote one myself but by the side of yours it is no good at all.

What do you think? Should the singing of the Service for the Dead, back stage, be sung by a church choir or the theatre chorus? Does Ivan Alex. Vsevoloisky know that a first class choir is needed for the opera? I would prefer the choir to sing back stage in the fifth scene.

I kiss you.

Modest's play *The Symphony* (see Letter 521) was accepted by the Malyi Theatre in Moscow. He was at this time preparing a copy of the libretto of *The Queen of Spades* for the Censor. On 17 March he enclosed part of a letter from Chekhov: 'In about two weeks' time,' wrote Chekhov, 'my book *The sombre people* is coming out, with a dedication to Piotr Illich. I am ready to stand guard at the door of Piotr Illich's house night and day so great is my respect for him. He takes second place in Russian art only to Tolstoi who has been at the very top for long now. (The third place I give to Riepin the painter, and take the ninety-eighth place for myself.) I have for a long time been cherishing the daring desire to dedicate something to your brother. This dedication would, I hoped, be a partial expression at least of the infinite appreciation which I – a scribbler – feel for his enormous talent and which, being completely unmusical, I do not know how to express on paper.'

[548] TO MODEST TCHAIKOVSKY   [Florence]
                                                23 March–4 April 1890

Dear Modia!

I am exhausted by this piano score. But the end is near and where I will go (from here) I do not know, but will let you know by telegram. I am glad that

The Symphony is placed. Goreva's wish to buy it has helped, for Pchelnikov will now take an interest in the play. In the end this is the best solution.

You cannot imagine what happiness Chekhov's words about me give me. I will write to him as soon as I am back to normal! I am well, but get easily tired and cannot write long letters. Money received and just in time.

Yours

P. Tchaikovsky

[549]   TO MODEST TCHAIKOVSKY   Florence
                                       26 March–7 April 1890

At last, Modia dear, I am leaving Florence. I finished the third Act and sent it off to Moscow yesterday *(Klavierauszug)*. I wondered where I should go! Actually I do not want to go anywhere except to Russia, but at last I have decided to try Rome. I am doing this more for Nazar's sake than mine, as I very much want to show him Rome. As to not going straight to Russia it is, as I told you before, because of my wish to bring back at least part of the full score; also I have heard that they want to put *Charodeika* on again, which was a fiasco before Lent, and I am afraid that they will involve me. However, I shall see. If I get the same kind of impression of Rome as I have of Florence, I shall return to Russia at once. Frolovskoie seems like heaven to me.

Today, for the first time after nine weeks of work, I have done nothing. All the morning I was at the Uffizi and enjoyed myself immensely; but not the same things as the rest of humanity. Whatever effort I ever made, I must honestly say that I could never understand classical paintings, and that they leave me completely indifferent. I understand that others, to whom they bring real pleasure, are able to appreciate them; but as for me I don't think much of all these *chef-d'oeuvres*. On the other hand, I found a real source of pleasure, very much to my taste, in the entrance to the Pitti Palace. Once, when I was quite ill I crawled there and managed to get interested, but then I did not stay long as I was not feeling well enough. Today, however, I spent more than two hours studying the portraits of various princes, kings, popes and other historical figures. It seems that no one but me has ever looked at them; yet they are terribly interesting. Some stand, some sit, looking alive, surrounded by appropriate settings. I found an excellent portrait of Ivan Principe Czomodanov Ambasciatore Moscovito there. Quite life-like! There is also a wonderfully well preserved portrait of Catherine I [Empress of Russia] and many others. In the Tribuna there are some changes. I well remember that my *Endimion* by Guercino (my favourite painting), was downstairs next to the *Holy Family* by Michelangelo. Now it is upstairs with Cranach's horrors. Why? I do not understand. It would have been better to hang the unattractive *Holy Family* there. The rest is as it was.

I am delighted that *Lizaveta Nikolaevna* is going to be repeated. It only shows that really good things swim up again. And *The Benefactor* is also coming back. It is a pity that the endings of both plays are bad. I hope that the end of *The Symphony* will not spoil it. Personally I like it; it is a true ending, not for the sake of effect, but the natural consequence of the characters and actions of the play. But will the end be interesting enough for the audience? It is not too late to consult the stage directors Fedorov and Davydov. What do you think, Modia? The news concerning Volodia Napravnik has upset me very much. News about student disorders have been published in the papers here for some time, but as no one has ever written to me about them I thought they had been invented. Now I know that it is true. I have, from afar, begun to feel more vividly and strongly the truth about what is going on at home and have often felt sorrow when reading about it all. However, letters could be opened so I prefer to keep silent on politics.

Modia! You will have some trouble and expense with the case I am sending today *(grande vitesse)* with books, music and warm clothes. If you are short of money when it arrives, borrow some from Kolia and I will pay him back when I come. When I questioned Nazar yesterday he said that as yet he has not been homesick. Generally speaking he is very pleased with his stay abroad. We are great friends. Did I have to be angry with him even once? Only when I was tired and irritable after working I occasionally got angry when he got into depths of philosophy from which there was no way out. This desire for serious thought without any proper knowledge is pathetic. Nazar is an outstanding individual, with remarkably high qualities of soul: a wonderfully good person.

After which I embrace you. I shall stay, on the advice of my present host, at the Hôtel Molaro. Will let you know by telegraph.

Kiss Kolia and Bob.

Yours

P.T.

Anna Merkling seems to be slightly hurt, do be kind to her.

Charodeika had one performance in Moscow, at the Bolshoi Theatre, on 2 February 1890. The staging was bad, the audience indifferent, and the work was not repeated.

The political condition of Czarist Russia is often hinted at in Tchaikovsky's letters. In this letter one does not have to read between the lines to appreciate the distaste with which a liberal-minded patriot like Tchaikovsky regarded the repressive policies carried out by K. P. Pobedonostsev (see Letter 542), a member of the State Council and Secular Head of the Church in the reign of Alexander III. All political dissent was stamped on; the press was censored; universities were entirely without independence; trade unions, although suppressed with difficulty, were forbidden. At the same time much industrial expansion was taking place and communications, through extended railways, improving.

Rome
27 March–8 April 1890
Via Gregoriana
Hôtel Molaro

I left at 11.00 last night. It was a cold night and I slept badly. The hotel staff saw us off and they were near to crying. I have chosen the Hôtel Molaro on the recommendation of our host from the Hôtel Washington and also because I like little hotels. At first, Nazar and I were lodged in a huge, deceptively luxurious suite – not at all comfortable – but now a charming little apartment is free at the top of the house and we have moved into it. I am very pleased with it. Judging by the cheerful mood which I was in when I left the house, and sniffed the well-remembered Roman air, and saw all the places I knew so well, I understood that I had been a fool not to have settled in Rome from the start. But I must not blame poor blameless Florence which, I do not know why, I came to hate so much, when on the contrary, I ought to be deeply grateful for having had the opportunity to write my *Queen of Spades* without any interference.

Rome has changed very much. Much of it is quite unrecognizable. For instance, the second half of the Via del Tritino has become wide and grand, and does not lead to the Trevi, but straight into the Corso. But, in spite of all these changes, I am extremely pleased to be back in this dear city. To this feeling is added a sad realization of the years for ever gone, and of N. D. Kondratiev now also gone into eternity, and Massalitinov too, who followed him. I think of Nikolai Dimitrievich all the time; it is sad, it moves me to tears, but for some reason it also brings pleasure. I went, of course, to the Via Nic. Tolentino, but looked in vain for the old man, who, do you remember, always sat and looked out of the window. The Costanzi building has become gloomy and dark, probably because all the windows are shuttered and the gates are tightly closed. Do you remember that Via Gregoriana? It leads to the Via Capo le Case, two steps away from the Sistine – you must know it well. The garden at the Post Office is lovely. I took Nazar to his friend Karl [Palen's valet] where he stayed all day. He is in raptures over Rome. I see you and Kolia in my mind at every step. It is a pleasure to imagine you here, as you are sure to come back; but poor Kondratiev will never see Rome again. I visited the Cathedral of St Peter and the Pantheon, but haven't yet seen the Forum.

It has been raining all day. I start working tomorrow and will stay here for three weeks. Hope to finish the first act, with God's help. My dear, dear Rome!

I embrace you.

P.T.

In Rome I love you and Kolia more than ever. Thought of Kolia when I passed the Café Venezia.

TO ANATOLI TCHAIKOVSKY　　　　Rome
29 March–10 April 1890

My Golubchik Tolia!

It is true that I write very rarely, but you do not spoil me with letters either.
I often feel lonely and worried without letters from you. I did not write only
because my work made me so tired that I had to renounce all letter writing.
Did I tell you that my opera is finished and that even the piano score and the
vocal parts have been sent to Moscow for printing? Now, in Rome, I have
started on the orchestration. I want to bring at least one fully orchestrated
Act back to Russia. But this is pleasant work. Easy and practically finished.
I was not feeling very well in Florence lately, it may have been a chill but
I think that the real reason was the piano score. I love composing and
orchestrating but the job of writing it out is real punishment. I could not let
anyone else do it as no one would be able to understand my rough drafts. Now,
thank God, I am perfectly well and am enjoying Rome. Florence is an excessively
boring town, and devoid of all attractions; it is good for a few days, no more.

Since my last visit Rome has greatly changed; for the best, of course, but I
miss the old Rome! Spring has come, the flowering apricot trees remind me
of Tiflis where in my soul I long to be. My heart contracts at the thought that
it is a whole year ago since I sailed from Marseilles. I wish I could do it again,
but honestly, it is impossible. Alexei writes that all the woods in Frolovskoie
have been felled. This will compel me to leave it as quickly as possible and, if
alive and well, I am certain to visit you at the end of the summer. Korganov's
death has made me very sad. I knew about it from the papers but still hoped
it was not true. Now, after Kokodek's letter, which took over a month to
reach me, it is a fact.

Send your letters now to Frolovskoie, I will be back there in three weeks' time.

I embrace Tata and Pania. I kiss you.

P.T.

TO MODEST TCHAIKOVSKY　　　　Rome
3–15 April 1890

I have been here a week, and have had time to get used to my new surroundings.
I am very pleased with the apartment, service, and food, and often think
I should have come here before. It is quite absurd that I spoiled my stay in
Italy by choosing Florence, the most boring of towns. How can one compare
it to Rome! I go for walks every day, and every time with great pleasure. On
Sunday I took a cab to the Via Appia and got so engrossed in my walk there
that I started work an hour and a half late. I still cannot get used to the
terrific changes in Rome.

It is just as old citizens told us, that Rome has lost a great deal of its charm since the Popes stopped ruling, I too am displeased with the changes, for Rome is more and more losing its character of cosiness and simplicity which gave it its main charm. All the same, there is plenty of beauty and interest around. The Forum (work on which was started when we were last here), has been greatly enlarged and excavated, but the new ruins are not very interesting. The greatest change has happened in the Piazza Colonna as a result of the enlargement of the Via Appia. On the last day of my visit I shall go to the Vatican for the sake of Antinoüs.

I feel much happier here, but to be honest all I think about is the wonderful happiness and bliss of returning home! ! ! Only two more weeks of self-imposed exile from my Fatherland. I fear even to seriously dream about it! . . .

P. T.

Tchaikovsky had been present at a performance arranged by Sgambati in honour of Liszt's 70th birthday, in Rome, on 6 December, 1881.

[553]   TO MODEST TCHAIKOVSKY   Rome
                                                 7–19 April 1890

For two days running I have been in a bad humour even in despair, and have lost both appetite and any desire to work etc. The Palens have announced all over Rome that I am here, and the first to arrive was Alexei Golitzin. It cannot be helped, I like him very much and, even after the first moment of horror at seeing a new face, I was glad to see him. But immediately after him Sgambati appeared, I managed to give the instruction that I was receiving no one, and he was not allowed in, but he left a note and a ticket for a quartet recital, for the next morning, at which my first quartet was to be played. This has brought me to absolute despair which proves how wild I have become. I had to go to the quartet recital, listen to a mediocre – not to say a bad – performance, go to the artists' room with Sgambati in view of all the gaping audience, and mutter polite trivialities, etc. I must say, though, that Sgambati – knowing that I am a solitary person and working hard – says he does not want to intrude and will not invite me to his house. But he begged me to come next Friday to hear his quartet. (The same we heard when Liszt was present.) All the same, the pleasure of my stay in Rome is quite poisoned. Today I had to go and see off the Palens, who showed me the most inexplicable but touching attention; I met Izvolsky, the Princess Shcherbatova and another Prince there, who invited me to come and taste a kulebiaka [chicken pie]. . . . Disgusting! I do not know if I will be able to stand another week, although I am terribly anxious to finish what I had planned. The quartet was a big success, and the papers were full of praise. Well! The papers here praise everything. Oh! The sooner home the better! Fancy, I have pains in my stomach at the mere thought of travelling home. Everybody is leaving, and it will be difficult to get seats.

I kiss and embrace you.
P. Tchaikovsky

[554] TO ANATOLI, AND PRASKOVIA TCHAIKOVSKAIA

Rome
17–29 April 1890

My dears, Tolia and Pania!

I do not think there have ever been lazier correspondents than you two. I have not had any news from you for over a month, and the only reason I am not worried is that if anything has been amiss I would have heard from Petersburg. Leaving for Russia today. I spent three very pleasant weeks in Rome but only because I knew I would soon be leaving for home. In any case I like Rome much better than Florence. I arrived here not quite recovered from my Florentine illness and looking thinner and paler than usual. But I have completely recovered here.

Alexei Golitzin and the Palens were struck by my poor looks when I arrived, but the same Alexei Golitzin back from Naples, where he went for a few days, was astonished how quickly I had managed to get better. The Palens have been too kind for me to behave coldly and I even saw them off. A. Golitzin found out from them that I am here. These are the only people I met; I got rid of all the rest in no uncertain manner. Unfortunately I had to go to a quartet recital where my quartet was played. I have orchestrated half my opera here. Still there is plenty more work to do; orchestrating the other half and correcting the piano score. But, in any case, I will be in Tiflis in August and stay until November.

At the very end of the month I will be in Frolovskoie (shall celebrate my birthday in Petersburg), and there expect a letter from you.

After which I embrace you most lovingly.

P. Tchaikovsky

[555] TO MODEST TCHAIKOVSKY

Frolovskoie
5 May 1890

It's my fourth day here . . . the house is unrecognizable. The hall (which is also dining-room and study) has become a really beautiful room, thanks to the addition of my furniture, and Ziloty's, but it looks darker. The other rooms have also been improved by things from Moscow; the rooms generally do not look as bare and cold as before. On the other hand it is horrible outside the house! All the forest – absolutely all of it – is gone and the rest of it is coming down now. No nice walks left! ! My God, how the disappearance of woods completely changes the character of a place and how sad it is! ! ... I could have said that everything is the same as before, but for this nightmare of the disappearance of a forest! ! All those dear shady nooks which were here last year are now bare and bald. We are sowing the flowers. Working twice as much, for during working hours I work, during the rest of the time I correct the proofs. ...

P. *Tchaikovsky*

Shall write only a little until the proofs are finished.

On March 1, having declined to conduct six concerts during the coming season, Tchaikovsky resigned his directorate of the Russian Musical Society, in Moscow. The Society had continued to lose members and Tchaikovsky had no wish to become involved with the inner political machinations either of that or the Conservatoire. Safonov was a somewhat ruthless if efficient administrator.

The sextet for strings, *Souvenir of Florence* (Op. 70) was written in June. (See Letter 565.)

[556] TO ANATOLI TCHAIKOVSKY   [Frolovskoie]
                                                  5 May 1890

Golubchik Tolia!

Having arrived here I found two letters from you. Thank you. I had a very pleasant time in Petersburg. ... My birthday was celebrated at the Davydovs with all the relatives. On your and Modest's birthday he gave a dinner (all those came who signed the telegram to you) and I left for Moscow at 8 o'clock, where I went for a few hours to see Yurgenson on business. I did not go to the Conservatoire. The further away it gets the more indignant I am over the matter which caused me to resign my directorship, and the boldness and insolence of Safonov (which, in the critical state the Conservatoire is at the moment, is actually a good thing). Let him rule, but I have no desire to show myself there.

I can imagine how Baranov's death upset you. It is sad when such dear people die. And for what reason? But to this question there is no answer. Formerly the disappearance of younger people from the face of the earth practically killed me. Now I have grown used to it. After shedding a few tears and thinking that all is 'nothing but dead grass' love of life surges up again.

At the moment I am in a period of exceptional love of life, and am proud of having finished an important work. However, perhaps it only seems to me that *The Queen of Spades* is a good opera. Of course I cannot be sure, but at the moment, I am positive that it will have a brilliant future. In Rome I had time to finish orchestrating the first half of the opera, and now I have started on the second half. Then I want to make some sketches for a sextet for strings, and at the end of July, or the beginning of August, I will go to Kamenka and then to you. I think no one is staying here this summer. Modest will only pass through on his way to Grankino. The Laroches wanted to come for the whole summer but are now crying off. They decided not to stay in Petersburg.

All the woods have been felled in Frolovskoie, and not a tree is left. When Alexei took the house in winter they said nothing about it. I am being advised to take a house in Zarskoie Selo, where I may try to settle. In any case my links with Moscow have been broken, and I am much more attracted to Peter. . . . Had a letter from M. M. Ippolitov-Ivanov and answered it. I will be sorry for him if he gets the post of opera conductor in Moscow. Korsov alone will spoil his life! But do not say anything for fear of frightening him.

This is between ourselves.
I kiss and embrace you. Regards and kisses to everybody. It will be interesting to see Vladimir Dimitrievich after Tiflis.

P. Tchaikovsky

[557] TO MODEST TCHAIKOVSKY   [Frolovskoie]
                                                14 May 1890

Modia!

I am sure that Yurgenson will agree to your wish to get as much for the libretto as Shpajinsky. About the translation of Oulibishev's work – I beg you to read it through carefully and correct all the literary mistakes. Where you are not sure about musical questions mark with a cross. I will look through them, correct them, and then send it to the publishers.

Nothing of importance has happened. I walked to Maidanovo and passed several pleasant hours with Novichikha. I like to have a good laugh with her now and then. All her dachas have been taken, thanks to Zakharin who recommends them and praises the lovely air there. Friends came to see me: Kashkin, Ziloty and Piotr Ivanovich. As usual we had plenty of drinks. Ziloty who is responsible for the corrections in *The Queen of Spades* admires it greatly. I must say, though, that he always admires my compositions. Work is not moving very fast for, what I am doing now, the orchestration of scenes 4–5 needs enormous attention and effort.

I saw Bob in my dreams today and because of this I have an irresistible desire to see him. Maybe I will come to see him at the end of May, otherwise he will slip away before I come. Please let me know about Kolia's and Bob's exams. Why cannot Mania come and see me?

I embrace you.

P. Tchaikovsky

Frolovskoie
                                                12 June 1890

Modia!

I would have written before but I just could not remember the address at
Grankino. After you left, Bob came and stayed for three days. Soon after he
left I completed the opera and then for two days was occupied in putting it
in order – i.e. marking the pages, sewing them together, and binding them.
The last was done by Alexei. Then, on Friday, 8 June, I took it to Moscow
to P. I. Yurgenson. That means that the opera was written between 19 January
and 8 June – i.e. in all, 4½ months.

I always had the feeling that Benkendorf is lacking in understanding. He makes
me shudder with his letters. In the first letter he said that the Grand Duke
Vladimir Alexandrovich asks me to make a duet for two cornet-à-pistons out
of the ballet, with military band accompaniment! ! ! ! ! Then he asks me to
go with him to the country to visit Figner. When I wrote back explaining that
I could not fulfil the G.D.'s wish he answered that the G.D. does not mind
but that he, Benkendorf, is displeased at my not saying anything about our
visit to Figner, and what do I mean by that? Extraordinary! One could think
he lives on the moon! The devil take him!

In Moscow for two days I had a pleasant time with Batasha and Kashkin.
Today is dedicated to letter writing. Starting the Sextet tomorrow. So glad
that you are happy in Grankino and that your work is getting on successfully.

I embrace you both and also Nazar and tell him that I have finished the opera.

I kiss Nara and Zaichik.

P. Tchaikovsky

Frolovskoie, near Klin
                                                12 June 1890

... Tolia, I do not advise you to go to Kamenka in August. If you can get a
whole month's leave you'd better take it in December. Then you can go to
Kamenka for a week and from there to Petersburg for the first performance
of *The Queen of Spades*. I have finished the opera and feel that it is extremely
good (although I should not boast) and the stage sets will be magnificent. If
you count on meeting me, for God's sake do remember not to try to do so – it
will upset me. I cannot at the moment say when I shall go to Kamenka!

My plans are to go to the Urals and see Alapaievo, Ekaterinburg, and then
down the Volga, to the Caspian Sea, and to you. You can be perfectly sure
that I will be in Tiflis not later than 1 September. My visit to Kamenka will
depend upon how the composition I am starting tomorrow gets on. If it goes

well I shall go to Kamenka in July, then come back, make a trip to Nijny-Novgorod Fair, and on from there. So I cannot promise to be in Kamenka in August.

I finished the opera on 8 June and sent it off on the same day. I went to Moscow, and spent three pleasant days with Yurgenson, Batasha and Kashkin. Bob stayed with me for three days, on the way to Kamenka. Do you know, in spite of the forests having been cut down I feel happy in Frolovskoie. Solitude at certain times is so important and restful that I may keep Frolovskoie after all. If I had about 25,000 [roubles] I could buy it now. I have definitely decided to put some money away this winter and, who knows, when an old man, maybe I will at last become a land-owner.

I had a letter from Ippolitov-Ivanov saying that his *Azra* is being produced in Tiflis in October. This will be frightfully interesting. In general I think of Tiflis with delight. . . .

I kiss you.

P. Tchaikovsky

As a child Tchaikovsky had lived in Alapaievo, mentioned above, (see p. 1).

[560]   TO MODEST TCHAIKOVSKY   [Frolovskoie]
                                                  15 June 1890

At last I have your proper address. I addressed my last letter according to the stamp on the envelope and it may not reach you at all. Do not make yourself write a Foreword if you do not feel like it. I do not need it but you might, to save you from abuse. You are right when you say that it is difficult to find the appropriate style in which to express it with simplicity and clarity without any particular wish to make an impression. I have usually written awful nonsense without shame and cannot think about my Forewords to Gevaert's *Orchestration* and the *Handbook on Harmony*. When you have written it let me have a look at it; I am very sensitive about the right tone. But if, after serious consideration you decide not to write a Foreword I will not object. I think of Oulibishev with disgust, but it cannot be helped. I hope you marked everything you want me to correct, as I don't want to read the whole thing. Now I hope you have started on your play. . . .

We have a period of rains with frightful heat here, and it is what we call 'steaming'. It makes me feel so sleepy and weak that I can scarcely move my hand over the paper. But perhaps it is the fault of the sextet. I started working on it three days ago and am writing with difficulty, handicapped by lack of ideas and the new form. One needs six independent but at the same time homogeneous voices. This is frightfully difficult. Haydn never managed to conquer this problem and never wrote anything but quartets for

Kammermusik. Most probably I am tired. If I notice that it continues to go on like this I shall stop for a time. I do want to come and see you, but later. A lot depends on my sextet.

Tolia asked for your address, I sent it to him. He wants you to meet him in August in Kamenka. I embrace both of you and also Nazar and Nara.

P. Tchaikovsky

[561] TO ANATOLI TCHAIKOVSKY   Frolovskoie
19 June 1890

I do not understand Golubchik, Tolia, why you have not had any letters from me for so long and got worried. I do not write very often but regularly. Everything is in order. I am composing a sextet now and am very pleased to be in solitude as this is a difficult composition, a new one, and isolation is the right thing in this case. Am perfectly well. No time to write properly any more as Alexei told me too late that someone was going up to town. Will write again in a day or two.

I kiss you.

P. Tchaikovsky

[562] TO MODEST TCHAIKOVSKY   [Frolovskoie]
21 June 1890

Modia!

You gave such an idyllic description of Grankino in your last letter that I felt a great desire to go there. It is a quiet nook, far away from anywhere, and I remember the beauty of the steppe towards evening. All the same I will not be able to come before the end of July, and fear that by then you will have left. Please, wait until I come.

I do not wonder at all that you sometimes find it difficult to write your comedy. To write a literary work is not as easy as to compose music. In the case of the latter it is sufficient to be in the proper mood; in your work you have to think, and to invent. Only the chatter that goes in newspapers can be easily scribbled down. I am composing a sextet also with great effort; but this is because to me it is a completely unknown form of composition. It is not that I want to compose some music, and then arrange it to be played by six instruments; but a *sextet* – I mean six independent voices – it must be so written that it could be nothing but a sextet.

A few days ago Yurgenson, Kashkin and Batasha stayed a whole day and night! I played them the first act of the opera in the evening and the two others the next day. They all praised it. Do you know it must really be good, because in certain places I can't play because I feel I am going to cry. Figner wrote that he is impatiently waiting for his part, and would like to come and rehearse it with me; but I told him that I will come to him.

I shall not celebrate my Name Day, no one has been invited, and perhaps I will go to Moscow instead. The weather is glorious, I do not remember such a summer. Not many mushrooms though, except on the little island where you can always find 'red' ones. Bob does not write. Glad that Kolia has found an interesting occupation. And with this, nothing more to say. I embrace you both. Please do not send a telegram on my Name Day.

P. Tchaikovsky

Wonderful how early everything is blooming and has ripened. All the flowers are in full bloom, strawberries are coming to an end, the raspberries are ripe, the dahlias are in flower and the asters are starting to bloom.

[563]   TO ANATOLI TCHAIKOVSKY   Frolovskoie, near Klin
                                              21 June 1890

My dear, my lonely Vice-Governor!

I can vividly imagine what a burning furnace Tiflis must be, when even here I sleep badly at night because of the heat. All the same I would love to find myself in Tiflis even for one day. All the most important things about me you know; i.e. that the opera is finished, and that I am deep in the composition of another work – a sextet. As soon as I have the sketches ready (in about a month's time) I shall start my wanderings. I have no definite plans, nor have I yet decided about Kamenka. I have a great desire to take a trip down the Volga and on the Caspian Sea.

On the day your telegram came, Yurgenson, Kashkin and Batasha were visiting me here. I played them my opera from start to finish. They are delighted. I must say that I also like this opera more than any of the others and sometimes I have to stop playing because I am so overwhelmed by emotion and want to cry! My God! Surely I am not mistaken? We shall see. . . .

The summer is wonderful; I have never experienced one like it here. It is as warm as it was in 1885 but without a drought. Now and again a thunderstorm comes over, clears the air and the vegetation, and then it is sunny and warm again. And now I embrace you with all my love. A 'Bezeshka' for Kokodeks. He would have preferred a pink or a grey one but my finances are not brilliant at the moment. My love to Panichka. What is her address? I would like to write to her.

P. Tchaikovsky

TO MODEST TCHIAKOVSKY

Modia dear!

Your Foreword to the libretto is to hand. I find it too long-winded and think, moreover, that you should not say 'I' but use the third person throughout – 'The author of the libretto . . .' 'I' is reminiscent of the style of newspaper reporters. So, having been advised by Kashkin, I have slightly shortened your libretto and changed the pronoun. I also added why Liza has been promoted to the title of Princess. So all is well now. . . .

The summer here is really wonderful. The flowers are abundant. Plenty of everything. Yesterday, half an hour before dinner when I went for a stroll I found several lovely white mushrooms.

You want to know when I will come. I cannot say exactly as I do not know when I am to conduct for Zet. In any case do whatever you have planned to do, without bothering about me, and if you have decided to leave for the Caucasus, I shall put up with it. I finished my sextet yesterday. For the time being I am very pleased with it; I hope you will be as pleased with your comedy. I have a feeling it will be a success.

Am in a great hurry. I embrace you and Kolia. Regards to Nazar and Nara. Am expecting Laroche any day now.

P. Tchaikovsky

TO MODEST TCHAIKOVSKY

Modia!

Oulibishev's manuscript has arrived. Will see to it as soon as all my sketches for the sextet are completed. I am more and more captivated by it and getting more indifferent to *The Queen of Spades*. Kashkin and I have shortened and brushed up your Foreword and it is perfect now.

I am going to Moscow today, dining at Yurgenson's tomorrow – his Saint's Day, and on the day after shall go to see Figner at his country place. The poor fellow broke his shoulder when he fell off his horse (I do not think it is bad) and implores me to visit him, and to look through his part, with which he is enraptured. From Figner's I shall return home and then – what next? Honest to God, I don't know. I have no desire to leave Frolovskoie and yet want to come and see you, and go to Kamenka, and take a trip down the Volga, and even go to Paris to clear up the complications with MM Detroyat and Gallet.

I am bothered by them as they are expecting an opera from me and the Eden Theatre has promised to produce it at once. On the other hand, I want to suggest that they translate and produce *The Queen of Spades* for which service I am prepared to relinquish your author's rights in the libretto and my rights in the music – i.e. the revenue from the performances – to them. It is a serious matter and I do not want to miss this opportunity. According to the theatre intendant's letter he is ready to put the opera on at once. So I think of Paris and at the same time must conduct at Zet's in Petersburg. No idea what to do. In any case I beg you and Kolia not to be hampered by my possible visit, for, who knows, I may not come at all.

Ah! Modia, my sextet is wonderful and the fugue at the end is charming. Terrific, how pleased I am with myself.

I kiss you both.

P. Tchaikovsky

No sound from Laroche.

I daily bring large quantities of white mushrooms home.

[566] TO MODEST TCHAIKOVSKY   [Frolovskoie]
                                        10 July 1890

Dear Modia!

I returned from my visit to Figner the day before yesterday. He is in raptures over his part, and talks about it with tears in his eyes – a good sign! He already knows some of it and has convinced me that he is clever and understanding. All his ideas about the part coincide with mine. There is only one thing that upsets me a little; he wants the Brindisi to be transposed down a tone, explaining quite rightly that at the end of the opera he can't sing this at the high pitch I have given, without being afraid of letting out a croak. It will have to be done. Medea also knows her part, and is also delighted, and it must be arranged that she – and not Mravina – sings the part at the first performance. It is important for she and Figner have rehearsed it beautifully and it will naturally be easier and better if she sings.

His estate is a real wonder: the memory of the terrace where they have their meals – especially in the evening – remains with me like a lovely dream. I stayed there a day and a night. His shoulder is better but when he, Kashkin and I went for a walk (I took the latter with me) Figner slipped, fell, and hurt it. The pain was so intense that he became white as a sheet and could not say a word for quite a long time. Both he and his wife are awfully nice. All the same I returned home with great pleasure. You would gasp at the sight of all the flowers I have in the garden.

I am definitely coming to see you at the beginning of August. The journey to Paris is only a flitting whim. Sapelnikov is back. Had one letter from him here. . . .

I kiss you and Kolia. Had a charming letter from him! Did he get my answer? Not a breath or sound from Laroche.

Yours

P.T.

[567] TO ANATOLI TCHAIKOVSKY   [Frolovskoie]
                                                 2 August 1890

Tolia!

Today I returned from Petersburg where I stayed a week, living at Laroche's. I went to Zarskoie, Peterhof, Terioky in Finland – at [Sophia] Menter's, in Ozerky, and to Arkadia, and on the whole had a very pleasant time. . . .

Laroche spent the summer in a very silly way. He sat in Petersburg, glum and penniless, when he could have come and stayed with me. . . . I returned to put all my business in order before leaving and – what is more important – to correct the proofs of *The Queen of Spades*. I leave here on the 6th; and Moscow on the 9th. We shall see each other in about a month's time, so do not bother to write. I shall tell you all about my stay in Petersburg in person. Am taking the usual route or over Taganrog to Batum. Not quite sure. Keep well and my regards to Panichka!

I kiss you hard

Yours

P. Tchaikovsky

[568] TO MODEST TCHAIKOVSKY   Tiflis
                                                 15 September 1890

I fear that Kolia, hoping that you get news from me, rarely writes, and I in my turn do not write often enough. A week has passed; our living quarters are excellent – a completely separate apartment, with everything we need, including a tea service. The time passes quickly: I try to work a little in the morning but am interrupted all the time and doubt if anything will come of it.

As yet I have not seen anyone but from today social life has begun with a dinner at the Persian Consulate. We often go to the opera where I have a special free seat. There are a few singers with beautiful voices: the tenor, Koshitz, is particularly good, and I will recommend him to the directors of the Imperial Theatres. After the theatre we go to the Krujok [the Circle] which is still in its summer premises which I like. . . .

Kiss Bob.

P. Tchaikovsky

Am studying Ippolitov-Ivanov's *Azra*, which will soon be given here. The music is often charming but the subject awful.

At the end of September Tchaikovsky had a letter from Mme von Meck in which she explained that because of family problems she had to economize and to discontinue his allowance. Tchaikovsky never replied to this letter. Lev Davydov, aware of his brother-in-law's considerable income from his music, and knowing that circumstances could alter, had for some time tried to persuade him to give up his von Meck allowance.

[569] TO MODEST TCHAIKOVSKY   [Tiflis]
10 October 1890

Modia!

Just got your telegram with the question about a flat. I do not know if Yurgenson has told you about the change in my budget? Maybe my letter has not yet reached him. I had a letter from [Mme] N. F. von Meck saying that she has lost all her money and cannot let me have her yearly allowance any more. This is something I never expected, for I was absolutely certain that it was to continue for ever! I did not get all that upset about my diminished resources, but. . . . However, I will talk about the feelings that Nadezhda Filaretovna's action have aroused in me when I see you. I will try and live less *en grand*, and so won't keep the flat in Petersburg but have a permanent room at the former Znamensky Hotel.

I had your letter from Moscow today which we had been impatiently waiting for. It is a pity that the fifth Act does not please the audience as the others do, but all the same it is clear that the play was a real success. I am sure that this success will gradually increase. I like what Iv[an] Iv[anov] said in his article. Let's see what Flerov will say in his. Here all is quiet. Kolia passes all his days at the Argutinskys compiling the catalogue. Ziloty is here. He gave two good concerts – actually there were three but he had to stop half-way through the third because the piano was bad. He gave the audience the option of having their money back or of coming back next day. They all came. On the 20th I am conducting a concert at the theatre. We are leaving on the 22nd, and shall stay in Frolovskoie for a few days, joining you at the beginning of November.

Have finished my ballad but it is impossible to orchestrate it. Disturbed all the time.

I embrace you.

P. Tchaikovsky

Modest's play had been quite favourably reviewed in the journal *Russkie Vedomosty* by Ivan Ivanov. In respect of his brother's misfortune Modest wrote: 'The news about your money matters has quite upset me. It is not the loss of 6000 roubles (after all, if you stop my allowance you will not lose very much) but the slight to your pride that is upsetting me.'

The concert of the Tiflis Russian Musical Society was an immense success. The programme included the first Suite, a movement from the Piano Sonata (Op. 37), played by I. M. Matkovsky, songs from *Eugene Onegin* sung by P. A. Koshitz, the Serenade for Strings, a paraphrase from *Onegin* (by P. A. Pabst) and *Romance* (Op. 51 no. 5), songs sung by I. Y. Sokolov, and the Concert Overture 1812.

The symphonic ballad, *Voevoda* (Op. 78), continued to make slow progress. Later in the year Rimsky-Korsakov wanted Tchaikovsky to conduct its first performance at a St Petersburg concert at the beginning of 1891, but, protesting an inability to finish the work, he felt unable to accede to the request.

[570]   TO MODEST TCHAIKOVSKY   Tiflis
                                                                 16 October 1890

Dear Modia!

Our stay in Tiflis is coming to an end. Tomorrow I have a rehearsal of the symphony concert, another in two days' time, and the concert itself on the 20th. Leaving on the 22nd. I will stop at Ippolit's on the way not to hurt his feelings. Kolia wants to go straight on and I think it will be safe to let him travel alone from Rostov to Peter[sburg]. It is a pity to leave, the weather is indescribable. Two days ago, on Pania's birthday we went to have dinner at one of my favourite places outside the town. We had dinner in the fresh air and a frightfully gay time. However, I am tired of perpetual parties and the silly life, and think with great pleasure about several days of peace in Frolovskoie.

Do not pay any attention to the attack on your *Symphony* in the *Novoe Vremia*. Surely you must know from experience how useless attacks of this kind are. One can get angry at them, but one must not be afraid that they will influence the public. If what *Novoe Vremia* says is true, that you have shortened the play, I am glad. I mean, to have cut the fifth Act out completely. If you remember I was always against the fifth Act. But what have you done instead, I would like to know. The first ending, i.e. 'Milochka! Save me!' I do not like either. All these endings! They are at the bottom of it!

I sent you a telegram asking you not to look for a flat, but you will do me a favour, Modinka, by going to the former Znamensky Hotel and seeing if there is a nice corner room convenient for me and Alexei. . . .

I embrace you.

P. Tchaikovsky

[571]   TO PRASKOVIA VLADIMIROVNA TCHAIKOVSKAIA
                                                                 Taganrog
                                                                 27 October 1890

Panichka!

This is my second day in Taganrog; the journey was pleasant and comfortable. I arrived in Vladikavkaz at 3 o'clock, had an excellent dinner, and went to the theatre in the evening. I saw the operetta *Birds of Song*, and sat through one Act admiring the local 'Kokodekses' making eyes at, and blowing kisses to, the very unattractive chorus girls. The train was crammed full of a group of tourists – Germans and their women. First, they yelled all the time and prevented one from sleeping; second, they smoked their stinking cigars; and third, they tried to talk to me in German and then in French. In Rostov we got into a train and arrived here at twelve. Ippolit is well, Sophia too. . . .

I could not refuse Ippolit to stay another day, so we only leave tomorrow. Today Ippolit showed Kolia and me the attractions of Taganrog.

How are you existing, poor dear, without seeing your joy, your precious, incomparable, adored, grey-haired, old, dear, gorgeous one.

Your

Petia Mila!!!

Regards to Kokodeks. Thousand kisses to Tata. Read in all the papers on the journey that P. I. Tchaikovsky is very ill.

On 29 November Modest wrote to his brother: 'About the Finale of *The Queen of Spades*, I do not at all understand why everybody insists on a change; they want to embellish the end after Hermann's suicide, making his death more sentimental. What do you think?' In the end no changes were made.

On 3 October Modest's *The Symphony*, with Ermolova, had opened at the Malyi Theatre in Moscow, and on 3 November, with Savina, it began a run in St Petersburg.

[572]   TO MODEST TCHAIKOVSKY   Frolovskoie
                                            2 November 1890

Modia!

I do not insist upon the Znamensky Hotel, but without really knowing why I like it. Maybe because I hate the Europeiskaia which is much too central and vulgar. Surely in this enormous Znamensky Hotel there must be cheaper but still comfortable rooms. In any case I certainly don't want to pay 300 roubles. Could you see if by chance there is something nice in the Belle-Vue Pension, opposite Ekaterina's monument? A kitchen is not important. Or rooms anywhere else except for the Europeiskaia which I definitely don't want. Remember that Alesha is with me. The price – 150 roubles and not more than 200. I would like the rooms to be booked in advance. Forgive me that I bother you with all this.

I shall talk over the finale of *The Queen of Spades* in person. I would hate to agree to any additions; I fear that it is Figner who wants them, something like the last aria in *Lucia* with interruptions – last agony hiccups and such like. But this is out of the question!!!

I can't say how wonderful it is to be in Frolovskoie. Shall expect a telegram tomorrow about your *Symphony*. Arriving next Thursday. A kiss for Bob and Kolia.

P.T.

[573] TO PRASKOVIA VLADIMIROVNA TCHAIKOVSKAIA
[Petersburg]
21 November 1890
Hotel Rossia

My very dear Panichka!

Thank you for your sweet letter. I would love to answer in the same way but I am in the middle of rehearsals and have very little time of my own. I have excellent and quite separate rooms. The rent is 200 roubles a month.

Life is one continual rush. I even got to such a state of exhaustion that the doctor had to be called, who made me take medicine and drink Vichy Water and my hand which hurt me in Tiflis is hurting again. On Dr Bertenson's instructions a masseur comes to me every morning. The opera is getting on quite well, and there are only two weeks before the first night. The production and sets are going to be lavish, the performance excellent!

Have seen only a few members of the family. Saw Modest's play, which is very nice and very successful. What I mean is, that when it is on the theatre is always full. Brother Nikolai Illich lives a great way off, and I only once went to see him. For now that is all I have to say.

Tell Kokodeks [Kolia Peresleny] that I got his kind letter and will answer soon. Kind regards to all our friends. How awful about the earthquake. Cannot write any more.

I kiss and embrace you and my sweet Tatka.

Yours

P.T.

[574] TO MODEST TCHAIKOVSKY
Kiev
13 December 1890

... Rehearsals every day. It is difficult to describe what I go through at having again to be present at an opera production, and this in a small and comparatively poor theatre. However, everyone is trying hard, and the production is going to be as brilliant as is possible. Medvedev is best of all. The others are not so good as those at Petersburg. Medvedev is no Figner, but his great quality is that he is musical. I am sure of him because I know he will always be in tune and keep to the rhythm. The Intermedia looks a bit poor. This was to be expected. The ballet here consists of four pairs. The orchestra also pitiful compared with Petersburg, but not so much in quality as in quantity. They play very nicely.

I pass practically all my time in theatrical circles. I mean, after rehearsals I have dinner with Prianishnikov in the pleasant company of Pribyk and others not known to you but very nice people. Then I go and have a nap and by 7.30 I am in my box at the theatre. Yesterday I heard Tartakov in *The Demon* for the first time. *Mignon* is on today ... tomorrow two rehearsals and an amateur concert which I have promised to attend.

But I would much prefer to be in Frolovskoie than here.

I embrace you and Kolia.

P. Tchaikovsky

[575] TO MODEST TCHAIKOVSKY   Kiev
                                                                   21 December 1890

Modia!

No letters either from Petersburg or Moscow! It cannot be that there are none. I am expecting some from abroad which will tell me if I am going to conduct in Germany, America, and so on. Please ask at the Hotel Rossia if there are any letters there. If there are, send them to Klin, in the Province of Moscow. I am going to Kamenka tomorrow but shall not stay long. The day before yesterday was the first night of *The Queen of Spades*. One cannot compare the exhilarating reception here with that in Petersburg. I get ovations here every day. But I am so exhausted with it all that I have no strength to write properly. The performance is very good, but naturally it seems a bit poor after Peter.

I am terribly tired, and suffering, and lonely. Not knowing about the future also worries me. Should I give up tours and concerts abroad, or not? Is it wise to accept the offer of the directorship when the sextet has proved that I am going downhill? My head is empty and I have no desire to work. *Hamlet* is a heavy burden.

The second performance of *The Queen* is tonight. Another prima donna is singing for whose sake I stayed on.

I embrace you and Kolia.

P. Tchaikovsky

TO MODEST TCHAIKOVSKY   Kamenka
                                                      1 January 1891

Modia!

You addressed two letters to Klin and not here; didn't I tell you that I was
going to Kamenka for a few days? – Never mind. I was here from the 23rd
until today. Tonight I am leaving for Moscow and Frolovskoie *via* Kharkov.
I enjoyed being here but all efforts to work were unsuccessful. Either one
has to go to the big house, or chat and play piano duets with Bob, or just do
nothing. . . . We celebrated the New Year last night at the big house, and
enjoyed ourselves.

I will stay for two days in Moscow, to hear Arensky's *Dream on the Volga*.
Shall be at home on the 6th. Cannot understand at all what has happened to
Anatoli and what letter from Pania kept him in Petersburg. He said in his
telegram that he would write, but there was no letter.

Are you thinking about *King René's Daughter?* What will happen in the
end is that I will go to Italy to compose; I need the libretto at the end of
January. And what about the ballet? I want to stay in Frolovskoie about three
weeks.

Please write to Frolovskoie.

I kiss you and Kolia.

P. Tchaikovsky

How delightful is Chekhov's short story [*Gusev*] in the Christmas Number of
the *Novoe Vremia*.

[577] TO MODEST TCHAIKOVSKY   [Frolovskoie]
                                                      6 January 1891

Modia!

I have returned home after a day in Moscow . . . Guitry and his cursed *Hamlet*
were in my way. I hate Guitry now – although it's my own fault, only do not
tell him that. I have not yet started to work, and have a mass of letters to
answer. Besides, today, all sorts of reasons were in the way including the two
priests – one from here, the other from Maidanovo. Anatoli asked Yurgenson
where I was going to be today. Yurgenson said here. So I thought he was
coming and ordered a good dinner, but neither he nor Taneev, who promised
to come, appeared. Tolia is probably coming soon. Why not come with him
for at least a day? I have many things to discuss with you. And if you brought
Laroche with you I would be very, very pleased.

Besides the money you expect from your *Symphony* you may count upon a
fifth share in *The Queen of Spades*. Only I do not want to touch the money
from the theatre before the end of January. I must also give you 100 roubles

from Leva which I had from him for my journey and he asked that it should be passed on to you. If you need any money for your journey with Laroche ask Kolia to lend you some. I want to see you very much. Bring with you *King René's Daughter* and my theatrical photographs. . . .

I kiss you, Kolia, Bob.

Also kiss Yuri.

P. Tchaikovsky

Do not forget that on Thursday the 10th I am going up to Moscow to hear Arensky's opera and on Friday the 11th shall be home for dinner.

Kong René's Datter (*King René's Daughter*), Henrik Hertz (1798–1879), written in 1845 was translated into almost every European language, and into Russian by Zvantsev. Modest made the libretto of Piotr's last opera *Yolanta* (Op. 69) from this play. Modest's career as playwright was beginning to blossom, and his *A Hangover* was performed at the Alexandrinsky Theatre in St Petersburg. Piotr began the composition of his opera in July and finished it in November. In January, however, he was protesting his inability to go abroad because of its claims. He was also working on the music for *The Nutcracker* (from A. Dumas's *Casse-Noisette*, which in turn was based on E. T. A. Hoffman's *Nussknacker und Mäusekönig*). Tchaikovsky refused to conduct some concerts at this time, according to Modest on account of neuralgic pains in the arm.

He did, however, direct a concert of the Women's Patriotic Society in St Petersburg on 3 February. On 6 February *Hamlet*, starring Guitry, was performed at the Mikhailovsky Theatre in the city, with Tchaikovsky's incidental music.

[578]   TO MODEST TCHAIKOVSKY   Klin–Frolovskoie
                                                 [11 January 1891]

Dear Modia!

I shall be very glad for you to come on the 18th; but even more so if you bring Laroche. Yesterday I went to Moscow to hear Arensky's *Dream on the Volga*. Some of the scenes are so lovely that I was moved to tears. The one of the dream is especially wonderful. I immediately wrote a letter to Vsevoloisky recommending the opera for Petersburg.

The telegraph exists to muddle people up. Yesterday thanks to a muddle over a telegram I had a disagreeable misunderstanding with Tolia. I understood that he was coming today, left some important business behind and arrived back in the morning, and – he did not come!!

I have definitely refused to conduct in Budapest, Frankfurt, and Mainz, and have sent my refusal to Wolff to go to America. All these sacrifices are for the sake of the Petersburg Theatre. But what if I do not get any inspiration? I am in such a mood, at the present, that I am inclined to think I won't have any. . . . *Hamlet* is getting on. But what a disgusting job! ! ! Oh, Lord, how I want to see Guittemans.

I embrace you, Kolia, Bob, Ouka.

Yours

P. Tchaikovsky

Yuri has risen in my esteem.

[579] TO ANATOLI TCHAIKOVSKY

Klin
22 January 1891

Tolia!

How upset I was that because of Alexei and me you missed the fast train! Please forgive me! Since you left nothing special has happened except that the frost is over. Today is one degree below freezing point. Modest and Laroche are here, and this morning they both went to Moscow for a day. Modest went to see Savina in his *Symphony*. I have finished *Hamlet* and sent it off, and now am busy correcting the full score of *The Queen of Spades*. At the end of the week I go to Petersburg for final talks with the directors about the opera and ballet.

After that I thought it would be wiser and less expensive not to go abroad but to stay here for two months and work hard. But I will go to America in April. I have received all particulars about what and how I am going to do there. Plenty to do, good pay, and it would be wrong to miss an opportunity which may not come again. Am waiting with impatience for news from you and from Kamenka. How did you find them there?

Am sending photographs together with this letter. My sweet Pania I kiss very hard. Ask Tata about numbers.

I embrace you.

P. Tchaikovsky

Tata – Tatiana – Anatoli's little daughter was being taught to count by her uncle Piotr, who took great pleasure in this self-imposed task.

[580] TO PRASKOVIA VLADIMIROVNA TCHAIKOVSKAIA

Petersburg
29 January 1891

. . . Came here on business and also to conduct at a concert arranged by the Grand Duchess Ekaterina Mikhailovna. As usual, the first day went very pleasantly but yesterday the invitations started to come and I am being torn to pieces. I will stay about two weeks. Then back to Frolovskoie and work, and America at the end of March. I shall work for the whole summer and in the autumn again go to Tiflis. No special news here. Modest is brushing up his play which will be on for Savina's Benefit. Generally speaking he is on the up-grade and has become the purveyor of fashionable plays in Petersburg. I am staying at the Hotel Rossia . . . that is all I have to say. I embrace you, Tata, Tolia, Kokodeks.

Regards to everybody. How do you like my photographs? Would you like one?

I kiss you.

P. Tchaikovsky

[581]   TO ANATOLI TCHAIKOVSKY   Frolovskoie
                                                   12 February 1891

Dear Tolia!

I have just returned from Petersburg where I stayed for two weeks and when I got back here I found your letter. You ask about America. I am invited to conduct at three concerts which will take place in connection with the opening of a new Concert Hall in New York. At one of them I shall conduct a symphony, at another the Piano Concerto, and at the third a chorus. The first concert will be on 6 May (new style) but I have promised to be there ten days earlier, and so must arrive about 12 April (our style). I shall leave about the 20th; the fee they offer me is quite sufficient – 2,500 dollars (about 3,000 roubles) and I shall go with pleasure as I am very interested in the journey itself. Back home in June. It may be that I will conduct at a big concert in Paris before my trip to America.

In Petersburg I conducted the Patriotic Concert with great success. At the theatre they have behaved like pigs to *The Queen of Spades*; for no reason at all they took it off altogether after the 12th performance. They pretended it was because of Figner's refusal to sing with anyone but his wife. I did not show myself there at all, but wrote a letter to Vsevoloisky today, protesting at the way in which they have offended me. However – to hell with them, and if they want me to write a ballet and an opera for next season I shall only agree if they let me have an official guarantee to protect me from the whims of the performers.

On the whole I was rather bored in Petersburg and am glad to be here again. Everybody liked my music to *Hamlet*, composed for Guitry's Benefit. Guitry was wonderful. Shall go to Peter in a week's time to see Modest's play.

Yours

P. Tchaikovsky

TO MODEST TCHAIKOVSKY

Frolovskoie
25 February 1891

Modia!

Are you homesick for your Fatherland and your nearest ones as I am when I am abroad? If so, I think you will be pleased to get this short note. I hope that you have stopped worrying about the failure of your *Hangover*. The play has immense qualities and provided you change the end it is sure to gain recognition. The long article in the *Novoe Vremia* was not at all hostile. I did not read any of the other papers. I am working with all my might and am beginning to get reconciled to the subject of the ballet. I think that I will have finished the major part of the first act before I leave. . . . I am going to Moscow on 1 March, to Petersburg on the 2nd, and to Paris on the 5th or 6th, but I will stop for a day or two in Berlin.

I hope you will wait for me in Paris. Go to Italy when I leave for America. . . . Tell the Béliards to have a room ready for me on 20 March, it does not matter on what floor. I kiss and embrace you! Kiss Vassia!

Yours

P. Tchaikovsky

[583] TO PRASKOVIA VLADIMIROVNA TCHAIKOVSKAIA

Frolovskoie
25 February 1891

My very dear Panichka!

Why do you live so far away! It makes me sad sometimes to think what a distance separates us. But in spite of Tolia's bad luck and his, and probably your, temporary coolness towards Tiflis I continue to love it passionately and my sweetest dream is to stay with you in the autumn. Meanwhile I am on the eve of a long journey, for on 1 March I will stay a day in Moscow, go to Petersburg on the 2nd, and on the 5th or 6th to Paris. I will have to stay there for two or three weeks because I am conducting a big concert. Directly after this concert I take the steamer at Le Havre and sail for America. From there I shall return straight to the country in June and work with great energy. After this spate of work (a ballet and an opera for next season) I will love having a good rest with you in Tiflis. At the moment I am hard at it drafting the rough sketches for the ballet. A few days ago I went to Petersburg to see Modest's play and to ask for an explanation from Vsevoloisky with whom I almost quarrelled. The fact is that, thanks to Figner's and Kondratiev's intrigues (not actually against me), *The Queen of Spades* – after twelve full performances at increased prices – has been temporarily taken out of the repertoire. This seemed to me both stupid and very offensive, and to ease my conscience and express my feelings I wrote Vsevoloisky a letter, polite in tone but actually very brusque. He was very hurt at first, but later both by letter and in conversation an explanation was forthcoming and we are friends as before.

Modest's play has good qualities but the end was too negative and gloomy for it to have any success. Modest would have been frightfully upset if it had not happened on the eve of his journey abroad which he was looking forward to so much, and he got over the fiasco quite well. He must be in Paris by now....

Yours

P. Tchaikovsky

[584] TO ANATOLI TCHAIKOVSKY   Berlin
8–20 March 1891

Golubchik Tolia!

Your letter was delivered to me at the moment when I was getting into the train for Paris, and I read it with lively interest. That was a wonderful ball the general's wife [i.e. Praskovia] gave! God! How I wish I had been there! ! ! !

I stayed only three days in Petersburg, but managed to see all the relatives, who, thank God, are all well and hearty. Have promised the directors that I will write a ballet and an opera for next season but have warned them that my trip to America may prevent me from accomplishing so difficult a task. I will try to work on the boat. Even on my way here I composed bits of the ballet. The main thing is to get rid of the ballet; as to the opera I am so fascinated by it that if I could have two weeks of peace I would be sure to finish it on schedule. We shall see! I was so tired from my journey that I decided to stay a night in Berlin. Tomorrow I am off to Paris where I will feel happy; for Modest and Sapelnikov are there, both of whom I shall be very glad to see again. On the 5th I am conducting a big concert in Paris, at the same Colonne Hall where I appeared three years ago. Soon afterwards I shall board the steamer. I will write to you both from Paris and America; and I beg you to write to New York: P. Tchaikovsky, Steinway Hall, New York, U.S.A.

May it please God that your service complications will be cleared, but I personally shall be sorry if you leave Tiflis.

Imagine what a curious person Katerina Ivanovna Sinelnikova Laroche is! She is coming with me to America – I mean on the same boat. I do not know if I ought to be glad or sorry, but most probably glad to have someone I know on board; tell Kokodeks to wait a little bit for the allowance. Please, embrace Panichka, and Tata, whose letter charmed me, as hard as you can.

I kiss you!

P. Tchaikovsky

TO VLADIMIR DAVYDOV   Paris
                                           15–27 March 1891

I have been here five days! Only after seeing those who know all about what
is taking place I found out what is in store for me. Colonne accepted an offer
from Petersburg to conduct three concerts there and, not knowing what to do
with the 23rd of the season here, asked me to conduct. The whole programme
consists of my works. The concert will be not on the Sunday coming but the
next one; that is on 5 April (24 March), as usual at the Colonne Hall where
I conducted three years ago.

All the American business is settled. On 6 April (25 March) I leave Paris. As yet
I do not know where. I shall work on the ballet and on the 18th (6 April) I
embark on the large transatlantic liner and travel to New York. The cabin is
booked, and I will be alone. Nothing more to say about me. . . .

Paris is interesting and full of life, and everybody is kind and charming. There
is nothing unpleasant in store for me, but this does not stop my soul from
being in torture. Finished! No more of all these travels for me.

I often see Menter and Sapelnikov. Modest is blooming. I embrace you a
thousand times.

P. Tchaikovsky

Modest wrote about meeting Piotr in Paris. 'It was,' he said, 'the first time I saw
him abroad not private but as a touring artiste. This meeting left a gloomy impression. He did not let me know the time of his arrival and I only found out that he
had come when I returned to the hotel. He was asleep; the servant told me he had
given orders not to be disturbed. This in itself was a bad sign, for he so much loved
the first hours of reunion. We only met in the morning. Piotr showed hardly any
pleasure and all he said was that, he wondered why – since I had no commitments
there – I did not go back to Russia. I saw him in Paris then, as shown in Kuznezov's
portrait at the Tretiakov Gallery, with a cold, dismal look in his eyes, red through
nervous strain and with a sarcastic smile on his lips.' (The daughter-in-law of Mme
von Meck considered this account by Modest exaggerated and complained that the
Kuznezov painting (see pp. 530, 531) was not a true likeness: translator.)
    At the Colonne Concert on 5 April (western style) Tchaikovsky's programme
contained the third Suite, the Second Piano Concerto (soloist Sapelnikov), the
Melancholy Serenade, Op. 26 (soloist I. Wolff), Andante Cantabile from the first string
quartet, *The Tempest*, the *Slavonic March*, and some songs.
    Modest received a telegram when he was in Paris telling him of the death of his
sister Alexandra Illinishna Davydova. He came to Rouen to tell Piotr, but his
courage failed him. He left Rouen suddenly without informing his brother of their
loss and returned to St Petersburg. Piotr found out of their sister's death from the
newspapers.

Rouen
30 March–11 April 1891

Golubushka Pania!

I got your letter when I was still in Paris but could not find any time to
answer. I have come here for a rest and solitude after Paris. I will not say
anything about the concert as I am sure you will know about it from the
papers. All I can say is that it was very successful and for several days I
attracted the attention of the Paris public. The rehearsals and the concert
troubled and tired me very much but this sort of fatigue is very pleasant. It
was all the dinners and receptions I had to attend which were awful!!!
I swear that it is going to be the last time that I agree to all this tiring and
boring business – I mean that from now on I am going to stick permanently
at home. At the bottom of my heart there is such an immense longing for my
Fatherland, so much impatience to be home again, that I find no words to
describe it.

I will stay here another six days, then Modest, Sapelnikov and Menter will
join me, to see me off to Le Havre, where I shall board the steamer next
Saturday 18 April (6th old style). I will telegraph from New York as promised.
Modest is still in Paris and is not going to Italy. Did I tell you that I have been
kicked out of Frolovskoie and that, for the time being I want to live again in
Maidanovo? For the winter (after Tiflis where I intend to go in the autumn)
I think of moving to Petersburg. Once in Paris I met yóur brother-in-law Kolia
in the street, but he pretended not to see me.

Forgive me my dove, that this letter is so short but I have about thirty letters
to answer today.

Yours

P. Tchaikovsky

Coming straight home from America; hope to be back at the beginning of June
or even earlier.

[Rouen]
3–15 April 1891

Dear Modia!

After you left my tortures and sufferings rose in a crescendo and yesterday
evening I reached a crisis, which ended in my writing a long letter to I. A.
Vsevoloisky. Now I am rid of a heavy burden and after three days of madness
feel quite well. The real reason for my despair was that I have been making
vigorous but vain efforts to work. Nothing came out but muck and *Casse
Noisette* and *King René's Daughter* turned into terrifying feverish nightmares,

so hateful that I don't dare to describe them. I was tortured by the realization that I could not properly fulfil the task I had undertaken, and the idea of perpetual strain on the way to America, as well as there and on the way back turned into a formidable, deadly apparition.

It would be difficult to describe all I went through and I do not remember having ever been so unhappy. As a background to all my tortures as a composer one has also to add my longing for my Fatherland which I foresaw, and am never without when out of Russia. Last night I realized that it was impossible to go on in this way, and in the morning I wrote a long letter to Vsevoloisky begging him not to be angry with me if I have the ballet and opera ready only for the season of 1892–93. Now all that weight is off my mind. Honestly, why should I force and torture myself and how can anything good come out of such an effort? I am in such a state of mind that I have started to hate *King René's Daughter*; when on the contrary I ought to love her! ! !

In short I must go to America free of the burden of a task beyond my strength, otherwise I shall go mad. I wrote to Vsevoloisky in a feverish state of mind, and even now, writing to you, I am trembling. No! To the devil all strain, rush and spiritual torture. I feel that I can make a *chef-d'oeuvre* out of *King René's Daughter*, but not in these circumstances. The reason for my letter to you is to ask you to go and see Vsevoloisky and beg him not to be angry with me. If he will not understand my reasons for putting the work off (they all think that all I need is to sit down for five minutes and the opera is written), explain to him that I am really not in a proper state to keep my promise, that I have been exhausted by my feelings in Paris, that I will have to go through the same experiences in America and so on. Am going back to Paris for a bit of fun.

Cannot say anything about Rouen as all I saw was the picture gallery which I liked very much. The weather is cold and grey. On the whole Rouen is not attractive. I went to the theatre *(Musette)*, but not for long. You are lucky, you are back in Russia now.

I embrace you, Bob and Kolia.

Oh! What a mountain has fallen off my shoulders!

P. Tchaikovsky

[588] TO MODEST TCHAIKOVSKY Paris
5–17 April 1891
[on Hotel Terminus paper]

Modia!

After having sent off my letter to Vsevoloisky yesterday I went to Paris. On my way to Menter I went to a book-stall I know in the Passage de l'Opéra and bought a *Novoe Vremia*. On the last page I read that Sasha is dead – I rushed out as if pursued by stinging bees. Reached Menter and Vassia much later. How lucky that they were there. I stayed the night with them. Tonight I am leaving for Rouen and Le Havre.

At first I thought it my duty to leave everything and go back to Petersburg but then I realized it could not help and besides I would have had to return the 5,000 francs advance, lose the rest and the ticket. No, I am going to America. I am suffering very much – I fear for Bob although I know that in youth one stands up to sorrow much more easily; but it is Leva and Nata I am especially sorry for. These two must suffer indescribably. And so, off to Rouen today, tomorrow to Le Havre and at 5 pm on Saturday I shall be at sea. Today I sent a telegram to Kolia; for God's sake write all details to New York. More than ever these last two days I feel an absolute lack of capacity to describe the 'Confitürenberg' [last scene of *The Nutcracker*] in music.

I embrace all of you.

P. Tchaikovsky

I do not live in the Hotel Terminus, am in the café by chance.

Modest wrote from St Petersburg: 'I came to Rouen to tell you the sad news of Sasha's death, but seeing the state you were in I was too sorry to upset you even more when you looked so sad and lonely. So after a walk in town I decided to let you take the trip without knowing of our great loss. As for myself, I could not think of staying in Paris at such a moment. . . . We arrived here at the same time as Sasha's coffin and only had time to change before meeting the sad procession and accompany Sasha to the Lavra [the great monastery]. Both your letters made me very unhappy; I blame myself for hiding from you why I left Paris so suddenly; but I hated to let you cross the ocean with this sorrow in your heart when you looked so sad already.'

[589]   TO MODEST TCHAIKOVSKY   [at sea]
6–18 April 1891
9 in the evening

I am going to write a diary which I shall send you on my arrival in New York. Please keep it as I intend to write an article based on it.

I left Paris the day before yesterday. Vassia, Menter and Konius saw me off. Stayed the night in hateful Rouen and in the morning I packed and at 2 o'clock left for Le Havre. I boarded the steamer direct from the railway station and went to my cabin. The steamer is one of the colossal and luxurious ones. I had dinner in town, roamed around a bit, and returned to the ship at 10 o'clock. Up till now, thinking about the journey, the excitement in anticipation of it, the prospect of being at sea – all this occupied my thoughts. But when I found myself in my cabin, I never felt as unhappy as I did at that moment. I am upset that I did not get any answer from Kolia and do not understand why.

Probably the usual telegram mix-up but it was awful leaving without news from Petersburg. Katerina Ivanovna was not on the boat yesterday.

I passionately wanted her to be there, and hoped, when going to bed, that she would arrive with the special boat train. Today (I woke up late, at 8.00), when the ship was already at sea, I came out of my cabin certain that I would find her among the passengers . . . but alas! She is not here. For a long time I hoped she would appear; that she had been sleeping late. How I wished that were so!!! No, without exaggeration, I never felt so miserable, lonely, and unhappy! The thought that I had another week at sea, that I can only get news in New York, frightens me. I curse this journey. The steamer is wonderfully luxurious, a real floating palace! Not too many passengers, and only 90 in the first class. The order of the day is as follows:

At 7.00 in the morning tea or coffee is served in your cabin if you wish. Breakfast from 9.00–11.00 when, after taking your seat, you may ask for as many different dishes as you like, and there are ten on the menu. Lunch at 1.30 is as plentiful as breakfast. I refused it but it seems I was the only one. At 5.30 dinner – very tasty and also a lot of it. I am at a table with an American family, which is inconvenient and boring.

A tragedy happened at 5 o'clock which made an awful impression both on me and the other passengers. I was downstairs when there was a sudden whistle, a lot of running and scurrying about, and a boat was lowered. Rushing upstairs I heard what had happened – a young man from the second class had suddenly taken out his wallet and – after writing a few words in it and leaving it on deck – had jumped overboard. A lifebelt was thrown down, and the boat went to look for him; but nothing appeared on the surface and half an hour later the boat returned and the steamer went on. The wallet had 35 francs in it and the note written in a very unclear hand. (I read the note and was the first to decipher it as it was written in German and the passengers are all Americans and French.) 'Ich bin unschuldig, der Bursche weint. . .'; the rest was scribbled and quite illegible. From what the passengers said the young man had attracted everybody's attention by his queer behaviour and it was decided he must have been out of his mind.

After dinner I roamed round the deck and the desire for company was so strong that I went down to the second class, and there found the *commis-voyageur* [commercial traveller] with whom I came from Rouen, a very talkative and jolly type. I found him, and chatted for a while, but this did not make it easier for me.

The weather is lovely. The sea is calm and the steamer is moving so smoothly that you forget you are at sea. Have just passed the lighthouse at the western end of England. This is the last bit of land until we reach New York.

If the circumstances of my trip had been different, if what has, had not happened, and if I had a companion (like Katerina Ivanovna for example) I could really enjoy it all. All the same I do not understand why Kolia did not answer. Leaving Rouen, I asked that the text of the telegram should be sent to me on the boat, but I did not get it. Which means that two days elapsed since I had sent mine! ! ! The most impossible and frightful things come into my mind and I worry, specially about Bob.

7–19 April
8 in the evening

In the morning it started to roll, and gradually became so bad that, now and again, I get very frightened. What is reassuring is that the majority of the passengers have made the crossing many times and are not a bit afraid of what I fear, i.e. to be wrecked. Moreover, only a few of the passengers so far are afraid of feeling sea-sick. As to myself I do not worry about it at all as I do not even feel a hint of it. The waiter whom I asked about the roll said that it is simply *une mer un peu grosse*, but what is it going to be like when it becomes *très grosse*! ! The sea is beautiful and when I am free of my fear I enjoy the wonderful sight. Three enormous gulls interested me (could they be albatrosses?) which follow us and I am told are going to do so until the *Terre Neuve*. How then do they rest, and where are they at night? I read all day as there is nothing else to do. Composition disgusts me, and an awful anguish still gnaws at me. When I tried to pour out my feelings to my acquaintance, the *commis-voyageur*, he said: 'Eh bien, à votre âge c'est assez naturel', which offended me very much. This does not prevent him from being a nice and jolly fellow and I chatted with him and his friends several times today. The waiter from the smoking lounge offered to bet how many miles we had done up to 12 o'clock. I gave him the agreed 5 francs and at 12.14 he brought me back fifty. I had won! How, I really don't know. At dinner I had to keep up a conversation with an unsympathetic Frenchwoman who sits opposite to me. Still another week at sea. Better not describe what I feel. All I know is that this is for the last time. . . . No – at my age one ought to stay at home, near to one's dearest ones. The thought that I am so far away is killing me. All the same, thank God, I am perfectly well. Yesterday a 'Miss' was singing Italian songs so disgustingly and with such arrogance that I wondered why no one was rude to her.

8–20 April

The night was very pleasant. When everybody went to bed I walked for a long time on deck, in my coat (which takes the place of a dressing-gown) and slippers. The wind was falling and when I went down it had become much calmer. Today the weather is sunny, but the wind which started at midday is gradually getting stronger. The rolling has changed to pitching but the ship is so large that very few passengers are ill. I am not afraid any more but I feel a slight hint of sea-sickness.

The friendship between the French *commis-voyageur*, his friends, and myself is growing. (All of them are travelling second class.) They are jolly and amusing, and I feel much more at ease with them than with the important and pompous first-class passengers. One of my new friends is the son of a rich 'Fishing King' who fishes for cod on the *Terre Neuve*. He, talking in a very curious French patois told me all about cod-fishing. They have several sailing

vessels which go out to sea to fish for many months (just like the author
Pierre Loti describes it). This young man is only eighteen and has been on
such expeditions several times and has had many experiences. At their invitation
I went to the second class where they brought in a poor emigrant, going to
America, with his trained monkey which showed us its tricks.

My head and heart are in quite a queer state. I am beginning to get calmer
and do not think at all about what is worrying me, I mean about home and
all my nearest and dearest. I force myself to think only about the steamer, how
to kill time by reading, walking, chatting with the Frenchmen, eating, and –
most of all – watching the sea which today, for instance, all lit up by the
sun, is wonderfully beautiful. The sunset was magnificent. In this way I do not
feel to be myself but another person, sailing on the seas and living for the
present moment. Sasha's death and all the attendant thoughts of her
that are torturing and painful are like a memory from a distant past which
I push away from me without much effort, and then I can think again about
the interests of this other one who, in me, is travelling to America. The first-class
passengers whom I am always meeting are not at all interesting. They are all
very vulgar male and female Americans, very smartly dressed, but not at all
attractive. The most interesting of the party is a Canadian bishop and his
secretary. He went to Rome to receive the Pope's blessing. Yesterday morning
he conducted a Low Mass in a special cabin which I attended. The sea is
getting rougher and rougher. But I understand now that in the middle of the
ocean it cannot be calm and am getting used to it. Off to bed.

9–21 April 1891

At night it became so rough that I woke up frightened, my heart thumping
hard, and feeling feverish. But a good glass of brandy soon calmed me down.
I got into my coat and slippers and went up on deck; the night was beautiful,
lovely. When I saw everything was absolutely normal I understood there was
no reason for anxiety. If there had been any danger the ship's company would
have been on the alert. The ocean did not look menacing but it did look
alarming, and at the same time infinitely beautiful in the bright rays of the
full moon. Then I went down and slept peacefully till the morning.

In the morning the sea became calmer and only a light swell was left. We
entered the Gulf Stream; you can feel it because the weather turns as warm as
in summer, and all day long the passengers were enjoying themselves. I must
add that we also have several hundred emigrants mostly from the Alsace. As
soon as the weather gets fine they organize a dance and it is fun watching
them dancing, accompanied by a mouth-organ. The emigrants do not look sad
at all. There are also six prostitutes of the lowest sort on board, engaged by
a 'gentleman' who trades in them and who is accompanying them. One of
them is quite attractive and my second-class passenger friends take it in turns
to use her charms. But the girls look miserable, poor and hungry. My best
friend (commis-voyageur) is successfully paying court to a second-class lady
passenger and has already a proper affair with her. When the couple disappear

into the men's cabin his friends take in turns to look after her little son. Just now all this jolly crowd invited me to the second class and the *commis-voyageur* entertained me and the others by singing *grivoise* couplets, satirizing the French law courts; all this was done with so much humour that I could not help laughing heartily.

The unattractive lady who is my neighbour at dinner and with whom I am obliged to talk, happens to be the wife of a member of the Boston orchestra. Consequently the conversation today became musical. For a musician she told me quite interesting things about the Boston concerts and the musical life there.

Today we met several sailing boats, a huge whale which was blowing a gorgeous fountain and a *cachalote*. But I missed both.

                                        10–22 April 1891

I thought I was immune to sea sickness; apparently not. In the night the weather got gradually worse and when I got up at 7 o'clock it was quite bad and the sea very rough but it did not prevent my watching the great ocean waves with admiration. But later it became worse and worse and at 2 o'clock it seemed so frightful that I expected us to perish at any moment; but of course there was no question of perishing. It is the most natural, bad Atlantic weather. Not only the captain and his helpers but all the waiters look upon it as the most ordinary occurrence. But I who judged the ocean according to Mediterranean standards, thought it was hell. Everything seemed to be cracking up, first we were sinking into an abyss, then we were flying up into the clouds, it was impossible even to think of going up on deck, as the wind blows you off your feet . . . in one word it was frightful.

Many of the passengers are sick but there are quite a few who do not care, even play the piano, or cards or what not.

At breakfast I had no appetite. Then I felt sickish and at dinner I could not look at my food without disgust. I was told that I would feel better by the evening but it got worse. . . . Something very disagreeable has happened. My purse with 460 francs in gold has been stolen from the drawer over my bed. I think it must be the *garçon*. I reported the matter to *M. le Commissaire*. A notice has been hung up. But I am certain of the theft. It is lucky I have some more money with me. At one moment I feel sick, then I do not; but on the whole I feel rotten. It is getting even rougher. Impossible to sleep. Coffee and brandy are my only food today.

                                        11–23 April 1891

The night was horrid. It threw one from side to side so much that it was impossible to sleep. Every time I tried to doze off I was woken up by a strong jolt. In the morning it became calmer and up to four it was quite possible. However at breakfast, I could not swallow even a morsel. Then another calamity threatened: as we neared the *Bancs de Sables* near *Terre Neuve*, as usually happens here – we ran into a thick fog. This is what one fears most

at sea for even a collision with a small sailing boat means ruin. We go dead
slow and every thirty seconds the siren sounds – a contraption which lets out
a frightening bellow like the roar of a colossal tiger. It affects one's nerves
badly. However, at this moment, as I am writing, the fog is thinning and the
siren howls less. The passengers have found out who I am and all sorts of
people come up now and ask me if I am really me. After which compliments
and conversations start up. Acquaintances have multiplied to such an extent
that I cannot find a place for a solitary walk. Wherever I go someone at once
comes up and starts talking. What is more, they all want me to play. I refuse
– but I shall have to play something on the horrid upright piano to get rid of
them. The only thoughts I have are: 'When will it all end and when shall I be
home again?' I do not have any other thoughts at all today. I count the days,
dream about the moment of bliss when I shall go home. The fog is going but
the pitching is starting again. Not a sign of my purse.

> 12–24 April 1891
> 8 in the evening

Definitely impossible to write. Since yesterday I am suffering. A terrific
hurricane is blowing; they say it was forecast by the meteorological observatory.
It is something awful! Much worse for me, a beginner, than for many of the
passengers who do not seem to care at all. I have been told this will continue
until New York. I am suffering more in mind than in body – I am just frightened
and horrified.

> 8 in the evening
> 13–25 April 1891

After I had finished writing I went up to the *fumoir* where usually in the
evening there are plenty of passengers smoking, drinking, playing cards or
dominoes etc. This time there were only a few and they looked worried. I had
a glass of punch and went back to my cabin. The storm was getting worse; to
lie down was impossible. I sat down on the corner of my bunk and tried not
to think about what was going on – but how can you stop thinking about it with
all the noise, crashes, convulsive leaps of the whole ship and the desperate
howling of the wind which you cannot deafen in any way.

I sat in this way for a long time and what I felt (what went on in my soul) is
difficult to describe. A nasty experience! Then I began to notice that the storm
was weakening; that the awful jolts when the screw comes out of the water
and a frightful, impossible shudder starts, do not happen so much any more;
that the howling and whistling of the wind is less horrible. . . . I went to sleep
in the same position. I had been sitting between my travelling case and the
cabin wall. I woke up at 5.00 am the storm was abating and I went to sleep
again – this time peacefully. In the morning I was told that we had been in an
exceedingly severe hurricane, the sort that happens very rarely. It was at its
height at 10.00 pm. From this morning the weather gradually improved and by
12.00 it became quite fine. At 2 o'clock the long expected pilot appeared at last.
All the passengers came out to watch him, as he waited for us in his tiny boat.
The steamer stopped and the pilot was taken on board. We have another

twenty-four sailing hours. We shall be several hours late because of the storm. I am very glad that the crossing is coming to an end at last. A longer stay on the ship would have been unbearable. Especially now that everybody knows me, wants to talk to me, and the only place I can hide is in my cabin. Besides, they nag me to play something and start discussing music. Oh God! When will all this end? I have decided to leave New York on 30 April–12 May on a German boat. With God's help I shall be in Petersburg about 10 May or a little later! ! ! ! ! !

New York
15–27 April

The rest of the journey was quite ordinary; the nearer we came to New York the more nervous, sorrowful and frightened I became and more and more sorry that I had undertaken this mad trip. Maybe, when everything is happily over I shall remember it with pleasure but at the moment it means nothing but suffering. Before entering New York there are unending formalities with the Customs and with landing permits. A long interrogation takes place. At last at 5.30 we landed. I was met with great courtesy by four gentlemen and a lady and they took me at once to the hotel. Here I told Mr Maurice Reno that I wanted to leave on 12 May. He said that this would be impossible, as a special concert has been arranged for the 18th which Wolff had not mentioned. When all the people left I walked up and down the rooms (there are two of them), shedding copious tears. I had asked for my freedom for the whole of the evening and had got rid of an invitation to dinner and a reception. After taking a bath (bath, lavatory, and wash-stand with hot and cold water, are in every room), and changing, I had dinner downstairs with distaste, and went for a walk along Broadway. A queer street, with one-storey houses standing between others of nine storeys. Very interesting! ! ! I returned home and cried again. As it always happens after these tearful attacks, the old cry-baby slept like one dead and woke up refreshed, but with a fresh supply of tears welling up in his eyes.

Thank you for the telegram – it brought great relief.

Modia, give this letter to read to anyone you wish and then send it over to Tolia, and ask him to return it to me. Who knows, I may after all write an article.

I embrace all of you.

P. Tchaikovsky

Am sending a cutting from today's *New York Herald*.

The New York Herald of 27 April, 1891, carried a short biography of Tchaikovsky and his photograph.

In New York he participated in four concerts, in connection with the opening of Carnegie Hall, and in one each in Baltimore and Philadelphia. The programmes included the Coronation March, the third suite, the First Piano Concerto (soloist, Adele Aus der Ohe), the Serenade for Strings and the chorus 'The Legend'.

A minute ago I had letters from Modia, Annette, and Yurgenson. I just do not know how to say what letters mean to me in my present circumstances. I was infinitely glad.

I am keeping a diary day by day and when I return will let all of you read it – so I shall not go into details now. All I can say is that New York, American customs, American hospitality, the town itself, and the wonderful comfort of the houses, are all very much to my liking, and if I were younger I would probably have felt great pleasure in being in this interesting country. But all I do is suffer – a punishment softened somewhat by congenial circumstances. All the same all I am yearning for is home, home, home! ! ! ! There is some hope that I shall be able to leave on the 12th.

Everybody is petting, entertaining, and fussing over me, and it appears I am much better known in America than in Europe.

At first when I heard this I imagined it was only exaggerated courtesy, but now I see that this is not the case. Some of my works which are unknown in Moscow are being played here several times a season, and whole articles and critical notices are written about them (e.g. *Hamlet*). Here I am a much more important person than in Russia. Isn't that odd? ! ! ! The orchestral players greeted me enthusiastically at the rehearsal (so far there has only been one).

Now a few words about New York itself:

It is a huge city, not beautiful but very original. Some of the houses have only one floor, others up to eleven, and one house (a new hotel that has just been built) is seventeen storeys high. In Chicago they went even further; one of the houses there has 21 floors! ! !

These high buildings are the result of New York being situated on a narrow peninsula, surrounded by water on three sides. As it cannot expand in width it has to grow in height. I have been told that in ten years time all the buildings will have at least ten floors. But out of all the arrangements in New York that would most please you, is that every apartment has a toilet room with a lavatory, bath, and wash-basin, and both the bath and the basin have constant hot and cold water. Splashing in my bath in the morning I always think of you. There is electric and gas lighting. Candles are not used at all. If one needs something one does not ask for it in the way one does in Europe – here you ring and say what you want into a tube hanging near the bell. Or if someone downstairs wants to see you, they ring you and tell you through the tube who is there and what they want. This is rather awkward for me as I do not know English. No one, except the staff, uses the stairs. The lift never stops working, running up and down at a terrific speed, taking in and putting out the hotel guests.

Except for the unique way the houses in the main street alternate between being quite small or huge, what attracts your attention is that there is not much noise in the streets, nor are they very crowded. This is because there are very few cabs and horse-carriages about. The traffic consists mostly of trams, or a real railway, which has branches through the whole of this enormous city. In the morning the entire population rushes to the east [south] – downtown – which is that part of the city where all the business premises are situated, and in the evening everyone goes uptown and home. One lives as in London, in apartments each of which has several narrow floors.

This will do for the present. Shall write soon again to one of you. I embrace you my dear, also Modest and Kolia. How much longer – oh – how much longer?

Yours

P. Tchaikovsky

[591] TO ANATOLI TCHAIKOVSKY   New York
                                              21 April–3 May 1891

I am not going to write very much about my stay here as I shall bring back my diary which will be sent to you as soon as it has been read by the relatives in Petersburg. I am pampered, spoiled, and made a great fuss of here; but in spite of it I am homesick and apart from rare moments of solitude I am in perpetual suffering. Fortunately, however, this is not affecting my health. By the time this letter reaches you I shall have begun my return journey as I have booked on a steamer that sails on 9–21 May. If only this happy moment could come sooner! ! ! As soon as I start on my journey home a mountain will fall off my shoulders. I meet many people, see all the sights, wonder at American enterprise and the size of all their undertakings. At the rehearsals the orchestra and choir received me enthusiastically. Sometimes I do manage to have a few hours of solitude and somehow continue to carry on this miserable existence. A journey like this is not for me, or at my age! My only consolation are letters from Russia.

Thank God that Leva, the children and Nata are bearing their great loss so bravely. I kiss and embrace you all as hard as I can. From this far distance my heart burns specially brightly with love for all my dearest and nearest.

Yours

P. Tchaikovsky

[592] TO MODEST TCHAIKOVSKY   [New York]
                                              27 April–9 May 1891

Modia!

I find it more difficult every day to find time for letter-writing. When I have a free moment in the morning I write my diary. Today my New York performances come to an end. Up to now I have had enormous success, especially with my Suite. The press is singing my praises as I never even hoped to be praised in Russia. The ladies collect in crowds during the intervals and at the end of a concert gape at me, and some come up to express their admiration. Everybody is wonderfully kind; time is beginning to fly, and I hope that in just over a week I shall be able to sail.

The next two days are going to be very tiring, without a moment of freedom; but on Monday I am off to the Niagara Falls alone. After that I shall have to travel from town to town and hope that time will pass even quicker until my departure. I had a very pleasant birthday – especially the second part. In the morning I had a trembling fit before conducting my Suite at the Matinée Concert, but it was a terrific success and afterwards I managed to get rid of all invitations and remained alone for the rest of the day. Two Russian ladies who live here came to see me yesterday, and one of them upset me so much by her Russian appearance and way of speaking that I burst into tears which – when I think of it – makes me awfully ashamed of myself. This shows you how I would have appreciated the presence of K. I. Laroche, from whom I had a very kind letter yesterday. On the whole I cannot complain of any lack of letters. Thank you all. Brother Kolia has written a charmingly kind letter. There is a strong possibility of my being invited here for next season, and I have been offered very good terms. Should I accept? If I do I shall bring Ziloty and Sapelnikov with me.

Please pass on the second letter to Brother Kolia. I hope you will all wait for me in Peter. Ask Kolia not to leave before I return. Good-bye! I embrace you all. Tell Bob I have received his charming one.

Yours

P. Tchaikovsky

Modest wrote to his brother: 'Your cooled feelings towards *Yolanta* have very much upset me. I fear that it is my fault, and I do not find strength to continue this work – everything seems so bad that I have lost the desire to finish it. I will, of course, finish it, but with much more effort than if I knew you were pleased with me.'

[593]   TO MODEST TCHAIKOVSKY   New York
                                        29 April–11 May 1891

Modia!

I have just received your letter of the 26th. Where did you get the idea that I have become cool towards *Yolanta*. It is because I am more than ever in love with her that I put her off until next year. I want to make a *chef d'oeuvre* out of her, and I can, but to do so I must not hurry. When could I have done it

properly? You can answer this yourself. It would have been too great a strain (before now), and the result would have been an inferior work.
Going to Niagara now. No time to write any more. I kiss and embrace you.

P. Tchaikovsky

[594]   TO MODEST TCHAIKOVSKY   Utica
                                                             On the way to Niagara
                                                             29 April–11 May 1891

I had no time this morning to say that you misunderstood my letters from Rouen to you and Vsevoloisky. More than ever I am in love with the subject of *Yolanta* and your libretto is excellent. But when I was in Rouen I was depicting soldiers, dolls, gingerbread characters, etc., in music and saw that I had still a lot of work to do on the ballet and that I could only start on the opera when I had finished that. I realized that either on my way to America, or when I was there, and even on my way back, I would not have the opportunity to work. I also realized that I would become desperate knowing the impossibility of finishing the work I had accepted. That was when I stopped loving *Yolanta*, so as to be able to love her passionately again later on. As soon as I had made my decision I loved *Yolanta* again. You will see; I shall write an opera to make everyone cry – but only for the 1892–93 season.

I am writing this letter in the buffet-car – the only place where you are allowed to smoke. There are also small desks here where you can write telegrams and letters. The train is going at a terrific speed and it is difficult to write. The comforts and amenities of American trains are wonderful, but in some ways ours are better. No stops at all here. You sit, and sit, and get tired of sitting. Shall describe them properly in my diary. Had lunch in the restaurant car. It was long and plentiful, but bad, which is usual everywhere here. I embrace you. Tonight at 10 o'clock I shall be in Niagara.

P. Tchaikovsky

[595]   TO VLADIMIR DAVYDOV   New York
                                                             2 May 1891

Things have gone so far that it is quite impossible to write letters. Not a free moment, and I scarcely manage to write my diary. I made a trip to Niagara. As soon as I returned I had to visit one Mayer at his country house and pay some visits in the few free hours I had left. Then I was invited out to lunch. Altogether I have been frightfully busy, and I am completely numb with exhaustion. Tonight I have to be at a big dinner, and then leave at midnight for Baltimore; tomorrow a rehearsal and concert there, the day after that Washington, then Philadelphia, then two days here, where all my time is already booked, and at last, on the morning of the 21st, I leave. Oh God! Will I ever come to that happy moment! ! !

492

In about a week after you receive this letter I will be with you! ! ! This seems an unattainable, impossible happiness! I try to think of it as little as possible, to have enough strength to stand up to the last insufferable days. But in spite of all I feel that I shall remember America with love. Everybody has been wonderfully kind.

Here are a few newspaper cuttings. Shall bring many more with me. I think that you will all much prefer reading my diary than getting only short news from my letters.

I embrace you all.

P. Tchaikovsky

In only one week! ! !

[596]   TO ANATOLI TCHAIKOVSKY   Atlantic Ocean
                                                      14–26 May 1891

Golubchik Tolia!

I am sitting in my cabin, writing to you on the sixth day at sea. No details about my stay in America, for, as I told you before you will have my diary soon after this letter reaches you. I can only say that in spite of exhaustion, strain, and an immense output of effort, I am perfectly well and even think that this trip was very good for my health. The impressions I bring are very pleasant as I enjoyed great success there and was spoiled by everyone. They insisted that I should come again next winter, and the terms would be most profitable; but I want to live quietly in Russia for at least a year and not go anywhere except to the Caucasus, if you are still there in the autumn. I am expecting news about your work and position in a fever of impatience.

They assured me in New York that there cannot be bad weather at sea in May. However, to my dismay I experienced a very bad storm that lasted for two days. Now, thank God, it has calmed down. I cannot express my intense longing for home, and I count the days and hours left until I reach Russia.

It is Tuesday today, and 3 o'clock in the afternoon! On Friday morning I shall be in Hamburg and will send off this letter at once; on the same evening I continue my journey to Petersburg where I hope to be in the evening of Sunday the 19th. Write to Maidanovo (Klin, Province of Moscow).

I embrace you very, very hard. Also Panichka, Tata and Kokodeks.

Yours

P. Tchaikovsky

[597] TO IPPOLIT TCHAIKOVSKY   Klin
District of Moscow
29 May 1891

Dear friend Ippolit!

I am sure that you and Sonia would like to know where and how I am. I hasten
to let you know that I returned home today. I left New York on 9–21 May and
was at sea for only 7½ days. Both journeys were without any complications in
spite of storms each way. From Hamburg (I sailed on a German boat), I
travelled straight to Petersburg where I passed 8 very pleasant days. Although
I was most perfectly received in New York, and in spite of having seen much
in America that was interesting I longed to get back home and cannot say how
happy I was when I found myself in Russia. Now I am going to work hard – I
have to compose a ballet and an opera for the 1892–3 season and also write
several other works which are already planned. . . .

I am back in Maidanovo. Health excellent. I embrace you and kiss Sonia's
hand. Tassia too I hug to my heart.

Yours

P. Tchaikovsky

[598] TO MODEST TCHAIKOVSKY   [Maidanovo]
17 June 1891

Thank you for your letter. I'm glad that you feel happy in Grankino. I am also
content, but work does not progress as fast as before. Different obstacles get
in my way. Yesterday, for example, Simon appeared for the whole day to play
his opera which, to tell the truth, is very interesting. In the evenings I
sometimes go to play vint with Novikova who is back and whom I was very
pleased to see. It seems that I like Novichikha much more than I thought I did.
Alexei is getting better and the weather is lovely. Letters smother me, and
they too take time away from my work. Have stopped drinking vodka and am
frightfully pleased that I can get on without this poison. If I only could get
used to smoking less! ! !

I embrace you and Kolia.

Yours

P. Tchaikovsky

A. Y. Simon's opera *Rolla* (Op. 40, libretto by A. M. Nevsky) was first performed at
the Bolshoi Theatre, on 29 April 1892. Tchaikovsky attended several rehearsals.

TO VLADIMIR DAVYDOV

Town of Klin
District of Moscow
25 June 1891

Bob!

As promised I can report that I finished the sketches for the ballet yesterday evening. You remember how, when you were here, I boasted that I had only about five days work left. How wrong I was, for I barely managed it in two weeks. No! the old man is definitely deteriorating. Not only is his hair thinning and as white as snow; not only is his teeth falling out and refusing to chew; not only is his sight deteriorating and his eyes getting tired; not only are his legs beginning to drag – but the only faculty he has is beginning to fade and disappear. The ballet is much worse than *The Sleeping Beauty*. Of this there is no doubt. It remains to be seen what the opera will be like.

If I come to the conclusion that I can only serve *du réchauffé* at my musical banquets I shall definitely stop composing.

And so the ballet is finished. The next three days I shall correct all sorts of piano scores – of old and reissued works – and on the 28th, the day before my Saint's day, I shall go off to Petersburg where I plan to stay about three days. On my return I will get going on *King René's Daughter*. We will see how it goes. The pattern of my life has been the same as usual. In the evenings I sometimes play vingt at Novikova's or at Mme Gourko's – a very nice lady who lives here. I do it because I get very tired if I read in the evenings – it always results in a frightful headache. But unless I read I don't know how else to kill time at night. This (I mean headaches as a result of solitude), is becoming a serious obstacle to life in the country, which made me decide to look for a place to live that was not in the suburbs of Petersburg but in the town itself. In general I think it would be simpler to settle in Petersburg for good. Just the possibility alone to be able to see more of you is so vitally important for me. I would love to know what you are doing. Write at least a few words. . . .

Embrace your father hard from me. Yurka and Nata also.

Yours

P. Tchaikovsky

TO ANATOLI TCHAIKOVSKY

[Maidanovo]
8 July 1891

Golubchik Tolia!

Just imagine! Back home I found twenty-seven letters which I have been answering and answering without stopping. So do not be surprised if this is short and don't be angry that I did not visit you in Reval during all the time I was in Peter. I had to attend to a lot of formalities concerning my pension – a lengthy procedure. As soon as I have finished answering all my letters – some of them business ones (about a second visit to America with a church choir) – I will get down to the opera seriously. If all goes well I hope to finish the sketches in a month and then it will be possible to take a trip to Reval. From what you and Sania [Litke] say I can judge that you will like it in Reval in spite of many difficulties which you have already mentioned. I think all one has to do is to behave with caution and tact; and as you are by nature very tactful you will easily manage to get out of every difficulty. Government Service is that sort of thing where you, sometimes, have to *faire bonne mine au mauvais jeu*. It cannot be helped. I am sure you would be interested to read Valuev's diary which is being published in the *Russkaia Starina*. He was for a time Governor of the Baltic provinces and gives many interesting details. At that time Suvorov ruled there, 'an absolute idiot with a liberal lining'. Even Pobedonoszev's attitude is better than Suvorov's.

I embrace you, will write again soon.

Yours

P. Tchaikovsky

Count P. A. Valuev (1814–90) became Minister of the Interior in 1861 after having administered Latvia, Lithuania and Estonia. He played a considerable part in the Great Reforms initiated by Alexander II, and was a prime mover in the intention to establish a consultative assembly – which was, however, frustrated by the assassination of the Czar in 1881 – Valuev's Diary for the years 1847–60 was published in *Russkaia Starina* (*Old Russia*) in 1890. Alexander Suvorov, grandson of the famous general of that name, was Governor of the Western Provinces in 1848.

In the last two years of his life Tchaikovsky was much interested in the works of Spinoza, especially the *Correspondence* (pub. by Preobrajensky, in St Petersburg, in 1891) and the *Ethics* (pub. by Preobajensky, in Moscow, in 1892. These works with Tchaikovsky's annotations are in his library at Klin.

[601] TO LEV DAVYDOV   [Maidanovo]
                                                           11 July 1891

... I would love to come to Kamenka in August, but fear that it will take time off *Yolanta* which is going to take two months more to finish. I'm not looking for sympathy or understanding, but quite honestly I really seem to be at a turning point in my creative work. My opera goes on lazily, with difficulty; and what is worst of all, I notice at every step that I am repeating myself. *Du réchauffé!* ! ! ! But in any case I shall finish it and if I then see that things are not as they were I shall definitely stop composing. I shall always find something else to do.

I embrace you with all my might.

Yours

P. Tchaikovsky

I have started to seriously study Spinoza and bought a mass of books about him and his works. The more I read the more I admire that man.

[602] TO VLADIMIR DAVYDOV

Klin, District of Moscow
22 July 1891

I am definitely coming to Kamenka, for I feel from your letter that you would like me to come, and also because I have a great desire to see you. Everything depends upon *Yolanta*. Up till now it was going very slowly, partly because of the corrections I had to make on the full score of *Onegin* which Yurgenson is re-publishing. It had a lot of my own mistakes and a multitude of Yurgenson's, and it was a job that poisoned my life. At last it came to an end, and I took the score to Moscow. So I can now give all my attention to the opera. Please tell Modest that the deeper I dive into the work the more pleased I am with his libretto. Very well done and the poetry is sometimes quite beautiful.

And so, when I can enjoy a peaceful and undisturbed period for composition to the full, when the work has progressed so far that my heart can be at rest, or – even better still – when, with God's help, it is completely finished – which I hope will be in about three weeks time; then I'll go to Kamenka. On my way I will stay with Nikolai Illich where I am awaited with some impatience. Kokodeks (I mean Kolia Peresleny) stayed here a whole week. As he immediately got to know all the residents in the dachas and spent all day with them, appearing only at meals, he was not in the least in my way and I enjoyed his stay very much. A very jolly and nice person. We went also to Moscow together.

You are not at all like an empty suitcase. There are plenty of things in it but they are still kept in disorder and it will take time to decide and sort out those that are important. However, stop worrying, for it will all sort itself out. Enjoy your youth and learn to cherish time; the longer I live the more frightened I get at the aimless dissipation of this priceless element of life. This rather high-flown sentence is nothing more than the advice to *read as much as possible*. You have an excellent gift of assimilating what you have read, I mean, you do not forget it but put it away in a sort of mental store-room until you need it. I do not possess such a store-room. To be honest – no memory at all. Am sending several numbers of the *Fliegende Blätter*.

I embrace you, my idol!

P.T.

Ask Modia to write about his impressions of Kamenka.

[603] TO MODEST TCHAIKOVSKY

[Maidanovo]
25 July 1891

It is a long time since I have written to you Modia! And this in spite of having plenty to do with you. The libretto is excellent. There is only one fault, but that is not of your doing. I find that between the duet about 'Light' and the end there is not enough music, only explanations of the action. I fear that this will be dull; but I may be mistaken. I did not start from the beginning but from the scene between Yolanta and Vaudemont. You did the scene very well and the music could have been magnificent; but it seems to me that my composition at that point is not up to standard. What is disgusting is that I have started to repeat myself and a lot in this scene reminds me of *Charodeika*??!!

However we shall see. I am more and more assailed by doubts, but I do not think it is a general decline. What I ought to do is to leave the theatre for a time and write symphonies, piano pieces, quartets, and so on. I am tired of writing ballets and operas, but that does not mean I am finished. I hope not. It is funny, when I was composing the ballet I thought it was no good but was sure that I would do something good with the opera; and now it seems to me that the ballet is good but the opera nothing much. You know yourself how it is; composers make mistakes in assessing their own works during the act of composition, yet what seems bad to them actually is quite good.

A sad occurrence! When I went to bed yesterday I wanted to wind my watch and found it was not there. It must have been stolen by a clever and bold thief who had studied my habits, for the only time when the watch could have been taken was when I was taking my after-dinner walk and Alexei was resting in his room. Everything possible has been done and long telegrams describing the watch have been sent to Moscow. I had an awful night, for I love this watch [a gift from Mme von Meck] like a human being.

I also feel ashamed for Bob's sake, for I have left it to him in my Will. Last winter I was going to give it to him and now I am very sorry that I did not do so.

No definite plans in view before finishing the opera. All I have decided upon is to visit brother Kolia and Kamenka even if it is for a short time. Embrace Bob and all the others.

Yours

P. Tchaikovsky

Tchaikovsky had just received a copy of the *Revue des deux Mondes*, for January 1891, with an article by André Chevrillon, 'Dans l'Inde'.

[604] TO VLADIMIR DAVYDOV   [Maidanovo]
                                                   1 August 1891

Today I am sending you, my Golubchik, a very good number of the *Fliegende Blätter*. Rudia must have arrived by now so if you do not understand any of it he will explain. I am reading in your Chevrillon about Ceylon and cannot share your enthusiasm. The latest French writers have begun to write in an awfully

affected manner. I mean an affectation of simplicity nearly as irritating as all
the noisy phrases, epithets, and antitheses, of Victor Hugo. All that your
favourite describes – actually not without talent and quite life-like – could be
told in simple, ordinary language, and not in short, unfinished sentences or
long periods with embellishments and an unnatural use of subjects, predicates,
compliments etc. It is very easy to parody these gentlemen, for instance:

> Une serviette de table négligemment attachée à son cou, il dégustait . . .
> tout alentout des mouches, avides, grouillantes, d'un noir inquiétant,
> volaient. . . . Nul bruit sinon un claquement de machoirs énervant. . . . Une
> odeur moite, fétide, écoeurante, lourde, répandait un je ne sais quoi
> d'animal, de carnacier dans l'air. Point de lumière. . . . Un rayon de soleil
> couchant pénétrant comme par hasard dans la chambre nue et basse éclairait
> par-ci par-là tantôt la figure blême du maître engurgitant sa soupe tantôt
> celle du valet moustachu, à trait kalmouks, stupide et rampant. . . . On
> devinait un idiot servi par un idiot . . . 9 heures. . . . Un morne silence
> régnait. . . . Les mouches fatiguées, somnolentes devenues moins agiles se
> dispersaient. . . . Et là-bas dans le lointain par la fenêtre on voyait une lune,
> grimaçante, énorme, rouge, surgir sur l'horizon embrasé. . . . Il mangeait
> toujours. . . . Puis l'estomac bourré, la face écarlate, l'oeil hagard, il se leva
> et sortit . . . etc. etc.

I have described my tonight's supper; if I am not mistaken, it is Zola – the
son of a bitch – who has invented this style of writing.

My work has suddenly started to get on well, now I know that *Yolanta* is not
going to stick her face in the mud. Has Rudia arrived? Has Modest left?

Embrace and give my regards to everybody.

Yours

P. Tchaikovsky

[605] TO MODEST TCHAIKOVSKY   Maidanovo
                                                  7 August 1891

Although the day of my departure to Ukolovo and Kamenka is coming nearer
Yolanta is still not finished. I shall probably have to postpone it until my
return, which will be much better than spoiling it by hurrying and finishing
it badly. Anyhow there will not be much left to do. I am now writing the scene
between the King and Ebn-Haky. After that, all I have to do is the scene in
which Robert and Vaudemont arrive and wake up Yolanta. The duet and all
the rest is written. These last few days I have been in the proper kind of mood
and have written without effort and with pleasure. I have changed a few of
the words, for the sake of my rhythm, which did not fit your rhymes. But this
will only be in the *Klavierauszug*. In the published libretto it will be as you
wrote it. For instance when Laura and Brigitta sing about flowers it goes this
way:

Here are the cornflowers and the kingcups,
here mimosas
as well as roses
and flowering stocks.
Lilies of the valley, lilies of spring,
common balsam
and white jasmine,
all full of aroma.

I dare make the statement that this number is really good and will please
everybody. On the whole I am now pleased with myself. What do you think – I
have promised to be in six places: (1) At the Peterhof again (important for the
dinner with Stachelberg). (2) In Reval. (3) At the Bazilevskys (Sasha is
imploring me in a very sweet letter to come). (4) In Ukolovo. (5) In Kamenka.
(6) In Taganrog. Also I have half promised Kashkin that I will invite him to
come in August, and I have also invited Annette to come then. Then Menter and
Vassia expect me in the autumn and I have promised you and Kolia to stay
in Grankino. How am I going to manage? I honestly do not know. However,
two things are certain: Ukolovo and Kamenka. I hope to be in Kamenka about
the 20th. There is also the fact that I shall have to go to Hamburg in
September!!! Judging by your letter the disappearance of my watch has not
made any impression upon any of you.

Good-bye.

P. Tchaikovsky

Anatoli Tchaikovsky was transferred this year from Tiflis to Reval (now Tallin), in
Estonia, where he was also Vice-Governor. Tchaikovsky met the impressionist poet
A. A. Fet (real name, Shenshin: 1820–92) on 18 August, in token of which the poet
subsequently presented him with a poem. On 5 September Tchaikovsky finished
Yolanta and began the scoring of *Voievoda*, in Moscow.

[606]   TO ANATOLI TCHAIKOVSKY   [Maidanovo]
                                         2 September 1891

My dear Tolia!

I have just returned home. Very pleased with my trip. I very much enjoyed
Ukolovo and life at Kolia's. I had four charming days there. We went to the
Korennaia Pustyn (Monastery) and one day we visited Fet. This was my first
meeting with him and I thought him very interesting. He has the reputation of
being silly and this has made him as famous as his poetry, but I did not
notice anything of that kind. The garden is wonderful.

From Kolia's I went to Kamenka. You were there recently so there is nothing
new to say. The weather was awful – impossibly hot, stuffy, dusty and dry.
No! Our north is definitely more attractive. Everybody was well. Modest is

there too. He has written a play [see p. 515], which is interesting and clever, but as it concerns only the Petersburg *beau monde* it is not of general interest. From there I hurried back home. I stayed one day in Moscow correcting proofs. The celebrations of the 25th anniversary of the Moscow Conservatoire are taking place but I did not stay for them because of my present awkward relationship with them.

I found the most boring but urgent work waiting for me here. I must correct the score of *The Queen of Spades* for Hamburg as soon as possible. I am writing to Pania to say that I will not be able to be in Moscow and will suggest that she comes here for a day. I cannot say for sure when I shall go to Hamburg, but I shall have to be in Peter in the near future and shall certainly come to Reval for a day or two.

Forgive this haste. Masses of letters and business.

Yours

P. Tchaikovsky

[607]   TO ANATOLI TCHAIKOVSKY   [Maidanovo]
                                        22 September 1891

My dear Tolia!

It would be interesting to know about Pania's move to Reval, how you have settled there, and how she likes the town? . . . I hope, with God's help, to come there but cannot say exactly when. My movements are at a standstill; not only because of my work, but because I have to be in Moscow for the production of *The Queen of Spades* and also because I am extremely short of cash. I have to wait for money to accumulate from the theatres; but unfortunately, first the poor little Grand Duchess died (and there was Court mourning), then the artists were ill and *Onegin* has not been on either in Moscow or in Petersburg. All the same I reckon that I shall get plenty of money from the theatres this year.

I have just finished my symphonic ballad *Voievoda*, and am very pleased with it. You must, without fail, come to Petersburg for the concert of the Musical Society which I am conducting. It will be in November.

Laroche is staying with me. He sleeps, eats, plays piano duets with me and – nothing more. Have started to orchestrate the opera. The weather is heavenly. Laroche begs to be remembered to you. I embrace you and kiss Pania's and Tania's little hands.

Yours

P. Tchaikovsky

TO ANATOLI TCHAIKOVSKY [Maidanovo]
1 October 1891

Tolia!

Forgive me that I have been so long in answering your letter. I am hard at
work and also had to go to Moscow on business. I fear, Tolia, that unless
something extraordinary happens I shall not be able to see you before the
middle of November. At the moment my time is very precious as I must finish
the orchestration of both the ballet and the opera this winter. At the same
time, from 15 October I shall have to be in Moscow for the rehearsals of *The
Queen of Spades* which is to be performed on 28 October. On 6 November
I am conducting a concert arranged by Ziloty and on the 23rd I conduct in
Petersburg. Between these two last dates I shall come to see you in Reval for
a few days. It is funny that now that you are so much nearer to me I see you
just as rarely as when you lived in Tiflis. But I reckon this is to be my last
winter in the country. Next year I shall settle in Petersburg and then it will
be possible to see each other really often. . . .

Laroche is still here; all he does is eat and sleep. But I greatly appreciate his
presence, for he reads to me in the evenings – a real rest, relaxation, and help
to the headaches which I get towards the evening if I have worked hard.

I embrace you all with all my love.

Yours

P. Tchaikovsky

Pania! I kiss your hands.

I also kiss my sweet Tatochka.

P.T.

TO MODEST TCHAIKOVSKY [Maidanovo]
7 October 1891

Modia!

Since you left nothing new has happened. I am hard at work. Mania [Laroche]
is doing nothing. He is very gloomy, and has never been as bad as this before.
It is quite obvious that he wants to work and earn something but cannot. All
my efforts to make him dictate to me as before came to naught. My attempts
to bring pressure on him twice brought tears and absolute despair.

I wish at least one of the three of you would write. However, I too am being
lazy. Another week here then to Moscow. Will conduct my *Voievoda* there on
6 November. Shall not come to Petersburg before the date of the concert there.

And now, good-bye!

P. Tchaikovsky

[610] TO MODEST TCHAIKOVSKY

Maidanovo
20 October 1891

Modia!

You probably imagine me in Moscow when I am still here. As usual things in Moscow are never done on time. They have not sent for me as the rehearsals will only start at the end of next week, and if it had not been for Colonne and his wife, who wrote me a charming letter begging me to come to his concert, I could have stayed here and worked for much longer. In spite of working hard as usual I still have quite a lot to do on *Yolanta*. (Actually the name Yolanta is wrong: it is a French name and ought to be Iolande.) Mania made such a dismal impression with his hypochondria that I not only do not miss him but find it a relief that I have not got to look at a deeply unhappy man whom I cannot help any more. . . .

Tell me honestly, would you like to come to Moscow for *The Queen of Spades*. If you do I will gladly pay for your fare and lodging. What if you also brought Kolia and Bob? If I do not get a letter from you today I shall send a telegram.

I kiss and embrace you all.

P. Tchaikovsky

[611] TO ANATOLI TCHAIKOVSKY

Moscow
27 October 1891

My dear Tolia!

It is very difficult to write letters. My head is in a whirl from the usual bustle that takes place during the staging of an opera, but the rehearsals are coming on very well. Sionizkaia is singing Liza (I find her better than Medea) but Medvedev — Hermann will not be as good as Figner. All the others are on the same level (as in St Petersburg); the stage sets inferior, but not bad. My concert in Petersburg will take place not on 23 November but on 14 December, which necessitates a change in my plans. I shall go to Petersburg on 7 November and to you on the 9th or 10th for a day or two. I do want to have at least a glimpse of you.

For God's sake arrange my incognito as carefully as possible. Afterwards, I shall go back to the country to work for three weeks and then we shall see each other again.

I embrace you with all my strength. No more today, I must hurry to a rehearsal.

P. Tchaikovsky

The Moscow premiere of *The Queen of Spades* took place at the Bolshoi Theatre on 4 November. The conductor was I. K. Altany; the cast was: Hermann — Medvedev,

Tomsky – Korsov, Prince Elezky – Khokhlov, Liza – Sionizkaia, Countess – Krutikova. After the performance the composer was fêted and presented with laurel wreaths. (Cf. Letters 572–3.)

On 6 November Ziloty conducted the first performance of the symphonic poem *Voievoda*. While it was in rehearsal Tchaikovsky felt that it was not a good work, and that the players thought so too. Although the first night audience gave no hint of lack of appreciation, he asked for the score and tore it up, saying, 'One must not write such muck'. He also asked that the parts should be collected and brought to him. Ziloty, however, managed to effect the preservation of the parts, so that the work was reconstituted after the composer's death.

[612]   TO ANATOLI TCHAIKOVSKY   Moscow
                                                 8 November 1891

My dear Tolia!

Circumstances have changed – I shall have to conduct in Petersburg on 1 December at a charity concert in aid of the starving. If I went to Petersburg and Reval now it would take too much time and, as I would have to return to Maidanovo after my journey to you, it would be too expensive – I must be careful with money just now. Also I have become so tired with all the worries about the opera and the concert that I felt quite ill yesterday, and I must rest in the country and finish the orchestration of the opera. What I mean is, that I shall come to Reval two weeks later than I intended, about 25 November. I long with all my heart to come and see you and am very upset that I had to postpone my trip but it cannot be otherwise. Please forgive me and don't be cross that I did not keep my promise.

The Queen of Spades was very successful. The ensemble is above praise; Altany wonderful; the stage sets sumptuous and only a little inferior to those in Petersburg. I liked Sionizkaia best of all. Medvedev was good but the memory of Figner will spoil anyone else's performance. It was all a great success. The performance took place on 3 November and the concert on the 6th, and there was great applause. My new composition, *Voievoda*, is no good and I am going to destroy it. I fear that this is a sign of the decline of my powers, although I must say that Taneev who is doing the *Klavierauszug* of my opera said it is very good.

I have stayed for another three days for the sake of the artists who are giving a dinner in my honour. On Sunday I go home, and shall rest, work a little, and after finishing the opera come to see you.

Forgive for writing hurriedly but, although I am well again, I still feel very tired.

P. Tchaikovsky

I kiss you. I press Tata and Pania to my heart.

Maidanovo
14 December 1891

I leave for Moscow today and on Monday for Kiev, Warsaw, and so on. Note the following addresses:

(1) Up to 23 December I am staying in Kiev. *Address:* Grand Hotel.

(2) Until 3 January – Warsaw. *Address*: Europeiskaia Gostiniza [European Hotel].

(3) About 7–20 January (our style), in Hamburg. *Address:* Hofrat Pollini, für P. Tchaikovsky, Hamburg.

(4) From 22 January to 1 February in Prague. *Address:* Hotel de Saxe, Praga, Böhmen.

In the interval between Hamburg and Prague I will go to Amsterdam and the Hague. Anyway I will write in transit. Tomorrow I shall find out from Yurgenson how much you are entitled to from the performances and will send the money through Osip Ivanovich. But as you will give this away and I am afraid that you will need money during the holidays I want you, in case of emergency, to take 100 roubles from Osip Ivanovich. If you don't want to go yourself send Nara. Forgive me for it being so little but I am planning to buy a house in Klin and shall need all the money I can lay my hands on. Alexei and I went to have a look at the house yesterday. We liked it, and I do want to purchase it and have a corner of my own. I shall never be able to buy an estate.

From next winter I definitely want to live in Petersburg during the winter months but at the same time to have my own home in Klin (my own corner). Do not worry about the beauties of nature. Maidanovo is also nothing special. I shall have many more possibilities of pleasant walks in Klin. Also, after I am gone, I want to leave Alexei at least some sort of home.

Back to your business transactions. You can now copy out the libretto, send it to Yurgenson, and ask for a good fee. I am enclosing the libretto for you to do this. On my return I shall receive more money both from Petersburg and Moscow and will give you something over and above the usual sum. In case you get very short of money during my absence ask for some from Osip Ivanovich. I beg you not to be afraid to say when you want money. You know very well that I find it more of a pleasure to help than just a duty towards a near relative. . . .

I have absolutely no wish to go anywhere. I have orchestrated the Introduction to *Yolanta* and have redone the sextet in the rough. I shall copy out all the corrections on my journey. The next letter will be to Bob, then to Kolia.

A thousand kisses to them and everybody else.

P. Tchaikovsky

TO MODEST TCHAIKOVSKY [Moscow]
16 December 1891

I do not understand why there is no answer to the telegram I sent yesterday
to Bob. He probably replied to Klin! My fault, I ought to have added that I
would wait for the answer in Moscow. As a result I will have to leave without
knowing the outcome of the rehearsal. Yurgenson has asked for my fee for
the performance but nothing is ever done here as simply and quickly as in
Petersburg. There can easily be a delay. So do not wonder why he has not sent
your money at once.

I spent the whole of yesterday at Taneev's, putting *Yolanta* in order, and she
is quite finished now. But Moscow makes me glum. Good-bye. Expecting news
from you in Kiev.

P. Tchaikovsky

Mascagni's *Cavalleria rusticana*, a prize-winning one-act opera, was first performed
in Rome on 17 May 1890 and it quickly commanded attention throughout Europe. On
31 December 1891 Tchaikovsky wrote to N. Konradi: 'Yesterday I saw the celebrated
Cavalleria rusticana for the first time. This opera is very interesting both as regards
the music and the choice of subject. Let Modia find me a subject as good as this.'

[615] TO MODEST TCHAIKOVSKY Warsaw
3 January 1892

Can only write a few words about myself. My concert took place yesterday
at the Warsaw Theatre. The orchestra, which has learned to like me, played
beautifully. Barzevich played my concerto with extraordinary brilliance and
Friede sang perfectly. I visit the Friede family – extremely likable people –
every day. On the day before yesterday Grossmann gave a gala dinner in my
honour. The Polish Countesses were charming and kind to me, and everybody,
more or less, fêted me. With the exception, that is, of Gourko who took no
notice of me. Fania [Tchaikovsky] appeared yesterday. I am on the whole very
pleased but this does not prevent me from feeling bored and wishing to get
back home. Off to Hamburg in three hours time. I shall have to conduct
Onegin myself since Pollini insists on it.

I embrace and kiss with love all of you.

P. Tchaikovsky

Go to the theatre every night. Twice saw *Cavalleria Rusticana*. Makes a strong
impression. Went also to the drama theatre. Very good acting.

[616]   TO VLADIMIR DAVYDOV   Hamburg
                                                          7–19 January 1892

... Arrived the day before yesterday. Travelled in fear because Pollini
insisted that I should stay with him and I hate not living in an hotel. It was
lucky for me that one of his guests got stuck at his house with influenza and
there was no room for me.

I spent the evening with Pollini and had supper with him. The only rehearsal
took place yesterday and the performance was today. The opera had been
perfectly rehearsed and quite nicely produced, but because of the changes in
the recitatives which result from the use of the German text I could not help
making mistakes, and in spite of everyone trying to persuade me I refused to
conduct for fear of spoiling everything. Besides, the German conductor is not
second-rate but quite a genius and is longing to conduct the first night.
I heard him direct a wonderful performance of *Tannhäuser*.

The singers, orchestra, Pollini, stage directors, conductor (his name is Mahler),
are all in love with *Eugene Onegin*; but I still wonder if the Hamburg public
will be immediately attracted by it. There are quite a lot of funny things in the
way it is being staged, in the costumes, sets etc.; most comic is the way in
which the mazurka is danced in the third scene – this is impossible to describe.
The singer who has the part of Tatiana is charming. Baritone nothing special,
tenor so-so; the choruses are good, the orchestra excellent. Tomorrow evening
at 11.00 I go straight to Paris to try and kill time in a pleasant way before
going to Holland.

So I shall be in Paris about (I say 'about' because I am not quite sure if I will
leave tomorrow) 10–22 January in the evening and shall stay nearly two weeks.
I want to try to live there incognito and work on my sextet. According to our
style, on the 29th and 30th I shall conduct in Holland and leave for home on
the 31st. Oh joy! Oh, happiness!

I shall write tomorrow or the day after about the first night. I embrace you
uncountable times.

My address: Paris, 14 Richepanse.

Yours

P.T.

[617]   TO ANATOLI, AND PRASKOVIA TCHAIKOVSKAIA
                                                          Hamburg
                                                          8–20 January 1892

My dears, Pania and Tolia!

Although Pania has probably left Reval by now, here is the news in brief. My
Warsaw concert was a great success and in general, I have been very much
[*lacuna*]. . . . I arrived here from there after a day in Berlin. On the day after

507

I arrived there was a rehearsal which I conducted. As this was the only rehearsal, and the German text troubled me, I refused to conduct on the first night for fear of making a blunder. Besides, the conductor here is excellent and can only improve the performance. Concerning the musical side the performance is very good. As to the staging and the sets – all one can say is that they are quite tolerable, though there were a few funny things about the costumes and sets. Tatiana is charming, graceful and very attractive. Onegin has a good voice. Lensky is also not bad at all. The orchestra and chorus are first class. I had considerable success. I was called out after each scene; but without enthusiasm – more with a hint of coldness and distrust.

Today I am going straight to Paris, where I shall stay about two weeks. From there to Holland and in the very beginning of February I shall be back in Russia.

I kiss and embrace you without end.

P.T.

[618] TO MODEST TCHAIKOVSKY   Paris
                                        10–22 January 1892

Yesterday I arrived in Paris to the great astonishment and delight of the Béliards. Both they and all their staff are well and happy. I shall try to live as I did nine years ago, absolutely incognito. I spent the evening with Ziloty and his wife who are also here in Richepanse. Today I had lunch with them and then returned to my rooms where I am answering all the letters which have accumulated, and which are the reason for my writing only a short one to you just to give you the news. I presume Tolia and Pania are in Petersburg; let them know I am well and content. I am going to the Palais Royal tonight. For the most part I intend to spend my time at the theatres and in amusing myself as much as possible – to deaden the ever-present intense longing to return home.

I embrace you all.

P.T.

Pollini is determined to produce *Yolanta* next season. He is delighted with the choice of the subject.

[619] TO VLADIMIR DAVYDOV   Paris
                                        12–24 January 1892

I feel an awful fool. Here I have another two weeks without anything to help me kill time. I thought this would be easier in Paris than anywhere else but, except for the first day, I have been bored. Since yesterday I do not know what to think up to be free of the worry and boredom that come from idleness. Correcting the text which I have brought with me will not occupy me for more than two or three days. If it were not for Sapelnikov and Menter, who would be frightfully hurt if I did not go to Holland, I would fly straight back home with delight. However, it cannot be done, and I must be patient. Luckily Sasha and Vera Ziloty are here at the same hotel. If it were also not for them I could not have held out. Am still keeping my incognito.

On my way here I hoped to enjoy the Paris theatres but in spite of excellent acting and an amusing plot the very first performance (of *M. l'Abbé* at the Palais Royal) made me feel bored and dejected and it was with an effort that I stayed to the end. Last night I went to the Folies Bergère (a sort of huge café chantant), and also felt frightfully bored. The Russian clown Durov showed 230 trained rats.

It is curious how the Parisians show their love of Russia. You will find nothing Russian in any concert, opera-house, or theatre, and whilst *Esclarmonde* is being produced at home the only sign of Russophilism in art here is the clown Durov with 230 rats!!!

This makes me furious; to be truthful, partly because of my own interests. Why, for example, does not Colonne, who is now at the head of the Grand Opera, produce *The Queen of Spades* or a ballet? He discussed this with me in the autumn and, so he said, because of this invited Petipas. All empty words. Petipas has been invited not for my ballet but for a new French one. Say: 'Foo! What a shame to be so envious and petty!' It is indeed.

For want of something better to do I am now reading the *Bête humaine* by Zola, which I did not dare read before. I do not understand how one can take Zola seriously and think of him as a great writer. What could be more impossible and false than the foundation of this novel? There are some scenes where reality is described truly and vividly; but the substance itself is so false that one cannot — even for a moment — take a lively interest in the actions and circumstances of the characters. It is just a criminal novel like Gaboriau's spiced with obscenities. However, if you have not read it I need not go into details.

I often think of you and see you in my dreams, usually looking sad and depressed. This has added a feeling of compassion to my love for you and makes me love you even more. Oh God! How I want to see you this very minute. Write me a letter from College during some boring lecture and send it to this address (14, Rue Richepanse). It will still reach me as I am staying here for nearly two weeks.

I embrace you with mad tenderness.

Yours

P. Tchaikovsky

Tchaikovsky found the tour too much and, refusing to go to Holland, returned to Maidonovo by way of St Petersburg. Anatoli Tchaikovsky was in Samara on his way to the district of Tobolsk, in Siberia, where he was to represent the special committee set up to consider aid for the starving. See Letter 612. The condition of the peasantry of Russia at this time was desperate. In the process of industrialization rural economy had been neglected. Some peasants had left the land, and had lost contact with those they had left behind, to seek work in the factories. The zemstvos (local councils elected on limited franchise) in the country were now under the most rigorous control, as was every other aspect of communal life. The famine of 1891 which affected the twenty most fertile provinces of Russia was of great severity, and in its wake came a wave of cholera (see Letters 628, 629, 670). Thousands of people died and distress was universal. Not only was the central government unable to cope with a situation which it did not acknowledge to exist; it also forbade voluntary bodies to be constituted to render aid. So great was the outcry, however, that this edict had to be revoked. There were hundreds of welfare committees, on one of which Anatoli was called to serve.

[620] TO ANATOLI TCHAIKOVSKY   Maidanovo
                                                 9 February 1892

I was very happy, dear Tolia, to get your letter from Samara. I read it with lively interest and gave it to Modest, who is staying here on his way, to read. It is a pity you could not come but I understand that it was a little complicated. As for me, I am living in Maidanovo with real pleasure and enjoy the best winter month of the year. I adore these clear frosty days when the sun begins to give some little warmth and when you can feel a hint of spring.

My work is going on so well that the full score of the ballet is ready and Modest is taking it to Petersburg today. Volodia Napravnik is staying with me and is a very nice guest. He is working hard for his examinations and is busy for longer hours than I. His being musical is very pleasant since in the evenings I enjoy playing piano duets with him, or making him play my favourite pieces.

I have taken a house in Klin for my future abode. I do not know if you will remember it – it is Sacharov's house, large, comfortable, and on the main road to Moscow outside Klin. I have decided to go on living here in the provinces and to rent a furnished flat in Petersburg for about three months in the year. I feel I must have a place in the country or what is an equivalent in Klin, to know that when I need it I always have at my disposal a quiet corner in which to work. An additional fact of importance is that I am used to Klin. The view from the house is delightful and the garden is quite large enough; maybe later I shall buy the house. My finances, thank God, are brilliant. In Moscow *The Queen of Spades* was played to full houses on 19 occasions. What with all my other operas and taking Petersburg into account I shall collect a considerable amount of money. I want to try and put some money away. . . .

Going to Moscow now with Volodia to show him the town during Shrovetide. At the end of the second week of Lent I shall go to Petersburg.

I embrace you hard.

P. Tchaikovsky

Tchaikovsky moved into the house at Klin (now the Tchaikovsky Museum) on 5 May. On 13 January, 1894, his valet Alexei Sofronov, who had inherited the contents of the house, bought it from Sakharov. He kept the composer's rooms as they had been in his lifetime and thus began the establishment of the museum on a private basis.

[621] TO ANATOLI TCHAIKOVSKY   Maidanovo
                                                        22 February 1892

My dear Tolia!

I am quite shameless writing so rarely and waiting for your answers. You are sure to be in need of news and I ought to have written long ago. I am well, thank God, and continue to work hard, and my work is getting on well. Volodia Napravnik is still here. He is a very pleasant guest, even-tempered and gentle. In the evenings he is my precious partner in piano duets, an occupation I like even more than playing vingt. He is working very assiduously. At Shrovetide we went to Moscow for four days. Imagine, during the week there were five performances of my operas, i.e. *Onegin* twice and *The Queen of Spades* three times. What do you think of that!!! I have made a lot of money this season, and hope to put some away for a rainy day.

Unfortunately I shall have to endure a most disagreeable experience in April. Wanting to help Prianishnikov and his company, who are coming to Moscow for the spring season, I promised to conduct three operas (*Faust, Demon, Onegin*); this will compel me to live a whole month in Moscow, to tear myself away from my work, and to spend a lot of money. In the middle of the week (i.e. on Wednesday of the coming week) I am going to Petersburg for 10 days. Why no letters from you for so long? Yakovlev assured me that you are being appointed Governor in Tobolsk. Is it true? Well, I have nothing against it. Shall come to visit you.

I kiss you.

P.T.

The scent of spring is in the air.

[622] TO ANATOLI TCHAIKOVSKY   Maidanovo
                                                        23 March 1892

How shameful it is that I write to you so seldom, my dear Tolia. This is explained by my orchestrating my ballet at full speed to have it ready for Easter. Pania has probably written all about my stay in Petersburg. From there [I came] back home [where] I have been spending my time as usual; with the difference, that two of my nephews – Bob and Sania – are staying with me. They are working for their examinations and are as busy as I am. Soon we shall all leave – the boys for Petersburg, and I, probably, straight to Moscow. I shall conduct (I do not know if you have heard) several times for the Prianishnikov's private opera. Modest and Kolia left yesterday, for abroad. While I am in Moscow Alexei will move all my belongings to my new home in Klin. Again I don't remember if I told you that I have taken a house near Klin on the main road to Frolovskoie. The house is large, pleasant, and comfortable. I shall have excellent rooms there, my own garden and absolutely no neighbours. I am very pleased with this move for Maidanovo makes me sicker and sicker. . . .

Your letter is extremely interesting. We read it all together and were both sorry for you and envied you. This is real work! And I am sure you will remember it all your life. How many people you have the possibility to save and feed! Well done Tolia! Honestly I am very happy and proud that you got this assignment. I kiss you my dear.

P. Tchaikovsky

When he was in Kiev Tchaikovsky had promised the manager of a private opera company, I. P. Prianishnikov, that he would help the company if the opportunity arose. Now he agreed to conduct *Faust*, A. Rubinstein's *The Demon*, and *Eugene Onegin,* but wrote to Ippolitov-Ivanov: 'It will be difficult, disagreeable, even silly – after all what sort of opera conductor am I? But it cannot be helped.' But when Tchaikovsky appeared at the desk on the first of his four appearances he was greeted thunderously by orchestra and audience alike, and it was some minutes before he could begin to conduct.

[623] TO MODEST TCHAIKOVSKY   Moscow
                                               6 April 1892

It is really a shame that I have not written to you for so long, my dear Modia! When I arrived in Moscow today I hoped to answer some letters, one of which was yours but I dived at once into the turmoil of Moscow and returned home so tired that I could not write at all. I am only sending a few words. It was very nice in Petersburg but you have heard about it from Sania and Bob. I left yesterday feeling quite sad. I have already been at my new place of work. First rehearsal tomorrow. Will start with *Faust* which I studied thoroughly in Petersburg, and shall conduct for the first time on the Tuesday of St Thomas's week [second week after Easter]. Just now I visited Pania who feels frightfully lonely, and also went to see the von Mecks. Invitations from all sides besides rehearsals and shows, I feel that I am going to have an awful month. . . .

Your letter made me happy. I am glad you are enjoying yourself but *I do not envy you at all*. Better to suffer, as I am going to here in Moscow, than be out of Russia. I embrace you and dear Nikolai.

P. Tchaikovsky

Shall write short letters but more often.

TO MODEST TCHAIKOVSKY Moscow
14 April 1892

Modia!

For God's sake forgive me – such a mad time that it is impossible to write.
Rehearsals (have not yet conducted because some of the artists are ill),
corrections, friends, etc. do not give me one moment of peace. Am hurrying
with proof corrections of *Yolanta*, and it takes up all my spare time. Hard
times for me but am perfectly well.

Yours

P. Tchaikovsky

I embrace you both.

Will write, word of honour, in a few days.

TO MODEST TCHAIKOVSKY Moscow
20 April 1892

My conscience tortures me that I do not write at all, but honestly I have no
time. Although I am very well I spend my time full of anguish, disgust, and
passionate desire for the end. The stupid thing is that for the last two weeks I
have tired myself out with rehearsals, and am nervous, worried to death, and
as yet I have not conducted. Today I shall conduct *Faust* for the first time.
I spend money irrationally, visitors annoy me, as do petitioners, invitations
etc. etc. Just as I lived with you in November, except that the weather now is
gorgeous and I doubly wish to leave Moscow. I have been very busy too with
the corrections of *Yolanta*, which is now ready. The opera is coming out in
a few days. . . .

Where and how I shall pass the month of May I do not know. I kiss you both
with love.

Yours

P. Tchaikovsky

The Prianishnikov Opera is quite successful but the good weather affects the
box-office.

TO ANATOLI TCHAIKOVSKY Moscow
23 April 1892

My dear Tolia!

I have written so rarely from Moscow because I counted on Pania writing to
you often. I, for my part, have been exhausted both by conducting and by
correcting *The Nutcracker* which I must hand over to the theatre at the end of
April. You cannot imagine how I hated the rash promise I gave to Prianishnikov;

this took a lot of my time, made me stay in town nearly a whole month, and spend a frightful amount of money. Moscow, in my case, is an impossible town; for it seems everyone tries to pester me with invitations and visits, while some insist that I listen to, or play through their operas, or other works, or listen to their singing. What is worst of all, some try to get money out of me in one way or another. All I can say is that this month in Moscow has been like an awful nightmare. Up till now I have conducted *Faust* and *Demon*. *Onegin* comes next.

I see Pania often. She is such a dear. She and Tata are my only consolation.

I kiss you with love.

Yours

P. Tchaikovsky

Congratulations to your 42nd birthday – and I am 52 the day after tomorrow.

On 24 April Tchaikovsky went to a performance of Modest's *The Symphony*, and met Maria Ermolova during the interval.

[627]   TO MODEST TCHAIKOVSKY   Peter
2 May 1892

Dear Modia!

I am here for the third day. My Moscow tortures finished with my conducting *Onegin* and there was, of course, much applause. Also concerning Moscow: a week ago I went with Pania to see your *Symphony*, beautifully played at the Malyi Theatre. Illinsky is charming, especially in the fifth Act. Yes! In the fifth; and I have come to the conclusion that you should not have changed the end of the play, and if I was one of those who advised you, I repent. I did not like Ermolova very much in this role but the other actors were magnificent. I meet the 'theatrical people' here all the time and discussions about *Yolanta* and its cast take place every day. Skompskaia has been invited. . . .

On my way here from Moscow I stopped for a few hours in Klin to christen Georgy Alexeevich Sofronov who was born on 24 April; the boy is sweet, strong and healthy. I have already moved to Klin. Alexei has arranged my rooms very nicely. I never had such a lovely room in my life before. It is real summer in Moscow, and all is green; but here it is cold, with not one leaf out. Yesterday I went to the magnificent funeral of Gresser. Am going home for three weeks, tomorrow. Shall write to Kolichka as soon as I am back.

P. Tchaikovsky

During May Tchaikovsky began work on a symphony in E flat, but the sketches produced to this end – which were in some state of completion by October – did not satisfy him. (See Letter 654.) Almost a year later they were used as the basis of the one movement Third Piano Concerto (Op. 75), and the Finale for Piano and Orchestra (Op. 79) put into practicable form by Taneev after Tchaikovsky's death.

At the beginning of June Tchaikovsky went abroad with Vladimir Davydov, first to Berlin, then to Paris and finally to Vichy. On 7 July he was back in St Petersburg and four days later in Klin.

As usual Modest's activities as dramatist aroused interest, and reference is made below to his comedy, *A Day in St Petersburg* which was to be performed for Savina's Benefit at the Alexandrinsky Theatre on 23 November. Flaubert's *Correspondance* (III, 1854–69) was studied in great detail and underlinings of many passages are conspicuous in the extant copy of the work at Klin. In a letter to Feydeau, who asked Flaubert to tell him about his work on *Salambo*, Flaubert wrote: 'No my friend, this would upset me. You would start criticizing and your criticism would irritate me the more it was just.' Against this Tchaikovsky wrote: 'Just like me.'

[628]   TO MODEST TCHAIKOVSKY   Klin
                                                 17 July 1892

Forgive me that I have not written for so long. It will be a week tomorrow since I saw Bob off. At home I found everything in order; the flowers, which before I left were only peeping out of the earth, have grown and are a lovely sight. During the day I often wander round the garden and enjoy looking at them. This makes me think that I could, maybe, make a good gardener. Egor Alexeevich Sofronov (the baby) has grown wonderfully and improved in appearance. Katia is obviously a very good wet-nurse. Now he has started teething, and his crying reaches me sometimes; but I do not mind at all for these sounds bring life into the prosaic and rather tedious routine of my life.

I continue to be pleased with the house. I found a mass of proofs here, as both the opera and ballet scores, and all their various parts are being published at the same time, and I had to check them all myself. I have decided not to continue working on my symphony as long as I have not finished all the other work. I often get angry with Piotr Ivanovich who as always has everything disorganized and in a muddle. I have not yet seen the badly published libretto, but if it is very bad I shall have to insist that they republish.

I am sorry that your comedy made no impression and is scenically no good. Why do you think so? However, authors never can judge their own work properly. In this respect Flaubert's letters are very interesting; I am reading them with great interest. It seems to me that there has never been a more likable figure in the world of art. He seems to be a hero, a martyr to art. And how clever! I have found in his writings wonderful answers to some of my thoughts on the Deity and religion. No news from Anatoli. I hope your fears of cholera have disappeared. I do not know up till now when I shall leave. Shall not be able to on 20 August because of all the proofs.

I embrace you and Kolia. When are you off to Verbovka?

Yours

P. Tchaikovsky

Moscow
30 July 1892

Modia!

You are angry with P. I. Yurgenson and he with you. It appears that you have
been sent the proofs [of the *Yolanta* libretto] and have not returned them yet.
It must be a misunderstanding. You may make such corrections and alterations
as you wish. I came to Moscow for Tretiakov's funeral. His death has upset
me much more than I imagined. It is not a happy time generally. I am sorry
for poor Anatoli. Although he does not complain about his fate it must be
frightening in a town full of cholera, with a very despotic and unsympathetic
Governor and chief. I do not know when I am going to Verbovka? All I know
is that I have to correct proofs without end and then I shall see. I too am
reading the *Débâcle* [E. Zola, 1892] and have admired it so far.

Good-bye, it is time to go to church for the Service for the Dead and the
funeral.

I embrace you.

P. Tchaikovsky

Klin
2 August 1892

Just received your letter with the text for Figner's aria. It is very good and I
will compose the music to it but not now – after I have finished my proofs.
All the same, send the continuation, my Golubchik; as I am not quite sure
that the number of lines will be sufficient.

It is not worth mentioning the disorder at Yurgenson's – quite impossible to
understand how the machine still works. . . .

I had three days in Moscow. S. M. Tretiakov left his enormous fortune to his
son with 40,000 a year to his wife for life. I was present when Alexeev the
executor arrived with the Will to see V. D. Konshin. Vladimir Dimitrievich
was very displeased that Sergei Mikhailovich did not leave anything to his
comparatively poor sister Hartung, and in his anger called the deceased a Pig!!!

It is now clear that I will not go to Grankino, and probably shall not go
anywhere. I have still a lot of proof correcting to do. And you? Will you go to
Verbovka? If Bob stays there until the 15th I may go there in September.
I embrace you, and thank you for the excellent verses.

Yours

P. Tchaikovsky

My dear Golubchik!

I have just received your letter, and was terribly pleased to hear that you are in a happy state of mind. Could it be that one of my letters to you has been lost? I did not write very often but I did write. With all my soul I long to join you, and think about it all the time. But what can I do? There are more and more complications and more work every day. Nothing of the sort has ever happened before. I am tied to my table all day, and forced to do everything myself as I have lost all faith in everybody else. At the same time I have to correct the scores of both my large compositions, all the transcriptions – including the German editions – and also have to make a simplified piano score of the ballet. This last job would have been a nuisance if it had not been for the thought that it will be easier for you to play it. So the public at large will be grateful to you for an easy version for piano.

I am obliged to go to Moscow very frequently to clear up all kinds of misunderstandings, and everyone is rushing me. The most important thing that has happened is this: I have received such a charming and flattering invitation from the Vienna Exhibition to conduct at a concert that I found it impossible to refuse. My publishers and my manager Pollini also want me to accept, for as yet Vienna has behaved in a very unfriendly manner towards me; even despising me. Both they and I find this a good opportunity to change this attitude. And so, about 5 September (our style) I must be in Vienna. Now I am hoping, if I manage to finish all my work by the 20th or 24th to go to Vienna by way of Verbovka and stay a few days with you. But Emma [Jenton] is upsetting this plan. She has taken a job in Simbirsk, is going there at the beginning of September, and implores me to see her before she leaves. Her letter has touched me greatly and I do want to do as she asks. I have already written to the Maslovs, Nikolai Ilyich, and Annette Merkling, that I am not coming (although I would also have liked to go there).

So all I can say is that it is impossible for me to leave before I have finished all my business in Moscow.

I embrace you to suffocation! ! !

P.T.

[632]   TO VLADIMIR DAVYDOV

I have just received the Paris photographs from Yurgenson and have told him to send four of them to you. I was so glad to see what a good likeness they were that I nearly started crying in the presence of Yurgenson. All this proof correction had completely destroyed all other feelings and thoughts and it had to be this little incident which made me feel again how strong my love for you is. I came here because another set of proofs had to be done for the foreign publication of *Yolanta*. Yurgenson forgot to send me the necessary material which meant that I had to go for it myself. I stayed here only a few hours and am now going back to Klin. If I decide to go to Vienna via Verbovka it will be at the very end of August and I will not be able to stay more than a few days, as the first rehearsal of the concert will be on 6 September. Oh God! How I want to see you.

I embrace you.

P. Tchaikovsky

What if both *Yolanta* and *Shchelkunchik* [*Nutcracker*], for whose sake I am suffering so much, are muck?

[633] TO VLADIMIR DAVYDOV   Klin (still here)
                                               28 August 1892

Am still sticking here. But at last, tomorrow, I shall finish everything I had to do. I think that if it had not been for my orderly and moderate way of living, exercise, and good hygienic conditions, I would have gone mad over this work. Anyway, I am like a madman, not feeling or understanding anything. Even all my dreams are about something which has to be corrected, and about sharps and flats which are not doing what they ought, with the result that something frightening, torturing, fatal, is bound to happen. I never imagined that such torture was in store for me when I was staying with you in Vichy. I could not anticipate it as none of my previous operas and ballets have been published before their performance.

In your last little letter you invite me to stay in Verbovka after Vienna. I would love to. But I have an idea that Menter, who is coming to my Vienna concert, will want to take me back with her to her castle, and I have already been deceiving her for the last three years. Moreover I am interested to see this great wonder, as people call it. Besides, I shall see very little of you in Verbovka, as I will get there just before you have to leave.

Well! We shall see.

If only you would write at least a few words to Vienna. Address: Goldenes Lamm, Praterstrasse. I do not like to reproach you, but you do write very rarely and yet you could keep me informed about many interesting things. However, if it is your creative work that is taking all your time I take back what I have just said. Modest is in Moscow. I am going there after tomorrow, and on the 1st through Petersburg (where I have some business to attend to) to Vienna. In any case at the end of September we shall see each other in Petersburg.

Good-bye, my Golubchik.

Yours

P. Tchaikovsky

[634] TO MODEST TCHAIKOVSKY   Vienna
                                                                7–19 September 1892

Why the hell am I accepting these foreign invitations? Just boredom and torture. But this time I seem to have done something absolutely idiotic. I was warned by someone that the hall where I shall have to conduct is no more than a huge restaurant; but I did not believe it because in the letters inviting me it was described as a 'Grosse Musikhalle'.

Yesterday, on arrival there was nobody to meet me but I was not offended. On the contrary I was very pleased. After changing I went straight to the Exhibition. It was Sunday, a lovely day and there were crowds of people and plenty of interesting things to see; then I went to look at the 'Musikhalle'. A concert was on. Well, it was just as I had been told – the 'Musikhalle' is a huge restaurant, stuffy from lack of air and the fumes of cheap oil and other cooking ingredients. I decided at once to insist that the tables should be removed and the 'Bierhalle' turned into a Concert Hall, otherwise I would refuse to conduct. At the moment I am expecting the gentleman who organizes the concerts and shall be extremely firm with him.

I wonder if I will have time to go to Kamenka and take you with me.

                                                                Vienna
                                                                10 September

Gutmann agreed to take the tables away, but first tried to assure me that the tables and the sausages and beer would not be in the way. On the same day Sapelnikov and Menter arrived, and since then we have been together all the time. Had rehearsals yesterday, one from 9–12 the other from 4.30–6. The orchestra is not bad but extraordinarily small. During the rest of the day, after thinking all things over and expecting the concert to be cheap and insignificant, I suddenly decided to run away and Menter was delighted. Two hours after the rehearsal I sent Gutmann my refusal and we, Menter, Sapelnikov and I left for Itter. Travelled all night. Arrived in the castle at 9 o'clock in the morning. It is grand, heavenly, beautiful and I am glad I came.

I embrace you all.

P.T.

I started to write this letter to Bob, who is in Kamenka, three days ago but I think it would be better to address it to Peter[sburg].

Itter
                                                    15–27 September 1892

Although not many days are left until my return I'd better let you have a few
words from me. as the Vienna papers say that I am ill and I fear that the
Russian ones could exaggerate my illness, which would be completely wrong as
I am perfectly well and enjoying life. Itter lives up to its reputation. It is a
devilishly beautiful nest. I shall report all particulars about the castle and the
life here in person. We lead a very regular life here, for my sake. My rooms
(a whole floor to myself) are lovely but are a mixture of luxury and bad taste.
Magnificent furniture, a gorgeous bed with incrustations, and a cheap oleograph
on the wall next to it. But what does it matter? The important thing is that
the country around is lovely. Also there is absolute, quiet, unruffled peace; no
sign of guests; and my hosts – Menter and Vassia – are charming. All I can say
is, that I have not for a very long time felt so contented as I do here. I shall
stay another five days. Then, by way of Salzburg (where I will stay for the sake
of the Mozarteum) and Prague (where I shall stay for *The Queen of Spades*), on
to Petersburg where I hope to appear about the 25th on the shores of the
Fontanka [a street beside a Neva tributary].

What upsets me is that I do not get any letters or newspapers from Russia
and do not know anything about you.

Has Bob arrived? Has Volodia arrived? I embrace you all.

P. Tchaikovsky

[636]   TO MODEST TCHAIKOVSKY   Itter
                                                    22 September – 4 October 1892

Yesterday just as we were getting into the carriage to go with Menter and
Sapelnikov to Salzburg, and then to Prague, a telegram was brought from
Schubert, the Director of the Prague opera. It said that *The Queen of Spades*,
which was to be performed on the 8th, was postponed for three days. So we
decided to stay here for another three days. This has upset me not because I do
not like it here – quite the contrary, Itter is charming – but because, thanks to
my stupid instructions, I have not had any news from Russia for more than
two weeks and am frightfully in need of it. All in all I want to get home as
soon as possible, and get rid of Prague, where I am sure to have plenty of
boring and exhausting hours.

I embrace all of you: you, Kolia, Bob and I hope Volodia. I shall telegraph
from Prague to find out if you are all alive and well.

P.T.

TO ANATOLI TCHAIKOVSKY

My dear friend Tolia!

I have just arrived home and found your letter of 21 September. I left Prague
a week ago the day after the first performance of *The Queen of Spades*. It went
off very well and had a very enthusiastic reception. On the next day I said
good-bye to Menter and Sapelnikov and arrived on Saturday morning in
Petersburg where I passed four very pleasant days. All the near relatives were
there and all are well and happy. . . .

On Thursday of next week the hundredth performance of *Eugene Onegin* takes
place. I shall not be there as I must stay at home for at least two weeks and
work again at proof corrections and also write the additional aria for Figner
in *Yolanta*. Then I shall go to Petersburg for a month to be there for the
Yolanta and *Nutcracker* rehearsals; I have been told that the first night is to
be in the middle of November, but I doubt it very much, I reckon it will be at
the end of November. . . .

I kiss and embrace you.

P. Tchaikovsky

[638] TO MODEST TCHAIKOVSKY

[Klin]
12 October 1892
in the evening

Thank you, my dear Modia for your letter. I am sending a photograph for kind
Levkeeva. Please, add her initials before her family name. Unfortunately all
the portraits I have are on a black background and there is nowhere to make
an appropriate inscription. That is why I have not written anything specially
sweet on it. Tell her that as soon as I am in Petersburg I shall get a photograph
on a white background and will write on it a proper declaration of my love.
Am hard at work. The aria for Figner is written and despatched. I am now
composing the symphony, and it will be ready in the rough very soon. My
house is cosy and warm. But I seem to feel lonely in the evenings and long
for Petersburg and No. 24 Fontanka. The day after tomorrow I go to Moscow
for the competition.

A week ago we enjoyed Svobodin's performance as Muromsky and where is he
now?

Good-bye. I embrace Kolia, Volodia, Bob and you.

P. Tchaikovsky

Tchaikovsky had written an additional aria for Vaudemont in *Yolanta*. He attended
the auditions of conductors for the Malyi Theatre, from which Andrei Arends was

selected. P. M. Svobodin, an actor much appreciated by Tchaikovsky for his performances in *Krechinsky's Wedding* and Molière's *Tartuffe*, had recently died at the age of forty-two while playing the leading role in Ostrovsky's *The Jokers* at the Mikhailovsky Theatre.

[639] TO ANATOLI TCHAIKOVSKY

[Petersburg]
11 November 1892
Grand Hotel

I have the honour to report to your Excellency that I have not written for a long time as it has been difficult to find time for this purpose. Have been here two weeks. Rehearsals every day, first of the opera then of the ballet, but things are going a bit slow. I think that the ballet and opera will not be on before 8 December and I shall be obliged to stick it out here a whole month. I am living at the Grand Hotel in a cosy room where I am very comfortable. Time passes quickly but although it is neither tedious nor jolly it is quite fruitless, and it is impossible to think about work. Modest is worried, his play *A Day in Petersburg* is to be produced soon, with Yuleva in the leading role. . . . I saw in the papers that Baranov has left for Petersburg. Will he return in time for the first night of *Yolanta*? I'll let you know when it is going to be. How are you and how is Pania's health? Write here and also tell me when you will be able to come.

I embrace you, my dear Tolia! I kiss Pania and Tania.

Yours

P. Tchaikovsky

[640] TO ANATOLI TCHAIKOVSKY

Petersburg
24 November 1892
Grand Hotel

Tolia, Golubchik!

Just a few words. . . . Modest's play was on yesterday. It was an awful flop; something I actually expected as it is too complicated for the audience of the Alexandrinsky Theatre. But it will do Modest good. Chasing unattainable aims prevents him from doing his proper work – I mean writing plays for the theatre in conventional form. Rehearsals for *Yolanta* and the ballet never seem to end. The Emperor is probably coming on the 5th and the first night for the public will be the 6th. Are you coming? Shall I keep a seat?

I embrace and kiss you all.

In a frightful hurry – sorry!

Yours

P. Tchaikovsky

TO ANATOLI TCHAIKOVSKY   [Petersburg]
                                                                9 December 1892

My dear Tolia!

The opera and the ballet were both very successful. On the day before the first
night there was a rehearsal with the Emperor present. He was delighted and
sent for me to his box and said a whole lot of kind words. The production and
settings are magnificent, even too magnificent in the ballet – all this luxury
tires the eyesight. Shall write again today or tomorrow and let you know all
the details.

For the moment I embrace you all.

P. Tchaikovsky

The Czar was polite about both *Yolanta* and *The Nutcracker*. Apart from the composer
very few other people were, and the critics exercised themselves in destroying both.
   This journey was to give opportunity to visit Fanny Dürbach, governess to the
Tchaikovskys in Votkinsk from 1844–48.

[642]   TO ANATOLI TCHAIKOVSKY   Petersburg
                                                                10 December 1892

How many times did I try to write to you, my dear Tolia, but it is only today
that I have found the opportunity to report at least briefly on my plans.

Today is the fourth day that the whole of the Petersburg Press is occupied in
attacking my latest progenies – one newspaper after another. But I am
completely indifferent to it all, being certain that my day will come. Although
all these attacks do not upset me I have been in an awful mood these last
days, which is always the usual aftermath of the finish of a big work. When
you live for a long time full of expectations of something important a sort of
apathy appears when, at last, this has been realized; this also accompanies a
revulsion against work, a feeling of void, and of the futility of all aspiration.
Also I was upset about having to go abroad. I ought to go from here straight
to Hamburg and Schwerin for the production of *Yolanta*; next to Brussels to
conduct at a concert; then to Odessa, and from there to Petersburg to conduct
for the Musical Society.

In addition to my present aversion to foreign countries I also suffer at the
thought of again living through all the vicissitudes of a composer on account
of *Yolanta*. I was already beginning to feel really desperate but then I realized
that I am not compelled to go to Hamburg and Schwerin, and that they can
very well do without me. This restored my peace, and now my plan is as
follows: the day after tomorrow – the 12th – I am going to Berlin. There
I shall decide where to go for a rest (most probably to Nice); then on
29 December–10 January I shall be in Brussels; from there on the 3–15th

I shall go to Paris for about three days, then to Montbéliard to see Mlle Fanny; and about 10–22 January I will be in Odessa, where I am conducting one or two concerts.

At the end of January I shall be in Petersburg. After that I shall settle in Klin for a long time but shall definitely visit you in Nijny during Lent. Write to Brussels – poste restante. Anyway, I will let you know from Berlin where I am going before Brussels. . . .

I kiss and embrace you all a thousand times.

P. Tchaikovsky

[643]   TO VLADIMIR DAVYDOV   [Berlin]
                                          14–26 December 1892

Nothing could have been worse than my journey from Berlin to Eidkunden. I travelled in that same disgusting railway carriage you and I travelled in this summer. It was uncomfortable and dirty; the doors didn't close; the bell never stopped ringing; and – to crown it all – the stove was out of order and we slept in a temperature of four or even three degrees [Centigrade] and – as the pipes were frozen – it was impossible to wash. Struve lodged complaints at every big station we passed through. So cleverly did I avoid him that, although he was next to me, we did not meet even once. In Eidkunden I changed for an excellent warm carriage. I stayed in a first class hotel. My state of mind on the journey was and is now absolutely awful. I praise myself for not having gone to Hamburg, and at the same time torture myself with the thought that I did not keep my promise to both Pollini and the Director of the Theatre in Schwerin.

My itinerary will be as follows: tomorrow to Basle, where I shall stay a day or two. From there I'll go to Montbéliard to keep my promise to Mlle Fanny at last; shall stay there for a day and then on to Paris, where I will be for about five or six days until it's time to go to Brussels.

If you write at once I will get your letter in Paris but as you are busy and I do not want to disturb your studies, show this letter to Kolia and beg him to write and tell me everything that has happened since I left, and also ask Sania to write. Then send this letter to Modest in Klin and let him write to Paris too to let me know how he is faring in my home. Where is Anatoli? I am sorry we missed each other. If he is in Petersburg I beg him to write to Paris. I think of you all incessantly and all I dream of is to be back in Russia. Have the frosts continued to be so fierce? How sick I am of Berlin and foreign countries! ! ! Good-bye, my Golubchik, I embrace you, Kolia, Volodia (if he does not hate writing letters too much, ask him also to write to Paris), Modia, Tolia, Sania, Koka [Litke] etc. etc. etc.

P. Tchaikovsky

My address: (1) 14, Rue Richepanse, Paris. (2) Hôtel de Suède, Bruxelles.

TO VLADIMIR DAVYDOV   Berlin
16–28 December 1892

I am still sitting in Berlin. I haven't got enough energy to leave – especially as there is no hurry. These last days I have been considering and reflecting on matters of great importance. I looked perfectly objectively through my new symphony and was glad that I had neither orchestrated it nor launched it; it makes a quite unfavourable impression. I mean the symphony has been written just for the sake of writing something – there is nothing either attractive or interesting in it. I have decided to throw it out and forget it. The decision is irrevocable and I am glad I made it. But, does it mean that I am completely dried up? That is the question I have been worrying about these last three days. Maybe I could still summon up inspiration to write programme music but pure music – i.e. symphonic and chamber music – I ought not to write any more. On the other hand, to live without work which absorbs time, thoughts and strength, is very dull. What must I do? Forget about composing? Too difficult to say. So here I am, thinking, and thinking, and thinking, and not knowing what to decide. Whatever happens these last three days were unhappy ones.

I am however, quite well, and have at last decided to leave for Basle tomorrow. You wonder why I am writing about all this to you? Just an irresistible longing to chat with you. What a pity that I did not ask you and all the others to write to me here; I would have had some interesting letters and known all about what you are doing. I pass the day in quite a novel way. That is, I sit nearly all day in my wonderfully comfortable room and wander round the streets in the evenings. The weather is quite warm. I can picture you sitting in your room, scented nearly to suffocation, working at your college exercises. How I would love to be in that dear room! Give my love to everybody.

I embrace you.

P. Tchaikovsky

If only I could give way to my secret desire, I would leave everything and go home.

TO PRASKOVIA VLADIMIROVNA TCHAIKOVSKAIA
Basle
18–30 December 1892

My dear Panichka!

I have no news at all about Tolia so I am writing today, and will you please send this letter over to him if he is away. I am perfectly well but suffer frightfully from boredom and loneliness. It's the last time in my life that I will go abroad alone. Tomorrow I am going to Montbéliard to see Mlle Fanny, and a day later to Paris where I have to pay a mass of visits to members of the Académie who have elected me as one of their colleagues. On 2–14 January

I have a concert in Brussels. From there I will go straight to Odessa where I will be obliged to stay for some time.

I shall return to Moscow at the end of January and if I hear that you are still in Nijny [-Novgorod] I shall certainly come to see you. I have managed to get my finances into such a bad state that I am drowning in debts. So I am going to sit in Klin and not go anywhere far until I am in credit again.

I shall see Emma in Paris. She left Petersburg just before me, very sad and upset. It would be most desirable to get news from you in Odessa where I will arrive at the beginning of January.

With all my love I press you and Tata to my heart.

If Tolia is at home tell him that I was very upset to leave without seeing him, but I could not wait.

Yours

P. Tchaikovsky

[646] TO MODEST TCHAIKOVSKY   Basle
                                                 19–31 December 1892

I only want to write about my complaints, which drive me to tears. It is quite extraordinary that I have not gone mad and been made ill by distress of a phenomenal nature. As this psychopathic state asserts itself with every stay abroad and gets worse every time I go, I will definitely not go anywhere alone any more – even for a short time. Tomorrow this state of mind will pass, and a less painful one will take its place. I am going to Montbéliard with – I must honestly say – a feeling of unnatural fear, even horror, as if I were about to step into the realms of death to meet people who have long disappeared from the scene. Then to Paris where I shall pay official visits to my co-academicians and will probably dive into the whirlwind of affairs in Paris. This will be definitely better. In Brussels I will again have no time for distress. After that to Odessa, which is nearly home, and where I shall be happy to meet Vassia. Only separation teaches one to realize how much one loves one's own people. . . .

How I envy you! How you must enjoy your rest away from Petersburg. Shall only stay one night and two days in Montbéliard and hope to get letters from you in Paris.

Basle is disgusting and boring.

Regards to everybody.

P. Tchaikovsky

I embrace you.

TO NIKOLAI ILYICH TCHAIKOVSKY Paris
22 December 1892–
3 January 1893

My very dear Ilyich!

I am writing this under the influence of my trip to Montbéliard, quite certain
that it would interest you to know about my meeting with Mlle Fanny. I let
her know when I was coming from Basle, so as not to upset the old lady too
much by my unexpected appearance. On 1 January (new style, on 20 December,
according to ours), I arrived in Montbéliard at 3 o'clock and went straight to
see Fanny. She lives in a small street in the little town, which is so quiet that
it could in this respect compete with one of our little provincial towns. The
house, which has only six rooms in all, has three floors (with two rooms on
each) and belongs to her and her sister; they were both born and lived in this
house all their lives. When in answer to my knock I heard the word: 'Entrez!'
and entered, Fanny met me and I recognized her at once. Although she is
70 now, she looks much younger, and has – however queer it may seem –
actually changed very little. The same red face, brown eyes, hair scarcely grey
and magnificent teeth (unless they are false). The only thing is, she has grown
much fatter. I was afraid that there would be tears and scenes, but not at all.
She received me as if we had parted only a year ago, with joy, kindness, and
great simplicity.

I understood at once why both our parents and all of us loved her so much.
She is a wonderfully sympathetic, straightforward, clever, extremely kind and
honest person. Unending reminiscences of the past started at once and a whole
stream of the most interesting details about our childhood days – Mamasha
[Mother] and all of us; then she showed me our copy books (yours, mine and
Venichka's), my compositions, your letters and mine; but what was most
important, several letters from Mamasha. I cannot describe what a delightful,
and magical feeling I had listening to her stories, reading all these letters and
looking at all the copy books. The past was reborn so vividly in all its details
that it seemed to me that I could hear the voices of Mamasha, Venichka,
Khamit, Arisha, Akulina and all the others. I had, for instance, completely
forgotten Khamit but now when she reminded me of him, and what he looked
like, and told me how he adored Papasha and us children, I saw him as if he
were alive. Just like Sestritza [sister] Nastasia Vassilievna [Popova] she lives in
memories of the past with the difference that in the case of Sestritza everything
is in a muddle and it is sometimes difficult to understand what she means;
whereas in Fanny's case everything has the breath of truth and life. This is
because when she returned to Montbéliard she lived a quiet, monotonous life for
forty years and the memories of her youth, so very different from the life in
Montbéliard, stayed in her mind quite unspoiled. There were moments when
I returned into the past so vividly that it became weird, and at the same time
sweet, and we both had to keep back our tears.

In answer to her question which of my brothers I love best I answered in a

vague way, saying that I love them all – this made her a bit angry and she
said that I must love you, the comrade of my childhood more than the others,
and I suddenly felt that this was true and that I dearly love you, the comrade
of my childhood joys. I stayed with her from 3 o'clock until 8 and never
noticed the time go by. The whole of the next day I was with her all the time,
except that she sent me out to have dinner, saying honestly that her and her
sister's fare was too miserable and that she did not dare share it with me.
I was obliged to make two calls with her on her nearest friends and relatives
who had been hoping for a long time to meet me. She gave me a lovely letter
from Mamasha where she writes with special love about you. I will show you
the letter. She and her sister live very simply but quite comfortable and cosy.
Her sister also lived many years in Russia and even speaks Russian quite well.
They both still give lessons and the whole town knows them; they have been
teaching all the intelligentsia for many years and have the love and the respect
of everybody there.

In the evening I kissed Fanny and gave her a great hug, and left promising to
come again one day. If I am not mistaken she had been hurt by our long
indifference but, out of pride, did not want to write first. However, there were
no reproaches, on the contrary she reproached herself for having been too
reserved.

And this, my dear Ilyich, is a full report about my visit to Montbéliard.

I embrace you and Olia and George. Regards to Martha.

P. Tchaikovsky

[648]   TO MODEST TCHAIKOVSKY   Paris
                                        24 December 1892–
                                        5 January 1893

I have just received your letter and see from it that I did not get the first one
(sent to Brussels). The Klin Post is the damnedest in the world. At last, dear
Modia, I have stopped indulging in mad despair and distress. This is my third
day here; I am suffering from the cold and feeling a bit sad; all I think about
is getting home as quickly as possible. However, the Béliards, my walks, the
restaurants, and the theatres, give me some pleasure. My first evening here
I went to see *M. Coulisset*. I do not understand Parisian taste. The play is
charming, Guittemans and Boisselet wonderful, the audience obviously enjoys
it and laughs till it cries; but the theatre is half empty and the takings bad! ! !
The sets are gorgeous. I think there is more taste and inventiveness here than
in Petersburg. The first act takes place at a ball, but this ball is much better
presented than in *A Day in Petersburg*. As in your play it ends with a
cotillion rushing into the hall with a troika group in front, and how charmingly
it is done! And how elegant all the guests look in comparison to the Petersburg
actors. I was extremely pleased. Last night I went to see *Lysistrata*. The play
shows talent, it is amusing and full of ribaldry, but at times it is boring. Guitry

was vulgar and I did not like him; Réjane on the other hand was the height of perfection.

Before coming to Paris I was in Montbéliard for two days. I described all the details of the meeting there to Nikolai Ilyich. It would interest you less and it is difficult to say the same thing twice. I had an extremely vivid, enchanting, fairy-like impression. It was as if I was back in the forties for a couple of days. Fanny looks young, just the same as she did, and as she lives entirely in memories of the past in Votkinsk, and looks upon the bygone days as Sestriza does, I relived everything most vividly. Stories never ending. I saw a lot of my copy-books, my compositions, and even the sketch of the chemist's shop. She read me a lot of letters from Mamasha, Zina, Lida (in perfect French), my own, Kolia's, Venichka's etc. Mamasha's letters are specially precious. She has left all this to me, and for the time being has made me a gift of one of Mamasha's letters, which I will show you.

When we met, Fanny did not make any scenes, nor cry; she did not pass any remarks about how I looked, but behaved just as if we had seen each other a year ago. But during the two days I was there, as we read all the old letters and remembered old days we had to try to keep back our tears. When she asked me which of my brothers I loved best and did not give a direct answer she got angry and said that I must surely love Kolia, the comrade of my childhood years, more than any of you; and suddenly I realized that I do love Kolia, if not more than the others then differently and in any case very dearly, because he was my companion in childhood.

The boys (Kolia and Sania) spoil you with letters but, in spite of my requests, have only written a joint one to me. I had a telegram from Hamburg saying that *Yolanta* was a great success. Do not torture yourself thinking that it is because of you I am not in Klin. I had to go abroad in any case.

Yours

P.T.

Fanny Dürbach sent all the material relating to the Tchaikovskys in her possession to Modest after Piotr's death, and it was used in his biography of his brother. At this juncture Modest was thinking that Piotr had gone abroad simply to leave him in solitude in the house at Klin.

On 2–14 January Tchaikovsky conducted an all-Tchaikovsky concert in Brussels: the third Suite, the First Piano Concerto (soloist F. Rummel), the *Nutcracker* Suite, Waltz and Elegy from the Serenade for Strings, the *1812* overture, and some piano pieces and songs.

In an article in the *Figaro* of 8 January, Lamoureux, who had been conducting in Moscow and St Petersburg, was praised at the expense of German conductors (especially von Bülow). The same article also attacked Anton Rubinstein. On 13 January Tchaikovsky wrote a letter in defence of von Bülow and Rubinstein to the *Paris*. Soon afterwards Lamoureaux sent a letter to the newspapers protesting against the tone of the offending article. All of this had to compete for space in the newspapers with the scandals concerning the Panama Canal which led to the imprisonment of its designer, Ferdinand de Lesseps, and his son.

[649] TO MODEST TCHAIKOVSKY   Paris
                                                4–16 January 1893

Thank you, Modinka, for all your letters some of which I had here, and some in Brussels. I came back here yesterday on the day after my brilliant concert there. The orchestra was good, even very good, but not sufficiently disciplined. Everyone was charming and kind to me. This did not make things any easier, and resulted in my suffering double in Brussels, from nervous strain and distress.

During the interval Gevaert, as President of the Artists' Benevolent Society, publicly thanked me in front of the whole orchestra and was altogether most kind. As the concert was given on behalf of the Society I refused to accept any fee, which greatly impressed the artists. All the same I was delighted to leave Brussels where Mackar and Noël were pestering me. Ziloty did not come with me to Brussels as Vera was having her confinement just at that time. Everything went well. In spite of the Panama, my letter about Lamoureux and his successes in the *Figaro*, published in *Paris*, is creating a sensation here.

I am leaving in three days. Shall have to devote them to farewell visits, an occupation which makes my heart contract just at the mere thought of it.

Please write to Odessa at the Hôtel London.

I embrace you! Sasha Ziloty has just come in to fetch me down to dinner.

Yours

P. Tchaikovsky

Best regards to all my nearest.

From Paris Tchaikovsky went to Odessa where he conducted three concerts, supervised the production of *The Queen of Spades*, attended several banquets in his honour, and sat to N. D. Kuznezov for the portrait (see page 531) now in the Tretiakov Gallery in Moscow.

[650] TO MODEST TCHAIKOVSKY   Kamenka
                                                28 January 1893

I still address my letters to Klin although by now you must already be in Peter. After all I did not manage to keep my promise, and write more fully about everything from Odessa. I never before got so tired conducting for I had to conduct at five concerts. On the other hand, however, I was never so highly praised and so well received. It is a pity that you have not got any Odessa papers. If you had you could have judged with how much exaggeration the

Odessa people speak of my achievements. There were many intolerable hours (for example, the grand dinner at the English Club), but also many happy ones. If only I could have at least a tenth of the adulations bestowed in Odessa in the Capitals! But this seems impossible and apparently it should not be. I need to have faith in myself again, and this has been badly shattered of late. It seems to me that my role is finished for good.

Everything seems very consoling here, but Sestritza has become weaker, and Nata looks older and thinner. At the big house everything is in order and everybody seems to be looking happier than last year. I shall stay here three or four days and then go straight back to Klin. In Lent I shall come to Petersburg for financial reasons. This year has not brought me much, surely I must get something at Shrovetide. Modia, please ask Kolia not to be angry if I am a little late in repaying my debt. If you have returned to Petersburg by now, write to Klin and tell me all about the people in your flat and about yourself. I long to come and see you but first I must return to normal in Klin before I come.

I embrace you.

P. Tchaikovsky

The painter Kuznezov in Odessa has painted a wonderful portrait of me. I hope he will have time to send it to the Peredvijnaia Exhibition.

Modest replied to this letter: 'How can a man who has just shown two wonderful *chef d'oeuvres* to the world say this? What is interesting is that on the day I received your letter I read in the *Figaro* reminiscences of someone who was present at a conversation between Verdi (who was then fifty-one) and Auber (eighty-one) in 1863. The former said with bitterness that he was finished and would never compose again in order not to let the public know his talent had come to an end. Auber replied that he, on the contrary, was composing with all the zest of a young man. Now the eighty-one year old Verdi is full of inspiration and you have taken the part of Verdi before he had written *Aida*, the *Requiem*, and *Otello*. I know this mood of yours will pass, but I still find it a shame that such thoughts come into your head, and that you suffer from them even if only for a short time.'

[651]   TO ANATOLI TCHAIKOVSKY   Kamenka
                                                          29 January 1893

Tolia!

Please, do not be angry because I haven't written. I tried to do so a thousand times from Odessa but there was no time to spare for letters. I stayed there two weeks and conducted three concerts of the Musical Society – two for charity – and also attended the two first performances of *The Queen of Spades* as well as many of its rehearsals. Nowhere else have people ever made such a fuss of me, and in every possible and splendid way. At the end I was utterly exhausted. But after sleeping a day and a night in the train I arrived in Kamenka feeling perfectly well. Do you know, although I grumble at these journeys I think they do me good. All the same, I have a deep craving for solitude, so I shall go straight to Klin from here.

About the middle of February I have to conduct the Musical Society Concert in aid of the Society funds, and it will be after this that I shall visit you in Nijny. I also ought to go to Petersburg. After all this I will settle down for a long stretch in Klin and work. My finances this year have been in a deplorable state. I shall have to sit quietly at home and will not be able to make the proposed trip to England at the beginning of June. I came to Kamenka in the first place to see the old ladies; one of them – Nastasia Vassilievna, or Sestriza – almost died recently, so I was very happy to find them hale and hearty. I am staying in Leva's empty house with the two old spinsters Nata and Sestriza, and have been here for three days. Am leaving for Klin tomorrow. In about two weeks and a half I shall be with you. I embrace you.

Kiss Pania and Tatochka.

Yours

P. Tchaikovsky

[652]   TO MODEST TCHAIKOVSKY   Klin
                                                5 February 1893

Thank you, Golubchik Módia, for your letters. I did not have a pleasant journey from Kamenka to Klin. I was really ill on the way, and to the horror of the other passengers I became delirious and had to stop in Kharkov. But, as usual, after a good night's rest and a dose of castor oil I woke up perfectly well. I think it was the result of Nata's rich food. As my funds ran short I was obliged to ask for help from Slatin, the Director of the Kharkov Department of the Musical Society, and in consequence I shall have to conduct in Kharkov during Lent. Slatin and his wife were so kind and sweet that I couldn't possibly refuse. I did not stop in Moscow, and only telegraphed Yurgenson to meet me and he brought me your letters.

I have a terrible longing to come to Petersburg to be with you now, at once, but reason makes me postpone this journey for two weeks. I conduct in Moscow on 14 February and must be there for rehearsals in a week's time. But I simply must come to my senses first. Besides, I haven't got any money at all. Osip Ivanovich will get my money during the first week of Lent and then I will appear at the end of the second week equipped with a sum of money which, if not very large, will at least be respectable, and shall put all our finances in order. Thank you for raising my morale in respect of composition – we shall see. Meanwhile, think about a libretto in your free moments. Something both original and touching! ! !

To make some money, I am for the time being going to compose songs, and pieces for the piano, then the symphony that has been recently planned; after that an opera and then finish. But the subject of the opera must really attract me; I do not want *The Merchant of Venice*. If it had not been for the longing to go to Petersburg it would be like paradise here; the weather today is wonderful – clear and windless; but letters, letters and letters!!! No end to them. Will have to sit and write all day.

I embrace you all.

P. Tchaikovsky

I shall be obliged to visit Volodia Shilovsky next week. It upsets and frightens me. Tell me, has he changed very much. What are the symptoms of dropsy? I fear tears and fear this meeting in general. Is there no hope at all? Please, Golubchik, answer my question. Am very interested to know of *The Prejudices*.

On 14 February Tchaikovsky was to conduct a concert of the Russian Musical Society in Moscow, for the first time for three years. Safonov, the Director, asked him to overlook the misunderstanding that had caused a breach and Tchaikovsky took the olive branch offered to him. His programme was: the Overture-Fantasy *Hamlet* (Op. 67), now performed for the first time in Moscow; the Concert Fantasy for Piano and orchestra (soloist Taneev); and the *Nutcracker* Suite (Op. 71a).

Between 7 and 22 April the 18 piano pieces of Op. 72 were composed, and between 23 April and 5 May the six songs of Op. 73 to words by D. M. Rathaus. Meanwhile Tchaikovsky was working with intensity on the sketches of the Sixth Symphony. These were completed on 24 March. Beginning on 19 July, he orchestrated the work in a month.

Modest wrote of the dying condition of V. S. Shilovsky, his brother's old pupil and friend. Modest also wrote of his own new play, *The Prejudices*.

[653] TO ANATOLI TCHAIKOVSKY   Klin
                                                10 February 1893

Golubchik Tolia!

I shall come next week either on Tuesday or Wednesday. But I must warn you that I shall not stay for long, not more than three days. All my thoughts are now full of my new composition (a symphony) and it is difficult for me to tear myself away from this task. I think my very best composition is coming to life. I must finish it as quickly as possible, for I have a multitude of other work, and also a journey to London and Cambridge in the near future! Also when back from Nijny I shall have to stay about two days in Petersburg. And so to a very near meeting.

I embrace you.

P. Tchaikovsky

Klin
11 February 1893

If you do not want to write, at least spit on a piece of paper, put it in an
envelope, and send it to me. You are not taking any notice of me at all. God
forgive you – all I wanted was a few words from you.

I am going to Moscow tonight. The concert will be on the 14th. On the 15th
I shall be going to Nijny-Novgorod for about three days and from there straight
to Petersburg. About the end of the second week in Lent, therefore, I shall be
with you

I want to tell you about the excellent state of mind I'm in so far as my works
are concerned. You know that I destroyed the symphony I had composed and
partly orchestrated in the autumn. And a good thing too! There was nothing
of interest in it – an empty play of sounds, without inspiration. Now, on my
journey, the idea of a new symphony came to me, this time one with a
programme, but a programme that will be a riddle for everyone. Let them try
and solve it. The work will be entitled *A Programme Symphony* (No. 6),
Symphonie à Programme (No. 6) *Eine Programmsinfonie* (Nr. 6). The programme
of this symphony is completely saturated with myself and quite often during
my journey I cried profusely. Having returned I have settled down to write
the sketches and the work is going so intensely, so fast, that the first movement
was ready in less than four days, and the others have taken shape in my head.
Half of the third movement is also done. There will still be much that is new
in the form of this work and the finale is not to be a loud *allegro*, but the
slowest *adagio*. You cannot imagine my feelings of bliss now that I am
convinced that the time has not gone forever, and that I can still work. Of
course, I may be wrong, but I do not think so. Please, do not tell anyone,
except Modest.

I purposely address the letter to the College, so that no one shall read it.
Does all this really interest you? It sometimes seems to me that you are not
interested at all and that you have no real sympathy for me. Good-bye, my
dear. Please, kiss Svechin, Rudia and Boris [Pleshii]. You see how much Svechin
is in my good graces.

Yours

P. Tchaikovsky

Consistently friendly to young composers, Tchaikovsky often put himself out to
encourage talent. Thus on 15 February he went to the first performance of the
orchestral suite *Child Life* (Op. 1) by G. E. Konius, a pupil of Taneev and Arensky.
He had already known the work in its piano version. Having heard it in orchestral
form, conducted by Safonov, he wrote an enthusiastic article for the *Russian Annals*,
but never sent it to the editor. He also suggested to Belaiev that the work should
be published.

Klin
28 February 1893

Please, Golubchik Modia, do the following errand for me. Go to the photographer of the Imperial Theatres and order:

1. A large portrait for Ziloty. If there is one ready take it away and send it at once to Ziloty in Paris.
2. Twelve dozen cabinet size portraits on white background. When they are ready they should be sent to O. I. Yurgenson who will pay for them and send them to me. Please, do this at once.

The Konius composition which I went to Moscow to hear surpassed all my expectations. Some of the numbers are extremely original and charming. Its only fault is that it is too long. I persuaded him to shorten it and end it differently.

My head aches just as much as it did in Petersburg; but first, I have got used to it and know how not to make it worse; while second, I am not at all worried as my appetite is excellent. I sleep well and know that – as has happened before – it will pass of its own accord. If it does not I shall ask Vassily Bertenson for help. Just returned from the Liturgy at the Cathedral.

Good-bye! I have masses of letters to write, but I'll make them short ones to everybody because of my head.

A thousand kisses to all of you.

Yours

P. Tchaikovsky

News came of the intention of Tchaikovsky's brother-in-law to re-marry, his fiancée being E. N. Olkhovsky, a niece of the composer. On 7 March there was a concert at which Napravnik's incidental music for A. K. Tolstoi's *Don Juan* (1891) and the *Nutcracker* Suite were played, the composers conducting.

Klin
4 March 1893

Golubchik Tolia!

Forgive my long silence. After Nijny I went to Moscow then to Klin to the Law Courts (the [alleged] thief was acquitted and that was quite right, for there was definitely no evidence that he was the thief). Then several days in Petersburg, back here for five days, and now today I am going to Moscow and Kharkov. I will be back in the sixth week of Lent, but haven't yet decided when I shall come to see you. At the court hearing, what with the disgust [I felt], the stuffiness [of the room], my pity for the poor boy, and the anger I felt for the Novikovs and the local police I developed a nervous headache which has not left me, even for a minute, since then. Only yesterday it started to get better; as I have had these headaches before I did not worry and continued working.

This present journey will make me completely well again, for a change is the best cure. In Peter I heard some news which will astonish you as much as it has me. . . .

Leva is going to marry Katia Olkhovsky. It is still a secret so do not tell it to anyone besides Pania.

Modest has written an excellent play. I mean that, and it is no exaggeration; it has a quite original plot and the language is good and full of character. I think it will be enormously successful.

Today I really felt the spring coming. I fear that I may be held back by the spring high waters on my way back from Kharkov.

I kiss you, Pania and Tata.

Yours

P. Tchaikovsky

[657]   TO MODEST TCHAIKOVSKY   Moscow
                                                 8 March 1893

Your letter with one from Leva enclosed was forwarded to me today. Leva's letter is very touching and I am deeply sorry for him. I wonder if he has any slight regrets about his decision? But no retreat is possible.

Just think, fourteen days after my head started aching and I decided that it would go on hurting for ever, the pain *suddenly* went. It made me indescribably happy as it was getting impossible and had completely spoiled my stay in Klin. Here I am busy with Napravnik, I mean that I pass all my time with him and Olga Eduardovna – not only at rehearsals – and I do not find it at all irksome. There was a sort of quarrel between him and Taneev, to whom Eduard Franzevich behaved in the proud and condescending manner as of a general to a subordinate, so that Taneev was offended and wrote a sharp letter to Napravnik. Napravnik's behaviour to Taneev was disgusting, but I remembered that long ago he behaved to me in this same 'principal to subordinate' way, and then felt ashamed. Now after an explanation to Taneev he has apologized. Taneev's concert yesterday was successful but the takings were not very good. We were both presented with silver wreaths. After the concert Baron Medem gave us supper at the Hermitage.

Am going to Kharkov the day after tomorrow. The second part of the sixth and the first half of the seventh week of Lent I shall stay in Klin. Then to Petersburg where I long to go. Thank you for doing my errand.

I kiss you all.

P. Tchaikovsky

TO MODEST TCHAIKOVSKY [Klin]
19 March 1893

Last night I returned home from Kharkov, where there were endless
celebrations, and I am very tired. All the same, it was very nice, and the
occasion was nearly as successful as the one in Odessa. On my way back I only
stayed a few hours in Moscow. Here I ran into real winter; I think it is probably
no better where you are. Now I shall be busy finishing the sketches of the
finale and scherzo of my new symphony. On Friday in Holy Week I am coming
to you and I am happy at the thought of it. Forgive for so little news – we
shall see each other soon. . . .

P. Tchaikovsky

[659] TO VLADIMIR DAVYDOV [Klin]
11 April 1893

Up till now I have been doing my duty very punctiliously: I bear one musical
progeny each day. But these children of mine are premature and mediocre.
I have no desire at all to create, and do so only for money. All I try to ensure
is that they should not be too bad. Please tell Modia that I am very upset that
my letter, in which I praised his *Nal and Damayanti*, has been lost. The devil
only knows how this happens! However, maybe it reached him after all. I find
this libretto very well made, but the subject – too far from real life – does not
attract me. What I need is a subject like. . . . More than ever I am angry with
the weather and am 'en froid' with the high authorities.

I embrace you a thousand times.

P. Tchaikovsky

Nal and Damayanti, a story of Hindu origin, did not appeal to Tchaikovsky, but
Modest's libretto was used by Arensky, whose opera of that name was produced in
1899.

[660] TO VLADIMIR DAVYDOV [Klin]
15 April 1893

I am continuing to concoct my musical pancakes, the tenth one is being done
today. The extraordinary thing is that the more cooking I do the easier it gets
and I find more pleasure in doing it. At the beginning it went slowly and the
first two or three [pieces] were entirely the result of an effort of will, but now
I cannot stop my thoughts, and they come one after another at all times of
the day. If I and my publisher could [agree] I would live a whole year in the
country to work *à la Leikin*, and he would publish all this mass of music. He
would then pay all the fees and I could then earn 36,000 roubles in one year.
It would not be bad!

The Kharkov photographs and portraits arrived today. They are all wonderfully good, especially the large one. I shall bring them for you to see. Meanwhile here is a cabinet portrait for you. My dear, how is your examination going? Why is no one writing? How is Apukhtin? Ask Uncle Modia to write! Here is another idea that has been born for a *Polka de Salon* (*à Mr George Tschaikovsky [sic]*).

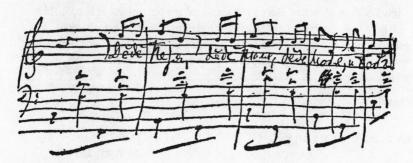

I kiss and embrace you,

Yours

P. Tchaikovsky

In Moscow in February the nineteen year old Rachmaninov, a student at the Conservatoire, had presented Tchaikovsky with a copy of his Op. 3 piano pieces. Tchaikovsky also heard several rehearsals and the first performance of Rachmaninov's opera *Aleko* (libretto from Pushkin's poem *The Gypsies* by V. Nemirovich-Dantshenko). This had been composed as an examination exercise and it was very successful. Tchaikovsky thought that since it was a one-act piece it could go into the same programme as his *Yolanta*. When, however, the two works were coupled together it was Tchaikovsky's that proved the failure.

Tchaikovsky was attracted to the subject of *Undine* (otherwise the subject of operas by Lortzing, E. T. A. Hoffmann, Mori and Sporck) from youth, and considered it as subject for opera in 1878 (see p. 164, and Letter 66) and for ballet in 1886 (see Letter 440). Modest now again suggested it and sent a libretto to his brother which he had written in fact for Rachmaninov. He wrote: 'I still hope . . . that you will use the libretto yourself. . . .I doubt if Rachmaninov, however talented he is, will write the opera.' Rachmaninov did not write the opera.

The author Nikolai Alexandrovich Leikin produced cheap novels at great speed and thereby accumulated a fortune. The suggestion that he wrote à la Leikin was not calculated to please a high-minded young author.

[661] TO MODEST TCHAIKOVSKY　　　　　　　　　　Klin
　　　　　　　　　　　　　　　　　　　　　　　　　17 April 1893

My poor Modinka!

Although it is very upsetting I have to disillusion you. The libretto is excellently planned, everything important has been used, as far as possible the poetry has been kept intact, there is nothing superfluous, much of what you have added over and above Zhukovsky's text is also very effective; but, all the same, I cannot compose *Undine*. There are several reasons for this. First, however cleverly you have done the libretto much of what attracts me in the poem is not there. For example; the drive in a cart, the hammering down of the well and other details (you have not put in the 'sympathetic padre') are absent, while because of the stage requirements what you have done in some places has lost its poetic meaning. For instance, the scene in which she comments as the knight dies must take place in his room, by the bed, in solitude. All the charm of the episode is lost by your having it in the presence of everybody, in the square. It might make it impressive but its poetic meaning is lost. And how can one put into a libretto the moment at which I had to cry last time I read it? I mean the scene during the knight's funeral when she turns into a stream and runs round the grave, never to be separated from his precious body. What I mean is, that in spite of your skill, *Undine*, whom I love so much, and who touches me so deeply, cannot be represented on the stage. And as far as a conventionally operatic, more or less prosaic, *Undine* is concerned, I have already written it once. This is the most important reason for my inability to use this subject again. In that other *Undine* composed long ago, there were good, deep-felt moments, and if I tried again I could not recapture the same freshness of feeling. On the other hand, some of it was absolutely awful; as for instance: 'Now all is ready in the temple for us, the marriage crowns are waiting.' It is so horrible that I hate even to think about the banquet scene. I could say more about it but had better discuss it with you in person. For the present all I can say is that I do not feel the inspiration that one ought to have to start a large new work. For God's sake look for, or yourself invent, a subject – but not a fantastic one; better something like *Carmen* or *Cavalleria rusticana*. Why not just write a libretto for Rachmaninov and not bother about putting it into verse. Let someone else write the poetry from your plot.

Please, my Golubchik, do not get upset and angry.

I embrace you.

P. Tchaikovsky

Am sending the libretto to Rachmaninov.

[662]   TO MODEST TCHAIKOVSKY   Moscow
                                                22 April 1893

Alas, dear Modia it seems that I will not be able to write thirty piano pieces. I composed eighteen in fifteen days and brought them to Moscow today. But now, I shall have to stay here for four days (a show at the Conservatoire, I have promised a morning to the Sinodalny Choir, my birthday festivities with friends, etc.). Then I want to make a trip to Nijny and on 29th Rachmaninov's *Aleko* has its first performance, which means that I shall not get back home before 30 April. And on 10 May I have to leave for abroad. But as I wish most intensely to pass a few days with all of you, I shall probably be in Petersburg on the 3rd. Perhaps I may have time to compose a few more songs.

What a muddle it is with poor Emma. I forced her to stay an extra day in Petersburg, so that she could see me in Moscow on Friday. But I thought that the Conservatoire performance was to be on Friday whereas it takes place today. However, it does not matter.

23 April

Yesterday I went to the dress rehearsal of the Conservatoire performance; it was the second act of *Orpheus* and the *Matrimonio segretto*. *Orpheus* was not very well performed, but Cimarosa's opera, which is charming, was excellently done. All the singers were pupils of Lavrovskaia who proved what a good teacher she is. Then I had dinner at the Hermitage and in the evening went with Kashkin and Poplavsky to the Malyi Theatre. We saw [Sardou's] *Patrie*. In spite of clever effects this is a very French play, and it would have been dull if it had not been for Ermolova being absolutely heavenly. Then I went to the Hermitage again, where I ate, drank, and played cards with a number of friends and returned home at 4 a.m. It seemed quite extraordinary to pass a day of this kind after my peaceful life in Klin. I have already spent the money for half of my songs.

I embrace you all.

P. Tchaikovsky

[663]   TO MODEST TCHAIKOVSKY   Berlin
                                               15–27 May 1893

Golubchik Modia!

I am not going to describe my journey nor say anything about my present state of mind.

I am frightened at the thought that after London and Cambridge I shall be obliged to pass through Paris to see Ziloty on business, then to Itter where I will also have to discuss business matters, and after that go to Grankino and Ukolovo to see the Maslovs. Travelling – I mean a journey by train – makes me so sick that I think of all these movements with horror. My soul is in turmoil – would it not be better not to go anywhere and return straight back to Klin? I do want to go to Grankino but if I have to orchestrate the symphony during the summer, put the concerto in order and also orchestrate it, is it not better to go straight back to Klin? On the other hand my heart longs for Grankino. . . .

I implore you all to write to London.

I embrace you.

Yours

P. Tchaikovsky

TO ANATOLI TCHAIKOVSKY

London
17–29 May 1893

Golubchik Tolia!

I am frightfully sorry, I promised to write from Petersburg but did not. I had several disagreeable days in Petersburg. Having started on my journey in a happy state of mind less than an hour later I was attacked by that maddening, indescribable, depression which now pursues me every time I go abroad. This torturing mood has not left me for a minute since I left and is even growing *crescendo*. It is definitely the last time I am going to [go abroad]. All my thoughts are centred on the wish that it will end as quickly as possible so that I can return. I will not come straight back, but via Paris where I shall stay a day or two (I have to see Ziloty there on behalf of the Petersburg Musical Society to persuade him to take the post of professor at the Conservatoire). From there to the Tirol where I intend to stay three days at Menter's, and then to Grankino. I promised this to Bob and, besides, I have a great desire to stay a few days in that charming steppe country. From Grankino I will go to see Nikolai Ilyich and then home at last. At the end of the summer I intend to visit you and we will then go to see Pania together.

I arrived in London this morning. I do not like this ugly town. I found a room with difficulty, for all the hotels are full. The concert will be on 20 May–1 June, and then I shall have to remain idle here for a week. On the 11th and 12th the celebrations take place in Cambridge and on the 13th (our 1 June) back home. I think of you, my dears, all the time. It is only in a far land, when separated, and oppressed by solitude and depression that I feel how great my love is for all of you.

Beg dear Emma to write.

I kiss Pania and Tata.

Yours

P. Tchaikovsky

TO VLADIMIR DAVYDOV

London
17–29 May 1893

I am writing to you with a voluptuous pleasure. The thought that this paper is going to be in your hands fills me with joy and brings tears to my eyes. Is it not curious that I voluntarily inflict upon myself all these tortures? What the devil do I want it all for? Several times yesterday, on my way, I wanted to run away; but somehow I felt ashamed to return empty-handed. Yesterday my tortures reached such a pitch that I lost both appetite and sleep and this happens very rarely. I am suffering not only from anguish and distress which cannot be expressed in words (in my new symphony there is a place which I think expresses it very well) but also from a vague feeling of fear and the devil only knows what else. The physical symptoms are pains at the bottom of my bowels, and aching and weakness in the legs. So, definitely, this is the last time I am going through all this. From now on I shall agree to go anywhere only for a very large sum of money and not for more than three days. Just think, I have to stick here for another two weeks, which seem an eternity!!!

Arrived tonight. Three hours crossing over a calm sea. Found a room with difficulty, the 'season' is on now, and all the hotels are full up. London is a loathsome town; I can never find anything here. No men's lavatories; no money exchange offices; it was with difficulty that I found a hat to fit my head. When I arrived at the hotel I met the Paris pianist Diémer who is now living here and to my astonishment was very glad to see him! He is, after all, an old acquaintance and has always been kind to me. Consequently I was obliged to go to his 'recital' – i.e. a matinée concert – straight after my arrival.

Saint-Saëns is participating in the concert I am conducting. After the matinée I went to see the organizer of the concert to fix the time of rehearsal. Now I am in a hurry to write to you. I have by now forgotten all my waverings which I mentioned in my letter from Berlin, and if you do not change your plans I shall go to Paris from Cambridge to see Ziloty, to Itter (I shall like this), and then I hope to be in Grankino about the 15th. After Cambridge at the end of all the excitement, on the way home, I shall not suffer any more from depression. . . .

Yours

P. Tchaikovsky

[666] TO MODEST TCHAIKOVSKY   London
                                          3 June 1893

Thank you, dear Modia, for both letters. Letters help very much to keep up my energy which is perpetually ready to fail. The concert was brilliant, i.e. according to the general opinion. I enjoyed a real triumph, so that Saint-Saëns who appeared after me rather suffered from my extraordinary success. This, of course, is very nice but what a punishment the life here is during the 'Season'! All my lunches and dinners are booked and everything takes so much time. Yesterday the Directors gave a dinner to Saint-Saëns and myself at the Westminster Club. The opulence and elegance were extraordinary, but we sat down at 7 and got up at 11.30 (without exaggeration). Besides all this, every day one has to be at afternoon concerts, for they come and invite you, and it is difficult to refuse. Today I had to lunch with Sarasate who was wonderfully nice to me.

It is difficult to give an idea about the traffic on the London streets. Last time I came here it was bad weather and I could not get any real idea of it. The devil only knows what it is like – with all the beautiful harnesses and trappings – and one does not know where to look. I have just returned from afternoon tea with the Ambassador's wife. She looks just like a cook but has a friendly and kind face. Sazonov the secretary is very nice; but what crowds of people I have to meet here. And how all this tires me!! Every morning I wake up suffering and unhappy, then get into a hazy state with only one thought in my mind, that all this should end as soon as possible!!

In Cambridge I shall keep a diary giving a full account of everything. It seems that the whole ceremony is most curious. Grieg is ill – all the others are coming. . . .

I embrace you.

P. Tchaikovsky

At a Philharmonic Concert on 2 June (western style) Tchaikovsky's Fourth Symphony was performed in London for the first time. Saint-Saëns's Second Piano Concerto (1868), with the composer as soloist, was also included in the programme. *The Musical Times* supported Tchaikovsky's own estimate of his popularity, observing that the symphony 'went straight to the heart of the audience, who, applauding long and loudly, would have heard it again with pleasure'.

[667]   TO MODEST TCHAIKOVSKY   London
                                          10 June 1893

I suppose this letter will find you already in Peter. Forgive me, Golubchik, for being so lazy about writing. Honestly, there's no time to write! A devilish life! Not one pleasant moment – fear, sadness, exhaustion, disgust, etc. But at last the end is near. However I must be fair and say that I have met many charming people here and much kindness has been shown to me. All the future Doctors [of Music] have arrived, except for Grieg who is ill. As well as Saint-Saëns I like Boïto; Bruch, on the other hand, is a disgustingly pompous figure. The day after tomorrow I go to Cambridge. I shall not stay in a hotel, but in rooms offered to me by one Dr Maitland, who sent me a most courteous letter of invitation. I only stay there one night. On the day we arrive there will be a concert and a banquet, and the [degree] ceremony will take place on the next day. All will be at an end at 4 o'clock and I shall travel straight back to Paris. From there through Switzerland to the Tirol to see Menter, and then on to Grankino.

I definitely approve your visiting the Optina Pustyn and even envy you; but where will you stay? I have a feeling that you will return to Grankino when I will be there.

I embrace you.

P. Tchaikovsky

In order to celebrate the Jubilee of the University Musical Society a group of eminent foreign composers was invited to Cambridge, each to be honoured with the Mus. D. degree and also at a concert at which he should direct one of his works. The programme included: Bruch, 'The banquet with the Phaeacians', from *Odysseus* (Op. 41); Saint-Saëns, Fantasia for Piano and Orchestra, *Africa* (first performance in England); Boïto, Prologue, *Mefistofele*; Tchaikovsky, Symphonic Poem, *Francesca da Rimini* (Op. 32); Grieg, *Peer Gynt* Suite (Op. 46). The programme also included C. V. Stanford's Ode, *East to West* (Op. 52). Stanford was the retiring conductor of the Society, and Professor of Music. Grieg was prevented from being present by illness.

After the concert there was a dinner at King's College. Among those present was a first year student from Trinity College, Ralph Vaughan Williams, who was friendly with Professor and Mrs F. W. Maitland, with whom Tchaikovsky stayed at the West Lodge of Downing College.

[668]   TO ANATOLI TCHAIKOVSKY   Paris
                                                  3–15 June 1893

I arrived here yesterday and found your letter waiting for me, my dear Tolia! If you only knew how I had to suffer in London and Cambridge! I cannot find words to say how glad I am that it is at an end and that everything went off quite smoothly.

The solemnities which took place at our investiture altogether lasted two days. I had to stay in rooms prepared for me by one of the professors and not at an hotel. It would have been awkward if the professor had not happened to be a delightful person and a great lover of everything Russian. His wife completely charmed me by her kindness. A concert was given on the day of our arrival at which we all conducted our own compositions. *Francesca* was successful and met with great applause. After the concert there was a grand dinner and an even grander reception. The degree ceremony took place on the next day. At 11.30 we all met in a special hall where all the University Professors and Directors were present for our investiture with our Doctors' gowns. The gown is white silk bordered with velvet and you wear a black velvet hat. Then the Master of Ceremonies placed us in the appropriate order and we proceeded across the huge courtyard to the hall of the University Senate. A large crowd watched the procession, and an Indian Rajah attracted the greatest attention by the precious stones worth several millions that adorned his dress. He received a Doctor's degree for having done much in his country for the enlightenment of his people. As soon as we were seated a Latin speech was pronounced in honour of each one of us in turn, by the public orator.

During this speech one had to stand in front of the rostrum without moving, very difficult. The students who filled the gallery in accordance with the centuries-old tradition, during the speeches, screamed, squeaked, whistled, behaved in a scandalous way and you have to suffer all this without a wink. After the speech, the Master of Ceremonies, carrying his mace, takes you up to the Chancellor who pronounces a Latin formula which means: 'In the name of the Father, the Son and the Holy Spirit I pronounce you to be a Doctor.'

After which the procession returned in the same order to the first hall. Half an hour later – a solemn luncheon took place at the end of which, again according to ancient tradition everybody had to drink out of an enormous ancient goblet which is passed along all the tables. Then there was a reception given by the [Vice-] Chancellor's wife and at four o'clock I left for London.

The same evening I gave a dinner to some of my new London friends and at eight o'clock the next morning I left for Paris. Only here I recovered a bit from the three weeks of nervous strain and fatigue. After the enormous traffic in the London streets, Paris seems like a desert. Write now to Grankino (Government of Poltava, District of Constantinograd, P.O. Novo-Nikolaevka).

I embrace and kiss you, my dear. Tell Emma I shall write to her soon and thank her for her letter.

Yours

P. Tchaikovsky

Other honorary degrees were awarded to the Maharajah of Bhaonagar, Lord Herschell, Field Marshal Lord Roberts, Julius Zupitza, a German philologist and famous scholar in the field of English literature, and Standish O'Grady, an expert in the province of ancient literature of Ireland. See *Cambridge University Reporter*, 16 June 1893, p. 1074. A photograph of Tchaikovsky taken by Mrs Maitland is reproduced in 'A Cambridge Occasion', Jill Vlasto, *The Musical Times*, July 1968, pp. 616–18.

The following letter was addressed to Modest, c/o B. V. Plessky (son of V. A. Plessky, business manager of the Kamenka estates), at the Optina Pustyn – a monastery in the province of Vologota, West of Lake Belo, in the north of Russia. The monastery was a frequent place for retreats. Modest was staying nearby.

[669]   TO MODEST TCHAIKOVSKY   Paris
                                         6–18 June 1893

How is it, Modia, that you've forgotten to send me your address? Although I do not quite know where to address my letter I am taking a risk and writing to Boris, asking him to forward it to you. This is my fourth day in Paris, resting after my London and Cambridge exploits. I have written all about Cambridge to Kolia, sorry I mean Tolia, and asked him to send my letter over to you. But please allow me not to repeat it all. It would take too long and I have a terrific attack of laziness intensified by the frightful heat.

Everything went off quite happily, and there were lots of curious details. I was most richly dressed; the wife of the professor at whose house I stayed in Cambridge took a photograph of me, which she promised to send to me, and then I shall send it to you. Without staying long in London I arrived here longing for solitude and peace. I enjoyed the first two days but now I'm beginning to get bored. Tomorrow I am going to visit Menter, and about five

days later travel to Grankino. How awful it is to have to travel in summer!!!
However, it's no matter so long as I get back to Russia as soon as possible!
I went once to the theatre here to see *Surprises du divorce* where Duris has
taken Joly's place but isn't half as good. I also heard Yvette Guilbert once.
How strange all this must seem to you where you are – at the Optina
Monastery!!! Tolia is very hurt that you don't want to visit them. Do go
there even if not for long. Anyway, I hope to see you soon in Grankino.

I embrace you and Boris.

Yours

P. Tchaikovsky

[670] TO ANATOLI TCHAIKOVSKY   Grankino
         19 June 1893

After four days and four nights in a train I finally arrived in Grankino last
night. It is odd but the beauties of the Tirol where I stayed for a week at
Menter's did not give me half the pleasure that I had at the sight of the
unending steppe across which I had to drive yesterday from the railway
station. Say what you like, but the Russian countryside appeals to me much
more than all the beauty-spots in Europe that are praised so much. Besides,
instead of the usual droughts there has been plenty of rain here and the crops
and grasses are wonderfully rich! I found Kolia, Bob, his friend and all of them
happy and well. I too feel really happy in this charming country wilderness.
On the way here I heard of the death of Karl Karlovich Albrecht. Although
I was expecting it as I knew his illness was incurable I shed tears over my dear
Karlusha. Kostia Shilovsky also died quite recently. Now I have to expect the
death of Lelia Apukhtin whose dropsy is also incurable. Thank God, that there
is no word of cholera and that you will not have to go through last year's
apprehensions.

Write a few words here. The address is – Government of Poltava, District of
Constantinograd, P.O. Novo-Nikolaevka.

I embrace you.

P. Tchaikovsky

[671] TO MODEST TCHAIKOVSKY   Grankino
         23 June 1893

... I have been five days. The journey from Itter was very tiring. (I was,
I must say, pleased at staying in Itter for six days.) Spent four nights on the
train. But from Alexeevka till this minute I always enjoy myself as you usually
do. The drive from Alexeevka [station] to Grankino was absolutely wonderful,
for – thanks to the rain – the steppe is beautiful. Halfway there Nazar was

waiting for me with tea. Arrived at 5 o'clock at their tea time. I think everybody was pleased to see me. Life here is very pleasant. . . .

But it rains too much and this is a bit frightening for the crops. We drove once to Skalonovska and went once to Juchikha to catch crabs — otherwise we are leading a regular life. Unfortunately it will soon come to an end. My visit here in Kamenka, thanks to a misunderstanding, has been turned into an intrigue, and it has been said that I am trying to influence Bob against his father. He is being bombarded by letters and reproaches. He even hid one of Miss Eastwood's letters from me, it was so full of abuse. Curious! ! In any case, we shall leave at the end of the month, in a week's time. They will go to Verbovka and I to brother Nikolai Ilyich.

I hope to be at home about the 15th. I embrace you. Do, please, Modia dear, think of a libretto for me. I want to write an opera in winter.

Yours

P. Tchaikovsky

[672] TO ANATOLI TCHAIKOVSKY   Ukolovo
6 July 1893
[Nikolai Tchaikovsky's Estate]

My dear friend Anatosha!

I arrived in Ukolovo yesterday after a rather tiring journey, as I had to drive the eighty versts from Kursk in the heat. As I did not want to sit and wait for hours for the next train which stops at the Korennaia Pustyn I decided to hire a carriage. I enjoyed the drive very much for the country here is beautiful. . . . Ukolovo and the whole of southern Russia are glorious this summer. Thanks to an abundance of rain the vegetation is wonderfully lush. I shall stay here for another five days until Olga's Saint's Day and then go to Klin. I must honestly say that I long to live at home for a time. Besides, I must start the instrumentation of two new large works, the Symphony (with which I am very pleased) and the Piano Concerto. I have been composing both during this winter and spring then finished the sketches in Grankino and now must hurry and finish everything for September.

I do want to visit you but it will be only at the end of the summer when at least half of the instrumentation will be ready.

I embrace you, my dear.

P. Tchaikovsky

TO ANATOLI TCHAIKOVSKY   [Klin]
19 July 1893

My very dear Tolia!

Last night I returned home at last, a bit later than I expected, for I had an attack of diarrhoea, cured as usual by a dose of castor oil. Stayed in Moscow only one day. Everything is perfect here and I am very happy that I can start working. Unfortunately I will first have to answer thirty letters which have also been waiting for me. I went to see Anna Leontievna in Moscow. She is quite well off and looks perfectly contented as much as she can be after the death of her husband whom she really loved. Karlusha died of an attack of angina pectoris with other complications. You wonder what he lived on? Actually his pension was very large but unfortunately diminished by his debts.

Do you know that both Kostia and Volodia Shilovsky died this summer, one after the other. Volodia left all his money to his wife who deserved it as she was, probably, his only real friend. Do not expect many letters from me now, my Golubchik, for I must work hard and not move from here until the end of August. Then I will come and see you.

I have the most pleasant memories of my visit to Ukolovo. What wonderful people Kolia and Olia are, and George is also a dear.

I kiss you.

P. Tchaikovsky

On 19 July Tchaikovsky wrote to V. L. Davydov that he was starting on his new symphony. A playful reference to the 'Fourth Suite' is to a group of young friends – Vladimir and Yuri Davydov, N. G. Konradi and five others – who acquired this as a collective nickname. One day Piotr told his brother Modest that he intended to compose a Fourth Suite. 'Why,' said Modest, 'do you want to compose a Fourth Suite when you already have one.' He thereupon gave the composer a photograph of himself with the above mentioned young men. The photograph is to be seen in the Museum in Klin.

[674] TO MODEST TCHAIKOVSKY   Klin
22 July 1893
10 o'clock, evening

I have not yet thanked you, Golubchik Modia, for your letter about your impression of Verbovka. It arrived three days ago. I enjoyed reading it but what upsets me in your letters is that when I read them my lonely life in Klin seems cheerless and I long so much to be there with you all. On the other hand I can only work properly at home. I have now dived deep into my symphony; the further I get with the instrumentation the more difficult it becomes. Twenty years ago I used to go full speed ahead and it came out very well. Now I have become cowardly and unsure of myself. For instance, today I sat the whole day over two pages – nothing went as I wanted it to. All the same, work is progressing and I could never have done as much anywhere else but at home.

Thanks to Alexei's efforts my house has taken on a very smart look. Everything has been repaired, the toilet is new and bright; there are masses of flowers in the garden, the paths are cleared, and there are new fences and gates too. I am excellently fed, and Alexei has not yet started to grumble. Egorushka is sweet – in one word, everything is perfect.

All the same, when I am not at work I feel bored and long for Verbovka, actually not Verbovka itself but to join my dear Fourth Suite. Of late I have noticed that after long journeys, and meeting many people, I feel bored alone at home. This will probably stop after a time. But I am again invited to go abroad and may go in a month's time – but not for long.

Pollini wrote a letter imploring me to be sure to come for the revival of *Yolanta* on 8 September. As he is both conductor and director he also wants personally to discuss the production of *The Queen of Spades* this season.

Had a desperate letter from Napravnik; he wants your address and complains that he has lost two weeks of work, waiting for the libretto [of *Dubrovsky*]. I sent him your address by telegraph but do not understand what has happened. . . .

P. Tchaikovsky

[675]   TO VLADIMIR DAVYDOV   Klin
                                                       3 [2?] August 1893

In my last letter to Modest I complain that you don't want to know me, and now he is silent too, and all links with your crowd are completely broken. . . .

What makes me sad is that you take so little interest in me. Could it be that you are positively a hard egotist? However, forgive me, I won't pester you again. The symphony which I was going to dedicate to you (not so sure that I shall now) is getting on. I am very pleased with the music but not entirely satisfied with the instrumentation. It does not come out as I hoped it would. It will be quite conventional and no surprise if this symphony is abused and unappreciated – that has happened before. But I definitely find it my very best, and in particular the most sincere of all my compositions. I love it as I have never loved any of my musical children.

My life is unvaried, and I often feel bored in the evenings, but I must not complain – the most important thing at the moment is my symphony, and it is only at home that I can work really properly.

My life is greatly enriched by the presence of my godson, a wonderfully attractive child. At the end of August I shall have to go abroad for a week. If I were sure that you would still be in Verbovka in September I would love to come at the beginning of the month. But I know nothing about you.

I embrace you with all my love.

P. Tchaikovsky

The godson referred to above was the child of Tchaikovsky's servant Alexei.

[676]   TO ANATOLI TCHAIKOVSKY   [Klin]
                                                12 August 1893

... My work is getting on very well, although I cannot write as fast as before. Not because I'm getting feebler through old age but because of being much more exacting with myself, and I've lost my former self-confidence.

I am very proud of my symphony and think it my very best work. I would like Pania to stay a little longer in the country as I shall not be able to come and see you before the beginning of September. However, if I don't stay with you in the country I shall spend a few weeks with you in town, if bad weather makes Pania leave the country earlier. Forgive this short letter. I fear overwork, as I have no other time but late at night to write letters.

I embrace you.

P. Tchaikovsky

[677]   TO ANATOLI TCHAIKOVSKY   Klin
                                                20 August 1893

Dear Tolia!

Circumstances compel me to postpone my trip to Nijny so that I will probably not come before 10 September; the fact is that I have to go to Hamburg on business. As I broke my promise to the director of the Hamburg opera to come to the first performance of *Yolanta* last year, I gave him my word to come this year. Now he writes that *Yolanta* is going to be on again on 8 September (27 August our style) and he implores me to come. I cannot refuse. He also asks me to come and state my requirements for the production of *The Queen of Spades* which is also going to be produced in the near future. So today I am off to Petersburg and from there to Hamburg. Then I shall return to Petersburg where I have some business to attend to for myself and Modest and Bob.

Kolia has found it a disadvantage to go on living with Modest and has chucked him out, although politely, if without much ceremony. Now Modest is going to settle down with Bob. I must help them for without me they will not be able to manage and as long as all is not settled and decided I shall stay in Petersburg. Then I can come and see you and stay with you, either in the country or in town, at least for eight days. Golubchik, write so that I get your letter at the beginning of September (address: 24 Fontanka). Where ought I to go, to Nijny or to the country? I shall not go home as Katia, Alexei's wife, will be having her baby then. Please forgive that I did not keep my word as promised. Have finished my symphony and worked with great effort to have it ready in time. I embrace you with love. As I am exhausted from hard work I think it will do me good to go away. At this moment the last rites of the church are being given to Lelia Apukhtin who has just died.

P. Tchaikovsky

During the final stages of composition of the Sixth Symphony the brothers Konius were staying with Tchaikovsky, the one assisting with annotations of the violin parts, the other busy playing through the piano duet score of the work.

[678] TO VLADIMIR DAVYDOV   Klin
                                                    20 August 1893

Not knowing how long you were going to stay in Verbovka the question about my going there became very complicated. I have to be in Petersburg at the beginning of September for the Music Society concerts. They want me to be present at their meeting and Petersen so insistently asked me to fix a day that, having decided that you and Modest will already be in Petersburg at the end of August, I told them that I shall be at their service at the beginning of September. Also Anatoli has been expecting me to come for quite a long time and wishes me to find them still in the country, where they will be staying until 15 September. This I promised to do before I got your telegram. All this means that I will not be able to come to Verbovka in the first half of September. In any case when I'm back from abroad and in Petersburg, I shall know from Modest about your removal to a new flat and how life is going to be settled. (This worries me and concerns me very much.) A letter from Anatoli will also be waiting for me in Petersburg. According to what he says I will decide either to join him at once or to go to Verbovka for a few days.

In any case we shall see each other soon.

P. Tchaikovsky

As I am writing this Lelia Apukhtin is taken to the place of his last rest!! Although I have been expecting it, it is still painful and frightening. He was once my nearest friend.

[679] TO MODEST TCHAIKOVSKY   [Klin]
                                                    9 September 1893

Modia!

I am leaving now to join Tolia! Have you seen Nazar? He stayed in Klin with
Alexei (not knowing he could miss you). I took the plays myself and gave
them to Ilyinsky. (Chernevsky was busy.) Write if you have found a flat and
also, if there is anything new? My address is: Vtorovo, Nijny-Novgorod
Railway, Mikhailovskoie Village. If your *Prejudices* is off, send a telegram.

Good-bye. Shall arrive on the 17th.

P. Tchaikovsky

[680] TO ANATOLI TCHAIKOVSKY   Moscow
                                                    20 September 1893

Golubchik!

Forgive me, but I have completely forgotten to send you a telegram about
Modest's play in time. The play is well acted but has great faults in its
construction – it is much too lengthy. As is usual with him the first three acts
are interesting, but the last one bad; and this spoils the whole effect. In spite
of this the play was a sensation because Ermolova for the first time played an
older woman. All the actors were good. As well as Ermolova, Medvedeva was
excellent. There are touching moments and the second act is vivacious and
amusing. Modest was well received and no one hissed, I think that this play
will bring good returns. . . .

I embrace you. Write to Klin. Remember with pleasure my stay in
Mikhailovskoie.

Yours

P. Tchaikovsky

[681] TO MODEST TCHAIKOVSKY   [Moscow]
                                                    24 September 1893

At last I have received news about the birth of a daughter to Alexei Ivanovich
Sofronov. But for some reason he does not allow me to return before the 25th,
i.e. tomorrow, Saturday.

These last days I have been frightfully bored and, for no reason at all, developed
an exceptional longing for solitude. Am sitting in my hotel room and have not
seen anyone but the servant. Longing to get home, to work and live a normal
life.

Shall probably get some news from you in Klin. My most important worry now is to have you properly settled. As long as everything is not in order in your life I shall be happy. Has Mülbach given you some money? I am in agony, fearing that he has not done so. If he hasn't I shall take immediate steps. I went to the third performance of your *Prejudices* and am definitely of the opinion that it needs a lot of cutting. It was excellently acted. Even Shchepkina was good.

And so expecting news from you, good-bye, Golubchik, Modia. I embrace Bob and Volodia.

P. Tchaikovsky

EPILOGUE

by Galina von Meck

There were two more letters to his nearest relatives; one to his brother Anatoli and one to his nephew V. L. Davydov both dated 27 September; in his letter to the latter he said: 'Started the instrumentation of the piano concerto but the work is taking time.' In his letter to his brother he mentions the dates of the concerts when the Sixth Symphony would be played: in Petersburg on 16 October; in Moscow on 4 December. But it was not the composer's fate to live until the second concert. On 10 October he came to Petersburg for the rehearsals and stayed at his brother Modest's flat. On 16 October the Sixth Symphony was given for the first time, conducted by the composer.

'I am prouder of this Symphony than of any other of my compositions,' wrote Tchaikovsky to P. I. Yurgenson on 18 October. Three days later the composer came back home seemingly very upset by something – we shall never really know what – and not feeling very well. He asked his brother for a glass of water. When told that he would have to wait for the water to be boiled (Petersburg water not being fit to drink unboiled as the town stood on boggy ground) he ignored his brother's protests, went into the kitchen, filled a glass of water from the tap and drank it, saying something like: 'Who cares anyway!'

That same evening he felt quite ill; the doctor who was sent for the next morning diagnosed cholera, which was then ever-present in Petersburg. Three days later the composer died in great agony.

I am not going here into full details about these last days of Tchaikovsky's life. There were, besides his brother Modest and the doctor, several other people present and the interpretation of some of the things said by the dying man in his agony, according to what I know from the composer's nephew, young Count Alexander Litke (Sania Litke) who was present, was completely different from the way his brother Modest related them. Anyway, the curse which Modest said was meant for my grandmother, Nadezhda von Meck, could not possibly have been directed towards her as Modest wanted it to be thought.

For the world in general Tchaikovsky is one of the great composers of the nineteenth century; but nothing that has been written about him in the innumerable biographies has conveyed the real personality of the man as we – the young generation – especially the Mecks – knew him or knew of him from those who were most intimate with him.

What we had heard from our parents and also from his childhood friend and cousin Annette Merkling was about 'Uncle Piotr' – he was never called anything else. Uncle Piotr, the kind, considerate, very charming and humane member of our family (although I did not know him personally, as he died when I was a baby), has always been not just a myth but a living person to me.

Avdotia Yakovlevna (Bakhireva, A. V.)
Alexander (Tarnavich, A.)
Alexander Mikhailovich (Lipport, A. M.)
Alexandra Vladimirovna (Alexeeva, A. V.)
Alexandra Valerianovna (Panaeva, A.V.)
Alexandrova Elizaveta Mikhailovna (Tchaikovskaia, E.M.)
Alesha, Alexei (Sofronov, A. I.)
Alesha (Davydov, A. V.)
Alina (Konradi, A. I.)
Amalia (Litke, A. V.)
Anatosha, Anatoshka (Tchaikovsky, A. I.)
Anna Leontievna (Albrecht, A. L.)
Annette (Merkling, A. P.)
Annia, Aniuta (Meck, A. L. von)

Batasha (Hubert, A. I.)
Bob, Bobik (Davydov, V. L.)
Boris (Plessky, B. V.)
Bun, the (Tchaikovskaia, E. M.)

Dina (Sangursky, G. M.)

Egor (Sofronov, G. A.)
Elizaveta Sergeevna, Lizaveta (Davydova, E. S.)
Elizaveta Vassilievna (Davydova, E. V.)
Emma (Jenton, E.)

Fania (Tchaikovsky, M. P.)
Fedotikha (Fedotova, G. N.)
Feklusha (Sofronova, F. G.)
Flegont (Bisterfeld, F. K.)
Fofa (Ershova, S. A.)

George (Tchaikovsky, G. N.)
Glamsha (Glama-Meshcherskaia, A. Y.)
Grisha (Sangursky, G. M.)

Ilenka (Tchaikovsky, I. P.)
Ivan Mikhailovich (Lipport, A. M.)

Karl Yulvich (Davydov, K. Y.)
Karlusha (Albrecht, K. K.)
Katerina Ivanovna (Sulmenieva, E. I.)
Katerina Vassilievna (Peresleny, E. V.)
Katia, Aunt (Alexeeva, E. A.)
Katia (Gorodezkaia, E. F.)
Katia (Shobert, E. V.)
Katia (Sofronova, E.)
Koka (Litke, K. N.)
Kokodeks, Kolia (Peresleny, N. V.)
Kolia, Kolichka, Kolinka (Konradi, N. H.)
Kolia (Konshin, N. V.)

Kolia (Meck, N. K. von)
Kolia (Rimsky-Korsakov, N. A.)
Konstantinov (Lazary, K. N.)
Kostia (Shilovsky, V. S.)
Kotik (Kotek, Y. Y.)

Lelia (Apukhtin, A. N.)
Lenka (Sofronov, A. I.)
Leva (Davydov, L. V.)
Lida (Olkhovskaia, L. V.)
Liza, Aunt (Shobert, E. A.)
Lizaveta Mikhailovna (Tchaikovskaia, E. M.)
Lizaveta Vassilievna (Davydova, E. V.)

Malia (Litke, A. V.)
Mania (Laroche, H. A.)
Mamasha (Tchaikovskaia, A. A.)
Mary (Kondratieva, M. S.)
Mashura, Mashurochka (Foss, M. E.)
Mikhailov (Sheller-Mikhailov, A. K.)
Mina (Hahn, W. V.)
Misha (Sofronov, M. I.)
Mitiuk, Mitia (Davydov, D. L.)
Mödia, Modichka, Modinka, Modka, Modosha (Tchaikovsky, M. I.)

Nadezhda Mikhailovnona (Hartung, N. M.)
Nastasia Vassilievna, Nata (Popova, A. V.)
Nata, Natalia Andreevna (Plesskaia, N. A.)
Nazar (Litrov, N.)
Nikolai Vassilievich (Davydov, N. V.)
Nikolai Dmitrievich (Kondratiev, N. D.)
Nikolai Lvovich (Bochechkarov, N. L.)
Niks (Litke, N. F.)
Novishikha (Novikova, N. V.)

Olga, Olia (Tchaikovskaia, O. S.)
Ouka (Davydov, Y. L.)

Panaishna (Panaeva, A. V.)
Panechka, Panichka, Pania, Paniusha (Tchaikovskaia, P. V.)
Papasha (Konshin, V. D.)
Papasha, Papochka (Tchaikovsky, I. P.)
Petia (Henke, P. E.)
Piotr Ivanovich (Yurgenson, P. I.)
Piotr Vassilievich (Davydov, P. V.)
Pyshka (Tchaikovskaia, E. M.)

Rina (Rimsky-Korsakov, N. A.)
Roman Efmovich (Depichenko, R. E.)
Rostislav (Tolstoi, F. M.)
Rudia (Bukaperden, R.)

Sania, Plemianik (Litke, A. N.)
Sasha, Sania, Sashura, Sanichka (Davydova, A. I.)
Sasha, Sashenka (Karzova, A. P.)
Sasha (Meck, A. K. von)
Sasha Gudim, Gudim (Levkovich, A.)
Sasha (Ziloty, A. I.)
Sergei Mikhailovich (Tretiakov, S. M.)
Sestnitza (Popova, A. N.)
Sofia Alexandrovna (Ershova, S. A.)
Sofia Vassilievna (Davydova, S. V.)
Sofia Mikhailovna (Lipport, S. M.)
Sonia (Tchaikovskaia, S. P.)

Tania (Davydova, T. L.)
Tania, Taniusha, Tassia, Tata, Tatiana, Tatochka,
    Tatussia (Tchaikovskaia, T. A.)
Tassia (Davydova, N. L.)
Tolia, Toliasha, Tolichka, Tolka (Tchaikovsky,
    A. T.)

Tota (Tchaikovskaia, T. A.)

Vassily Vassilievich (Pisarev, V. V.)
Vassia (Sapelnikov, V. L.)
Velina (Velinskaia, F. N.)
Venichka (Alexeev, V.)
Vera (Rimskaia-Korsakova, V. L.)
Vera Vasilievna (Butakova, V. V.)
Vera Nikolevna (Tretiakova, V. N.)
Vladimir Dimitrievich (Konshin, V. D.)
Vladimir Andreevich (Plessky, V.)
Voladia (Napravnik, V. E.)
Volodia (Davydov, V. L.)
Volodia (Shilovsky, V. S.)

Yasha (Hartung, J. F.)

Zina, Zinochka (Tchaikovskaia, Z. I.)

BIOGRAPHICAL INDEX

Abaza, Julia Fedorovna (d. 1915), singer and wife of a Government Minister, 193, 195

Abdul-Hamid II, Sultan (1842–1918), 112

Adam, Mme, 395, 396

Adamov, Vladimir Stepanovich (1833–1877), student at Law College until 1858, Steward of Imperial Household (1872), later Departmental Head in Ministry of Justice, 26, 51, 52, 101

Adlerberg, Alexander Vladimirovich (1818–1888), Minister, 227

Agafon, Alexander, N. G. Rubinstein's valet, 24, 58, 59, 71

Agar, Marie Léonide Charvin (1832–1891), French actress, 191

Akim, A. I., Tchaikovsky's servant, 175, 177, 181, 182, 187, 195, 239, 240

Akulina, cook for Tchaikovsky family in Votkinsk, 527

Aladina, 94

Albert, Eugène Francis Charles d' (1846–1932), Scottish pianist and composer, 301, 371, 372

Albrecht, Anna Leontievna, wife of K. K. Albrecht, 32, 33, 548

Albrecht, Karl (Konstantin) Karlovich (1836–1893), violinist and professor Moscow Conservatoire, 24, 32, 33, 41, 58, 83, 124, 127, 139, 141, 146, 171, 175, 253, 272, 285, 293, 363, 376, 423, 546, 548

Alexander I, Czar (1777–1825), 345

Alexander II, Czar (1818–1881), 2, 28–29, 153, 233, 260

Alexander III, Czar (1845–1894), 260, 288, 292, 293, 315, 316, 318, 383, 399, 409, 425, 428, 454, 496, 522, 523

Alexander, Grand Duke, 30

Alexander, King of Macedonia, 42

Alexeev, Nikolai Alexandrovich (1848–1893), director Russian Musical Society, Moscow section, 285, 286, 516

Alexeev, Vendikt, son of employee at Votkinsk, 527

Alexeeva, Alexandra Vladimirovna (née Konshina), sister of Praskovia V. Tchaikovskaia, 342

Alexeeva, Ekaterina Andreevna, aunt of Tchaikovsky on maternal side and singer, 16

Alferaky, Achilles Nikolaevich (1846–1919), composer, 241

Alcpeus, Ivan Samoilovich (1824–1904), Law School director, 26

Altany, Ippolit Karlovich (1846–1919), conductor of opera Bolshoi Theatre Moscow, 326, 336, 337, 338, 368, 370, 503, 504

Amici, boy singer and later guitar teacher in Rome, 231, 235

Ampère, Jean Jacques (1800–1864), French author 231

Apukhtin, Alexei Nickolaevich (1844–1893), poet, 25, 26, 30, 34, 40, 79, 101, 102, 143, 191, 194, 239, 240, 241, 314, 346, 538, 546, 551

Apukhtin, Andrei Nikolaevich, brother of preceding, 34, 79

Arensky, Antonin Stepanovich (1861–1906), composer, 311, 340, 341, 474, 534; *Dream on the Volga*, 437, 474

Argutinsky family, whose head was Mayor of Tiflis, 468

Arnold, Yuri Karlovich (1811–1898), theoretician, critic, composer, 52

Arseniev, Nikolai Sergeevich (1830–1903), Vice-President Moscow district law courts, 36

Artôt, Désirée (1835–1907), French mezzo-soprano, 39, 40, 42, 43, 44, 45, 47, 48, 53, 54, 55, 57, 76, 98, 103, 382, 390, 416, 444

Assiere, Mikhail Andreevich, cousin of Tchaikovsky, 114

Auber, Daniel François Esprit (1782–1871), French composer, director Paris Conservatoire from 1842, 531; *Le domino noir*, 42, 43, 55

Auer, Leopold Semionovich (1845–1930), violinist and professor St. Petersburg Conservatoire, 88, 92, 95, 150, 240, 241, 269, 270, 338, 380

Augier, Guillaume Victor Emile (1820–1889), French author and satirist, 191, 214

Ave-Lallemant, Theodor von, Chairman Hamburg Philharmonic Society, 386, 388, 417

Averkiev, Dmitri Vassilievich (1836–1905), dramatist, 240, 268

Azanchevsky, Mikhail Pavlovich, composer, and director St. Petersburg Conservatoire 1871–1876, 101

Azeev, Evstafi Stepanovich (1851–1918), church music director and composer, 344

Bach, Johann Sebastian (1685–1750), 266, 332

Baikova, 76

Bakhireva, Ardotia Yakovlevna (d. 1880), governess to A. I. and M. I. Tchaikovsky, 7, 9, 24

Bakmetiev, Nikolai Nikolaevich (1847–1909), secretary of *Russkaia Mysl*, 297, 298

Balakirev, Mily Alexeevich (1837–1910), composer, 34, 48, 50, 51, 52, 53, 56, 57, 58, 59, 64, 282, 283, 305, 319, 326

Balzek, Berta, singing professor, 31

Baranov, Nikolai Mikhailovich (1837–1901),

559

Khokhlov, Pavel (1854–1919), baritone Bolshoi Theatre, 370, 372

Khomiakov, Alexei Stepanovich (1804–1860), poet, 361

Khvostova, Alina Alexandrovna, soprano, 60, 62

Kisselev, Alexei, 276

Klenovsky, Nikolai Semenovich (1857–1915), conductor, composer, assistant director for first performance *Eugene Onegin*, 400, 406, 409

Klimenko, Ivan Alexandrovich, architect, friend of Tchaikovsky, 36, 38, 40, 52

Klimenko, Mikhail, assistant to P. Y. Yurgenson, recommended by Tchaikovsky, 52, 277

Klimentova, Maria Nikolaevna, soprano Bolshoi Theatre, 251, 370

Klindworth, Karl (1830–1916), pupil of Liszt, pianoforte professor Moscow Conservatoire, 67, 109, 252, 316, 416

Kniajevich, Antonin, acquaintance of P. Tchaikovsky, 108

Kokorev, Vassily Alexeevich (1817–1889), Moscow hotel proprietor, 19, 283

Kologrivov, Vassily Alexeevich (1829–1875), musician, an organiser of Russian Musical Society, 28

Komissarov, Osip Ivanovich (1838–1892), hatmaker, prevented assassination of Alexander II, 29

Kommisarjevsky, Fedor Petrovich (1838–1905), tenor, professor Moscow Conservatoire, 227

Kondatriev, Gennadyi Petrovich (1835–1905), baritone and stage director Marinsky Theatre, 477

Kondatriev, Nikolai Dmitrievich (c. 1830–1887), land-owner in Kharkov Province, friend of P. Tchaikovsky, 68, 74, 83, 87, 88, 93, 97, 101, 102, 103, 122, 136, 165, 168, 175, 199, 226, 236, 261, 262, 269, 270, 271, 275, 276, 292, 319, 323, 376, 377, 402, 418, 455

Kondatrieva, Maria Sergeevna, wife of previous, 274, 276, 280, 319, 323

Konius, Georgi Eduardovich (1862–1933), composer, musicologist, 482, 534, 535

Konius, Lev Eduardovich (b. 1871), pianist, 551

Konius, Yuli Eduardovich (1869–1942), violinist, 551

Konradi, Alina Ivanovna (1849–1932), wife of following, 125, 187, 271, 295

Konradi, Herman Karlovich (1833–1882), manager of estates in Ukraine, father of following, 99, 101, 102, 107, 114, 125, 154, 234, 238, 239, 248, 257, 446

Konradi, Nikolai Hermanovich (1868–1923), deaf and dumb pupil of M. I. Tchaikovsky, 99, 101, 102, 105, 106, 107, 109, 110, 114, 120, 124, 125, 126, 132

Konshin, Nikolai Dmitrievich (d. 1915), Moscow textile merchant, father-in-law of A. I. Tchaikovsky, 292, 342, 345, 404, 516

Konshin, Nikolai Vladimirovich, brother-in-law of A. I. Tchaikovsky, 480

Konshin, Vladimir Vladimirovich, brother-in-law of A. I. Tchaikovsky, 326

Konshina, Praskovia, 271, 273, 275

Konstantin Konstantinovich, Grand Duke (1858–1916), poet, amateur pianist, Vice-President Russian Musical Society, President Academy of Science, 239, 240, 241, 259, 362

Konstantin Nikolaevich, Grand Duke (1827–1892), President Russian Musical Society, 80, 105, 239, 240, 241, 242

Korganov, Gennadi Ossipovich (1858–1890), pianist and composer, 348, 456

Korolenko, Vladimir Galaktionovich (1853–1921), author, 331, 332

Korsov, Gottfried (1845–1920), baritone St. Petersburg, and after 1882 Moscow Imperial Theatre, 370, 460, 504

Koshitz, Pavel Alexandrovich (1868–1940), tenor Bolshoi Theatre, 467, 469

Kossmann, Bernhard (1822–1910), German violinist, professor Moscow Conservatoire 1866–1870, 32, 34

Kotek, Yosif Yosifovich (1855–1885), violinist, protégé of N. F. von Meck, 114, 120, 121, 122, 126, 129, 150, 151, 152, 154, 155, 156, 157, 158, 159, 160, 163, 171, 174, 178, 186, 190, 198, 202, 218, 228, 269, 270, 283, 314, 315, 316, 317, 318, 321, 390

Kotzebue, counsellor at Russian Embassy, Paris, 395

Kozlova, Mme, 11, 227

Kraevsky, Andrei Alexandrovich (1810–1889), editor of *Golos*, 94, 95

Kraus, Gabriela (1842–1906), soprano at Paris Opera, 89, 212

Kross, Gustav Gustavovich (1831–1885), pianist, friend of Tchaikovsky at St. Petersburg Conservatoire, 331

Krutikova, Alexandra Pavlovna (1851–1919), mezzo-soprano Bolshoi Theatre, 101, 250, 370, 371, 504

Kushnik, Mme, singer, 142

Kuzmin, General, 7

Kuznezov, Nikolai Dmitrievich (1850–1930), painter, 479, 530, 531

Lachner, Franz (1803–1890), Austrian composer, friend of Schubert, 66

Lalo, Edouard (1823–1892); *Le roi d'Ys*, 422, *Symphonie espagnole*, 150

Lamary, French actor, 301

Lamoureux, Charles (1834–1899), French violinist and conductor, 356, 529, 530

Landrol, Joseph Alexandre (1828–1888), French actor, 319

Langer, Eduard Leontievich (1835–1892), pianist, professor Moscow Conservatoire, 89

Lanin, Piotr Nikolaevich, a director Russian Musical Society, Moscow, 24

Laroche, Anastasia Petrovna (née Sushkina), first wife of H. A. Laroche, 37, 52

Laroche, Ekaterina Ivanovna (née Sinelnikova), second wife of following, 297, 308, 376, 405, 478, 483, 491, 492

Laroche, Hermann Augustovich (1845–1906), music critic, professor St. Petersburg (1872–79) and Moscow (1883–86) Conservatoires, 17, 19, 20, 25, 28, 33, 34, 35, 36, 37, 40, 41, 42, 43, 48, 49, 52, 61, 62, 68, 70, 77, 78, 83, 91, 93, 95, 101, 102, 103, 107, 108, 109, 110, 141, 143, 153, 171, 172, 185, 187, 194, 197, 211

Laroche, Zinaida Hermanovna, daughter of preceding, translator of Oulibishev's *Mozart*, 52, 403

Lassalle, Jean Louis (1847–1909), French baritone, 319

Laub, Ferdinand (1832–1875), violinist, professor Moscow Conservatoire, 32, 34, 56, 83, 96, 305, 404, 418

Durossova, Princess, 395
Dussatov, Dmitri Andreevich (1849–1913), tenor Bolshoi Theatre, 370, 371

Pabst, Pavel Augustovich (1854–1897), pianist, professor Moscow Conservatoire, 313, 469
Pachulsky, Vladislav Albertovich, violinist, secretary and son-in-law to N. F. von Meck, 178, 218, 224, 287, 311
Padilla y Ramos, Mariano (1842–1906), baritone, husband of D. Artôt, 48, 390
Palen, Konstantin Ivanovich, Count (1833–1912), Minister of Justice 1867–78, Member of Council of State, 433, 434, 439, 444, 455, 457, 458
Palmerston, Lord (1784–1865), British statesman, 1
Panaeva, Alexandra Valerianovna (1853–1942), well-known in society as a singer, 142, 143, 144, 146, 148, 151, 154, 181, 227, 240, 241, 249, 366, 369
Pasca, French comedy actress, 290
Pasdeloup, Jules (1819–1887), French conductor, organiser of popular classical concerts, 217, 227
Patti, Adelina (1843–1919), Italian soprano, 8, 75, 127
Pavel, Exarch of Georgia, 349
Pavlovna, Grand Duchess Elena (1806–1873), founder of Russian Musical Society, 14, 49
Pavlovskaia, Emilia Karlovna (1853–1935), soprano Marinsky Theatre, 122, 327, 366, 374
Pchelnikov, Pavel Mikhailovich (1851–1913), manager of Moscow head office, Imperial Theatres, 321, 328, 329, 330, 338, 453
Pechkovskaia, Natalia Nikolaevna (1850–1930), mistress of P. I. Yurgenson, 403
Peresleny, Ekaterina Vassilievna (1822–1898), elder sister of L. V. Davydov, 30, 43, 60, 61, 70
Peresleny, Nikolai Vladimirovich, nephew of L. V. Davydov, civil servant, 273, 330, 333, 347, 348, 349, 350, 401, 410, 464, 470, 471, 476, 478, 493, 497
Perfilier family, 292
Perrault, Charles (1628–1703), author of Contes de ma mère l'oye, 406
Perugino, Pietro (1446–1524), Italian painter, 193
Petersen, Pavel Leontievich (1831–1895), a director of Russian Musical Society, 551
Petipa, Marius Ivanovich (1822–1910), ballet master and teacher, 367, 406, 509
Petrovsky, Sergei Alexandrovich (1846–1917), succeeded Katkov as editor Moskovskie Vedomosty, 427
Piccioli, Luigi (1812–1868), Italian singing-teacher, 3, 9, 11, 16, 17, 18
Pichugin, friend of Tchaikovsky, 26
Piotr Gerasimovich, butler at Kamenka, 78–9
Pisarev, Vassily Vassilievich, engineer, friend of Tchaikovsky family, 4, 5, 6, 7, 9
Pisemsky, Alexei Feofilaktovich (1820–1881), novelist and playwright, 23, 25, 259
Platonova, acquaintance of Tchaikovsky, in Florence, 430
Pleshcheev, Alexei Nikolaevich (1825–1893), poet, member of Petrashevsky group, arrested 1849, sentenced to serve in army, 25, 51, 52, 255, 314
Plesskaia, Natalia Andreevna, grand-daughter of a Decembrist, friendly with Davydov family, 169, 199, 232, 272, 295, 298
Plessky, Vladimir Andreevich, financial manager of Kamenka estates, 267, 545; family of, 113,

122
Plessky, Boris Vladimirovich, son of preceding, on staff of newspaper, 534, 545, 546
Plevako, Fedor Nikiforovich (1842–1908), lawyer, 405, 407
Plusch, Yakov Alexandrovich (d. 1916), theatre critic, translator, 249
Pobedonoszev, Konstantin Petrovich, (1827–1906), secular head of church synod, 303, 306, 496
Podobedova, Ekaterina Ivanovna, (d. 1888), actress Alexandrinsky Theatre, St. Petersburg 1857–82, 4
Pollini, Bernhard (1838–97), director Hamburg Opera House, 506, 507, 508, 517, 524, 549
Polonsky, Yakov Petrovich (1819–98), poet, 87, 215, 326, 331, 425
Poplavsky, Ulian Ignatievich (b. 1871), cellist, 540
Popova, Anastasia Vassilievna (1807–94), daughter of V. V. Popova, née Tchaikovsky, 69, 70, 527, 531, 532
Porokhovshchikova, Nadezhda Petrovna, wife of General S. A. Porokhovshchikov and cousin of Tchaikovsky, 101
Postels, Alexander Filippovich (1801–1871), naturalist and professor College of Law, 33
Potekhin, Alexei Antipovich (1829–1908), author of peasant drama, Fate and Sorrow, 274
Potekhin, Nikolai Antipovich (1824–1896), playwright, 260, 359, 360, 362
Potulov, Nikolai Mikhailovich (1810–1873), composer of church music, 264
Pravdin, Osip Andreevich (1847–1921), actor Malyi Theatre, 426
Prianishnikov, Ippolit Petrovich (1847–1921), baritone Marinsky Theatre and theatrical manager, 472, 511, 512, 513
Pribyk, Yosif Viacheslavovich (1853–1936), opera conductor, 472
Prokhorova-Manrelli, Ksenia Alexeevna (1836–1902), soprano Marinsky Theatre 1863–66, 56
Pugachov, Emelian Ivanovich (1726–1775), leader of Cossack rebellion, proclaimed himself Emperor Piotr III, issued manifesto liberating serfs, 399
Pushkin, Alexander Sergeevich (1799–1837), 2, 117, 118, 119, 139, 251, 266, 399, 428, 442, 538
Pyleev, 240

Raab, Wilhelmina Ivanovna (1848–1917), soprano Marinsky Theatre, 227, 249
Rachel, Elize (1821–1858), French actress, 237
Rachinsky, Sergei Alexandrovich (1836–1902), professor of botany, educationist, librettist, 59
Rachmaninov, Sergei Vassilievich (1873–1943), Aleko, 538, 539
Racine, Jean Baptiste (1639–1699), 237; Andromaque, 190
Radecky, musician, 318
Raievskaia, Ludmila, singer, 135, 138, 141, 143
Rassokhin, Sergei Fedorovich, Moscow bookseller, 332, 336
Rathaus, Daniel Maximovich (b. 1868), poet, 533
Rater (Bütner), Hamburg music publisher, 384, 403
Ravel, Maurice (1875–1937), 244
Raymond, H. (b. 1844), French actor, 299
Razmadze, Alexander Solomonovich (1845–1896), music historian and critic, 89, 108
Réaumur, René (1683–1757), scientist, 106

INDEX OF PLACES